SEEING JESUS

BIBLE ENCOUNTER STUDY GUIDE

ENCOUNTER THE WORD

with Marilyn Hickey

Marilyn & Sarah
marilynandsarah.org
MARILYN HICKEY MINISTRIES P.O. Box 6598 Englewood, CO 80155-6598

Unless otherwise indicated, all Scriptures quoted in this volume are from the King James Version of the Bible.

SEEING JESUS
MARILYN HICKEY BIBLE ENCOUNTER

Printed in the United States of America

ISBN # 978-0-9830274-2-3

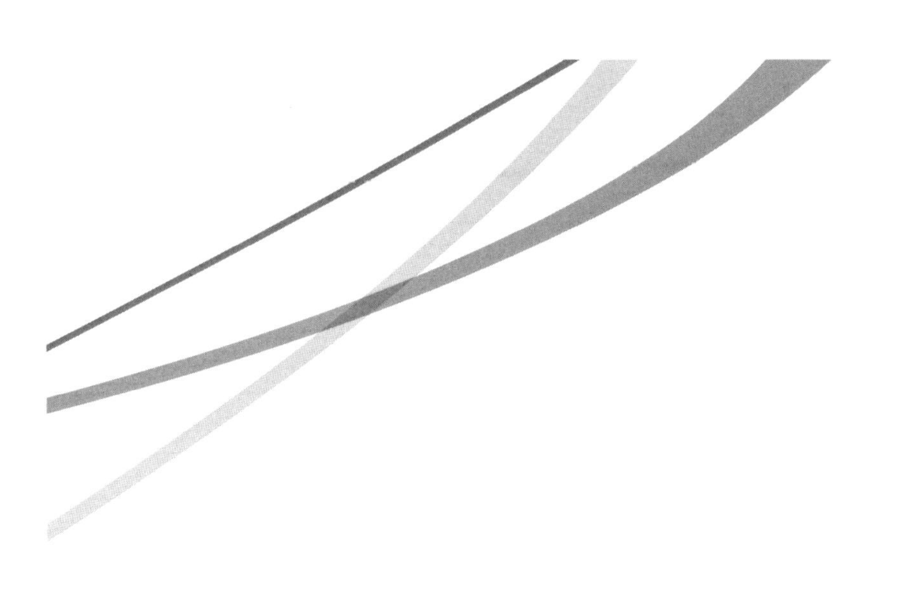

"And beginning at Moses and all the prophets, (Jesus) expounded unto them in all the scriptures the things concerning himself" **(Luke 24:27).**

"But we all, with open face beholding as in a glass the glory of the Lord, are changed into the same image from glory to glory, even as by he Spirit of the Lord. Therefore seeing we have this ministry, as we have received mercy, we faint not" **(II Corinthians 3:18-4:1).**

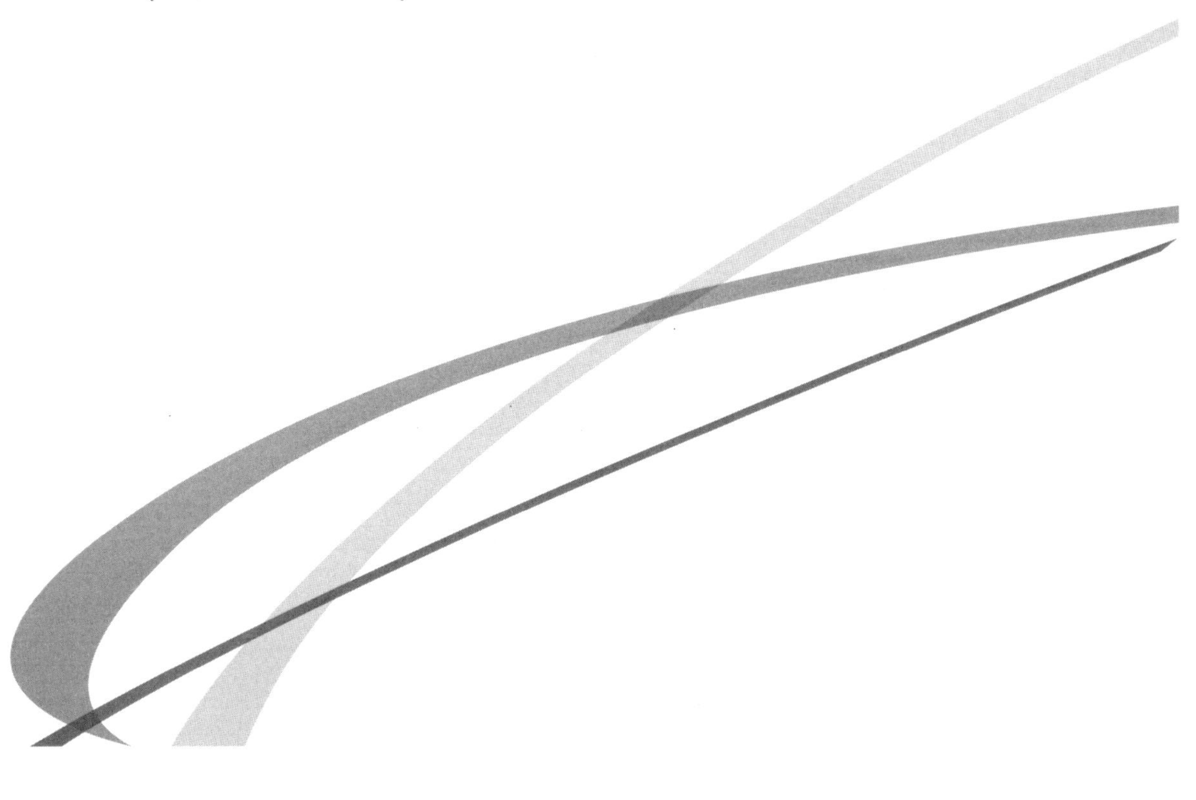

SEEING JESUS BIBLE ENCOUNTER

TABLE OF CONTENTS

MARILYN HICKEY BIBLE ENCOUNTER

"SEEING JESUS IN EVERY BOOK OF THE BIBLE"

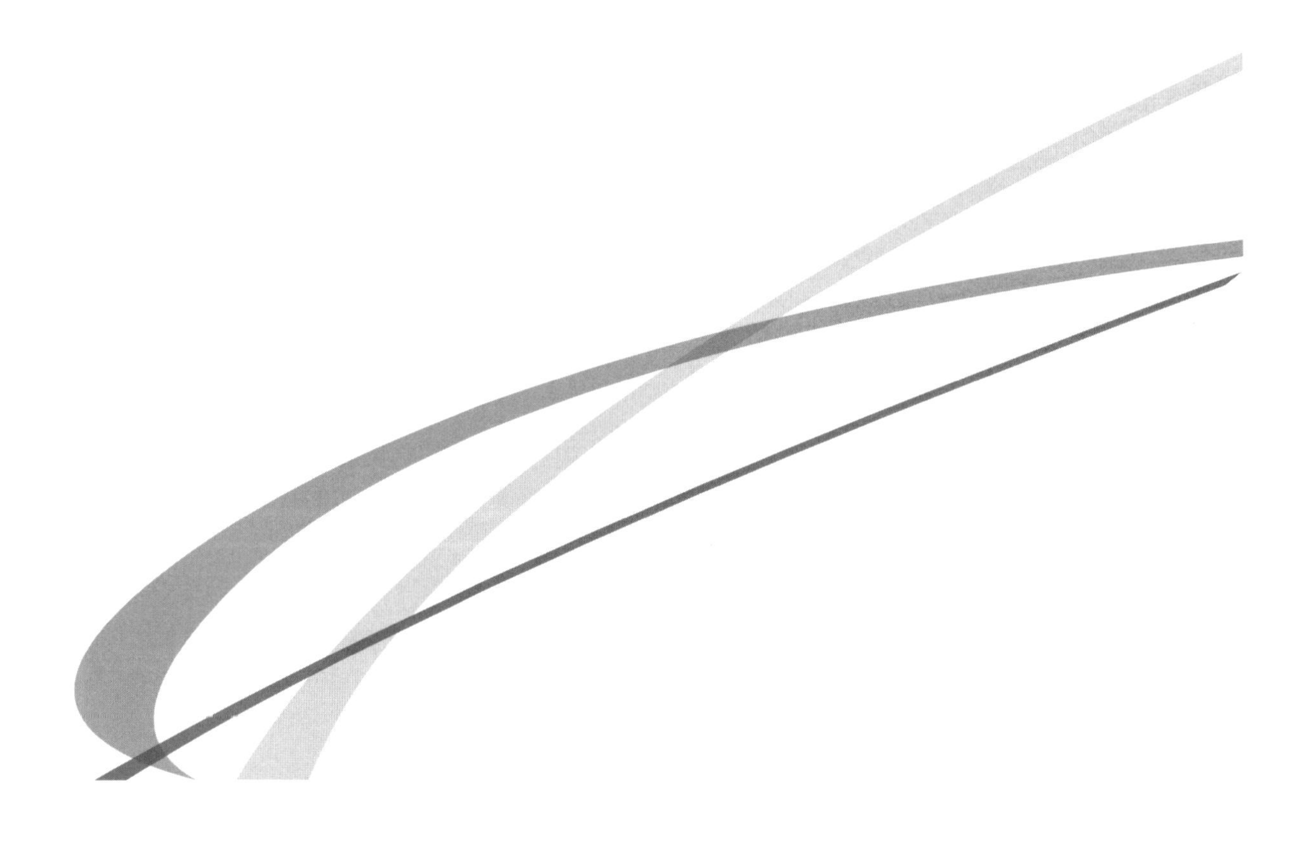

INTRODUCTION

The Bible is one of your best friends! It is a library composed of 66 books. There are 39 books in the Old Testament and 27 books in the New Testament.

It is said that in the British Navy there is a red thread within each rope, running the length of the rope, which identifies it as belonging to the Royal Navy. In similar fashion the Cross and blood of Jesus run from Genesis to Revelation, identifying our Redeemer in each book.

It is believed that there were 30 men who, under the direction of the Holy Spirit, were involved in the writing of our Bible.

The purpose of the Old Testament was to *prepare the way* for a Redeemer. The purpose of the New Testament was to *prepare a people* to receive the Redeemer.

In the New Testament we have the manifestation of the Redeemer and His manifestation through His people. Jesus can be seen as a prophet, a priest, and a king. Man needs a prophet to *reveal* God, a priest to *redeem* him from sin, and a king to *rule* his life.

The first revelation God gave was an oral revelation. The first written revelation was through Moses. The following scriptures all refer to the Word being written:

"And the LORD said unto Moses, Write this for a memorial in a book, and rehearse it in the ears of Joshua: for I will utterly put out the remembrance of Amalek from under heaven" **(Exodus 17:14)**.

"And Moses wrote their goings out according to their journeys by the commandment of the LORD; and these are their journeys according to their goings out" **(Numbers 33:2)**.

"And it shall be, when he sitteth upon the throne of his kingdom, that he shall write him a copy of this law in a book out of that which is before the priests the Levites" **(Deuteronomy 17:18)**.

"This book of the law shall not depart out of thy mouth; but thou shalt meditate therein day and night, that thou mayest observe to do according to all that is written therein: for then thou shalt make thy way prosperous, and then thou shalt have good success" **(Joshua 1:8)**.

"And Joshua wrote these words in the book of the law of God, and took a great stone, and set it up there under an oak, that was by the sanctuary of the LORD" **(Joshua 24:26).**

"Then Samuel told the people the manner of the kingdom, and wrote it in a book, and laid it up before the LORD. And Samuel sent all the people away, every man to his house"
(I Samuel 10:25).

"And all the people gathered themselves together as one man into the street that was before the water gate; and they spake

NOTES

NOTES

unto Ezra the scribe o bring the book of the law of Moses, which the LORD had commanded to Israel" **(Nehemiah 8:1)**.

"Bind up the testimony, seal the law among my disciples. To the law and to the testimony: if they speak not according to this word, it is because there is no light in them" **(Isaiah 8:16, 20)**.

"Take thee a roll of a book, and write therein all the words that I have spoken unto thee against Israel and against Judah, and against all the nations, from the day I spake unto thee, from the days of Josiah, even unto this day" **(Jeremiah 36:2)**.

"In the first year of his reign I Daniel understood by books the number of the years, whereof the word of the LORD came to Jeremiah the prophet, that he would accomplish seventy years in the desolations of Jerusalem" **(Daniel 9:2)**.

In the New Testament the Letters were read in the assemblies:

"I charge you by the LORD that this epistle be read unto all the holy brethren" **(I Thessalonians 5:27)**.

"And if any man obey not our word by this epistle, note that man, and have no company with him, that he may be ashamed" **(II Thessalonians 3:14)**.

The letters were exchanged among the churches:

"And when this epistle is read among you, cause that it be read also in the church of the Laodiceans; and that ye likewise read the epistle from Laodicea" **(Colossians 4:16).**

NOTE: The gospels, Acts, and Revelation were probably written after the epistles.

The arrangement of the books in the Bible shows God's pattern in REVEALING JESUS, our Redeemer:

1. Genesis to Deuteronomy - Revelation
2. Joshua to Esther - Preparation
3. Job to Song of Solomon - Aspiration
4. Isaiah to Malachi - Expectation
5. Matthew to John - Manifestation
6. Acts to Epistles - Realization
7. Revelation - Culmination

Why is "Seeing Jesus in Every Book of the Bible" so important to you?

1. You will see Jesus and His love for you in every book.
2. You will make practical applications in your life.
3. You will recognize the unity of the Bible, noting the relationship of the books to one another.
4. You will demonstrate God's supernatural power in your life.
5. You will gain mastery of the factual content of the Bible.

It will take spiritual discernment to perceive what God has for YOU in this "Seeing Jesus In Every Book of the Bible" series:

"But the natural man receiveth not the things of the Spirit of God: for they are foolishness unto him: neither can he know them, because they are spiritually discerned" **(I Corinthians 2:14).**

"But we all, with open face beholding as in a glass the glory of the Lord, are changed into the same image from glory to glory, even as by the Spirit of the Lord" **(II Corinthians 3:18).**

NOTES

GENESIS

GOD'S RELATIONSHIP TO TWO GROUPS OF PEOPLE	
HUMAN RACE	**FAMILY OF ABRAHAM**
Creation: **1,2** Fall: **3-5** Flood:**6-9** Nations: **10,11**	Abraham: **11-25** Isaac: **21-26** Jacob: **27-36** Joseph: **37-50**
LOCATION: Fertile Crescent	Canaan/Egypt
OVERVIEW: Seed plot for all major doctrines, including redemption through shed blood	Historical record of God's covenant with the Jewish nation
TIME: Approximately 2000 years	300 years

FAST FACTS

AUTHOR AND SETTING:

Moses; Fertile Crescent, Israel, Egypt

PURPOSE:

Genesis is the seed plot for all major doctrines found in the Bible - including redemption through shed blood. Here we see man's creation, his fall through sin, and God's plan of redemption through one nation and one man - Jesus Christ.

SEEING JESUS:

There are four major prophecies about Jesus in *Genesis*: (1) 3:15; (2) 9:24-27; (3) 12:3, 22:8, 14; (4) 49:10. Joseph's life, betrayal, and position as "savior" of the Hebrew people is a major "type" of Jesus.

THEME VERSE:

Genesis 3:15

NOTES

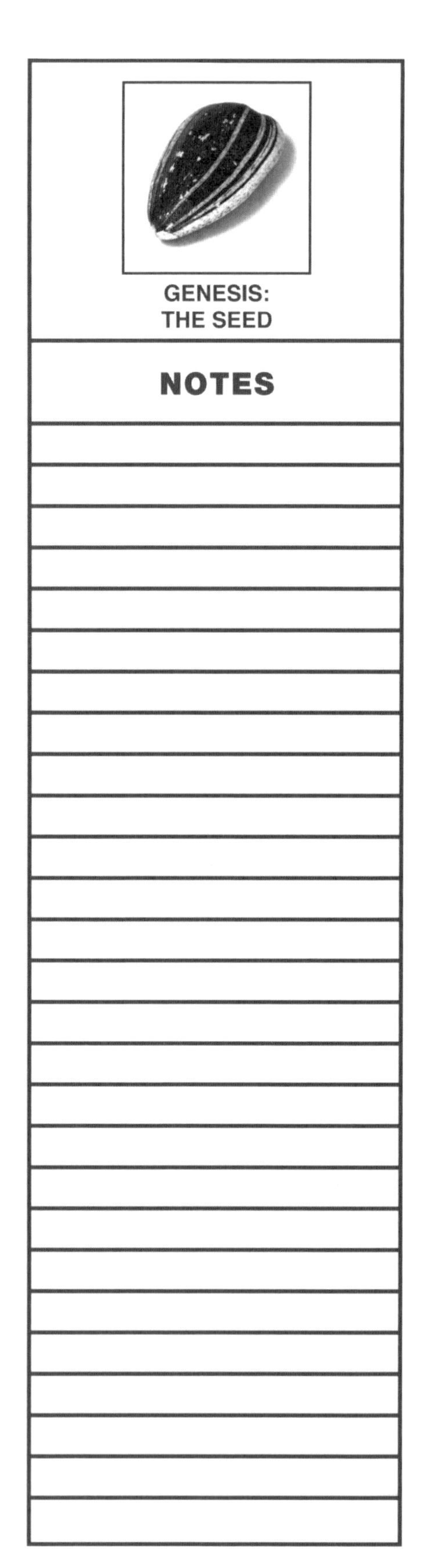

SEEING JESUS IN GENESIS

AUTHOR & SETTING

There is no doubt that Moses authored the first five books of our Bible. In Exodus 17:14 God commanded Moses to write a book, and we know from Exodus 24:4 that Moses did write a book. Jesus speaks of the "book of Moses" in Mark 12:26. Acts 7:22 tells us that Moses was ***"...learned in all the wisdom of the Egyptians and was might in words and in deeds."*** Moses had much time in the wilderness to hear from God and record His words.

Genesis opens in the Garden of Eden somewhere in what we now call the Fertile Crescent. From there Abraham is called into Israel. The Jews eventually end up in Egypt as slaves following Joseph's death.

OVERVIEW

We are going to study the Bible together, and we are going to do what was prophesied to Daniel that "many" would do:

"But thou, O Daniel, shut up the words, and seal the book, even to the time of the end: many shall run to and fro, and knowledge shall be increased" **(Daniel 12:4).**

The portion of this Hebrew scripture that says *"...many shall run to and fro, ..."* basically means "to walk through the pages with your fingers." God was way ahead of the Yellow Pages! And as we walk through the pages of the Bible, *"...knowledge shall be increased"* just as was promised to Daniel.

OVERVIEW OF THE OLD TESTAMENT:

The word ***testament*** means "a covenant or agreement." In the Old Testament there are 5 books of the law, 12 books of history, 5 books of poetry, 5 major prophets, and 12 minor prophets:

HISTORICAL	POETICAL	PROPHETICAL
Law	Job	***Major***
Genesis	Psalms	Isaiah
Exodus	Proverbs	Jeremiah
Leviticus	Ecclesiastes	Lamentations
Numbers	Song of Solomon	Ezekiel
Deuteronomy		Daniel
History		***Minor***
Joshua		Hosea
Judges		Joel
Ruth		Amos
I Samuel		Obadiah
II Samuel		Jonah
I Kings		Micah
II Kings		Nahum
I Chronicles		Habakkuk
II Chronicles		Zephaniah
Ezra		Haggai
Nehemiah		Zechariah
Esther		Malachi

Genesis is the introduction to the Pentateuch (five volumes).

God gave His revelation progressively.

Genesis is the "seed plot" of the Bible. It is the book of beginnings.

Genesis presents the beginning of everything but God!

JESUS REFERRED TO *GENESIS*:

"And he answered and said unto them, Have ye not read, that he which made them at the beginning made them male and female" **(Matthew 19:4).**

"But as the days of Noah were, so shall also the coming of the Son of man be. For as in the days that were before the flood they were eating and drinking, marrying and giving in marriage, until the day that Noah entered into the ark" **(Matthew 24:37,38).**

"And they said, Moses suffered to write a bill of divorcement, and to put her away. And Jesus answered and said unto them, For the hardness of your heart he wrote you this precept. But from the beginning of the creation God made them male and female" **(Mark 10:4-6).**

"Therefore also said the wisdom of God, I will send them prophets and apostles, and some of them they shall slay and persecute: That the blood of all the prophets, which was shed from the foundation of the world, may be required of this generation; From the blood of Abel unto the blood of Zacharias,..." **(Luke 11:49-51).**

"And as it was in the days of Noe, so shall it be also in the days of the Son of man. They did eat, they drank, they married wives they were given in marriage, until the day that Noe entered into the ark, and the flood came, and destroyed them all. Likewise also as it was in the days of Lot; they did eat, they drank, they bought, they sold, they planted, they builded; But the same day that Lot went out of Sodom it rained fire and brimstone from heaven, and destroyed them all" **(Luke 17:26-29).**

THERE ARE FOUR DIVINE INSTITUTIONS IN THE BOOK OF GENESIS:

1. Volition
2. Marriage
3. Family
4. Nations

IT WILL HELP US TO UNDERSTAND THE ENTIRE BIBLE IF WE KEEP IN MIND THE FOLLOWING DISPENSATIONS:

1. Gentiles (Genesis 1-11)
    a. Attack on volition (Adam and Eve)
    b. Attack on the family (Cain and Abel)
    c. Attack on marriage (Genesis 6)
    d. Attack on nationalism (Genesis 11:1-6)
2. Age of the Jews (Genesis 12)
3. Age of the Church (Acts 1)
4. Millennium (Revelation 20:4)

NOTES

NOTES

SEEING JESUS IN GENESIS

Christ is the key which unlocks the Word: *Jesus said, "Search the scriptures; for in them ye think ye have eternal life: and they are they which testify of me"* **(John 5:39).**

Genesis testifies of Christ!

There are four major prophecies about Jesus in *Genesis*:

1. *"And I will put enmity between thee and the woman, and between thy seed and her **seed**; it shall bruise thy head, and thou shalt bruise his heel"* **(Genesis 3:15).**

Adam was a type of Jesus:

"Nevertheless death reigned from Adam to Moses, even over them that had not sinned after the similitude of Adam's transgression, who is the figure of him that was to come" **(Romans 5:14).**

Adam was the head of the old creation; Christ is the head of the new creation.

Melchizedek was a type of Jesus:

1. *"Without father, without mother, without descent, having neither beginning of days, nor end of life; but made like unto the Son of God abideth a priest continually"* **(Hebrews 7:3).**

2. *"And Noah awoke from his wine, and knew what his younger son had done unto him. And he said, Cursed be Canaan; a servant of servants shall he be unto his brethren. And he said, Blessed be the LORD God of Shem; and Canaan shall be his servant. God shall enlarge Japheth, and **he shall dwell in the tents of Shem**; and Canaan shall be his servant"* **(Genesis 9:24-27).**

3. *"And I will bless them that bless thee, and curse him that curseth thee: and **in thee shall all families of the earth be blessed.** And Abraham said, My son, God will provide **himself a lamb** for a burnt offering: so they went both of them together. And Abraham called the name of that place Jehovah-jireh: as it is said to this day, In the mount of the LORD it shall be seen"* **(Genesis 12:3, 22:8, 14).**

4. *"The sceptre shall not depart from Judah, nor a lawgiver from between his feet, until **Shiloh** come; and unto him shall the gathering of the people be"* **(Genesis 49:10).**

THEME VERSE

"And I will put enmity between thee and the woman, and between thy seed and her seed; it shall bruise thy head and thou shalt bruise his heel" **(Genesis 3:15).**

OUTLINE

(Refer to maps on pages A3, A4, and A5 in the APPENDIX.)

I. GENESIS RECORDS GOD'S RELATIONSHIP TO TWO GROUPS OF PEOPLE:

A. THE HUMAN RACE - Genesis 1-11

1. CREATION - Genesis 1,2

a. Creation was the work of the Father, the Son, and the Holy Spirit:

i. *"And God said, Let **us** make man in **our** image, after **our** likeness..."* **(Genesis 1-26).**

ii. *"And **God** said, ...and there was..."* **(Genesis 1:3)**

iii. *"For by him* **[Jesus]** *were all things created, that are in heaven, and that are in earth..."* **(Colossians 1-16).**

iv. *"And the earth was without form, and void; and darkness was upon the face of the deep. And the **Spirit** of God moved upon the face of the waters"* **(Genesis 1:2).**

2. THE FALL - Genesis 3-5

a. The same temptations faced Adam and Jesus.

b. The substitutionary death of Jesus is seen in **Genesis 3:21:** *"Unto Adam also and to his wife did the LORD God make coasts of skins ad clothed them."* (There was shedding of blood)

c. Cain's murder of Abel was Satan's first attempt to destroy the Seed

d. Abel was the first to offer a lamb. (There was shedding of blood)

3. THE FLOOD - Genesis 6-9

a. Jesus spoke of the flood (Matthew 24:37-39); He is our Ark provided by the Father.

b. Arks mentioned in Scripture: Noah's ark, the "ark"that baby Moses floated in to hide from the Egyptians, the Ark of the Covenant, and the "ark of his testament" in heaven (Revelation 11:19).

c. Noah offered a blood sacrifice following the flood (Genesis 8:20).

4. THE NATIONS - Genesis 10,11

a. The nations began with Shem, Ham, and Japheth (Genesis 9:24,25). Shem was the Father of the Jews, the lineage of Jesus, the Messiah.

B. THE COVENANT FAMILY OF ABRAHAM - GENESIS 12-50

1. ABRAHAM - Genesis 12-20

a. Jesus was the seed of Abraham: *"Now to Abraham and his seed were the promises made. He saith not, And to seeds, as of many; but as of one, And to thy seed, which is Christ"* **(Galatians 3:16).**

NOTES

NOTES

2. ISAAC - Genesis 21-26

a. Abraham and Isaac are a picture of the Father and the Son (Romans 4). Jesus was offered as the Lamb of God for the sin of the world.

3. JACOB - Genesis 27-36

a. Jacob saw the ladder of God (Genesis 28:12), a picture of the Lord Jesus Christ - the link between heaven and earth.

4. JOSEPH - Genesis 37-50

a. Joseph is a picture of the Son sold into bondage to redeem His family.

b. Jacob prophesied of Shiloh - the coming redeemer (Genesis 49:10).

NOTES

GENESIS QUOTED IN THE NEW TESTAMENT.

Genesis 1:27 (Genesis 5:2)
So God created man in his own image, in the image of God created he him; male and female created he them.

Matthew 19:4
And he answered and said unto them, Have ye not read, that he which made them at the beginning made them male and female.

Mark 10:6
But from the beginning of the creation God made them male and female.

****

Genesis 2:2
And on the seventh day God ended his work which he had made; and he rested on the seventh day from all his work which he had made.

Hebrews 4:4
For he spake in a certain place of the seventh day on this wise, And God did rest the seventh day from all his works.

****

Genesis 2:7
And the LORD God formed man of the dust of the ground, and breathed into his nostrils the breath of life; and man became a living soul.

I Corinthians 15:45
And so it is written, The first man Adam was made a living soul; the last Adam was made a quickening spirit.

****

Genesis 2:24
Therefore shall a man leave his father and his mother, and shall cleave unto his wife: and they shall be one flesh.

Matthew 19:5
And said, for this cause shall a man leave father and mother, and shall cleave to his wife: and they twain shall be one flesh?

Mark 10:7,8
For this cause shall a man leave his father and mother, and cleave to his wife; And they twain shall be one flesh: so then they are no more twain, but one flesh.

I Corinthians 6:16
What? Know ye not that he which is joined to an harlot is one body? For two, saith he, shall be one flesh.

Ephesians 5:31
For this cause shall a man leave his father and mother, and shall be joined unto his wife, and they two shall be one flesh.

****

Genesis 5:2
Male and female created he them; and blessed them, and called their name Adam, in the day when they were created.

Matthew 19:4
And he answered and said unto them, Have ye not read, that he which made them at the beginning made them male and female.

Mark 10:6
But from the beginning of the creation God made them male and female.

****

Genesis 5:24
And Enoch walked with God: and he was not for God took him.

Hebrews 11:5
By faith Enoch was translated that he should not see death; and was not found, because God had translated him: for before his translation he had this testimony, that he pleased God.

****

Genesis 12:1
Now the Lord had said unto Abram, Get thee out of thy country, and from thy kindred, and from thy father's house, unto a land that I will shew thee.

Acts 7:3
And said unto him, Get thee out of thy country and from thy kindred, and come into the land which I shall shew thee.

****

Genesis 12:3 (Genesis 22:18, 26:4, 28:14)
And I will bless them that bless thee, and curse him that curseth thee: and in thee shall all families of the earth be blessed.

Acts 3:25
Ye are the children of the prophets, and of the covenant which God made with our fathers, saying unto Abraham, And in thy seed shall all the kindreds of the earth be blessed.

Galatians 3:8
And the scripture, foreseeing that God would justify the heathen through faith, preached before the gospel unto Abraham, saying, in thee shall all nations be blessed.

****

Genesis 12:7 (Genesis 12:7, 17:8, 48:4)
And the Lord appeared unto Abram, and said, Unto thy seed will I give this land: and there builded he an altar unto the LORD who appeared unto him.

Acts 7:5
And he gave him none inheritance in it, no, not so much as to set his foot on: yet he promised that he would give it to him for a possession, and to his seed after him, when as yet he had no child.

****

Genesis 13:15 (Genesis 12:7, 17:8, 48:4)
For all the land which thou seest, to thee will I give it, and to thy seed for ever.

Acts 7:5
And he gave him none inheritance in it, no, not so much as to set his foot on: yet he promised that he would give it to him for a possession, and to his seed after him, when as yet he had no child.

****

Genesis 15:5 (Genesis 22:17)
And he brought him forth abroad, and said, Look now toward heaven, and tell the stars, if thou be able to number them: and he said unto him, So shall thy seed be.

Hebrews 11:12
Therefore sprang there even of one, and him as good as dead, so man as the stars of the sky in multitude, and as the sand which is by the sea shore innumerable.

Romans 4:18
Who against hope believed in hope, that he might become the father of many nations, according to that which was spoken, So shall thy seed be.

****

Genesis 15:6 (Genesis 12:7, 13:15, 17:8, 48:4)
And he believed in the LORD; and he counted it to him for righteousness.

Acts 7:5
And he gave him none inheritance in it, no, not so much as to set his foot on: yet he promised that he would give it to him for a possession, and to his seed after him, when as yet he had no child.

Romans 4:3
For what saith the scripture? Abraham believed God, and it was counted unto him for righteousness.

Romans 4:9
Cometh this blessedness then upon the circumcision only, or upon the uncircumcision also? For we say that faith was reckoned to Abraham for righteousness.

Romans 4:22
And therefore it was imputed to him for righteousness.

Galatians 3:6
Even as Abraham believed God, and it was accounted to him for righteousness.

James 2:23
And the scripture was fulfilled which saith, Abraham believed God, and it was imputed unto him for righteousness: and he was call the Friend of God.

****

Genesis 15:13
And he said unto Abram, Know of a surety that thy seed shall be a stranger in a land that is not their's, and shall serve them; and they shall afflict them four hundred years.

Acts 7:6
And God spake on this wise, That his seed should sojourn in a strange land; and that they should bring them into bondage, and entreat them evil four hundred years.

****

Genesis 15:14
And also that nation, whom they shall serve, will I judge: and afterward shall they come out with great substance.

Acts 7:7
And the nation to whom they shall be in bondage will I judge, said God: and after that shall they come forth, and serve me in this place.

****

Genesis 17:5
Neither shall thy name any more be called Abram, but thy name shall be Abraham; for a father of many nations have I made thee.

Romans 4:17,18
(As it is written, I have made thee a father of many nations,) before him whom he believed, even God, who quickeneth the dead, and calleth those things which be not as though they were. Who against hope believed in hope, that he might become the father of many nations, according to that which was spoken, So shall thy seed be.

****

Genesis 17:8 (Genesis 12:7,13:15, 48:4)
And I will give unto thee, and to thy seed after thee, the land wherein thou art a stranger, all the land of Canaan, for an everlasting possession; and I will be their God.

Acts 7:5
And he gave him none inheritance in it, no, not so much as to set his foot on: yet he promised that he would give it to him for a possession, and to his seed after him, when as yet he had no child.

****

Genesis 18:10
And he said, I will certainly return unto thee according to the time of life; and, lo, Sarah thy wife shall have a son. And Sarah heard it in the tent door, which was behind him.

Romans 9:9
For this is the word of promise, At this time will I come, and Sarah shall have a son.

****

Genesis 21:10
Wherefore she said unto Abraham, Cast out this bondwoman and her son: for the son of this bondwoman shall not be heir with my son, even with Isaac.

Galatians 4:30
Nevertheless what saith the scripture? Cast out the bondwoman and her son: for the son of the bondwoman shall not be heir with he son of the freewoman.

****

Genesis 21:12
And God said unto Abraham, Let it not be grievous in thy sight because of the lad, and because of thy bondwoman; in all that Sarah hath said unto thee, hearken unto her voice; for in Isaac shall thy seed be called.

Romans 9:7
Neither, because they are the seed of Abraham, are they all children: but, in Isaac shall thy seed be called.

Hebrews 11:18
Of whom it was said, That in Isaac shall thy seed be called.

****

Genesis 22:17 (Genesis 15:5)
That in blessing I will bless thee, and in multiplying I will multiply thy seed as the stars of the heaven, and as the sand which is upon the sea shore; and thy seed shall possess the gate of his enemies.

Hebrews 6:14
Saying, Surely blessing I will bless thee, and multiplying I will multiply thee.

****

Genesis 22:18 (Genesis 12:3, 26:4, 28:14)
And in thy seed shall all the nations of the earth be blessed; because thou hast obeyed my voice.

Acts 3:25
Ye are the children of the prophets, and of the covenant which God made with our fathers, saying unto Abraham, And in thy seed shall all the kindreds of the earth be blessed.

Galatians 3:8
And the scripture, foreseeing that God would justify the heathen through faith, preached before the gospel unto Abraham, saying, in thee shall all nations be blessed.

****

Genesis 25:23
And the LORD said unto her, Two nations are in thy womb, and two manner of people shall be separated from thy bowels; and the one people shall be stronger than the other people; and the elder shall serve the younger.

Romans 9:12
It was said unto her, The elder shall serve the younger.

****

Genesis 26:4 (Genesis 12:3, 22:18, 28:14)
And I will make thy seed to multiply as the stars of heaven, and will give unto thy seed all these countries; and in thy seed shall all the nations of the earth be blessed.

Acts 3:25
Ye are the children of the prophets, and of the covenant which God made with our fathers, saying unto Abraham, And in thy seed shall all the kindreds of the earth be blessed.

Galatians 3:8
And the scripture, foreseeing that God would justify the heathen through faith, preached before the gospel unto Abraham, saying, in thee shall all nations be blessed.

****

Genesis 28:14 (Genesis 12:3, 22:18, 26:4)
And thy seed shall be as the dust of the earth, and thou shalt spread abroad to the west, and to the east, and to the north, and to the south: and in thee and in thy seed shall all the families of the earth be blessed.

Acts 3:25
Ye are the children of the prophets, and of the covenant which God made with our fathers, saying unto Abraham, And in thy seed shall all the kindreds of the earth be blessed.

Galatians 3:8
And the scripture, foreseeing that God would justify the heathen through faith, preached before the gospel unto Abraham, saying, in thee shall all nations be blessed.

****

Genesis 48:4 (Genesis 12:7, 13:15, 17:8)
And said unto me, Behold, I will make thee fruitful, and multiply thee, and I will make of thee a multitude of people; and will give this land to thy seed after thee for an everlasting possession.

Acts 7:5
And he gave him none inheritance in it, no, not so much as to set his foot on: yet he promised that he would give it to him for a possession, and to his seed after him, when as yet he had no child.

EXODUS

INTRODUCING THE LAW		
REDEMPTION FROM EGYPTIAN BONDAGE	**GOD REVEALS HIS LAWS**	**EVERYTHING HAS SPIRITUAL SIGNIFICANCE**
Bondage: **1** Deliverer: **2-4** Judgment: **5-10** The Passover: **11-13** Red Sea & Wilderness: **14-16**	The Holy Law: **19-24** 3 Parts of the Law: **20-24**	Tabernacle & priesthood: **25-40**
LOCATION: Egypt	Mount Sinai	Wilderness
OVERVIEW: Suffering of the Israelites in Egypt	God's holy plan for His people	Putting God's laws into action
TIME: 430 years	2 months	10 months

FAST FACTS

AUTHOR AND SETTING:

Moses; Egypt, wilderness, and desert

PURPOSE:

Exodus focuses on redemption and deliverance, paralleling the exciting history of the Israelites with the preparation for Christ's mission on earth.

SEEING JESUS:

There are no direct prophecies about Jesus in ***Exodus***, but His *person* was represented in several ways: (1) the Passover lamb; (2) the manna (Bread of Life); (3) our spiritual Rock; (4) our deliverer; (5) our sacrifice; and (6) our great high priest. Moses was a "type" of Christ in his leadership roles as prophet, priest, and king/ruler.

THEME VERSE:

Exodus 15:13

NOTES

EXODUS:
PASSOVER LAMB

NOTES

SEEING JESUS IN EXODUS

AUTHOR & SETTING

We know that Moses wrote the book of *Exodus* for a number of reasons: (1) Portions of *Exodus* are directly attributed to Moses - Exodus 24:3,4; (2) In the New Testament Philip credits Moses with writing *Exodus* - John 1:45; and (3) Jesus attributes Exodus 20:12 to Moses - Mark 7:10.

Exodus was no doubt written by Moses during the forty years of wilderness wanderings.

OVERVIEW

God gave His revelation progressively; in *Genesis* God introduced us to the covenant family of Abraham. *Exodus* tells the story of that family becoming a nation, being delivered from Egypt, and receiving God's law. "Family" is an important word to God! *Exodus* also tells us about the nation's ceremonies and worship.

The two most important chapters in this book are Exodus 12 and Exodus 20: the Passover and the law.

SEEING JESUS IN EXODUS

There are many foreshadowings of Jesus in *Exodus*:

"Now all these things happened unto them for ensamples: and they are written for our admonition, upon whom the ends of the world are come" **(I Corinthians 10:11)**

The Passover
"Purge out therefore the old leaven, that ye may be a new lump, as ye are unleavened. For even Christ our Passover is sacrificed for us" **(I Corinthians 5:7).**

The manna:
"And Jesus said unto them, I am the bread of life: he that cometh to me shall never hunger..." **(John 6:35).**

The water from the smitten rock:
"And did all drink the same spiritual drink: for they drank of that spiritual Rock that followed them: and that Rock was Christ" **(I Corinthians 10:4).**

The prophet:
"The LORD thy God will raise up unto thee a Prophet from the midst of thee, of thy brethren, like unto me; unto him ye shall hearken" **(Deuteronomy 18:15).**

Each of the seven feasts:
1. **Passover**
2. **Unleavened bread**
3. **First fruits**
4. **Pentecost**
5. **Trumpets**
6. **Day of Atonement**
7. **Tabernacle**

The High Priest:
"Seeing then that we have a great high priest, that is passed into the heavens, Jesus the Son of God, let us hold fast our profession. For we have not an high priest which cannot be touched with the feeling of our infirmities; but was in all points tempted like as we are, yet without sin. Let us therefore come boldly unto the throne of grace, that we may obtain mercy, and find grace to help in the time of need" **(Hebrews 4:14-16).**

"But Christ being come an high priest of good things to come, by a greater and more perfect tabernacle, not made with hands, that is to say, not of this building" **(Hebrews 9:11).**

NOTES

THEME VERSE

"Thou in thy mercy hast led forth the people which thou hast redeemed: thou hast guided them in they strength unto thy holy habitation" **(Exodus 15:13).**

OUTLINE

(Refer to maps on pages A3 and A6 in the APPENDIX)

I. **REDEMPTION FROM EGYPTIAN BONDAGE -** EXODUS 1-18

A. **Five Terms Are Used:**

1. **BONDAGE -** Exodus 1

a. The whole Bible is a story of deliverance.

b. Jesus is our deliverer:

i. *"Jesus answered them, Verily, Verily, I say unto you, whosoever committeth sin is the servant of sin. If the Son therefore shall make you free, ye shall be free indeed"* **(John 8:34,36).**

ii. *"But Christ being come an high priest of good things to come, by a greater and more perfect tabernacle, not made with hands, that is to say, not of this building; Neither by the blood of goats and calves, but by his own blood he entered in once into the holy place, having obtained eternal redemption for us"* **(Hebrews 9:11,12).**

2. **DELIVERER -** Exodus 2-4

a. Jesus, the deliverer, the I AM, introduced Himself to Moses and called him to be a deliverer:

i. *"And God said unto Moses, I AM THAT I AM: and he said, Thus shalt thou say unto thechildren of Israel, I AM hath sent me unto you"* **(Exodus 3:14).**

ii. *"By faith Moses, when he was come to years, refused to be called the son of Pharaoh's daughter; choosing rather to suffer affliction with the people*

NOTES

of God, than to enjoy the pleasures of sin for a season; esteeming the reproach of Christ greater riches that the treasures in Egypt: for he had respect unto the recompence of the reward" **(Hebrews 11:24-26).**

3. JUDGMENT - Exodus 5-10

a. God performed miracles of judgments on the gods of Egypt.

4. THE PASSOVER - Exodus 11-13

a. The slaying of the firstborn:

i. *"And ye shall keep it up until the fourteenth day of the same month: and the whole assembly of the congregation of Israel shall kill it in the evening. And they shall take of the blood, and strike it on the two side posts and on the upper door post of the houses, wherein they shall eat it"* **(Exodus 12:6, 7).**

ii. *"Purge out therefore the old leaven, that ye may be a new lump, as ye are unleavened. For even Christ our passover is sacrificed for us"* **(I Corinthians 5:7).**

iii. *"But with the precious blood of Christ, as of a lamb without blemish and without spot"* **(1 Peter 1:19).**

b. The blood applied:

i. *"And the blood shall be to you for a token upon the houses where ye are: and when I see the blood, I will pass over you, and the plague shall not be upon you to destroy you, when I smite the land of Egypt"* **(Exodus 12:13).**

ii. *"The next day John seeth Jesus coming unto him, and saith, Behold the Lamb of God which taketh away the sin of the world"* **(John 1:29).**

c. Ten Passovers in the Bible:

1. Egypt - Exodus 12
2. Wilderness - Numbers 9:5
3. Under Joshua - Joshua 5:10
4. Under Hezekiah - II Chronicles 30:13-22
5. Under Josiah - II Kings 23:21
6. Upon return from Babylon - Ezra 6:19
7. Jesus as a boy - Luke 2:41
8. First during Jesus' ministry - John 2:13
9. Second during Jesus' ministry - John 6:4
10. Last supper - Matthew 26:17

5. RED SEA AND WILDERNESS - Exodus 14-18

a. God took them through the Red Sea and gave them manna and water in the wilderness:

i. *"By faith they passed through the Red Sea as by dry land: which the Egyptians assaying to do were drowned"* **(Hebrews 11:29).**

ii. *"Our fathers did eat manna in the dessert; as it is written, He gave them bread from heaven to eat"* **(John 6:31).**

iii. *"And had rained down manna upon them to eat, and had given them of the corn of heaven"* **(Psalms 78:24).**

iv. *"The people asked, and he brought quails, and satisfied them with the bread of heaven"* **(Psalms 105:40).**

v. *"And did all drink the same spiritual drink: for they drank of that spiritual Rock that followed them: and that Rock was Christ"* **(I Corinthians 10:4).**

II. LAW - Exodus 19-2

A. The Law is Holy:

1. *"Wherefore the law is holy, and the commandment holy, and just, and good"* **(Romans 7:12).**

B. There Are Three Parts to the Law - (Exodus 20; Deuteronomy 5):

1. Judgments

2. Statutes

3. Ordinances

C. The Law of the Bondslave and Jesus:

1. *"Then his master shall bring him unto the judges; he shall also bring him to the door, or unto the door post; and his master shall bore his ear through with an aul; and he shall serve him for ever"* **(Exodus 21:6).**

D. Jesus Quoted From the Law:

1. *"Jesus said unto him, Thou shalt love the Lord thy God with all thy heart, and with all thy soul, and with all thy mind This is the first and great commandment. And the second is like unto it, Thou shalt love thy neighbour as thyself. On these two commandments hang all the law and the prophets"* **(Matthew 22:37-40).**

III. TABERNACLE AND PRIESTHOOD - EXODUS 25-40

A. Everything Had Spiritual Significance:

1. *"The Holy Ghost this signifying, that the way into the holiest of all was not yet made manifest, while as the first tabernacle was yet standing: which was a figure for the time then present, in which were offered both gifts and sacrifices, that could not make him that did the service perfect, as pertaining to the conscience; which stood only in meats and drinks, and divers washings, and carnal ordinances, imposed on them until the time of reformation. But Christ being come an high priest of good things to come, by a greater and more perfect tabernacle, not made with hands, that is to say, not of this building; Neither by the blood of goats and calves, but by his own blood he entered*

NOTES

NOTES

in once into the holy place, having obtained eternal redemption for us" **(Hebrews 9:8-12).**

B. Jesus Is Our Sacrifice and Great High Priest:

1. *"But this man (Jesus), because he continueth ever, hath an unchangeable priesthood"* **(Hebrews 7:24).**
2. **Moses The Intercessor and Jesus**

C. The Layout of the Furniture in the Tabernacle is in the Shape of a Cross.

EXODUS QUOTED IN THE NEW TESTAMENT.

Exodus 1:8
Now thee arose up a new king over Egypt, which knew not Joseph.

Acts 7:18
Till another king arose, which knew not Joseph.

****

Exodus 2:13-15 (Exodus 3:2)
And when he went out the second day, behold, two men of the Hebrews strove together: and he said to him that did the wrong, Wherefore smitest thou thy fellow? And he said, Who made thee a prince and a judge over us? intendest thou to kill me, as thou killedst the Egyptian? And Moses feared, and said, Surely this thing is known. Now when Pharaoh heard this thing, he sought to slay Moses. But Moses fled from the face of Pharaoh, and dwelt in the land of Midian: and he sat down by a well.

Acts 7:27-30
But he that did this neighbour wrong thrust him away, saying, Who made thee a ruler and a judge over us? Wilt thou kill me, as thou didst the Egyptian yesterday? Then fled Moses at this saying, and was a stranger in the land of Madian, where he begat two sons. And when forty years were expired, there appeared to him in the wilderness of mount Sina an angel of the Lord in a flame of fire in a bush.

Acts 7:35
This Moses whom they refused, saying, Who made thee a ruler and a judge? the same did God send to be a ruler and a deliverer by the hand of the angel which appeared to him in a bush.

****

Exodus 2:14
And he said, Who made thee a prince and a judge over us? intendest thou to kill me, as thou killedst the Egyptian? And Moses feared, and said, Surely this thing is known.

Acts 7:27
But he that did his neighbour wrong thrust him away, saying, Who made thee a ruler and a judge over us?

Acts 7:35
This Moses whom they refused, saying, Who made thee a ruler and a judge? the same did God send to be a ruler and a deliverer by the hand of the angel which appeared to him in a bush.

****

Exodus 3:2 (Exodus 2:13-15)
And the angel of the LORD appeared unto him in a flame of fire out of the midst of a bush: and he looked, and behold, the bush burned with fire, and the bush was not consumed.

Acts 7:27-30
But he that did this neighbour wrong thrust him away, saying, Who made thee a ruler and a judge over us? Wilt thou kill me, as thou didst the Egyptian yesterday? Then fled Moses at this saying, and was a stranger in the land of Madian, where he begat two sons. And when forty years were expired, there appeared to him in the wilderness of mount Sina an angel of the Lord in a flame of fire in a bush.

Acts 7:35
This Moses whom they refused, saying, Who made thee a ruler and a judge? the same did God send to be a ruler and a deliverer by the hand of the angel which appeared to him in a bush.
****

Exodus 3:5, 7, 8, 10
And he said, Draw not nigh hither: put off thy shoes from off thy feet, for the place wheron thou standest is holy ground. And the LORD said, I have surely seen the affliction of my people which are in Egypt, and have heard their cry by reason of their taskmasters; for I know their sorrows; And I am come down to deliver them out of the hand of the Egyptians, and to bring them up out of that land unto a good land and a large, unto a land flowing with milk and honey; unto the place of the Canaanites, and the Hittites, and the Amorites, and the Perizzites, and the Hivites, and the Jebusites. Come now therefore, and I will send thee unto Pharaoh, that thou mayest bring forth my people the children of Israel out of Egypt.

Acts 7:33-34
Then said the Lord to him, Put off thy shoes from thy feet: for the place where thou standest is holy ground. I have seen, I have seen the affliction of my people, which is in Egypt, and I have heard their groaning, and am come down to deliver them. And now come, I will send thee into Egypt.

****

Exodus 3:6 (Exodus 3:15)
Moreover he said, I am the God of thy father, the God of Abraham, the God of Isaac, and the God of Jacob. And Moses hid his face; for he was afraid to look upon God.

Matthew 22:32
I am the God of Abraham, and the God of Isaac, and the God of Jacob? God is not the God of the dead, but of the living.

Mark 12:26
And as touching the dead, that they rise: have ye not read in the book of Moses, how in the bush God spake unto him, saying, I am the God of Abraham, and the God of Isaac, and the God of Jacob?

Luke 20:37
Now that the dead are raised, even Moses shewed at the bush, when he calleth the Lord the God of Abraham, and the God of Isaac, and the God of Jacob.

Acts 7:32
Saying, I am the God of thy fathers, the God of Abraham, and the God of Isaac, and the God of Jacob. Then Moses trembled, and durst not behold.

****

Exodus 3:12
And he said, Certainly I will be with thee; and this shall be a token unto thee, that I have sent thee: When thou hast brought forth the people out of Egypt, ye shall serve God upon this mountain.

Acts 7:7
And the nation to whom they shall be in bondage will I judge, said God: and after that shall they come forth, and serve me in this place.

****

Exodus 3:15 (Exodus 3:6)
And God said moreover unto Moses, Thus shalt thou say unto the children of Israel, The Lord God of your fathers, the God of Abraham, the God of Isaac, and the God of Jacob, hath sent me unto you: this is my name for ever, and this is my memorial unto all generations.

Matthew 22:32
I am the God of Abraham, and the God of Isaac, and the God of Jacob? God is not the God of the dead, but of the living.

Mark 12:26
And as touching the dead, that they rise: have ye not read in the book of Moses, how in the bush God spake unto him, saying, I am the God of Abraham, and the God of Isaac, and the God of Jacob?

Luke 20:37
Now that the dead are raised, even Moses shewed at the brush, when he calleth the Lord the God of Abraham, and the God of Isaac, and the God of Jacob.

Acts 7:32
Saying, I am God of thy fathers, the God of Abraham, and the God of Isaac, and the God of Jacob. Then Moses trembled, and durst not behold

****

Exodus 9:16
And in very deed for this cause have I raised thee up, for to shew in thee my power; and that my name may be declared throughout all the earth.

Romans 9:17
For the scripture saith unto Pharaoh, Even for this same purpose have I raised thee up, that I might shew my power in thee, and that my name might be declared throughout all the earth.

****

Exodus 12:46 (Numbers 9:12; Psalms 34:20).
In one house shall it be eaten; thou shalt not carry forth ought of the flesh abroad out of the house; neither shall ye break a bone thereof.

John 19:36
For these things were done, that the scripture should be fulfilled, A bone of him shall not be broken.
Exodus 13:2 (Exodus 13:12,15; Numbers 3:13, 8:17)
Sanctify unto me all the firstborn, whatsoever openeth the womb among the children of Israel, both of man and of beast: it is mine.

Exodus 13:2 (Exodus 13:12,15; Numbers 3:13, 8:17)
Sanctify unto me all the firstborn, whatsoever openeth the womb among the children of Israel, both of man and of beast: it is mine.

Luke 2:23
(As it is written in the law of the Lord, Every male that openeth the womb shall be called holy to the Lord.)

****

Exodus 13:12,15 (Exodus 13:2; Numbers 3:13, 8:17)
That thou shalt set apart unto the LORD all that openeth the matrix, and every firstling that cometh of a beast which thou hast; the males shall be the LORD'S. And it came to pass, when Pharoah would hardly let us go, that the LORD slew all the firstborn in the land of Egypt, both the firstborn of man, and the firstborn of beast: therefore I sacrifice to the LORD all that openeth the matrix, being males; but all the firstborn of my children I redeem.

Luke 2:23
(As it is written in the law of the Lord, Every male that openeth the womb shall be called holy to the Lord.)

****

Exodus 16:4,15 (Psalms 78:24; Nehemiah 9:15)
Then said the LORD unto Moses, Behold, I will rain bread from heaven for you; and the people shall go out and gather a certain rate every day, that I may prove them, whether they will walk in my law, or no. And when the children of Israel saw it, they said one to another, It is manna: for they wist not what it was. And Moses said unto them, This is the bread which the LORD hath given you to eat.

John 6:31
Our fathers did eat manna in the desert; as it is written, He gave them bread from heaven to eat.

****

Exodus 16:18
And when they did mete it with an omer, he that gathered much had nothing over, and he that gathered little had no lack; they gathered every man according to his eating.

II Corinthians 8:15
As it is written, He that had gathered much had nothing over; and he that had gathered little had no lack.

****

Exodus 19:5,6 (Isaiah 43:20:21)
Now therefore, if ye will obey my voice indeed, and keep my covenant, then ye shall be a peculiar treasure unto me above all people: for all the earth is mine: And ye shall be unto me a kingdom of priests, and an holy nation. These are the words which thou shall speak unto the children of Israel.

I Peter 2:9
But ye are a chosen generation, a royal priesthood, an holy nation, a peculiar people; that ye should shew forth the praises of him who hath called you out of darkness into his marvelous light.

****

Exodus 19:12,13
And thou shalt set bounds unto the people round about, saying, Take heed to yourselves, that ye go not up into the mount, or touch the border of it: whosoever toucheth the mount shall be surely put to death: There shall not a hand touch it, but he shall surely be stoned, or shot through whether it be beast or man, it shall not live: when the trumpet soundeth long, they shall come up to the mount.

Hebrews 12:20
(For they could not endure that which was commanded, And if so much as a beast touch the mountain, it shall be stoned, or thrust through with a dart.)

****

Exodus 20:11 (Psalms 146:6)
For in six days the LORD made heaven and earth, the sea, and all that in them is, and rested the seventh day: wherefore the LORD blessed the Sabbath day, and hallowed it.

Acts 4:24
And when they heard that, they lifted up their voice to God with one accord, and said, Lord, thou art God, which hast made heaven, and earth, and the sea, and all that in them is.

Acts 14:15
And saying, Sirs, why do ye these things? We also are men of like passions with you, and preach unto you that ye should turn from these vanities unto the living God, which made heaven, and earth and the sea, and all things that are therein.

Revelation 10:6
And sware by him that liveth forever and ever, who created heaven, and by the things that therein are, and the earth, and the things that therein are, and the sea, and the things which are therein, that there should be time no longer.

****

Exodus 20:12
Honor thy father and thy mother: that thy days may be long upon the land which the LORD thy God giveth thee.

Matthew 15:4
For God commanded, saying, Honour thy father and mother: and, He that curseth father or mother, let him die the death.

Matthew 19:19
Honour thy father and thy mother: and, Thou shalt love thy neighbour as thyself.

Mark 7:10
For Moses said, Honour thy father and thy mother; and, Whoso curseth father or mother, let him die the death.

Mark 10:19
Thou knowest the commandments, Do not commit adultery, Do not kill, Do not steal, Do not bear false witness, Defraud not, Honour thy father and mother.

Luke 18:20
Thou knowest the commandments, Do not commit adultery, Do not kill, Do not steal, Do not bear false witness, Honour thy father and thy mother.

Ephesians 6:2,3
Honour thy father and mother; which is the first commandment with promise; That it may be well with thee, and thou mayest live long on the earth.

James 2:8,11
If ye fulfill the royal law according to the scripture, Thou shalt love thy neighbour as thyself, ye do well. For he that said, Do not commit adultery, said also, Do not kill. Now if thou commit no adultery, yet if thou kill, thou art become a transgressor of the law.

****

Exodus 20:13-16 (Deuteronomy 5:16-18)
Thou shalt not kill. Thou shalt not commit adultery. Thou shalt no steal. Thou shalt not bear false witness against thy neighbour.

Matthew 5:21, 27, 43
Ye have heard that it was said by them of old time, Thou shalt not kill; and whosoever shall kill shall be in danger of the judgment: Ye have heard that it was said by them of old time, Thou shalt not commit adultery: Ye have heard it hath been said, Thou shalt love thy neighbour, and hate thine enemy.

Matthew 19:18, 19
He saith unto him, Which? Jesus said, Thou shalt do no murder, Thou shalt not commit adultery, Thou shalt not steal, Thou shalt not bear false witness, Honour thy father and thy mother: and, Thou shalt love thy neighbour as thyself.

Mark 10:19
Thou knowest the commandments, Do not commit adultery, Do not kill, Do not steal, Do not bear false witness, Defraud not, Honour thy father and mother.

Luke 18:20
Thou knowest the commandments, Do not commit adultery, Do not kill, Do not steal, Do not bear false witness, Honour thy father and thy mother.

Romans 13:9
For this, Thou shalt not commit adultery, Thou shalt not kill, Thou shalt not steal, Thou shalt not bear false witness, Thou halt not covet; and if there be any other commandment, it is briefly comprehended in this saying, namely Thou shalt love thy neighbour as thyself.

****

Exodus 20:17 (Deuteronomy 5:21)
Thou shalt not covet thy neighbour's house, thou shalt not covet thy neighbour's wife, nor his manservant, nor his maidservant, nor his ox, nor his ass, nor any thing that is thy neighbour's.

Romans 7:7
What shall we say then? Is the law sin? God forbid. Nay, I had not known sin, but by the law: for I had not known lust, except the law had said, Thou shalt not covet.

Romans 13:9
For this, Thou shalt not commit adultery, Thou shalt not kill, Thou shalt not steal, Thou shalt not bear false witness. Thou shalt not covet; and if there by any other commandment, it is briefly comprehended in this saying, namely, Thou shalt love thy neighbour as thyself.

****

Exodus 21:17
And he that curseth his father, or his mother, shall surely be put to death.

Matthew 15:4
For God commanded saying, Honour thy father and mother and, He that curseth father or mother, let him die the death.

Mark 7:10
For Moses said, Honour thy father and thy mother; and, Whoso curseth father or mother, let him die the death.

****

Exodus 21:24 (Leviticus 24:20; Deuteronomy 19:21)
Eye for eye, tooth for tooth, hand for hand, foot for foot.

Matthew 5:38
Ye have heard that it hath been said, An eye for an eye and a tooth for a tooth.

****

Exodus 22:28
Thou shalt not revile the gods, nor curse the ruler of thy people.

Acts 23:5
Then said Paul I wist not, brethren, that he was the high priest; for it is written, Thou shalt not speak evil of the ruler of thy people.

****

Exodus 24:8
And Moses took the blood, and sprinkled it on the people, and said, Behold the blood of the covenant, which the LORD hath made with you concerning all these words.

Hebrews 9:20
Saying, This is the blood of the testament which God hath enjoined unto you.

****

Exodus 25:40
And look that thou make them after their pattern, which was shewed thee in the mount.

Hebrews 8:5
Who serve unto the example, and shadow of heavenly things as Moses was admonished of God when he was about to make the tabernacle for See, saith he, that thou make all things according to the pattern shewed to thee in the mount.

****

Exodus 32:1
And when the people saw that Moses delayed to come down out of the mount, the people gathered themselves together unto Aaron, and said unto him, Up, make us gods, which shall go before us; for as for this Moses, the man that brought us up out of the land of Egypt, we wot not what is become of him.

Acts 7:40
Saying unto Aaron, Make us gods to go before us; for as for this Moses, which brought us out of the land of Egypt, we wot not what is become of him.

****

Exodus 32:6
And they rose up early on the morrow, and offered burnt offerings, and brought peace offerings; and the people sat down to eat and to drink, and rose up to play.

I Corinthians 10:7
Neither be ye idolaters, as were some of them; as it is written, The people sat down to eat and drink, and rose up to play.

****

Exodus 32:23 (Exodus 32:1)
For they said unto me, Make us gods, which shall go before us: for as for this Moses, the man that brought us up out of the land of Egypt, we wot not what is become of him.

Acts 7:40
Saying unto Aaron, Make us gods to go before us; for as for this Moses, which brought us out of the land of Egypt, we wot not what is become of him.

****

Exodus 33:19
And he said, I will make all my goodness pass before thee, and I will proclaim the name of the LORD before thee: and will be gracious to whom I will be gracious, and will shew mercy on whom I shew mercy.

Romans 9:15
For he saith to Moses, I will have mercy on whom I will have mercy, and I will have compassion on whom I will have compassion.

LEVITICUS

APPROACH TO GOD			
SACRIFICE & PRIESTHOOD	**CEREMONIAL CLEANSING**	**HOLINESS OF GOD'S PEOPLE**	**SACRED SEASONS & VOWS**
Sacrifices: **1-7** Priesthood: **8-10**	Food: **11** Mothers: **12** Leprosy: **13,14** Body issues: **15** Day of Atonement: **16**	Setting apart: **17** Moral Conduct: **18-20** Priests & Offerings: **21,22**	Feasts & Seasons: **23-27**
LOCATION: Camped at the foot of Mt. Sinai			
OVERVIEW: Sacrifice is the basis of all true worship	Distinguishing between right & wrong, good & bad	Holiness is morality & separation from evil	Checkpoints in the path to holiness
TIME: 1 month			

FAST FACTS

AUTHOR AND SETTING:

Moses; camped at the foot of Mount Sinai

PURPOSE:

The theme of *Leviticus* is learning to live in relationship with the holy God Himself. But to obtain holiness man was required to perform sacrifices for the covering of his sins.

SEEING JESUS:

Jesus is represented in many ways in *Leviticus*: (1) as each of the five sacrifices; (2) as a priest - frequently compared to Aaron, the first High Priest; and (3) as the fulfillment of the feats and festivals..

THEME VERSE:

Leviticus 19:2

NOTES

LEVITICUS:
THE HIGH PRIEST

NOTES

SEEING JESUS IN LEVITICUS

AUTHOR & SETTING

Jesus told us that Moses was the author of *Leviticus* when He commanded the cleansed leper to *"...offer the gift that Moses commanded, ..."* (Matthew 8:4). This is a reference to *Leviticus* 13. Moses probably wrote this book while the Israelites were camped at the foot of Mt. Sina

OVERVIEW

Leviticus is not the Hebrew title assigned to this third book of the Pentateuch. The original title is *Wayyiqra*, meaning "he called," and is the first word of the Hebrew text. The Greek Septuagint called this book *Leuitikon*, meaning "that which pertains to the priests," and from this the Latin Vulgate derived *Leviticus*. The book of *Leviticus* is especially powerful because it is the book that teaches us how to approach God. The New Testament book of Hebrews quotes much from *Leviticus*.

In this book there are laws that deal with sacrifices. A sacrifice is the basis of all true worship. Man is guilty and unclean. He needs a sacrifice to free him from his guilt and to cleanse away his defilement. First God got Israel out of Egypt; now God is getting Egypt out of Israel!

SEEING JESUS IN LEVITICUS

Jesus is seen in the five sacrifices, the seven feasts, and the priesthood:

THERE WERE FIVE SACRIFICES:

The whole burnt offering (Leviticus 1:1-17, 6:8-13). This was an individual expression of devotion, thanksgiving, and worship. The burnt offering met the needs of a redeemed people, and it was their approach to the Savior. This sacrifice could consist of a bull, sheep, goat, pigeon, or turtledove. It speaks to us of Christ's total commitment to give Himself for us.

The meal offering (Leviticus 2:1-16, 6:14-23). This was a voluntary offering of thanksgiving, and it could be offered as fine flour or cooked into bread or wafers. It was something that man had done; grain required man's diligent cultivation. By this act the offerer acknowledged that his benefits came from and through the aid and goodness of God. Jesus became poor that we might be rich; He offered Himself.

The peace offering (Leviticus 3:1-17, 7:11-38). This was an offering of a consecrated sacrificial animal which the people joyfully ate together. Their celebration declared, "We have peace with God." The peace offering was food for the priest and the worshiper. This sacrifice represents

Christ Who was the sacrificial victim for our salvation as well as the source of our spiritual sustenance

"And as they were eating, Jesus took bread, and blessed it, and brake it, and gave it to the disciples, and said, Take, eat; this is my body" **(Matthew 26:26).**

By daily feeding on the Word of Christ, we live and grow into life eternal, and we experience His peace.

The sin offering (Leviticus 41-5, 13,14, 6:24-30). The sin offering was required because man had sinned. Man's forgiveness involved his repentance and his reliance upon an atonement. When we repent, we have to trust in Christ's atonement. The purpose of the sin offering was to restore the priest, the congregation, the ruler, and the common man. Jesus Christ is our effectual sin offering. We have boldness, therefore, to enter into the holy place by the blood of Jesus.

The trespass offering (Leviticus 5:14-6:7, 7:1-10). The trespass offering had two sections: it was for a trespass against the Lord or a trespass against man. This sacrifice was always a ram of the flock. Jesus shed His blood that we might be reconciled to God and reconciled to one another when we trespass against each other.

THERE WERE SEVEN FEAST DAYS:

Passover: This was strictly a family feast held in the homes of the people. Aliens, travelers, or hired servants could participate. Originally, the Israelites killed a lamb and applied the blood to the doors of their homes so that the death angel would pass over their houses. Christ is our Passover Lamb (I Corinthians 5:7). This feast shows the power of the *lamb* for deliverance from death.

Unleavened bread: For seven days no leaven was permitted in the house of the Israelites. Leaven is a symbol of corruption. That's why Paul told the Corinthians to purge out the leaven (I Corinthians 5:1-8). Jesus was without spot and without sin; He had no leaven.

First fruits: This observance involved the bringing of the first sheaves of grain to the priest who would wave it before the Lord and offer burnt offerings with meal and drink offerings. It symbolized that the whole harvest belonged to the Lord. Our first fruits belong to God. Jesus was the first fruit - He was the first to arise from the dead. Death could not hold Him because He was sinless.

Pentecost: This prefigured the ministry of the Holy Spirit. This feast was marked by the offering of raised bread such as we eat daily, and the priest also waved these loaves before the Lord. We are reminded of Jesus Who came to be among us, providing us with daily bread from heaven for

NOTES

NOTES

our spiritual sustenance. He then returned to heaven and sent the Holy Spirit to us.

Trumpets: The trumpet is often used to symbolize the voice of God. This is symbolic of the trumpet which will be blown at the return of Jesus Christ.

Day of Atonement: The Day of Atonement was extremely important. It was nine days after the Hebrew New Year and was the most solemn day of all. It was to be a day of fasting - a day of humbling one's self before God for all of Israel. Israel was a separated people showing forth the complete salvation God provided through Jesus Christ. Jesus is our atonement. Detailed instructions were given in Leviticus 16 for the observance of this day.

Tabernacles: Two weeks after the Day of Atonement, the Israelites began a weeklong celebration known as the Feast of Tabernacles. During this feast the people dwelt in the fields in tabernacles or booths to celebrate the fact that God had brought them through the wilderness into their own land. It was a joyous time. This celebration allows us to look ahead to Jesus' coming back as the One Who was pierced for us in the Day of Atonement and as the One Who will live among us.

The priesthood: The priesthood was established in *Leviticus.* Originally God wanted the entire nation to be priests. The priesthood was eventually comprised of the tribe of Lev Chapter nine shows how the Levites began their ministry and also how they received their instructions and requirements for offering sacrifices for themselves as well as for the people. Following instructions brought God's blessings. They were to distinguish between the clean and the unclean. Jesus is our high priest:

"Seeing then that we have a great high priest, that is passed into the heavens, Jesus the Son of God, let us hold fast our profession. For we have not an high priest which cannot be touched with the feeling of our infirmities; but was in all points tempted like as we are, yet without sin. Let us therefore come boldly unto the throne of grace, that we may obtain mercy, and find grace to help in time of need" **(Hebrews 4:14-16).**

"But Christ being come an high priest of good things to come, by a greater and more perfect tabernacle, not made with hands, that is to say, not of this building" **(Hebrews 9:11).**

THEME VERSE

"Speak unto all the congregation of the children of Israel, and say unto them, Ye shall be holy: for I the Lord your God am holy" **(Leviticus 19:2).**

OUTLINE

(Refer to maps on pages A3 and A6 in the APPENDIX)

I. **APPROACH TO GOD -** LEVITICUS 1-10

A. **Two Essentials to Approach - Sacrifice and Priesthood**

1. **Sacrifices -** Leviticus 1-7
2. **Priesthood -** Leviticus 8-10
   a. Blood on priests' ear, thumb, toe - Leviticus 8:23
3. **Jesus is the offering and offerer.**

B. **Five Offerings - Burnt, Meal, Peace, Sin, Trespass**

1. **Four are animal sacrifices -** Hebrews 10:1-14
2. **They symbolize the work of Jesus Christ.**
3. **Christ is our high priest, and we are a royal priesthood:**
   a. *"But ye are a chosen generation, a royal priesthood, an holy nation, a peculiar people; that ye should shew forth the praises of him who hath called out of darkness into his marvelous light"* **(I Peter 2:9).**
4. **You cannot worship apart from the altar (Christ our sacrifice) -** Abihu and Nadab - Leviticus 10.

II. **CEREMONIAL CLEANSING -** LEVITICUS 11-16

A. **God Teaches His People How to Make a Distinction.**

1. **Cleansing of food -** Leviticus 11
2. **Cleansing in motherhood -** Leviticus 12
3. **Cleansing of leprosy -** Leviticus 13,14
4. **Cleansing of bodily issues -** Leviticus 15
5. **National cleansing - Day of Atonement -** Leviticus 16
   a. Key chapter in the Bible
   b. "Scapegoat" in the Hebrew is azazel. It is taken from the Hebrew: aze (goat) and azal (depart).

III. **HOLINESS OF GODS PEOPLE -** LEVITICUS 17:22

1. ***Holiness* Means "To Set Apart."**
2. **God's Standard of Moral Conduct -** Leviticus 18-20
3. **Separation of Priests and Offering -** Leviticus 21,22

IV. **SACRED SEASONS AND VOWS -** LEVITICUS 23-27

1. **Leviticus 23 Lists Feasts and Sacred Seasons.**
2. **The Day of Atonement was a fast.**
3. **Jubilee -** Leviticus 25:1-7
   a. Jesus is our jubilee!

NOTES

LEVITICUS QUOTED IN THE NEW TESTAMENT

Leviticus 11:44 (Leviticus 19:2, 20:7)
For I am the LORD your God: ye shall therefore sanctify yourselves, and ye shall be holy; for I am holy: neither shall ye defile yourselves with any manner of creeping thing that creepeth upon the earth.

I Peter 1:16
Because it is written, Be ye holy; for I am holy.

****

Leviticus 12:8
And if she be not able to bring a lamb, then she shall bring two turtles, or two young pigeons: the one for the burnt offering, and the other for a sin offering: and the priest shall make an atonement for her, and she shall be clean.

Luke 2:24
And to offer a sacrifice according to that which is said in the law of the Lord, A pair of turtledoves, or two young pigeons.

****

Leviticus 18:5
Ye shall therefore keep my statutes, and my judgments: which if a man do, he shall live in them: I am the LORD.

Galatians 3:12
And the law is not of faith: but, The man that doeth them shall live in them.

****

Leviticus 19:2 (Leviticus 11:44, 20:7)
Speak unto all the congregation of the children of Israel, and say unto them, Ye shall be holy: for I the LORD your God am holy.

I Peter 1:16
Because it is written: Be ye holy; for I am holy.

****

Leviticus 19:12 (Numbers 30:2, Deuteronomy 23:21)
And ye shall not swear by my name falsely, neither shalt thou profane the name of thy God: I am the LORD.

Matthew 5:33
Again, ye have heard that it hath been said by them of old time, Thou shalt not forswear thyself, but shalt perform unto the Lord thine oaths.

****

Leviticus 19:18
Thou shalt not avenge nor bear any grudge against the children of thy people, but thou shalt love thy neighbour as thyself: I am the LORD.

Matthew 5:43
Ye have heard that it hath been said, Thou shalt love thy neighbour, and hate thine enemy.

Matthew 19:19
Honour thy father and thy mother: and, Thou shalt love thy neighbour as thyself.

Matthew 22:39
And the second is like unto it, Thou shalt love thy neighbour as thyself.

Mark 12:31, 33
And the second is like, namely this, Thou shalt love thy neighbour as thyself. There is none other commandment greater than these. And to love him with all the heart, and with all the understanding, and with all the soul, and with all the strength, and to love his neighbour as himself, is more than all whole burnt offerings and sacrifices.

Luke 10:27
And he answering said, Thou shalt love the Lord thy God with all thy heart, and with all thy soul, and with all thy strength, and with all thy mind; and thy neighbour as thyself.

Romans 13:9
For this, Thou shalt not commit adultery, Thou shalt not kill, Thou shalt not steal, Thou shalt not bear false witness, Thou shalt not covet; and if there be any other commandment, it is briefly comprehended in this saying, namely, Thou shalt love thy neighbour as thyself.

Galatians 5:14
For all the law is fulfilled in one word, seen in this; Thou shalt love thy neighbour as thyself.

James 2:8
If ye fulfill the royal law according to the scripture, Thou shalt love thy neighbour as thyself, ye do well.

****

Leviticus 20:7 (Leviticus 11:44; Leviticus 19:2)
Sanctify yourselves therefore, and be ye holy: for I am the LORD your God.

I Peter 1:16
Because it is written, Be ye holy; for I am holy.

****

Leviticus 24:20 (Exodus 21:24; Deuteronomy 19:21)
Breach for breach, eye for eye, tooth for tooth; as he hath caused a blemish in a man, so shall it be done to him again.

Matthew 5:38
Ye have heard that it hath been said, An eye for an eye, and a tooth for a tooth.

****

Leviticus 26:12
And I will walk among you, and will be your God, and ye shall be my people.

II Corinthians 6:16
And what agreement hath the temple of God with idols? for ye are the temple of the living God; as God hath said, I will dwell in them, and walk in them; and I will be their God, and they shall be my people.

NUMBERS

WANDERING THROUGH THE WILDERNESS		
FROM SINAI TO KADESH-BARNES	**FROM KADESH THROUGH WILDERNESS & BACK**	**HOLINESS OF GOD'S PEOPLE**
The faithless generation: **1-12**	Sin & Rebellion: **13-19**	The next Generation: **20-36**
LOCATION: Sinai / Kadesh-barnea / Moab		
OVERVIEW: Disobedience produces penalties	Wanderings are the result of sin	The death of a generation
TIME: 40 years		

FAST FACTS

AUTHOR AND SETTING:

Moses; the wilderness

PURPOSE:

The Israelites learned about the consequences of disbelief and disobedience to God. Their sins condemned an entire generation. Two census of the Israelites were taken here: the first to organize themselves after their years of slavery; the second to prepare them for battle.

SEEING JESUS:

A picture of the Crucifixion is clearly seen in the bronze serpent on the stake (21:4-9). Jesus is also seen as the rock which quenched thirst (20:11); as the sacrificial "red heifer" (19); and as the Bread of Life (manna - 11:6)

THEME VERSE:

Numbers 6:27

NOTES

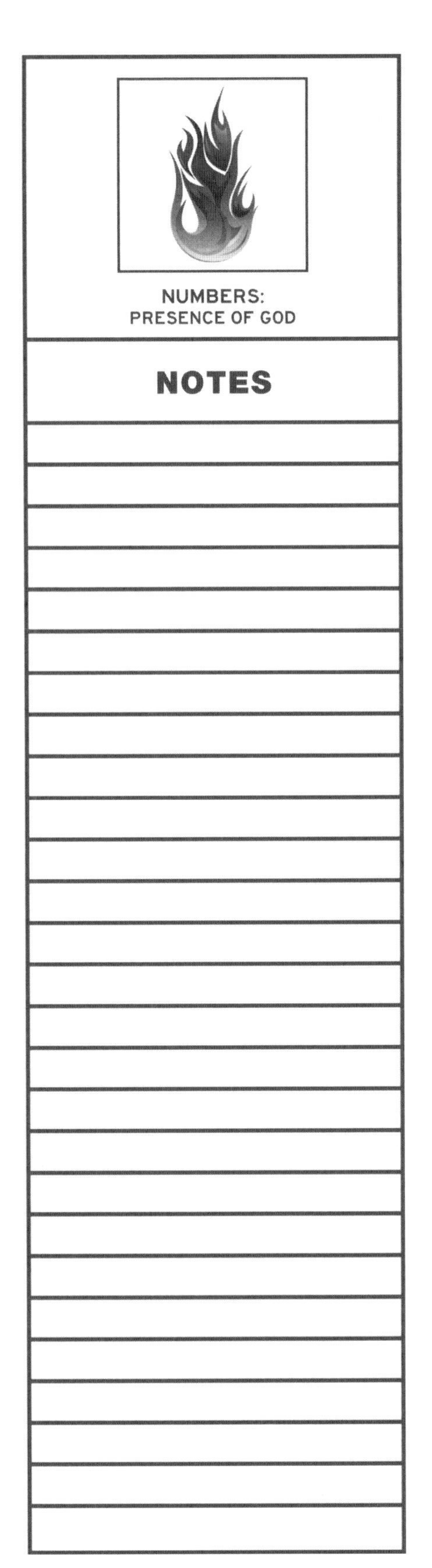

SEEING JESUS IN NUMBERS

AUTHOR AND SETTING

It is obvious by now that Moses wrote the entire Pentateuch - the first five books of the Bible. Numbers 33:2 is the clearest testimony of Moses' authorship of *Numbers*. It was no doubt written during the Israelites' forty years of wilderness wanderings.

OVERVIEW

Numbers takes its name from the two numberings or censuses taken of the Israelites in chapters 1 and 26. It has been called the Book of Divine Discipline.

The central location of events in the book is Kadesh-barnea. This is the great camping place after Sinai just before the attempt to enter the Holy Land.

The census in chapter 1 was taken the second year, the second month after leaving Egypt. It was taken to let the Israelites know exactly who they were, where they were, and what tribes had what numbers. It was a very important census after their long stay in Egypt as slaves.

The Hebrew name for *Numbers* is "in the wilderness." The Israelites spent 38 years in the wilderness.

There have been some who call this the book of murmuring. It is easy to see why when we read this book and even other parts of the Bible:

"Thou carriest them away as with a flood; they are as a sleep: in the morning they are like grass which groweth up. In the morning it flourisheth, and groweth up; in the evening it is cut down, and withereth. For we are consumed by thine anger, and by thy wrath are we troubled. Thou hast set our iniquities before thee, our secret sins in the light of thy countenance. For all our days are passed away in thy wrath: we spend our years as a tale that is told. The days of our years are threescore years and ten; and if by reason of strength they be fourscore years, yet is their strength labour and sorrow: for it is soon cut off, and we fly away **(Psalms 90:5-10).**

Psalms 90 and 91 were penned by Moses, and they certainly reflect the Israelites' circumstances during this time.

The first numbering was simply a census so they knew how many there were. The second numbering was for war and land allotment. Also, there was a second Passover (Numbers 9:1-14); if, through absence or ceremonial uncleanness, they could not eat the first Passover, the law provided for eating it a month later.

HERE IS A DIGEST OF THE ORDER OF THE MARCH:

1. The cloud lifts from the Tabernacle (Numbers 10:11). Aaron steps out and says, *"The LORD bless thee, and keep thee: The LORD make his face shine upon thee, and be gracious unto*

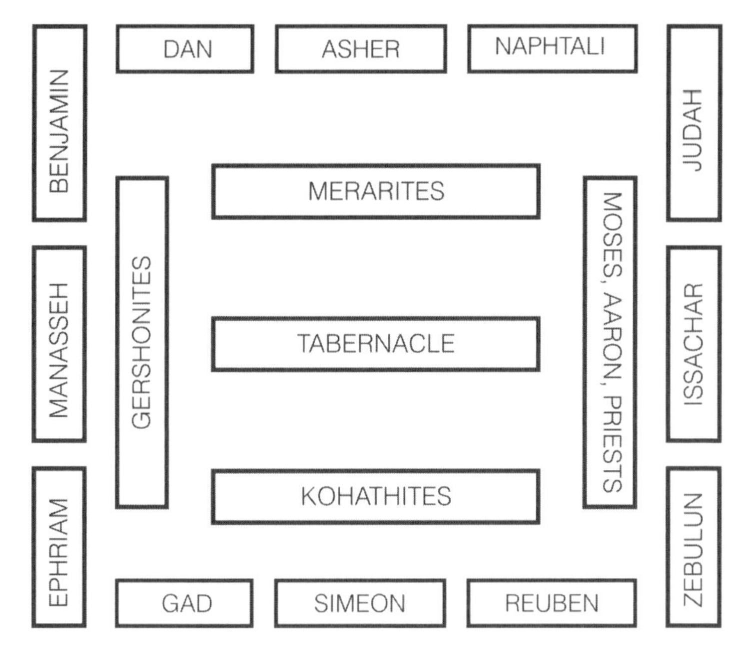

thee: The LORD lift up his countenance upon thee, and give thee peace" **(Numbers 6:24-26).**

This came at the time of the morning sacrifice. The name of Jehovah was put on the people. The divine signal was given - the cloud moved; the human signal was given - the trumpets blew.

2. The order of the march: Judah, Issachar, Zebulun, Reuben, Simeon, Gad, Ephraim, Manasseh, Benjamin, Dan, Asher, and Naphtal

3. Aaron went into the Holy of Holies and covered the Ark of the Covenant. Aaron and his sons covered up every one of the holy things in a prescribed way.

4. The Gershonites, part of the tribe of the Levites, took charge of the curtains. They had wagons with two oxen, each to help carry luggage.

5. Then Eleazar and Ithamar took charge of the sacred oil and special things of that kind.

6. Then the Merarites took down the heavy parts of the tent and carried them on wagons pulled by oxen.

7. Next the Kohathites came and took what Aaron had covered. Four men took the Ark. It was kept directly under the cloud:

"And they departed from the mount of the LORD three days' journey: and the ark of the covenant of the LORD went before them in the three days' journey, to search out a resting place for them" **(Numbers 10:33)**

Next Moses said, *"...Rise up, LORD, and let thine enemies be scattered; and let them that hate thee flee before thee"* **(Numbers 10:35).**

NOTES

NOTES

8. Moses and Aaron followed the Ark with trumpets blowing. Judah was on the east, with Issachar and Zebulun following with 186,000 armored men. The Gershonites and Merarites followed.

9. Then the trumpets blew a second alarm, and the tribes on the south side, Reuben, Gad, and Simeon, with an army of 151,450 men, rode after them. The Kohathites followed with the holy things. Eleazar, Ithamar, and the sons of Aaron led.

10. The third trumpet alarm blew, and a crowd on the west moved. These were Ephraim, Manasseh, and Benjamin with a total of 108,600 men.

11. The trumpet blew for the north, and Dan, Naphtali, and Asher moved.

12. The Israelites stopped when the cloud stopped. God was the captain of this expedition. When the Ark stopped, Moses and Aaron stopped.

13. Judah took its position on the east. The Gershonites and Merarites came with the curtains and set up the poles. The people never saw the sacred things.

14. Then out marched Reuben's corps and camped on the south. The Kohathites placed the furniture in the Tabernacle.

15. On the west, Ephraim, Manasseh, and Benjamin camped.

16. On the north, Dan, Naphtali, and Asher camped.

17. Aaron alone west in to uncover the Holy of Holies.

18. The cloud came down and settled. Moses said these words: *"...Return, O LORD, unto the many thousands of Israel"* **(Numbers 10:36).**

19. Following this came the evening sacrifices - that was the way the march progressed and ended.

THE DISTANCE FROM SINAI TO KADESH-BARNEA WAS ABOUT 150-200 MILES, WHICH WOULD BE AN ELEVEN DAYS' JOURNEY. THREE GREAT SINS CULMINATED IN A GREATER SIN AT KADESH-BARNEA:

• **The first sin** was that during the first three days, from Marah to Sinai, the people murmured. God sent a sign (Numbers 11:1); the place was called *Taberah*.

• **The second sin** was the lustful appetite of the multitude (Numbers 11:32-34). God gave them meat and named that place *Kibroth-hattaavah*, which means "graves of gluttony" because many of the Israelites gorged themselves and died there.

• **The third sin** was Miriam and Aaron's speaking against Moses. Miriam received leprosy but was later healed.

In Numbers 13-15 are recorded the events at Kadesh-barnea. The time was probably July when they sent out the spies. This was the idea of the people:

"And ye came near unto me every one of you, and said, We will send men before us, and they shall search us out the land, and bring us word again by what way we must go up, and into what cities we shall come" **(Deuteronomy 1:22).**

Numbers 16-19 records the Israelites' wandering.

THREE BREACHES OF THE COVENANT:

• **The first breach** of the covenant was the worship of the golden calf.

• **The second breach** was receiving the evil report. They said they wanted to return to Egypt, which was, of course, their place of bondage. God's response is recorded in Numbers 14:11-35.

• **The third breach** was the revolt of Korah - Numbers 16.

Korah, a descendant of Levi, challenged Moses' leadership, claiming that Moses had exalted himself above the people.

With Korah were gathered 250 princes of Israel (Numbers 16:2). They claimed rights to the same priestly functions as Levites. They provided themselves with censors. Moses called for the test. He called the princes to bring their censors, and then a fire from God came out and destroyed them - an earthquake destroyed the rest. The rebellion spread, and 14,000 were killed by the plague. The people began to fall to pieces with despair. Moses then called for the rods, and Aaron's rod budded.

Three famous Reubenites, whose camp was next to Korah's, complained that Moses hadn't taken them into the land. Their murmuring became very contagious. They aligned themselves with Korah.

In Numbers 18 we see the provision for the Levites. In Numbers 19 is the cleansing from the defilement of their sins - the beautiful story of the red heifer.

The description of the events in Numbers 19 typifies the change of the carnal mind, the imparting of the new nature, and the cleansing of the defilement of sin - regeneration.

The red heifer was taken outside of the camp and killed. Not a white hair could be on it. It was burned with red cedar wood - signifying blood. Threads of scarlet were thrown signifying blood. This is a beautiful picture of Jesus Christ.

The ashes were mixed with rainwater - making liquid lye. It was kept on hand at all times. A bunch of hyssop, whose wood was red, was used for sprinkling blood. Here is a beautiful picture of Jesus Christ and the new nature we receive by accepting Him.

Ezekiel 36:26 says, *"...I will take away the stony heart out of your flesh, and I will give you an heart of flesh."*

Hebrews 9:13,14 says, *"For if the blood of bulls and of goats, and the ashes of an heifer sprinkling the unclean, sanctifieth to the purifying of the flesh: How much more shall the blood of Christ, who through the eternal Spirit offered himself without*

NOTES

NOTES

spot to God, purge your conscience from dead works to serve the living God?"

For 38 years the Israelites did not perform circumcisions; after crossing the Jordan, Joshua circumcised them. In Amos 5 and Acts 7 we learn that they made no sacrifices. There was a total suspension of the covenant. The Levites, however, kept their worship.

Numbers 20 records the stopping place of the Ark. The Israelites had to reassemble where they broke the covenant. Miriam dies at the place where she committed sin, and there the Israelites committed yet another sin; they murmured for water. Moses struck the rock instead of speaking to it.

Numbers 20:10,11: *"And Moses and Aaron gathered the congregation together before the rock, and he said unto them, Hear now, ye rebels; must we fetch you water out of this rock? And Moses lifted up his hand, and with his rod he smote the rock twice: and the water came out abundantly, and the congregation drank, and their beasts also."*

Numbers 27:14: *"For ye rebelled against my commandment in the desert of Zin, in the strife of the congregation, to sanctify me at the water before their eyes: that is the water of Meribah in Kadesh in the wilderness of Zin."*

Deuteronomy 1:37: *"Also the LORD was angry with me for your sakes, saying, Thou also shalt not go in thither."*

Deuteronomy 3:26,27: *"But the LORD was wroth with me for your sakes, and would not hear me: and the LORD said unto me, Let it suffice thee; speak no more unto me of this matter."*

Psalms 106:33: *"Because they provoked his spirit, so that he spake unadvisedly with his lips."*

The Edomites refused to allow Israel to pass through their land. The Israelites made a long circuit going through the valley of Arabah, and Aaron died at Mount Hor. His clothes were placed on his sons.

In Numbers 21 the Canaanites came out and fought with the Israelites at the same place where they were defeated before - but this time Israel won.

After journeying from Mount Hor, Israel began to murmur again, and God sent fiery serpents among them. Moses lifted up the brazen serpent which, of course is another beautiful picture of Jesus Christ as presented in John chapter three.

At Beer, the princes dug the well, and water was supplied.

Next, we come to Bashan and get a description of Og.

In Numbers 24 Balaam appeared with the intention of cursing the Israelites just before they were to cross over to Jericho, but you can't curse what God has blessed!

Numbers 25 recorded the idolatry of the people. The ones responsible were killed and hung up in the sight of all the people. People were dying like flies in the plague. Phinehas appeared and stopped the sin; it was counted to him for righteousness.

In Numbers 26,27 a second numbering occurred. This was for war and land allotment. The tribe of Simeon had fearfully decreased.

Numbers 31 is devoted to war against Midian. This was a result of Balaam's counsel. Only 1,000 were taken from each tribe. A priest, not a general, commanded them. It was a destruction wrought by God. The spoils were devoted to God because it was God's war. Midian was smitten all the way to the Euphrates. Sihon and Og had been destroyed. Moab, Amon, and Edom were incapable of war. Much land east of the Jordan was captured; it was excellent grazing ground.

In Numbers 32 two-and-a-half tribes asked for this grazing land. Reuben, Gad, and the half tribe of Manasseh received it.

Numbers 33 shows the whole itinerary from Egypt to Jordan.

Numbers 34 is devoted to a description of the border.

Numbers 35 is devoted to the Levite cities and the refuge cities. How beautiful these cities are, for they are cities set on a hill. Jesus is our refuge. He is set on a hill that we might flee unto Him. We are like cities set on a hill too. The light never went out in these cities because when men were in darkness, they needed a light they could run toward. Jesus is our light. We run toward Him. The light in us also causes others to run toward us. These cities of refuge are one of the greatest pictures in the Old Testament of the light of Jesus Christ.

SEEING JESUS IN NUMBERS

We have already discussed many types and shadows of Jesus; here are some others:

1. The bronze serpent - Numbers 21:4-9 (John 3:13)
2. The Rock that followed them - I Corinthians 10:4.
3. The manna - John 6:31-33
4. The Star that rises out of Jacob - Numbers 24:17.

THEME VERSE

"And they shall put my name upon the children of Israel; and I will bless them" **(Numbers 6:27).**

OUTLINE

(Refer to maps on pages A3 and A6 in the APPENDIX)

I. FROM SINAI TO KADESH-BARNEA - NUMBERS 1-12 (SEE THEIR MURMURING IN NUMBERS 11,12).

NOTES

NOTES

A. **Law of Nazarite Vow -** Numbers 6 - Example: Samson, Samuel, John the Baptist

B. **Aaronic Benediction -** Numbers 6:24-27

1. God gives full credit to each man.

II. **FROM KADESH THROUGH THE WILDERNESS AND BACK TO KADESH -** NUMBERS 13-19

A. **Wilderness Wanderings Are the Result of Sin and Disobedience.**

B. **Korah's Rebellion -** Numbers 16:

1. *"Woe unto them! For they have gone in the way of Cain, and ran greedily after the error of Balaam for reward, and perished in the gainsaying of Core"* **(Jude 11).**

2. **Aaron's rod that budded -** God's seal on Aaron's priesthood - Numbers 17

III. **FROM KADESH TO JORDAN -** NUMBERS 20-36

A. **The Death of a Generation** (Psalms 90):

1. *"Because all those men which have seen my glory, and my miracles, which I did in Egypt and in the wilderness, and have tempted me now these ten times, and have not hearkened to my voice; Surely they shall not see the land which I swore unto their fathers, neither shall any of them that provoked me see it"* **(Numbers 14:22,23).**

B. **Sin of Moses -** Numbers 20:

1. *"(Now the man Moses was very meek, above all the men which were upon the face of the earth)"* **(Numbers 12:3).**

2. *"And Moses lifted up his hand, and with his rod he smote the rock twice: and the water came out abundantly, and the congregation drank, and their beasts also. And the LORD spake unto Moses and Aaron, Because ye believed me not, to sanctify me in the eyes of the children of Israel, therefore ye shall not bring this congregation into the land which I have given them"* **(Numbers 20:11,12).**

C. **Death of Aaron -** succeeded by Eleazar

D. **Brazen serpent:**

1. *"And as Moses lifted up the serpent in the wilderness, even so must the Son of man be lifted up: That whosoever believeth in him should not perish, but have eternal life"* **(John 3:14,15).**

E. **Victory Over Sihon and Og** (Psalms 136)

F. **Account of Balaam:**

1. *"Which have forsaken the right way, and are gone astray, following the way of Balaam the son of Bosor, who loved the wages of unrighteousness"* **(II Peter 2:15).**

2. *"Woe unto them! For they have gone in the way of Cain, and ran greedily after the error of Balaam*

for reward, and perished in the gainsaying of Core" **(Jude11).**

3. *"Ye adulterers and adulteresses, know ye not that the friendship of the world is enmity with God? whosoever therefore will be a friend of world is the enemy of God"* **(James 4:4).**
4. *"But I have a few things against thee, because thou hast there them that hold the doctrine of Balaam, who taught Balac to cast a stumblingblock before the children of Israel, to eat things sacrificed unto idols, and to commit fornication"* **(Revelation 2:14).**

G. **Second Numbering of the People -** Numbers 26

1. **Inheritance of the daughters of Zelophehad -** Numbers 27,36; Joshua 17:3
2. **Two and one-half tribes settle east of Jordan** (Reuben, Gad, and half of Manasseh).

H. **Moses prepared for his death and appointed Joshua -** Numbers 27.

I. **Summary of Israel's Journey -** Numbers 33

J. **Cities of refuge appointed** (Hebrews 6:19,20)

K. **Numbers closes with the mention of the inheritance of the daughters of Zelophehad -** Numbers 36:6-12.

NOTES

NUMBERS QUOTED IN THE NEW TESTAMENT

Numbers 3:13
(Exodus 13:2, 13:12,15; Numbers 8:17)
Because all the firstborn are mine for on the day that I smote all the firstborn in the land of Egypt I hallowed unto me all the firstborn in Israel, both man and beast; mine shall they be: I am the LORD.

Luke 2:23
(As it is written in the law of the Lord, Every male that openeth the womb shall be called holy to the Lord.)

****

Numbers 8:17 (Exodus 13:2, 13:12,15; Numbers 3:13)
For all the firstborn of the children of Israel are mine, both man and beast: on the day that I smote every firstborn in the land of Egypt I sanctified them for myself.

Luke 2:23
(As it is written in the law of the Lord, Every male that openeth the womb shall be called holy to the Lord.)

****

Numbers 9:12 (Exodus 12:46: Psalms 34:20)
They shall leave none of it unto the morning, nor break any bone of it: according to all the ordinances of the Passover they shall keep it.

John 19:36
For these things were done, that the scripture should be fulfilled, A bone of him shall not be broken.

****

Numbers 30:2 (Leviticus 19:12; Deuteronomy 23:21)
If a man vow a vow unto the LORD, or swear an oath to bind his soul with a bond; he shall not break his word, he shall do according to all that proceedeth out of his mouth.

Matthew 5:33
Again, ye have heard that it hath been said by them of old time, Thou shalt not forswear thyself, but shalt perform unto the Lord thine oaths.

DEUTERONOMY

LEARNING FROM HISTORY			
A REVIEW OF HISTORY	**RESUME OF THE LAW**	**PALESTINIAN COVENANT**	**DEATH OF MOSES**
First sermon: **1-4**	Second sermon: **40-26**	Third sermon: **27-30**	Exhortation & blessngs: **31-34**
LOCATION: The plains of Moab - due east of Jericho & the Jordan River			
OVERVIEW: On disobedience	Review of Mosaic Law	Blessings & Curses	Moses' last words
TIME: 1 month			

FAST FACTS

AUTHOR AND SETTING:

Moses; on the plains of Moab - the Israelites ready to enter the Promised Land

PURPOSE:

Moses was the greatest leader his people had known. In *Deuteronomy* he preaches three sermons - his last words to them. The first sermon is historyand looks backward, the second looks inward, and the third sermon looks forward.

SEEING JESUS:

The most obvious reference to Christ - *Deuteronomy 18:15.* Moses is a type of Christ as the deliverer of His people from the bondage of sin.

THEME VERSE:

Deuteronomy 11:1

NOTES

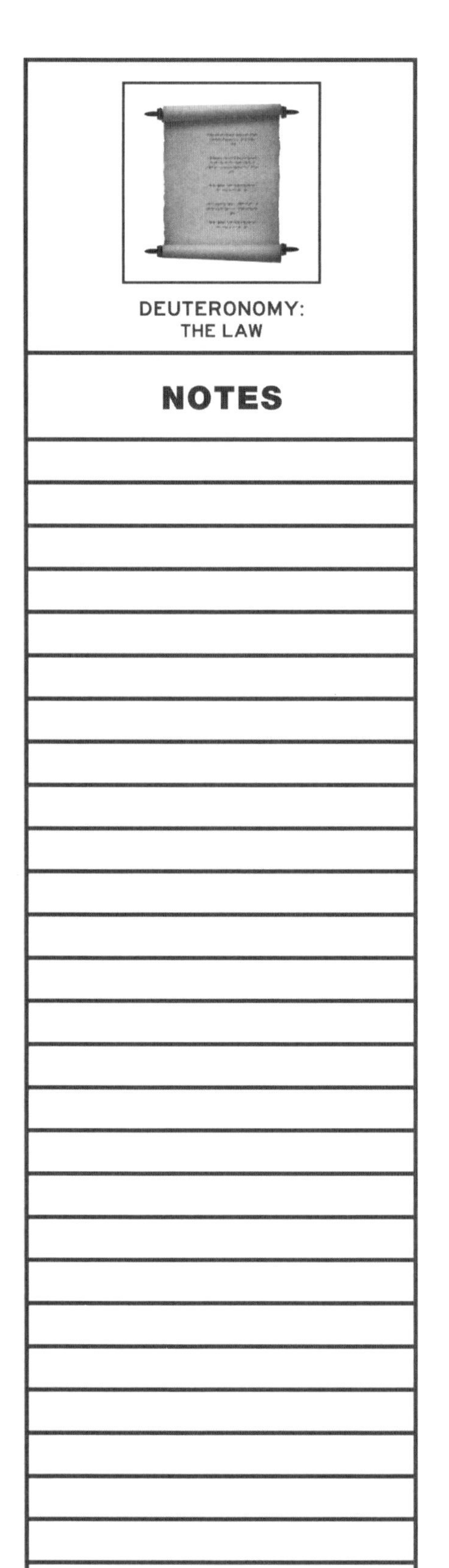

SEEING JESUS IN DEUTERONOMY

AUTHOR AND SETTING

Deuteronomy is the last of the five books of Moses known as the Pentateuch. The Jews referred to these books as the writings of Moses. Jesus confirmed their Mosaic authorship in John 5:46,47.

The entire book of *Deuteronomy* covers only one month's time. The Israelites were camped in the plains of Moab by the river Jordan where they received this second giving of the law.

OVERVIEW

The Hebrew title of *Deuteronomy* is "the Message." *Deuteronomy* means "the second law." Moses rehearsed the wilderness wanderings and gave a summary of the law to the generation who grew up in the wilderness. The greater part of the book consists f the orations of Moses shortly before his death. They were delivered in the plains of Moab by the river Jordan. The one who spoke was the one who, forty years earlier, had said he couldn't speak well:

***"And Moses said unto the LORD O my LORD, I am not eloquent, neither heretofore, nor since thou has spoken unto thy servant: but I am slow of speech, and of a slow tongue"* (Exodus 4:10).**

How interesting hat this was being taught while Balaam was trying to curse Israel. (See Numbers 22-24.)

Jesus quotes from *Deuteronomy* during His temptation in the wilderness (Matthew 4). Use the Word to defeat the devil!

Deuteronomy is a dissertation on obedience. It is made up of three sermons. The first sermon, consisting of chapters 1-4, gives history and warning. The second sermon is long, chapters 4-26, and is a review of the Mosaic law. The third sermon, chapters 27-30, lists the blessings and cursing of the law and, of course, Moses' last sermon. He certainly didn't run out of breath, did he? Chapters 31-34 deal with his death. Chapter 32 is a death song; chapter 33 is a death blessing; and chapter 34 is Moses' death.

In the first month of the Hebrew calendar Miriam died, in the fifth month Aaron died, and in the eleventh month Moses died. Moses laid the foundation of doctrine for action. The first sermon is history and looks backward; the second sermon looks inward; and the third sermon on the covenant looks forward.

Of all the Old Testament books, the Psalms and *Deuteronomy* are the most-often quoted books by Jesus. *Deuteronomy* is quoted a number of times in the New Testament by Jesus:

***"Master, which is the great commandment in the law? Jesus said unto him, Thou shalt love the Lord thy God with all thy heart, and with all thy soul, and with all thy mind"* (Matthew 22:36,37).**

SEEING JESUS IN DEUTERONOMY

Moses clearly spoke of Christ's First Advent in Deuteronomy 18:15:

"The LORD thy God will raise up unto thee a Prophet from the midst of thee of thy brethren, like unto me; unto him ye shall hearken."

Moses, the mighty deliver of the Israelites, is a type of Christ in His role as our deliverer from the bondage of sin.

THEME VERSE

"Therefore thou shalt love the LORD thy God, and keep his charge, and his statues, and his judgments, and his commandments, always" **(Deuteronomy 11:1).**

OUTLINE

(Refer to maps on pages A3 and A6 in the APPENDIX.)

I. **A REVIEW OF HISTORY: THE FIRST SERMON -** DEUTERONOMY 1-4

In the Hebrew Bible this book opens with the words: *"These be the words..."* **(Deuteronomy 1:1).**

A. **The Israelites Could Have Entered the Promised Land in Just Eleven Days:**

"(There are eleven days' journey from Horeb by the way of mount Seir unto Kadesh-Barnea.)" **(Deuteronomy 1:2)**.

Numbers records that on the twelfth day after they came to Mount Sinai they could have entered the Promised Land. Instead they disbelieved God.

1. **Dispatching spies from Kadesh-barnea**
2. **Long years in the wilderness**
3. **Conquest of Sihon and Og**
4. **God's refusal to let Moses go into the Promised Land -** Deuteronomy 3:23-26

B. **These Words Are Used Throughout the Book: "Hear and Do."**

1. **The first address was followed by setting apart (Deuteronomy 4:41-43) three of the six cities of refuge listed in Joshua 20.**

II. **RESUME OF THE LAW -** DEUTERONOMY 4-26

Jesus quoted from *Deuteronomy*: *"But he answered and said, it is written, Man shall not live by bread alone, but by every word that proceedeth out of the mouth of God"* **(Matthew 4:4).**

NOTES

NOTES

"And he humbled thee, and suffered thee to hunger, and fed thee with manna, which thou knewest not, neither did thy fathers know that he might make thee know that man doth not live by bread only, but by every word that proceedeth out of the mouth of the LORD doth man live" **(Deuteronomy 8:3).**

"Jesus said unto him, it is written again, Thou shalt not tempt the Lord thy God" **(Matthew 4:7).**

"Ye shall not tempt the LORD your God, as ye tempted him in Massah" **(Deuteronomy 6:16).**

"Then saith Jesus unto him, Get thee hence, Satan: for it is written, Thou shalt worship the Lord thy God, and him only shalt thou serve" **(Matthew 4:10).**

"Thou shalt fear the LORD thy God; him shalt thou serve, and to him shalt thou cleave, and swear by his name" **(Deuteronomy 10:20).**

A. They Disobeyed and Followed Sinful Practices of the Canaanites.

B. Special Lessons:

1. **His providence -** Deuteronomy 8:2-5
2. **Support for ministry:**
   a. *"Take heed to thyself that thou forsake not the Levite as long as thou livest upon the earth"* **(Deuteronomy 12:19).**
3. **Warning against bribery:**
   a. *"Thou shalt not wrest judgment; thou shalt not respect persons, neither take a gift: for a gift doth blind the eyes of the wise, and pervert the words of the righteous"* **(Deuteronomy 16:19).**
4. **Brotherhood and charity -** Deuteronomy 22
5. **Honest weights of measurements -** Deuteronomy 25:13-15
6. **Mount Gerizim and Mount Ebal -** Deuteronomy 27, 28
   a. This is a beautiful picture - if we chose Jesus, we take His blessings, and if we refuse, we receive the curses. Only one could take those curses, the One who sacrificed Himself for us.
7. **The willing bond slave:**
   a. *"And it shall be, if he say unto thee, I will not go away from thee; because he loveth thee and thine house, because he is well with thee; Then thou shalt take an aul, and thrust it through his ear unto the door, and he shall be thy servant for ever. And also unto thy maidservant thou shalt do likewise"* **(Deuteronomy 15:16,17).**

b. There is no question that this is Jesus Christ. He was willing to be a slave for us because He loved His Father, His wife, and His children. His wife, of course, would be Israel and the gentiles; the children would be the church.

8. Two or three witnesses:

a. *"At the mouth of two witnesses, or three witnesses, shall he that is worthy of death be put to death; but at the mouth of one witness he shall not be put to death"* **(Deuteronomy 17:6).**

b. *"If I bear witness of myself, my witness is not true. There is another that beareth witness of me; and I know that the witness which he witnesseth of me is true. Ye sent unto John, and he bare witness unto the truth. But I receive not testimony from man; but these things I say, that ye might be saved. He was a burning and a shining light: and ye were willing for a season to rejoice in his light. But I have greater witness than that of John: for the works which the Father hath given me to finish, the same works that I do, bear witness of me, that the Father hath sent me. And the Father himself, which hath sent me, hath borne witness of me. Ye have neither heard his voice at any time, nor seen his shape. And ye have not his word abiding in you: for whom he hath sent, him ye believe not. Search the scriptures; for in them ye think ye have eternal life and they are they which testify of me"* **(John 5:31-39).**

9. Instructions concerning a king - Deuteronomy 17:14-20)

10. Warning against demonism - Deuteronomy 18:9-14

11. Prediction about a prophet - Deuteronomy 18:15-19

a. *"For Moses truly said unto the fathers, A prophet shall the Lord your God raise up unto you of your brethren, like unto me; him shall ye hear in all things whatsoever he shall say unto you. And it shall come to pass, that every soul, which will not hear that prophet, shall be destroyed from among the people"* **(Acts 3:22,23).**

b. *"And they asked him, What then? Art thou Elias? And he saith, I am not. Art thou that prophet? And he answered, No"* **(John 1:21).**

c. *"Then those men, when they had seen the miracle that Jesus did, said, This is of a truth that prophet that should come into the world"* **(John 6:14).**

d. *"Many of the people therefore, when they heard this saying said, Of a truth this is the Prophet"* **(John 7:40).**

12. Mosaic law of divorce - Deuteronomy 24:1-4 (Parallel: Matthew 19:3-12; I Corinthians 7:12-15)

NOTES

NOTES

III. PALESTINIAN COVENANT - DEUTERONOMY 27-30

A. History: This gives a forecast of the history of Israel. This covenant foretold the dispersion because of disobedience. It also foretells of their future repentance and conversion, the return of the Lord, and restoration of their land - it was a *conditional covenant.* Abraham's covenant was *unconditional.*

IV. THE CLOSE OF MOSES' LIFE - THE THREE GREAT ORATIONS CONTAIN HISTORY, LAW, AND COVENANT - DEUTERONOMY 31-34

A. Deuteronomy 31 - The Book; Deuteronomy 32 - The Song; Deuteronomy 33 - The Blessings; Deuteronomy 34 - The Death of Moses.

B. God Told Moses to Write the Law in a Book, and Jesus Attested to the Fact That He Had Done So:

1. *"For had ye believed Moses, ye would have believed me: for he wrote of me"* **(John 5:46).**

2. This law was to be kept at the place of worship and was to be read in the hearing of all Israel, every sabbatical year at the Feast of Tabernacle. (See Deuteronomy 31:9-12).

C. The Song Commemorates the Lord As the Rock - Deuteronomy 32.

1. David did the same - Psalms 18:2.

2. The song of Moses in Revelation - Revelation 15.

D. Moses' Blessing on the Tribes - Deuteronomy 33

1. The casting of lots

2. Noah's blessings - Genesis 9

3. Jacob's blessings - Genesis 49

a. *"The eternal God is thy refuge, and underneath are the everlasting arms: and he shall thrust out the enemy from before thee; and shall say, Destroy them"* **(Deuteronomy 33:27).**

b. *"Blessed be the God and Father of our Lord Jesus Christ, who hath blessed us with all spiritual blessings in heavenly places in Christ"* **(Ephesians 1:3).**

E. Deuteronomy 34 Was Probably Written by Joshua:

1. *"And there arose not a prophet since in Israel like unto Moses, whom the LORD knew face to face"* **(Deuteronomy 34:10).**

2. *"And he said unto them, These are the words which I spake unto you, while I was yet with you, that all things must be fulfilled, which were written in the law of Moses, and in the prophets, and in the psalms, concerning me"* **(Luke 24:44).**

F. God's Word Goes On:

1. *"And Joshua the son of Nun was full of the spirit of wisdom; for Moses had laid his hands upon him: and* *the children of Israel hearkened unto him, and did as the Lord commanded Moses"* **(Deuteronomy 34:9).**

Jesus quoted more from *Deuteronomy* and Psalms than any books of the Old Testament. Certainly *Deuteronomy* shows the picture of the *coming prophet*, the Lord Jesus Christ.

NOTES

DEUTERONOMY QUOTED IN THE NEW TESTAMENT

Deuteronomy 4:35
Unto thee it was shewed, that thou mightest know that the LORD he is God; there is none else beside him.

Mark 12:32
And the scribe said unto him, Well, Master, thou hast said the truth: for there is one God; and there is none other but he.

****

Deuteronomy 5:16-20 (Exodus 20:12-16)
Honour thy father and thy mother, as the LORD thy God hath commanded thee; that thy days may be prolonged, and that it may go well with thee, in the land which the LORD thy God giveth thee. Thou shalt not kill. Neither shalt thou commit adultery. Neither shalt thou steal. Neither shalt thou bear false witness against thy neighbour.

Matthew 5:21,27,43
Ye have heard that it was said by them of old time, Thou shalt not kill; and whosoever shall kill shall be in danger of the judgment: Ye have heard that it was said by them of old time, thou shalt not commit adultery. Ye have heard that it hath been said, Thou shalt love thy neighbour, and hate thine enemy.

Matthew 15:4
For God commanded, saying, Honour thy father and mother: and, He that curseth father or mother, let him die the death.

Matthew 19:18,19
He saith unto him, Which? Jesus said, Thou shalt do no murder, Thou shalt not commit adultery, Thou shalt not steal, Thou shalt not bear false witness, Honour thy father and thy mother: and, Thou shalt love thy neighbour as thyself.

Mark 7:10
For Moses said, Honour thy father and thy mother; and, Whoso curseth father or mother, let him die the death.

Mark 10:19
Thou knowest the commandments, Do not commit adultery, Do not kill, Do not steal, Do not bear false witness, Defraud not, Honour thy father and mother.

Luke 18:20
Thou knowest the commandments, Do not commit adultery, Do not kill, Do not steal, Do not bear false witness, Honour thy father and thy mother.

Romans 13:9
For this, Thou shalt not commit adultery, Thou shalt not kill, Thou shalt not steal, Thou shalt not bear false witness, Thou shalt not covet; and if there be any other commandment it is briefly comprehended in this saying, namely, Thou shalt love thy neighbour as thyself.

James 2:11
For he that said, Do not commit adultery, said also, Do not kill. Now if thou commit no adultery, yet if thou kill, thou art become a transgressor of the law.

****

Deuteronomy 5:21 (Exodus 20:17)
Neither shalt thou desire thy neighbor's wife, neither halt thou covet thy neighbor's house, his field or his manservant or his maidservant his ox, or his ass, or anything that is thy neighbour's.

Romans 7:7
What shall we say then? Is the law sin? God forbid. Nay, I had not known sin, but by the law: for I had not known lust, except the law had said, Thou shalt not covet.

Romans 13:9
For this, Thou shalt not commit adultery, Thou shalt not kill, Thou shalt not steal, Thou shalt not bear false witness, Thou shalt not covet; and if there be any other commandment, it is briefly comprehended in this saying, namely, Thou shalt love thy neighbor as thyself.

****

Deuteronomy 6:4
Hear, O Israel: The LORD our God is one LORD.

Mark 12:29
And Jesus answered him, The first of all the commandments is, Hear, O Israel; The Lord our God is one Lord.

Mark 12:32,33
And the scribe said unto him, Well, Master, thou hast said the truth: for there is one God; and there is none other but he.

****

Deuteronomy 6:5
And thou shalt love the LORD thy God with all thine heart, and with all thy soul, and with all thy might.

Matthew 22:37
Jesus said unto him, Thou shalt love the Lord thy God with all thy heart, and with all thy soul, and with all thy mind.

Mark 12:30
And thou shalt love the Lord thy God with all thy heart, and with all thy soul, and with all thy mind, and with all thy strength: this is the first commandment.

Mark 12:33
And to love him with all the heart, and with all the understanding, and with all the soul, and with all the strength, and to love his neighbor as himself, is more than all whole burnt offerings and sacrifices.

Luke 10:27
And he answering said, Thou shalt love the Lord thy God with all thy heart, and with all thy soul, and with all strength, and with all thy mind; and thy neighbor as thyself.

****

Deuteronomy 6:13
Thou shalt fear the LORD thy God, and serve him, and shalt swear by his name.

Matthew 4:10
Then saith Jesus unto him, Get thee hence, Satan: for it is written, Thou shalt worship the Lord thy God, and him only shalt thou serve.

Luke 4:8
And Jesus answered and said unto him, Get thee behind me, Satan: for it is written, Thou shalt worship the Lord thy God, and him only shalt thou serve.

****

Deuteronomy 6:16
Ye shall not tempt the LORD your God, as ye tempted him in Massah.

Matthew 4:7
Jesus said unto him, It is written again, Thou shalt not tempt the Lord thy God.

Luke 4:12
And Jesus answering said unto him, It is said, Thou shalt not tempt the Lord thy God.

****

Deuteronomy 8:3
And he humbled thee, and suffered thee to hunger, and fed thee with manna, which thou knewest not, neither did thy fathers know; that he might make thee know that man doth not live by bread only, but by every word that proceedeth out of the mouth of the LORD doth man live.

Matthew 4:4
But he answered and said, It is written, Man shall not live by bread alone, but by every word that proceedeth out of the mouth of God.

Luke 4:4
And Jesus answered him, saying, It is written, That man shall not live by bread along, but by every word of God.

****

Deuteronomy 9:19
For I was afraid of the anger and hot displeasure, wherewith the LORD was wroth against you to destroy you. But the LORD hearkened unto me at that time also.

Hebrews 12:21
And so terrible was the sight, that Moses said, I exceedingly fear and quake.

****

Deuteronomy 13:5 (Deuteronomy 17:7, 19:19, 22:24, 24:7)
And that prophet, or that dreamer of dreams, shall be put to death; because he hath spoken to turn you away from the LORD your God, which brought you out of the land of Egypt, and redeemed you out of the house of bondage, to thrust thee out of the way which the LORD thy God commanded thee to walk in. So shalt thou put the evil away from the midst of thee.

I Corinthians 5:13
But them that are without God judgeth. Therefore put away from among yourselves that wicked person.

****

Deuteronomy 17:7 (Deuteronomy 13:5, 19:19, 22:24, 24:7)
The hands of the witnesses shall be first upon him to put him to death, and afterward the hands of all the people. So thou shalt put the evil away from among you.

I Corinthians 5:13
But them that are without God judgeth. Therefore put away from among yourselves that wicked person.

****

Deuteronomy 18:15
The LORD thy God will raise up unto thee a Prophet from the midst of thee, of thy brethren, like unto me; unto him ye shall hearken.

Acts 3:22
For Moses truly said unto the fathers, A prophet shall the Lord your God raise up unto you of your brethren, like unto me; him shall ye hear in all things whatsoever he shall say unto you.

Acts 7:37
This is that Moses, which said unto the children of Israel, A prophet shall the Lord your God raise up unto you of your brethren, like unto me; him shall ye hear.

****

Deuteronomy 19:15
One witness shall not rise up against a man for any iniquity, or for any sin, in any sin that he sinneth: at the mouth of two witnesses, or at the mouth of three witnesses, shall the matter be established.

Matthew 18:16
But if he will not hear thee, then take with thee one or two more, that in the mouth of two or three witnesses

every word may be established.

II Corinthians 13:1
This is the third time I am coming to you. In the mouth of two or three witnesses shall every word be established.

****

Deuteronomy 19:19 (Deuteronomy 13:5, 17:7, 22:24, 24:7)
Then shall ye do unto him, as he had thought to have done unto his brother: so shalt thou put the evil away from among you.

I Corinthians 5:13
But them that are without God judgeth. Therefore put away from among yourselves that wicked person.

****

Deuteronomy 19:21 (Exodus 21:24; Leviticus 24:20)
And thine eye shall not pity; but life shall go for life, eye for eye, tooth for tooth, hand for hand, foot for foot.

Matthew 5:38
Ye have heard that it hath been said, An eye for an eye, and a tooth for a tooth.

****

Deuteronomy 21:23
His body shall not remain all night upon the tree, but thou shalt in any wise bury him that day; (for he that is hanged is accursed of God;) that thy land be not defiled, which the LORD thy God giveth thee for an inheritance.

Galatians 3:13
Christ hath redeemed us from the curse of the law, being made a curse for us: for it is written, Cursed is every one that hangeth on a tree.

****

Deuteronomy 22:24 (Deuteronomy 13:5, 17:7, 19:19, 24:7)
Then ye shall bring them both out unto the gate of that city, and ye shall stone them with stones that they die; the damsel, because she cried not, being in the city; and the man, because he hath humbled his neighbour's wife so thou shalt put away evil from among you.

I Corinthians 5:13
But them that are without God judgeth. Therefore put away from among yourselves that wicked person.

****

Deuteronomy 23:21 (Leviticus 19:12; Numbers 30:2)
When thou shalt vow a vow unto the LORD thy God, thou shalt not slack to pay it: for the LORD thy God will surely require it of thee; and it would be sin in thee.

Matthew 5:33
Again, ye have heard that it hath been said by them of old time, Thou shalt not forswear thyself but shalt perform unto the Lord thine oaths.

****

Deuteronomy 24:1
When a man hath taken a wife and married her, and it come to pass that she find no favor in his eyes, because he hath found some uncleanness in her: then let him write her a bill of divorcement, and give it in her hand, and send her out of his house.

Matthew 5:31
It hath been said, Whosoever shall put away his wife, let him give her a writing of divorcement.

Matthew 19:7
They say unto him, why did Moses then command to give a writing of divorcement, and to put her away?

Mark 10:4
And they said, Moses suffered to write a bill of divorcement, and to put her away.

****

Deuteronomy 24:7 (Deuteronomy 13:5, 17:7, 19:19, 22:24)
If a man be found stealing any of his brethren of the children of Israel, and maketh merchandise of him, or selleth him; then that thief shall die, and thou shalt put evil away from among you.

I Corinthian 5:13
But them that are without God judgeth. Therefore put away from among yourselves that wicked person.

****

Deuteronomy 25:4
Thou shalt not muzzle the ox when he treadeth out the corn.

I Corinthians 9:9
For it is written in the law of Moses, Thou shalt not muzzle the mouth of the ox that treadeth out the corn. Doth God take care for oxen?

I Timothy 5:18
For the scripture saith, Thou shalt not muzzle the ox that treadeth out the corn. And, The labourer is worthy of his reward.

****

Deuteronomy 25:5
If brethren dwell together, ad one of them die, and have no child, the wife of the dead shall not marry without unto a stranger: her husband's brother shall go in unto her, and take her to him to wife, and perform

the duty of an husband's brother unto her.

Matthew 22:24
Saying, Master, Moses said, If a man die, having no children, his brother shall marry his wife, and raise up seed unto his brother.

Mark 12:19
Master, Moses wrote unto us, If a man's brother die, and leave his wife behind him, and leave no children, that his brother should take his wife, and raise up seed unto his brother.

Luke 20:28
Saying, Master, Moses wrote unto us, If any man's brother die, having a wife, and he die without children, that his brother should take his wife, and raise up seed unto his brother.

****

Deuteronomy 27:26
Cursed be he that confirmeth not all the words of his law to do them. And all the people shall say, Amen.

Galatians 3:10
For as many as are of the works of the law are under the curse: for it is written, Cursed is every one that continueth not in all things which are written in the book of the law to do them.

****

Deuteronomy 29:4 (Isaiah 29:10)
Yet the LORD hath not given you an heart to perceive, and eyes to see, and ears to hear, unto this day.

Romans 11:8
(According as it is written, God hath given them the spirit of slumber, eyes that they should not see, and ears that they should not hear;) unto this day.

****

Deuteronomy 30:12-14
It is not in heaven, that thou shouldest say, Who shall go up for us to heaven, and bring it unto us, that we may hear it, and do it? Neither is it beyond the sea, that thou shouldest say, Who shall go over the sea for us, and bring it unto us, that we may hear it, and do it. But the word is very nigh unto thee, in thy mouth, and in thy heart, that thou mayest do it.

Romans 10:6-8
But the righteousness which is of faith speaketh on this wise, Say not in thine heart, Who shall ascend into heaven? (that is, to bring Christ down from above:) Or, Who shall descent into the deep? (that is, to bring up Christ again from the dead.) But what saith it? The word is nigh thee, even in thy mouth, ad in thy heart: that is, the word of faith, which we preach.

****

Deuteronomy 31:6
Be strong and of a good courage, fear not, nor be afraid of them; for the LORD thy God, he it is that doth go with thee; he will not fail thee, nor forsake thee.

Hebrews 13:5
Let your conversation be without covetousness; and be content with such things as ye have: for he hath said, I will never leave thee, nor forsake thee.

****

Deuteronomy 32:21
They have moved me to jealousy with that which is not God; they have provoked me to anger with their vanities: and I will move them to jealousy with those which are not a people; I will provoke them to anger with a foolish nation.

Romans 10:19
But I say, Did not Israel know? First Moses saith, I will provoke you to jealousy by them that are no people, and by a foolish nation I will anger you.

****

Deuteronomy 32:35,36
To me belongeth vengeance, and recompense; their foot shall slide in due time: for the day of their calamity is at hand, and the things that shall come upon them make haste. For the LORD shall judge his people, and repent himself for his servants, when he seeth that their power is gone, and there is none shut up, or left.

Romans 12:19
Dearly beloved, avenge not yourselves, but rather give place unto wrath: for it is written, Vengeance is mine; I will repay, saith the Lord.

Hebrews 10:30
For we know him, that hath said, Vengeance belongeth unto me, I will recompense, saith the Lord. And again, The Lord shall judge his people.

****

Deuteronomy 32:43
Rejoice, O ye nations, with his people: for he will avenge the blood of his servants, and will render vengeance to his adversaries, and will be merciful unto his land, and to his people.

Romans 15:10
And again he saith Rejoice, ye Gentiles, with his people.

JOSHUA

ENTERING THE PROMISED LAND	
A REVIEW OF HISTORY	**DIVIDING THE LAND**
Preparations: **1-5** Conquering Jericho: **6-8** Southern Campaign: **9,10** Northern Campaign: **11,12**	Reuben, Gad, Manasseh: **13,14** Judah: **15** Ephraim & Manasseh: **16,17** Tabernacle & remaining tribes: **18,19** Cities of refuge: **20** Levi: **21-23** Joshua's Challenge: **24**
LOCATION: Canaan - both sides of the Jordan River	
OVERVIEW: Taking the land is no easy task	Sharing the land is no easy task
TIME: 7-year conquest	8 years

FAST FACTS

AUTHOR AND SETTING:

Joshua; The Promised Land

PURPOSE:

The purpose of *Joshua* was to show that God was faithful to give His people the Promised Land.

SEEING JESUS:

Joshua is the Old Testament equivalent for *Yeshua*, Jesus. Joshua was a courageous man who strongly led his people; his life was another "type" for Jesus Himself - Who was also identified through Rahab's "scarlet cord" (Joshua 2:21).

THEME VERSE:

Joshua 1:8

NOTES

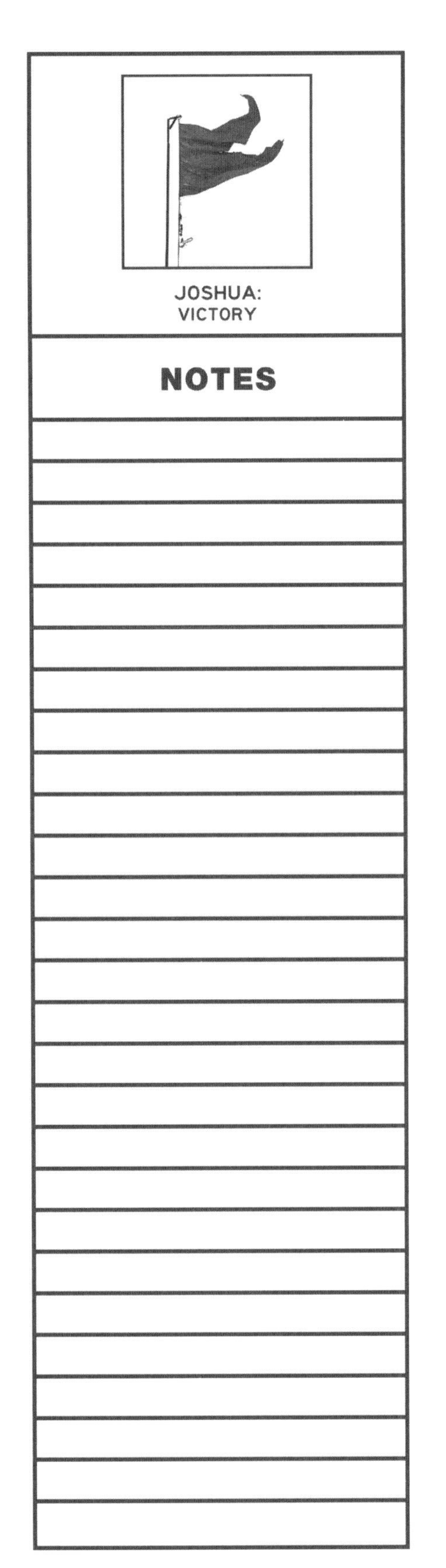

SEEING JESUS IN JOSHUA

AUTHOR & SETTING

There's no question that Joshua wrote this book:

"And Joshua wrote these words in the book of the law of God, and took a great stone, and set it up there under an oak, that was by the sanctuary of the LORD" **(Joshua 24:26).**

From *Joshua 24:26* it appears that Joshua wrote this book after the division of the land among the tribes.

OVERVIEW

Joshua and Judges are marked with tragedy and triumph. Joshua conquered Canaan in three campaigns. However, the tribes did not fully possess all the territory allotted and drive out all the Canaanites.

Following are references about Joshua which are found in the New Testament:

"Which also our fathers that came after brought in with Jesus into the possession of the Gentiles, whom God drave out before the face of our fathers, unto the days of David" **(Acts 7:45).**

"For if Jesus had given them rest, then would he not afterward have spoken of another day" **(Hebrews 4:8).**

"By faith the walls off Jericho fell down, after they were compassed about seven days. By faith the harlot Rehab perished not with them that believed not, when she had received the spies with peace" **(Hebrews 11:30,31).**

"Likewise also was not Rahab the harlot justified by works, when she had received the messengers, and had sent them out another way?" **(James 2:25).**

The purpose of the book is to show that God is faithful to give His people the Promised Land.

A short history of the man Joshua:

Joshua appeared in the battle with Amalek in Exodus 17; on Mount Sinai with Moses in Exodus 24; and came down from the mountain in Exodus 32.

Joshua was concerned with the prophesying of Eldad and Medad in Numbers 11. He was sent out as a spy in Numbers 13. His ordination was in Numbers 27. Deuteronomy 31 shows his charge from Jehovah. He is called *Hoshea* in Moses' song in Deuteronomy 32:44.

Joshua succeeded Moses in Deuteronomy 34. Joshua was of the tribe of Ephraim ad was a general and minister to Moses. His farewell address is somewhat similar to that of Moses, Samuel, and Paul.

SEEING JESUS IN JOSHUA

Joshua's name is the Hebrew for of *Jesus*. Joshua's role in bringing the Children of Israel into rest within the Promised Land is a type of Christ who leads us into true rest (see Hebrews 3,4). Rahab and the scarlet cord are a clear picture of salvation through the blood of Jesus. We also see an Old Testament appearance of Jesus in **Joshua 5:13-15.**

Joshua took the Promised Land and gave his people rest. The people on this land were the descendants of Ham. The Canaanites surpassed the land allotted to them.

The division of the nations is given three times.

Canaan means "low landers." *Amorites* means "high landers." The Hittites were descendants of Heth.

Abraham bought the field of Machpelah from Heth.

The Jebusites occupied the whole territory which included Jerusalem. Jerusalem derives its name from this tribe (Joshua 18:16,28).

The Philistines were on the Mediterranean coast.

The Amalekites settled in the wilderness of Arabia.

The Phoenicians were Tyre and Sidon.

At Gilgal the Lord rolled away the reproach of Egypt.

THEME VERSE

"This book of the law shall not depart out of thy mouth; but thou shalt meditate therein day and night, that thou mayest observe to do according to all that is written therein: for then thou shalt make thy way prosperous, and then thou shalt have good success" **(Joshua 1:8).**

OUTLINE

(Refer to maps on pages A3, A6, and A7 in the APPENDIX.)

I. **CONQUEST OF THE LAND -** JOSHUA 1-12

A. **Preparation for Conquest -** Joshua 1-5

1. **The successful conquest was faith in action:**

a. *"Blessed be the God and Father of our Lord Jesus Christ, who hath blessed us with all spiritual blessings in heavenly places in Christ"* **(Ephesians 1:3).**

b. *"Put on the whole armour of God, that ye may be able to stand against the wiles of the devil"* **(Ephesians 6:11).**

NOTES

NOTES

c. *"For if Jesus had given them rest, then would he not afterward have spoken of another day"* **(Hebrews 4:8).**

2. **Rahab:**

a. *"By faith the harlot Rahab perished not with them that believed not, when she had received the spies with peace"* **(Hebrews 11:31).**

b. *"Likewise also was not Rahab the harlot justified by works, when she had received the messengers, and had sent them out another way?"* **(James 2:25).**

B. Circumcision and Passover - Spiritual Preparation - Joshua 5

1. **The captain of the host:**

a. *"And it came to pass, when Joshua was by Jericho, that he lifted up his eyes and looked, and, behold, there stood a man over against him with his sword drawn in his hand: and Joshua went unto him, and said unto him, Art thou for us, or for our adversaries? And he said, Nay; but as captain of the host of the LORD am I now come. And Joshua fell on his face to the earth, and did worship, and said unto him, What saith my lord unto his servant? And the captain of the LORD'S host said unto Joshua, Loose thy shoe from off thy foot; for the place whereon thou standest is holy. And Joshua did so"* **(Joshua 5:13-15).**

b. *"For it became him, for whom are all things, and by whom are all things, in bringing many sons unto glory, to make the captain of their salvation perfect through sufferings. For both he that sanctifieth and they who are sanctified are all of one: for which cause he is not ashamed to call them brethren"* **(Hebrews 2:10,11).**

c. *"And I fell at his feet to worship him. And he said unto me, See thou do it not: I am thy fellowservant, and of thy brethren that have the testimony of Jesus: worship God: for the testimony of Jesus is the spirit of prophecy"* **(Revelation 19:10).**

2. **The captain of the host is Jesus Christ.**

C. Conquest of Jericho and Ai - Joshua 6-8

1. **A parade was used:**

a. *"For I am not ashamed of the gospel of Christ for it is the power of God unto salvation to every one that believeth; to the Jew first, and also to the Greek"* **(Romans 1:16).**

b. *"For the preaching of the cross is to them that perish foolishness; but unto us which are saved it is the power of God"* **(I Corinthians 1:18).**

c. *"By faith the walls of Jericho fell down, after they were compassed about seven days"* **(Hebrews 11:30).**

2. **Account of Achan**

a. Achan could have enjoyed the spoils of Ai - I John 1:9.

D. **Completion of the Southern Campaign -** Joshua 9,10

1. **Gibeonites**

a. *"And all these kings and their land did Joshua take at one time, because the LORD God of Israel fought for Israel. And Joshua returned, and all Israel with him, unto the camp to Gilgal"* **(Joshua 10:42,43).**

E. **Northern campaign -** Joshua 11,12

1. **The long campaign to conquer kings in the northern part of the land - Joshua 11.**
2. **If the Canaanites had submitted, they would have been spared.**
3. **This first main division closes with the list of conquered kings.**

II. **DIVISIONS OF THE LAND - A RECORD OF THE DIVISION AND THE FINAL INSTRUCTIONS OF JOSHUA -** JOSHUA 13-24

A. **Review is Given of the Territories of Reuben, Gad, and Manasseh -** Joshua 13.

1. **Special attention is given to Caleb.**

B. **Judah is Portioned -** Joshua 15.

C. **Ephraim and the Half Tribe of Manasseh -** Joshua 16,17

D. **Setting Up the Tabernacle at Shiloh and the Record of Division the Other Seven tribes -** Joshua 18,19

E. **Cities of Refuge -** Joshua 20

F. **Forty-eight Cities Were Set Apart as Living Quarters for the Tribe of Levi:**

1. *"And the LORD gave them rest round about, according to all that he sware unto their fathers: and there stood not a man of all their enemies before them; the LORD delivered all their enemies into their hand. There failed not ought of any good thing which the LORD had spoken unto the House of Israel; all came to pass"* **(Joshua 21:44,45).**
2. **Account of altar**

G. **Joshua's Challenge -** Joshua 24

1. **The bones of Joseph**

JOSHUA QUOTED IN THE NEW TESTAMENT: NOT FOUND

NOTES

JUDGES

GOD INTERVENES TO PREVENT ISRAELITE DESASTERS		
FIDELITY & INFIDELITY	**GOD'S INTERVENTION**	**SPECIAL DELIVERERS**
Briefly obedient: **1,2**	Jehovah steps in: **2**	Through cycles of rest & oppression: **3-16**
LOCATION: The Promised Land		
OVERVIEW: Opportunity for a total victory was lost through disobedience	God knew in advance what would happen	People brave and wise rose up to help their nation
TIME: 490 years		

FAST FACTS

AUTHOR AND SETTING:

Samuel; the Promised Land

PURPOSE:

The story of Israel from the death of Joshua to the time of Samuel is one of military deliverers and rulers, those who functioned under the Holy Spirit's anointing. The Israelites alternated between serving God and departing from Him.

SEEING JESUS:

A *judge* is defined as a "savior and ruler, a spiritual guide and political deliverer" - an apt description for Jesus Christ. The 15 judges (13 in *Judges*, 2 in *I Samuel*) present a cumulative picture of Jesus as the ultimate prophet, priest, and king.

THEME VERSE:

Judges 21:25

NOTES

JUDGES:
RIGHTEOUS JUDGE

NOTES

SEEING JESUS IN JUDGES

AUTHOR & SETTING

Ancient Hebrew tradition states that Samuel wrote this book. It was probably written around the time of King Saul.

OVERVIEW

The book of *Judges* emphasizes military deliverers and rulers. A summary of the action of this book is contained in the second chapter. The Israelites served the Lord during the period mentioned in Judges 2:7:

"And the people served the LORD all the days of Joshua, and all the days of the elders that outlived Joshua, who had seen all the great works of the LORD, that he did for Israel."

In the succeeding generation they departed:

***"And also all that generation were gathered unto their fathers: and there arose another generation after them, which knew not the LORD, nor yet the works which he had done for Israel"* (Judges 2:10).**

In distress they turned unto the Lord:

***"Nevertheless the LORD raised up judges, which delivered them out of the hand of those that spoiled them"* (Judges 2:16).**

There are four key words in this book: sin, punishment, repentance, and deliverance. Tragic to say, the general tendency was downward.

There are 13 judges mentioned in the book of *Judges*:

12 men and 1 woman. There are four other judges who are not mentioned in this book: Samuel, Eli, Joel, and Abijah.

Judges covers a period from the time of Joshua to King Saul - 490 years.

THE KEY THOUGHT: Every man did what was right in his own eyes - Judges 17:6, 21:25.

THE BOOK SHOWS THE ISRAELITES GENERAL FAILURES:

1. They turned from a central place of worship (Gideon and Abimelech).
2. The failure of the priesthood
3. The loss of national unity which had been established under Joshua (Deborah and Barak):
    a. Joshua was appointed to the conquest of the national land with the national army.
    b. The allotment of the territory to nine-and-a-half tribes.
    c. The renewal of the covenant
    d. The establishment of a central place of worship.

SEEING JESUS IN JUDGES

Undoubtedly, Jesus is seen as the angel in Judges 2:1, which was the same messenger as in the book of Joshua before Joshua went in to take the promised Land. *Angel* also means "messenger."

Certainly every deliver who was raised up showed a picture of Jesus Christ being the deliverer for any man who will turn unto Him and cry unto Him in the time of his trouble.

Jesus can also be seen in the parable mentioned in Judges 9:7-15.

THEME VERSE

"In those days there was no king in Israel: every man did that which was right in his own eyes" **(Judges 21:25).**

OUTLINE

Refer to map on page A8 in the APPENDIX

I. **ORDER OF EVENTS -** JUDGES 1-2:5

A. **Short Period of Fidelity - Judges 1:6-10**

B. **History Reveals Itself: history shows how, in disobedience to God, each one of the nine-and-a-half tribes west of the Jordan failed to destroy the remnant of the Canaanites and made terms with the nations.**

1. **JUDAH AND SIMEON:**

a. *"And the LORD was with Judah; and he drove out the inhabitants of the mountain; but could not drive out the inhabitants of the valley, because they had chariots of iron"* **(Judges 1:19).**

b. *"And Judah went with Simeon his brother, and they slew the Canaanites that inhabited Zephath, and utterly destroyed it. And the name of the city was called Hormah. Also Judah took Gaza with the coast thereof, ad Askelon with the coast thereof, and Ekron with the coast thereof"* **(Judges 1:17,18).**

2. **BENJAMIN:**

a. *"And they gave Hebron unto Caleb, as Moses said: and he expelled thence the three sons of Anak. And the children of Benjamin did not drive out the Jebusites that inhabited Jerusalem; but the Jebusites dwell with the children of Benjamin in Jerusalem unto this day"* **(Judges 1:20,21).**

3. **EPHRAIM:**

a. *"And the house of Joseph, they also went up against Bethel: and the LORD was with them. And the house of Joseph sent to descry Bethel. (Now the*

NOTES

NOTES

name of the city before was Luz.) And the spies saw a man come forth out of the city, and they said unto him, Shew us, we pray thee, the entrance into the city, and we will shew thee mercy. And when he shewed them the entrance into the city, they smote the city with the edge of the sword; but they let go the man and all his family. Neither did Ephraim drive out the Canaanites that dwelt in Gezer; but the Canaanites dwelt in Gezer among them" **(Judges 1:22-25,29).**

4. **MANASSEH (WEST)**
   a. *"Neither did Manasseh drive out the inhabitants of Bethshean and her towns, not Taanach and her towns, nor the inhabitants of Dor and her towns, nor the inhabitants of Ibleam and her towns, nor the inhabitants of Megiddo and her towns: but the Canaanites would dwell in that land"* **(Judges 1:27).**
5. **ZEBULUN:**
   a. *"Neither did Zebulun drive out other inhabitants of Kitron, nor the inhabitants of Nahalol; but the Canaanites dwelt among them, and became tributaries"* **(Judges 1:30).**
6. **ASHER:**
   a. *"Neither did Asher drive out the inhabitants of Accho, nor the inhabitants of Zidon, nor of Ahlab, nor of Achzib, nor of Helbah, nor of Aphik, nor of Rehob: But the Asherites dwelt among the Canaanites, the inhabitants of the land: for they did not drive them out"* **(Judges 1:31,32).**
7. **NAPHTALI:**
   a. *"Neither did Naphtali drive out the inhabitants of Bethshemesh, nor the inhabitants of Bethanath; but he dwelt among the Canaanites, the inhabitants of the land: nevertheless the inhabitants of Bethshemesh and of Bethanath became tributaries unto them"* **(Judges 1:33).**
8. **DAN:**
   a. *"And the Amorites forced the children of Dan into the mountain: for they would not suffer them to come down to the valley"* **(Judges 1:34).**

C. **The Third Event: was the appearance of an angel from Gilgal (where Joshua had seen him) to rebuke unfaithful tribes - Judges 2:1-6.**

D. **General Apostasy: the two-and-one-half tribes east of the Jordan River were also involved in idolatry.**

II. **GENERAL STATEMENTS CONCERNING JEHOVAH'S INTERVENTION -** JUDGES 2:6-3:4

III. **STORIES OF SPECIAL DELIVERERS -** JUDGES 3-16

A. **OTHNIEL** (Judges 3:7-11)

1. **Eight years of oppression - Mesopotamians**

2. **Forty years of rest**

B. **EHUD** (Judges 3:12-30)

1. **Eighteen years of oppression - Moabites, Ammonites, Amalekites**
2. **Eighty years of rest**

C. **SHAMGAR** (Judges 3:31)

1. **Oppression by the Philistines**

D. **DEBORAH AND BARAK** (Judges 4,5)

1. **Twenty years of oppression - Jabin, King of Hazor (Canaanites)**
2. **Forty years of rest**

E. **GIDEON** (Judges 6-8)

1. **Seven years of oppression - Midianites**
2. **Forty years of rest**

F. **TOLA** (Judges 10:1,2)

1. **Oppression by Abimelech**
2. **Twenty-three years rest**

G. **JAIR** (Judges 10:3-5)

1. **Twenty-two years rest**

H. **JEPHTHAH** (Judges 10:6-12:7)

1. **Eighteen years of oppression - Amon and Philistines**
2. **Six years of rest**

I. **IBZAN** (Judges 12:8-10)

1. **Seven years of rest**

J. **ELON** (Judges 12:11,12)

1. **Ten years of rest**

K. **ABDON** (Judges 12:13-15)

1. **Eight years of rest**

L. **SAMSON** (Judges 13-16)

1. **Forty years of oppression - Philistines**
2. **Twenty years of rest**

IV. **GENERAL CONDITIONS -** JUDGES 17-21

ADDITIONAL FACTS ABOUT JUDGES

Some of the finest literature comes from this book.

Jabin is the name of a dynasty like the pharaohs of Egypt.

The conditions in Deborah's time were terrible:

1. Highways unoccupied
2. No leaders
3. They chose a new god.

NOTES

NOTES

4. War in the gates
5. They were disarmed - only two tribes responded: Naphtali and Zebulun.

The sun, moon, and stars helped Joshua and then Deborah.

Some were decreed Nazarites from the womb: Samson, Samuel, John the Baptist, and the Rechabites.

THERE WERE FOUR INSTANCES OF FORSAKING JEHOVAH AS KING:

1. Micah established an independent "house of gods," with an independent ephod, image, and priesthood (Judges 17:5,6).
2. Dan left his assigned lot and set up an independent priesthood at Laish (Judges 18:27,30).
3. A story equaling Sodom and Gomorrah (Judges 19:1, 22-26).
4. The crafty way of getting wives (Judges 20:1-18, 26-28).
5. Dan was eliminated from the catalog of tribes in Revelation 7:4-8 (probably for acts at Laish).
6. The Levite was right in asking for revenge for his concubine to keep the land clean.

There are basically five Spirit-filled judges in this book. One of them is *Othniel* which means "force of God." The Hebrew indicates he was a Spirit-filled man.

When you study the Hebrew, it says Othniel was filled with the Spirit before the occasion of his battle with Chushan-rishathaim but received a special anointing for this occasion. Although filled with the Spriit, Othniel needed the special anointing for the occasion.

Deborah was a Spirit-filled judge. The wording in the Hebrew indicates that the Spirit of God carried her into her occasions, and there's no question that the Holy Spirit carried her through a miraculous battle with a supernatural victory.

Another Spirit-filled judge was Gideon. The Hebrew indicates that he was clothed in the Spirit. He seemed to have so many holes of unbelief that the Spirit *had* to clothe him to make him the deliverer that e so needed to be.

The next Spirit-filled judge we read about is Jephthah. He had the same anointing as Othniel. Jephthah was not filled with the Spirit for the occasion, but was *already* filled with the Spirit and was specially anointed to win the battle.

Lastly, we read of Samson. The wording in the Hebrew indicates that the Spirit would break in upon him from occasion to occasion and give him supernatural strength.

Three judges who moved by faith are listed in the Hebrew 11: Deborah, Jephthah, and Samson. These were people who heard God's Word and acted in faith.

The long-suffering of God is certainly portrayed in this book. Jesus is the watching messenger at the beginning of the book.

In Judges 9:8 we read the first allegory in the Bible and perhaps the most ancient parable. An allegory is a story with a meaning other than the literal one - a story to illustrate truth in which one thing is said and something else is meant. Here the trees are spoken of as persons holding a convocation to elect a king over them.

Jotham's interpretation and application of this allegory to the anointing of one like Abimelech makes clear the purpose of the speech. Certainly it is prophetic.

The olive tree is the spiritual heritage of the Jews. The fig tree is their national heritage. The vine, of course, is Jesus Christ, and the bramble is the Antichrist.

Study these verses: Judges 9:8-15. They are a picture of the history of Israel through revelation.

JUDGES QUOTED IN THE NEW TESTAMENT: NOT FOUND

NOTES

RUTH

REVERSING THE CURSE			
DISOBEDIENCE	**FAITHFULNESS**	**REDEMPTION**	**REWARD**
Cursings & Blessings: **1**	Seeking favor: **2**	Claiming redemption: **3**	Receiving redemption: **4**
LOCATION: Bethlehem & Moab	Bethlehem	Bethlehem	Bethlehem
OVERVIEW: Naomi & her family start with wrong motives	Ruth's faithfulness brings attention to their needs	How to catch a husband!	Boaz as kinsman-redeemer
TIME: 30 years			

FAST FACTS

AUTHOR AND SETTING:

Samuel; Moab, Bethlehem

PURPOSE:

A picture of the Messiah and the gentile Church, Ruth's story reveals redemption through the "kinsman-redeemer" and stresses God's providential rewards for faithfulness.

SEEING JESUS:

A "kinsman-redeemer" must: 1. Be related by blood to those he redeems; 2. Be able to pay the redemption; 3. Be willing to redeem; 4. Be free himself. Jesus typifies each of these requirements!

THEME VERSE:

Ruth 2:12

NOTES

RUTH:
KINSMAN REDEEMER

NOTES

SEEING JESUS IN RUTH

AUTHOR & SETTING

It is believed that Samuel wrote this book. The events of *Ruth* took place in the early days of Judges; in Ruth 4:21,22 we read the fact that Boaz was the son of Salmon (Matthew 1:5) who married Rahab the harlot of Jericho. If Salmon married Rahab soon after the conquest of Jericho, the events had to occur at least during the first fifty to seventy-five years of the 490 years from Joshua to Saul.

OVERVIEW

The name *Ruth* means "friend or companion." The name Boaz means "in Him is strength." Ruth is the story of one woman's love and friendship to Naomi and to Naomi's God.

Two books of the Bible are named after women: Ruth and Esther. Ruth is found in the lineage of Jesus Christ (Matthew 1:5).

This book belongs to the period of the Judges, and it is a picture of the Messiah and the gentile Church.

Moab certainly had a poor beginning because the Moabites came out of the incestuous relationship of Lot with his daughters. One of the sons was Moab:

"Thus were both the daughters of Lot with child by their father. And the firstborn bare a son, and called his name Moab: the same is the father of the Moabites unto this day"
(Genesis 19:36,37).

They were idolaters and worshiped an idol called *Chemosh*, which means a "dunghill deity":

"Then did Solomon build an high place for Chemosh, the abomination of Moab, in the hill that is before Jerusalem, and for Molech, the abomination of the children of Ammon. Because that they have forsaken me, and have worshipped Ashtoreth the goddess of the Zidonians, Chemosh the god of the Moabites..."
(I Kings 11:7,33).

In God's eyes Moab was a cursed place, and He did not want a Moabite entering into His congregation until the tenth generation (Deuteronomy 2:9-11).

The Moabites' territory was east of the Dead Sea and south of the River Arnon (Numbers 21:11-29).

Moses was buried in Moab (Deuteronomy 34).

We find the Moabites' oppression of Israel in Judges 3:12-30.

Later David made them subject to Israel:

"And he smote Moab, and measured them with a line, casting them down to the ground; even with two lines measured he to put to death, and with one full line to keep alive. And so the Moabites became David's servants, and brought gifts" **(II Samuel 8:2).**

"Then Moab rebelled against Israel after the death of Ahab" **(II Kings 1:1; see also II Kings 3:4-26).**

David refers to the Moabites in the Psalms - God said that Moab was His '"*washpot*" (Psalms 60:8 108:9).

There is no question that Moab will be in the fulfillment of future prophecy: Isaiah 15,16,25:10; Jeremiah 48; Ezekiel 25; Daniel 11:41; and Zephaniah 2:8,9.

Modern-day Jordan would be a part of ancient Moab.

SEEING JESUS IN RUTH

Boaz is a beautiful picture of Jesus Christ, our Kinsman-Redeemer. Jesus came in the flesh, was tempted in all ways as we are (He had to be the Son of *Man*), yet was without sin and paid the price with a perfect, sinless life - shedding His blood to be our sacrificial Lamb. He paid what was needed.

The *kinsman-redeemer* is certainly a picture of Jesus:

"But if the man have no kinsman to recompense the trespass unto, let the trespass be recompensed unto the LORD, even to the priest; beside the ram of the atonement, whereby an atonement shall be made for him" **(Numbers 5:8).**

THEME VERSE

The LORD recompense thy work, and a full reward be given thee of the LORD God of Israel, under whose wings thou art come to trust" **(Ruth 2:12).**

OUTLINE

I. **RUTH MADE HER DECISION -** CHAPTER 1

A. **13 Famines: there were basically 13 famines listed in the Old Testament. Famines came as judgments when God's people were worshiping idols. It was certainly not a time to leave and go into Moab, which was considered a cursed place. However, Elimelech, his wife Naomi, and his two sons left Bethlehem-Judah, which means "a house of bread and a place of praise," and came into Moab, a cursed place.**

NOTES

NOTES

B. Don't Leave God's Place of Blessing: It is bad to leave God's blessed places even though a famine is present and go into a cursed place.

C. Elimelech's Sons: one of Elimelech's sons was Mahlon, which means "sick." The other son was Chillon, which means "consumption." If they were already sickly, to take them outside of God's blessed place was asking for trouble.

D. In Addition: these two men married Moabite girls. This was forbidden by law:

1. *"Neither shalt thou make marriages with them; thy daughter thou shalt not give unto his son, nor his daughter shalt thou take unto thy son"* **(Deuteronomy 7:3).**

2. *"An Ammonite or Moabite shall not enter into the congregation of the LORD; even to their tenth generation shall they not enter into the congregation of the LORD for ever"* **(Deuteronomy 23:3).**

E. Naomi's Losses: Naomi lost her sons and her husband in the cursed place. In ten years she had a great deal of tragedy.

F. Naomi's Decision: when she heard that the famine was over in Bethlehem-Judah, she made a decision to return to the "house of bread and place of praise." Anytime we come back to the Word of God and to the place of praise, God can create a new beginning for us because we are then in a blessed place.

G. Naomi Prepares To Leave: as Naomi prepared to leave, both her daughters-in-law wanted to go with her. Her words to her daughters-in-law are certainly spiritual (Ruth 1:9). Though she had been in a cursed place, Naomi had never lost her faith in a living God. However, she had become very bitter, and her concept of God was affected:

1. *"...for it grieveth me much for your sakes that the hand of the LORD is gone out against me"* **(Ruth 1:13).**

H. Disobeying God's Word: when we disobey God's Word, sin comes against us, and sin brings death. It is not God Who is against us but our sin that brings a harvest of death against us.

I. Reverse the Curse: Ruth's words absolutely reversed the curse in her life and turned her situation around. This undoubtedly is the theme of the book:

1. *"And Ruth said, Intreat me not to leave thee, or to return from following after thee: for whither thou goest, I will go; and where thou lodgest, I will lodge: thy people shall be my people, and thy God my God: Where thou diest, will I die, and there will I be buried: the LORD do so to me, and more also, if ought but death part thee and me"* **(Ruth 1:16,17).**

J. Naomi's Return: when Naomi returned to Bethlehem she again recalled her bitterness and her past wounds. She said, "Call me not Naomi, but call me Mara," which means "bitter."

K. Naomi Speaks of the Almighty: Naomi spoke of the One Who had dealt bitterly with her as the *"Almighty"* (1:20). *Almighty* is the Hebrew word *El Shaddai*, which means the "the God Who is more than enough."

L. Naomi's New Beginning: she may have left and come home empty, but she is about to be full again! El Shaddai is always mentioned when death has occurred and there is no way out except God to bring resurrection life. El Shaddai is the God of resurrection.

II. RUTH GLEANED IN THE FIELD - CHAPTER 2

A. Arrival in Bethlehem: when they arrived in Bethlehem, they began to pray for God's grace and favor (Ruth 2:2). *Grace* and *favor* are the same word.

B. Ruth Finds Favor: Ruth must glean in the fields, but only within the fields belonging to the tribe of her dead husband. It is there that she truly had an answer to prayer and found grace or favor in the eyes of Boaz:

1. *"Then she fell on her face, and bowed herself to the ground, and said unto him, Why have I found grace in thine eyes, that thou shouldest take knowledge of me, seeing I am a stranger?"* **(Ruth 2:10).**

C. Ruth Worships the Lord God: we read also that Ruth had a reputation for having come to a living God - she is no longer a worshiper of the idol Chemosh but a worshiper of the Lord God of Israel:

1. *"The LORD recompense thy work, and a full reward be given thee of the LORD God of Israel, under whose wings thou art come to trust"* **(Ruth 2:12).**

D. Boaz Blesses Ruth: Ruth continued to ask for favor, and Boaz secretly began to bless her.

III. RUTH CLAIMED THE RIGHT TO BE REDEEMED - CHAPTER 3.

A. Naomi Advises Ruth: In chapter three, Naomi began to tell her daughter-in-law how to catch a husband. She told her to take a bath, to put on perfume, and to put on a new dress (Ruth 3:3).

B. A Marriage Request: when Ruth lay down at the feet of Boaz, she was basically making a marriage request. She asked him to spread his skirt over his handmaiden because he was a near-kinsman. In a Jewish wedding a man puts his robe around his bride, saying that he will be her covering. Ruth was asking Boaz to be her covering.

NOTES

NOTES

IV. RUTH RECEIVES HER REDEMPTION - CHAPTER 4

A. Boaz Proves Himself: In order for Boaz to marry Ruth he had to prove that he was a kinsman so that he could redeem the land for her dead husband. Boaz also had to have the money to buy the land that belonged to her husband.

B. Boaz, the Kinsman-Redeemer: such a man was not only the one to redeem but also the one to take vengeance for a slain relative:

1. *"And they shall be unto you cities for refuge from the avenger; that the manslayer die not, until he stand before the congregation in judgment"* **(Numbers 35:12).**

2. *"Lest the avenger of the blood pursue the slayer, while his heart is hot, and overtake him, because the way is long, and slay him; whereas he was not worthy of death, inasmuch as he hated him not in time past. Then the elders of his city shall send and fetch him thence, and deliver him into the hand of the avenger of blood, that he may die"* **(Deuteronomy 19:6,12; see also Joshua 20:3-9).**

C. Selling an Inheritance: when a Hebrew was forced to sell his inheritance because of poverty, the nearest relative was to redeem it for him:

1. *"If thy brother be waxen poor, and hath sold away some of his possession, and if any of his kin come to redeem it, then shall he redeem that which his brother sold"* **(Leviticus 25:25).**

D. The Kinsman-Redeemer: In case one acted as a kinsman-redeemer of one who had died without a son, he was obliged to marry the widow. Should he refuse to take possession of the property, he was not under obligation to marry the widow. Boaz had no right to redeem the property until the nearest kinsman refused.

E. Seven basic steps: there were seven basic steps in kinsman redemption:

1. **Getting witnesses to confirm every transaction between all parties involved as possible redeemers** (Ruth 4:2)
2. **Agreement on which man shall be the redeemer** (Ruth 4:3-6)
3. **Taking off of the shoe of the one who gives his right of redemption to another as a witness that he gives up such rights** (Ruth 4:7,8)
4. **Redemption of the inheritance itself** (Ruth 4:9)
5. **Marriage between the redeemer and the wife of the dead husband in order to raise up seed to continue his name** (Ruth 4:10).
6. **Confession of witnesses to the transaction** (Ruth 4:11)

7. **Blessing of the married couple** (Ruth 4:11)

F. **Not a Fixed Law: the number of witnesses of the kinsman-redeemer were not a fixed law, but usually ten men were chosen as witnesses. The law required two or three witnesses and allowed any other number above this:**

1. *"Whoso killeth any person, the murderer shall be put to death by the mouth of witnesses: but one witness shall not testify against any person to cause him to die"* **(Numbers 35:30).**
2. *"At the mouth of two witnesses, or thee witnesses, shall he that is worthy of death be put to death; but at the mouth of one witness he shall not be put to death. The hands of the witnesses shall be first upon him to put him to death, and afterward the hands of all the people. So thou shalt put the evil away from among you"* **(Deuteronomy 17:6,7).**
3. *"One witness shall not rise up against a man for any iniquity, or for any sin, in any sin that he sinneth: at the mouth of two witnesses, or at the mouth of three witnesses, shall the matter be established"* **(Deuteronomy 19:15).**
4. *"But if he will not hear thee, then take with thee one or two more, that in the mouth of two or three witnesses every word may be established"* **(Matthew 18:16).**
5. *"But found none: yea, though many false witnesses came, yet found they none. At the last came two false witnesses"* **(Matthew 26:60).**
6. *"This is the third time I am coming to you. In the mouth of two or three witnesses shall every word be established"* **(II Corinthians 13:1).**
7. *"Against an elder receive not an accusation, but before two or three witnesses"* **(I Timothy 5:19).**
8. *"He that despised Moses' law died without mercy under two or three witnesses"* **(Hebrews 10:28).**

G. **Witnesses: In the matter of witnesses to the death, burial, and Resurrection of Christ and His teaching, there were twelve witnesses or six times more than the number required by law to confirm anything:**

1. *"Beginning from the baptism of John, unto that same day that he was taken up from us, must one be ordained to be a witness with us of this resurrection"* **(Acts 1:22).**
2. *"This Jesus hath God raised up, whereof we all are witnesses"* **(Acts 2:32).**
3. *"And killed the Prince of life, whom God hath raised from the dead; whereof we are witnesses"* **(Acts 3:15).**
4. *"And with great power gave the apostles witness of the resurrection of the Lord Jesus: and great grace was upon them all"* **(Acts 4:33).**

NOTES

NOTES

5. *"And we are his witnesses of these things; and so is also the Holy Ghost, whom God hath given to them that obey him"* **(Acts 5:32).**

6. *"And we are witnesses of all things which he did both in the land of the Jews, and in Jerusalem; whom they slew and hanged on a tree: Him God raised up the third day, and shewed him openly; Not to all the people, but unto witnesses chosen before of God, even to us, who did eat and drink with him after he rose from the dead"* **(Acts 10:39-41).**

H. Only Two Witnesses: In future tribulation only two witnesses will be sent to men (Revelation 11:1-11).

I. Ruth and Boaz's Child: remember, the child that would be born of Ruth and Boaz would not have Boaz's name but her dead husband's name. That would make Naomi a grandmother when it would have been impossible since she had a dead husband and two dead sons! El Shaddai, the God of resurrection, would make her a grandmother in an impossible situation.

J. Naomi's Grandson: her grandson would be a restorer of her life and a nourisher of her old age. Her daughter-in-law, who had come to put her trust in El Shaddai, would be better to her than seven sons. Naomi became the baby-sitter of *Obed*, which means "a worshiper of God." Her grandson would be in the lineage of King David and in the lineage of Jesus Christ.

K. A Picture of Our Redeemer: there is no question that the book of Ruth shows the picture of our Redeemer as well as any book of the Bible.

L. Naomi Abundantly Blessed: Naomi had come home *empty*, but she would leave this life *full* because of El Shaddai.

RUTH QUOTED IN THE NEW TESTAMENT: NOT FOUND

I SAMUEL

SAMUEL, SAUL, AND DAVID - THREE CHOSEN MEN		
A PROPHET & JUDGE - GOD'S CHOICE	**A KING - THE PEOPLE'S CHOICE**	**A NEW KING - GOD'S CHOICE**
Samuel: **1-7**	Saul: **8-15**	David: **16-31**
LOCATION: The Promised Land		
OVERVIEW: A barren wife asks God for a son.	Saul's reign, disobedience, & rejection.	David's anointing, wandering, & suffering.
TIME: 100 years		

FAST FACTS

AUTHOR AND SETTING:

Samuel; Israel, Judah

PURPOSE:

Samuel writes a prophetically oriented history of Israel's early monarchy. Because their sinful nature found it easier to follow an earthly king, the Israelites were reluctantly granted a monarch of their popular choice - but man's wisdom never exceeds God's wisdom, and this promising reign ended in bitterness and failure.

SEEING JESUS:

The person of Jesus is revealed both in Samuel - prophet, priest, and judge; and in David - shepherd and king.

THEME VERSE:

I Samuel 2:9

NOTES

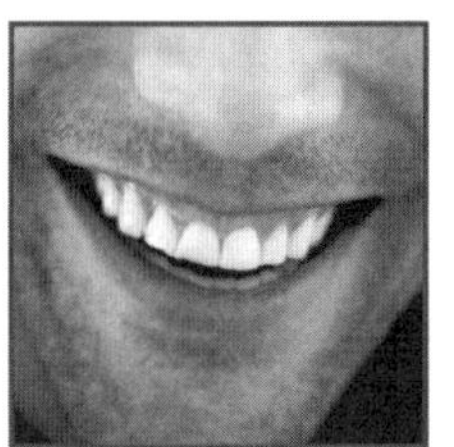

I SAMUEL:
THE PROPHET

NOTES

SEEING JESUS IN I SAMUEL

AUTHOR & SETTING

First Chronicles 29:29 mention the "book of Samuel," and Talmudic tradition attributes *I Samuel* to this prophet. Another writer no doubt added details of Samuel's death in I Samuel 25:1 and the events in II Samuel.

OVERVIEW

Men are called in unique and unusual ways. Moses was prepared to deliver Israel from Egypt and for the giving of the law. Samuel was prepared to guide a government-by-judges to a government-by-kings. Most important Samuel established a school of prophets. These prophets were the mouthpieces of God to kingly and national conscience. For five hundred years they were the orators, the poets, the historians, and the reformers of both the northern and the southern kingdoms.

Samuel was born at Ramathaim-zophim. He lived, died, and was buried there. He belonged to the tribe of Levi but was not a descendant of Aaron. Eli was a descendant of Aaron but not Eleazar. When Eli's descendants all died, the priesthood went back to Aaron's eldest son Zadok.

Samuel's mother Hannah greatly desired a son; Samuel's birth came out of her great faith and desire before God to have a son. *Samuel* means "asked of God".

I'm sure that Hannah never dreamed that her vow and her gift of her son to the Lord would bring such a high "interest rate" to Israel as well as to the Body of Christ:

"Therefore also I have lent him to the LORD; as long as he liveth he shall be lent to the LORD. And he worshipped the LORD there" **(I Samuel 1:28).**

You never give unto the Lord that it isn't recompensed unto you again:

"And the LORD visited Hannah, so that she conceived, and bare three sons and two daughters. And the child Samuel grew before the LORD"
(I Samuel 2:21).

As a young child Samuel was committed to be a priest in the household of Eli - an ungodly household. But Hannah's commitment of her son kept him under the supernatural guidance of God during those years.

Eli lost his priesthood as well as his sons because he esteemed his sons more than he esteemed God. There is no question that Eli knew God's voice, but he didn't listen.

Samuel leaned God's voice, and he listened.

Eli died with a broken neck as well as a broken heart. He judged Israel for forty years (I Samuel 4:18).

The Ark would go into captivity, but certainly God's presence would not stay in captivity.

The people turned to Samuel for an answer and cried out for him to pray for them:

"And the children of Israel said to Samuel, Cease not to cry unto the LORD our God for us, that he will save us out of the hand of the Philistines" **(I Samuel 7:8).**

There was a miraculous victory of the Israelites over the Philistines at this time:

"And as Samuel was offering up the burnt offering, the Philistines drew near to battle against Israel: but the LORD thundered with a great thunder on that day upon the Philistines, and discomfited them; and they were smitten before Israel. Then Samuel took a stone, and set it between Mizpeh and Shen, and called the name of it Ebenezer, saying, Hitherto hath the LORD helped us" **(I Samuel 7:10,12).**

Samuel led Israel as a prophet and a judge, but the people wanted a king like the nations around them. Although God had a time for a king, the people of Israel demanded a king before God's timing. Samuel felt very rejected by their demands, but God spoke to him and said, "They have not rejected you, Samuel. They have rejected Me." However, because of the cry of the people, God had Samuel anoint Saul to be their king. God gave Saul another heart, and the Spirit of God came upon him:

"And it was so, that when he had turned his back to go from Samuel, God gave him another heart: and all those signs came to pass that day. And when they came thither to the hill, behold, a company of prophets met him; and the Spirit of God came upon him, and he prophesied among them" **(I Samuel 10:9,10).**

The first record of the kingdom of Israel was written by Samuel:

"Then Samuel told the people the manner of the kingdom, and wrote it in a book, and laid it up before the LORD. And Samuel sent all the people away, every man to his house" **(I Samuel 10:25).**

Saul, however, did not esteem his anointing and thereby lost it through disobedience. God turned to David, and Samuel was directed to anoint him. Samuel was not to look upon David's outward appearance because God was looking upon David's heart.

It is interesting that after I Samuel 16, with the anointing of God upon him, David killed a giant (I Samuel 17). The anointing upon David's life certainly made him a giant in God and a giant-killer.

David esteemed highly the anointing upon his own life, but he also esteemed the anointing upon Saul's life and refused to touch God's anointed. For nine years Saul harassed David and attempted to kill him, but David would not retaliate because of

NOTES

NOTES

God's anointing upon Saul's life.

David ended up in the position as the king of Israel. It was God's anointing that put him there and certainly God's anointing that kept him there.

One of the greatest blessings that would come to David, as well as all the kings of Israel, would be the prophets. They came out of the school of the prophets that Samuel began.

Samuel's greatest ministry was at the end of his life. When he started the school of the prophets, it produced every major prophet that we read about. They became the spiritual power behind every throne.

Jezebel tried to wipe out the school of prophets, but this school brought the whole nation to repentance. These prophets were "live wires"; whoever touched them was burned!

God's thoughts on kings:

1. A government-by-king was God's thought.
2. God did not give the Israelites a king like other nations, because the king would be his choice.
3. The kingdom of Israel would have a written charter (Deuteronomy 17:14-20).
4. The king would be appointed by Jehovah - not elected by the people.
5. The kingship didn't necessarily go to the oldest heir.

The prophet was to make known God's choice. For example Solomon, although not the eldest son of David, was chosen to be king. This safeguarded the people from tyranny.

God first showed Samuel that Saul was to be the king. At Mizpah the choice was made known publicly (I Samuel 10:17-21).

Saul was qualified by the Holy Spirit.

Saul did not begin to fall until he made God his enemy.

David made God his friend. David was a man after God's own heart.

The key to David's great success was that he was never whipped on the inside.

SEEING JESUS IN I SAMUEL

Mary and Hannah's songs (Luke 1 and I Samuel 2) were both about the Lord's anointed. Hannah was the first one to call the Lord "anointed," which is the word *Messiah*. Until this time no one had known of God's deliverer as *Messiah*. How beautiful that she and Mary would receive the revelation of the Messiah - the Lord's anointed One.

In her song Hannah mentions the Messiah:

"The adversaries of the LORD shall be broken to pieces; out of heaven shall he thunder upon them: the LORD shall judge the ends of the earth; and he shall give strength unto his king, and exalt the horn of his anointed" **(I Samuel 2:10).**

Samuel and Jesus are both described in the same terms during their childhood:

"And the child Samuel grew on, and was in favour both with the LORD, and also with men" **(I Samuel 2;26).**

"And Jesus increased in wisdom and stature, and in favour with God and man" **(Luke 2:52).**

When God spoke to Samuel, He revealed Himself as a Messiah - not only as He had to Hannah, but now to her son:

"And I will raise me up a faithful priest, that shall do according to that which is in mine heart and in my mind: and I will build him a sure house; and he shall walk before mine anointed forever" **(I Samuel 2:35).**

THEME VERSE

"He will keep the feet of his saints, and the wicked shall be silent in darkness; for by strength shall no man prevail" **(I Samuel 2:9).**

OUTLINE

(Refer to map on page A8 in the APPENDIX.)

I. **SAMUEL - THE PROPHET AND JUDGE -** I SAMUEL 1-7

A. **Comparison of Elkanah's Two Wives**

1. **Barren Hannah asked God for a son.**
2. **Hannah named her son Samuel ("asked of God").**
3. **Her prophetic prayer mentions the word Messiah for the first time.**
4. **The song of Mary in Luke 1 contains echoes of Hannah's song.**

B. **Contrast of Eli and His Sons:**

NOTES

NOTES

1. **God pronounced judgment because of Eli's lack of discipline:** *"For I have told him that I will judge his house for ever for the iniquity which he knoweth; because his sons made themselves vile, and he restrained them not"* **(I Samuel 3:13).**

2. **The actions of Eli's sons caused men to despise God's offerings:** *"Wherefore the sin of the young men was very great before the LORD: for men abhorred the offering of the LORD"* **(I Samuel 2:17).**

3. **They used the Ark as a fetish for battle with the Philistines.**

4. **God brought judgment on Philistine idols (I Samuel 5). Later, they beat the Philistines at Ebenezer ("the stone of the help") saying, *"...Hitherto hath the LORD helped us"* (I Samuel 7:12).**

II. KING SAUL'S REIGN, DISOBEDIENCE, AND REJECTION - I SAMUEL 8-15

A. Saul's Selection To Be King - I Samuel 8-12

1. **After his selection and victory at Jabesh-gilead the nations rallied around him.**

2. **He intruded into the priest's office -** I Samuel 13:8-10:

   "But now thy kingdom shall not continue: the LORD hath sought him a man after his own heart, and the LORD hath commanded him to be captain over his people, because thou hast not kept that which the LORD commanded thee" **(I Samuel 13:14).**

3. **Saul was corrected again in the treatment of the Amalekites -** I Samuel 15:22.

III. DAVID'S ANOINTING, WANDERING, AND SUFFERING - I SAMUEL 16-31

A. David is Seen First As a Shepherd - I Samuel 16,17.

B. Next David is Seen As a Military Leader and Official in Saul's Court - I Samuel 18,19.

C. David is Finally Seen As a Fugitive - I Samuel 20:31.

1. **Twice David spared Saul's life.**

D. Saul and His Sons: The book closes with the death of Saul and his sons. His reign started with promise but ended with bitterness and failure:

1. *"And afterward they desired a king: and God gave unto them Saul the son of Cis, a man of the tribe of Benjamin, by the space of forty years"* **(Acts 13:21).**

I SAMUEL QUOTED IN THE NEW TESTAMENT

I Samuel 13:14 (Psalms 89:20)
But now thy kingdom shall not continue: the LORD hath sought him a man after his own heart, and the LORD hath commanded him to be captain over his people, because thou hast not kept that which the LORD commanded thee.

Acts 13:22
And when he had removed him, he raised up unto them David to be their king; to whom also he gave testimony, and said, I have found David the son of Jesse, a man after mine own heart, which shall fulfill all my will.

II SAMUEL

DAVID THE KING	
KING OF JUDAH & HEBRON	**KING OF ALL ISRAEL**
Preparations: **1-4**	Nation United: **5-10** David's Troubles: **11-19** David's Solutions: **20-24**
LOCATION: Judah	All Israel
OVERVIEW: Saul's son Fights David God's anointed	Ruling and entire nation through repentance and faith
TIME: 40 years - halfway between Abraham & Christ	

FAST FACTS

AUTHOR AND SETTING:

Part authorship by Samuel; Israel

PURPOSE:

Second Samuel offers a candid portrait of the strengths and weaknesses of David's 40-year reign as he built Israel into a powerful nation. The only person honored as "a man after God's own heart," the very humanity of David offers hope for redemption to all people; for ***"...all have sinned, and come short of the glory of God"*** **(Romans 3:23).**

SEEING JESUS:

David is an important Old Testament type of Christ. Many of the promises made to David are fulfilled in Jesus. In the New Testament Jesus is called *"the son of David"* (Matthew 21:9).

THEME VERSE:

II Samuel 23: 2

NOTES

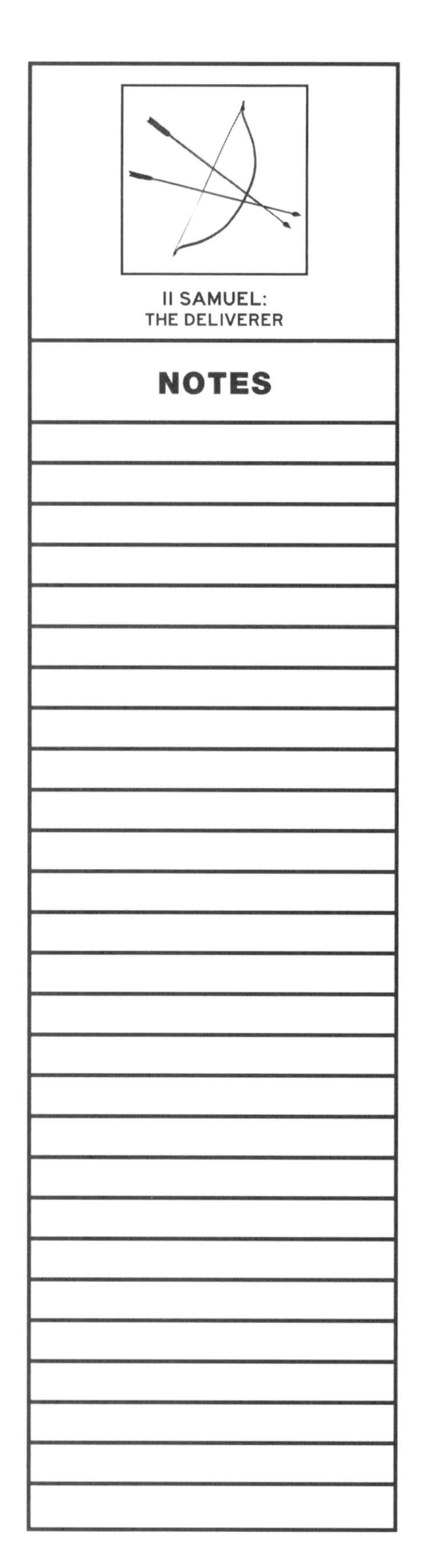

SEEING JESUS IN II SAMUEL

AUTHOR & SETTING

An unnamed prophet close to Samuel (and no doubt trained by him) wrote this continuing history of David.

OVERVIEW

The history of David is given against the background of three prophets: Samuel, Nathan, and Gad.

In I Samuel we saw the record of the failure of Israel under Eli, Saul, and Samuel. The restoration of order through David is given in ***II Samuel.*** David is the choice of God for ruler of His people. This book records the full establishment of the kingdom of Israel with Jerusalem as the political and religious center. The making of the Davidic covenant as the basis of all earthly kingdom truth (I Samuel 7:1-29) is also found in ***II Samuel.***

We see the full conquest of the enemies of Israel (II Samuel 3:1, 5:17-25, 8:1-15). We see David's sin and repentance (II Samuel 11:1-12:24). We see the family troubles of David (II Samuel 13:1-14:33). We see the rebellion of Absalom (II Samuel 15-19:43). We see the last days of David (II Samuel 20:1-24:25).

CERTAINLY DAVID WAS PREPARED TO BE A KING THROUGH:

1. **His shepherd life**
2. **His fleeing from Saul**

As David began his reign he brought unity into the nation after seven-and-a-half years. He provided a central place of worship. He destroyed the backbone of the enemy. He organized a civil service, and he organized the priesthood.

He was anointed at Bethlehem and Hebron. Psalms 133 was probably written by him in relationship to the anointing. Jerusalem had been the city of Melchizedek. On Mount Moriah Abraham had offered his son.

David warred against the Ammonites, the Philistines, the Syrians of Zobah, the Syrians of Damascus, the Moabites, and the Edomites.

David knew that God was on his side:

1. He was never the aggressor with Saul.
2. He never lost a battle.
3. He filled up boundaries promised to Abraham.
4. The spoils of war were consecrated to Jehovah.
5. His alliance with Hiram made him safe on his Mediterranean border.
6. He had men who, like himself, were giant killers.

David's administration:

1. Joab was over his host.
2. Jehoshaphat was his recorder.
3. Zadok and Ahimelech were his priests.
4. Seraiah was his scribe.
5. Benaiah was over the Cherethites and the Pelethites.
6. David's sons were chiefs

Psalms 38 and 51 were written about David's sins.
Psalms 32 expresses the joy of forgiveness.

The nations of Moab, Ammon, and Edom conspired to destroy David but were not successful.

SEEING JESUS IN II SAMUEL

In I Samuel we saw the faith and revelation of Hannah. She believed God for a son and named him *Samuel*, which means "asked of God." Hannah also received the first revelation of Jesus as the Messiah - the Anointed One. In *II Samuel* we will see the preparation for the coming of this Messiah in the Davidic line. The books of I and II Chronicles also lean heavily upon this.

David knew Jesus in an intimate way. He even recorded, in Psalms 22, the very words that the Messiah would speak on the Cross. David knew soul-cleansing that only Jesus could give.

THEME VERSE

"The Spirit of the LORD spake by me, and his word was in my tongue" **(II Samuel 23:2).**

OUTLINE

I. **DAVID - KING OVER JUDAH AND HEBRON -** II SAMUEL 1-4

A. **Civil War Began Between Ish-bosheth and David.**

1. **After Abner deserted Ish-bosheth, the tide of the war turned in David's favor.**

2. **Ish-bosheth was killed.**

II. **DAVID - KING OVER THE WHOLE NATION OF ISRAEL IN JERUSALEM -** II SAMUEL 5-24

A. **Victories of King David -** II Samuel 5-10

1. **Davidic covenant -** II Samuel 7

a. This, of course, pictures the Messiah Who would come through David's line.

B. **The Account of His Troubles and Sins -** II Samuel 11-24

1. **Sin with Bath-sheba**

a. Repentance - Psalms 32, 51

b. Influence on sons Amnon, Absalom, and Adonijah

2. **David's numbering of Israel**

3. **The book closes with the purchasing of the threshing floor of Araunah.**

a. This was later the site of Solomon's temple.

4. **David was a man of faith.**

a. His song in chapter 22 is a version of Psalms 18.

NOTES

II SAMUEL QUOTED IN THE NEW TESTAMENT.

II Samuel 7:12,13 (Psalms 89:4,34, 132:11)
And when thy days be fulfilled, and thou shalt sleep with thy fathers, I will set up thy seed after thee, which shall proceed out of thy bowels, and I will establish his kingdom. He shall build an house for my name, and I will establish the throne of his kingdom forever.

Acts 2:30
Therefore being a prophet, and knowing that God had sworn with an oath to him, that of the fruit of his loins, according to the flesh, he would raise up Christ to sit on this throne.

****

II Samuel 7:14
I will be his father, and he shall be my son. If he commits iniquity, I will chasten him with the rod of men, and with the stripes of the children of men.

Hebrews 1:5
For unto which of the angels said he at any time, Thou art my Son, this day have I begotten thee? And again, I will be to him a Father, and he shall be to me a Son?

****

II Samuel 22:3 (Isaiah 8:17,18)
The God of my rock; in him will I trust: he is my shield, and the horn of my salvation, my high tower, and my refuge, my saviour; thou savest me from violence.

Hebrews 2:13
And again, I will put my trust in him. And again, Behold I and the children which God hath given me.

****

II Samuel 22:50 (Psalms 18:49)
Therefore I will give thanks unto thee, O LORD, among the heathen, and I will sing praises unto thy name.

Romans 15:9
And that the Gentiles might glorify God for his mercy; as it is written, For this cause I will confess to thee among the Gentiles, and sing unto thy name.

NOTES

I KINGS

SOLOMON & THE DIVIDED KINGDOM	
LIFE & REIGN OF SOLOMON	**DIVIDED KINGDOM**
The establishing of Solomon: **1,2** The wisdom of Solomon: **3** The glory of Solomon: **4-8** The fall of Solomon: **9-11**	Division of the kingdom: **12-14** Reigns of various kings: **15,16** Ahab & Elijah: **16-22** Jehoshaphat in Judah: **22** Ahaziah in Israel: **22**
LOCATION: Jerusalem - capital of the united kingdom of Israel	Samaria - capital of Israel; Jerusalem - capital of Judah
OVERVIEW: A man who knew how to amass and creatively use wealth lost all because of sinfulness	A house divided does not stand
TIME: 40 years	945 B.C. (74 years)

FAST FACTS

AUTHOR AND SETTING:

Jeremiah; Israel/Judah

PURPOSE:

First Kings shows that the welfare of Israel and Judah depended upon the faithfulness of the people and their king. The lives of the kings were used to teach basic principles: (1) man cannot rule himself without the help of God; (2) kings depended upon faithfulness to God to be good administrators; (3) if kings disregarded God, so did their people; and (4) observance of God's laws produces blessing, but disobedience is followed by judgment.

SEEING JESUS:

Solomon typified Jesus Christ in many ways; his wisdom, fame, glory, wealth, and honor foreshadow Christ's wisdom and kingdom.

THEME VERSE:

I Kings 9:4,5

NOTES

II KINGS

COLLISION COURSE WITH CAPTIVITY	
DIVIDED KINGDOMS	**SURVIVING KINGDOMS**
Elisha: **1-8** Kings of Israel & kings of Judah: **8-16** Fall of Israel: **17**	Hezekiah & evil kings: **18-21** Josiah & evil kings: **22-24** Fall of Judah: **24, 25**
LOCATION: Israel, Assyria	Judah, Babylonia
OVERVIEW: 19 consecutive evil kings rule in Israel - great prophets rise to avert destruction.	Godly kings occasionally emerge in Judah, but sin outweighed righteousness
TIME: 130 years	150 years

FAST FACTS

AUTHOR AND SETTING:

Jeremiah; Israel/Judah

PURPOSE:

Second Kings records the pivotal events in the careers of the kings of Israel and Judah and shows how rebellion against God led to the failure and overthrow of the monarchy. Among many great prophets who arose during these dismal years, Elijah and Elisha stand out as strong men of God.

SEEING JESUS:

God remained faithful to His covenant with David by protecting his lineage through which Jesus Christ eventually came. Elisha typifies Jesus - emphasizing grace, life, and hope.

THEME VERSE:

II Kings 23:27

NOTES

I CHRONICLES

REVIEWING DAVID'S KINGDOM	
DAVID'S ANCESTRY	**DAVID'S KINGDOM**
Genealogical tables: **1-9**	David takes the throne: **10-12** Retrieving the Ark of the Covenant: **13-17** David's victories: **18-20** Materials for the Temple: **21-27** David's final days: **28,29**
LOCATION: Fertile Crescent	Israel
OVERVIEW: Reinforcing the direct descent of Jesus Christ from Adam through David	Putting military and political events into a religious significance
TIME: 4000 - 500 B.C.	30 years

FAST FACTS

AUTHOR AND SETTING:

Ezra; Israel

PURPOSE:

Ezra wrote *I Chronicles* to reveal God's faithfulness and continuing purpose for His people. While *I Chronicles* does not deny human failures, it emphasizes the Messianic line, the Temple, and spiritual reforms.

SEEING JESUS:

God promised David that He would *"...settle him (David's ultimate offspring, Jesus Christ) in mine house and in my kingdom forever: and his throne shall be established for evermore" (I Chronicles 17:14).*

THEME VERSE:

I Chronicles 17:11-14

NOTES

II CHRONICLES

GODLY KINGS & REFORMERS	
THE TEMPLE IS CONSTRUCTED	**THE TEMPLE IS DESTROYED**
Solomon's accession: **1** The Temple is built: **2-7** Glory of Solomon's reign: **8,9**	Dividing the kingdom: **10-13** Judah's kings: **14-35** Fall of Judah: **36**
LOCATION: Jerusalem	Judah
OVERVIEW: While obeying God's laws, the kingdom prospers.	When disobedience interferes, the kingdom collapses in spite of faithful men's efforts
TIME: 40 years	400 years

FAST FACTS

AUTHOR AND SETTING:

Ezra; Judah

PURPOSE:

The Tabernacle and the Temple were the center of Israel's identity as a nation. After the Temple was destroyed and later rebuilt, the prophet wrote this book to encourage people to accept the new Temple and to remind them of their true calling and God's faithfulness.

SEEING JESUS:

While the throne of David had been destroyed during this period, the line of David remained...and Christ's fulfillment can be seen in the genealogies of *Matthew 1* and *Luke 3*. Also, the Temple is a type of Christ Himself *(Matthew 12:6; John 2:19; Revelation 21:22)*.

THEME VERSE:

II Chronicles 20:15

NOTES

KINGS & CHRONICLES:
RECORD BOOKS

NOTES

SEEING JESUS IN KINGS & CHRONICLES

AUTHOR & SETTING

We are not told specifically who wrote *I* and *II Kings* or *I* and *II Chronicles*. Many believe that Jeremiah was the author of the Kings and that Ezra was the author of the *Chronicles*. The *Kings* are written in a similar style as the book of Jeremiah, and the same is true of the style of writing in the *Chronicles* and Ezra. Jewish tradition holds to this opinion also.

OVERVIEW

Originally the books of *Kings* were one volume, as were the books of *Chronicles*. In Hebrew *Kings* was titled *Melechim* or "*Kings*" and *Chronicles* was titled *Dibere Hayyamin*, meaning "The Words of the Days." The division of the books came when the Septuagint was translated. We are going to cover the four books together and look at Israel's crucial years leading up to the captivity of both kingdoms and the eventual fulfillment of God's promise to bring them back into the Promised Land after 70 years.

These histories were written by contemporary prophets of the day including Nathan, Ahijah, Iddo, Isaiah, and Jeremiah. It is supposed that Jeremiah later compiled Kings and that Ezra compiled *Chronicles*. The books of *Kings* present a political history of Israel and Judah while the *Chronicles* relate a moral and religious history.

The books of *Kings* and *Chronicles* cover the period of Israel's kings before and after the kingdom was divided. This history includes a span of approximately 450 years. The book of *II Chronicles* covers the same time span as *I* and *II Kings*. A chronological view of these four books would begin with *I Chronicles* and end with *II Chronicles*.

First Chronicles gives a genealogy from Adam to David, records the death of Saul, and relates details of the Davidic kingdom, ending with David's death. The book of *II Chronicles* begins with Solomon's reign and the building of the Temple. It concludes after Judah's 70 years of captivity with the proclamation of Cyrus, king of Persia, which allowed the Jews to return to Jerusalem to rebuild the Temple.

The book of *I Kings* begins with the death of King David and the anointing of his son Solomon to be his successor. This book includes the division of the kingdom after Solomon's death and ends with the reign of Jehoshaphat in Judah and Ahaziah in Israel. The succession of kings is picked up in *II Kings* with the death of Ahaziah and the reign of Jehoram. *Second Kings* includes the Babylonian captivity and ends with Evil-Merodach king of Babylon releasing Judah's king Jehoiachin from prison.

SEEING JESUS IN KINGS & CHRONICLES

David, of course, is a type of Christ, and Solomon is certainly a type of Christ. The wisdom of Solomon points to Christ Who is made wisdom to us (I Corinthians 1:30). Jesus, in Matthew 12:42, spoke of Himself as "greater than Solomon." Jesus also made a comparison between His physical body ("Destroy this temple" - John 2:19-with Solomon's Temple). Elisha is also a type of Christ, the miracle worker.

Our Lord Jesus can be seen throughout the books of *Kings* and *Chronicles* in the lives of godly kings such as David, Solomon, Jehoshaphat, Hezekiah, and Josiah. King David, especially, was a man after God's own heart (I Samuel 13:14). The prophets were all forerunners of the great Prophet, Jesus Christ. Isaiah had tremendous revelations of the coming Savior in His First and Second Advents. Each of the other prophets added their portion of revelation concerning the Messiah to complete God's preparation for bringing Jesus into the world. As we behold Jesus in *Kings* and *Chronicles* during those turbulent times, let's be ever mindful of God's Hand directing the destiny of men and of nations to accomplish His divine purpose.

ORDER OF EVENTS

Upon the death of Saul, his son Ishbosheth was made king over all of Israel except the tribe of Judah. God had told David to go to Hebron where he was anointed king over the tribe of Judah to which he belonged. The civil war which resulted between the two factions ended when Ishbosheth was assassinated, much to David's displeasure.

David was then elected king over all of Israel, and he immediately sought to unite the southern and northern regions by conquering the city of Jebus - later known as Jerusalem. Its location on the border between the southern tribe of Judah and the northern tribes made it an ideal place to set up the capital of the united kingdom.

After David established his residence at Jerusalem, he began to strengthen the worship of God. David transferred the Ark of the Covenant to a tent tabernacle he constructed in Jerusalem. Sacrifices were offered, musicians appointed, and there was constant ministry at the Ark.

David was not happy that he lived in a beautiful house built of cedar wood while Gods Ark resided within the curtain walls of a tent. Instead of David building a house for God, however, God promised to build David's house by establishing his descendant as king over Israel. It was this descendant, Solomon, who would build God's house.

NOTES

NOTES

Chapter 21 of *I Chronicles* records David's sin in numbering the people of Israel. God had promised Abraham that his descendants would be *"...as the stars of the heaven, and as the sand which is upon the sea shore;..."* **(Genesis 22:17).** David's actions showed distrust of the divine promise, or perhaps the information gathered was to be used for unjust taxation of the people. Either way, God judged David and Israel:

"And God was displeased with this thing; therefore he smote Israel" **(I Chronicles 21:7).**

David's heart was soon turned back to the Lord, and David began to gather the materials for the Temple. He further organized worship and the priest's duties.

First Chronicles ends with the coronation of Solomon and the death of King David. Solomon's reign can be divided into four parts:

1. **The beginning** of Solomon's reign
2. **The Wisdom** of Solomon
3. **The glory** of Solomon
4. **The fall** of Solomon

Solomon's desire for wisdom pleased God. Along with granting Solomon wisdom, God promised him riches, wealth, and honor.

One of the high points in Solomon's life was the dedication of the Temple. The glory of the Lord so filled the house *"...that the priests could not stand to minister by reason of the cloud: for the glory of the LORD had filled the house of God"* **(II Chronicles 5:14).**

This same glory filled those who were present in the Upper room on the day of Pentecost: *"And they were all filled with the Holy Ghost, and began to speak with other tongues, as the Spirit gave them utterance"* **(Acts 2:4).** The apostle Paul would later write, *"Know ye not that ye are the temple of God, and that the Spirit of God dwelleth in you?"* **(I Corinthians 3:16).**

The glory of the Lord, however, did not remain with Solomon. Eventually he violated God's charter for Israel's kings found in Deuteronomy 17:14-20:

1. **Solomon** multiplied horses.
2. **Solomon** multiplied wives.
3. **Solomon** multiplied wealth.
4. **Solomon** heavily taxed the people.
5. **Solomon** took foreign wives.

Upon Solomon's death, the united kingdom was split by the rebellion of the ten northern tribes because Solomon's son Rehoboam refused to lighten his father's oppressive practices of forced labor and high taxes. Thus began the succession of kings over the separated kingdoms known as Judah and Israel, along with the rise of God's prophets calling both sides to repentance and obedience to God's ways. Because the people failed to heed the words of the prophets, the people of both nations were led captive until God fulfilled His promise to return them to the Promised Land after 70 years of captivity

ADDITIONAL FACTS ON KINGS AND CHRONICLES

Not one of Israel's 19 kings was considered *right* in the eyes of God, while 8 of Judah's kings are said to have done that which was right in the eyes of the Lord.

The only kings to rule over Judah came from David's lineage. In Israel, however, there were nine different dynasties:

1. Jeroboam and his son Nadab (killed)
2. Baasha and his son Elah (killed)
3. Zimri (burned himself)
4. Omri and three successors: Ahab, Ahaziah, and Jehoram
5. Jehu (the longest dynasty of the northern kings) killed the seed of Omri and was succeeded by Jehoahaz, Jehoash, Jeroboam II, and Zechariah.
6. Shallum (ruled one month)
7. Menahem and his son Pekahiah (killed)
8. Pekah (killed)
9. Hoshea (taken into captivity)

Asa was the first king of Judah who followed after the ways of David. When Asa's son Jehoshaphat became king, he continued to walk and lead the people in godly ways:

1. Jehoshaphat walked in the ways of his father Asa and in the ways of David - I Kings 22:43, II Chronicles 17:3.
2. He sought not unto Baalim - II Chronicles 17:3.
3. His heart was lifted up in the ways of Jehovah - II Chronicles 17:6.
4. He took away the high places - II Chronicles 17:6.
5. He made abundant provision for the people's instruction in the Word - II Chronicles 17:7.
6. He established a judicial system - II Chronicles 19:5-7.
7. He did not isolate himself from the people - II Chronicles 18:2,3.
8. He organized a vast army - II Chronicles 17:13-19.

The results of Jehoshaphat's moral measures:

1. Jehovah established his kingdom - II Chronicles 17:5.
2. Fear fell on surrounding kingdoms - II Chronicles 17:10.
3. All Judah brought tribute - II Chronicles 17:5.
4. The Philistines brought tribute - II Chronicles 17:11.
5. Arabs brought tribute - II Chronicles 17:11.

Jehoshaphat's three errors:

He made affinity with Ahab king of Israel and married his son Jehoram to Ahab's daughter Athaliah - II Chronicles 18:1, 21:5,6; II Kings 8:26 (NAS "granddaughter of Omri").

He became involved in a war with Ahab against Syria - II Chronicles 18.

He joined himself with Ahab's son Ahaziah to build ships and go to Tarshish - II Chronicles 20:35-37.

NOTES

NOTES

Eventually there was war with the Moabites who joined with the Ammonites and the Edomites to attack Judah.

Jehoshaphat called a fast, and the prophet Jahaziel brought God's answer:

"And he said, Hearken ye, all Judah, and ye inhabitants of Jerusalem, and thou king Jehoshaphat, Thus saith the LORD unto you, Be not afraid nor dismayed by reason of this great multitude; for the battle is not yours, but God's" **(II Chronicles 20:15).**

Judah sang while God fought for them:

"And when they began to sing and to praise, the LORD set ambushments against the children of Ammon, Moab, and mount Seir, which were come against Judah; and they were smitten" **(II Chronicles 20:22).**

Omri was the sixth king of Israel. His 12 year reign is noteworthy because:

He established a 45-year dynasty and controlled the foreign policy of Judah. He dominated the throne of Judah for 12 years and attracted much attention from foreign countries.

He built a city, called Samaria, that was the rival to Jerusalem for 1,000 years.

He enacted statues of idolatry that corrupted the people of Israel for 200 years.

He brought in the worship of Baal by marrying his son Ahab to Jezebel.

He inaugurated a policy of alliance that affected the foreign policy of Judah.

Omri's son Ahab was the most wicked of all the northern kings:

"And Ahab the son of Omri did evil in the sight of the LORD above all that were before him. And it came to pass, as if it had been a light thing for him to walk in the sins of Jeroboam the son of Nebat, that he took to wife Jezebel the daughter of Ethbaal king of the Zidonians, and went and served Baal, and worshipped him. And Ahab made a grove; and Ahab did more to provoke the LORD God of Israel to anger than all the kings of Israel that were before him" **(I Kings 16:30,31,33).**

"But there was none like unto Ahab, which did sell himself to work wickedness in the sight of the LORD, whom Jezebel his wife stirred up. And he did very abominably in following idols, according to all things as did the Amorites, whom the LORD cast out before the children of Israel" **(I Kings 21:25,26).**

The reign of King Hezekiah over Judah was another spiritual high point in the period of the divided kingdom:

1. Hezekiah was a righteous king and a great poet (Isaiah 38). He revived the psalter of David. The first two books of psalms were used as songs in the Temple in the days of Hezekiah.

2. Hezekiah rebelled against Assyria and refused to pay the tribute that his father had begun. Sennacherib attacked them, and they had to pay the tribute. There was a crisis in Hezekiah's life (II Kings 20:1-11).

3. After Hezekiah had been reigning about 14 years, he became mortally ill. Hezekiah prayed, and God promised him 15 more years. The prophet Isaiah relayed God's message and told Hezekiah to go to the house of the Lord on the third day. God's confirmation of Hezekiah's recovery was an astounding miracle: the sun reversed its direction ten degrees!

4. Hezekiah received letters and a gift from the son of the king of Babylon during his recovery. Hezekiah showed them all the wealth of his treasure house. When Isaiah learned what had happened, he prophesied:

"...'Hear the word of the LORD. "Behold, the days are coming when all that is in your house, and all that your fathers have laid up in store to this day shall be carried to Babylon; nothing shall be left,"...'" **(II Kings 20:16,17 NAS).**

5. Hezekiah had great wealth and became involved in much building.

6. Assyria attacked again, as prophesied by Isaiah:

"In the same day shall the Lord shave with a razor that is hired, namely, by them beyond the river, by the king of Assyria, the head, and the hair of the feet: and it shall also consume the beard" **(Isaiah 7:20).**

"Now therefore, behold, the Lord bringeth up upon them the waters of the river, strong and many, even the king of Assyria, and all his glory: and he shall come up over all his channels, and go over all his banks: And he shall pass through Judah; he shall overflow and go over, he shall reach even to the neck; and the stretching out of his wings shall fill the breadth of thy land, O Immanuel" **(Isaiah 8:7,8).**

7. Hezekiah prepared well for the siege.

8. Isaiah prophesied the victory.

9. Judah won. Psalms 46-48 were written for this occasion.

10. Victory came because of faith.

THE PROPHETS

The real story of the time of the kings centers around God's prophets; they were the spiritual leaders in Judah and Israel.

Four prophets spoke during the reign of King David:

1. Gad told David to leave the cave Adullam and return to Judah - I Samuel 22:5.

2. Nathan rebuked David over his sin with Bath-sheba - I Samuel 12:1-14.

NOTES

NOTES

3. Zadok returned to Jerusalem after David fled from Absalom and was to report to David what happened there - II Samuel 15:27.

4. Heman was David's seer in matters related to God - I Chronicles 25:5.

Four prophets are mentioned during the time of Jeroboam king of Israel:

1. Ahijah prophesied of the rending of the kingdom into two tribes and ten tribes with Jeroboam as king over the ten tribes - I Kings 11:29-39.
2. A prophet known only as "a man of God" prophesied against the idol worship set up by Jeroboam - I Kings 13:1-10.
3. An "old prophet" deceived the man of God and caused his death - I Kings 13:11-32.
4. Iddo the seer prophesied against Jeroboam - II Chronicles 9:29.

God raised up other prophets in the northern kingdom:

1. Jehu condemned the wickedness of King Baasha - I Kings 16:1-4.
2. Elijah spoke God's Word during the reign of kings Ahab, Ahaziah, and Jehoram - I Kings 17-29,21; II Kings 1-2.
3. Elisha succeeded Elijah during the reign of Jehoram and performed many miracles - II Kings 2-9.
4. Micaiah prophesied of King Ahab's death - II Chronicles 18.
5. Jonah prophesied to Nineveh - Jonah 1-4.
6. Amos prophesied when Uzziah and Jeroboam II reigned - Amos 1:1.
7. Hosea prophesied during the days of kings Uzziah, Jotham, Ahaz, Hezekiah, and Jeroboam II - Hosea 1:1.
8. Oded convinced the Israelites to release Judaean captives in the days of King Ahaz - II Chronicles 28:1-15.

God also raised up prophets in the southern kingdom of Judah:

1. Shemaiah spoke to Solomon's son Rehoboam and told him not to attempt to reunite the country by force - II Chronicles 11:2-4.
2. Azariah blessed King Asa - II Chronicles 15:1-7.
3. Hanani was imprisoned for rebuking King Asa - II Chronicles 16:7-10.
4. Jahaziel promised King Jehoshaphat victory over his enemies - II Chronicles 20:14-17.
5. Eliezer spoke of God's dismay over the alliance of King Jehoshaphat with Israel's King Ahaziah - II Chronicles 20:37. (Each of the following prophets wrote books which are included in the Bible.)
6. Obadiah
7. Joel

8. Zechariah
9. Isaiah
10. Micah

In both kingdoms the prophets were the very life of the nation. They were historians, poets, reformers, orators - the voice of God to people and kings.

ELIJAH THE TISHBITE - (I Kings 17:1-21:29)

Elijah was one of the most dramatic personages in Biblical history. The books in the Bible which mention him are I Kings, II Chronicles, Malachi, Matthew, Mark, Luke, John, Romans, and James. His effective measures included:

1. Announcing a 3-1/2 year drought (his own nourishment coming from ravens and a widow)
2. Challenging King Ahab to bring the prophets of Baal together at Carmel and calling down fire from heaven upon the altar.
3. Confrontation with Ahab in Naboth's vineyard
4. The sick son of Ahab, Ahaziah, was rebuked and died.
5. The letter to Jehoram, the son of Queen Athaliah
6. The measure of perpetuity - he anointed Hazael to be king of Syria and commissioned Elisha as his successor.
7. He was translated.

Elijah was a man who stood against the world!

THE MIRACLES OF ELIJAH:

The miracle of the long drought - I Kings 17:1
The miracle of the ravens - I Kings 17:2-7
The miracle of the meal and oil - I Kings 17:8-16
The miracle of resurrection - I Kings 17:17-24
The miracle at Carmel - I Kings 18:1-39
The miracle of rain - I Kings 18:1,41-45
The miracle run - I Kings 18:46
The miracle of the angelic meal - I Kings 19:1-8
The miracle of God's manifestation - I Kings 19:9-18
The miracle of fire from heaven - II Kings 1:9-14
The miracle parting of the Jordan River - II Kings 2:8
The miracle of the double portion - II Kings 2:10
The miracle of translation - II Kings 2:11
The miracle of transfiguration - Luke 9:28-35

ELISHA

(II Kings 2:13-13:21; II Chronicles 21:1-20)
Elisha burned his bridges behind him. Elisha means "God the Saviour." Elijah's ministry was one of judgment; Elisha's ministry was one of mercy.

There were four schools of the prophets during Elijah's and

NOTES

NOTES

Elisha's time: Jericho, Bethel, Gilgal, and Mount Carmel. Elijah visited each one of them before his translation; Elisha visited them afterward. These schools had great influence for 500 years.

THE MIRACLES OF ELISHA:

Dividing the Jordan with the mantle - II Kings 2:12-14
Healing of bad springs at Jericho - II Kings 2:19-22
Sending of she-bears - II Kings 2:23-25
Water for three kings - II Kings 3:1-22
Multiplying of oil - II Kings 4:1-7
Son and life of Shunamite - II Kings 4:8-37
Healing of poisonous porridge - II Kings 4:38-41
Multiplying of loaves - II Kings 4:42-44
Healing of Naaman's leprosy - II Kings 5:1-19
Leprosy on Gehazi - II Kings 5:26,27
Axe to swim - II Kings 6:1-7
Revealing of secret of Syrian king - II Kings 6:12
Vision to the doubtful servant - II Kings 6:17
Blinding of Syrian host - II Kings 6:18
The Syrian host routed - II Kings 6:19,20
Foreseeing and foretelling seven years of famine - II Kings 8:1
Revelation of the heart of Hazael - II Kings 8:7-15
The miracle of Elisha's bones - II Kings 13:20,21

In addition to the prophets, there were wise women in the land:

1. Jael slew Sisera - Judges 4:1-22.
2. A woman dropped a millstone on Abimelech - Judges 9:52,53.
3. Abigail - I Samuel 25
4. Woman from Tekoa - II Samuel 14:2
5. Bath-sheba, along with David, encouraged Solomon to seek wisdom - Proverbs 1:8.

THE CAPTIVITY

Despite the prophets' warnings, Israel and Judah refused to live in obedience to God's ways. The resultant captivity accomplished five things:

1. It permanently cured the nation of idolatry.
2. It spiritualized religion - they could do without the externals.
3. Suffering was acute and real.
4. It enlarged their concept of God.
5. It gave them a clearer concept of the mission of Israel in God's plan.

THEME VERSES

"And if thou wilt walk before me, as David thy father walked, in integrity of heart, and in uprightness, to do according to all that I have commanded thee, and wilt keep m statutes and my judgments: Then I will establish the throne of thy kingdom upon Israel for ever, as I promised to David thy father, saying, There shall not fall thee a man upon the throne of Israel" **(I Kings 9:4,5).**

"And the LORD said, I will remove Judah also out of my sight, as I have removed Israel, and will cast off this city Jerusalem which I have chosen, and the house of which I said, My name shall be there" **(II Kings 23:27).**

"And it shall come to pass, when thy days be expired that thou must go to be with thy fathers, that I will raise up thy seed after thee, which shall be of thy sons; and I will establish his kingdom. He shall build me an house, and I will stablish his throne for ever. I will be his father, and he shall be my son: and I will not take my mercy away from him, as I took it from him that was before thee: But I will settle him in mine house and in my kingdom for ever: and his throne shall be established for evermore" **(I Chronicles 17:11-14).**

"...Thus saith the LORD unto you, Be not afraid nor dismayed by reason of this great multitude; for the battle is not yours, but God's" **(II Chronicles 20:15).**

OUTLINE

(Refer to maps on pages A7 ad A8 in the Appendix)

I. **GENEALOGICAL TABLES -** I CHRONICLES 1-9
   A. **Documents the Line of the Messiah**
      1. **God emphasizes men - not movements.**

II. **THE REIGN OF DAVID -** I CHRONICLES 10-29
   A. **Death of Saul**
      1. **Saul's son Ishbosheth became king over Israel -** II Samuel 2:8-11.
      2. **David, from the tribe of Judah, became king in Hebron over Judah -** II Samuel 2:1-7.
   B. **Civil War: after years of civil war, the untied kingdom passed to David upon the assassination of Ishbosheth -** II Samuel 4:1-5:5.
   C. **Jerusalem Made Capital**
   D. **David's' Mighty Men**
   E. **David's Religious Policies and Material Wealth**
   F. **The Transfer of the Ark**
   G. **David Desired To Build the Temple.**
   H. **Military Affairs**
   I. **David Numbered the people.**
   J. **Preparation for Future Temple**

NOTES

NOTES

1. **David collected material for the Temple.**
2. **David organized worship.**
3. **Priests divided into 24 orders.**

K. **Death of David**

L. **Solomon on the throne**

III. **THE REIGN OF SOLOMON -** I KINGS 1-11; II CHRONICLES 1-9

A. **Solomon's Prayer for Wisdom**

B. **Establishment of Ceremonies**

C. **Magnificence of the Temple**

D. **Solomon's Prayer**

1. **God appeared to Solomon again:**

a. *"And the LORD appeared to Solomon by night, and said unto him, I have heard thy prayers, and have chosen this place to myself for an house of sacrifice"* **(II Chronicles 7:12).**

E. **Solomon's Glory**

F. **Solomon's Disobedience**

1. **Solomon violated God's warnings in Deuteronomy 17:14-20.**

IV. **THE DIVIDED KINGDOM -** I KINGS 12- II KINGS 25; II CHRONICILES 10-36

A. **Solomon's Son Rehoboam: he divided the kingdom by refusing to lighten the forced labor, high taxes, and other oppressive practices of his father:**

1. *"And now whereas my father did lade you with a heavy yoke, I will add to your yoke: my father hath chastised you with whips, but I will chastise you with scorpions"* **(I Kings 12:11).**

B. **Jeroboam: a former servant of Solomon led the ten northern tribes of Israel in rebellion against the house of David in fulfillment of the prophet Ahijah's words:**

1. *"And he said to Jeroboam, Take thee ten pieces: for thus saith the LORD, the God of Israel, Behold, I will rend the kingdom out of the hand of Solomon, and will give ten tribes to thee"* **(I Kings 11:31).**

2. **Fearing the people of Israel would reunite under Rehoboam if they traveled to Jerusalem to worship, Jeroboam led Israel into idol worship at Dan and Bethel:**

a. *"Whereupon the king took counsel, and made two calves of gold, and said unto them, It is too much for you to go up to Jerusalem: behold thy gods, O Israel, which brought thee up out of the land of Egypt"* **(I Kings 12:28).**

I KINGS QUOTED IN THE NEW TESTAMENT.

I Kings 19:10 (I Kings 19:14)
And he said, I have been very jealous for the Lord God of hosts: for the children of Israel have forsaken thy covenant, thrown down thine altars, and slain thy prophets with the sword; and I, even I only, am left; and they seek my life, to take it away.

Romans 11:3
Lord, they have killed thy prophets, and digged down thine altars; and I am left alone, and they seek my life.

***

I Kings 19:14 (I Kings 19:10)
And he said, I have been very jealous for the Lord God of hosts: for the children of Israel have forsaken thy covenant, thrown down thine altars, and slain thy prophets with the sword; and I, even I only, am left; and they seek my life, to take it away.

Romans 11:3
Lord, they have killed thy prophets, and digged down thine altars; and I am left alone, and they seek my life.

***

I Kings 19:18
Yet I have left me seven thousand in Israel, all the knees which have not bowed unto Baal, and every mouth which hath not kissed him.

Romans 11:4
But what saith the answer of God unto him? I have reserved to myself seven thousand men, who have not bowed the knee to the image of Baal.

II KINGS, I AND II CHRONICLES QUOTED IN THE NEW TESTAMENT: NOT FOUND

NOTES

THE DIVIDED KINGDOM

JUDAH	ISRAEL
South	NORTH
Capital: Jerusalem	Capital: Samaria
Two Tribes	Ten Tribes
(945-586 B.C.)	(945-721 B.C.)

JUDAH

REHOBOAM (B)
945-928
I KINGS 12:1
II CHRONICLES 10:1

ABIJAM (B)
928-926
I KINGS 15:1
II CHRONICLES 13:1

ASA (G)
926-886
I KINGS 15:9
II CHRONICLES 14:1

JEHOSHAPHAT (G)
886-864
I KINGS 22:41
II CHRONICLES 17:1

JEHORAM (B)
865-858
I KINGS 22:50
II CHRONICLES 21:1

AHAZIAH (B)
859-858
II KINGS 8:24
II CHRONICLES 22:1

QUEEN ATHALIAH (B)
858-852
II KINGS 11:1,3
II CHRONICLES 22:10,12

JEHOASH (JOASH) (G)
852-813
II KINGS 11:21
II CHRONICLES 24:1

AMAZIAH (G)
812-784
II KINGS 14:1
II CHRONICLES 25:1

PROPHETS (Judah)

OBADIAH

JOEL

DATES

940
930
920
910
900
890
880
870
860
850
840
830
820
810

PROPHETS (Israel)

ELIJAH

ELISHA

DYNASTIES (Israel)

1

JEROBOAM I (B)
945-924
I KINGS 12:20
II CHRONICLES 10:17

NADAB (B)
925-924
I KINGS 15:25

2

BAASHA (B)
924-901
I KINGS 15:28

ELAH (B)
901-900
I KINGS 16:8

3

ZIMRI (B)
900
I KINGS 16:15

4

OMRI (B)
900-889
I KINGS 16:23

AHAB (B)
889-870
I KINGS 16:29

AHAZIAH (B)
870-869
I KINGS 22:40

JEHORAM (B)
869-858
II KINGS 3:1

5

JEHU (B)
858-831
I KINGS 19:16
II KINGS 9:13
II CHRONICLES 22:7

JEHOAHAZ (B)
830-814
II KINGS 13:1

JEHOASH (B)
816-798
II KINGS 13:10

THE DIVIDED KINGDOM

JUDAH

UZZIAH (AZARIAH) (G)
799-748
II KINGS 15:1
II CHRONICLES 26:1

JOTHAM (G)
747-732
II KINGS 15:32
II CHRONICLES 27:1

AHAZ (B)
732-717
II KINGS 15:38
II CHRONICLES 28:1

HEZEKIAH (G)
727-698
II KINGS 18:1
II CHRONICLES 29:1

MANASSEH (B)
697-642
II KINGS 21:1
II CHRONICLES 33:1

AMON (B)
642-640
II KINGS 21:19
II CHRONICLES 33:21

JOSIAH (G)
640-609
II KINGS 22:1
II CHRONICLES 34:1

JEHOAHAZ (B)
608
II KINGS 23:31
II CHRONICLES 36:1

JEHOIAKIM (B)
608-598
I KINGS 23:36
II CHRONICLES 36:4

JEHOIACHIN (B)
598
II KINGS 24:6
II CHRONICLES 36:9

PROPHETS

MICAH
ISAIAH
NAHUM
ZEPHANIAH
HABAKKUK
JEREMIAH

DATES

800
790
780
770
760
750
740
730
720
710
700
690
680
670
660
650
640
630
620
610
600

ISRAEL

PROPHETS

JONAH
AMOS
HOSEA

DYNASTIES

5
JEROBOAM (B)
798-762
I KINGS 14:16

ZECHARIAH (B)
762
II KINGS 14:29

6
SHALLUM (B)
761
II KINGS 15:10,13

7
MENAHEM (B)
761-751
II KINGS 15:14,17

PEKAHIAH (B)
750-748
II KINGS 15:23

8
PEKAH (B)
748-729
II KINGS 15:25,27
ISAIAH 7:1

9
HOSHEA (B)
728-721
II KINGS 15:30

In 732 B.C. after conquering Damascus, the Assyrians under Tiglath-Pileser attacked Israel, led the tribes of Gad, Reuben, and Manasseh captive to Mesopotamia, and demanded tribute from the remaining tribes.

Ten years later (722 B.C.) upon the death of Tiglath-Pileser, Israel refused to continue paying tribute. Assyria responded by attacking Samaria and led the rest of the 10 tribes captive.

THE DIVIDED KINGDOM

JUDAH			ISRAEL	
	PROPHETS	DATES	PROPHETS	DYNASTIES
ZEDEKIAH (B) 597-586 II KINGS 24:17 II CHRONICLES 36:11	EZEKIEL	590 580 570		
Babylon rose in power until it conquered the Assyrians and placed Judah under tribute (605 B.C.). King Jehoiakim rebelled, leading to the eventual conquering of Jerusalem in 597 B.C. and to the Babylonian captivity of 70 years (dated from the first deportation around 606 B.C.).	DANIEL	560 550		
There were 3,023 taken captive in the seventh year of Nebuchadnezzar (Jeremiah 52:28) and 7,000 taken captive in the eighth year (II Kings 24:12,16), a total of around 10,000.				
Cyrus the Persian conquered Babylon in 539 B.C.		540		
Decree of Cyrus (538 B.C.) allowed Jews to return, led by Zerubbabel.		530		
Temple begun (536 B.C.) Building stopped (534 B.C.) Building renewed (520 B.C.) Building finished (516 B.C.)	ZECHARIAH HAGGAI	520 510 500		
Second return under Ezra (457 B.C.) Third return under Nehemiah (444 B.C.)	MALACHI	430		

KEY: (G) = Good(B) = Bad

Chart compiled from -
Edward Reese, THE REESE CHRONOLOGICAL BIBLE, 1977.
John W. Walton, CHRONOLOGICAL AND BACKGROUND CHARTS OF THE OLD TESTAMENT, 1978.

EZRA

REESTABLISHING GOD'S PEOPLE	
RESTORING THE TEMPLE	**REFORMING THE PEOPLE**
The return under Zerubbabel: **1-6**	The return under Ezra: **7-10**
LOCATION: Babylonia to Jerusalem	
OVERVIEW: The decree of Cyrus released the Israelites from their captivity	As a priest, Ezra helps bring repentance and deliverance to his people
TIME: 79 years	

FAST FACTS

AUTHOR AND SETTING:

Ezra; Babylonia to Jerusalem

PURPOSE:

Ezra tells of the return to Jerusalem of two groups of Israelites after their release from captivity. The first group returned with Zerubbabel and restored the Temple. The second group retuned with Ezra who restored the people to godly behavior.

SEEING JESUS:

The book of *Ezra* typifies Christ's work of restoration.

THEME VERSE:

Ezra 3:11

NOTES

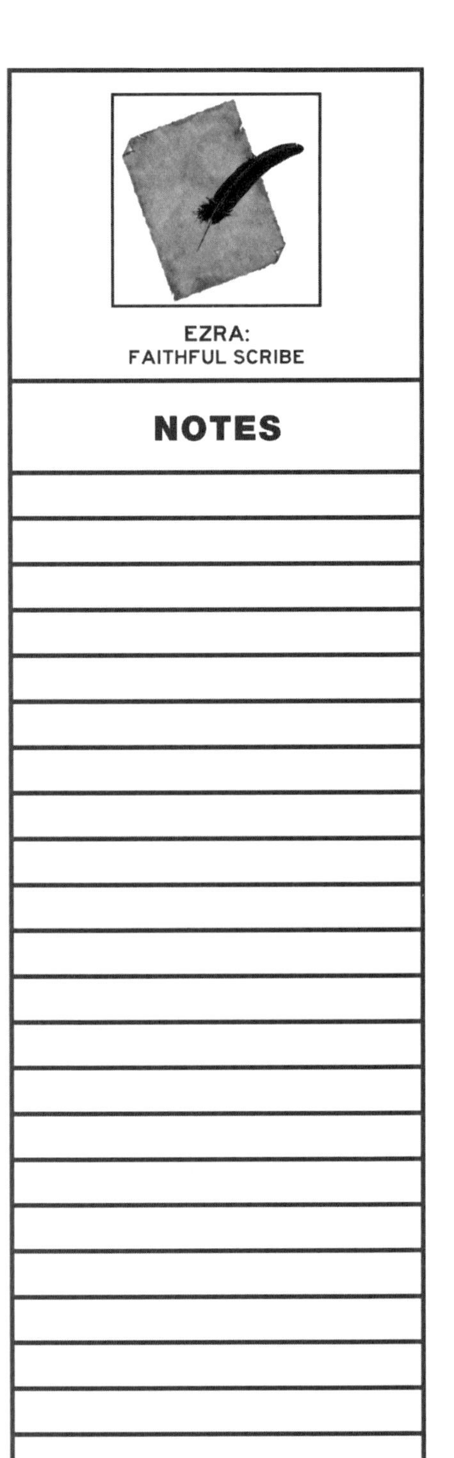
EZRA:
FAITHFUL SCRIBE

NOTES

SEEING JESUS IN EZRA

AUTHOR & SETTING

This book bears the name of Ezra, the priest and scribe whose history is recorded in the latter part of the book. Ezra was a descendant of Aaron through Eleazar, and as a scribe, he had extensive knowledge of the books of Moses - Genesis through Deuteronomy. Ezra is also said to have written I and II Chronicles.

OVERVIEW

The book of *Ezra* covers 79 years, and in this period there were six Persian kings. *Ezra* gives the account of the reestablishment of God's people in the land. The name *Ezra* means "help," and he certainly was a help to those who returned to rebuild the walls of the Temple.

The return of the Israelites to the Promised Land began with the wonderful decree of the Persian king Cyrus who signed the decree allowing the Israelites to leave Babylon. Ezra lists the heads of the families who traveled back to Jerusalem: the first thing they did was to set up an altar for worship, make arrangements for sacrifices, and begin in earnest to rebuild the Temple.

Opposition came immediately from the Samaritans and from the older Jews who were discouraged because the foundation of the Temple was not nearly as great as Solomon's Temple. The people at one time actually stopped building because a new king signed a decree ordering them to stop. This new decree came because of the pressures of the Samaritans. These were dark and difficult times. The people stopped building for 14 years, but God raised up two prophets - Haggai and Zechariah - who with the Word and the power of the Holy Spirit stirred up Joshua (KJV *Jeshua*), the priest, and Zerubbabel, the governor. At this time a new king searched and found the original decree of Cyrus, and the people were allowed to finish building.

Ezra tells of the return of two groups of Israelites: the first group returned with Zerubbabel and restored the Temple. The second group retuned with Ezra, and he restored the people to godly behavior. Many who had taken foreign wives repented and made a covenant to put them away. Moral delinquencies had crept in, the people were lax, and the foreign marriages that had been contracted had to be broken. *Ezra* also preserved the genealogy. Ezra brought revival to a new country, and he traveled 800 miles to do it! In our day we think nothing of that, but in his day it was a horrendous journey. It took a miracle to get him there.

There were many immediate provisions given to Ezra by the favor of King Artaxerxes. The king gave him gold and silver for purchasing animals for sacrifice. Any money that was left over could be used as Ezra pleased. Vessels that had been taken by Nebuchadnezzar were to be returned to Jerusalem. If there was more money needed. Ezra was at liberty to draw from the king's treasure house. The treasurers beyond the river were also required to give him all the money he needed. Also there was to be no restrictions on salt. (In addition, Ezra could stay in the Promised Land or return.) It was a miracle.

There were long-term provisions as well. Priests and Levites were excused from taxation. Ezra was empowered to appoint magistrates and judges in order to enforce and teach God's law. Whoever refused to obey could be punished by death, banishment, confiscation of goods, or imprisonment.

It was no wonder that Ezra and the people broke into such a song of thanksgiving at the laying of the Temple foundation. Ezra certainly enforced the law, and it was the rigidity of the law that was enforced that preserved the nation.

SEEING JESUS IN EZRA

God's promises of a Messiah necessitated keeping David's descendants alive and in the Promised Land. The first return of the captives from Babylon was led by Zerubbabel (Ezra 1-6). A descendant of David through Solomon, Zerubbabel was an ancestor of Joseph, through whom Jesus earned the right to be called the "Son of David." Christ's work of restoration is beautifully seen in the book of *Ezra*.

THEME VERSE

"And they sang together by course in praising and giving thanks unto the LORD; because he is good, for his mercy endureth for ever toward Israel. And all the people shouted with a great shout, when they praised the LORD, because the foundation of the house of the LORD was laid" **(Ezra 3:11).**

OUTLINE

(Refer to maps on pages A9, A10, A11, and A12 in the APPENDIX.)

I. **THE RETURN UNDER ZERUBBABEL -** EZRA 1-6
   - A. **The Book Opens with the Decree of Cyrus.**
   - B. **The Leaders of the People of Judah Return From Captivity With Zerubbabel.**
   - C. **The People Begin to Rebuild the Temple Under the Prophesying of Haggai & Zechariah.**

II. **THE RETURN OF EZRA -** EZRA 7-10
   - A. **Ezra, a Priest, Traced His Ancestry Back to Aaron.**
   - B. **His Ministry Was Spiritual.**
   - C. **There was great Repentance Among the People.**

EZRA QUOTED IN THE NEW TESTAMENT: NOT FOUND

NOTES

NEHEMIAH

RESTORATION & RENEWAL		
REBUILDING THE WALL	**SPIRITUAL REVIVAL**	**REBUILDING JERUSALEM**
Nehemiah, the great administrator: **1-7**	Leaders sign a covenant: **8-10**	Ceremony of dedication: **11-13**
LOCATION: Jerusalem		
OVERVIEW: Opposition fails to stop construction	Faithfulness abounds within protective walls	Religious renewal
TIME: 20 years		

FAST FACTS

AUTHOR AND SETTING:

Nehemiah; Jerusalem

PURPOSE:

Nehemiah was a man of prayer; and his powerful, persistent prayers accomplished great things. God's hand was obvious in the establishment of His people in their homeland.

SEEING JESUS:

Nehemiah contains a picture of God's power of restoration through the work of Jesus Christ. Nehemiah's prayer life foreshadows he prayer ministry of Jesus while He was on earth and also as our great high priest in heaven.

THEME VERSE:

Nehemiah 6:3

NOTES

NEHEMIAH:
RESTORER & REBUILDER

NOTES

SEEING JESUS IN NEHEMIAH

AUTHOR & SETTING

Nehemiah was born of Jewish parents who had been taken as captives to Babylon. His parents must have done a marvelous job of teaching him of their historical and religious heritage; when he heard that the walls of Jerusalem were broken down nearly 100 years after the first Jewish captives had returned, he mourned for many days and prayed to God (Nehemiah 1:5-11). Nehemiah was a contemporary with Ezra who may have had a hand in writing this book. In the Hebrew Old Testament, the books of Ezra and *Nehemiah* are one continuous book.

Nehemiah means "comforter." There were about twelve years separating *Nehemiah* and Ezra. Nehemiah knew men, and he knew the affairs of men. His brother Hanani told him that the walls were broken down and that the people were afflicted. The news had a tremendous affect on Nehemiah.

Nehemiah could not show his sadness to the king because the law stated that you could never go into the king's presence with a depressed expression on your face: you had to go in looking happy and joyful. But the king recognized that Nehemiah was discouraged, and Nehemiah prayed and asked favor from the Lord. There is no question that God gave Nehemiah supernatural favor, because the king sent Nehemiah forth to build the walls that there might be protection around the newly built Temple.

The king not only sent Nehemiah forth and gave him long periods to build the walls, but he also gave him much wealth and supplies in order to do it.

OVERVIEW

Nehemiah was a great man of prayer. He prayed over every situation, including the retribution of his enemies, and then went forward. There are nine major prayers in the book of *Nehemiah.* It is a powerful book on prayer. Nehemiah prayed again and again, and each time God gave him the victory.

There were many problems that Nehemiah encountered. The number-one problem, of course, was that the walls were down. When he arrived in the city, he immediately met the harassment of Sanballat, Tobiah, and other Arabians and Samaritans. The root meaning of *Sanballat* means "Satan." Satan will oppose us in anything we are called upon to do for God.

Nehemiah was a very wise man. He took a journey at night around those broken walls and broken gates. He surveyed the situation and then rallied the people to a job that he said their God would help them to accomplish. Nehemiah strengthened the hands of the people. He strengthened their image; for remember, they had been an enslaved people, and now they were to be a free people doing great and mighty things in the name of God. Nehemiah assigned them to the walls and the gates nearest to where they lived. Everything was done in a very orderly manner. There's no question that Nehemiah must have had an organizational-motive gift.

The enemy continued to harass Nehemiah, even threatening to kill the people while they worked on the wall. Nehemiah simply reorganized the people and had part of them work on the wall while the other part stood with weapons on the ground for protection.

There was also strife from within their own ranks. Although unusually high usury rates were forbidden by Moses, the people were being charged exorbitant interest by their own relatives and those of their own tribes. Nehemiah had to settle family disputes over usury. Nehemiah had been trained as an orderly of the court, and he seemed o be very aware of trickery.

Next the enemy tied spreading false religious claims: they said that a prophetess had told them that Nehemiah was there to set himself as a king again and cause the Jews to rebel. The enemy did everything possible to get him to come down from the wall, but Nehemiah and his crews worked day and night to complete the wall. Nehemiah said he didn't even take his clothes off except to wash them on occasion. Food was brought to them at the working site, and they completed the walls in 52 days.

Nehemiah's major statement that I love so much is, "I am doing a great work. How can I come down?" God calls us to do a great work. How can we come down when Satan besieges us, people falsely accuse us, and we are attacked again and again? We can't! We must finish what God has called us to do.

When the walls were built Nehemiah set up the doors and appointed singers and Levites to serve before the Lord. He appointed his own brother over the city. He gave instruction about opening and closing the city gates. He found the book of genealogy recorded in Ezra 2, which helped to organize those who returned from the captivity.

When the law was read (Nehemiah 8) a great revival began. Ezra read the law and the Levites explained it. Three hours were spent in reading the law and three hours were spent in confessing sin. The leading men of the nation signed a covenant signifying their obedience to God. When they dedicated the walls, Nehemiah took a company and went one direction, and Ezra took a company and went the other direction. The walls were so broad that they marched and met on them. After the dedication Nehemiah appointed Temple officers, treasurers, and singers. Then, according to the book of Moses, the foreigners were separated from Israel.

Nehemiah went back to Persia for one year. When he retuned the people were backslidden. Did he give up? No way! He threw out Eliashib and Tobiah and cleansed the Temple, ordering their potion to be given to the Levites who were suffering hardship. He enforced the Sabbath laws, and he compelled the Jews to put away their foreign wives. (Ezra had

NOTES

NOTES

dealt with this before: He covered himself with a mantle and wept.) Nehemiah cursed the Jews and pulled their hair and beards. Backing Nehemiah, though, was the authority - not only of our great and loving heavenly Father - but also the authority of the king of Persia. Nehemiah chased away the son-in-law of Sanballat, the grandson of the high priest.

Nehemiah closed the book saying, *"...Remember me, O my God, for good"* (Nehemiah 13:31). When we read the book of Nehemiah, we have to say, "He was a man who did good by the power of the Holy Spirit and obedience to the Word."

SEEING JESUS IN NEHEMIAH

Like Ezra, Nehemiah's work of restoration of the walls of Jerusalem foreshadows the work of Jesus in restoring man to God though the Cross. The wonderful prayers of Nehemiah also remind us of the prayer ministry of Jesus.

THEME VERSE

"And I sent messengers unto them, saying, I am doing a great work, so that I cannot come down: why should the work cease, whilst I leave it, and come down to you?" **(Nehemiah 6:3).**

OUTLINE

(Refer to maps on pages A9, A10, A11, and A12 in the APPENDIX.)

I. THE COMING OF NEHEMIAH TO JERUSALEM AND THE REBUILDING OF THE WALL - NEHEMIAH 1-7

  A. Nehemiah Was the Great Administrator.

II. SPIRITUAL REVIVAL - NEHEMIAH 8-10

  A. Leading Men Signed a Covenant Signifying Their Obedience to God.

III. REBUILDING JERUSALEM - NEHEMIAH 11-13

  A. Ceremony of the Dedication of the Walls

  B. Restoration of Temple Worship

  C. Renewal of Battle Against Sin

  D. Two-fold Separation.

NEHEMIAH QUOTED IN THE NEW TESTAMENT.

Nehemiah 9:15 (Psalms 78:24: Exodus 16:4,15)
"And gavest them bread from heaven for their hunger, and broughtest forth water for them out of the rock for their thirst, and promisedst them that they should go in to possess the land which thou hadst sworn to give them.

John 6:31
"Our fathers did eat manna in the desert; as it is written, He gave them bread from heaven to eat."

NOTES

ESTHER

A MIRACULOUS DELIVERANCE		
A NEW QUEEN IS CHOSEN	**ANTI-SEMITISM EXPOSED**	**FROM RAGS TO RICHES**
Esther becomes queen: **1,2**	Haman's plot spoiled: **3-7**	Mordecai comes to prominence: **8-10**
LOCATION: Persia		
OVERVIEW: A beauty contest	A potential massacre	A wise man helps the king
TIME: 10 years		

FAST FACTS

AUTHOR AND SETTING:

Esther, Mordecai, or Ezra; Persia

PURPOSE:

The devil had a plan to exterminate the Jews in Babylon. The book of *Esther* shows the miraculous deliverance of the Jews from this attempted extermination.

SEEING JESUS:

Esther, like Jesus, was the savior and advocate of her people.

THEME VERSE:

Esther 4:14

NOTES

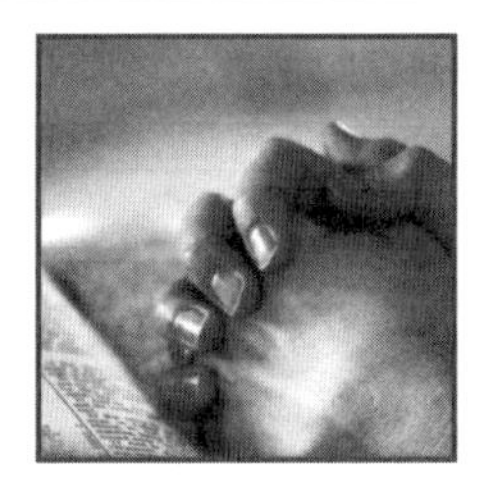

ESTHER:
INTERCESSOR

NOTES

SEEING JESUS IN ESTHER

AUTHOR & SETTING

Mordecai has been suggested as the author of this book. Because it fits between chapters 6 and 7 of Ezra, it is possible that Ezra may have written Esther's story. The events in *Esther* take place in Persia while, far away, the first group of Jewish exiles are just settling in their homeland.

OVERVIEW

The devil had a plan to exterminate the Jews held captive in Babylon. The book of *Esther* shows the miraculous deliverance of the Jews from this extermination.

The name *Esther* means "a star." Certainly she was a bright and shining star in the plan of God to save His people. The book of *Esther* shows that God swings big doors on little hinges.

The narrative begins with a wife who refuses to submit to her husband. Vashti would not allow herself to be shown as a piece of furniture or beautiful "property" to a group of leering men. When she refused to appear before her husband's male guests, Ahasuerus, king of Shusan, or ancient Persia, divorced Vasht

In order to keep women in submission, a law was passed according to the language of every people that every man should bear rule in his own house:

***"For he sent letters into all the king's provinces, into every province according to the writing thereof, and to every people after their language, that every man should bear rule in his own house, and that it should be published according to the language of every people"* (Esther 1:22).**

King Ahasuerus held a "Miss Universe" contest and women came from all over the civilized world to become a candidate for his bride. *Hadassah* was Esther's original name, and it means "a myrtle tree."

Mordecai, a Benjamite, had brought up Hadassah, his orphaned first cousin. They were in Shushan as a result of the Babylonian captivity of Israel.

Esther was a very beautiful woman, and Mordecai entered her in the contest.

The book of *Esther* is a book of favor, because whatever Esther did, she came out with favor. She became the next queen.

Haman is the villain of the story. He was an Agagite-ancient enemies of the Jews. He became enraged because Mordecai would not bow to him. He hatched a plot to kill every Jew in order to get even with Mordeca Haman was a man of tremendous pride and arrogance.

Mordecai called upon Esther to be the deliverer of her people but told her that if she didn't respond, God had someone else who would:

"For if thou altogether holdest thy peace at this time, then shall there enlargement and deliverance arise to the Jews from another place; but thou and thy father's house shall be destroyed: and who knoweth whether thou art come to the kingdom for such a time as this?" **(Esther 4:14).**

Esther entered into fasting before she approached the king in order to have favor, which was granted her. Esther invited the king twice for dinner and told him the truth about Haman's hatred of the Jews and his plot to destroy them. Esther told her husband that she, too, was a Jewess!

Haman's plot to kill Mordecai came upon his own head - he was hung upon the very gallows that he had prepared for Mordecai!

Mordecai was promoted to a high position within the Persian government, and thousands and thousands of Jews saw their plight turned around - which was nothing short of a miracle.

It is thought that Mordecai was one of the men who went back to Israel with Ezra to help rebuild the Promised Land (Ezra 2:2).

This book is the only book in the Bible that does not mention the name of God or Lord one time. In the ancient Hebrew text, however, there were five places where the name of God was hidden, being abbreviated JHVH (for *Jehovah*) four times and EHYEH (for *I AM* that *I AM*) once. These letters were used as acrostics in certain statements. They were originally larger than the rest of the text so that they stood out boldly on the scroll.

Statements wherein these letters occur in the Hebrew text:

1. *"And when the king's decree which he shall make shall be published throughout all his empire, (for it is great,) all the wives shall give to their husbands honour, both to great and small"* **(Esther 1:20).**

2. *"And Esther answered, If it seem good unto the king, let the king and Haman come this day unto the banquet that I have prepared for him"* **(Esther 5:4).**

3. *"Then answered Esther, and said, My petition and my request is"* **(Esther 5:7).**

4. *"Yet all this availeth me nothing, so long as I see Mordecai the Jew sitting at the king's gate"* **(Esther 5:13).**

These four verses show the name Jehovah (JHVH) written in large capital letters above the scriptures.

5. *"Then the king Ahasuerus answered and said unto Esther the queen, Who is he, and where is he, that durst presume in his heart to do so?"* **(Esther 7:5).**

This verse is where the acrostic EHYEH was used.

God has a way of showing up when His people call upon His name. He gives them miraculous deliverance.

NOTES

NOTES

Esther is a beautiful story of *I AM* that *I AM* - Who without a doubt is Jesus Christ! Jesus was in control of the circumstances and the situation of His people.

In the gospel account of the soldiers coming to take Jesus away, He said "I AM," and the soldiers fell backward. When He came upon the scene in Esther's time, the Persians fell backward and I AM delivered His people.

This is one of two books of the Bible named after a woman (Ruth and Esther).

SEEING JESUS IN ESTHER

Like Jesus, Esther was a mediator for her people (I Timothy 2:5). Esther was willing to lay down her life for her people (Esther 4:16); Jesus, of course, was not only willing, but did so!

THEME VERSE

"For if thou altogether holdest thy peace at this time, then shall there enlargement and deliverance arise to the Jews from another place; but thou and thy father's house shall be destroyed: and who knoweth whether thou art come to the kingdom for such a time as this?" **(Esther 4:14).**

OUTLINE

(Refer to map on page A11 in the APPENDIX.)

I. **HOW ESTHER CAME TO BE QUEEN** - ESTHER 1,2

II. **HOW HAMAN PLOTTED TO DESTROY THE JEWS AND WAS SPOILED -** ESTHER 3-7

III. **HOW MORDECAI CAME TO PROMINENCE IN THE KINGDOM -** ESTHER 8-10

A. **This book, chronologically, should be located between the sixth and seventh chapters of Ezra. The author could have been Esther or Mordeca**

B. **Esther was beautiful but not spoiled by her beauty - she used her beauty in a right way.**

C. **She was not spoiled by position - she remained loyal to Mordeca**

D. **She didn't lose her spirituality in a wicked court - she practiced fasting.**

E. **She knew how to manage the king - she outwitted Haman.**

F. She was the savior of her people.

G. She was talented, brave, shrewd, and certainly a *womanly* woman.

H. Most of all Esther was a godly woman.

ESTHER QUOTED IN THE NEW TESTAMENT: NOT FOUND

NOTES

JOB

WILLING SUBMISSION				
PROLOGUE	**CONTROVERSY**	**MANY WORDS OF MEN**	**ANSWERS FROM GOD**	**EPILOGUE**
Heaven: **1,2**	Discussion: **3-31**	Opinion: **32-37**	Depending on God: **38-41**	God's reward: **42**
LOCATION: The land of Uz (southeast of Dead Sea)				
OVERVIEW: Testing Satan's theory	Hypocrite or sinner?	The dubious value of suffering	God asks questions	God delights to bless
TIME: 2000 B.C. (Before Israel's exodus from Egypt)				

FAST FACTS

AUTHOR AND SETTING:

Possibly Moses; land of Uz (southeast of Dead Sea)

PURPOSE:

The main purpose of *Job* is to give us light concerning human suffering through calamities and sickness. Satan is also clearly identified as the author of such misery. Job's experience teaches us the value of patience (James 5:11).

SEEING JESUS:

There is no question that Job knew about Jesus: *"For I know that my redeemer liveth, and that he shall stand at the latter day upon the earth"* **(Job 19:25).**

THEME VERSE:

Job 4:3,4

NOTES

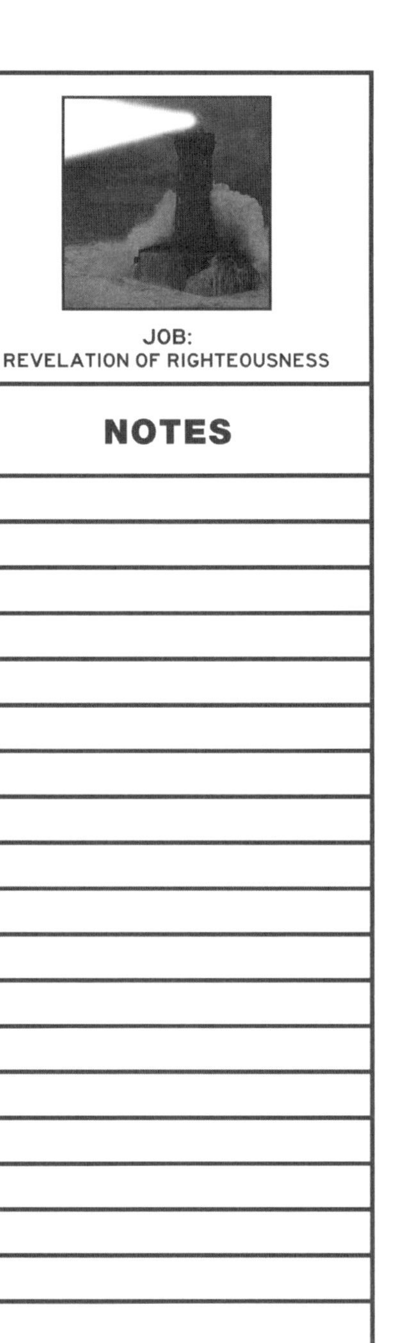

SEEING JESUS IN JOB

AUTHOR & SETTING

Many feel that Moses wrote this book. No doubt Job and Moses lived at the same time in the vast wilderness section of the country from Arabia-Petra to the Persian Gulf. For 40 years Moses was in this part of the world herding the flocks of Jethro, priest of Midian. Job and Moses could have spent time together.

According to Genesis 46:13, Job was the son of Issachar and the grandson of Jacob:

"And the sons of Issachar; Tola, and Phuvah, and Job, and Shimron."

The events of *Job* probably took place in the latter part of the 430-year period of the dispensation of promise. Judging from the time of the birth of Jacob's son, we suppose that Job died about 15 years before the exodus from Egypt.

Issachar was born when Jacob was about ninety years of age, and Job was born when Issachar was about twenty years of age. Job was around seventy years of age when he experienced his trial, and he lived 140 years after that:

"After this lived Job an hundred and forty years, and saw his sons and his sons' sons, even four generations" **(Job 42:16).**

The events described in this book took place in the land of Uz. It is certain that Job lived before the giving of the *law* because there is no mention made of Jewish rights, manners, customs, religious ceremonies, priesthood, festivals, fasts, Sabbaths, or anything else commanded in the Mosaic Law.

The references to God in this book make it clear that Job's revelations of God were the same as those which prevailed in the days of Abraham, Isaac, Jacob, and Israel before the giving of the *law*.

Job is the one who offered sacrifices as the head of his family and on behalf of his children just as Noah (Genesis 8:20), Abraham, and the other pre-law patriarchs (Genesis 5:9-11, 12:1-13).

OVERVIEW

The main purpose of this book is to give us light concerning human suffering through calamities and sickness. The book records the reasonings of ordinary men concerning these experiences, but God identifies Satan as the author of such misery. Job's experiences certainly teach the value of patience (James 5:10), and reveal God as the deliverer of His people when He is called upon to help in time of need.

The name *Almighty* God or El Shaddai-the God Who is more than enough in the time of trial - is used again and again in this book. It appears in Job 5:17; 6:4, 14; 8:3, 5; 11:7; 13:3; 15:25; 21:15, 20; 22:17, 23, 25, 26; 24:1; 27:1, 10, 11, 13; 29:5; 31:2, 35; 32:8; 33:4; 34:10, 12; 35:13; 37:23; and finally in 40:1!

If ever a man had a revelation of the God Who is more than enough - the Lord Jesus Christ - it is Job! He also saw Jesus as a mediator:

"Neither is there any daysman betwixt us, that might lay his hand upon us both" **(Job 9:33).**

Job, Psalms, Proverbs, Ecclesiastes, and Song of Solomon are called poetic books which means, basically, that poetry is the style of these books. Hebrew poetry has a sense rhythm known as parallelism. The three most common parallelisms are synonymous, antithetic, and synthetic.

Job is highly complimented as a man of prayer in Ezekiel 14:14, 20:

"Though these three men, Noah, Daniel, and Job, were in it, they should deliver but their own souls by their righteousness, saith the Lord GOD. Though Noah, Daniel, and Job, were in it, as I live, saith the Lord GOD, they shall deliver neither son nor daughter; they shall but deliver their own souls by their righteousness."

SEEING JESUS IN JOB

There is no question that Job knew about Jesus:

"For I know that my redeemer liveth, and that he shall stand at the latter day upon the earth: And though after my skin worms destroy this body, yet in my flesh shall I see God: Whom I shall see for myself, and mine eyes shall behold, and not another; though my reins be consumed within me" **(Job 19:25-27).**

This is one of the greatest revelations of resurrection because of the redemption of Jesus Christ in the whole Bible.

THEME VERSES

"Behold, thou hast instructed many, and thou hast strengthened the weak hands. Thy words have upholden him that was falling, and thou hast strengthened the feeble knees" **(Job 4:3, 4).**

OUTLINE

Job is written in five parts. The first and the last parts are prose. The three in-between parts are written in poetry.

I. PROLOGUE-WHAT TOOK PLACE IN HEAVEN JOB 1,2

- **A. Satan's Theory Was That Job Served God Because God Blessed Him.**
- **B. Two Tests Come to Job.**
- **C. Three Friends Arrive: Eliphaz, Bildad, and Zophar**

II. THE CONTROVERSY OF JOB AND HIS FRIENDS - JOB 3-31

NOTES

NOTES

A. Three Cycles of Discussion

1. First cycle - Job 3-14

a. Their basic conclusion was that Job's suffering was because he was a sinner.

b. Bildad called Job a hypocrite:

i. *"So are the paths of all that forget God; and the hypocrite's hope shall perish"* **(Job 8:13).**

c. Zophar called Job a liar:

i. *"Should thy lies make men hold their peace? and when thou mockest, shall no man make thee ashamed?"* **(Job 11:3).**

2. Second cycle - Job 15-21

a. Bildad spoke most sternly.

3. Third cycle - Job 22-31

a. Eliphaz accused Job of infinite iniquities:

i. *"Is not thy wickedness great? and thine iniquities infinite?"* **(Job 22:5).**

III. THE WORDS OF ELIHU - JOB 32-37

A. Elihu Stood by and Listened. Then he stated that suffering is remedial.

1. He believed that Job had accused God unjustly.

2. Some suffering is penal.

3. Some suffering is remedial.

IV. THE ANSWER OF THE LORD - JOB 38-41

A. The Lord Answered Job - but With Questions.

B. Job's Discovery. He did not need to know "Why?" if he knew God.

V. EPILOGUE-THE REWARD OF THE LORD - JOB 42

A. God Delights in Giving to his Own:

1. *"And the LORD turned the captivity of Job, when he prayed for his friends: also the LORD gave Job twice as much as he had before"* **(Job 42:10).**

2. *"Behold, we count them happy which endure. Ye have heard of the patience of Job, and have seen the end of the Lord; that the Lord is very pitiful, and of tender mercy"* **(James 5-11).**

JOB QUOTED IN THE NEW TESTAMENT.

Job 5:13
He taketh the wise in their own craftiness: and the counsel of the forward is carried headlong.

1 Corinthians 3:19
For the wisdom of this world is foolishness with God. For it is written, He taketh the wise in their own craftiness.

****

Job 41:11
Who hath prevented me, that I should repay him? whatsoever is under the whole heaven is mine.

Romans 11:35
Or who hath first given to him, and it shall be recompensed unto him again?

NOTES

PSALMS

GOD'S SONG BOOK				
GOD'S SOVEREIGNTY	**REDEMPTION**	**SANCTUARY**	**ISRAEL'S HISTORY**	**THE SCRIPTURE**
Genesis	Exodus	Leviticus	Numbers	Deuteronomy
Book I: **1-41**	Book II: **42-72**	Book III: **73-89**	Book IV: **90-106**	Book V: **107-150**
LOCATION: Middle East				
OVERVIEW: Compiled by David	Compiled by David	Compiled by Hezekiah	Compiled by Ezra	Compiled by Ezra
TIME: Written over a period of 1,000 years				

FAST FACTS

AUTHOR AND SETTING:

David, Asaph, the sons of Korah, Heman, Ethan, Moses, Solomon, and other anonymous authors; Middle East

PURPOSE:

Psalms teaches doctrine...provides guidance for emotions and feelings...expounds on the names and nature of God Himself—they are the ultimate in musical expression!

SEEING JESUS:

Jesus is seen clearly throughout the *Psalms*, most notably in *Psalms 22*, where the very words He uttered on the Cross were prophesied over 1000 years earlier

THEME VERSE:

Psalms 1:3

NOTES

PSALMS:
PRAISE

NOTES

SEEING JESUS IN PSALMS

AUTHOR & SETTING

Psalms provides guidance for emotions and feelings. It really is God's song book! The word *psalm* means "a poem to be sung to a stringed instrument." This book is actually a collection of psalms. There are many authors: 73 probably came from the heart of David, while 12 came from Asaph, 12 are attributed to the sons of Korah, 1 to Heman, 1 to Ethan, 2 to Moses, 2 to Solomon, and the others are anonymous.

OVERVIEW

***Psalms* is divided into five books:**

1. **Book one** is Psalms 1-41—Genesis—Sovereignty of God.
2. **Book two** is Psalms 42-72—Exodus—Redemption of God.
3. **Book three** is Psalms 73-89—Leviticus—Sanctuary of God.
4. **Book four** is Psalms 90-106—Numbers—History of God.
5. **Book five** is Psalms 107-150—Deuteronomy—Word of God.

The entire book is marked by an introduction and a doxology: Psalms 1 forms the introduction to the whole book, and psalms 150 is the doxology of the whole book.

Books one and two of *Psalms* were compiled by David. Book three was compiled by Hezekiah, and books four and five were compiled by Ezra.

The *Psalms* are also grouped according to the uses of the names of God:

1. **Psalms 1-41** are Jehovah psalms.
2. **Psalms 42-83** are Elohim psalms.
3. **Psalms 84-150** are Jehovah psalms.

Some psalms were arranged as companion psalms in groups of two, three, or more. For example, Psalms 2 and 3 go together; Psalms 22, 23, and 24 go together; Psalms 113-118 go together.

They were also arranged for liturgical purposes to be used on special occasions. There are some psalms without titles which are called orphan psalms.

There are also the penitential psalms such as Psalms 6, 32, 38, 51, 102, 130, and 143. There are alphabetical psalms—Psalms 9, 10, 25, 34, 37, 111, 112, 119, and 145. There are hallelujah psalms—Psalms11-13, 115-117, 135, and 146-150. Psalms 113-118 are called the Hallel psalms.

The psalms teach doctrine. They teach about the throne of grace and how to approach it by sacrifice, prayer, and praise. They teach the covenant which is the basis of all worship. They give the assertions of both the innocent and the guilty. They show the pardon of sin and justification. Without question they reveal the Messiah. They reveal the future life—pro and con. They show us how to pray and cry out for mercy.

The New Testament quotes from *Psalms* more than any one book of the Bible.

The psalms that were written for special occasions are interesting: Psalms 127 was written when Solomon built the Temple. When the Israelites were taken into captivity by Nebuchadnezzar, they wrote Psalms 137. The Israelites said they could not respond and sing a song as requested by their captors when they dwelt in a strange land. The revival of Israel's hope is seen in Psalms 102 and Psalms 85:10.

David, the greatest psalmist, psalmed on his special occasions: he psalmed during his crises, he psalmed during the highlights of his life, and he psalmed when he desperately needed an answer from God. He seemed to know how to center in and hear from God.

The book of *Psalms* is absolutely marvelous for every believer. There is not a believer who can read one psalm without his or her life being deeply affected by the strengths, the emotions, and the heart cry contained in the psalm.

Sometimes when you sing a psalm, you may find your spirit is lifted in the same way as the psalm must have lifted the one who first received it from God!

SEEING JESUS IN PSALMS

Jesus is seen perhaps in the boldest way in Psalms 22 where the very words that He uttered on the Cross were prophesied over a thousand years before He uttered them. You can certainly behold Jesus in Psalms!

THEME VERSES

"And he shall be like a tree planted by the rivers of water, that bringeth forth his fruit in his season; his leaf also shall not wither; and whatsoever he doeth shall prosper" **(Psalms 1:3).**

OUTLINE

I. **GOD'S SOVEREIGNTY -** PSALMS 1-41
II. **REDEMPTION -** PSALMS 42-72
III. **THE SANCTUARY -** PSALMS 73-89
IV. **ISRAEL'S HISTORY -** PSALMS 90-106
V. **THE SCRIPTURE -** PSALMS 107-150

NOTES

PSALMS QUOTED IN THE NEW TESTAMENT.

Psalms 2:1, 2
Why do the heathen rage, and the people imagine a vain thing? The kings of the earth set themselves, and the rulers take counsel together, against the LORD, and against his anointed, saying, Let us break their bands asunder, and cast away their cords from us.

Acts 4:25, 26
Who by the mouth of thy servant David hast said, Why did the heathen rage, and the people imagine vain things? The kings of the earth stood up, and the rulers were gathered together against the Lord, and against his Christ.

****

Psalms 2:7
I will declare the decree: the LORD hath said unto me, Thou are my son; this day have I begotten thee.

Acts 13:33
God hath fulfilled the same unto us their children, in that he hath raised up Jesus again; as it is also written in the second psalm, Thou art my Son, this day have I begotten thee.

Hebrews 1:5
For unto which of the angels said he at any time, Thou art my son, this day have I begotten thee? And again, I will be to him a Father, and he shall be to me a Son?

Hebrews 5:5
So also Christ glorified not himself to be made an high priest; but he that said unto him, Thou art my Son, today have I begotten thee.

****

Psalms 2:8,9
Ask of me, and I shall give the heathen for thine inheritance, and the uttermost parts of the earth for thy possession. Thou shalt break them with a rod of iron; thou shalt dash them in pieces like a potter's wheel.

Revelation 2:26, 27
And he that overcometh, and keepeth my works unto the end, to him will I give power over the nations: And he shall rule them with a rod of iron; as the vessels of a potter shall they be broken to shivers: even as I received of my Father.

****

Psalms 4:4
Stand in awe, and sin not: commune with your own heart upon your bed, and be still. Selah.

Ephesians 4:26
Be ye angry, and sin not: let not the sun go down upon your wrath.

****

Psalms 5:9 (Isaiah 59:7, 8)
For there is no faithfulness in their mouth; their inward part is very wickedness; their throat is an open sepulchre; they flatter with their tongue.

Romans 3:13
Their throat is an open sepulchre; with their tongues they have used deceit; the poison of asps is under their lips.

****

Psalms 6:8
Depart from me, all ye workers of iniquity; for the LORD hath heard the voice of my weeping.

Matthew 7:23
And then will I profess unto them, I never knew you: depart from me, ye that work iniquity.

Luke 13:27
But he shall say, I tell you, I know you not whence ye are: depart from me, all ye workers of iniquity.

****

Psalms 8:2
Out of the mouth of babies and sucklings hast thou ordained strength because of thine enemies, that thou mightiest still the enemy and the avenger.

Matthew 21:16
And said unto him, Hearest thou what these say? And Jesus saith unto them, Yea; have ye never read, Out of the mouth of babes and sucklings thou hast perfected praise?

****

Psalms 8:4-6
What is man, that thou art mindful of him? And the son of man, that thou visitest him? For thou hast made him a little lower than the angels, and hast crowned him with glory and honour. Thou madest him to have dominion over the works of thy hands; thou hast put all things under his feet.

Hebrews 2:6-8
But one in a certain place testified, saying, What is man, that thou art mindful of him? or the son of man, that thou visitest him? Thou madest him a little lower than the angels; thou crownedst him with glory and

honour, and didst set him over the works of thy hands: Thou hast put all things in subjection under his feet. For in that he put all in subjection under him, he left nothing that is not put under him. But now we see not yet all things put under him.

****

Psalms 8:6
Thou madest him to have dominion over the works of thy hands; thou hast put all things under his feet.

1 Corinthians 15:27
For he hath put all things under his feet. But when he saith all things are put under him, it is manifest that he is excepted, which did put all things under him.

****

Psalms 10:7 (Isaiah 59:7, 8)
His mouth is full of cursing and deceit and fraud: under his tongue is mischief and vanity.

Romans 3:14
Whose mouth is full of cursing and bitterness.

****

Psalms 14:1-3
The fool hath said in his heart, There is no God. They are corrupt, they have done abominable works, there is none that doeth good. The LORD looked down from heaven upon the children of men, to see if there were any that did understand, and seek God. They are all gone aside, they are all together become filthy: there is none that doeth good, no, not one.

Romans 3:10-18
As it is written, There is none righteous, no, not one: There is none that understandeth, there is none that seeketh after God. They are all gone out of the way, they are together become unprofitable; there is none that doeth good, no, not one. Their throat is an open sepulcher; with their tongues they have used deceit; the poison of asps is under their lips: Whose mouth is full of cursing and bitterness: Their feet are swift to shed blood: Destruction and misery are in their ways: And the way of peace have they not known: There is no fear of God before their eyes.

****

Psalms 16:8-11
I have set the LORD always before me: because he is at my right hand. I shall not be moved. Therefore my heart is glad, and my glory rejoiceth: my flesh also shall rest in hope. For thou wilt not leave my soul in hell; neither wilt thou suffer thine Holy One to see corruption. Thou wilt shew me the path of life: in thy presence is fullness of joy; at thy right hand there are pleasures for evermore.

Acts 2:25-31
For David speaketh concerning him, I foresaw the Lord always before my face, for he is on my right hand, that I should not be moved: Therefore did my heart rejoice, and my tongue was glad; moreover also my flesh shall rest in hope: Because thou wilt not leave my soul in hell, neither wilt thou suffer thine Holy One to see corruption. Thou hast made known to me the ways of life; thou shalt make me full of joy with thy countenance. Men and brethren, let me freely speak unto you of the patriarch David, that he is both dead and buried, and his sepulcher is with us unto this day. Therefore being a prophet, and knowing that God had sworn with an oath to him, that of the fruit of his loins, according to the flesh, he would raise up Christ to sit on his throne; He seeing this before spake of the resurrection of Christ, that his soul was not left in hell, neither his flesh did see corruption.

****

Psalms 16:10
For thou wilt not leave my soul in hell; neither wilt thou suffer thine Holy One to see corruption.

Acts 13:35
Wherefore he saith also in another psalm, Thou shalt not suffer thine Holy One to see corruption.

****

Psalms 18:49 (II Samuel 22:50)
Therefore will I give thanks unto thee, O LORD, among the heathen, and sing praises unto thy name.

Romans 15:9
And that the Gentiles might glorify God for his mercy; as it is written, For this cause I will confess to thee among the Gentiles, and sing unto thy name.

****

Psalms 19:4
Their line is gone out through all the earth, and their words to the end of the world. In them hath he set a tabernacle for the sun.

Romans 10:18
But I say, Have they not heard? Yes verily, their sound went into all the earth, and their words unto the ends of the world.

****

Psalms 19:9
The fear of the LORD is clean, enduring for ever: the judgments of the LORD are true and righteous altogether.

Revelation 19:2
For true and righteous are his judgments: for he hath judged the great whore, which did corrupt the earth with her fornication, and hath avenged the blood of his servants at her hand.

****

Psalms 22:1
My God, my God, why hast thou forsaken me? why art thou so far from helping me, and from the words of my roaring?

Matthew 27:46
And about the ninth hour Jesus cried with a loud voice, saying, Eli, Eli, lama sabachthani? That is to say, My God, my God, why hast thou forsaken me?

Mark 15:34
And at the ninth hour Jesus cried with a loud voice, saying, Eloi, Eloi, lama, sabachthani? which is, being interpreted, My God, my God, why hast thou forsaken me?

****

Psalms 22:18
They part my garments among them, and cast lots upon my vesture.

John 19:24
They said therefore among themselves; Let us not rend it, but cast lots for it, whose it shall be: that the scripture might be fulfilled, which saith, They parted my raiment among them, and for my vesture they did cast lots. These things therefore the soldiers did.

****

Psalms 22:22
I will declare thy name unto my brethren in the midst of the congregation will I praise thee.

Hebrews 2:12
Saying, I will declare thy name unto my brethren, in the midst of the church will I sing praise unto thee.

****

Psalms 24:1 (Psalms 50:12)
The earth is the LORD's, and the fullness thereof; the world, and they that dwell therein.

1 Corinthians 10:26
For the earth is the Lord's, and the fullness thereof.

****

Psalms 31:5
Into thine hand I commit my spirit: thou hast redeemed me, O LORD God of truth.

Luke 23:46
And when Jesus had cried with a loud voice, he said, Father, into thy hands I commend my spirit: and having said thus, he gave up the ghost.

****

Psalms 32:1, 2
Blessed is he whose transgression is forgiven, whose sin is covered. Blessed is the man unto whom the LORD imputeth not iniquity, and in whose spirit there is no guile.

Romans 4:7, 8
Saying, Blessed are they whose iniquities are forgiven, and whose sins are covered. Blessed is the man to whom the Lord will not impute sin.

****

Psalms 34:12-16
What man is he that desireth life, and loveth many days, that he may see good? Keep thy tongue from evil, and thy lips from speaking guile. Depart from evil, and do good; seek peace, and pursue it. The eyes of the LORD are upon the righteous, and his ears are open unto their cry. The face of the LORD is against them that do evil, to cut off the remembrance of them from the earth.

1 Peter 3:10-12
For he that will love life, and see good days, let him refrain his tongue from evil, and his lips that they speak no guile: Let him eschew evil, and do good; let him seek peace, and ensue it. For the eyes of the Lord are over the righteous, and his ears are open unto their prayers: but the face of the Lord is against them that do evil.

****

Psalms 34:20 (Exodus 12:46; Numbers 9:12)
He keepeth all his bones: not one of them is broken.

John 19:36
For these things were done, that the scripture should be fulfilled, A bone of him shall not be broken.

****

Psalms 35:19 (Psalms 69:4)
Let not them that are mine enemies wrongfully rejoice over me: neither let them wink with the eye that hate me without a cause.

John 15:25
But this cometh to pass, that the word might be fulfilled that is written in their law, They hated me without a cause.

****

Psalm 36:1 (Isaiah 59:7, 8)
The transgression of the wicked saith within my heart, that there is no fear of God before his eyes.

Romans 3:18
There is no fear of God before their eyes.

****

Psalms 40:6-8
Sacrifice and offering thou didst not desire; mine ears hast thou opened: burnt offering and sin offering hast thou not required. Then said I, Lo, I come: in the volume of the book it is written of me, I delight to do thy will, O my God: yea, thy law is within my heart.

Hebrews 10:5-9
Wherefore when he cometh into the world, he saith, Sacrifice and offering thou wouldest not, but a body hast thou prepared me: In burnt offerings and sacrifices for sin thou hast had no pleasure. Then said I, Lo, I come (in the volume of the book it is written of me,) to do thy will, O God. Above when he said, Sacrifice and offering and burnt offerings and offering for sin thou wouldest not, neither hadst pleasure therein: which are offered by the law; Then said he, Lo, I come to do thy will, O God. He taketh away the first, that he may establish the second.

****

Psalms 41:9
Yea, mine own familiar friend, in whom I trusted, which did eat of my bread, hath lifted up his heel against me.

John 13:18
I speak not of you all: I know whom I have chosen: but that the scripture may be fulfilled, He that eateth bread with me hath lifted up his heel against me.

****

Psalms 44:22
Yea, for thy sake we are killed all the day long; we are counted as sheep for the slaughter.

****

Romans 8:36
As it is written, For thy sake we are killed all the day long; we are accounted as sheep for the slaughter.

****

Psalms 45:6, 7
Thy throne, O God, is for ever and ever: the scepter of thy kingdom is a right sceptre. Thou lovest righteousness, and hatest wickedness: therefore God, thy God, hath anointed thee with the oil of gladness above thy fellows.

Hebrews 1:8, 9
But unto the Son he saith, Thy throne, O God, is for ever and ever: a sceptre of righteousness is the sceptre of thy kingdom. Thou hast loved righteousness, and hated iniquity; therefore God, even thy God, hath anointed thee with the oil of gladness above thy fellows.

****

Psalms 48:2 (Isaiah 66:1)
Beautiful for situation, the joy of the whole earth, is mount Zion, on the sides of the north, the city of the great King.

Matthew 5:35
Nor by the earth; for it is his footstool: neither by Jerusalem; for it is the city of the great King.

****

Psalms 50:12 (Psalms 24:1)
If I were hungry, I would not tell thee: for the world is mine and the fullness thereof.

1 Corinthians 10:26
For the earth is the Lord's, and the fullness thereof.

****

Psalms 51:4
Against thee, thee only, have I sinned, and done this evil in thy sight: that thou mightiest be justified when thou speakest, and be clear when thou judgest.

Romans 3:4
God forbid: yea, let God be true, but every man a liar; as it is written, That thou mightiest be justified in thy sayings, and mightiest overcome when thou art judged.

****

Psalms 53:1-3 (Psalms 14:1-3)
The fool hath said in his heart, There is no God. Corrupt are they, and have done abominable iniquity: there is none that doeth good. God looked down from heaven upon the children of men, to see if there were any that did understand, that did seek God. Every one of them is gone back: they are altogether become filthy; there is none that doeth good, no, not one.

Romans 3:10-18
As it is written, There is none righteous, no, not one: There is none that understandeth, there is none that seeketh after God. They are all gone out of the way, they are together become unprofitable; there is none that doeth good, no, not one. Their throat is an open sepulcher; with their tongues they have used deceit; the poison of asps is under their lips: Whose mouth is full of cursing and bitterness: Their feet are swift to shed blood: Destruction and misery are in their ways: And the way of peace have they not known: There is no fear of God before their eyes.

****

Psalms 62:12 (Proverbs 24:12)
Also unto thee, O Lord, belongeth mercy: for thou renderest to every man according to his work.

Matthew 16:27
For the Son of man shall come in the glory of his Father with his angels; and then he shall reward every man according to his works.

Romans 2:6
Who will render to every man according to his deeds.

****

Psalms 68:18
Thou hast ascended on high, thou hast led captivity captive: thou hast received gifts for men; yea, for the rebellious also, that the LORD God might dwell among them.

Ephesians 4:8
Wherefore he saith, When he ascended up on high, he led captivity captive, and gave gifts unto men.

****

Psalms 69:4 (Psalms 35:19)
They that hate me without cause are more than the hairs of mine head: they that would destroy me, being mine enemies wrongfully, are mighty: then I restored that which I took not away.

John 15:25
But this, cometh to pass, that the word might be fulfilled that is written in their law, They hated me without a cause.

****

Psalm 69:9
For the zeal of thine house hath eaten me up; and the reproaches of them that reproached thee are fallen upon me.

John 2:17
And his disciples remembered that it was written, The zeal of thine house hath eaten me up.

Romans 15:3
For even Christ pleased not himself; but, as it is written, The reproaches of them that reproached thee fell on me.

****

Psalm 69:22, 23
Let their table become a snare before them: and that which should have been for their welfare, let it become a trap. Let their eyes be darkened, that they see not; and make their loins continually to shake.

Romans 11:9, 10
And David saith, Let their table be made a snare, and a trap, and a stumbling block, and a recompence unto them: Let their eyes be darkened, that they may not see, and bow down their backs always.

****

Psalms 69:25 (Psalms 109:8)
Let their habitation be desolate; and let none dwell in their tents.

Acts 1:20
For it is written in the book of Psalms, Let his habitation be desolate, and let no man dwell therein: and his bishopric let another take.

****

Psalms 78:2
I will open my mouth in a parable: I will utter dark sayings of old.

Matthew 13:35
That it might be fulfilled which was spoken by the prophet, saying, I will open my mouth in parables; I will utter things which have been kept secret from the foundation of the world.

****

Psalms 78:24 (Exodus 16:4, 15; Nehemiah 9:15)
And had rained down manna upon them to eat, and had given them of the corn of heaven.

John 6:31
Our fathers did eat manna in the desert; as it is written, He gave them bread from heaven to eat.

****

Psalms 82:6
I have said, Ye are gods; and all of you are children of the most High.

John 10:34
Jesus answered them, Is it not written in your law, I said, Ye are gods?

****

Psalms 86:9
All nations whom thou hast made shall come and worship before thee, O Lord; and shall glorify thy name.

Revelation 15:4
Who shall not fear thee, O Lord, and glorify thy name? for thou only art holy: for all nations shall come and worship before thee; for thy judgments are made manifest.

****

Psalms 89:4, 34 (Psalms 132:11; II Samuel 7:12, 13)
Thy seed will I establish for ever, and build up thy throne to all generations. Selah. My covenant will I not break, nor alter the thing that is gone out of my lips.

Acts 2:30
Therefore being a prophet, and knowing that God had sworn with an oath to him, that of the fruit of his loins, according to the flesh, he would raise up Christ to sit on his throne.

****

Psalms 89:20 (I Samuel 13:14)
I have found David my servant; with my holy oil have I anointed him.

Acts 13:22
And when he had removed him, he raised up unto them David to be their king; to whom also he gave testimony, and said, I have found David the son of Jesse, a man after mine own heart, which shall fulfill all my will.

****

Psalms 90:4
For a thousand years in thy sight are but as yesterday when it is past, and as a watch in the night.

II Peter 3:8
But, beloved, be not ignorant of this one thing, that one day is with the Lord as a thousand years, and a thousand years as one day.

****

Psalm 91:11, 12
For he shall give his angels charge over thee, to keep thee in all thy ways. They shall bear thee up in their hands, lest thou dash thy foot against a stone.

Matthew 4:6 (Luke 4:10, 11)
And saith unto him, If thou be the Son of God, cast thyself down: for it is written, He shall give his angels charge concerning thee: and in their hands they shall bear thee up, lest at any time thou dash thy foot against a stone.

****

Psalms 94:11
The LORD knoweth the thoughts of man, that they are vanity.

I Corinthians 3:20
And again, The Lord knoweth the thoughts of the wise, that they are vain.

****

Psalms 95:7, 8
For he is our God; and we are the people of his pasture, and the sheep of his hand. Today if ye will hear his voice, Harden not your heart, as in the provocation, and as in the day of temptation in the wilderness.

Hebrews 3:7, 8
Wherefore as the Holy Ghost saith, To day if ye will hear his voice, Harden not your hearts, as in the provocation, in the day of temptation in the wilderness.

Hebrews 3:15
While it is said, To day if ye will hear his voice, harden not your hearts, as in the provocation.

Hebrews 4:7
Again, he limiteth a certain day, saying in David, To day, after so long a time; as it is said, To day if ye will hear his voice, harden not your hearts.

****

Psalms 95:9-11
When your fathers tempted me, proved me, and saw my work. Forty years long was I grieved with this generation, and said, It is a people that do err in their heart, and they have not known my ways: Unto whom I sware in my wrath that they should not enter into my rest.

Hebrews 3:9-11
When your fathers tempted me, proved me, and saw my works forty years. Wherefore I was grieved with that generation, and said, They do alway err in their heart; and they have not known my ways. So I sware in my wrath, They shall not enter into my rest.

Hebrews 4:3
For we which have believed do enter into rest, as he said As I have sworn in my wrath, if they shall enter into my rest: although the works were finished from

the foundation of the world.

Hebrews 4:5
And in this place again, If they shall enter into my rest.

****

Psalms 96:13
Before the LORD: for he cometh, for he cometh to judge the earth: he shall judge the world with righteousness, and the people with his truth.

Acts 17:31
Because he hath appointed a day, in the which he will judge the world in righteousness by that man whom he hath ordained; whereof he hath given assurance unto all men, in that he hath raised him from the dead.

****

Psalms 98
(The entire psalm!)

Luke 1:46-55
(Mary's Magnificat)

****

Psalms 102:25-27
Of old hast thou laid the foundation of the earth: and the heavens are the work of thy hands. They shall perish, but thou shalt endure: yea, all of them shall wax old like a garment; as a vesture shalt thou change them, and they shall be changed: But thou art the same, and thy years shall have no end.

Hebrews 1:10-12
And, Thou, Lord, in the beginning hast laid the foundation of the earth; and the heavens are the works of thine hands: They shall perish; but thou remainest; and they all shall wax old as doth a garment; And as a vesture shalt thou fold them up, and they shall be changed: but thou art the same, and thy years shall not fail.

****

Psalms 103: 17
But the mercy of the LORD is from everlasting to everlasting upon them that fear him, and his righteousness unto children's children.

Luke 1:50
And his mercy is on them that fear him from generation to generation.

****

Psalms 104:4
Who maketh his angels spirits; his ministers a flaming fire.

Hebrews 1:7
And of the angels he saith, Who maketh his angels spirits, and his ministers a flame of fire.

****

Psalms 104:12 (Ezekiel 17:23)
By them shall the fowls of the heaven have their habitation, which sing among the branches.

Matthew 13:32
Which indeed is the least of all seeds: but when it is grown, it is the greatest among herbs, and becometh a tree, so that the birds of the air come and lodge in the branches thereof.

Mark 4:32
But when it is sown, it growth up, and becometh greater than all herbs, and shooteth out great branches; so that the fowls of the air may lodge under the shadow of it.

Luke 13:19
It is like a grain of mustard seed, which a man took, and cast into his garden; and it grew, and waxed a great tree; and the fowls of the air lodged in the branches of it

****

Psalms 106:10
And he saved them from the hand of him that hated them, and redeemed them from the hand of the enemy.

Luke 1:71
That we should be saved from our enemies, and from the hand of all that hate us.

****

Psalms 107:9
For he satisfieth the longing soul, and filleth the hungry soul with goodness.

Luke 1:53
He hath filled the hungry with good things; and the rich he hath sent empty away.

****

Psalms 109:8 (Psalms 69:25)
Let his days be few; and let another take his office.

Acts 1:20
For it is written in the book of Psalms, Let his habitation be desolate, and let no man dwell therein: and his bishopric let another take.

****

Psalms 110:1
The LORD said unto my Lord, Sit thou at my right hand, until I make thine enemies thy footstool.

Matthew 22:44
The LORD said unto my lord, Sit thou on my right hand, till I make thine enemies thy footstool?

Matthew 26:64
Jesus saith unto him, Thou hast said: nevertheless I say unto you, Hereafter shall ye see the Son of man sitting on the right hand of power, and coming in the clouds of heaven.

Mark 12:36
For David himself said by the Holy Ghost, The LORD said to my Lord, Sit thou on my right hand, till I make thine enemies thy footstool.

Mark 14:62
And Jesus said, I am: and ye shall see the Son of man sitting on the right hand of power, and coming in the clouds of heaven.

Luke 20:42, 43
And David himself saith in the book of Psalms, The LORD said unto my Lord, Sit thou on my right hand, Till I make thine enemies thy footstool.

Luke 22:69
Hereafter shall the Son of man sit on the right hand of the power of God.

Acts 2:34, 35
For David is not ascended into the heavens: but he saith himself, The LORD said unto my Lord, Sit thou on my right hand Until I make thy foes thy footstool.

Hebrews 1:13
But to which of the angels said he at any time, Sit on my right hand, until I make thine enemies thy footstool?

Hebrews 10:12, 13
But this man, after he had offered one sacrifice for sins for ever, sat down on the right hand of God; From henceforth expecting till his enemies be made his footstool.

****

Psalms 110:4
The LORD hath sworn, and will not repent, Thou art a priest for ever after the order of Melchisedec.

Hebrews 5:6
As he saith also in another place, Thou art a priest for ever after the order of Melchisedec.

Hebrews 7:17, 21
For he testifieth, Thou art a priest for ever after the order of Melchisedec. (For those priests were made without an oath; but this with an oath by him that said unto him, The Lord sware and will not repent, Thou art a priest for ever after the order of Melchizedek.

****

Psalms 112:9
He hath dispersed, he hath given to the poor; his righteousness endureth for ever; his horn shall be exalted with honour.

II Corinthians 9:9
As it is written, He hath dispersed abroad; he hath given to the poor: his righteousness remaineth for ever.

****

Psalms 116:10
I believed, therefore have I spoken: I was greatly afflicted.

II Corinthians 4:13
We having the same spirit of faith, according as it is written, I believed, and therefore have I spoken; we also believe, and therefore speak.

****

Psalms 117:1
O praise the LORD, all ye nations: praise him, all ye people.

Romans 15:11
And again, Praise the Lord, all ye Gentiles; and laud him, all ye people.

****

Psalms 118:6
The LORD is on my side; I will not fear: what can man do unto me?

Hebrews 13:6
So that we may boldy say, The Lord is my helper, and I will not fear what man shall do unto me.

****

Psalms 118:22, 23
The stone which the builders refused is become the head stone of the corner. This is the LORD's doing; it is marvelous in our eyes.

Matthew 21:42
Jesus saith unto them, Did ye never read in the scriptures, The stone which the builders rejected, the same is become the head of the corner: this is the Lord's doing, and it is marvelous in our eyes?

Mark 12:10, 11
And have ye not read this scripture; The stone which the builders rejected is become the head of the corner: This was the Lord's doing, and it is marvellous in our eyes?

Luke 20:17
And he beheld them, and said, What is this then that is written, The stone which the builders rejected, the same is become the head of the corner?

Acts 4:11
This is the stone which was set at nought of you builders, which is become the head of the corner.

I Peter 2:7
Unto you therefore which believe he is precious: but unto them which be disobedient, the stone which the builders disallowed, the same I made the head of the corner.

****

Psalms 118:26
Blessed be he that cometh in the name of the LORD: we have blessed you out of the house of the LORD.

Matthew 21:9
And the multitudes that went before, and that followed, cried, saying, Hosanna to the son of David: Blessed is he that cometh in the name of the Lord; Hosanna in the highest.

Matthew 23:39
For I say unto you, Ye shall not see me henceforth, till ye shall say, Blessed is he that cometh in the name of the Lord.

Mark 11:9
And they that went before, and they that followed, cried, saying, Hosanna; Blessed is he that cometh in the name of the Lord.

Luke 13:35
Behold your house is left unto you desolated: and verily I say unto you, Ye shall not see me, until the time come when ye shall say, Blessed is he that cometh in the name of the Lord.

Luke 19:38
Saying, Blessed be the King that cometh in the name of the Lord: peace in heaven, and glory in the highest.

John 12:13
Took branches of palm trees, and went forth to meet him, and cried, Hosanna: Blessed is the King of Israel that cometh in the name of the Lord.

****

Psalms 132:11 (Psalms 89:4, 34; II Samuel 7:12, 13)
The LORD hath sworn in truth unto David; he will not turn from it; Of the fruit of thy body will I set upon thy throne.

Acts 2:30
Therefore being a prophet, and knowing that God had sworn with an oath to him, that of the fruit of his loins, according to the flesh, he would raise up Christ to sit on his throne.

****

Psalms 135:14
For the LORD will judge his people, and he will repent himself concerning his servants.

Hebrews 10:30
For we know him that hath said, Vengeance belongeth unto me I will recompense, saith the Lord. And again, The Lord shall judge his people.

****

Psalms 140:3 (Isaiah 59:7, 8)
They have sharpened their tongues like a serpent; adders' poison is under their lips. Selah.

Romans 3:13-18
Their throat is an open sepulchre; with their tongues they have used deceit; the poison of asps is under their lips: Whose mouth is full of cursing and bitterness: Their feet are swift to shed blood: Destruction and misery are in their ways: And the way of peace have they not know: There is no fear of God before their eyes.

****

Psalms 146:6 (Exodus 20:11)
Which made heaven, and earth, the sea, and all that therein is; which keepeth truth for ever.

Acts 4:24
And when they heard that, they lifted up their voice to God with one accord, and said, Lord, thou art God, which hast made heaven, and earth, and the sea, and all that in them is.

Acts 14:15
And saying, Sirs, why do ye these things? We also are men of like passions with you, and preach unto you that ye should turn from these vanities unto the

living God, which made heaven, and earth, and the sea, and all things that are therein.

Revelation 10:6
And sware by him that liveth for ever and ever, who created heaven, and the things that therein are, and the earth, and the things that therein are, and the sea, and the things which are therein, that there should be time no longer.

PROVERBS

SEEKING WISDOM					
WISDOM & FOLLY CONTRASTED	**BRIEF PROVERBS**	**WORDS OF WISDOM**	**MORE WORDS OF WISDOM**	**PROVERBS COPIED BY HEZEKIAH'S SCRIBES**	**THREE APPENDIXES**
Preparation for kingship: **1-9**	Poems which taught wisdom: **10-22**	Simple truths by which to live: **22-24**	Wisdom is "skillful living": **24**	Wisdom in relationships: **25-29**	Summarizing Wisdom: **30,31**
LOCATION: Judah					
OVERVIEW: Solomon's parents gave their son the very best training, including these lessons on wisdom for everyday living, composed in poetic, musical form. Solomon—known as the wisest man who ever lived—continued this method of instruction for his children...and for our benefit today.					
TIME: Written over a 250-year span around 800 B.C.					

FAST FACTS

AUTHOR AND SETTING:

Solomon, Agur, Lemuel; Judah

PURPOSE:

Proverbs was originally two-line poems set to music and taught to Solomon by his parents in preparation for kingship. Poetry was used to teach the wisdom of God's Word. You can base your life on this book of wisdom.

SEEING JESUS:

Jesus is the fullness of God's wisdom, and thus He is seen throughout this book; perhaps the best example is in 8:30, 31.

THEME VERSE:

Proverbs 2:6

NOTES

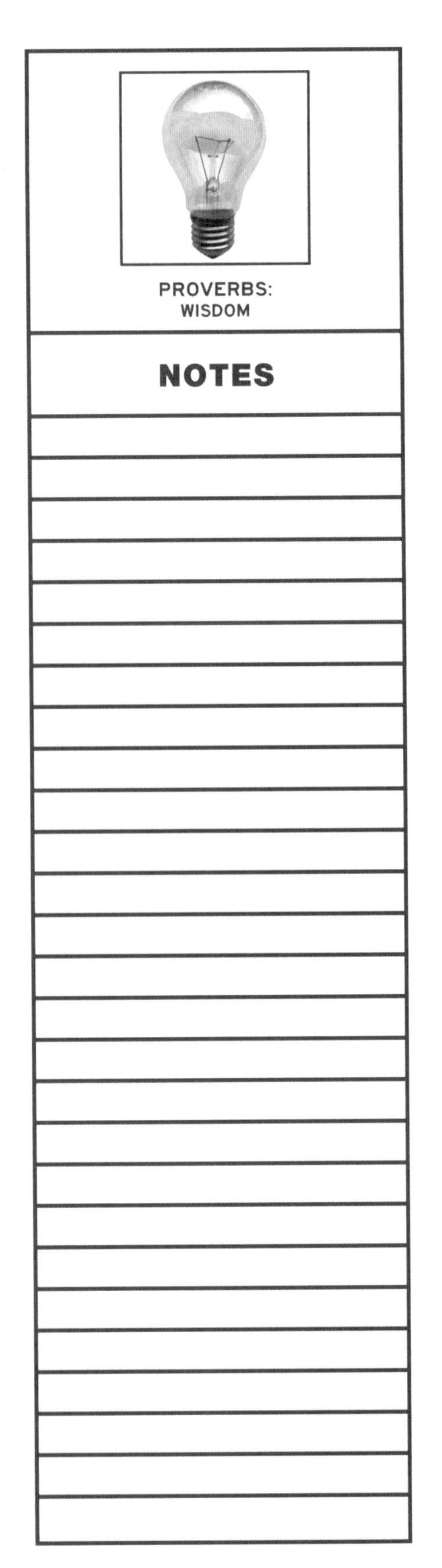

SEEING JESUS IN PROVERBS

AUTHOR & SETTING

The book of *Proverbs* was compiled in the 8th century B.C. The first ten chapters, which are ascribed to Solomon, reflect the teaching his parents gave him concerning wisdom. Solomon *"...spake three thousand proverbs: and his songs were a thousand and five"* **(I Kings 4:32).**

There is evidence in the Old Testament that there was a school of person who devoted themselves to the study and promotion of wisdom:

"To understand a proverb, and the interpretation; the words of the wise, and their dark sayings" **(Proverbs 1:6).**

"Bow down thine ear, and hear the words of the wise, and apply thine heart unto my knowledge" **(Proverbs 22:17).**

"These things also belong to the wise. It is not good to have respect of persons in judgment" **(Proverbs 24:23).**

"Which wise men have told from their fathers, and have not hid it" **(Job 15:18).**

According to Proverbs 25:1 "men of Hezekiah" compiled some of the proverbs.

OVERVIEW

Wisdom must be diligently sought. The essential teachings are moral and spiritual. All wisdom begins with the fear of God.

Proverbs was originally two-line poems set to music and taught to Solomon by his mother and father—probably when he was a teenager—in order to prepare him to be a wise king. Solomon was the father of this kind of literature. Remember, it was taught to him by his mother and father, David and Bath-sheba. Solomon loved his mother and father and gave both of them credit again and again in chapters one through ten.

Note the emphasis on wisdom:

Wisdom is justified by her works—Matthew 11:19.
Wisdom's method is to cry aloud—Proverbs 1:20.
Wisdom's appeal is to the simple and scoffers—Proverbs 1:22, 23.
Wisdom's rejection—Proverbs 1:24-32.
Wisdom's encouragement—Proverbs 1:33.
Wisdom is seen as a woman—Proverbs 1:20.

King David used poetry to teach Solomon the wisdom of God's Word. Solomon wrote down that poetry, which later became the book of *Proverbs*. You can base your life on this book of wisdom.

Proverbs was written basically in six different forms of *distich* meaning "two successive lines of verse regarded as a unit." Here are explanations and examples of these different forms of distich:

The synonymous distich: in this distich the first line offers a doctrine, which the second repeats. However, the second line uses different wording: *"The liberal soul shall be made fat: and he that watereth shall be watered also himself"* **(Proverbs 11:25).**

The antithetical distich: in this distich the first line is positive; the second line is negative: *"A sound heart is the life of the flesh: but envy the rottenness of the bones"* **(Proverbs 14:30).**

The synthetical distich: in this distich both lines express doctrine and have something in common that is neither antithetical nor synonymous. Both lines develop the subject: *"He that hideth hatred with lying lips, and he that uttereth a slander, is a fool"* **(Proverbs 10:18).**

The integral distich: in an integral distich the first line begins a thought; the second line completes that thought: *"The law of the wise is a fountain of life, to depart from the snares of death"* **(Proverbs 13:14).**

The parabolic distich: in a parabolic distich the first line illustrates the second line. The first line characteristically uses the word "as": *"As a jewel of gold in a swine's snout, so is a fair woman which is without discretion"* **(Proverbs 11:22).**

The comparative distich: in a comparative distich the first line expresses something better than that which is mentioned in the second line: *"Better is a dinner of herbs where love is, than a stalled ox and hatred therewith"* **(Proverbs 15:17).**

SEEING JESUS IN PROVERBS

Jesus is seen very beautifully in the book of *Proverbs*:

"Then I was by him, as one brought up with him: and I was daily his delight, rejoicing always before him; Rejoicing in the habitable part of his earth; and my delights were with the sons of men" **(Proverbs 8:30, 31).**

Proverbs 8 shows Jesus, the Son of God, in Creation.

We see Jesus again and again in the wisdom of *Proverbs*. For in Him dwells all the fullness of God's wisdom. Solomon knew that God had a Son and, of course, we know His name is Jesus:

"Who hath ascended up into heaven, or descended? who hath gathered the wind in his fists? Who hath bound the waters in a garment? Who hath established all the ends of the earth? What is his name, and what is his son's name, if thou canst tell?" **(Proverbs 30:4).**

Solomon was so programmed in God's wisdom by his mother and father that when he became a king and God asked him what he desired most, of course he cried out for wisdom. Jesus is God's wisdom, and He is made unto us wisdom **(I Corinthian 1:30).**

NOTES

NOTES

THEME VERSE

"For the LORD giveth wisdom: out of his mouth cometh knowledge and understanding" **(Proverbs 2:6).**

OUTLINE

I. **WISDOM AND FOLLY CONTRASTED -** PROVERBS 1:7-9:18

II. **COLLECTION OF BRIEF PROVERBS -** PROVERBS 10:1-22:16

III. **THE WORDS OF THE WISE -** PROVERBS 22:17-24:22

IV. **ANOTHER COLLECTION OF WORDS OF THE WISE -** PROVERBS 24:23-34

V. **ANOTHER GROUP OF PROVERBS COPIED BY HEZEKIAH'S SCRIBES -** PROVERBS 25-29

VI. **THREE APPENDIXES -** PROVERBS 30, 31

Proverbs 6:22 is one of the major themes of my life:

"When thou goest, it [the Word] shall lead thee; when thou sleepest, it shall keep thee; and when thou awakest, it shall talk with thee."

PROVERBS QUOTED IN THE NEW TESTAMENT.

Proverbs 3:11, 12
My son, despise not the chastening of the LORD; neither be weary of his correction: For whom the LORD loveth he correcteth; even as a father the son in whom he delighteth.

Hebrews 12:5, 6
And ye have forgotten the exhortation which speaketh unto you as unto children, My son, despise not thou the chastening of the Lord, nor faint when thou art rebuked of him: For whom the LORD loveth he chasteneth, and scourgeth every son whom he receiveth.

****

Proverbs 3:34
Surely he scorneth the scorners: but he giveth grace unto the lowly.

James 4:6
But he giveth more grace. Wherefore he saith, God resisteth the proud, but giveth grace unto the humble.

I Peter 5:5
Likewise, ye younger, submit yourselves unto the elder. Yea, all of you be subject one to another, and be clothed with humility: for God resisteth the proud, and giveth grace to the humble.

****

Proverbs 11:31
Behold, the righteous shall be recompensed in the earth: much more the wicked and the sinner.

I Peter 4:18
And if the righteous scarcely be saved, where shall the ungodly and the sinner appear?

****

Proverbs 24:12 (Psalms 62:12)
If thou sayest, Behold, we knew it not; doth not he that pondereth the heart consider it? And he that keepeth thy soul, doth not he know it? And shall not he render to every man according to his works?

Matthew 16:27
For the Son of man shall come in the glory of his Father with his angels; and then he shall reward every man according to his works.

Romans 2:6
Who will render to every man according to his deeds.

****

Proverbs 25:21, 22
If thine enemy be hungry, give him bread to eat; and if he be thirst, give him water to drink: For thou shalt heap coals of fire upon his head, and the LORD shall reward thee.

Romans 12:20
Therefore if thine enemy hunger, feed him; if he thirst, give him drink: for in so doing thou shalt heap coals of fire on his head.

****

Proverbs 26:11
As a dog returneth to his vomit, so a fool returneth to his folly.

II Peter 2:22
But it is happened unto them according to the true proverb, The dog is turned to his own vomit again; and the sow that was washed to her wallowing in the mire.

NOTES

ECCLESIASTES

SEARCHING FOR MEANING IN LIFE			
SEEKING VANITIES	**SEEKING ADVICE**	**CONTRASTING WISDOM & FOLLY**	**REPENTING FROM MAN'S WISDOM**
Education: **1** Entertainment: **2** Great Works: **2** Heritage: **2** Riches & Glory: **2** Philosophy: **3,4** Money: **5,6** Reputation: **7** Sex: **7**	Oppression & sins: **8**	Seeking God's Wisdom: **9,10**	Remembering the Creator: **11,12**
LOCATION: Jerusalem			
OVERVIEW: Although gifted with supernatural wisdom, as Solomon prospered materially, he turned his eyes from godly wisdom. But "the man who had everything" soon found that true happiness lay only in knowing God.			
TIME: Late in Solomon's life—around 945 B.C.			

FAST FACTS

AUTHOR AND SETTING:

Solomon; Jerusalem

PURPOSE:

Contrasting the emptiness of life—even a life filled with wealth and glory—apart from God, this poetic book serves to remind all of us that no truly successful man is a "self-made man," but that all good things come from God *(Ecclesiastes 2:24).*

SEEING JESUS:

Ecclesiastes convincingly portrays the emptiness and perplexity of life without a relationship with Jesus Christ. Only He can provide ultimate satisfaction, joy, and wisdom.

THEME VERSE:

Ecclesiastes 12:13, 14

NOTES

ECCLESIASTES:
PREACHER

NOTES

SEEING JESUS IN ECCLESIASTES

AUTHOR & SETTING

Like Proverbs, *Ecclesiastes* is a book of wisdom. *Ecclesiastes* records Solomon's reasonings under the sun while he was in a backslidden condition. It ends up, however, with his reasonings under the Son.

OVERVIEW

Ecclesiastes means "a preacher" This book shows the fallacy of thinking that earthly sins, pleasures, and pursuits are the chief end in life and the source of happiness. The final conclusion is that the whole of life is to fear God, to keep His commandments, and to live forever with Him. This is the chief thing in life and the only eternally rewarding thing. There is no question that this was Solomon's personal testimony!

When you try to live life under the sun, truly it is vanity of vanities. It is like going in circles—one generation passes away, and another comes along and does the same thing all over again.

At one time in Solomon's life, he had totally sought the wisdom of God. Wisdom was Solomon's heart cry. He'd been taught as a child to seek after God's wisdom by both his mother and father. The first ten chapters of Proverbs teach this.

Later, after he was crowned king, Solomon went to God and asked for wisdom to govern God's people. God was pleased with this. There is no question that Solomon received the wisdom of God. He received *sophia* wisdom, which is wisdom of ultimate things. He received *phronesis* wisdom which is practical wisdom of how to bring ultimate things to pass. He received *sunesis* wisdom which is the wisdom of putting two and two together.

After he prospered materially, Solomon began to turn his eyes away from godly wisdom. He turned to nine different things in order to bring happiness to his life (see Outline). He was the man who had everything, but he really had nothing when he forgot the wisdom of God.

Gold was abundant in Solomon's empire. It was said that it could be picked up like rocks in the street. When Solomon's annual income was given, it was beyond what any man could imagine. He was a man who even had apes and peacocks—but he was unhappy without God's wisdom.

In our outline we will see the nine things that Solomon tried in order to bring happiness to his own heart.

SEEING JESUS IN ECCLESIASTES

There is no question that Solomon knew the great Shepherd—Jesus Christ:

"The words of the wise are as goads, and as nails fastened by the masters of assemblies, which are given from one shepherd" **(Ecclesiastes 12:11).**

It would be the Shepherd's words that would hold Solomon in the time of his needs.

THEME VERSES

"Let us hear the conclusion of the whole matter: Fear God, and keep his commandments: for this is the whole duty of man. For God shall bring every work into judgment, with every secret thing, whether it be good, or whether it be evil" **(Ecclesiastes 12:13, 14).**

OUTLINE

I. **SOLOMON SOUGHT AFTER VANITIES TO SATISFY HIS HUNGER FOR HAPPINESS** - ECCLESIASTES 1-7.

A. **He Sought To Find Happiness in Education -** Ecclesiastes 1:12-18.

1. **He found that much learning was grief and the increase of knowledge multiplied sorrow -** Ecclesiastes 1:18.

B. **Solomon Sought After Entertainment -** Ecclesiastes 2:1-3.

1. **He found that entertainment was mad and mirth didn't accomplish anything -** Ecclesiastes 2:2.

C. **Then Solomon Sought After Great Works -** Ecclesiastes 2:4-6.

D. **He Sought After Possessions, Riches, and Glory -** Ecclesiastes 2:7-19.

1. **Yet, he hated his labor because he thought that he had not truly enjoyed it and that it would simply pass on to someone else.**

E. **Solomon Sought After an Heritage -** Ecclesiastes 2:21-26.

1. **He found this only to be vanity and vexation of spirit -** Ecclesiastes 2:17.

F. **He Sought After Philosophy and Human Reasoning -** Ecclesiastes 3:1-22.

NOTES

NOTES

1. **He came to a place where he no longer expected eternal life, and he got into humanism. He found no happiness there.**
2. **He spoke of advice; then he gave advice and instruction out of his pursuit of philosophy -** Ecclesiastes 4:1-5:9.

G. **He Sought for Money To Bring Happiness -** Ecclesiastes 5:10-6:12.

1. **He found that money can cause ulcers -** Ecclesiastes 6:2.

H. **He Sought for Reputation -** Ecclesiastes 7:1-25.

1. **He found reputation to be only foolishness and madness.**

I. **He Sought After Sex -** Ecclesiastes 7:26-29.

1. **He found no happiness in many women.**

II. **SOLOMON SPOKE OF THE VANITY OF OPPRESSION AND SINS AND GAVE ADVICE -** ECCLESIASTES 8.

III. **SOLOMON BEGAN TO LOOK FOR GOD'S WISDOM AND SAW THE CONTRAST BETWEEN WISDOM AND FOLLY -** ECCLESIASTES 9, 10.

IV. **REPENTANCE FROM EARTHLY WISDOM TO GODLY WISDOM -** ECCLESIASTES 11, 12.

A. **Solomon Remembered His Creator -** Ecclesiastes 12:1.

1. **He looked at the older years -** Ecclesiastes 12:3-7.

B. **Solomon's Heart Was Turned Totally to Godly Wisdom -** Ecclesiastes 12:9-14.

ECCLESIASTES QUOTED IN THE NEW TESTAMENT: NOT FOUND

SONG OF SOLOMON

THE PLAY: A DISSERTATION ON LOVE				
ACT I	**ACT II**	**ACT III**	**ACT IV**	**ACT V**
She longs for her lover: **1,2**	Solomon's magnificence: **3**	Courtship: **4-6**	Vows: **7**	Epilogue: **8**
LOCATION: Israel				
OVERVIEW: This long and beautiful play/song illustrates that God has designed one mate for each of us. God created the Shulamite woman for the shepherd-lover...just as He decreed one Lord—Jesus Christ—for His Bride, the Church.				
TIME: Early in Solomon's life				

FAST FACTS

AUTHOR AND SETTING:

Solomon; Jerusalem

PURPOSE:

The *Song of Solomon* is an analogy of the love relationship between God and the believer... and a dissertation on human love between the "right man" (Jesus Christ) and the "right woman" (the Bride of Christ).

SEEING JESUS:

Jesus is the great lover of our souls.

THEME VERSE:

Song of Solomon 1:3

NOTES

SONG OF SOLOMON:
LOVER & BRIDEGROOM

NOTES

SEEING JESUS IN SONG OF SOLOMON

AUTHOR & SETTING

Solomon is the author of this book but not the hero of it. He wrote about his failure, for the Holy Spirit makes a hero out of us when we are willing to admit we have failed. Solomon failed in his right-man, right-woman relationship. God designed the Shulamite woman for the shepherd-lover, not for Solomon.

OVERVIEW

This book is basically a five-act play which was originally sung. It contains three main characters: Solomon, the villain, is the basso-profundo or the bass; the Shulamite woman, the heroine, is the soprano; and the shepherd-lover, the hero, is the tenor. The supporting cast consists of the dancing queen or the wicked queen, who is probably an alto, and the virgins, who are the chorus. If we were to sing a song about Solomon today, it would be to the tune of "Dare To Be a Daniel" only the words would be "Don't Be a Solomon"!

The Song of Solomon is a dissertation on love—love toward God and love between right man and right woman. In the doctrine of right man, right woman we have an analogy between the Lord and the believer as responder to the Lord. It is the shepherd who represents the Lord Jesus Christ. Solomon is the villain and represents temptation and, in some parts of the book, evil. The right woman, of course, represents the Bride of Christ.

Solomon was a genius; he knew a great deal about botany, geography, geology, and spices. His language indicates a phenomenal understanding of these topics.

The Jewish concept of drama contained five acts; the Greek concept was three acts.

Act I (chapters 1;1-3;5) sets the foundation for the entire play. The Shulamite woman had fallen in love with the shepherd, of whom her brothers did not approve (her father was dead). Hoping to make their sister forget about her shepherd-lover, the brothers sent her to the northern part of the country to work in a vineyard. Solomon was on a visit to northern Israel and was traveling down the highway in one of his beautiful chariots; he saw the Shulamite woman, fell in love with her, and desired her for his harem.

We have to remember that the harem was composed of three categories: The first category included the *queens*. These were women who had a sexual relationship with Solomon-he had actually married them. Next were the *concubines* who also had a sexual relationship along with performing other tasks. They played music and carried on conversations, but they were not married to Solomon. Lastly, there were the virgins of the harem. They did all the sewing and cooking, arranged the furniture, and attended to the everyday work of the harem.

When the Shulamite volunteered for the harem, she was trying to get away from her brothers and get back to her shepherd-lover. The Shulamite approached one of Solomon's virgins and said that she wanted to enlist as a virgin of the harem. The virgins of the harem in this particular book are called the *daughters of Jerusalem*; they act as the chorus in the drama.

Solomon had other ideas for the Shulamite woman; Solomon wanted her to become his queen. A good deal of this book relates Solomon's efforts to persuade the Shulamite to become one of his queens.

Act II (chapters 3:6-3:11) has two purposes: (1) it shows Solomon arriving at the gates of Jerusalem; and (2) it describes Solomon's glamour and human glory. In short, he was a very attractive man!

Act III (chapters 4:1-7:9) takes place in the royal palace in Jerusalem. Solomon attempts to persuade the Shulamite woman to marry him. She refuses because of her love for the shepherd.

Act IV (chapters 7:10-8:4) also takes place in the royal palace. The shepherd-lover comes to deliver the Shulamite woman—his right woman. This is the rescue scene.

In Act V (chapter 8:5-14) the Shulamite woman returns home with her shepherd-lover and, of course, they live happily ever after. Here we see the right-man, right-woman relationship—everything falling into proper place. Gracious comments from her mother, neighbors, and the general public await the Shulamite woman when she arrives home.

SEEING JESUS IN SONG OF SOLOMON

Song of Solomon opens with the Shulamite woman speaking of the kisses of her shepherd-lover (Song of Solomon 1:2). This was a courtship; she and the shepherd-lover were very much in love, and she dreamt of his kisses. The Shulamite was completely occupied with her shepherd-lover. Because she had centered her thoughts on her lover, she was able to resist the temptations of the king. We need to follow her example and focus our thoughts on our Lord Jesus Christ in order to overcome temptations.

This long and beautiful song illustrates that God has designed one mate for each of us. God designed the shepherd-lover for the Shulamite woman. God has also given us one Lord to rule and reign in our lives—the Lord Jesus Christ.

Jesus is the great lover of our souls. Our Lord kisses us through Bible doctrine; He has thousands and thousands of kisses stored up. The more we are in His Word, the more we will feel His presence.

NOTES

NOTES

THEME VERSE

"Because of the savour of thy good ointments thy name is as ointment poured forth, therefore do the virgins love thee"
(Song of Solomon 1:3)

OUTLINE

I. **THE SHULAMITE LONGS FOR HER LOVER -** SONG OF SOLOMON 1:1-3:5

II. **SOLOMON'S MAGNIFICENCE -** SONG OF SOLOMON 3:6-11

III. **THE COURTSHIP -** SONG OF SOLOMON 4:1-7:9

IV. **THE VOWS -** SONG OF SOLOMON 7:10-8:4

V. **THE EPILOGUE -** SONG OF SOLOMON 8:5-14

SONG OF SOLOMON QUOTED IN THE NEW TESTAMENT: NOT FOUND

ISAIAH

THE EVANGELICAL PROPHET		
PROPHECIES OF JUDGMENT	**HISTORICAL INTERLUDE**	**PROPHECIES OF PEACE**
Rebukes & promises: **1-6** Immanuel: **7-12** Foreign prophecies: **13-23** 1st judgment: **24-27** Zion's woes: **28-34** 2nd judgment: **35**	Invasion: **36, 37** The king's sickness: **38,39**	Purpose of peace: **40-48** Prince of peace: **49-57** Program of peace: **58-66**
LOCATION: Israel & surrounding nations		
OVERVIEW: There must be judgment & repentance	As a court-trained historian, Isaiah accurately recorded events	A right relationship with God brings comfort and peace
TIME: 63 years of prophetic work around 740 B.C.		

FAST FACTS

AUTHOR AND SETTING:

Isaiah; Israel and surrounding nations

PURPOSE:

Isaiah is a "miniature" Bible: the first division has 39 chapters—the number of Old Testament books—and emphasizes judgment; the second division has 27 chapters—the number of New Testament books—and stresses grace. Isaiah brought judgment and comfort to God's people, then and now.

SEEING JESUS:

We learn much about Jesus Christ throughout *Isaiah*: His virgin birth (7:14, 9:6); the King Who reigns in righteousness (32:1); the great Shepherd (40:11); the servant (42:1); the man of sorrows bearing our sins (53:3,7); and more.

THEME VERSE:

Isaiah 1:18

NOTES

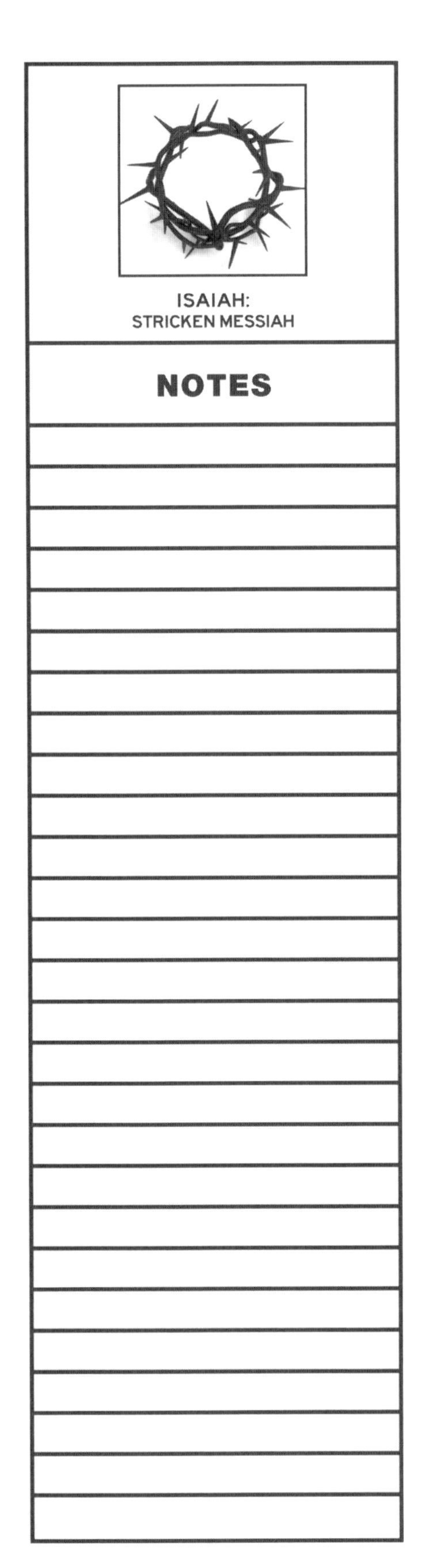

SEEING JESUS IN ISAIAH

AUTHOR & SETTING

Isaiah means "the salvation of Jehovah." His name is a summary of this book. He is called the evangelical prophet because he presents Jesus and the plan of redemption more completely than any other prophet. Isaiah is called "the Saint Paul of the Old Testament." His wife was a prophetess; he had two sons, Shear-jashub and Maher-shalal-hash-baz.

His official position was a historiographer of the Hebrew court during the reigns of Jotham and Hezekiah. He wrote the accounts of Jotham and Hezekiah in the book of Kings. He was a prophet, a preacher, a psalmist, an instructor, an intercessor, an evangelist, and a seer.

His prophetic call covered the reigns of five kings: Uzziah, Jotham, Ahaz, Hezekiah, and Manasseh. Although Isaiah was certainly alive during the reign of Hezekiah's son Manasseh, the book of Isaiah doesn't mention Manasseh.

Critics have tried to say that Isaiah only wrote the first 39 chapters of this book, but the New Testament book of John attributes both Isaiah 6:9 and Isaiah 53:1 to Isaiah (see John 12:38-41).

OVERVIEW

Isaiah had sixty-three years of prophetic work. He was uncompromising with the kings with whom he dealt. Isaiah was the Moses of his day. He brought God's final offer of mercy to Judah. When they refused, Isaiah brought the message of doom, exile, and desolation.

Isaiah showed that selfishness, greed, and oppression crush the helpless. The wicked are joined together, they are full of falsehood and vanity; they put darkness for light and light for darkness; they are conceited; they become wise in their own eyes, and strong drink keeps them inflamed.

Isaiah is quoted frequently in the New Testament:

"That it might be fulfilled which was spoken by Esaias the prophet, saying" **(Matthew 4:14).**

"That it might be fulfilled which was spoken by Esaias the prophet, saying, Himself took our infirmities, and bare our sicknesses" **(Matthew 8:17).**

"That it might be fulfilled which was spoken by Esaias the prophet, saying" **(Matthew 12:17).**

"He said, I am the voice of one crying in the wilderness, Make straight the way of the Lord, as said the prophet Esaias" **(John 1:23).**

"These things said Esaias, when he saw his glory, and spake of him" **(John 12:41).**

"And when they agreed not among themselves, they departed, after that Paul had spoken one word, Well spake the Holy Ghost by Esaias the prophet unto our fathers, Saying, Go unto this people, and say, Hearing ye shall hear, and shall not understand; and seeing ye shall see, and not perceive: For the heart of this people is waxed gross, and their ears are dull of hearing, and their eyes have they closed; lest they should see with their eyes, and hear with their ears; and understand with their heart, and should be converted, and I should heal them" **(Acts 28:25-27).**

"Esaias also crieth concerning Israel, Though the number of the children of Israel be as the sand of the sea, a remnant shall be saved: And as Esaias said before, Except the Lord of Sabaoth had left us a seed, we had been as Sodoma, and been made like unto Gomorrha" **(Romans 9:27, 29).**

"But they have not all obeyed the gospel. For Esaias saith, Lord, who hath believed our report? But Esaias is very bold, and saith, I was found of them that sought me not; I was made manifest unto them that asked not after me" **(Romans 10:16, 20).**

"And again, Esaias saith, There shall be a root of Jesse, and he that shall rise to reign over the Gentiles; in him shall the Gentiles trust" **(Romans 15:12).**

(See also Luke 4:16-21 and Acts 8:26-33.)

During Isaiah's life, Assyria swallowed up Israel and Judah was attacked. Basically, Uzziah and Jotham were good kings. Revival time came during Hezekiah's reign.

There are two divisions to the book. In the first part are thirty-nine chapters, the number of books in the Old Testament. In the second part are twenty-seven chapters, the number of books in the New Testament.

The first part of Isaiah contains *judgment* from God, and the second part is *comfort* from God.

SEEING JESUS IN ISAIAH

There is much about Jesus in this wonderful book:

"Therefore the Lord himself shall give you a sign; Behold, a virgin shall conceive, and bear a son, and shall call his name Immanuel" **(Isaiah 7:14).**

"Nevertheless the dimness shall not be such as was in her vexation, when at the first he lightly afflicted the land of Zebulun and the land of Naphtali, and afterward did more grievously afflict her by the way of the sea, beyond Jordan, in Galilee of the nations. The people that walked in darkness have seen a great light: they that dwell in the land of the shadow of death, upon them hath the light shined" **(Isaiah 9:1, 2).**

NOTES

NOTES

SEEING JESUS IN ISAIAH - *continued*

"For unto us a child is born, unto us a son is given: and the government shall be upon his shoulder: and his name shall be called Wonderful, Counsellor, The mighty God, The everlasting Father, The Prince of Peace" **(Isaiah 9:6).**

"And there shall come forth a rod out of the stem of Jesse, and a Branch shall grow out of his roots: And the spirit of the LORD shall rest upon him, the spirit of wisdom and understanding, the spirit of counsel and might, the spirit of knowledge and of the fear of the LORD" **(Isaiah 11:1,2).**

"Therefore thus saith the Lord GOD, Behold, I lay in Zion for a foundation a stone, a tried stone, a precious corner stone, a sure foundation: he that believeth shall not make haste" **(Isaiah 28:16).**

"Behold, a king shall reign in righteousness, and princes shall rule in judgment" **(Isaiah 32:1).**

"The voice of him that crieth in the wilderness, Prepare ye the way of the LORD, make straight in the desert a highway for our God. Every valley shall be exalted, and every mountain and hill shall be made low: and the crooked shall be made straight, and the rough places plain: And the glory of the LORD shall be revealed, and all flesh shall see it together: for the mouth of the LORD hath spoken it" **(Isaiah 40:3-5).**

"He shall feed his flock like a shepherd: he shall gather the lambs with his arm, and carry them in his bosom, and shall gently lead those that are with young" **(Isaiah 40:11).**

"Behold my servant, whom I uphold; mine elect, in whom my soul delighteth; I have put my spirit upon him: he shall bring forth judgment to the Gentiles. He shall not cry, nor lift up, nor cause his voice to be heard in the street. A bruised reed shall he not break, and the smoking flax shall he not quench: he shall bring forth judgment unto truth. He shall not fail nor be discouraged, till he have set judgment in the earth: and the isles shall wait for his law" **(Isaiah 42:1-4).**

"I the LORD have called thee in righteousness, and will hold thine hand, and will keep thee, and give thee for a covenant of the people, for a light of the Gentiles" **(Isaiah 42:6).**

"I gave my back to the smiters, and my cheeks to them that plucked off the hair: I hid not my face from shame and spitting" **(Isaiah 50:6).**

"He is despised and rejected of men; a man of sorrows, and acquainted with grief: and we hid as it were our faces from him; he was despised, and we esteemed him not" **(Isaiah 53:3).**

SEEING JESUS IN ISAIAH - *continued*

"He was oppressed, and he was afflicted, yet he opened not his mouth: he is brought as a lamb to the slaughter, and as a sheep before her shearers is dumb, so he openeth not his mouth" **(Isaiah 53:7).**

"The Spirit of the Lord GOD is upon me: because the LORD hath anointed me to preach good tidings unto the meek; he hath sent me to bind up the brokenhearted, to proclaim liberty to the captives, and the opening of the prison to them that are bound" **(Isaiah 61:1).**

THEME VERSE

"Come now, and let us reason together, saith the LORD: though your sins be as scarlet, they shall be as white as snow; though they be red like crimson, they shall be as wool" **(Isaiah 1:18).**

OUTLINE

I. **PROPHECIES OF JUDGMENT** - ISAIAH 1:2-35:10
   - A. **Book of Rebukes and Promises** - Isaiah 1:2-6:13
   - B. **Book of Immanuel** - Isaiah 7-12
   - C. **Book of Foreign Prophecies** - Isaiah 13-23
   - D. **First Book of Judgment** - Isaiah 24-27
   - E. **Book of Zion-a Book of Woes** - Isaiah 28-34
   - F. **Second Book of Judgment** - Isaiah 35

II. **HISTORICAL INTERLUDE** - ISAIAH 36-39
   - A. **Sennacherib's Invasion** - Isaiah 36, 37
   - B. **Hezekiah's Sickness and Babylonian Embassy** - Isaiah 38, 39

III. **PROPHECIES OF PEACE** - ISAIAH 40-66
   - A. **Theology - the Purpose of Peace** - Isaiah 40-48
   - B. **Soteriology - the Prince of Peace** - Isaiah 49-57
   - C. **Eschatology - Program of Peace** - Isaiah 58-66

The last twenty-seven chapters-one grand Messianic poem-is subdivided into three books. The first and second book close with: *"There is no peace, saith the Lord, unto the wicked"* **(Isaiah 48:22)** and:*"There is no peace, saith my God, to the wicked"* **(Isaiah 57:21).**

Here is the historical distribution of Isaiah's prophecies:

1. **During the reign of Uzziah** - Isaiah 1-5
2. **During the reign of Jotham** - Isaiah 6
3. **During the reign of Ahaz** - Isaiah 7:1-14:27
4. **First half of Hezekiah's reign** - Isaiah 14:28-39:8
5. **Second half of Hezekiah's reign** - Isaiah 40-66

NOTES

ISAIAH QUOTED IN THE NEW TESTAMENT.

Isaiah 1:9
Except the LORD of hosts had left unto us a very small remnant, we should have been as Sodom, and we should have been like unto Gomorrah.

Romans 9:29
And as Esaias said before, Except the Lord of Sabaoth had left us a seed, we had been as Sodoma, and been made like unto Gomorrha.

****

Isaiah 5:1, 2
Now will I sing to my wellbeloved a song of my beloved touching his vineyard. My wellbeloved hath a vineyard in a very fruitful hill: And he fenced it, and gathered out the stones thereof, and planted it with the choicest vine, and built a tower in the midst of it, and also made a winepress therein: and he looked that it should bring forth grapes, and it brought forth wild grapes.

Matthew 21:33
Hear another parable: There was a certain householder, which planted a vineyard, and hedged it round about, and digged a winepress in it, and built a tower, and let it out to husbandmen, and went into a far country.

Mark 12:1
And he began to speak unto them by parables. A certain man planted a vineyard, and set an hedge about it, and digged a place for the winefat, and built a tower, and let it out to husbandmen, and went into a far country.

****

Isaiah 6:9, 10 (Jeremiah 5:21, Ezekiel 12:2)
And he said, Go, and tell this people, Hear ye indeed, but understand not; and see ye indeed, but perceive not. Make the heart of this people fat, and make their ears heavy, and shut their eyes; lest they see with their eyes, and hear with their ears, and understand with their heart, and convert, and be healed.

Matthew 13:14, 15
And in them is fulfilled the prophecy of Esaias, which saith, By hearing ye shall hear, and shall not understand; and seeing ye shall see, and shall not perceive: For this people's heart is waxed gross, and their ears are dull of hearing, and their eyes they have closed; lest at any time they should see with their eyes, and hear with their ears, and should understand with their heart, and should be converted, and I should heal them.

Mark 4:12
That seeing they may see, and not perceive; and hearing they may hear, and not understand; lest at any time they should be converted, and their sins should be forgiven them.

Mark 8:18
Having eyes, see ye not? and having ears, hear ye not? and do ye not remember?

Luke 8:10
And he said, Unto you it is given to know the mysteries of the kingdom of God: but to others in parables; that seeing they might not see, and hearing they might not understand.

John 12:40
He hath blinded their eyes, and hardened their heart; that they should not see with their eyes, nor understand with their heart, and be converted, and I should heal them.

Acts 28:26, 27
Saying, Go unto this people, and say, Hearing ye shall hear, and shall not understand; and seeing ye shall see, and not perceive: For the heart of this people is waxed gross, and their ears are dull of hearing, and their eyes have they closed; lest they should see with their eyes, and hear with their ears, and understand with their heart, and should be converted, and I should heal them.

****

Isaiah 7:14
Therefore the Lord himself shall give you a sign; Behold, a virgin shall conceive, and bear a son, and shall call his name Immanuel.

Matthew 1:23
Behold, a virgin shall be with child, and shall bring forth a son, and they shall call his name Emmanuel, which being interpreted is, God with us.

****

Isaiah 8:12, 13
Say ye not, A confederacy, to all them to whom this people shall say, A confederacy; neither fear ye their fear, nor be afraid. Sanctify the LORD of hosts himself; and let him be your fear, and let him be your dread.

I Peter 3:14
But and if ye suffer for righteousness' sake, happy are ye: and be not afraid of their terror, neither be troubled.

****

Isaiah 8:14 (Isaiah 28:16)

And he shall be for a sanctuary; but for a stone of stumbling and for a rock of offence to both the houses of Israel, for a gin and for a snare to the inhabitants of Jerusalem.

Romans 9:33
As it is written, Behold, I lay in Sion a stumblingstone and rock of offence: and whosoever believeth on him shall not be ashamed.

I Peter 2:6, 8
Wherefore also it is contained in the scripture, Behold, I lay in Sion a chief corner stone, elect, precious: and he that believeth on him shall not be confounded. And a stone of stumbling, and a rock of offence, even to them which stumble at the word, being disobedient: whereunto also they were appointed.

****

Isaiah 8:17, 18 (II Samuel 22:3)
And I will wait upon the LORD, that hideth his face from the house of Jacob, and I will look for him. Behold, I and the children whom the LORD hath given me are for signs and for wonders in Israel from the LORD of hosts, which dwelleth in mount Zion.

Hebrews 2:13
And again, I will put my trust in him. And again, Behold I and the children which God hath given me.

****

Isaiah 9:1, 2
Nevertheless the dimness shall not be such as was in her vexation, when at the first he lightly afflicted the land of Zebulun and the land of Naphtali, and afterward did more grievously afflict her by the way of the sea, beyond Jordan, in Galilee of the nations. The people that walked in darkness have seen a great light: they that dwell in the land of the shadow of death, upon them hath the light shined.

Matthew 4:15, 16
The land of Zabulon, and the land of Nephthalim, by the way of the sea, beyond Jordan, Galilee of the Gentiles; The people which sat in darkness saw great light; and to them which sat in the region and shadow of death light is sprung up.

Luke 1:79
To give light to them that sit in darkness and in the shadow of death, to guide our feet into the way of peace.

****

Isaiah 10:22, 23 (Hosea 1:10)
For though thy people Israel be as the sand of the sea, yet a remnant of them shall return: the consumption decreed shall overflow with righteousness. For the Lord GOD of hosts shall make a consumption, even determined, in the midst of all the land.

Romans 9:27, 28
Esaias also crieth concerning Israel, Though the number of the children of Israel be as the sand of the sea, a remnant shall be saved: For he will finish the work, and cut it short in righteousness: because a short work will the Lord make upon the earth.

****

Isaiah 11:5 (Isaiah 59:17)
And righteousness shall be the girdle of his loins, and faithfulness the girdle of his reins.

Ephesians 6:14, 15
Stand therefore, having your loins girt about with truth, and having on the breastplate of righteousness; And your feet shod with the preparation of the gospel of peace.

****

Isaiah 11:10
And in that day shall be a root of Jesse, which shall stand for an ensign of the people; to it shall the Gentiles seek: and his rest shall be glorious.

Romans 15:12
And again, Esaias saith, There shall be a root of Jesse, and he that shall rise to reign over the Gentiles; in him shall the Gentiles trust.

****

Isaiah 22:13
And behold joy and gladness, slaying oxen, and killing sheep, eating flesh, and drinking wine: let us eat and drink; for to morrow we shall die.

I Corinthians 15:32
If after the manner of men I have fought with beasts at Ephesus, what advantageth it me, if the dead rise not? let us eat and drink; tor to morrow we die.

****

Isaiah 25:8
He will swallow up death in victory; and the Lord GOD will wipe away tears from off all faces; and the rebuke of his people shall he take away from off all the earth: for the LORD hath spoken it.

I Corinthians 15:54
So when this corruptible shall have put on incorruption, and this mortal shall have put on

immortality, then shall be brought to pass the saying that is written, Death is swallowed up in victory.

****

Isaiah 26:11
LORD, when thy hand is lifted up, they will not see: but they shall see, and be ashamed for their envy at the people; yea, the fire of thine enemies shall devour them.

Hebrews 10:27
But a certain fearful looking for of judgment and fiery indignation, which shall devour the adversaries.

****

Isaiah 27:9 (Isaiah 59:20, 21; Jeremiah 31:33, 34)
By this therefore shall the iniquity of Jacob be purged; and this is all the fruit to take away his sin; when he maketh all the stones of the altar as chalkstones that are beaten in sunder, the groves and images shall not stand up.

Romans 11:26, 27
And so all Israel shall be saved: as it is written, There shall come out of Sion the Deliverer, and shall turn away ungodliness from Jacob: For this is my covenant unto them, when I shall take away their sins.

****

Isaiah 27:13 (Joel 2:1; Zechariah 2:6)
And it shall come to pass in that day, that the great trumpet shall be blown, and they shall come which were ready to perish in the land of Assyria, and the outcasts in the land of Egypt, and shall worship the LORD in the holy mount at Jerusalem.

Matthew 24:31
And he shall send his angels with a great sound of a trumpet, and they shall gather together his elect from the four winds, from one end of heaven to the other.

****

Isaiah 28:11, 12
For with stammering lips and another tongue will he speak to this people. To whom he said, This is the rest wherewith ye may cause the weary to rest; and this is the refreshing: yet they would not hear.

I Corinthians 14:21
In the law it is written, With men of other tongues and other lips will I speak unto this people; and yet for all that will they not hear me, saith the Lord.

****

Isaiah 28:16 (Isaiah 8:14)
Therefore thus saith the Lord GOD, Behold, I lay in Zion for a foundation a stone, a tried stone, a precious corner stone, a sure foundation: he that believeth shall not make haste.

Romans 9:33
As it is written, Behold, I lay in Sion a stumblingstone and rock of offence: and whosoever believeth on him shall not be ashamed.

Romans 10:11
For the scripture saith, Whosoever believeth on him shall not be ashamed.

I Peter 2:6, 8
Wherefore also it is contained in the scripture, Behold, I lay in Sion a chief corner stone, elect, precious: and he that believeth on him shall not be confounded. And a stone of stumbling, and a rock of offence, even to them which stumble at the word, being disobedient: whereunto also they were appointed.

****

Isaiah 29:10 (Deuteronomy 29:4)
For the LORD hath poured out upon you the spirit of deep sleep, and hath closed your eyes: the prophets and your rulers, the seers hath he covered.

Romans 11:8
(According as it is written, God hath given them the spirit of slumber, eyes that they should not see, and ears that they should not hear;) unto this day.

****

Isaiah 29:13
Wherefore the Lord said, Forasmuch as this people draw near me with their mouth, and with their lips do honour me, but have removed their heart far from me, and their fear toward me is taught by the precept of men.

Matthew 15:8, 9
This people draweth nigh unto me with their mouth, and honoureth me with their lips; but their heart is far from me. But in vain they do worship me, teaching for doctrines the commandments of men.

Mark 7:6, 7
He answered and said unto them, Well hath Esaias prophesied of you hypocrites, as it is written, This people honoureth me with their lips, but their heart is far from me. Howbeit in vain do they worship me, teaching for doctrines the commandments of men.

****

Isaiah 29:14
Therefore, behold, I will proceed to do a marvelous work among this people, even a marvelous work and

a wonder: for the wisdom of their wise men shall perish, and the understanding of their prudent men shall be hid.

I Corinthians 1:19
For it is written, I will destroy the wisdom of the wise, and will bring to nothing the understanding of the prudent.

****

Isaiah 35:5, 6 (Isaiah 58:6, 61:1)
Then the eyes of the blind shall be opened, and the ears of the deaf shall be unstopped. Then shall the lame man leap as an hart, and the tongue of the dumb sing: for in the wilderness shall waters break out, and streams in the desert.

Luke 4:18
The Spirit of the Lord is upon me, because he hath anointed me to preach the gospel to the poor; he hath sent me to heal the brokenhearted, to preach deliverance to the captives, and recovering of sight to the blind, to set at liberty that are bruised.

Luke 7:22
Then Jesus answering said unto them, Go your way, and tell John what things ye have seen and heard; how that the blind see, the lame walk, the lepers are cleansed, the deaf hear, the dead are raised, to the poor the gospel is preached.

****

Isaiah 40:3
The voice of him that crieth in the wilderness, Prepare ye the way of the LORD, make straight in the desert a highway for our God.

Matthew 3:3
For this is he that was spoken of by the prophet Esaias, saying The voice of one crying in the wilderness, Prepare ye the way of the Lord, make his paths straight.

****

Isaiah 40:3-5
The voice of him that crieth in the wilderness, Prepare ye the way of the LORD, make straight in the desert a highway for our God. Every valley shall be exalted, and every mountain and hill shall be made low: and the crooked shall be made straight, and the rough places plain: And the glory of the LORD shall be revealed, and all flesh shall see it together: for the mouth of the LORD hath spoken it.

Matthew 3:3
For this is he that was spoken of by the prophet Esaias, saying, The voice of one crying in the wilderness, Prepare ye the way of the Lord, make his paths straight.

Mark 1:3
The voice of one crying in the wilderness, Prepare ye the way of the Lord, make his paths straight.

Luke 3:4-6
As it is written in the book of the words of Esaias the prophet, saying, The voice of one crying in the wilderness, Prepare ye the way of the Lord, make his paths straight. Every valley shall be filled, and every mountain and hill shall be brought low; and the crooked shall be made straight, and the rough ways shall be made smooth; And all flesh shall see the salvation of God.

John 1:23
He said, I am the voice of one crying in the wilderness, Make straight the way of the Lord, as said the prophet Esaias.

****

Isaiah 40:6-8
The voice said, Cry. And he said, What shall I cry? All flesh is grass, and all the goodliness thereof is as the flower of the field: The grass withereth, the flower fadeth: because the spirit of the LORD bloweth upon it: surely the people is grass. The grass withereth, the flower fadeth: but the word of our God shall stand for ever.

I Peter 1:24, 25
For all flesh is as grass, and all the glory of man as the flower of grass. The grass withereth, and the flower thereof falleth away: But the word of the Lord endureth for ever. And this is the word which by the gospel is preached unto you.

****

Isaiah 40:9 (Isaiah 62:11; Zechariah 9:9)
O Zion, that bringest good tidings, get thee up into the high mountain; O Jerusalem, that bringest good tidings, lift up thy voice with strength; lift it up, be not afraid; say unto the cities of Judah, Behold your God!

Matthew 21:5
Tell ye the daughter of Sion, Behold, thy King cometh unto thee, meek, and sitting upon as ass, and a colt the foal of an ass.

John 12:15
Fear not, daughter of Sion: behold, thy King cometh, sitting on an ass's colt.

****

Isaiah 40:13
Who hath directed the Spirit of the LORD, or being his counselor hath taught him?

Romans 11:34
For who hath known the mind of the Lord? Or who hath been his counselor?

I Corinthians 2:16
For who hath known the mind of the Lord, that he may instruct him? But we have the mind of Christ.

****

Isaiah 41:8 (Genesis 15:6)
But thou, Israel, art my servant, Jacob whom I have chosen, the seed of Abraham my friend.

Romans 4:3
For what saith the scripture? Abraham believed God, and it was counted unto him for righteousness.

Romans 4:9
Cometh this blessedness then upon the circumcision only, or upon the circumcision also? for we say that faith was reckoned to Abraham for righteousness.

Romans 4:22
And therefore it was imputed to him for righteousness.

Galatians 3:6
Even as Abraham believed God, and it was accounted to him for righteousness.

James 2:23
And the scripture was fulfilled which saith, Abraham believed God, and it was imputed unto him for righteousness: and he was called the Friend of God.

****

Isaiah 42:1-4
Behold my servant whom I uphold; mine elect, in whom my soul delighteth; I have put my spirit upon him: he shall bring forth judgment to the Gentiles. He shall not cry, nor lift up, nor cause his voice to be heard in the street. A bruised reed shall he not break, and the smoking flax shall he not quench: he shall bring forth judgment unto truth. He shall not fail nor be discouraged, till he have set judgment in the earth: and the isles shall wait for his law.

Matthew 12:18-21
Behold my servant, whom I have chosen; my beloved, in whom my soul is well pleased: I will put my spirit upon him, and he shall shew judgment to the Gentiles. He shall not strive, nor cry; neither shall any man hear his voice in the streets. A bruised reed shall he not break, and smoking flax shall he not quench, till he send forth judgment unto victory. And in his name shall the Gentiles trust.

Romans 15:12
And again, Esaias saith, There shall be a root of Jesse, and he that shall rise to reign over the Gentiles; in him shall the Gentiles trust.

****

Isaiah 42:6 (Isaiah 49:6)
I the LORD have called thee in righteousness, and will hold thine hand, and will keep thee, and give thee for a covenant of the people, for a light of the Gentiles.

Luke 2:32
A light to lighten the Gentiles, and the glory of thy people Israel.

Acts 13:47
For so hath the Lord commanded us, saying, I have set thee to be a light of the Gentiles, that thou shouldest be for salvation unto the ends of the earth.

****

Isaiah 43:20, 21 (Exodus 19:5, 6)
The beast of the field shall honour me, the dragons and the owls: because I give waters in the wilderness, and rivers in the desert, to give drink to my people, my chosen. This people have I formed for myself; they shall shew forth my praise.

I Peter 2:9
But he are a chosen generation, a royal priesthood, an holy nation, a peculiar people; that ye should shew forth the praises of him who hath called you out of darkness into his marvellous light.

****

Isaiah 45:23
I have sworn by myself, the word is gone out of my mouth in righteousness, and shall not return, That unto me every knee shall bow, every tongue shall swear.

Romans 14:11
For it is written, As I live, saith the Lord, every knee shall bow to me, and every tongue shall confess to God.

Philippians 2:10
That at the name of Jesus every knee should bow, of things in heaven, and things in earth, and things under the earth.

****

Isaiah 49:6 (Isaiah 42:6)
And he said, It is a light thing that thou shouldest be my servant to raise up the tribes of Jacob, and to restore the preserved of Israel: I will also give thee for a light to the Gentiles, that thou mayest be my

salvation unto the end of the earth.

Acts 13:47
For so hath the Lord commanded us, saying, I have set thee to be a light of the Gentiles, that thou shouldest be for salvation unto the ends of the earth.

Luke 2:32
A light to lighten the Gentiles, and the glory of thy people Israel.

****

Isaiah 49:8
Thus saith the LORD, In an acceptable time have I heard thee, and in a day of salvation have I helped thee: and I will preserve thee, and give thee for a covenant of the people, to establish the earth, to cause to inherit the desolate heritages.

II Corinthians 6:2
(For he saith, I have heard thee in a time accepted, and in the day of salvation have I succoured thee: behold, now is the accepted time; behold, now is the day of salvation.)

****

Isaiah 52:5
Now therefore, what have I here, saith the LORD, that my people is taken away for nought? they that rule over them make them to howl, saith the LORD; and my name continually every day is blasphemed.

Romans 2:24
For the name of God is blasphemed among the Gentiles through you, as it is written.

****

Isaiah 52:7 (Nahum 1:15)
How beautiful upon the mountains are the feet of him that bringeth good tidings, that publisheth peace; that bringeth good tidings of good, that publisheth salvation; that saith unto Zion, Thy God reigneth!

Romans 10:15
And how shall they preach, except they be sent? as it is written, How beautiful are the feet of them that preach the gospel of peace, and bring glad tidings of good things!

Ephesians 6:15
And your feet shod with the preparation of the gospel of peace.

****

Isaiah 52:11 (Jeremiah 51:45)
Depart ye, depart ye, go ye out from thence, touch no unclean thing; go ye out of the midst of her; be ye clean, that bear the vessels of the LORD.

II Corinthians 6:17
Wherefore come out from among them, and be ye separate, saith the Lord, and touch not the unclean thing; and I will receive you.

****

Isaiah 52:15
So shall he sprinkle many nations; the kings shall shut their mouths at him: for that which had not been told them shall they see; and that which they had not heard shall they consider.

Romans 15:21
But as it is written, To whom he was not spoken of, they shall see: and they that have not heard shall understand.

****

Isaiah 53:1
Who hath believed our report? and to whom is the arm of the LORD revealed?

John 12:38
That the saying of Esaias the prophet might be fulfilled, which he spake, Lord, who hath believed our report? and to whom hath the arm of the Lord been revealed?

Romans 10:16
But they have not all obeyed the gospel. For Esaias saith, Lord, who hath believed our report?

****

Isaiah 53:4
Surely he hath borne our griefs, and carried our sorrows: yet we did esteem him stricken, smitten of God, and afflicted.

Matthew 8:17
That it might be fulfilled which was spoken by Esaias the prophet, saying, Himself took our infirmities, and bare our sicknesses.

I Peter 2:24, 25
Who his own self bare our sins in his own body on the tree, that we, being dead to sins, should live unto righteousness: by whose stripes ye were healed. For ye were as sheep going astray; but are now returned unto the Shepherd and Bishop of your souls.

****

Isaiah 53:7, 8
He was oppressed, and he was afflicted, yet he opened not his mouth: he is brought as a lamb to the slaughter, and as a sheep before her shearers is dumb, so he

openeth not his mouth. He was taken from prison and from judgment: and who shall declare his generation? for he was cut off out of the land of the living: for the transgression of my people was he stricken.

Acts 8:32, 33
The place of the scripture which he read was this, He was led as a sheep to the slaughter; and like a lamb dumb before his shearer, so opened he not his mouth: In his humiliation his judgment was taken away: and who shall declare his generation? for his life is taken from the earth.

****

Isaiah 53:9
And he made his grave with the wicked, and with the rich in his death; because he had done no violence, neither was any deceit in his mouth.

I Peter 2:22
Who did no sin, neither was guile found in his mouth.

****

Isaiah 53:12
Therefore will I divide him a portion with the great, and he shall divide the spoil with the strong; because he hath poured out his soul unto death: and he was numbered with the transgressors; and he bare the sin of many, and made intercession for the transgressors.

Luke 22:37
For I say unto you, that this that is written must yet be accomplished in me, And he was reckoned among the transgressors: for the things concerning me have an end.

****

Isaiah 54:1
Sing, O barren, thou that didst not bear; break forth into singing, and cry aloud, thou that didst not travail with child: for more are the children of the desolate than the children of the married wife, saith the LORD.

Galatians 4:27
For it is written, Rejoice, thou barren that bearest not; break forth and cry, thou that travailest not: for the desolate hath many more children than she which hath an husband.

****

Isaiah 54:13 (Jeremiah 31:33, 34)
And all thy children shall be taught of the LORD; and great shall be the peace of thy children.

John 6:45
It is written in the prophets, And they shall be all taught of God. Every man therefore that hath heard, and hath learned of the Father, cometh unto me.

****

Isaiah 55:3
Incline your ear, and come unto me: hear, and your soul shall live; and I will make an everlasting covenant with you, even the sure mercies of David.

Acts 13:34
And as concerning that he raised him up from the dead, now no more to return to corruption, he said on this wise, I will give you the sure mercies of David.

****

Isaiah 56:7 (Jeremiah 7:11)
Even them will I bring to my holy mountain, and make them joyful in my house of prayer: their burnt offerings and their sacrifices shall be accepted upon mine altar; for mine house shall be called an house of prayer for all people.

Matthew 21:13
And said unto them, It is written, My house shall be called the house of prayer; but ye have made it a den of thieves.

Mark 11:17
And he taught, saying unto them, Is it not written, My house shall be called of all nations the house of prayer: but ye have made it a den of thieves.

Luke 19:46
Saying unto them, It is written, My house is the house of prayer: but ye have made it a den of thieves.

****

Isaiah 57:19
I create the fruit of the lips; Peace, peace to him that is far off, and to him that is near, saith the LORD; and I will heal him.

Ephesians 2:17
And came and preached peace to you which were afar off, and to them that were nigh.

****

Isaiah 58:6 (Isaiah 35:5, 6; 61:1, 2)
Is not this the fast that I have chosen? to loose the bands of wickedness, to undo the heavy burdens, and to let the oppressed go free, and that ye break every yoke?

Matthew 11:5
The blind receive their sight, and the lame walk, the lepers are cleansed, and the deaf hear, the dead are raised up, and the poor have the gospel preached to them.

Luke 4:18, 19
The Spirit of the Lord is upon me, because he hath anointed me to preach the gospel to the poor; he hath sent me to heal the brokenhearted, to preach deliverance to the captives, and recovering of sight to the blind, to set at liberty them that are bruised, To preach the acceptable year of the Lord.

Luke 7:22
Then Jesus answering said unto them, Go your way, and tell John what things ye have seen and heard; how that the blind see, the lame walk, the lepers are cleansed, the deaf hear, the dead are raised, to the poor the gospel is preached.

****

Isaiah 59:7, 8 (Psalms 5:9, 10:7, 36:1, 140:3)
Their feet run to evil, and they make haste to shed innocent blood: their thoughts are thoughts of iniquity; wasting and destruction are in their paths. The way of peace they know not; and there is no judgment in their goings: they have made them crooked paths: whosoever goeth therein shall not know peace.

Romans 3:13-18
Their throat is an open sepulchre; with their tongues they have used deceit; the poison of asps is under their lips: whose mouth is full of cursing and bitterness: Their feet are swift to shed blood: Destruction and misery are in their ways: And the way of peace have they not know: There is no fear of God before their eyes.

****

Isaiah 59:17 (Isaiah 11:5)
For he put on righteousness as a breastplate, and an helmet of salvation upon his head; and he put on the garments of vengeance for clothing, and was clad with zeal as a cloak.

Ephesians 6:14, 15, 17
Stand therefore, having your loins girt about with truth, and having on the breastplate of righteousness; And your feet shod with the preparation of the gospel of peace; And take the helmet of salvation, and the sword of the Spirit, which is the word of God.

****

Isaiah 59:20, 21 (Isaiah 27:9; Jeremiah 31:33, 34)
And the Redeemer shall come to Zion, and unto them that turn from transgression in Jacob, saith the LORD. As for me, this is my covenant with them, saith the LORD; My spirit that is upon thee, and my words which I have put in thy mouth, shall not depart out of thy mouth, nor out of the mouth of thy seed, nor out of the mouth of thy seed's seed, saith the LORD, from henceforth and for ever.

Romans 11:26, 27
And so all Israel shall be saved: as it is written, There shall come out of Sion the Deliverer, and shall turn away ungodliness from Jacob: For this is my covenant unto them, when I shall take away their sins.

****

Isaiah 61:1, 2 (Isaiah 35:5, 6; 58:6)
The Spirit of the Lord God is upon me; because the LORD hath anointed me to preach good tidings unto the meek; he hath sent me to bind up the brokenhearted, to proclaim liberty to the captives, and the opening of the prison to them that are bound; To proclaim the acceptable year of the LORD, and the day of vengeance of our God; to comfort all that mourn.

Matthew 11:5
The blind receive their sight, and the lame walk, the lepers are cleansed, and the deaf hear, the dead are raised up, and the poor have the gospel preached to them.

Luke 4:18, 19
The Spirit of the Lord is upon me, because he hath anointed me to preach the gospel to the poor; he hath sent me to heal the brokenhearted, to preach deliverance to the captives, and recovering of sight to the blind, to set at liberty them that are bruised, To preach the acceptable year of the Lord.

Luke 7:22
Then Jesus answering said unto them, Go your way, and tell John what things ye have seen and heard; how that the blind see, the lame walk, the lepers are cleansed, the deaf hear, the dead are raised, to the poor the gospel is preached.

****

Isaiah 62:11 (Isaiah 40:9; Zechariah 9:9)
Behold, the LORD hath proclaimed unto the end of the world, Say ye to the daughter of Zion, Behold, thy salvation cometh; behold, his reward is with him, and his work before him.

Matthew 21:5
Tell ye the daughter of Sion, Behold, thy King cometh unto thee, meek, and sitting upon an ass, and a colt the foal of an ass.

John 12:15
Fear not, daughter of Sion: behold, they King cometh, sitting on an ass's colt.

****

Isaiah 64:4
For since the beginning of the world men have not heard, nor perceived by the ear, neither hath the eye seen, O God, beside thee, what he hath prepared for him that waiteth for him.

I Corinthians 2:9
But as it is written, Eye hath not seen, nor ear heard, neither have entered into the heart of man, the things which God hath prepared for them that love him.

****

Isaiah 65:1
I am sought of them that asked not for me; I am found of them that sought me not: I said, Behold me, behold me, unto a nation that was not called by my name.

Romans 10:20
But Esaias is very bold, and saith, I was found of them that sought me not; I was made manifest unto them that asked not after me.

****

Isaiah 65:2
I have spread out my hands all the day unto a rebellious people, which walketh in a way that was not good, after their own thoughts.

Romans 10:21
But to Israel he saith, All day long I have stretched forth my hands unto a disobedient and gainsaying people.

****

Isaiah 66:1
Thus saith the LORD, The heaven is my throne, and the earth is my footstool: where is the house that ye build unto me? And where is the place of my rest?

Matthew 5:35
Nor by the earth; for it is his footstool: neither by Jerusalem; for it is the city of the great King.

Acts 7:49, 50
Heaven is my throne, and earth is my footstool: what house will ye build me? Saith the Lord: or what is the place of my rest? Hath not my hand made all these things?

****

Isaiah 66:24
And they shall go forth, and look upon the carcases of the men that have transgressed against me: for their worm shall not die, neither shall their fire be quenched; and they shall be an abhorring unto all flesh.

Mark 9:44, 46, 48
Where their worm dieth not, and the fire is not quenched. Where their worm dieth not, and the fire is not quenched. Where their worm dieth not, and the fire is not quenched.

JEREMIAH

THE WEEPING PROPHET			
CALL OF THE PROPHET	**PROPHECIES AGAINST JUDAH & JERUSALEM**	**PROPHECIES AGAINST THE NATIONS**	**HISTORICAL APPENDIX**
Tearing down: **1**	God's Love & Judah's ingratitude: **2-45**	From Egypt to Babylon: **46-51**	Fall of Jerusalem: **52**
LOCATION: Judah			
OVERVIEW: Total dedication	Judah is threatened by Assyria	Judah is beseiged by Babylon	During captivity
TIME: About 40 years leading up to Jerusalem's conquest by Babylon in 586 B.C.			

FAST FACTS

AUTHOR AND SETTING:

Jeremiah; suburb of Jerusalem

PURPOSE:

Jeremiah was called to proclaim God's coming judgment on the unrepentant people of Judah. He also foretold of future restoration after 70 years' captivity *(Jeremiah 29:10)*

SEEING JESUS:

Jeremiah had asked God to make his eyes as a fountain of tears to weep over God's people. His heart of compassion is similar to the heart of Jesus Christ. Jesus is clearly seen as the coming shepherd and the righteous Branch (23:1-8) Who will bring in the New Covenant (31:31-34).

THEME VERSE:

Jeremiah 7:23, 24

JEREMIAH:
COMPASSION

NOTES

SEEING JESUS IN JEREMIAH

AUTHOR & SETTING

Jeremiah means "Yahweh establishes, appoints, or sends." Jeremiah was appointed by God to deliver God's message through parables, sermons, and object lessons.

This is one of the longest of the prophetic books. It was written by Jeremiah. He was a priest as well as a prophet. His native town was Anathoth in the area belonging to the tribe of Benjamin. Anathoth was one of the priestly cities about three miles north of the city of Jerusalem.

Jeremiah identifies himself as the son of Hilkiah. Perhaps Hilkiah was the high priest during the time of King Josiah.

OVERVIEW

Jeremiah was a young man when God called him:

"Then said I, Ah, Lord GOD! behold, I cannot speak: for I am a child" **(Jeremiah 1:6).**

At the command of God he remained unmarried:

"Thou shalt not take thee a wife; neither shalt thou have sons or daughters in this place" **(Jeremiah 16:2).**

The book covers 44 years. The greater part of the book was written by Baruch, Jeremiah's secretary or scribe.

Jeremiah 36 tells how Baruch came to write Jeremiah's prophecy. The first edition was burned. Jeremiah again dictated the prophecy to a scribe. This is the first 17 chapters of the book.

Jeremiah 52 is a repetition of II Kings 24.

Jeremiah prophesied *before* the fall of Jerusalem, *during* the fall of Jerusalem, and *after* the Babylonian destruction of Jerusalem.

Jeremiah is called the weeping prophet because he asked God to make his eyes as a fountain of tears to weep over God's people. The greatest compliment ever paid to Jeremiah was that they asked Jesus if He was the prophet Jeremiah.

Jeremiah's heart of compassion for his people is overwhelming and certainly shows the heart of Jesus Christ's compassion for His own people.

The general theme of Jeremiah is the backsliding of God's people in days of apostasy.

He was the first prophet who had continuous open warfare with his people. His messages repeatedly referred to the immediate Babylonian captivity, the return of Israel after 70 years, another worldwide dispersion, a final regathering of Israel at the end of this age, and the reign of Messiah over Israel forever **(Jeremiah 3:14-25, 7:1-7, 16:14-21, 17:21-26, 23:3-8, 31:31-40, and 32:26-37)**.

Jeremiah showed that the destiny of every man is determined by his conformity or lack of conformity to God and His plan.

After the fall of Jerusalem, Jeremiah prophesied against Egypt, Philistia, Moab, Ammon, Edom, Damascus, Arabia, Elam, and Babylon. Only Moab, Egypt, Ammon, and Elam were promised.

SEEING JESUS IN JEREMIAH

Jeremiah is one of the prophets who called Jesus the Branch:

"Behold, the days come, saith the LORD, that I will raise unto David a righteous Branch, and a King shall reign and prosper, and shall execute judgment and justice in the earth" **(Jeremiah 23:5).**

"In those days, and at that time, will I cause the Branch of righteousness to grow up unto David; and he shall execute judgment and righteousness in the land" **(Jeremiah 33:15).**

THEME VERSES

"But this thing commanded I them, saying, Obey my voice, and I will be your God, and ye shall be my people: and walk ye in all the ways that I have commanded you, that it may be well unto you. But the hearkened not, nor inclined their ear, but walked in the counsels and in the imagination of their evil heart, and went backward and not forward" **(Jeremiah 7:23, 24).**

OUTLINE

(Refer to map on page A11 in the APPENDIX.)

I. **THE CALL OF THE PROPHET** - JEREMIAH 1

   A. **God Called Jeremiah To Do More Tearing Down Than Building Up -** Jeremiah 1:10

      1. **But God promised Jeremiah courage.**

   B. **The Sign of God's Call Was the Almond Rod and the Seething Pot-the Sign of Babylonian Invasion.**

II. **PROPHECIES AGAINST JUDAH AND JERUSALEM -** JEREMIAH 2-45

   A. **Prophecies in the Book of Jeremiah: the prophecies are not entirely in chronological order.**

      1. **The sermons of Jeremiah 2-20 were given during the reign of Josiah and Jehoiakim.**

   B. **The Messages in Chapters 2 and 3: reminded Judah of God's love and rebuked them for ingratitude.**

   C. **The Second Message -** Jeremiah 3:6-6:30: warned against the great devastation that was coming from the north. Although Babylon was to the east of Judah, the invasion route was from the north.

NOTES

NOTES

D. **The Message at the Gate of the Lord's House -** Jeremiah 7:1-10, 25: the prophet warned of a coming exile. In Jeremiah 11 and 12 he reminded the nation of the broken covenant. In chapter 13, through the sign of the linen girdle, Jeremiah declared that Judah would not be spared even though some of the people had been very close to God.

E. **The Message on the Drought -** Jeremiah 14, 15 reminded the nation that such a natural phenomenon was a sign of judgment from God.

F. **God's Message Stating That Jeremiah Should Remain Unmarried -** Jeremiah 16-17:18 - was to be a personal sign to the nation.

G. **The Message About Breaking the Sabbath -** Jeremiah 17:19-27: violating the Sabbath brought judgment.

H. **The Word Concerning a Potter's Wheel -** Jeremiah 18-19:13. God showed his sovereignty over the nation.

I. **The Persecution of Jeremiah Followed -** Jeremiah 19:14-20:18.

J. **The Messages Predicting the Fall of Jerusalem Were Delivered at Different Periods -** Jeremiah 21-39.

K. **The Restoration Was Promised:**

   1. *"Behold, the days come, saith the LORD, that I will raise unto David a righteous Branch, and a King shall reign and prosper, and shall execute judgment and justice in the earth. In his days Judah shall be saved, and Israel shall dwell safely: and this is his name whereby he shall be called, THE LORD OUR RIGHTEOUSNESS"* **(Jeremiah 23:5-6).**

L. **Jeremiah 25 is a Great Prophecy of the Seventy Years of Captivity In Babylon. This is undoubtedly the prophecy which Daniel read later -** Daniel 9:2.

M. **In Jeremiah 31 God Mentioned the New Covenant:**

   1. *"Behold, the days come, saith the LORD, that I will make a new covenant with the house of Israel, and with the house of Judah"* **(Jeremiah 31:31, see also Hebrews 8:8-12).**

N. **Jeremiah 32 is the Sign of the Field Which Jeremiah Purchased. Jeremiah 33 is the great prophesy concerning the kingdom of the Messiah.**

O. **King Jehoiakim Tried to Burn the Prophecy of Jeremiah 36, but God's Word Abides.**

P. **Jeremiah's Imprisonment During the Period of the Siege of Jerusalem Almost Led to his Death.**

Q. **In Jeremiah 38, Jeremiah Was Rescued by Ebed-melech, the Ethiopian.**

R. **Jeremiah 39 Shows the Fall of Jerusalem and Captivity of Judah. The same facts are repeated in Jeremiah 52.**

S. **Jeremiah 40-45 Contains Prophecies Given After the Fall of Jerusalem. The remnant left on the land went to Egypt where Jeremiah was forcibly taken.**

T. **Jeremiah 45 is a Brief Message to Baruch, Jeremiah's Friend and Secretary.**

III. **THE PROPHECIES AGAINST THE NATIONS** - JEREMIAH 46-51

A. **The List Begins With Egypt and Closes With the Greatest Enemy of All: Babylon.**

IV. **HISTORICAL APPENDIX** - JEREMIAH 52

A. **This is a Historical Resume and Can Be Compared With Jeremiah 39 and II Kings 25:27-30.**

NOTES

JEREMIAH QUOTED IN THE NEW TESTAMENT.

Jeremiah 5:21 (Isaiah 6:9, 10; Ezekiel 12:2)
Hear now this, O foolish people, and without understanding; which have eyes, and see not; which have ears, and hear not.

Matthew 13:14, 15
And in them is fulfilled the prophecy of Esaias, which saith, By hearing ye shall hear, and shall not understand; and seeing ye shall see, and shall not perceive: For this people's heart is waxed gross, and their ears are dull of hearing, and their eyes they have closed; lest at any time they should see with their eyes, and hear with their ears, and should understand with their heart, and should be converted, and I should heal them.

Mark 4:12
That seeing they may see, and not perceive; and hearing they may hear, and not understand; lest at any time they should be converted, and their sins should be forgiven them.

Mark 8:18
Having eyes, see ye not? And having ears, hear ye not? and do ye not remember?

****

Jeremiah 6:16
Thus saith the LORD, Stand ye in the ways, and see, and ask for the old paths, where is the good way, and walk therein, and ye shall find rest for your souls. But they said, We will not walk therein.

Matthew 11:29
Take my yoke upon you, and learn of me; for I am meek and lowly in heart: and ye shall find rest unto your souls.

****

Jeremiah 7:11 (Isaiah 56:7)
Is this house, which is called by my name, become a den of robbers in your eyes? Behold, even I have seen it, saith the LORD.

Matthew 21:13
And said unto them, It is written, My house shall be called the house of prayer; but ye have made it a den of thieves.

Mark 11:17
And he taught saying unto them, Is it not written, My house shall be called of all nations the house of prayer? but ye have made it a den of thieves.

Luke 19:46
Saying unto them, It is written, My house is the house of prayer: but ye have made it a den of thieves.

****

Jeremiah 9:24
But let him that glorieth glory in this, that he understandeth and knoweth me, that I am the LORD which exercise lovingkindness, judgment, and righteousness, in the earth: for in these things I delight, saith the LORD.

I Corinthians 1:31 (II Corinthians 10:17)
That, according as it is written, He that glorieth, let him glory in the Lord.

II Corinthians 10:17
But he that glorieth, let him glory in the Lord.

****

Jeremiah 31:15
Thus saith the LORD; A voice was heard in Ramah, lamentation, and bitter weeping; Rachel weeping for her children refused to be comforted for her children, because they were not.

Matthew 2:18
In Rama was there a voice heard, lamentation, and weeping, and great mourning, Rachel weeping for her children, and would not be comforted, because they are not.

****

Jeremiah 31:33, 34 (Isaiah 54:13)
But this shall be the covenant that I will make with the house of Israel; After those days, saith the LORD, I will put my law in their inward parts, and write it in their hearts; and will be their God, and they shall be my people. And they shall teach no more every man his neighbor, and every man his brother, saying, Know the LORD: for they shall all know me, from the least of them unto the greatest of them, saith the LORD: for I will forgive their iniquity, and I will remember their sin no more.

John 6:45
It is written in the prophets, And thy shall be all taught of God. Every man therefore that hath heard, and hath learned of the Father, cometh unto me.

Hebrews 8:10, 12
For this is the covenant that I will make with the house of Israel after those days, saith the LORD; I will put my laws into their mind, and write them in their hearts: and I will be to them a God, and they shall be to me a people: For I will be merciful to their unrighteousness, and their sins and their iniquities will I remember no

more.

Hebrews 10:16, 17

This is the covenant that I will make with them after those days, saith the Lord, I will put my laws into their hearts, and in their minds will I write them; And their sins and iniquities will I remember no more.

****

Jeremiah 51:45 (Isaiah 52:11)

My people, go ye out of the midst of her, and deliver ye every man his soul from the fierce anger of the LORD.

II Corinthians 6:17

Wherefore come out from among them, and be ye separate, saith the Lord, and touch not the unclean thing; and I will receive you.

LAMENTATIONS

MOURNING FOR JERUSALEM				
DESOLATION & MISERY	**JEHOVAH'S ANGER WITH HIS PEOPLE**	**NATION'S COMPLAINT**	**ZION'S PAST & PRESENT**	**APPEAL FOR COMPASSION**
Jerusalem after capture: **1**	Cause of Jerusalem's overthrow: **2**	God's purpose: **3**	Remembering former days: **4**	Seeking restoration: **5**
LOCATION: A quarry north of Jerusalem on the road to Damascus				
OVERVIEW: In spite of years of disobedience—and repeated warnings—the Jewish people lost their beautiful city of Jerusalem. Here Jeremiah eloquently mourns its destruction. Lamentations presents Jeremiah's grief along with God's great sorrow, the depth of His love, and His willingness to forgive.				
TIME: Immediately following Jerusalem destruction in 586 B.C.				

FAST FACTS

AUTHOR AND SETTING:

Jeremiah; Jerusalem

PURPOSE:

While expressing God's sorrow along with his own, *Jeremiah* takes this opportunity to express God's faithfulness and to call His people to repentance. God again reminds them to trust in Him.

SEEING JESUS:

Centuries later Jesus weeps over the city of Jerusalem in the same fashion that Jeremiah did. But the city of Jesus' day was *physically* whole...it was for the Jews' *spiritual* ruin that He mourned. Like Jesus—Who was *"...a man of sorrows, acquainted with grief"* (Isaiah 53:5)—Jeremiah identified himself with human suffering.

THEME VERSE:

Lamentations 3:22, 23

NOTES

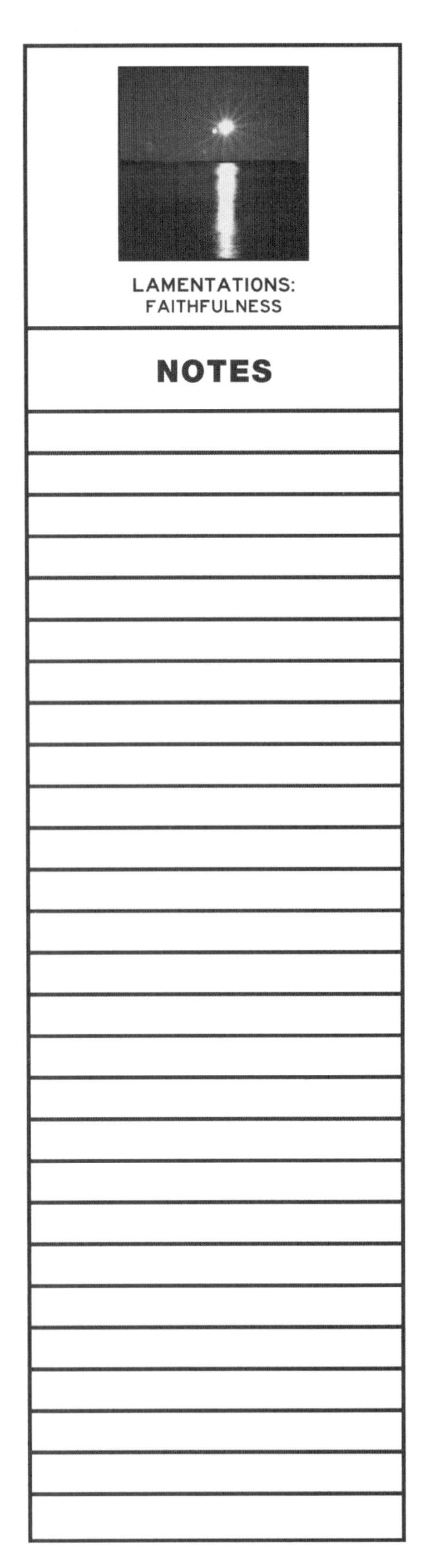

SEEING JESUS IN LAMENTATIONS

AUTHOR & SETTING

These lamentations were composed by Jeremiah in a quarry north of Jerusalem on the road to Damascus. With the exception of the last chapter, this book is an elegy in the form of an acrostic poem on the fall of Jerusalem.

This is a poetic book, a group of dirges or psalms of lamentations over the fall of the city of Jerusalem. It expresses the ever-increasing sufferings of the people of Jerusalem during the siege of Babylon. The horrors and bitterness of captivity to a pagan people increased at the stubbornness of their resistance.

This book is read on the anniversary of the fall of Jerusalem. It has been read for two thousand years at the western wall in Jerusalem.

OVERVIEW

There are 22 verses in chapters one and two. Chapter three has 66 verses, a multiple of 22. Chapters four and five are 22 verses each. In chapters one and two, each verse begins with a letter of the Hebrew alphabet. In chapter three they are grouped in three lines. They have a funeral cadence—a long line and a short line. These lamentations expressed the feeling of the people. There are basically three themes:

1. Jerusalem's holocaust
2. Confession of sin
3. God's restoration and faithfulness

Lamentations is probably the greatest elegy ever written. Jeremiah had a broader view than the people. He took all the known world in his horizon. He foresaw what was coming, and he gave advice to all nations. He was a very emotional man, and he prayed that his eyes would weep again and again. He laid bare his heart.

Jeremiah cursed the day he was born and considered leaving the ministry. His nature was one of surpassing strength. The Word of God was the very essence of his being. He was a figure cast in bronze and dissolved in tears. He had prophetic insight into humanity. He was also a sublime optimist; he prophesied restoration and saw the better age more clearly than any other prophet. He pictured a better covenant—a new dispensation.

His writing style resembles the style of Deuteronomy.

The first chapter of Lamentations describes the condition of the city after it was captured by the Babylonians. It certainly was in a condition of wretchedness.

The second chapter tells us the cause of the overthrow of Zion, or Jerusalem—sin had brought the judgment of God upon her.

The third lamentation declares God's purpose or design in this affliction. We see God's wonderful faith and mercy on us:

"It is of the LORD'S mercies that we are not consumed, because his compassions fail not. They are new every morning: great is thy faithfulness" **(Lamentations 3:22, 23).**

In the fourth lamentation Zion is portrayed as remembering the former days lamenting the contrast between what she was and what she is now. She describes her enemy.

The fifth and closing lamentation contains Zion's pathetic prayer:

"Turn thou us unto thee, O LORD, and we shall be turned; renew our days as of old" **(Lamentations 5:21).**

Throughout these songs we see not only the sorrow of Jeremiah the prophet, but we also see the sorrow of God Who did not rejoice in judgment but used judgment as an occasion for a call to repentance. God called His people to trust in Him.

SEEING JESUS IN LAMENTATIONS

Jeremiah prophesied of Jesus:

"Is it nothing to you, all ye that pass by: behold, and see if there be any sorrow like unto my sorrow which is done unto me, wherewith the LORD hath afflicted me in the day of his fierce anger. From above hath he sent fire into my bones, and it prevaileth against them: he hath spread a net for my feet, he hath turned me back: he hath made me desolate and faint all the day" **(Lamentations 1:12, 13).**

"All that pass by clap their hands at thee; they hiss and wag their head at the daughter of Jerusalem, saying, Is this the city that men call The perfection of beauty, The joy of the whole earth? All thine enemies have opened their mouth against thee: they hiss and gnash the teeth: they say, We have swallowed her up: certainly this is the day that we looked for; we have found, we have seen it" **(Lamentations 2:15,16).**

"I was a derision to all my people; and their song all the day" **(Lamentations 3:14).**

"Remembering mine affliction and my misery, the wormwood and the gall" **(Lamentations 3:19).**

"He giveth his cheek to him that smiteth him: he is filled full with reproach" **(Lamentations 3:30).**

NOTES

NOTES

THEME VERSES

"It is of the LORD's mercies that we are not consumed, because his compassions fail not. They are new every morning: great is thy faithfulness" **(Lamentations 3:22, 23).**

OUTLINE

I. **THE DESOLATION AND MISERY OF JERUSALEM -** CHAPTER 1

   A. **Verse 12 Expresses the Feelings of the Messiah and is also the Voice of Jerusalem Expressing Herself.**

   B. **She [Jerusalem] Acknowledged Jehovah's Righteousness and Prayed for Retribution on Her Foes.**

II. **JEHOVAH'S ANGER WITH HIS PEOPLE -** CHAPTER 2

III. **THE NATION'S COMPLAINT AND ITS GROUND FOR CONSOLATION -** CHAPTER 3

IV. **ZION'S PAST AND PRESENT CONTRASTED -** CHAPTER 4

   A. **Jeremiah's High-faith Victory:** *"His compassions fail not. They are new every morning:..."* **(Lamentations 3:22, 23).**

V. **A NATIONAL APPEAL FOR COMPASSIONATE REGARD -** CHAPTER 5

LAMENTATIONS OF JEREMIAH QUOTED IN THE NEW TESTAMENT: NOT FOUND

EZEKIEL

THE PROPHET OF VISIONS	
PROPHECIES BEFORE THE FALL OF JERUSALEM	**PROPHECIES AFTER THE FALL OF JERUSALEM**
Prophecies against Judah: **1-24** Prophecies against the nations: **25-32**	Predictions of new life: **33-37** Predictions against Gog & Magog: **38,39** Israel in the kingdom age: **40-48**
LOCATION: Babylon	
OVERVIEW: Ezekiel's very name means "God strengthens," and Ezekiel was a prophet who ministered to his people while in Babylonian bondage. He used prophecies, parables, signs, and symbols to dramatize God's message to His exiled people.	
TIME: 20 years (divided before and after Jerusalem's fall)	

FAST FACTS

AUTHOR AND SETTING:

Ezekiel; in Babylonian captivity

PURPOSE:

While Jeremiah was the prophet in Jerusalem who foresaw the captivity of Judah, Ezekiel was the prophet who arose while the Jews were in Babylonian captivity...and his visions stretched from horror to hope...condemning Judah's faithless leaders and godless foes. His overriding message, however, was the glory and supremacy of God: *"And they shall know that I am the LORD,..."* **(Ezekiel 6:10).**

SEEING JESUS:

Ezekiel was the first to receive the revelation of *Jehovah-Shammah*, meaning "the presence Who is always with us" (from Ezekiel 48:35: *"...the LORD is there"*). Jesus said, *"...I am with you always..."* **(Matthew 28:20).**

THEME VERSE:

Ezekiel 6:10

NOTES

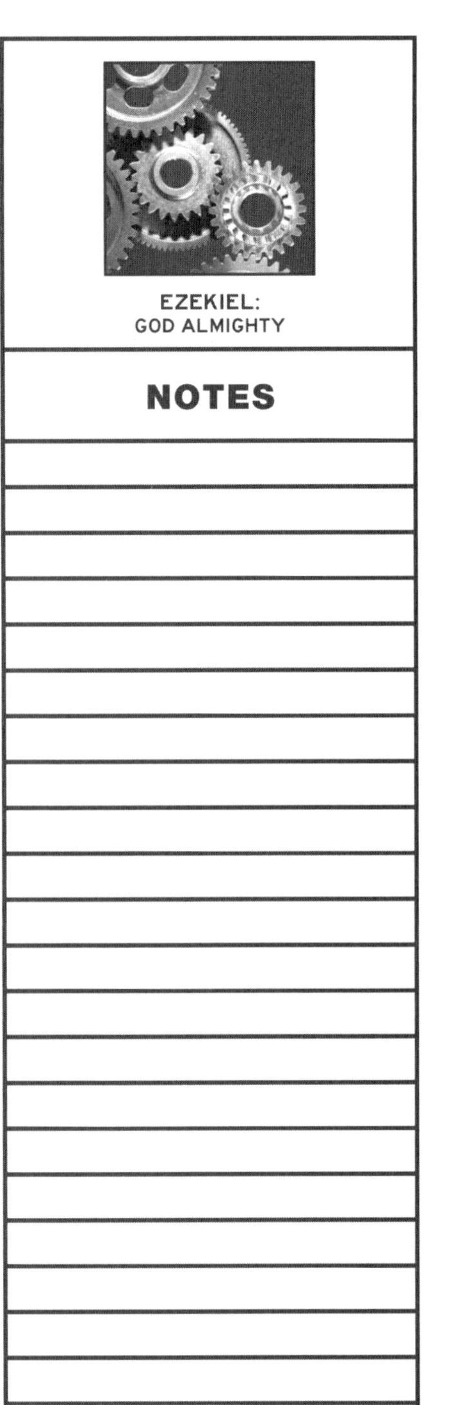

SEEING JESUS IN EZEKIEL

AUTHOR & SETTING

Ezekiel means "God strengthens." He was a descendant of Zadok, who traced his family to Aaron. He was a greatly educated and prepared priest.

In 597 B.C. Nebuchadnezzar besieged Jerusalem and King Jehoiachin surrendered. Seven thousand outstanding people were taken as captives to Babylon—Ezekiel was one of them. Ezekiel was a man of wealth who lived comfortably in Babylon by the river Chebar at a place called Telabib. The Israelites appeared to have a lot of freedom there. They were envious of those who were left in Israel (Judah) and felt that their property had been confiscated by them.

The people who were left in Jerusalem had religious pride and felt that they were more spiritual than those Israelites in captivity. Jeremiah preached the sermon of the figs to those who were left in Jerusalem (Jeremiah 24). Jeremiah probably had great influence over Ezekiel. Jeremiah had been a prophet for 30 years at the time of Ezekiel's captivity.

OVERVIEW

Ezekiel compared the ritual and ceremony of a rebellious people with the new heart of flesh and the pure spirit which God would give. The book of *Ezekiel* is very orderly, chronologically, and logically arranged.

Ezekiel's vision and call came on the fifth day of August in the fifth year of Jehoiachin's captivity. This first vision occurred by Chebar—an irrigation canal connecting the Tigris and Euphrates. This is the location of the Garden of Eden.

Isaiah saw the seraphim, which probably are the same as the cherubim that Ezekiel saw. (See Revelation 4, 5). They constitute God's executive force.

Man represents the highest form of created intelligence; the lion represents the highest form of courage; the ox represents the highest form of steadfastness and strength; and the eagle represents the highest form of vision and flight.

John, the revelator, and Ezekiel both ate the heavenly scroll in their visions. Ezekiel was assigned as a prophet of destruction to Israel. God revealed to Ezekiel that persecutions would come to him because of his message.

Ezekiel had one of the most unique ways of preaching of any of the prophets. Again and again he used visual aids to demonstrate his sermons. Some have called these "gimmicks"; nevertheless, these visual aids, along with the preaching of the sermon, caused the people to remember his message.

1. The tile: Ezekiel 4:1-2
2. The iron pan: Ezekiel 4:3

3. Lying on right and left side: Ezekiel 4:4-6
4. Arm bare and bound: Ezekiel 4:7-8
5. Eating unclean food: Ezekiel 4:9-17
6. Barber's razor: Ezekiel 5:1-4
7. Prophecy to the mountains of Israel: Ezekiel 6:1-3
8. Smiting hands and stamping feet: Ezekiel 6:11
9. Chain: Ezekiel 7:23-27
10. Moving from house: Ezekiel 12:1-7
11. Eating and drinking: Ezekiel 12:17, 18
12. Vine tree consumed: Ezekiel 15:1-5
13. Child: Ezekiel: 16:1-6
14. Fire in the forest of the south field: Ezekiel 20:45-49
15. Drawn sword: Ezekiel 21:1-5
16. Convulsive sighing: Ezekiel 21:6, 7
17. Sharp sword: Ezekiel 21:8-11
18. Howling and smiting: Ezekiel 21:12, 13
19. Smiting hands: Ezekiel 21:14-17
20. No mourning: Ezekiel 24:15-19

Ezekiel was given one of the greatest revelations of Jesus. It occurs in the last verse of chapter 48. The last words are "... *The LORD is there.*" This is JEHOVAH-SHAMMAH. Jesus said that He would never leave us nor forsake us—His presence is always with us; Ezekiel was the first to receive this revelation. Ezekiel meets the Lord and the Spirit in many ways in this book.

SEEING JESUS IN EZEKIEL

"Thus saith the Lord GOD; I will also take of the highest branch of the high cedar, and will set it; I will crop off from the top of his young twigs a tender one, and will plant it upon an high mountain and eminent: In the mountain of the height of Israel will I plant it: and it shall bring forth boughs, and bear fruit, and be a goodly cedar: and under it shall dwell all fowl of every wing; in the shadow of the branches thereof shall they dwell. And all the trees of the field shall know that I the LORD have brought down the high tree, have exalted the low tree, have dried up the green tree, and have made the dry tree to flourish: I the LORD have spoken it and have done it" **(Ezekiel 17:22-24).**

Jesus is seen as the true Shepherd in Ezekiel 34:11-31.

Undoubtedly, Ezekiel knew JEHOVAH-SHAMMAH—the Lord Jesus and His presence. Ezekiel knew the Lord as the great Shepherd Who would come and feed them.

NOTES

NOTES

THEME VERSE

"And they shall know that I am the LORD,..." **(Ezekiel 6:10).**

OUTLINE

(Refer to map on page A11 in the APPENDIX.)

I. **PROPHECIES GIVEN BEFORE THE FALL OF JERUSALEM** - EZEKIEL 1-32

A. **Prophecies Against Judah -** Ezekiel 1-24

1. **Ezekiel was sent to a rebellious nation** - Ezekiel 2
2. **He ate the book, showing he was filled with the Word** - Ezekiel 3.
3. **Through various signs he was showing the coming judgments** - Ezekiel 4, 5.
4. **A clear message of judgment is given** - Ezekiel 6, 7.
5. **In Ezekiel 8 he was taken to Jerusalem and saw the abomination.**
6. **Ezekiel saw the departing glory:**

a. *"Then did the cherubims lift up their wings, and the wheels beside them; and the glory of the God of Israel was over them above. And the glory of the LORD went up from the midst of the city, and stood upon the mountain which is on the east side of the city"* **(Ezekiel 11:22, 23).**

7. **The judgment was certain -** Ezekiel 12-19:

a. *"Son of man, when the land sinneth against me by trespassing grievously, then will I stretch out mine hand upon it, and will break the staff of the bread thereof, and will send famine upon it, and will cut off man and beast from it: Though these three men, Noah, Daniel, and Job, were in it, they should deliver but their own souls by their righteousness, saith the Lord GOD"* **(Ezekiel 14:13,14).**

8. **The sin of Judah was the cause of judgment** - Ezekiel 20-24.

a. There would be no more kings until the Messiah:

i. *"I will overturn, overturn, overturn it: and it shall be no more, until he come whose right it is; and I will give it him"* **(Ezekiel 21:27).**

9. **Further rehearsal of Israel's sin -** Ezekiel 22
10. **Story told of adulteresses Aholah (Samaria) and Ahollbah (Jerusalem) -** Ezekiel 23
11. **The parable of the boiling pot** (Ezekiel 24:3-6) **described the siege of Jerusalem.**
12. **Ezekiel was a sign to the people, and the death of Ezekiel's wife was also a sign:**

a. *"Son of man, behold, I take away from thee the desire of thine eyes with a stroke: yet neither shalt thou mourn nor weep, neither shall thy tears run down. So I spake unto the people in the morning: and at even my wife died; and I did in the morning as I was commanded"* **(Ezekiel 24:16, 18).**

B. **Prophecies Against the Nations -** Ezekiel 25-32

1. **Visitation on Gentile nations: Ammon, Moab, Edom, Philistia, Tyre, Sidon, and Egypt**.

II. **PROPHECIES GIVEN AFTER THE FALL OF JERUSALEM** - EZEKIEL 33-48

A. **Predictions of New Life -** Ezekiel 33-37

1. **God appointed Ezekiel to be the watchman of Israel.**
2. **The leaders were addressed as faithless shepherds.**
3. **Ezekiel pointed to a coming King:**

a. *"And I will set up one shepherd over them, and he shall feed them, even my servant David; he shall feed them, and he shall be their shepherd"* **(Ezekiel 34:23).**

4. **There was a cleansing and restoration of Israel:**

a. *"Then will I sprinkle clean water upon you, and ye shall be clean: from all your filthiness, and from all your idols, will I cleanse you. A new heart also will I give you, and a new spirit will I put within you: and I will take away the stony heart out of your flesh, and I will give you an heart of flesh. And I will put my spirit within you, and cause you to walk in my statutes, and ye shall keep my judgments, and do them"* **(Ezekiel 36:25-27).**

5. **The vision of the restoration of Israel** - Ezekiel 37:

a. *"And so all Israel shall be saved: as it is written, There shall come out of Sion the Deliverer, and shall turn away ungodliness from Jacob"* **(Romans 11:26).**

B. **Predictions Against Gog and Magog** - Ezekiel 38, 39

C. **Israel in the Kingdom Age** - Ezekiel 40-48:

1. *"It was round about eighteen thousand measures: and the name of the city from that day shall be, The LORD is there"* **(Ezekiel 48:35)**

NOTES

EZEKIEL QUOTED IN THE NEW TESTAMENT.

Ezekiel 12:2 (Isaiah 6:9, 10; Jeremiah 5:21)
Son of man, thou dwellest in the midst of a rebellious house, which have eyes to see, and see not; they have ears to hear, and hear not: for they are a rebellious house.

Matthew 13:14, 15
And in them is fulfilled the prophecy of Esaias, which saith, By hearing ye shall hear, and shall not understand; and seeing ye shall see, and shall not perceive: For this people's heart is waxed gross, and their ears are dull of hearing, and their eyes they have closed; lest at any time they should see with their eyes, and hear with their ears, and should understand with their heart, and should be converted, and I should heal them.

Mark 4:12
That seeing they may see, and not perceive; and hearing they may hear, and not understand; lest at any time they should be converted, and their sins should be forgiven them.

Mark 8:18
Having eyes, see ye not? and having ears, hear ye not? and do ye not remember?

****

Ezekiel 17:23 (Psalms 104:12)
In the mountains of the height of Israel will I plant it: and it shall bring forth boughs, and bear fruit, and be a goodly cedar: and under it shall dwell all fowl of every wing; in the shadow of the branches thereof shall they dwell.

Matthew 13:32
Which indeed is the least of all seeds: but when it is grown, it is the greatest among herbs, and becometh a tree, so that the birds of the air come and lodge in the branches thereof.

Mark 4:32
But when it is sown, it growth up, and becometh greater than all herbs, and shooteth out great branches; so that the fowls of the air may lodge under the shadow of it.

Luke 13:19
It is like a grain of mustard seed, which a man took, and cast into his garden; and it grew, and waxed a great tree; and the fowls of the air lodged in the branches of it.

****

Ezekiel 37:27 (Leviticus 26:12)
My tabernacle also shall be with them: yea, I will be their God, and they shall be my people.

II Corinthians 6:16
And what agreement hath the temple of God with idols? for ye are the temple of the living God; as God hath said, I will dwell in them, and walk in them; and I will be their God, and they shall be my people.

NOTES

DANIEL

THE VISIONARY PROPHET	
DANIEL'S HISTORY	**DANIEL'S VISIONS**
1st adventure: **1** Nebuchadnezzar's dream: **2** Three friends: **3** Humbling the king: **4** Wall writing: **5** Den of lions: **6**	Vision of 4 beasts: **7** Vision of the ram & the goat: **8** Vision of 70 weeks: **9** Vision of God's glory: **10-12**
LOCATION: Babylon / Persia	
OVERVIEW: Daniel was one of the few well-known Bible characters about whom nothing negative was ever written. His wisdom and divinely given interpretative abilities brought him into prominence in the courts of kings...and helped change the course of four nations. His life was characterized by purpose, prayer, perception, and power.	
TIME: 70 years from around 605-536 B.C.	

FAST FACTS

AUTHOR AND SETTING:

Daniel; Babylon/Persia

PURPOSE:

Daniel was given great prophetic visions of God's programs for the Gentiles and Jews from the days of Nebuchadnezzar until Christ's Second Coming. To the Jews who saw their city and Temple destroyed, *Daniel's* message of God's control over human governments was an encouragement to continue trusting in the Lord's sovereignty.

SEEING JESUS:

Daniel portrays Jesus as "the great stone" Who will crush earthly kingdoms (2:34, 35, 44); as *"the Son of Man"* Who is given dominion (7:13, 14); and as "the coming Messiah" (9:25, 26). He also had a vision of Jesus (10:5-9) which parallels Revelation 1;12-16.

THEME VERSE:

Daniel 2:47

NOTES

DANIEL:
FOURTH MAN IN THE FIRE

NOTES

SEEING JESUS IN DANIEL

AUTHOR & SETTING

In Matthew 24:15 Jesus attributes a quote from Daniel 9:27 to the prophet Daniel. In Daniel 12:4 Daniel is told to "seal the book" Daniel's authorship of this book is also confirmed by the Jewish Talmud. According to Daniel 1:4, Daniel had "*... no blemish, but well favoured, and skillful in all wisdom, and cunning in knowledge, and understanding science, and such as had ability in them to stand in the king's palace, and whom they might teach the learning and the tongue of the Chaldeans.*" More than that, Daniel was a man of purpose, prayer, perception, and power.

OVERVIEW

When Daniel was taken into captivity his captors changed his name to *Belteshazzar* which means "one whom Bel protects." But God had called him *Daniel* which means "God as judge." His captors might change his name, but they couldn't change his character. The same type of name change occurred with each of Daniel's friends:

Mishael means "like God." His name was changed to *Meshach* which means "agile" and referred to one of the Babylonian idols.

Azariah means "Jehovah aids." His name was changed to *Abednego* which means "the servant of Nebo" and referred to one of their major idols.

Hananiah means "Jehovah has favored." His name was changed to *Shadrach* which means "tender" and referred to a pagan idol.

Though the prince of the eunuchs changed the names of these Hebrew boys, he could not change their hearts, because they purposed in their hearts to serve the Lord.

In chapter one, verse eight, we read that "*...Daniel purposed in his heart...*" That was to be the beginning of one man literally changing four nations! Because Daniel and the other three Hebrew children *purposed* in their hearts to serve the Lord, God gave them knowledge and skill in learning and wisdom. Daniel had understanding in visions and dreams. Whenever we purpose or commit our hearts to God, He will reward us.

Once Daniel had purposed in his heart, he went to *prayer.* After Nebuchadnezzar dreamed a dream, he could find no wise man who could tell him the dream or its interpretation. Daniel and his friends, however, spent a night in prayer and received the revelation of the dream.

From prayer, Daniel went into *perception.* God gave him spiritual perception: God gave him the dream and its interpretation, which will involve the gentile nations until the time of the return of Jesus.

Daniel was also a man of *power.* After he had revealed the meaning of Nebuchadnezzar's dream, he was given power in the nation. Daniel had power under Nebuchadnezzar, in the reign of Belshazzar, in the reign of Darius, and in seeing the Israelites return from captivity to rebuild their land.

The book of *Daniel* is a book of winning over circumstances again and again. The foundation of it all was the *purpose* and *prayer* in Daniel's heart.

God disciplines people as well as nations (Hebrews 12:6). Israel would not have gone into captivity if, when God began His discipline upon them for their sins, they would have responded, confessed their sins, and repented. But with each cycle of discipline they simply hardened their hearts.

These cycles of discipline are found in Leviticus:

1. Leviticus 26:14-17
2. Leviticus 26:18-20
3. Leviticus 26:21-22
4. Leviticus 26:23-26
5. Leviticus 26:27-39

The fifth cycle occurs when people are taken into captivity. This is what happened to the nation of Israel - they were taken into captivity.

The northern kingdom was the first part of Israel to be taken into captivity. At the time of their fifth cycle of discipline they were destroyed as a nation by the Assyrians. Judah at that time was under the fourth cycle of discipline and would be destroyed by Babylon in the fifth cycle.

There are three strong messages given in the book of Daniel:

God blesses in adversity.
God rewards spiritual faithfulness.
God disciplines nations.

The first half of this book is historical. The second half is prophetic, with a foundation of some prophecies in the first six chapters.

This book is a key to future events. Daniel was taken from Judah in 606 B.C., and he was probably the same age as Ezekiel.

Daniel was a righteous man:

"Though these three men, Noah, Daniel, and Job, were in it, they should deliver but their own souls by their righteousness, saith the Lord GOD. Though Noah, Daniel, and Job, were in it, as I live, saith the Lord GOD, they shall deliver neither son nor daughter; they shall but deliver their own souls by their righteousness" **(Ezekiel 14:14, 20).**

NOTES

NOTES

SEEING JESUS IN DANIEL

Christ is the great stone Who will crush the kingdoms of this world-Daniel 2:34, 35, 44.

The Trinity is shown in the book of Daniel in a very unique way:

"The king answered unto Daniel, and said, Of a truth it is, that your God is a God of gods, and a Lord of kings, and a revealer of secrets, seeing thou couldest reveal this secret" **(Daniel 2:47).**

God the Father is seen in the words *"...God of gods..."* Jesus is seen in the words *"...Lord of kings..."* The Holy Spirit is seen in the words *"...a revealer of secrets..."*

Daniel foresaw the Second Advent of Jesus Christ:

"I saw in the night visions, and, behold, one like the Son of man came with the clouds of heaven, and came to the Ancient of days, and they brought him near before him. And there was given him dominion, and glory, and a kingdom, that all people, nations, and languages, should serve him: his dominion is an everlasting dominion, which shall not pass away, and his kingdom that which shall not be destroyed" **(Daniel 7:13,14).**

Jesus is the coming Messiah - Daniel 9:25, 26.

Daniel had another beautiful vision of Jesus:

"Then I lifted up mine eyes, and looked, and behold a certain man clothed in linen, whose loins were girded with fine gold of Uphaz: His body also was like the beryl, and his face as the appearance of lightning, and his eyes as lamps of fire, and his arms and his feet like in colour to polished brass, and the voice of his words like the voice of a multitude" **(Daniel 10:5, 6).**

THEME VERSE

"The king answered unto Daniel, and said, Of a truth it is, that your God is a God of gods, and a Lord of kings, and a revealer of secrets, seeing thou couldest reveal this secret"
(Daniel 2:47).

OUTLINE

(Refer to map on page A11 in the APPENDIX.)

I. **THE HISTORY OF DANIEL IN BABYLON** - DANIEL 1-6
   - A. **Daniels's First Adventure in Babylon** - Daniel 1
   - B. **Nebuchadnezzar's Dream** - Daniel 2
   - C. **Daniel's Three Friends** - Daniel 3

- D. **The Humbling of Nebuchadnezzar** - Daniel 4
- E. **Belshazzar and the Handwriting on the Wall** - Daniel 5
- F. **Daniel in the Den of Lions** - Daniel 6

II. **THE VISIONS OF DANIEL** - DANIEL 7-12

- A. **The Vision of the Four Beasts** - Daniel 7
- B. **The Vision of the Ram and the Goat** - Daniel 8
- C. **Daniel's Prayer and Vision of Seventy Weeks** - Daniel 9
- D. **Vision of the Glory of God** - Daniel 10-12

Daniel's life ended as it had begun - in purpose, prayer, perception, and power.

NOTES

DANIEL QUOTED IN THE NEW TESTAMENT.

Daniel 7:13
I saw in the night visions, and, behold, one like the Son of man came with the clouds of heaven, and came to the Ancient of days, and they brought him near before him.

Matthew 24:30
And then shall appear the sign of the Son of man in heaven: and then shall all the tribes of the earth mourn, and they shall see the Son of man coming in the clouds of heaven with power and great glory.

Matthew 26:64
Jesus saith unto him, Thou hast said: nevertheless I say unto you, Hereafter shall ye see the Son of man sitting on the right hand of power, and coming in the clouds of heaven.

Mark 13:26
And then shall they see the Son of man coming in the clouds with great power and glory.

Mark 14:62
And Jesus said, I am: and ye shall see the Son of man sitting on the right hand of power, and coming in the clouds of heaven.

Luke 21:27
And then shall they see the Son of man coming in a cloud with power and great glory.

Revelation 1:7
Behold, he cometh with clouds; and every eye shall see him, and they also which pierced him: and all kindreds of the earth shall wail because of him. Even so, Amen.

****

Daniel 11:31 (Daniel 12:11)
And arms shall stand on his part, and they shall pollute the sanctuary of strength, and shall take away the daily sacrifice, and they shall place the abomination that maketh desolate.

Matthew 24:15
When ye therefore shall see the abomination of desolation, spoken of by Daniel the prophet, stand in the holy place, (whoso readeth, let him understand).

Mark 13:14
But when ye shall see the abomination of desolation, spoken of by Daniel the prophet, standing where it ought not, (let him that readeth understand,) then let them that be in Judea flee to the mountains.

****

Daniel 12:3
And they that be wise shall shine as the brightness of the firmament; and they that turn many to righteousness as the stars for ever and ever.

Matthew 13:43
Then shall the righteous shine forth as the sun in the kingdom of their Father. Who hath ears to hear, let him hear.

****

Daniel 12:11 (Daniel 11:31)
And from the time that the daily sacrifice shall be taken away, and the abomination that maketh desolate set up, there shall be a thousand two hundred and ninety days.

Matthew 24:15
When ye therefore shall see the abomination of desolation, spoken of by Daniel the prophet, stand in the holy place, (whoso readeth, let him understand.)

Mark 13:14
But when ye shall see the abomination of desolation, spoken of by Daniel the prophet, standing where it ought not, (let him that readeth understand,) then let them that be in Judea flee to the mountains.

HOSEA

THE PROPHET OF UNCONDITIONAL LOVE	
THE PROPHET'S EXPERIENCE	**THE PROPHET'S MESSAGE**
Gomer & Hosea: **1** Gomer & Israel compared: **2** Gomer & restoration: **3**	Israel's sinfulness: **4,5** Israel's judgment: **6-10** Israel's restoration: **11-14**
LOCATION: Northern kingdom of Israel	
OVERVIEW: Hosea's personal life was tragic: his wife was an adulteress who spurned his faithful love. Finally he redeemed her from slavery, and she truly repented.	The nation of Israel was like the prophet's faithless wife. But God had promised to redeem His disobedient people from bondage. Both Israel and Gomer responded to unconditional love.
TIME: Around 750 B.C.—prior to the Assyrian captivity of the ten northern tribes	

FAST FACTS

AUTHOR AND SETTING:

Hosea; northern kingdom of Israel

PURPOSE:

Through the story of Hosea and Gomer, God gave Israel a visual-aid lesson of His unconditional love.

SEEING JESUS:

We clearly see the unconditional love of Jesus in Hosea's actions toward his wife. Jesus' flight to Egypt is prophesied *(Hosea 11:1)*, and the Messianic promise foreshadowing the Resurrection is given in *Hosea 13:14*.

THEME VERSE:

Hosea 14:1

NOTES

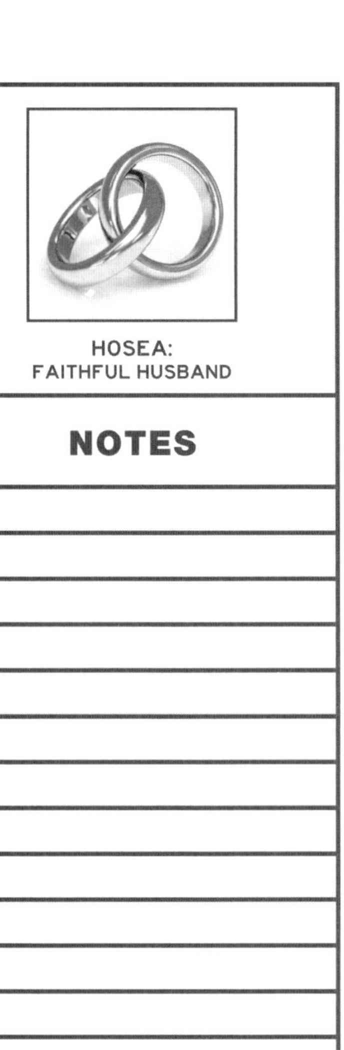

SEEING JESUS IN HOSEA

AUTHOR & SETTING

Hosea is the shortened form of *Jehoshea*, meaning "the Lord is my help." This shortened form means "Savior." Hosea was a prophet of the northern kingdom of Israel, but he also had messages for the southern kingdom or Judah. First he praised her—then he warned her.

Hosea prophesied in the days of Uzziah, Jotham, Ahaz, Hezekiah, and in the days of Jeroboam II. He lived to be a very old man. Hosea prophesied in the darkest time of Israel. Their political life was in a state of anarchy and misrule. There was one assassination after another and every kind of violence.

OVERVIEW

Hosea's life was to be a visual-aid lesson of God's unconditional love for Israel. He gave the message of Jehovah in three clearly marked elements:

1. **He showed the present in light of past love -** Hosea 11:1-11.
2. **He showed the present in light of present love -** Hosea 12:7-11
3. **He showed the present in light of future love -** Hosea 13:4-14.

Hosea's constant cry was for Israel to return to the Lord. Israel is seen as an unfaithful wife to the Lord. God will heal their backsliding; He will love them freely **(Hosea 14:4)**.

Hosea means "Jehovah is salvation." *Gomer* means "complete." When Hosea was commanded to take Gomer as his wife, she was a woman who had been delivered from whoredom. But after their first child Jezreel, Gomer began again to go back to her old life. *Jezreel* means "planted by God." Probably this child belonged to Hosea, but after Gomer began to live with other men they had two more children.

The first was a girl named Lo-ruhamah. *Lo* in front of a Hebrew name means "no" or "not." Her name means "I will no longer have mercy upon you." God was using Hosea's household as a picture to the whole nation of His marriage to the nation of Israel. She had played the whore; she had gone into spiritual idolatry. God would no longer have mercy upon her.

Gomer conceived again and had a little boy—*Lo-ammi*—meaning "you are not mine." With names like these, it is likely that these were not Hosea's children. They were the result of Gomer's whoredom, and she probably didn't know their father's identity.

In chapter two Hosea pleads with his children Ammi and Ruhamah to plead with their mother to come home. Notice that Hosea drops the *Lo* before their names which implies 'I will have mercy" and "you are mine." One believing mate sanctified the household. It is important for one person to stand in faith like Hosea. Likewise, we as Christians need to stand in faith for our nation to return to God.

Hosea sent his children to plead with their mother to come back, but she did not respond to their pleas. New wine and adultery take away our natural affection:

"Whoredom and wine and new wine take away the heart" **(Hosea 4:11).**

But God encouraged Hosea and told him that He would hedge Gomer's path about and would deal with her face to face. That is exactly what he did—because of Hosea's intercession, Gomer became repulsive to her lovers. When she was on the slave-block, offered for the small price of a gored bull, Hosea bought her back as his wife! He told her that she would not call him Baali—master—but she would call him Ishi-my husband. Though he owned her as a master, he would love her like a husband.

What was God saying to the nation of Israel through the picture of Gomer and Hosea? He would buy Israel back off the slave-block. That proved to be true—they returned from their captivity and were once again married to God and walked in righteousness.

Hosea is one of the most beautiful books of love in the whole Bible. Another key verse is **Hosea 4:6**:

"My people are destroyed for lack of knowledge: because thou has rejected knowledge, I will also reject thee, that thou shalt be no priest to me: seeing thou hast forgotten the law of thy God, I will also forget thy children."

What is the knowledge spoken of here? It is the knowledge of how much God loves us. How could we play spiritual idolatry when we have such a God Who loves us so much?

SEEING JESUS IN HOSEA

There is no question that Hosea gives many beautiful revelations of Jesus the Messiah:

1. Judah and Israel will have one head:

"Yet the number of the children of Israel shall be as the sand of the sea, which cannot be measured nor numbered; and it shall come to pass, that in the place where it was said unto them, Ye are not my people, there it shall be said unto them, Ye are the sons of the living God" **(Hosea 1:10).**

2. God will betroth both Israel and the gentiles in the same covenant:

"Plead with your mother, plead: for she is not my wife, neither am I her husband: let her therefore put away her whoredoms out of her sight, and her adulteries from between her breasts" **(Hosea 2:2).**

NOTES

NOTES

SEEING JESUS IN HOSEA—*continued*

"Afterward shall the children of Israel return, and seek the LORD their God, and David their king; and shall fear the LORD and his goodness in the latter days" **(Hosea 3:5).**

3. The picture of Jesus:

"When Israel was a child, then I loved him, and called my son out of Egypt" **(Hosea 11:1). (Quoted in Matthew 2:15)**

4. Jehovah's promise to restore Israel: (See Hosea 11:8-11.)
5. The Messianic promise foreshadowing the Resurrection:

"I will ransom them from the power of the grave; I will redeem them from death: O death, I will be thy plagues; O grave, I will be thy destruction: repentance shall be hid from mine eyes" **(Hosea 13:14).**

6. Messianic promise of Israel's final repentance and abundant blessings: **(See Hosea 14:1-8.)**

Hosea shows the unfailing love of Jesus Christ, our Bridegroom.

THEME VERSE

"O Israel, return unto the LORD thy God; for thou hast fallen by thine iniquity" **(Hosea 14:1).**

OUTLINE

I. THE PROPHET'S EXPERIENCE - HOSEA 1-3

- **A. The Picture of Gomer**
- **B. Israel's Many Sins**

II. THE PROPHET'S MESSAGE - HOSEA 4-14

- **A. Blessed Restoration:**
  - **1.** *"I will heal their backsliding, I will love them freely: for mine anger is turned away from him"* **(Hosea 14:4).**
- **B. Israel's Future Bond With the Messiah**

HOSEA QUOTED IN THE NEW TESTAMENT.

Hosea 1:6, 9, 10 (Hosea 2:23)
And she conceived again, and bare a daughter. And God said unto him, Call her name Lo-ruhamah: for I will no more have mercy upon the house of Israel; but I will utterly take them away. Then said God, Call his name Lo-ammi: for ye are not my people, and I will not be your God. Yet the number of the children of Israel shall be as the sand of the sea, which cannot be measured nor numbered; and it shall come to pass, that in the place where it was said unto them, Ye are not my people, there it shall be said unto them, Ye are the sons of the living God.

Romans 9:25
As he saith also in Osee, I will call them my people, which were not my people; and her beloved, which was not beloved.

Romans 9:26
And it shall come to pass, that in the place where it was said unto them, Ye are not my people; there shall they be called the children of the living God.

I Peter 2:10
Which in time past were not a people, but are now the people of God: which had not obtained mercy, but now have obtained mercy.

****

Hosea 2:23 (Hosea 1:6, 9, 10)
And I will sow her unto me in the earth; and I will have mercy upon her that had not obtained mercy; and I will say to them which were not my people, thou art my people; and they shall say, Thou art my God.

Romans 9:25
As he saith also in Osee, I will call them my people, which were not my people; and her beloved, which was not beloved.

I Peter 2:10
Which in time past were not a people, but are now the people of God: which had not obtained mercy, but now have obtained mercy.

****

Hosea 6:6
For I desired mercy, and not sacrifice; and the knowledge of God more than burnt offerings.

Matthew 9:13
But go ye and learn what that meaneth, I will have mercy, and not sacrifice: for I am not come to call the righteous, but sinners to repentance.

Matthew 12:7
But if ye had known what this meaneth, I will have mercy, and not sacrifice, ye would not have condemned the guiltless.

****

Hosea 11:1
When Israel was a child, then I loved him, and called my son out of Egypt.

Matthew 2:15
And was there until the death of Herod: that it might be fulfilled which was spoken of the Lord by the prophet, saying, Out of Egypt have I called my son.

****

Hosea 13:14
I will ransom them from the power of the grave; I will redeem them from death: O death, I will be thy plagues; O grave, I will be thy destruction: repentance shall be hid form mine eyes.

I Corinthians 15:55
O death, where is thy sting? O grave, where is thy victory?

JOEL

THE PROPHET OF *"...THE DAY OF THE LORD"*		
GOD'S JUDGMENTS	**VIEW FROM WITHIN**	**VIEW FROM WITHOUT**
Two Invasions: **1**	Warfare & Christ's return: **2**	Warfare of the enemy: **3**
LOCATION: Southern kingdom of Judah		
OVERVIEW: Historical Invasion	Prophetic Invasions	Judgments & restoration
TIME: Around 852 B.C. during the reign of King Jehoash (Joash)		

FAST FACTS

AUTHOR AND SETTING:

Joel; southern kingdom of Judah

PURPOSE:

The purpose of this book is to call Israel to repentance and to give an overall prophetic view of the history of Israel.

SEEING JESUS:

Joel depicted Jesus Christ as El Shaddai—the God Who is more than enough (*Joel 1:15*, "Almighty"). *Joel* also prophesied of the outpouring of the Holy Spirit, of which Jesus reminded His disciples in Acts 1:8.

THEME VERSE:

Joel 12:28, 29

NOTES

JOEL:
RESTORATION

NOTES

SEEING JESUS IN JOEL

AUTHOR & SETTING

Joel means "Jehovah is good." All that is known of this prophet is contained in this book. He was the son of Pethuel. It is suggested that he lived close to Jerusalem and the Temple because of his frequent references to Zion and the house of the Lord.

The book of *Joel* was written during a time of apostasy. This time is described in verse 5 of chapter 1:

"Awake, ye drunkards, and weep; and howl, all ye drinkers of wine, because of the new wine; for it is cut off from your mouth."

What caused the nation of Israel to fall away from Jehovah? They had gotten used to prosperity. There is nothing wrong with prosperity, but there is a danger in becoming prosperous if it causes you to take your eyes off the Lord.

Their prosperity was to have been used to establish the Lord's covenant—not to establish their lusts. It is the same today with us.

The Israelites had taken possession of the Promised Land. They had conquered their enemies and took the spoils of the different areas. But by the time of the end of the book of Joshua the Israelites were sitting down. They no longer wanted to conquer; they just wanted to rest on their laurels and enjoy their luxuries. Luxuries are nice, but they should not be enjoyed at the expense of the gospel.

OVERVIEW

By the time of the prophet Joel, the nation of Israel was enjoying tremendous prosperity—but the salt of the nation was losing its savor (Matthew 5:13). The nation was expending its time and energy in the pursuit of pleasure: drunkenness, carousing, and the like. Wine and liquor were the chief occupation of the people. Even their priests were getting drunk until a terrible plague came upon the nation.

When the plague hit Judah, it consisted basically of four types of locusts. They were called by different names:

Palmerworms
Locusts
Cankerworms
Caterpillars

These locusts invaded the land in the day of Joel. They were used as a warning to the people.

The first wave took the top of the stalks. The next devoured the stalk itself. The third wave came in and ate the stubble off the ground. The fourth and final wave actually destroyed the seed under the ground!

According to Joel, these insects devastated the economy of Israel.

From this judgment Joel gave two parallels so that the people would learn from this dreadful experience:

The first concerned the imminent invasion of the nation by Assyria which would come in like the locusts to invade the land.

Later on Joel talked about a second army that would attack. This second invasion will occur during the time of the Tribulation. This army will destroy the land as the locusts did and as the nation of Assyria had done.

Because this second invasion was to occur much later—at the end of this age—Joel commands the people to recount these events to their children and grandchildren (Joel 1:3). This is why the book of *Joel* is important in our day too.

Joel also prophesied of the outpouring of God's Spirit which would begin at Pentecost and continue on:

"And it shall come to pass afterward, that I will pour out my spirit upon all flesh; and your sons and your daughters shall prophesy, your old men shall dream dreams, your young men shall see visions: And also upon the servants and upon the handmaids in those days will I pour out my spirit: **(Joel 2:28, 29).**

"But this is that which was spoken by the prophet Joel; And it shall come to pass in the last days, saith God, I will pour out of my Spirit upon all flesh: and your sons and your daughters shall prophesy, and your young men shall see visions, and your old men shall dream dreams: And on my servants and on my handmaidens I will pour out in those days of my Spirit; and they shall prophesy" **(Acts 2:16-18).**

Joel literally described the battle of Armageddon in chapter 1 verses 15 through 20.

Joel gives us an overview from his time until the time of the establishing of the Millennium. Joel ends with the words *"...for the LORD dwelleth in Zion,"* and we Christians will dwell there also, ruling and reigning with our Lord for ever and ever. Amen!

The purpose of the book is to call Israel to repentance and give an overall prophetic view of the history of Israel.

Some important lessons from the book of Joel:

God's retribution for disobedience

God's forbearance shows that His mercy endureth forever.

God's blessings of the Holy Spirit

God's blessings of final victory for His cause and for His people

NOTES

NOTES

SEEING JESUS IN JOEL

There are three references to Jesus in Joel:

1. *Joel 1:15 speaks of the Almighty: **"Alas for the day! for the day of the LORD is at hand, and as a destruction from the Almighty shall it come."***

Almighty is El Shaddai, the God Who is more than enough—more than enough to meet all the needs of His people—but also more than enough to point His wrath upon those who will not repent. We see this picture of the great and terrible day of the Lord—with the outpouring of the wrath of the Almighty.

2. In Joel 2:28, 29 we see his prophecy of the outpouring of the Holy Spirit, which Jesus spoke of to His disciples in Acts 1:8. Jesus told them to tarry in Jerusalem until they would receive the outpouring of the Spirit. Joel knew of this outpouring, and he prophesied that Jesus would send it upon all flesh.

3. Jesus is seen as the judge of the nations in Joel 3:2, 12.

THEME VERSE

"And it shall come to pass afterward, that I will pour out my spirit upon all flesh; and your sons and your daughters shall prophesy, your old men shall dream dreams, your young men shall see visions: And also upon the servants and upon the handmaids in those days will I pour out my spirit" **(Joel 2:28, 29).**

OUTLINE

I. **GOD'S JUDGMENTS** - JOEL 1

  A. **Verses 1-5 describe the locusts' invasion.**

  B. **Verses 6-14 speak of what will occur in the next generation - the invasion of Assyria.**

  C. **Verses 15-20 describe the battle of Armageddon.**

II. **THE VIEW FROM WITHIN** - JOEL 2

  A. **Verses 1-14 present a view of the battle of Armageddon from *inside* the city of Jerusalem.**

  B. **Verses 15-32 have to do with the return of Christ.**

III. **THE VIEW FROM WITHOUT** - JOEL 3

  A. **Verses 1-21 present a view of the battle of Armageddon from *outside* the city and the enemies' camp.**

  Joel calls the people to repentance, fasting, and prayer. God promised to restore the years that the palmerworm, the locusts, the cankerworm, and the caterpillars had eaten.God was not referring to the invasion of palmerworms in Joel's day; He was referring to four armies:

1. **The Assyrians:** who came through and plundered Israel in the next generation after Joel.
2. **The locusts of the Babylonians:** who later invaded Israel and carried her people away into captivity for a period of seventy years.
3. **The cankerworms or Romans:** who invaded just after the time of Jesus.
4. **The caterpillars or the army:** which will invade Israel at the time of the battle of Armageddon.

Above all, God said that He would restore all those years. God will reverse the curse upon Israel.

OUTLINE OF "THE DAY OF JEHOVAH" IN JOEL:

I. THE PLAGUE OF INSECTS ON THE DAY OF THE LORD - JOEL 1:1-2:27

II. BLESSINGS AND JUDGMENTS IN THE LAST DAY - JOEL 2:28-3:21

A. Peter Quotes From Joel (Acts 2:16-23; Joel 2:28-32).

1. **Wonders in heaven and earth are to precede the great and terrible day of the Lord:**
   a. *"The sun shall be turned into darkness, and the moon into blood, before the great and the terrible day of the LORD come"* **(Joel 2:31).**
   b. *"The sun shall be turned into darkness, and the moon into blood, before that great and notable day of the Lord come"* **(Acts 2:20).**
2. **Salvation is offered to all who call upon the Lord's name.**

B. The Establishment of God's Kingdom Upon the Earth and His Ruling in Zion Forever and Ever.

NOTES

JOEL QUOTED IN THE NEW TESTAMENT

Joel 2:1 (Isaiah 27:13; Zechariah 2:6)
Blow ye the trumpet in Zion, and sound an alarm in my holy mountain: let all the inhabitants of the land tremble: for the day of the LORD cometh, for it is nigh at hand.

Matthew 24:31
And he shall send his angels with a great sound of a trumpet, and they shall gather together his elect from the four winds, from one end of heaven to the other.

****

Joel 2:10, 31
The earth shall quake before them; the heavens shall tremble: the sun and the moon shall be dark, and the stars shall withdraw their shining. The sun shall be turned into darkness, and the moon into blood, before the great and terrible day of the LORD come.

Matthew 24:29
Immediately after the tribulation of those days shall the sun be darkened, and the moon shall not give her light, and the stars shall fall from heaven, and the powers of the heavens shall be shaken.

Mark 13:24, 25
But in those days, after that tribulation, the sun shall be darkened, and the moon shall not give her light, And the stars of heaven shall fall, and the powers that are in heaven shall be shaken.

****

Joel 2:28-32
And it shall come to pass afterward, that I will pour out my spirit upon all flesh; and your sons and your daughters shall prophesy, your old men shall dream dreams, your young men shall see visions: And also upon the servants and upon the handmaids in those days will I pour out my spirit. And I will shew wonders in the heavens and in the earth, blood, and fire, and pillars of smoke. The sun shall be turned into darkness, and the moon into blood, before the great and the terrible day of the LORD come. And it shall come to pass, that whosoever shall call on the name of the LORD shall be delivered: for in mount Zion and in Jerusalem shall be deliverance, as the LORD hath said, and in the remnant whom the LORD shall call.

Acts 2:17-21
And it shall come to pass in the last days, saith God, I will pour out my Spirit upon all flesh: and your sons and your daughters shall prophesy, and your young men shall see visions, and your old men shall dream dreams: And on my servants and on my handmaidens I will pour out in those days of my Spirit; and they shall prophesy: And I will shew wonders in heaven above, and signs in the earth beneath; blood, and fire, and vapour of smoke: The sun shall be turned into darkness, and the moon into blood, before that great and notable day of the Lord come: And it shall come to pass, that whosoever shall call on the name of the Lord shall be saved.

Romans 10:13
For whosoever shall call upon the name of the Lord shall be saved.

NOTES

AMOS

THE PROPHET OF JUDGMENT		
JUDGMENT ON THE NATIONS	**PUNISHMENT OF ISRAEL FOR INIQUITY**	**VISIONS OF JUDGMENT**
Three transgressions: **1,2**	Luxury & social injustice: **3-6**	Locusts & fire: **7** Summer fruit: **8** The Lord on the altar: **9**
LOCATION: Israel		
OVERVIEW: Despite outward prosperity judgment is coming for sinful Israel.		
TIME: Around 780 B.C. during the reign of King Uzziah of Judah		

FAST FACTS

AUTHOR AND SETTING:

Amos; Tekoa (ten miles south of Jerusalem)

PURPOSE:

Although he lived in Judah, Amos prophesied of the coming judgment upon northern Israel because of the sinfulness of God's covenant people

SEEING JESUS:

Jesus Christ is the restorer of His people in the coming kingdom *(Amos 9:11-15)*.

THEME VERSE:

Amos 3:3

NOTES

AMOS:
PLUMB LINE

NOTES

SEEING JESUS IN AMOS

AUTHOR & SETTING

Amos means "a burden bearer." There is no question that he was a prophet with a great burden. He was an older contemporary of Hosea. His home was Tekoa—ten miles south of Jerusalem. His ministry, however, was not to the kingdom of Judah but to Israel—specifically to Bethel, which was the site of one of the golden calves that Jeroboam I had set up. Jeroboam literally turned the nation of Israel to idolatry.

Amos did not attend a prophet school; he received his prophecy while a herdsman on the farm. We know the exact timing of his calling:

"The words of Amos, who was among the herdsmen of Tekoa, which he saw concerning Israel in the days of Uzziah king of Judah, and in the days of Jeroboam the son of Joash king of Israel, two years before the earthquake" **(Amos 1:1).**

The earthquake that is mentioned here is also mentioned in Zechariah 14:5:

"And ye shall flee to the valley of the mountains; for the valley of the mountains shall reach unto Azal: yea, ye shall flee, like as ye fled from before the earthquake in the days of Uzziah king of Judah: and the LORD my God shall come, and all the saints with thee."

OVERVIEW

During the time of *Amos*, the northern kingdom had much luxury and indulgence because under Jeroboam II they really prospered.

The subject of this book is a heavy one—it is judgment:

1. The charge against Damascus: they threshed Gilead with instruments of iron. This judgment against Damascus was fulfilled with Tiglath-pileser who carried the people captive to Kir and slew Rezin (II Kings 16:9).

2. The charge against Philistia: they carried captive the whole people—neither age nor sex were spared—and delivered them over to Edom (II Chronicles 21:16, 28:18).

3. The judgment of the Philistines was complete destruction. Gaza was taken by Sennacherib, by Pharoah Neco, and by Alexander the Great. Ashdod was taken by Uzziah, by Sargon's chief Tartan, and by Psannetichus, king of Egypt They were finally destroyed by the Maccabees. Ashkelon was taken by Sennacherib, who also took Ekron (II Kings 18:8; Isaiah 14:29).

4. The charge against Phoenicia or Tyre was that they had delivered their captives to Edom in disregard of the covenant by Hiram to David and Solomon. It was fulfilled by the thirteen-year siege of Nebuchadnezzar and complete destruction by Alexander the Great.

5. The charge against Edom: perpetual hatred toward Jacob. Their two principal cities, Teman and Bozrah, were destroyed by Nebuchadnezzar.

6. The charge against Ammon: cruelty to the people of Gilead—probably under Hazael (II Kings 8:12, 10:32). Punishment was pronounced upon Ammon with the destruction of Rabbah and the exile of their kings and princes. It was fulfilled by Nebuchadnezzar.

7. The charge against Moab: they burned the bones of the king of Edom (II Kings 3:26, 27). Nebuchadnezzar conquered this country.

8. The charge against Judah: rejection of the law of Jehovah.

9. The charge against Israel basically was fourfold: (1) injustice; (2) hardness of heart toward the poor; (3) incest; and (4) luxury combined with idolatry. Their captivity was wrought by Shalmaneser, king of Assyria (II Kings 17:6).

Next Amos recalled incidents of the history of Israel. God was their defender and preserver **when** they humbled themselves and kept His law. He gave examples: (1) the destruction of Ammorites; (2) the deliverance from Egypt and forty years in the wilderness; and (3) God gave them prophets and Nazarites. But what did they do? They caused the Nazarites to drink, and they refused to let the prophets prophesy.

Amos stated *the Lord has spoken, therefore I prophesy*—and he invited the Philistines and Egyptians to see their downfall. This is basically a part of his first address—his first sermon.

The second sermon is in chapter 4, verses 1-3, and is Jehovah's warning to carousing women. Bashan was famous for its flocks and herds. These women were like the cattle - large, wanton, and headstrong.

Five distinct judgments follow: (1) a scarcity of food; (2) severe drought; (3) blasting and with mildew; (4) pestilence; and (5) destruction of cities. However, there was always hope for the remnant:

***"Hate the evil, and love the good, and establish judgment in the gate: it may be that the LORD God of hosts will be gracious unto the remnant of Joseph"* (Amos 5:15).**

In Amos 7:1-Amos 9:10, Amos has five visions:

(1) the locusts; (2) the fire; (3) the plumb line; (4) the basket of fruit; and (5) Jehovah Himself. After the plumb line was the interference of Amaiah, the priest of Bethel. He was an imposter, and he was reporting to Jeroboam II that Amos should be exiled. Amos declared God's call on him and prophesied against Amaziah.

Amos concluded his book with the prophecy of evangelical promises - Amos 9:11-15 - quoted in Acts 15:16:

NOTES

NOTES

"After this I will return, and will build again the tabernacle of David, which is fallen down; and I will build again the ruins thereof, and I will set it up."

"Behold, the days come, saith the LORD, that the plowman shall overtake the reaper, and the treader of grapes him that soweth seed; and the mountains shall drop sweet wine, and all the hills shall melt" **(Amos 9:13).**

Amos 9:14-15 is the return of the Jews, their conversion, and the ushering in of the Millennium—also extending the glorious kingdom of our Lord.

We could say this about Amos; he was a herdsman with no prophetic background but a strong call.

SEEING JESUS IN AMOS

Christ's work of restoration is clearly seen at the end of the book of Amos:

"In that day will I raise up the tabernacle of David that is fallen, and close up the breaches thereof; and I will raise up his ruins, and I will build it as in the days of old: That they may possess the remnant of Edom, and of all the heathen, which are called by my name, saith the LORD that doeth this. Behold, the days come, saith the LORD, that the plowman shall overtake the reaper, and the treader of grapes him that soweth seed; and the mountains shall drop sweet wine, and all the hills shall melt. And I will bring again the captivity of my people of Israel, and they shall build the waste cities, and inhabit them; and they shall plant vineyards, and drink the wine thereof; they shall also make gardens, and eat the fruit of them. And I will plant them upon their land, and they shall no more be pulled up out of their land which I have given them, saith the LORD thy God" **(Amos 9:11-15).**

THEME VERSE

"Can two walk together, except they be agreed?" **(Amos 3:3).**

OUTLINE

I. **JUDGMENT ON THE NATIONS -** AMOS 1, 2

A. **Judgment for Three Transgressions and for Four Repeated Sins Addressed:**

1. *"Thus saith the LORD; For three transgressions of Judah, and for four, I will not turn away the punishment thereof; because they have despised the law of the LORD, and have not kept his commandments, and their lies caused them to err, after the which their fathers have walked: Thus saith the LORD; For three*

transgressions of Israel, and for four, I will not turn away the punishment thereof; because they sold the righteous for silver, and the poor for a pair of shoes" **(Amos 2:4, 6).**

II. PUNISHMENT OF ISRAEL FOR INIQUITY - AMOS 3-6

A. Jeroboam I had begun the Idolatrous Sanctuaries at Dan and Bethel.

B. Luxury Was Accompanied by Social Injustices.

III. VISIONS OF JUDGMENT - AMOS 7-9

A. Locusts - Amos 7:1-3

B. Fire - Amos 7:4-6

C. Plumb Line - Amos 7:7-9

1. Prophet's experience at Bethel - Amos 7:10-17

D. Summer Fruit - Amos 8

E. Vision of the Lord Standing Upon the Altar - Amos 9:1-10

F. The Closing Prophecy is Referred to in James 5 - Judgments on the Wealthy. (See also Hosea 9:11-15; Acts 15:15-17).

ADDITIONAL FACTS ABOUT AMOS:
Some of the key verses in this book for us to remember:

Amos 3:3: *"Can two walk together, except they be agreed?"*

Amos 3:7: *"Surely the Lord GOD will do nothing, but he revealeth his secret unto his servants the prophets."*

Amos 4:12: *"Therefore thus will I do unto thee, O Israel: and because I will do this unto thee, prepare to meet thy God, O Israel."*

Amos 5:14: *"Seek good, and not evil, that ye may live: and so the LORD, the God of hosts, shall be with you, as ye have spoken."*

Amos 8:11, 12: *"Behold, the days come, saith the Lord GOD, that I will send a famine in the land, not a famine of bread, nor a thirst for water, but of hearing the words of the LORD: And they shall wander from sea to sea, and from the north even to the east, they shall run to and fro to seek the word of the LORD, and shall not find it."*

Amos 9:13-15: *"Behold, the days come, saith the LORD, that the plowman shall overtake the reaper, and the treader of grapes him that soweth seed; and the mountains shall drop sweet wine, and all the hills shall melt. And I will bring again the captivity of my people of Israel, and they shall build the waste cities, and inhabit them; and they shall plant vineyards, and drink the wine thereof; they shall also make gardens, and eat the fruit of them. And I will plant them upon their land, and they shall no more be pulled up out of their land which I have given them, saith the LORD thy God."*

NOTES

AMOS QUOTED IN THE NEW TESTAMENT.

Amos 5:25-27
Have ye offered unto me sacrifices and offerings in the wilderness forty years, O house of Israel? But ye have borne the tabernacle of your Moloch and Chiun your images, the star of your god, which ye made to yourselves. Therefore will I cause you to go into captivity beyond Damascus, saith the LORD, whose name is The God of hosts.

Acts 7:42, 43
Then God turned, and gave them up to worship the host of heaven; as it is written in the book of the prophets, O ye house of Israel, have ye offered to me slain beasts and sacrifices by the space of forty years in the wilderness? Yea, ye took up the tabernacle of Moloch, and the star of your god Remphan, figures which ye made to worship them: and I will carry you away beyond Babylon.

****

Amos 9:11, 12
In that day will I raise up the tabernacle of David that is fallen, and close up the breaches thereof; and I will raise up his ruins, and I will build it as in the days of old: That they may possess the remnant of Edom, and of all the heathen, which are called by my name, saith the LORD that doeth this.

Acts 15:16-18
After this I will return, and will build again the tabernacle of David, which is fallen down; and I will build again the ruins thereof, and I will set it up: That the residue of men might seek after the Lord, and all the Gentiles, upon whom my name is called, saith the Lord, who doeth all these things. Known unto God are all his works from the beginning of the world.

NOTES

OBADIAH

<table>
<tr><th colspan="3">PRIDE GOES BEFORE A FALL</th></tr>
<tr><td>DOOM OF EDOM</td><td>REASONS FOR JUDGMENT</td><td>PROMISE OF FUTURE DELIVERANCE</td></tr>
<tr><td>Rocky fortress: 1-6
Allies fail: 7
Wise & mighty men fail: 8,9</td><td>Emnity between brothers: 10-16</td><td>Jacob's house will possess: 17-21</td></tr>
<tr><td colspan="3">LOCATION: Edom—south of the Death Sea</td></tr>
<tr><td>OVERVIEW:
Edom's defeat</td><td>Warring brothers' fight continues</td><td>Israel's victory</td></tr>
<tr><td colspan="3">TIME: Edom's actual destruction came after the conquest of Judah by Babylon</td></tr>
</table>

FAST FACTS

AUTHOR AND SETTING:

Obadiah; small Judean town

PURPOSE:

Obadiah is a declaration of Edom's doom because of its cruelty toward Judah; a vivid example of the Golden Rule in negative operation: ***"...as you have done, it shall be done unto you"*** **(Obadiah 15).**

SEEING JESUS:

Jesus Christ can be seen as the judge of the nations *(Obadiah 15, 16)*, the Savior of Israel *(Obadiah 17-20)*, and the possessor of the kingdom *(Obadiah 21)*.

THEME VERSE:

Obadiah 4

NOTES

OBADIAH:
DELIVERER/MOUNTAIN TOP

NOTES

SEEING JESUS IN OBADIAH

AUTHOR & SETTING

Obadiah means "a worshiper of Jehovah." Little is known about this prophet. His book is the shortest book of the Old Testament. *Obadiah's* theme is judgment on Edom, the descendants of Esau (Genesis 36). The indictment of *Obadiah* was against Edom for its unbrotherly conduct toward Judah. The vision of Obadiah occurs after the invasion of Judah and the plundering of Jerusalem by the Philistines and Arabians. Many captives of the royal family were taken. This was during the reign of Jehoram II (II Chronicles 21:16-17; II Kings 8:20).

OVERVIEW

The geographical area of Edom was taken by Esau from the Horonites. These descendants of Esau, Jacob's brother, never lost an opportunity to show their dislike of Israel.

Joel 2:23-3:19 parallels *Obadiah*.

Obadiah 1, 2 is a summons to the nations to rise against Edom and bring her to desolation.

Obadiah 3, 4 is a description of her pride.

Three prophecies claim our attention:

1. The conquest of the Edomites by the heathen because of the Edomites' cruelty to the Jews at the time of their capture at Jerusalem by the Philistines and Arabians

2. A second conquest of the Edomites and their utter extermination by the Jews

3. The subsequent expansion of the Israelite nation and the triumphant glories of Zion

Nebuchadnezzar invaded Edom five years after the destruction of Jerusalem. The Chaldeans then took over Edom, and the Edomites moved into southern Judah. The fulfillment of the second prophecy, the conquest of Edom by the Jews, was by Judas Maccabeus. They were subjugated—they lost their nationality—and eventually were slain. Jehovah had spoken: and, none would remain.

What are the important lessons in this book? There are the following:

1. This is a lesson about a family feud.
2. Pride goeth before a fall.
3. This is a lesson of false confidence.
4. God's method of dealing out his wrath.
5. This is a lesson of hope in a dark hour.

SEEING JESUS IN OBADIAH

Who is Jesus in *Obadiah*, and where is He?

"But upon mount Zion shall be deliverance, and there shall be holiness; and the house of Jacob shall possess their possessions" **(Obadiah 17).**

"And saviours shall come up on mount Zion to judge the mount of Esau; and the kingdom shall be the LORD'S" **(Obadiah 21).**

Christ is also seen as judge of the nations in verses 15 and 16. In verses 17-20 He is seen as the Savior of Israel.

THEME VERSE

"Though thou exalt thyself as the eagle, and though thou set thy nest among the stars, thence will I bring thee down, saith the LORD" **(Obadiah 4).**

OUTLINE

I. **THE DOOM OF EDOM -** OBADIAH 1-9
   - A. **The Rocky Fortress Will Fail them -** Obadiah 3-6.
   - B. **Their Allies Will Fail Them -** Obadiah 7.
   - C. **Their Wise and Mighty Men Will Fail -** Obadiah 8, 9.

II. **THE REASONS FOR GOD'S JUDGMENT -** OBADIAH 10-16
   - A. **The Violent Story of Israel**
   - B. **The Aid They Gave: those who despoiled Israel (Edom's actual destruction came after the destruction of Judah by Babylon).**

III. **GOD'S PROMISE FOR FUTURE DELIVERANCE OF ISRAEL -** OBADIAH 17-21
   - A. **The House of Jacob Shall Possess Their Possessions.**

OBADIAH QUOTED IN THE NEW TESTAMENT: NOT FOUND

NOTES

JONAH

THE STUBBORN PROPHET			
DISOBEDIENCE	**PRAYER & DELIVERANCE**	**OBEDIENCE**	**COMPASSION & MERCY**
God speaks, but Jonah won't listen: **1**	A psalm-like prayer: **2**	Nineveh repents: **3**	A Jew learns compassion toward the gentiles: **4**
LOCATION: Mediterranean Sea; Nineveh			
OVERVIEW: Three great doctrines are taught in this book: resurrection, genuine repentance, and God's lovingkindness, Jonah was a patriotic Jew who didn't think the gentiles of Nineveh deserved God's mercy; Jonah's stubborn resistance to God's sovereign call on his life had dramatic consequences.			
TIME: During the reign of Jeroboam II—around 800 B.C.			

FAST FACTS

AUTHOR AND SETTING:

Jonah; Gath Hepher (in Galilee)

PURPOSE:

The power of God and His mercy in human affairs is richly illustrated in this book. The prophet learns that *"...Salvation is of the LORD"* (Jonah 2:9) and that His gracious offer extends beyond the Jews.

SEEING JESUS:

Jesus Himself authenticated this book (Matthew 12:40), which beautifully illustrates His death, His resurrection, and His commission to His disciples to *"...go ye into all the world, and preach the gospel to every creature"* (Mark 16:15).

THEME VERSE:

Jonah 2:8, 9

NOTES

JONAH:
MESSENGER MISSIONERY

NOTES

SEEING JESUS IN JONAH

AUTHOR & SETTING

Jonah means "a dove." Certainly this is a book with a tremendous message from the Holy Spirit. Jonah lived during the reign of Jeroboam II around 800 B.C. (II Kings 14;25). The book relates more of the experiences of the prophet than his message. Jesus authenticated this book:

"For as Jonas was three days and three nights in the whale's belly; so shall the Son of man be three days and three nights in the heart of the earth" **(Matthew 12:40).**

OVERVIEW

Nineveh, the capital of Assyrian empire, was on the Tigris River. Because of Jonah's message of destruction, the people of Nineveh repented temporarily, but Nahum tells of their later destruction.

These are three beautiful aspects to this book:

1. **To teach us** that salvation is also for the Gentiles
2. **To give a genuine lesson** on the repentance of the Ninevites and Jonah and to show God's forgiveness
3. **To typify Christ**

The occasion of the book was the moral corruption of Nineveh:

"Now the word of the LORD came unto Jonah the son of Amittai, saying, Arise, go to Nineveh, that great city, and cry against it; for their wickedness is come up before me" **(Jonah 1:1, 2).**

"Woe to the bloody city! It is all full of lies and robbery; the prey departeth not" **(Nahum 3:1).**

"This is the rejoicing city that dwelt carelessly, that said in her heart, I am, and there is none beside me: how is she become a desolation, a place for beasts to lie down in! every one that passeth by her shall hiss, and wag his hand" **(Zephaniah 2:15).**

There was a two-fold miracle—there was a moral and spiritual revival.

There are three great doctrines in this book:

1. Resurrection
2. Genuine repentance
3. God's loving-kindness

Nineveh was founded by Nimrod, a descendant of Ham:

"Out of that land went forth Asshur, and builded Nineveh, and the city Rehoboth, and Calah" **(Genesis 10:11).**

"And they shall waste the land of Assyria with the sword, and the land of Nimrod in the entrances thereof: thus shall he deliver us from the Assyrian, when he cometh into our land, and when he treadeth within our borders" **(Micah 5:6).**

Balaam prophesied about it:

"Nevertheless the Kenite shall be wasted, until Asshur shall carry three away captive. And ships shall come from the coast of Chittim, and shall afflict Asshur, and shall afflict Eber, and he also shall perish for ever" **(Numbers 24:22, 24).**

Assyria would carry Israel away captive—Greece would afflict Assyria:

"Assur also is joined with them: they have holpen the children of Lot. Selah" **(Psalms 83:8).**

This site is an historic reality. In II Chronicles 20:1-4 is an account of Syria under Shalmaneser II joining with Moab and Ammon against Israel under Jehoshaphat—at which time the Israelites were victorious. This is the beginning of a series of victories.

Nineveh was on the Tigris River and was built in the shape of a parallelogram. It was 60 miles around—a three-day journey through it. It had 60 walls and 1500 towers that were 200 feet high. It was destroyed by the combined forces of the Medes and Babylonians.

The Ninevites worshiped the fish god. Many stone images have been dug up with a man coming out of a fish's mouth. How like God to use the very thing they worshiped to show Himself as the true and living God.

Why didn't Jonah want to go to Nineveh? Basically—for four reasons:

1. His hatred of the Gentiles
2. The fear of God's mercy on them
3. Nineveh's growing strength
4. The ill-treatment of Israel at the hands of the Assyrians

Please note the reactions of the sailors to Jonah:

1. They feared Jehovah.
2. They made sacrifices.
3. They made vows.

Jonah's hymn is made up of quotes from the Psalms:

"And said, I cried by reason of mine affliction unto the LORD, and he heard me; out of the belly of hell cried I, and thou heardest my voice" **(Jonah 2:2).**

"In my distress I cried unto the LORD, and he heard me" **(Psalms 120:1).**

"For thou hadst cast me into the deep, in the midst of the seas; and the floods compassed me about: all thy billows and thy waves passed over me" **(Jonah 2:3).**

"Deep calleth unto deep at the noise of thy waterspouts: all thy waves and thy billows are gone over me" **(Psalms 42:7).**

NOTES

NOTES

"Then I said, I am cast out of thy sight; yet I will look again toward thy holy temple" **(Jonah 2:4).**
"For I said in my haste, I am cut off from before thine eyes: nevertheless thou heardest the voice of my supplications when I cried unto thee" **(Psalms 31:22).**

"The waters compassed me about, even to the soul; the depth closed me round about, the weeds were wrapped about my head" **(Jonah 2:5).**

"The sorrows of death compassed me,...The sorrows of hell compassed me about: the snares of death prevented me" **(Psalms 18:4, 5).**

"When my soul fainted within me I remembered the LORD: and my prayer came in unto thee, into thine holy temple" **(Jonah 2:7).**

"In my distress I called upon the LORD, and cried unto my God: he heard my voice out of his temple, and my cry came before him, even into his ears" **(Psalms 18:6).**

"When my spirit was overwhelmed within me, then thou knewest my path. In the way wherein I walked have they privily laid a snare for me" **(Psalms 142:3).**

"They that observe lying vanities forsake their own mercy" **(Jonah 2:8).**

"I have hated them that regard lying vanities: but I trust in the LORD. I will be glad and rejoice in thy mercy: for thou hast considered my trouble; thou hast known my soul in adversities" **(Psalms 31:6, 7).**

Please note three things about God's relationship to this ministry:

1. **God calls** by direct appeal to His ministers.
2. **God selects** the field of labor.
3. **God gives** the message.

The forty-day warning gave space for repentance.

After his "resurrection," Jonah preached to the Gentiles.

After His Resurrection, Christ gave His commission to the disciples to go to the Gentiles.

SEEING JESUS IN JONAH

It is easy to see Jesus in this book: the death and Resurrection of Jesus is *the* picture in the book of *Jonah.*

THEME VERSE

"They that observe lying vanities forsake their own mercy. But I will sacrifice unto thee with the voice of thanksgiving; I will pay that that I have vowed. Salvation is of the LORD" **(Jonah 2;8, 9).**

OUTLINE

I. **JONAH'S COMMISSION FROM THE LORD AND JONAH'S DISOBEDIENCE** - JONAH 1

II. **JONAH'S PRAYER AND DELIVERANCE** - JONAH 2

  A. **The Prayer is in the Form of a Psalm.**

III. **JONAH'S SECOND COMMISSION AND OBEDIENCE** - JONAH 3

  A. **Nineveh Repented:**

    1. *"The men of Nineveh shall rise in judgment with this generation, and shall condemn it: because they repented at the preaching of Jonas; and, behold, a greater than Jonas is here"* **(Matthew 12:41).**

IV. **GOD'S OBJECT LESSON IN COMPASSION AND MERCY** - JONAH 4

  A. **Jonah Was an Intense Patriot and Hated the Repentance of Nineveh.**

  B. **Three Prepared Things:**

    1. *"And the LORD God prepared **A GOURD**, and made it to come up over Jonah, that it might be a shadow over his head, to deliver him from his grief. So Jonah was exceeding glad of the gourd"* **(Jonah 4:6).**

    2. *"But God prepared **A WORM** when the morning rose the next day, and it smote the gourd that it withered"* **(Jonah 4:7).**

    3. *"And it came to pass, when the sun did arise, that God prepared **A VEHEMENT EAST WIND**; and the sun beat upon the head of Jonah, that he fainted, and wished in himself to die, and said, It is better for me to die than to live"* **(Jonah 4:8).**

  C. **God Revealed to Jonah Where His Mercy and Compassion Should Be.**

    1. **Jonah must have repented of his attitude because he wrote the book. He is the author and the hero of the book.**

JONAH QUOTED IN THE NEW TESTAMENT.

Jonah 1:17
Now the LORD had prepared a great fish to swallow up Jonah. And Jonah was in the belly of the fish three days and three nights.

Matthew 12:40
For as Jonas was three days and three nights in the whale's belly; so shall the Son of man be three days and three nights in the heart of the earth.

NOTES

MICAH

THE "POOR MAN'S" PROPHET		
WITNESS AGAINST ISRAEL	**FAILURES OF LEADERS**	**CONTROVERSY TO ALL PEOPLE**
Samaria to be destroyed: **1,2**	Princes, prophets, & priests: **3** Millennial kingdom: **4** The true ruler: **5**	Future restoration & blessing: **6** Repentance: **7**
LOCATION: Judah & Israel		
OVERVIEW: There are three distinct addresses beginning with "Hear." Micah's message of coming judgment was mainly to Jerusalem and Samaria—the two capitals of the divided kingdom		
TIME: 735-710 B.C.		

FAST FACTS

AUTHOR AND SETTING:

Micah; Judah

PURPOSE:

Micah warned of God's judgment upon sin and offered hope by speaking of God's deliverer (Jesus) to come and restore His people.

SEEING JESUS:

Micah 5:2 clearly predicted the birth of Christ—700 years before the fact.

THEME VERSE:

Micah 6:8

NOTES

MICAH:
EVERLASTING RULER

NOTES

SEEING JESUS IN MICAH

AUTHOR & SETTING

Micah means "like Jehovah." He was a contemporary of Isaiah. Micah's prophecy was given more than seven hundred years before Christ was born. Micah was a prophet in Judah, but the book deals primarily with Samaria and the Gentile nations—reproving them for their sins and warning of the judgment of captivity coming to Israel. Micah also saw the future restoration of the kingdom of the Messiah and the great events of the latter days.

OVERVIEW

These latter day prophecies were encouraging to the people who were under the judgment of the wrath of God. God had warned Israel many times regarding what would befall them if they continued in sin and rebellion, but they were backslidden and hard in their lifestyle. God was becoming less tolerant of their mock worship, ritualism, and sin. God would eventually bring them back to repentance and would give them an everlasting covenant, but it would be built on the grounds of fulfilling righteousness.

God wanted to bring Israel and all mankind back to the place of conformity to His eternal will and plan.

Micah was a contemporary of Hosea of the northern kingdom and of the great prophet Isaiah of the southern kingdom. They all prophesied during the reigns of King Jotham, King Ahaz, and King Hezekiah.

Isaiah belonged to a royal class; Micah belonged to a poor class. Isaiah ministered to kings; Micah ministered to poor people. Micah has been termed the "prophet of the poor."

Micah's preaching helped bring the reformation under Hezekiah. Isaiah dealt with political situations; Micah dealt with the moral, civil, and economic situations. This book is a compilation of Micah's sermons.

There are three distinct addresses beginning with, "Hear ye." Micah's message was mainly to Jerusalem and Samaria: "As goes the cities, so goes the country." *Micah* puts the source of all the evil in the two capitals.

Samaria was captured by Shalmaneser V. In Micah 1:8-16 we read of the distress of the prophet over the destructions. By the Spirit, Micah saw the Assyrians coming and taking the villages of his beloved plains. Micah's sympathy was with the poor and with the lowlands of Judah. Micah prophesied against the leaders who refused to listen to him.

In chapter two Micah, by the Spirit, saw the future restoration. Israel, led by their God, was to return from exile. Their sins are characterized in Micah 3:1-4. Micah attacked the false prophets; he addressed the heads and rulers of Jacob, the seers, the soothsayers, the diviners, the visionaries, the fortunetellers, and the class that lived by preying upon the people. The people had no answers from God.

The contrast between the false prophets and Micah is a contrast of character. The people would always scream out that the Temple would save them because God's presence was there; because of the Temple, nothing could happen to them—Micah 3;9-11. But Micah's reply was:
"Therefore shall Zion for your sake be plowed as a field, and Jerusalem shall become heaps,..." **(Micah 3:12).**

Micah's prediction of Zion's fate saved Jeremiah's life (Jeremiah 26:12-24).

SEEING JESUS IN MICAH

Micah prophesied the birthplace of Jesus:

"But thou, Bethlehem Ephratah, though thou be little among the thousands of Judah, yet out of thee shall he come forth unto me that is to be ruler in Israel; whose goings forth have been from of old, from everlasting" **(Micah 5:2).**

His prophecy is quoted in the New Testament:

"And thou Bethlehem, in the land of Juda, art not the least among the princes of Juda: for out of thee shall come a Governor, that shall rule my people Israel" **(Matthew 2:6).**

THEME VERSE

"He hath shewed thee, O man, what is good; and what doth the LORD require of thee, but to do justly, and to love mercy, and to walk humbly with thy God?" **(Micah 6:8).**

OUTLINE

The outline consists of the three messages that Micah preached. Each one began with "Hear."

I. **GOD'S WITNESS AGAINST ISRAEL (TO ALL PEOPLE) -** MICAH 1, 2
   A. **Judgment is Coming Because of Sin.**
   B. **Samaria Was To Be Destroyed.**
II. **THE FAILURES OF THE PRINCES** MICAH 3:1; **PROPHETS MICAH 3:5; AND PRIESTS** MICAH 3:11 **(TO ALL LEADERS)**
   A. **Zion Was To Suffer the Same Fate As Samaria.**
   B. **The Description of the Millennial Kingdom in Micah 4 is similar to Isaiah 2.**

NOTES

NOTES

C. **God Proclaimed the Coming of the True Ruler, the Messiah:**

1. *"But thou, Bethlehem Ephratah, though thou be little among the thousands of Judah, yet out of thee shall he come forth unto me that is to be ruler in Israel; whose goings forth have been from of old, from everlasting"* **(Micah 5:2).**

III. **THE LORD'S CONTROVERSY (TO ALL PEOPLE) -** MICAH 6, 7

A. **Hear the Lord's Controversy:**

1. *"Hear ye, O mountains, the LORD's controversy, and ye strong foundations of the earth: for the LORD hath a controversy with his people, and he will plead with Israel"* **(Micah 6:2).**

B. **Future Restoration and Blessing**

C. **The Book Closes With Israel's Soliloquy of Repentance** - Micah 7:7-20:

1. *"Rejoice not against me, O mine enemy: when I fall, I shall arise; when I sit in darkness, the LORD shall be a light unto me. Who is a God like unto thee, that pardoneth iniquity, and passeth by the transgression of the remnant of his heritage? He retaineth not his anger for ever, because he delighteth in mercy"* **(Micah 7:8, 18).**

MICAH QUOTED IN THE NEW TESTAMENT.

Micah 5:2
But thou, Bethlehem Ephratah, though thou be little among the thousands of Judah, yet out of thee shall he come forth unto me that is to be ruler in Israel; whose goings forth have been from of old, from everlasting.

Matthew 2:6
And thou Bethlehem, in the land of Juda, art not the least among the princes of Juda: for out of thee shall come a Governor, that shall rule my people Israel.

****

Micah 7:6
For the son dishonoureth the father, the daughter riseth up against her mother, the daughter in law against her mother in law; a man's enemies are the men of his own house.

Matthew 10:35, 36
For I am come to set a man at variance against his father, and the daughter against her mother, and the daughter in law against her mother in law. And a man's foes shall be they of his own household.

NAHUM

THE COMPASSIONATE PROPHET	
MAJESTY OF THE LORD	**JUDGMENT OF NINEVEH**
Character & power of God: **1**	Man joins with nature: **2,3**
LOCATION: Nineveh, capitol of Assyria	
OVERVIEW: Once the recipients of God's mercy and grace toward the gentiles (under Jonah), now 100 years later, the Ninevites had returned to sin and rebellion. They thought their high-walled, 200-towered city was impregnable . . . but they should have listened to Nahum!	
TIME: Around 640 B.C.	

FAST FACTS

AUTHOR AND SETTING:

Nahum; Judah

PURPOSE:

The Judeans who trusted in the Lord were comforted to hear of God's judgment upon the proud and brutal Assyrians *(Nahum 1:15, 2:2)*. God's retribution against wickedness is the theme of *Nahum*, although He is shown to be "slow to wrath" *(Nahum 1:2-8)*.

SEEING JESUS:

The compassion of the Lamb is seen in *Nahum 1:15*; the wrath of the Lamb is seen in *Nahum 1:6* (compare Revelation 6:16).

THEME VERSE:

Nahum 1:7,8

NOTES

NAHUM:
AVENGER

NOTES

SEEING JESUS IN NAHUM

AUTHOR & SETTING

Nahum means "compassionate." The only information we have about Nahum is that he was an "Elkoshite" (Nahum 1:1). Some scholars think Nahum was from the town of "Elkoshi," which was north of Nineveh. Other scholars believe that "Elkosh" was a city in Judah, which would explain Nahum's "good tidings" (Nahum 1:15) for Judah regarding the downfall of the cruel Assyrians and their capital city of Nineveh. Nahum prophesied of the destruction of Nineveh about a hundred years after Jonah's preaching. This prophecy is an accompaniment and counterpart to the book of Jonah.

Nineveh was destroyed as prophesied by both Nahum and Jonah. It was destroyed by the Medes and the Babylonians under Nabopolassar, the father of Nebuchadnezzar. Under the preaching of Jonah, Nineveh had repented; but the next generation had gone back into sin and rebellion against God. Now they would be destroyed.

It is not unusual that God used a prophet to deal with one complete gentile nation. For example, Obadiah dealt with Edom; similarly, Nahum dealt with Assyria.

OVERVIEW

Nahum prophesied that Nineveh would not arise a second time; the coming destruction would be the utter end of the capital of Assyria:

"What do ye imagine against the LORD? he will make an utter end: affliction shall not rise up the second time" **(Nahum 1:9)**

The Assyrians were known for their cruelty. Assyria was the empire founded by Asshur, the son of Shem – Genesis 10:11, 22. Assyria became the second world empire to oppress Israel in the times of the gentiles.

Of the 151 times the people of Assyrian empire are mentioned in the Scripture, 139 times the references are connected with the 175 years Israel was oppressed by them.

Assyria's national symbol is a lion – Jeremiah 50:17:18; Nahum 2:11-13.

The Antichrist shall be called an Assyrian because he will come from Assyrian territory— Isaiah 10:24; 14:24,25; 30:31; Micah 5:5,6. However, there is some good news for Assyria—they are to be blessed with Israel in the Millennium:

"And there shall be an highway for the remnant of his people, which shall be left, from Assyria; like as it was to Israel in the day that he came up out of the land of Egypt" **(Isaiah 11:16).**

"In that day shall there be a highway out of Egypt to Assyria, and the Assyrian shall come into Egypt, and the Egyptian into Assyria, and the Egyptian shall serve with the Assyrians. In that

day shall Israel be the third with Egypt and with Assyria, even a blessing in the midst of the land: Whom the Lord of hosts shall bless, saying, Blessed be Egypt my people, and Assyria the work of my hands, and Israel mine inheritance" **(Isaiah 19:23-25).**

In Nahum 1:15 we read:
"Behold upon the mountains the feet of him that bringeth good tidings, that publisheth peace! O Judah, keep thy solemn feasts, perform thy vows: for the wicked shall no more pass through thee; he is utterly cut off."

The same scripture was written earlier in Isaiah 52:7:
"How beautiful upon the mountains are the feet of him that bringeth good tidings, that publisheth peace; that bringeth good tidings of good, that publisheth salvation; that saith unto Zion Thy God reigneth!"

The above scripture from Isaiah is partially quoted in Romans 10:15:
"And how shall they preach, except they be sent? as it is written, How beautiful are the feet of them that preach the gospel of peace, and bring glad tidings of good things!"

In Nahum 2:3-6 we see a description of the coming battle over Nineveh. The shields of Nineveh's army were dyed red, and the soldiers wore scarlet military tunics. With their wheels the chariots struck sparks from the stones, which could have given the appearance of torches and flashes of lightning on the battlefield. These highly –polished chariots would jostle one another in the broad streets of Nineveh.

A flood would make the fall of the city possible. In the third year of the actual siege, the river Khusur and the canal to the Tigris running through the city became so swollen by constant rain that the overflow even washed away a portion of the wall. Through this break in the wall, the invaders entered to take over.

When the King of Nineveh saw this happening, he gave up and built a large funeral tower in the palace. He burned his concubines, eunuchs, and himself. The fate of the queen, however, remains unknown.

In Nahum 3 eight reasons are presented as to why Nineveh was destroyed:

1. It was a bloody city – known for violence and murder.
2. It was full of deceit.
3. It was full of robberies.
4. It was full of warring.
5. It was full of immorality.
6. It was full of witchcraft.
7. It was full of drunkenness.
8. It was full of extreme oppression.

In Nahum 3:8 we have a description of No, a city of Egypt. Assyria had conquered No and had taken the people into captivity. The city of No fell because of her immorality. Nineveh was no better; God said she would fall too. Assyria, evidently, had conquered both Egypt and Ethiopia.

NOTES

NOTES

There would be absolutely no remedy for the coming destruction:

"There is no healing of thy bruise; thy wound is grievous: all that hear the bruit of thee shall clap the hands over thee: for upon whom hath not thy wickedness passed continually?" **(Nahum 3:19).**

SEEING JESUS IN NAHUM

Christ's position as the judge of the nations is seen in Nahum 1:2-6.

We also see Jesus exercising God's will upon this city as the Lord of hosts:

"Behold, I am against thee, saith the LORD of hosts, and I will burn her chariots in the smoke, and the sword shall devour they young lions: and I will cut off thy prey from the earth, and the voice of thy messengers shall no more be heard" **(Nahum 2:13).**

THEME VERSE

"The LORD is good, a strong hold in the day of trouble; and he knoweth them that trust in him. But with an overrunning flood he will make an utter end of the place thereof, and darkness shall pursue his enemies" **(Nahum 1:7-8).**

OUTLINE

I. **THE MAJESTY OF THE LORD** - NAHUM 1
   - A. **This is the Poetic Section Describing the Character and Power of God.**
   - B. **God Won't Equip the Wicked** - Nahum 1:8.
   - C. **God is a Stronghold** - Nahum 1:7.

II. **THE JUDGMENT OF NINEVAH** - NAHUM 2,3
   - A. **Description of the Battle for Nineveh**
   - B. **It Was Brought to Doom:** by a collusion of the Medes and the Babylonians assisted by the swollen Tigris River.
   - C. **The Ninevites' Sins Brought Their Inevitable Punishment.**

Please note that God sent His grace before His wrath was sent. Jonah brought the message of grace, Nahum brought the message of wrath. *Jonah* means "love"; *Nahum* means "compassionate." God desired to have love and compassion upon this city, but she refused His love, so she experienced His judgment.

NAHUM QUOTED IN THE NEW TESTAMENT.

Nahum 1:15 (Isaiah 52:7)
Behold upon the mountains the feet of him that bringeth good tidings, that publisheth peace! O Judah, keep thy solemn feasts, perform thy vows: for the wicked shall no more pass through thee; he is utterly cut off.

Romans 10:15
And how shall they preach, except they be sent? as it is written, How beautiful are the feet of them that preach the gospel of peace, and bring glad tidings of good things!

Ephesians 6:15
And your feet shod with the preparation of the gospel of peace.

NOTES

HABAKKUK

THE PROPHET ON THE WATCHTOWER	
PROPHET'S COMPLAINT & GOD'S ANSWER	**PROPHET'S PRAYER**
The question: **1** The answer: **2**	The solution is in God: **3**
LOCATION: Judah	
OVERVIEW: A prophet, a preacher, and a poet, Habakkuk asked God for understanding about the prosperity of the wicked. He learned that both Israel and Babylon would be judged for their sins . . . but Babylon's triumph would be temporary.	
TIME: Around 600 B.C. during the reign of King Jehoiakim	

FAST FACTS

AUTHOR AND SETTING:

Habakkuk; Judah

PURPOSE:

Habakkuk struggled in his faith when he saw men flagrantly violating God's laws...and he asked God why He allowed growing iniquity to go unpunished. God's answers made it clear that, despite appearances, justice would be done. In the meantime, God's people would need to live by faith.

SEEING JESUS:

The word "salvation" appears three times (twice in *Habakkuk 3:13* and once in *Habakkuk 3:18*) and is the root word from which the name "Jesus" is derived (see Matthew 1:21). Jesus is also mentioned as "thine anointed" in *Habakkuk 3:13*.

THEME VERSE:

Habakkuk 2:14

NOTES

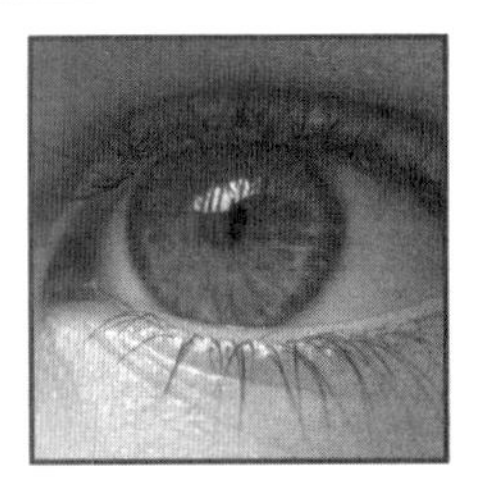

HABAKKUK:
VISION, HOPE

NOTES

SEEING JESUS IN HABAKKUK

AUTHOR & SETTING

Habakkuk means "embrace" or "to be embraced." There is no question that Habakkuk kept very close to God. This book was written during the reign of Jehoiakim. Babylon was a rising power. Habakkuk was not only a preacher, but he was also a sublime poet.

Jeremiah and Zephaniah also lived at this time. Zephaniah was spared from the evil leaders because he was a prince, and Jeremiah was rescued by friends.

Habakkuk seems to have lived in obscurity. Unlike Jeremiah and Zephaniah, Habakkuk did not warn the people of their sins. Instead, he dealt with the question of why God allowed evil to exist—why would God allow a sinful nation like Babylon to destroy Judah? Habakkuk stood on a watchtower to get his answer from God.

OVERVIEW

God gave Habakkuk an answer as to why a sinful nation like Babylon would be used to judge Judah; the answer came through a vision. God told him to write it on a tablet. The answer was that both Israel and Babylon would suffer for their sins—the triumph of Babylon was only temporary.

Habakkuk cried out against injustice and oppression: Habakkuk 1:2-4.

The Babylonians made their own strength their god and treated other nations as if they were fish to be caught. Habakkuk, however, expressed a high faith in God—Habakkuk 1:12-17.

Habakkuk spoke these important words:

"Behold, his soul which is lifted up is not upright in him: but the just shall live by his faith" **(Habakkuk 2:4).**

The righteous shall live by his faithfulness. The word *faithfulness* comes from the root meaning of the word *amen.* Faithfulness is life; sin is suicide.

There are five songs of woe:

1. The plunderer shall be plundered: Habakkuk 2:6-8.
2. A house built by evil gain shall witness against its owner: Habakkuk 2:9-11.
3. The capital built by blood shall be fed to the fire: Habakkuk 2:12-14.
4. The producer of drunkenness and shame shall in turn be put to shame: Habakkuk 2:15-17.
5. The gross idols of Babylon disappoint the idol maker: Habakkuk 2:18-20.

Habakkuk 3 is in the form of a poem picturing a theophany – God appearing on the horizon of history. *Habakkuk* celebrates the greatness of the Lord in His dealings and doings with His people. *Habakkuk* ends on a mountaintop of faith.

The book is a powerful and wonderful testimony of Habakkuk. The prophecy is a conversation between Habakkuk and God. It opens with Habakkuk's appeal to God to end injustice in the earth.

THE FIRST QUESTION:

"O Lord, how long shall I cry, and thou wilt not hear! even cry out unto thee of violence, and thou wilt not save!" **(Habakkuk 1:2).**

THE FIRST ANSWER:

"Behold ye among the heathen, and regard, and wonder marvelously: for I will work a work in your days, which ye will not believe, though it be told you" **(Habakkuk 1:5).**

THE SECOND QUESTION:

"Art thou not from everlasting, O LORD my God, mine Holy One? we shall not die. O LORD, thou hast ordained them for judgment; and, O might God, thou hast established them for correction. Thou art of purer eyes than to behold evil, and canst not look on iniquity: wherefore lookest thou upon them that deal treacherously and holdest thy tongue when the wicked devoureth the man that is more righteous than he?" **(Habakkuk 1:12,13).**

THE SECOND ANSWER:

"And the LORD answered me, and said, Write the vision, and make it plain upon tables, that he may run that readeth it" **(Habakkuk 2:2).**

The great answer that Habakkuk kept for his own heart is that the just shall live by faith:

"Behold, his soul which is lifted up is not upright in him: but the just shall live by his faith" **(Habakkuk 2:4).**

This is also quoted in the New Testament:

For therein is the righteousness of God revealed from faith to faith: as it is written, The just shall live by faith" **(Romans 1:17).**

"But that no man is justified by the law in the sight of God, it is evident: for, The just shall live by faith" **(Galatians 3:11).**

"Now the just shall live by faith: but if any man draw back, my soul shall have no pleasure in him" **(Hebrews 10:38).**

Perhaps one of the most encouraging answers that Habakkuk received was: *"For the earth shall be filled with the knowledge of the glory of the LORD, as the waters cover the sea"* **(Habakkuk 2:14).**

His poem, of course, was his prayer in Habakkuk 3. He closed by saying that the joy of the Lord was his strength (Habakkuk 3:17-19). He shows how the just shall live by faith: they will rejoice in God and not be moved by circumstances; they will not walk by sense-knowledge; they will walk and live by faith-knowledge.

We need desperately to embrace this truth.

NOTES

NOTES

SEEING JESUS IN HABAKKUK

"Salvation" is mentioned three times in this book:

"Thou wentest forth for the salvation of thy people, even for salvation with thine anointed; thou woundedst the head out of the house of the wicked, by discovering the foundation unto the neck. Selah. Yet I will rejoice in the LORD, I will joy in the God of my salvation" **(Habakkuk 3:13,18).**

Salvation is the root word from which *Jesus* is derived (as used in Matthew 1:21).

Jesus is also mentioned as the anointed in Habakkuk 3:13. There is no question that we see the Redeemer here.

THEME VERSE

"For the earth shall be filled with the knowledge of the glory of the LORD, as the waters cover the sea" **(Habakkuk 2:14).**

OUTLINE

I. **THE PROPHET'S COMPLAINT AND GOD'S ANSWER** - HABAKKUK 1,2

   A. **The Question:**

      1. *"Thou art of purer eyes than to behold evil, and canst not look on iniquity: wherefore lookest thou upon them that deal treacherously, and holdest thy tongue when the wicked devoureth the man that is more righteous than he?"* **(Habakkuk 1:13).**

   B. **Awaiting the Reply:**

      1. *"And the LORD answered me, and said, Write the vision, and make it plain upon tables, that he may run that readeth it"* **(Habakkuk 2:2).**

   C. **God Urges His People To Wait and Have Patience:**

      1. *"For the vision is yet for an appointed time, but at the end it shall speak, and not lie: though it tarry, wait for it; because it will surely come, it will not tarry"* **(Habakkuk 2:3).**

      2. *"But the LORD is in his holy temple: let all the earth keep silence before him"* **(Habakkuk 2:20).**

II. **THE PROPHET'S PRAYER** – HABAKKUK 3

   A. **He Would Recall His God's Past Works and His Own Confidence in the Lord.**

   B. **He Rejoices in God:**

      1. *"Yet I will rejoice in the LORD, I will joy in the God of my salvation"* **(Habakkuk 3:18).**

      2. *"Rejoice in the LORD always: and again I say, Rejoice"* **(Philippians 4:4).**

   C. **The Prophet Finds His Solution in God.**

HABAKKUK QUOTED IN THE NEW TESTAMENT.

Habakkuk 1:5
Behold ye among the heathen, and regard, and wonder marvelously: for I will work a work in your days, which ye will not believe, though it be told you.

Acts 13:41
Behold, ye despisers, and wonder, and perish: for I work a work in your days, a work which ye shall in no wise believe, though a man declare in unto you.

*****

Habakkuk 2:3,4
For the vision is yet for an appointed time, but at the end it shall speak, and not lie: though it tarry, wait for it; because it will surely come, it will not tarry. Behold, his soul which is lifted up is not upright in him: but the just shall live by his faith.

Hebrews 10:37,38
For yet a little while, and he that shall come will come, and will not tarry. Now the just shall live by faith: but if any man draw back, my soul shall have no pleasure in him.

Romans 1:17
For therein is the righteousness of God revealed from faith to faith: as it is written,The just shall live by faith.

Galatians 3:11
But that no man is justified by the law in the sight of God, it is evident: for, The just shall live by faith.

NOTES

ZEPHANIAH

THE REFORMING PROPHET		
JUDGMENT UPON JUDAH	**JUDGMENT UPON NATIONS**	**DELIVERANCE FOR JUDAH**
Appeal for escape: **1**	Gentile neighbors were about to experience God's crushing hand: **2**	After chastening comes blessing: **3**
LOCATION: Judah & surrounding nations		
OVERVIEW: Zephaniah's warnings of God's coming wrath contributed to an outward revival in Jerusalem during King Josiah's reign but did not change the sinfulness of the nation's leaders.		
TIME: Around 630 B.C. during the reign of King Josiah		

FAST FACTS

AUTHOR AND SETTING:

Zephaniah; Judah

PURPOSE:

Zephaniah's theme is similar to Joel's: "the day of the LORD" is coming. Wrath, fierce anger, and the fire of God's jealousy was about to descend upon Judah. A righteous remnant would survive; and all who called upon God, Jew or gentile, would be blessed.

SEEING JESUS:

Zephaniah concludes his book by writing wonderfully of Jesus the Messiah reigning in Zion *(Zephaniah 3:14-20).*

THEME VERSE:

Zephaniah 1:7

NOTES

ZEPHANIAH:
SAVIOR

NOTES

SEEING JESUS IN ZEPHANIAH

AUTHOR & SETTING

Zephaniah means "Jehovah hides." This is the only prophet who gives his ancestry for several generations. He had a direct connection with David. He was also a distant relative of Josiah, the king of his day. Zephaniah was the great-grandson of Hezekiah. He had a wide vision.

This prophecy was probably given around 630 B.C., making Zephaniah a contemporary of Jeremiah. Zephaniah was an 11th hour prophet.

OVERVIEW

Zephaniah's theme is very similar to Joel—the day of the Lord, the coming of the wrath, fierce anger, and the fire of God's jealousy. Zephaniah's prophecies of judgment were upon Judah.

The Chemarims (Zephaniah 1:4) were a group of idolatrous priests living during the time of Zephaniah. *Chemarim* means "darkness." Zephaniah identified different classes of sinners, different irreligious people, and backsliders. However, he gave the beautiful joys of restoration in Zephaniah 3:14-20. His vision is very similar to the other prophets.

The book makes it clear that Judah will have to consecrate herself to the will of God, or judgment will come. Zephaniah also encouraged the godly people, the remnant, that there would be a final, complete restoration under the Messiah—Jesus Christ.

Zephaniah opens with the message regarding immediate judgment upon Judah from Babylon. Zephaniah 2 talks about immediate judgment (by Babylon) upon the gentile nations of Philistia, Moab, Ammon, Ethiopia, and Assyria. Then the prophet returned to the immediate judgment upon Judah by Babylon and made predictions concerning Israel in the future day of the Lord. Zephaniah mentions the reign of the Messiah in Zephaniah 3:14-20.

"The LORD of hosts" seems to be the major title of the Lord in this book. *Zephaniah* makes comparisons as to what God has done to Assyria and Nineveh (Nahum 1:13, 14).

From Zephaniah 3:9 we learn that what was lost at Babel will be restored—one pure language. Please notice the *remnant* of Israel—there has always been a *remnant* of Jews who walked in faith, believed God's Word, and obeyed it.

The restoration of Israel is encouraging and spoken of again and again by every prophet:

"At that time will I bring you again, even in the time that I gather you: for I will make you a name and a praise among all people of the earth, when I turn back your captivity before your eyes, saith the LORD," **(Zephaniah 3:20)**

In Matthew 13:41 Jesus alludes to Zephaniah 1:3:

"The Son of man shall send forth his angels, and they shall gather out of his kingdom all things that offend, and them which do iniquity" **(Matthew 13:41).**

"I will consume man and beast; I will consume the fowls of the heaven, and the fishes of the sea, and the stumblingblocks with the wicked; and I will cut off man from off the land, saith the LORD" **(Zephaniah 1:3).**

Jesus also alluded to *Zephaniah* in Matthew 24:29:

"Immediately after the tribulation of those days shall the sun be darkened, and the moon shall not give her light, and the stars shall fall from heaven, and the powers of the heavens shall be shaken" **(Matthew 24:29).**

"That day is a day of wrath, a day of trouble and distress, a day of wasteness and desolation, a day of darkness and gloominess, a day of clouds and thick darkness" **(Zephaniah 1:15).**

Both of these references refer to the Second Coming; *Zephaniah* refers to the "day of the Lord" 23 times in only three chapters!

Zephaniah, Habakkuk, and Lamentations are all concerned with the fall of Jerusalem. Zephaniah delivered his message about 40 years *before* the fall of Jerusalem; Habakkuk delivered his message about 20 years *before* the fall; Jeremiah wrote Lamentations right *after* the destruction of Jerusalem.

SEEING JESUS IN ZEPHANIAH

The wonderful ending of this book is the Messiah and the picture of Jesus reigning in Zion:

"Sing, O daughter of Zion; shout, O Israel; be glad and rejoice with all the heart, O daughter of Jerusalem. The LORD hath taken away thy judgments, he hath cast out thine enemy: the king of Israel, even the LORD, is in the midst of thee: thou shalt not see evil any more. In that day it shall be said to Jerusalem, Fear thou not: and to Zion, Let not thine hands be slack" **(Zephaniah 3:14-16).**

NOTES

NOTES

THEME VERSE

"Hold thy peace at the presence of the Lord God: for the day of the LORD is at hand: for the LORD hath prepared a sacrifice, he hath bid his guests" **(Zephaniah 1:7).**

OUTLINE

I. **JUDGMENT UPON JUDAH** - ZEPHANIAH 1:1-2:3

A. **An Appeal to the Meek for Escape:**

1. *"Seek ye the LORD, all ye meek of the earth, which have wrought his judgment; seek righteousness, seek meekness: it may be ye shall be hid in the day of the LORD's anger"* **(Zephaniah 2:3).**

II. **JUDGMENT UPON THE NATIONS** - ZEPHANIAH 2:4–3:8

A. **Philistia on the West**

B. **Ammon and Moab on the East**

C. **Ethiopia on the South**

D. **Assyria on the North**

III. **ULTIMATE DELIVERANCE FOR JUDAH** - ZEPHANIAH 3:9-20

We see the principles of God's righteousness which must punish sin. We see God's grace for salvation to those who trust Him.

ZEPHANIAH QUOTED IN THE NEW TESTAMENT: NOT FOUND

HAGGAI

THE PROPHET OF PRIORITIES			
REBUKE FOR NEGLIGENCE	**CALL TO COURAGE**	**ADDRESS TO PRIESTS**	**WORD FOR ZERUBBABEL**
Lack of prosperity: **1**	Political & spiritual leaders: **2**	Separation: **2**	Symbol of Jesus Christ: **2**
LOCATION: Jerusalem			
OVERVIEW: *"But seek ye first the kingdom of God...and all these things shall be added unto you"* **(Matthew 6:33).** This was the same message which Haggai brought to his discouraged people, rallying them to accomplish their first purpose – to complete the rebuilding of the Temple – and to overcome the outward harassment and conflict against them.			
TIME: September 1, 520 B.C. (Haggai 1:1)	October 21, 520 B.C. (Haggai 2:1)	December 24, 520 B.C. (Haggai 2:10)	December 24, 520 B.C. (Haggai 2:20)

FAST FACTS

AUTHOR AND SETTING:

Haggai; Jerusalem

PURPOSE:

Sixteen years after returning from captivity, the Jews were slow to rebuild the Temple because their personal affairs interfered with God's work. *Haggai* preached a fiery series of sermons designed to stir up the nation to resume work on the Temple.

SEEING JESUS:

Haggai pointed to Jesus as the future glory for the Temple (*Haggai 2:1-9*), calling Him *"...the desire of all nations..."* **(Haggai 2:7).**

THEME VERSE:

Haggai 2:9

NOTES

HAGGAI:
STRENGTH

NOTES

SEEING JESUS IN HAGGAI

AUTHOR & SETTING

Haggai means "festal." He was a prophet who caused the Jews to really celebrate their return to the Promised Land. The books of Ezra and Nehemiah are the background of the prophecies of Haggai. When the people returned from Persia at the decree of Cyrus, the first thing they did was rebuild the Temple: they sought first the kingdom of God and His righteousness so that all things would be added unto them.

OVERVIEW

When the people began to rebuild the Temple, there were lots of harassments and conflicts against them. The Arabs and various tribes who had settled in Judah began to tell them they could never do it. This was frightening to the people who had spent seventy years in slavery and had just returned to their Promised Land. The older men who returned with them wept when they saw the foundation of this Temple compared to Solomon's Temple: it was nothing compared to the earlier Temple.

On top of that, the Arabs and other tribes who were dwelling on the land wrote to the new king of Persia and told him that he must stop the people from building their Temple because the Jews were rebellious and would rebel again. They new king issued a decree that the building had to stop.

It was a time of great discouragement. The people turned from building God's house and began to build their own houses. For 14 years nothing was done on the Temple, but God raised up Haggai and Zechariah at this time to encourage the people to complete the rebuilding of the Temple.

The Jews refused to be defeated. They sent a message back saying that Cyrus had given them a decree granting permission to build the Temple. The new king, King Darius, found that decree and not only gave them permission to finish the Temple, but he also sent provisions to help them and asked for their prayers for himself. When we walk in faith, God will cause the obstacles around us to fall.

At the prophesying of Haggai and Zechariah the people were so built up and cheered up and stirred up that they finished the Temple within four years. Haggai rebuked the people for living in their homes and being at ease while the house of God was lying in waste. He also gave a message to the leaders of the new nation of Israel urging them to be strong because God was with them to help them in all their problems. Haggai pointed to the day of future glory for the new Temple and also spoke of the future and the eternal glory of Jesus in Haggai 2:1-9.

God has always confirmed things in the mouth of two or three witnesses. Haggai and Zechariah were the two witnesses who prophesied and confirmed the messages of what the people were called to do. These two men, in their day, brought great faith and encouragement to the hearts of all Israel as well as encouraging us today.

In this book, we see that God blends the present and future by exhortation and promise.

SEEING JESUS IN HAGGAI

Twice Haggai refers to the future renovation of the heavens and earth by a great shaking at the end of the Millennium (Haggai 2:6, 20-23)—compare this with Hebrews 12:24-28; II Peter 3:5-13). Haggai beautifully refers to Jesus as *"...the desire of all nations..."* **(Haggai 2:7).**

Haggai 2:23 mentions Zerubbabel, who would hold a strategic place in the genealogy of Jesus:

"In that day, saith the LORD of hosts, will I take thee, O Zerubbabel, my servant, the son of Shealtiel, saith the LORD, and will make thee as a signet: for I have chosen thee, saith the LORD of hosts."

Zerubbabel became the *ring* which joined both Joseph and Mary's lineages together at one point in time (see Matthew 1:12; Luke 3:27).

THEME VERSE

"The glory of this latter house shall be greater than of the former, saith the LORD of hosts: and in this place will I give peace, saith the LORD of hosts" **(Haggai 2:9)**

OUTLINE

I. **FIRST MESSAGE - REBUKE FOR NEGLIGENCE AND CALL TO BUILD GOD'S HOUSE -** HAGGAI 1:1-15

   A. **This is Why They Had Not Been Prospering -** Haggai 1:9

   B. **It Brought Quick Response From the People -** Haggai 1:12-15

II. **SECOND MESSAGE - CALL TO BE COURAGEOUS AND STRONG -** HAGGAI 2:1-9

   A. **Zerubbabel Was the Political Leader and Joshua Was the Spiritual Leader of Jerusalem**

   B. **Haggai Called Upon Zerubbabel, Joshua, and the People: to be strong because of God's covenant and God's presence among them.**

NOTES

NOTES

1. This temple won't be as beautiful as Solomon's, but its glory will be greater because of the presence of the Son of God and His earthly ministry.

III. **THIRD MESSAGE - ADDRESSED TO PRIESTS -** HAGGAI 2:10-19

A. *"Thus saith the LORD of hosts; Ask now the priests concerning the law..."* **(Haggai 2:11).**

B. **Separate Yourselves Unto the Lord.**

IV. **FOURTH MESSAGE - A WORD FOR ZERUBBABEL -** HAGGAI 2:20-23

A. **He is Seen As a Prophetic Symbol of Jesus Christ:**

1. *"And I will overthrow the throne of kingdoms, and I will destroy the strength of the kingdoms of the heathen; and I will overthrow the chariots, and those that ride in them; and the horses and their riders shall come down, every one by the sword of his brother"* **(Haggai 2:22).**

B. **God Sent Encouragement.**

1. **God sent Haggai with the word of encouragement to the people, to the priests, to Zerubbabel, and to Joshua. Every man was stirred up, cheered up, and built up by the power of God's Spirit.**

HAGGAI QUOTED IN THE NEW TESTAMENT

Haggai 2:6
For thus saith the LORD of hosts; Yet once, it is a little while, and I will shake the heavens, and the earth, and the sea, and the dry land.

Hebrews 12:26
Whose voice then shook the earth: but now he hath promised, saying, Yet once more I shake not the earth only, but also heaven.

ZECHARIAH

<table>
<tr><th colspan="3">THE PRACTICAL PROPHET</th></tr>
<tr><th>EIGHT VISIONS</th><th>ABOUT FEASTING</th><th>END-TIME PROPHECIES</th></tr>
<tr><td>Myrtle trees: 1
Four horns & four carpenters: 1
Measuring Line: 2
Joshua, the high priest: 3
Candlestick & two olive trees: 4
Flying roll: 5
Woman & ephah: 5
Four horses: 6
Crowning of Joshua: 6</td><td>Fasting & feasting: 7
God is concerned with obedience: 8</td><td>Judgment upon nations: 9
The Messiah: 9
Destruction of Antichrist: 10-12
Cleansing Israel: 13
Coming kingdom of Christ: 14</td></tr>
<tr><td colspan="3">LOCATION: Jerusalem</td></tr>
<tr><td colspan="3">OVERVIEW: Zechariah's message was one of encouragement to continue rebuilding the Temple. He also prophesied of the First and Second Advents of Jesus and the millennial kingdom.</td></tr>
<tr><td colspan="2">TIME: 520-518 B.C.—one month after the Temple foundation was completed</td><td>480-470 B.C.—after the Temple was rebuilt</td></tr>
</table>

FAST FACTS

AUTHOR AND SETTING:

Zechariah; Jerusalem

PURPOSE:

Zechariah encouraged the Jews to continue rebuilding the Temple. As they were building the Temple, they were preparing the way for their Messiah to come.

SEEING JESUS:

Messianic purpose is clearly seen in *Zechariah*, where Jesus is portrayed as the "rider on the red horse" (*Zechariah 1:8*); the "wall of fire" (*Zechariah 2:5*); the "branch" (*Zechariah 3:8*); and more.

THEME VERSE:

Zechariah 1:3

NOTES

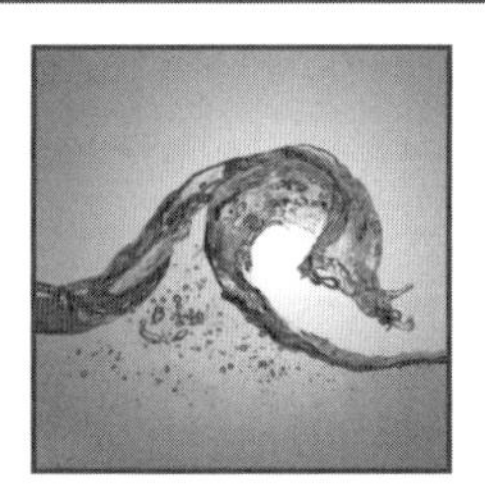

ZECHARIAH:
FOUNTAIN OF CLEANSING

NOTES

SEEING JESUS IN ZECHARIAH

AUTHOR & SETTING

Zechariah means "Jehovah remembers." Ezra mentions Zechariah along with Haggai:

"Then the prophets, Haggai the prophet, and Zechariah the son of Iddo, prophesied unto the Jews that were in Judah and Jerusalem in the name of the God of Israel, even unto them" **(Ezra 5:1).**

"And the elders of the Jews builded, and they prospered through the prophesying of Haggai the prophet and Zechariah the son of Iddo. And they builded, and finished it, according to the commandment of the God of Israel, and according to the commandment of Cyrus, and Darius, and Artaxerxes king of Persia" **(Ezra 6:14).**

Zechariah and Haggai began their ministries in the same year:

"In the eighth month, in the second year of Darius, came the word of the LORD unto Zechariah, the son of Berechiah, the son of Iddo the prophet..." **(Zechariah 1:1).**

"In the second year of Darius the king, in the sixth month, in the first day of the month, came the word of the LORD by Haggai the prophet..." **(Haggai 1:1).**

OVERVIEW

Zechariah had a practical message to the people about their obedience to God. His prophecy is more expansive than Haggai's prophecy. Zechariah's prophecy is very broad, including both the First and Second Advents and the millennial kingdom. He uses the title *"The LORD of hosts"* 52 times. It is a description of God as the leader and ruler of heavenly armies.

Chapters 1-8 of this book were written while the Temple was being built; chapters 9-14 were written after the Temple was completed.

SEEING JESUS IN ZECHARIAH

There are many references to Jesus in *Zechariah*:

1. The rider on the red horse—Zechariah 1:8
2. The wall of fire—Zechariah 2:5
3. The branch—Zechariah 3:8
4. The Lord of the whole earth—Zechariah 4:14
5. The branch and the two crowns—Zechariah 6:12,14
6. The king of Palm Sunday—Zechariah 9:9
7. The betrayed shepherd—Zechariah 11:12
8. The one who is pierced—Zechariah 12:10
9. The smitten one—Zechariah 13:7
10. The returning one—Zechariah 14:3, 4,9

THEME VERSE

"Therefore say thou unto them, Thus saith the LORD of hosts; Turn ye unto me, saith the LORD of hosts, and I will turn unto you, saith the LORD of hosts" **(Zechariah 1:3)**

OUTLINE

I. EIGHT VISIONS FOLLOWED BY THE SYMBOLIC CROWNING OF JOSHUA - ZECHARIAH 1-6

A. Eight Visions Were All Given in the Same Night:

1. **The man among the myrtle trees** (Zechariah 1:8-11) **represents God's displeasure with the heathen.**
2. **The four horns and four carpenters** (Zechariah 1:18-21) **represent the nations which scattered Judah and Israel and God's judgment upon the nations.**
3. **The man with a measuring line** (Zechariah 2:1) **represents a future enlargement and blessing for Jerusalem.**
4. **The cleansing of Joshua, the high priest,** (Zechariah 3:1-10) **represents future cleansing.**

a. The sinner's condition is seen...

i. Satan opposes him:
"And he shewed me Joshua the high priest standing before the angel of the LORD, and Satan standing at his right hand to resist him" **(Zechariah 3:1).**

ii. God has chosen him:
"And the LORD said unto Satan, The LORD rebuke thee, O Satan; even the LORD that hath chosen Jerusalem rebuke thee: is not this a brand plucked out of the fire?" **(Zechariah 3:2).**

iii. God's salvation leads to transformation:
"And he answered and spake unto those that stood before him, saying, Take away the filthy garments from him. And unto him he said, Behold, I have caused thine iniquity to pass from thee, and I will clothe thee with change of raiment. And I said, Let them set a fair mitre upon his head. So they set a fair mitre upon his head, and clothed him with garments. And the angel of the LORD stood by" **(Zechariah 3:4,5).**

iv. Service for God:
"And the angel of the LORD protested unto Joshua, saying, Thus saith the LORD of hosts; If thou wilt walk in my ways, and if thou wilt keep my charge, then thou shalt also judge my house, and shalt also keep my courts, and I will give thee places to walk among these that stand by" **(Zechariah 3:6,7).**

NOTES

NOTES

It is accomplished through the branch (Zechariah 3:8).

5. **The candlestick and the two olive trees** (Zechariah 4:1-14) **represent witnessing power.**
   a. Symbolic work of the Holy Spirit...
      i. *"Then he answered and spake unto me, saying, This is the word of the LORD unto Zerubbabel, saying, Not by might, nor by power, but by my spirit, saith the LORD of hosts"* **(Zechariah 4:6).**
   b. The two anointed ones were Zerubbabel (governor) and Joshua (high priest) - Zechariah 3,4.

   (The last three visions have to do with judgment.)

6. **Flying roll -** Zechariah 5:1-4
   a. God's law of bringing judgment on His people
7. **The woman and the ephah** (Zechariah 5:5-11) **represents God's judgment on elements of Babylon still remaining in His people (greedy commercialism).**
8. **Four judgments. God's judgments upon nations who perish through the destructive agency of the four horses -** Zechariah 6:1-8; Revelation 6:1-8.
   a. This section closes with the symbolic crowning of Joshua. It combines in one person the offices of king and priest.

II. **QUESTIONS CONCERNING FASTING -** ZECHARIAH 7,8
   A. **A Fast Can Be Turned Into a Feast.**
   B. **God is Concerned With Obedience.**

III. **END-TIME PROPHECIES -** ZECHARIAH 9-14
   A. **Judgment Upon the Nations and God's People.**
   B. **Well-known Prophecies:**
      1. **Christ enters Jerusalem as king -** Matthew 21:1-10:
         a. *"Rejoice greatly, O daughter of Zion; shout, O daughter of Jerusalem: behold, thy King cometh unto thee: he is just, and having salvation; lowly, and riding upon an ass, and upon a colt the foal of an ass"* **(Zechariah 9:9).**
      2. **Destruction of the Antichrist -** Zechariah 12
      3. **National cleansing of Israel -** Zechariah 13
      4. **Coming glory and kingdom of Christ -** Zechariah 14

ZECHARIAH QUOTED IN THE NEW TESTAMENT.

Zechariah 2:6 (Isaiah 27:13; Joel 2:1)
Ho, ho, come forth, and flee from the land of the north, saith the LORD: for I have spread you abroad as the four winds of the heaven, saith the LORD.

Matthew 24:31
And he shall send his angels with a great sound of a trumpet, and they shall gather together his elect from the four winds, from one end of heaven to the other.

* * * * * * * *

Zechariah 8:16
These are the things that ye shall do; Speak ye every man the truth to his neighbour; execute the judgment of truth and peace in your gates.

Ephesians 4:25
Wherefore putting away lying, speak every man truth with his neighbor: for we are members one of another.

* * * * * * * *

Zechariah 9:9 (Isaiah 40:9, 62:11)
Rejoice greatly, O daughter of Zion; shout, O daughter of Jerusalem: behold, thy King cometh into thee: he is just, and having salvation; lowly, and riding upon an ass, and upon a colt the foal of an ass.

Matthew 21:5
Tell ye the daughter of Sion, Behold, the King cometh unto thee, meek, and sitting upon an ass, and a colt the foal of an ass.

John 12:15
Fear not, daughter of Sion: behold, thy King cometh, sitting on an ass's colt.

* * * * * * * *

Zechariah 11:12, 13
And I said unto them, if ye think good, give me my price, and if not, forbear. So they weighed for my price thirty pieces of silver. And the LORD said unto me, Cast it unto the potter: a goodly price that I was prised at of them. And I took the thirty pieces of silver, and cast them to the potter in the house of the LORD.

Matthew 27:9,10
Then was fulfilled that which was spoken by Jeremiah the prophet, saying, And they took the thirty pieces of silver, the price of him that was valued, whom they of the children of Israel did value; And gave them for the potter's field, as the Lord appointed me.

* * * * * * * *

Zechariah 12:10
And I will pour upon the house of David, and upon the inhabitants of Jerusalem, the spirit of grace and of supplications: and they shall look upon me whom they have pierced, and they shall mourn for him, as one mourneth for his only son, and shall be in bitterness for him, as one that is in bitterness for his firstborn.

John 19:37
And again another scripture saith, They shall look on him whom they pierced.

Revelation 1:7
Behold, he cometh with clouds; and every eye shall see him, and they also which pierced him: and all kindreds of the earth shall wail because of him. Even so, Amen.

* * * * * *

Zechariah 13:7
Awake, O sword, against my shepherd, and against the man that is my fellow, saith the LORD of hosts; smite the shepherd, and the sheep shall be scattered: and I will turn mine hand upon the little ones.

Matthew 26:31
Then saith Jesus unto them, All ye shall be offended because of me this night: for it is written, I will smite the shepherd, and the sheep of the flock shall be scattered abroad.

Mark 14:27
And Jesus saith unto them, All ye shall be offended because of me this night: for it is written, I will smite the shepherd, and the sheep shall be scattered.

MALACHI

LAST VOICE BEFORE A 400-YEAR SILENCE		
BATTLE WITH SIN	**TWO MESSENGERS**	**THE REMNANT**
God's love for Israel: **1** Priestly sins: **1** People's sins: **2**	Forerunner of the Messiah: **3** Messenger of the covenant: **3**	The Sun of righteousness: **3,4**
LOCATION: Jerusalem		
OVERVIEW: Malachi proclaims the sinful condition of the Jews, warns of God's judgment, and promises relief in the coming of the Savior.		
TIME: Around 400 years before the birth of Christ		

FAST FACTS

AUTHOR AND SETTING:

Malachi; Jerusalem

PURPOSE:

Although directed toward Israel, *Malachi's* message is for any nation to heed: whether a nation prospers or falls depends on obedience to God's laws.

SEEING JESUS:

Jesus' First and Second Advents are clearly described in *Malachi 3:1-5*. *Malachi* foretells of the messenger (John the Baptist) who will prepare the way before the Lord (*Malachi 3:1*). He also prophesies of the ministry of Elijah and Moses before Jesus' Second Coming (*Malachi 3:17-4:6*).

THEME VERSE:

Malachi 3:17

NOTES

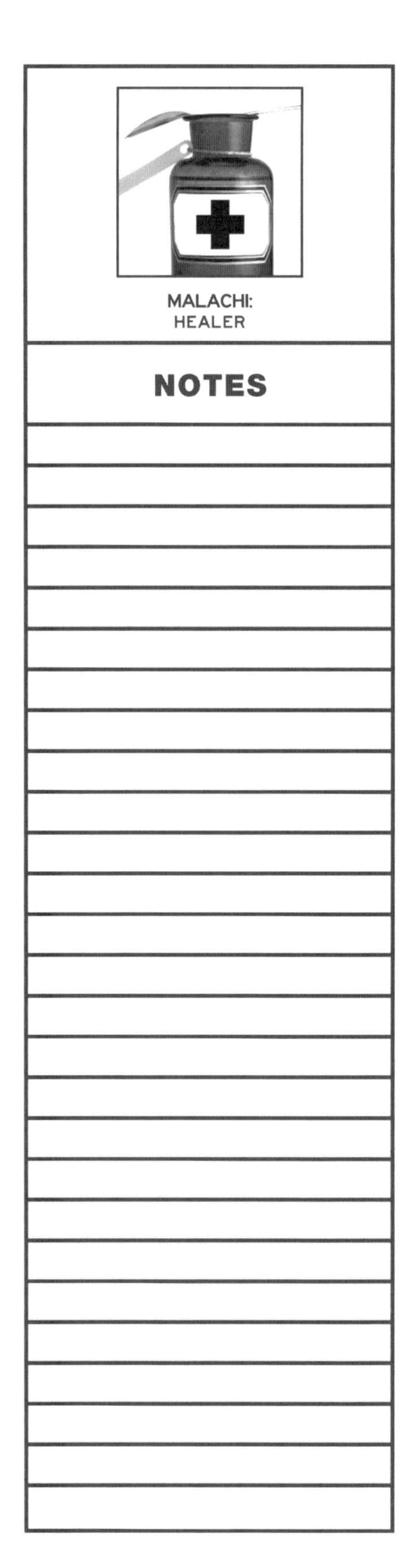

SEEING JESUS IN MALACHI

AUTHOR & SETTING

Malachi means "my messenger." Nehemiah and Malachi were contemporaries. Nehemiah wrote *historically* and Malachi wrote *spiritually* about this time period. They both faced the task of straightening out a generation which was against God and His Word.

The nation had just come through two hundred years of economic, spiritual, and governmental prosperity. After twelve years Nehemiah straightened out the nation politically (in 433 B.C.) and went back to Babylon (Nehemiah 5:14). When he left, the nation went downhill because of anarchy and religious formality without spiritual fervor.

Malachi described what happened when Nehemiah left. After an unknown period of time, Nehemiah returned to Jerusalem (Nehemiah 13:6,7). Nehemiah and Malachi became a team – one political and the other spiritual. This parallels Zerubbabel, the political leader, and Zechariah, the prophet.

OVERVIEW

The message of *Malachi* is twofold:

1. To the individual – tying him into the plan of God through regeneration.

2. To the nation – to heed God's Word of coming calamity and destruction.

By interpretation the message of this book is toward Israel, but by application the message is for any nation to heed. The Biblical principles for the preservation of any nation are found in *Malachi*. Each nation can either destroy itself or prosper according to Biblical law.

Under Haggai and Zechariah the second Temple was completed after Israel's return from captivity. There was a fantastic period of prosperity for almost 200 years except for a very short period of about 20 years (from 420 to 400 B.C.). The period of prosperity was the time of the writing of *Malachi*. But the nation had turned away from the Word, and destruction was coming quickly. The only thing that would save the nation was to heed the message of *Malachi*.

SEEING JESUS IN MALACHI

Malachi was the last prophet before John the Baptist. After Malachi there were four hundred years of silence. John introduced the One of whom the prophets spoke – Jesus Christ. Jesus is beautifully seen in this book in prophecies of the First and Second Advent (Malachi 3:1-5). We also see the ministry of Elijah and Moses preceding the Second Advent (Malachi 3:17-4:6).

Malachi, the messenger, speaks of several other messengers. In Malachi 2:7 the priest is called the messenger of the Lord of hosts – the high priest was to be God's messenger. Malachi 3:1 speaks of the messenger, John the Baptist, who will come and prepare the way of the Lord. Malachi also tells of the messenger of the new covenant which is Jesus Christ (Malachi 3:1). Lastly, in Malachi 4:5, he speaks of Elijah coming as a messenger before the great and terrible day of the Lord. This, undoubtedly, is the appearance of the two witnesses—Elijah and Moses—in Revelation 11:1-14. There are a number of messengers with tremendous messages in the book of *Malachi*—no wonder his name means "my messenger."

THEME VERSE

"And they shall be mine, saith the LORD of hosts, in that day when I make up my jewels; and I will spare them, as a man spareth his own son that serveth him" **(Malachi 3:17).**

OUTLINE

I. **BATTLE WITH SIN** - MALACHI 1-3
   - A. **God's Love for Israel** - Malachi 1:1-5
   - B. **The Sins of the Priest** - Malachi 1:6-2:9
   - C. **The Sins of the People** - Malachi 2:10-3:15

II. **TWO MESSENGERS** - MALACHI 3:1
   - A. **The Forerunner of Messiah**
     - 1. *"For this is he, of whom, it is written. Behold, I send my messenger before thy face, which shall prepare thy way before thee"* **(Matthew 11:10)**
   - B. **The Lord Jesus Christ - Messenger of the Covenant**

III. **THE REMNANT** - MALACHI 3:16 – 4:6
   - A. **Christ the Sun of Righteousness** - Malachi 4:2

     The book closes with great expectation.

NOTES

MALACHI QUOTED IN THE NEW TESTAMENT.

Malachi 1:2, 3
I have loved you, saith the LORD. Yet ye say, Wherein hast thou loved us? Was not Esau Jacob's brother? saith the LORD; yet I loved Jacob. And I hated Esau, and laid his mountains and his heritage waste for the dragons of the wilderness.

Romans 9:13
As it is written, Jacob have I loved, but Esau have I hated.

* * * * * * * *

Malachi 3:1
Behold, I will send my messenger, and he shall prepare the way before me: and the Lord, whom ye seek, shall suddenly come to his temple, even the messenger of the covenant, whom ye delight in: behold, he shall come, saith the LORD of hosts.

Matthew 11:10
For this is he, of whom it is written, Behold, I send my messenger before thy face, which shall prepare thy way before thee.

Mark 1:2
As it is written in the prophets, Behold, I send my messenger before thy face, which shall prepare thy way before thee.

Luke 1:76
And thou, child, shalt be called the prophet of the Highest: for thou shalt go before the face of the Lord to prepare his ways.

Luke 7:27
This is he, of whom it is written, Behold, I send my messenger before thy face, which shall prepare thy way before thee.

* * * * * * * *

Malachi 4:5,6
Behold, I will send you Elijah the prophet before the coming of the great and dreadful day of the LORD: And he shall turn the heart of the fathers to the children, and the heart of the children to their fathers, lest I come and smite the earth with a curse.

Luke 1:17
And he shall go before him in the spirit and power of Elias, to turn the hearts of the fathers to the children, and the disobedient to the wisdom of the just; to make ready a people prepared for the Lord.

NOTES

MARILYN HICKEY BIBLE ENCOUNTER

SEEING JESUS IN THE NEW TESTAMENT

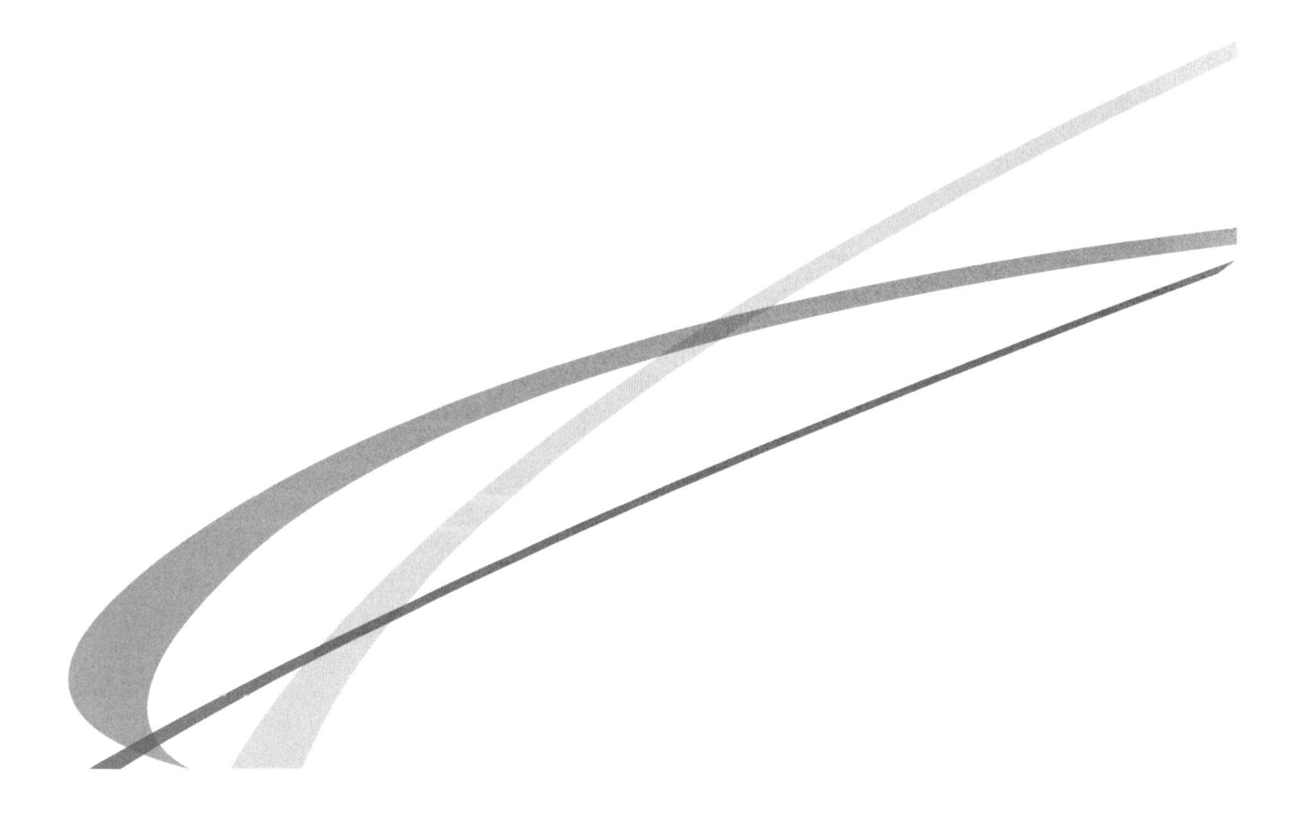

The Old Testament writings are an integrated part of the progressive revelation of redemption. It is estimated that there are about 300 direct quotations from the Old Testament in the New Testament. This means that the New Testament writers regarded the Christian religion as having its roots in the Old Testament.

The two Testaments are one revelation, and in both there is a single organic movement. The two dispensations are a unity. God divinely planned this from the beginning: the Old Testament quotations in the New Testament make this clear. The Bible is one because the history out of which it grew is one. The history is one because God is in the history, and God is one. This is made unmistakably plain in the epistle to the Hebrew (Hebrews 1:2).

The Old Testament was our Lord's Bible. Jesus quoted directly from 14 of these books. He quotes primarily from the books of Deuteronomy, Psalms, and Isaiah. Jesus made the assaults on the enemy from Deuteronomy (Matthew 4:1-11). He opened His ministry at Nazareth by quoting from a passage in Isaiah (Luke 4:14-19). And He quoted from the Psalms as He hung on the Cross (Mark 15:34). Christ laid great stress on the fulfillment of the prophecies of the Old Testament.

The New Testament is made up of 27 books and records the coming of Jesus Christ. There are 5 books of history (the 4 gospels and Acts), 21 epistles (Romans-Jude), and 1 book of prophecy (Revelation). They were written by eight or nine authors.

We will be looking at the synoptic gospels first. *Synoptic* comes from the two words, *sun opsis*, which means "to see together." The gospel of John is not included as a synoptic gospel because its presentation of Jesus is so different from the other three gospels. The first three gospels "see together" but each has a little different view of Jesus in His ministry.

Matthew depicts Jesus as a lion and shows Him as a coming King – the King of all kings. Mark depicts Him as an ox, symbolic of a servant – the One who came to be the Son of Man and came to be the servant of man. Luke depicts Jesus as a man. Jesus was tempted in all ways as we are; yet He did not yield to temptation. He was the perfect man. John depicts Him as an eagle, the Son of God, the divine One, the One Who lived high above all circumstances. The gospel writers all pictured Jesus from a different viewpoint, but each writer pictured Him as the one Lord of us all.

Sometimes we need to be the king of the situation. Jesus made us to be kings and priests in this life, but we always need to be servants. The apostle Paul said, ***"Let this mind be in you, which was also in Christ Jesus"*** (Philippians 2:5). That mind was the mind of a servant. We are to be serving men and women on the earth so that others can relate to us.

When we become so holy that sinners are afraid of us, afraid to talk to us and relate to us, we have lost our ability to witness and testify. Although we must relate to others, the Spirit of God in us causes us to soar high above our circumstances because we have world-overcoming faith.

NOTES

MATTHEW

JESUS: THE UNDISPUTED MESSIAH					
GENEALOGY & CHILDHOOD	**KINGDOM AT HAND**	**WITHDRAWL OF THE KING**	**REJECTION OF THE KING**	**PROPHECIES OF THE KING**	**FINAL DAYS**
Virgin birth: **1,2**	Early ministry: **3-13**	Teaching great doctrines: **14-18**	Jesus' last week: **19-23**	Climactic events: **24,25**	Fulfilling covenants: **26-28**
LOCATION: Bethlehem	Galilee	Galilee	Jerusalem	Jerusalem	Judea
OVERVIEW: Matthew - who would likely be an accountant or a banker today – sets out to connect the Old Testament prophecies concerning the Messiah with the life story of Jesus.					
TIME: About thirty-four years dated from around 4 B.C.					

FAST FACTS

AUTHOR AND SETTING:

Matthew, Israel

PURPOSE:

Matthew carefully documented the Messiahship of Jesus in His fulfillment of Old Testament prophecies. His purpose was to teach Jews everywhere that Jesus of Nazareth was the promised Messiah.

SEEING JESUS:

Matthew presents Jesus as the promised King of the Jews.

THEME VERSE:

Matthew 3:2,3

NOTES

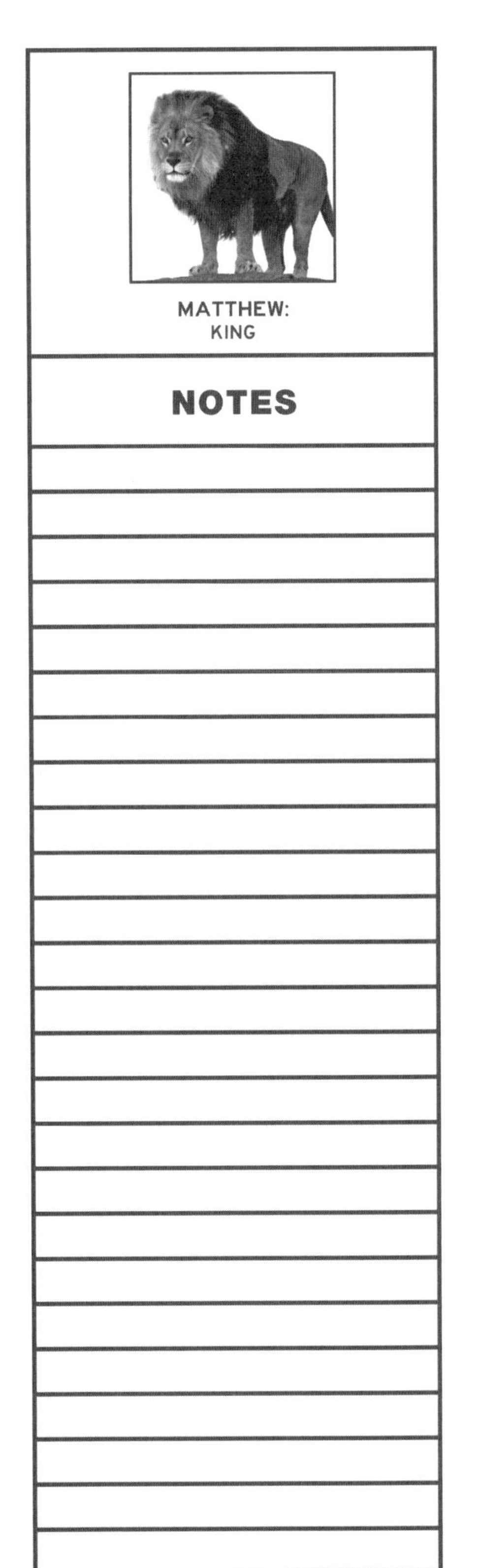

SEEING JESUS IN MATTHEW

AUTHOR & SETTING

Matthew means "the gift of Jehovah" and is the equivalent of the Greek *Theodore*. Before the call of Matthew to his apostolic office, his name was Levi. He was a customs' officer in the territory of Herod Antipas. As a Roman tax man, Matthew must have had some education and must have been acquainted with the Aramaic and Greek languages.

It was while Matthew was sitting at the toll office near Capernaum on the great west road from Damascus to the Mediterranean that Jesus called him. It is likely that the name *Levi* was changed to *Matthew* after Jesus called him. *Levi* was probably his Jewish name and *Matthew* was his Christian name (a name change similar to Simon Peter).

After he became an apostle, Matthew entertained Jesus at a feast where other invited guests included tax collectors and some persons who were regarded as sinners (Matthew 9:9-13). This event led Jesus to utter memorable words on self-righteousness, fasting and feasting, and the old and new dispensations.

OVERVIEW

Matthew's main themes are (1) the Messiah, (2) Israel, (3) the law, (4) the kingdom, and (5) prophecy. He presents four discourses of Jesus which end with the formula *"...when Jesus had finished..."* (Matthew 7:28, 13:53, 19:1 and 26:1). A fifth discourse in Matthew 23 does not follow the same formula.

Matthew, Mark, and Luke are considered the *syncoptic gospels* because of their similarities. The gospel of John presents a different look at Jesus. Matthew's intent was to teach Jews everywhere that Jesus of Nazareth was the promised Messiah. *Messiah* in Hebrew and *Christ* in the Greek mean "anointed." It was expected that the Messiah would unite in Himself the three important offices into which a member was inducted by the ceremonial function of pouring oil - namely the prophetic, the priestly, and the regal (prophet, priest, and king):

"And Jehu the son of Nimshi shalt thou anoint to be king over Israel: and Elisha the son of Shaphat of Abelmeholah shalt thou anoint to be prophet in thy room" **(I Kings 19:16).**

"And thou shalt anoint them, as thou didst anoint their father, that they may minister unto me in the priest's office: for their anointing shall surely be an everlasting priesthood throughout their generations" **(Exodus 40:15)**

"Then Samuel took a vial of oil, and poured it upon his head, and kissed him, and said, Is it not because the LORD hath anointed thee to be captain over his inheritance?" **(1 Samuel 10:1).**

Matthew's gospel shows that these hopes were fulfilled in Jesus. The genealogy (Matthew 1) shows His royal descent. The magi were looking for a king (Matthew 2:1,2). *Matthew* shows Jesus' prophetic ministry, His atoning death as a priest (His sacrifice), and His kingly anointing.

SEEING JESUS IN MATTHEW

In *Matthew* we behold Jesus as Israel's promised Messiah and King. Matthew quotes extensively from the Old Testament to prove that Jesus fulfills the prophecies concerning the promised Savior of the Jews.

THEME VERSE

"And saying, Repent ye: for the kingdom of heaven is at hand. For this is he that was spoken of by the prophet Esaias, saying, The voice of one crying in the wilderness, Prepare ye the way of the Lord, make his paths straight" **(Matthew 3:2,3).**

OUTLINE

(Refer to maps on pages A13 and A14 in the APPENDIX)

I. **GENEALOGY, BIRTH, AND CHILDHOOD OF THE KING –** MATTHEW 1,2

   A. **Virgin Birth Prophesied:**

      1. *"Therefore the Lord himself shall give you a sign; Behold, a virgin shall conceive, and bear a son, and shall call his name Immanuel"* **(Isaiah 7:14).**

      2. *"Behold, a virgin shall be with child, and shall bring forth a son, and they shall call his name Emmanuel, which being interpreted is, God with us"* **(Matthew 1:23)**

   B. **The Wise Men Arrive After a Period of Time.**

   C. **Flight Into Egypt**

II. **THE KINGDOM AT HAND -** MATTHEW 3-13

   A. **John the Baptist Declared Jesus King. Jesus was by Himself in the beginning of His ministry and later was accompanied by his disciples:**

      1. *"From that time Jesus began to preach, and to say, Repent: for the kingdom of heaven is at hand"* **(Matthew 4:17).**

   B. **The Laws of the Kingdom (Principles of Living) -** Matthew 5-7

   C. **Miracles Begin To Follow the King -** Matthew 8,9

   D. **Messengers for the Kingdom Sent Forth -** Matthew 10

   E. **Messengers Announce His Credentials -** Matthew 11, 12

   F. **Rejection of the King Foretold:**

      1. *"But the Pharisees said, He casteth out devils through the prince of the devils"* **(Matthew 9:34).**

      2. **Attack Intensified -** Matthew 12:24

   G. **Parables of the King -** Matthew 13

NOTES

NOTES

1. *"He answered and said unto them, Because it is given unto you to know the mysteries of the kingdom of heaven, but to them it is not given"* **(Matthew 13:11).**

2. **Chapter 13 closes with His rejection at Nazareth.**

III. **WITHDRAWAL OF THE KING IN VIEW OF HIS COMING REJECTION -** MATTHEW 14-18

A. **The Death of John the Baptist: this led Christ to retire from His ministry in the cities.**

1. **He fed 4000 (four gospels) -** Matthew 14:15-21.
2. **He warned against leaven -** Matthew 16:12.
3. **The great confession:**

a. *"And Simon Peter answered and said, "Thou art the Christ, the Son of the living God"* **(Matthew 16:16).**

b. Jesus announced His purpose to build His Church and predicted His death and Resurrection.

4. **The Transfiguration and coming millennial kingdom -** Matthew 17:1-13.
5. **He announced impending death -** Matthew 17:22, 23.
6. **He taught humility and forgiveness -** Matthew 18.

IV. **APPROACH OF KING TOWARD OFFICIAL REJECTION -** MATTHEW 19-23

A. **On the way to Jerusalem He Predicted His Death on the Cross -** Matthew 20:18,19.

B. **His Entrance Into the City (His Last Week) -** Matthew 21.

C. **He Answered Questions From Critics and Asked His Own Questions -** Matthew 22:41-46.

D. **Sharp Denunciation of Scribes and Pharisees as Hypocrites -** Matthew 23

1. **Sad lament over city of Jerusalem -** Matthew 23:37-39

V. **PROPHECIES OF THE KING –** MATTHEW 24,25

VI. **ARREST, TRIAL, DEATH, BURIAL, AND RESURRECTION OF THE KING -** MATTHEW 26-28

A. **Coming Forth From the Grave, He Fulfilled Both the Davidic and Abrahamic Covenants.**

B. **Gospel Closes With the Great Commission -** Matthew 28:18-20.

THE OLD TESTAMENT QUOTED IN MATTHEW.

Matthew 1:23
Behold, a virgin shall be with child, and shall bring forth a son, and they shall call his name Emmanuel, which being interpreted is, God with us.

Isaiah 7:14
Therefore the Lord himself shall give you a sign; Behold, a virgin shall conceive, and bear a son, and shall call his name Immanuel.

* * * * * * * * * *

Matthew 2:6
And thou Bethlehem, in the land of Juda, art not the least among the princes of Juda; for out of thee shall come a Governor, that shall rule my people Israel.

Micah 5:2
But thou, Bethlehem Ephratah, though thou be little among the thousands of Judah, yet out of thee shall he come forth unto me that is to be ruler in Israel; whose goings forth have been from of old, from everlasting.

* * * * * * * * * *

Matthew 2:15
And was there until the death of Herod; that it might be fulfilled which was spoken of the Lord by the prophet, saying, Out of Egypt have I called my son.

Hosea 11:1
When Israel was a child, then I loved him, and called my son out of Egypt.

* * * * * * * * * *

Matthew 2:18

In Rama was there a voice heard, lamentation, and weeping, and great mourning, Rachel weeping for her children, and would not be comforted, because they are not.

Jeremiah 31:15
Thus saith the LORD; A voice was heard in Ramah, lamontation, and bitter weeping; Rahel weeping for her children refused to be comforted for her children, because they were not.

* * * * * * * * * *

Matthew 3:3 (Mark 1:3; Luke 3:4; John 1:23)
For this is he that was spoken of by the prophet Esaias, saying, The voice of one crying in the wilderness, Prepare ye the way of the Lord, make his paths straight.

Isaiah 40:3
The voice of him that crieth in the wilderness, Prepare ye the way of the LORD, make straight in the desert a highway for our God.

* * * * * * * * * *

Matthew 4:4 (Luke 4:4)
But he answered and said, It is written, Man shall not live by bread alone, but by every word that proceedeth out of the mouth of God.

Deuteronomy 8:3
And he humbled thee, and suffered thee to hunger, and fed thee with manna, which thou knewest not, neither did thy fathers know; that he might make thee know that man doth not live by bread only, but by every word that proceedeth out of the mouth of the LORD doth man live.

* * * * * * * * * *

Matthew 4:6 (Luke 4:10,11)
And saith unto him, If thou be the Son of God, cast thyself down: for it is written, He shall give his angels charge concerning thee: and in their hands they shall bear thee up, lest at any time thou dash thy foot against a stone.

Psalms 91:11,12
For he shall give his angels charge over thee, to keep thee in all thy ways. They shall bear thee up in their hands, lest thou dash thy foot against a stone.

* * * * * * * * * *

Matthew 4:7 (Luke 4:12)
Jesus said unto him, It is written again, Thou shalt not tempt the Lord thy God.

Deuteronomy 6:16
Ye shall not tempt the LORD your God, as ye tempted him in Massah.

* * * * * * * * * *

Matthew 4:10 (Luke 4:8)
Then saith Jesus unto him, Get thee hence, Satan: for it is written, Thou shalt worship the Lord thy God, and him only shalt thou serve.

Deuteronomy 6:13
Thou shalt fear the LORD thy God, and serve him, and shalt swear by his name.

* * * * * * * * * *

Matthew 4:15,16 (Luke 1:79)
The land of Zabulon, and the land of Nephthalim, by the way of the sea, beyond Jordan, Galilee of the Gentiles; The people which sat in darkness saw great light; and to them which sat in the region and shadow of death light is sprung up.

Isaiah 9:1,2
Nevertheless the dimness shall not be such as was in her vexation, when at the first he lightly afflicted the land of Zebulun and the land of Naphtali, and afterward did more grievously afflict her by the way of the sea, beyond Jordan, in Galilee of the nations. The people that walked in darkness have seen a great light: they that dwell in the land of the shadow of death, upon them hath the light shined.

* * * * * * * * * *

Matthew 5:21 (Matthew 19:18; Mark 10:19; Luke 18:20; Romans 13:9; James 2:11)
Ye have heard that it was said by them of old time, Thou shalt not kill; and whosever shall kill shall be in danger of the judgment.

Exodus 20:13
Thou shalt not kill.

Deuteronomy 5:17
Thou shalt not kill.

* * * * * * * * * *

Matthew 5:27 (Matthew 19:18; Mark 10:19; Luke 18:20; Romans 13:9; James 2:11)
Ye have heard that it was said by them of old time, Thou shalt not commit adultery.

Exodus 20:14
Thou shalt not commit adultery.

Deuteronomy 5:18
Neither shalt thou commit adultery.

* * * * * * * * * *

Matthew 5:31 (Matthew 19:7; Mark 10:4)
It hath been said, Whosoever shall put away his wife, let him give her a writing of divorcement.

Deuteronomy 24:1
When a man hath taken a wife, and married her, and it come to pass that she find no favour in his eyes, because he hath found some uncleanness in her: then let him write her a bill of divorcement, and give it in her hand, and send her out of his house.

* * * * * * * * * *

Matthew 5:33
Again, ye have heard that it hath been said by them of old time, Thou shalt not forswear thyself, but shalt perform unto the Lord thine oaths.

Leviticus 19:12
And ye shall not swear by my name falsely, neither shalt thou profane the name of thy God: I am the LORD.

Numbers 30:2
If a man vow a vow unto the LORD, or swear an oath to bind his soul with a bond; he shall not break his word, he shall do according to all that proceedeth out of his mouth.

Deuteronomy 23:21
When thou shalt vow a vow unto the LORD thy God, thou shall not slack to pay it: for the LORD thy God will surely require it of thee; and it would be sin in thee.

* * * * * * * * * *

Matthew 5:35
Nor by the earth; for it is his footstool: neither by Jerusalem; for it is the city of the great King.

Isaiah 66:1
Thus saith the LORD, The heaven is my throne, and the earth is my footstool: where is the house that ye build unto me? and where is the place of my rest?

Psalms 48:2
Beautiful for situation, the joy of the whole earth, is mount Zion, on the sides of the north, the city of the great King.

* * * * * * * * * *

Matthew 5:38
Ye have heard that it hath been said, An eye for an eye, and a tooth for a tooth.

Exodus 21:24
Eye for eye, tooth for tooth, hand for hand, foot for foot.

Leviticus 24:20
Breach for breach, eye for eye, tooth for tooth: as he hath caused a blemish in a man, so shall it be done to him again.

Deuteronomy 19:21
And thine eye shall not pity; but life shall go for life, eye for eye, tooth for tooth, hand for hand, foot for foot.

* * * * * * * * * *

Matthew 5:43 (Matthew 19:19, 22:39, Mark 12:33; Luke 10:27; Romans 13:9; Galatians 5:14; James 2:8)
Ye have heard that it hath been said, "Thou shalt love thy neighbour, and hate thine enemy.

Leviticus 19:18
Thou shalt not avenge, nor bear any grudge against the children of thy people, but thou shalt love thy neighbour as thyself: I am the LORD.

* * * * * * * * * *

Matthew 7:23 (Luke 13:27)
And then will I profess unto them, I never knew you: depart from me, ye that work iniquity.

Psalms 6:8
Depart from me, all ye workers of iniquity; for the LORD hath heard the voice of my weeping.

Matthew 8:17
That it might be fulfilled which was spoken by Esaias the prophet, saying, Himself took our infirmities, and bare our sicknesses.

Isaiah 53:4
Surely he hath borne our griefs, and carried our sorrows: yet we did esteem him stricken, smitten of God, and afflicted.

* * * * * * * * * *

Matthew 9:13 (Matthew 12:7)
But go ye and learn what that meaneth, I will have mercy, and not sacrifice: for I am not come to call the righteous, but sinners to repentance.

Hosea 6:6
For I desired mercy, and not sacrifice; and the knowledge of God more than burnt offerings.

* * * * * * * * * *

Matthew 10:35,36
For I am come to set a man at variance against his father, and the daughter against her mother, and the daughter in law against her mother in law. And a man's foes shall be they of his own household.

Micah 7:6
For the son dishonoureth the father, the daughter riseth up against her mother, the daughter in law against her mother in law; a man's enemies are the men of his own house.

* * * * * * * * * *

Matthew 11:5 (Luke 4:18,19, 7:22)
The blind receive their sight, and the lame walk, the lepers are cleansed, and the deaf hear, the dead are raised up, and the poor have the gospel preached to them.

Isaiah 61:1
The Spirit of the Lord God is upon me; because the LORD hath anointed me to preach good tidings unto the meek; he hath sent me to bind up the brokenhearted, to proclaim liberty to the captives, and the opening of the prison to them that are bound.

* * * * * * * * * *

Matthew 11:10; (Luke 7:27)
For this is he, of whom it is written, Behold, I send my messenger before thy face, which shall prepare thy way before thee.

Malachi 3:1
Behold, I will send my messenger, and he shall prepare the way before me: and the Lord, whom ye seek, shall suddenly come to his temple, even the messenger of the covenant, whom ye delight in: behold, he shall come, saith the LORD of hosts.

* * * * * * * * * *

Matthew 11:29
Take my yoke upon you, and learn of me; for I am meek and lowly in heart: and ye shall find rest unto your souls.

Jeremiah 6:16
Thus saith the LORD, Stand ye in the ways, and see, and ask for the old paths, where is the good way, and walk therein, and ye shall find rest for your souls. But they said, We will not walk therein.

* * * * * * * * * *

Matthew 12:7 (Matthew 9:13)
But if he had known what this meaneth, I will have mercy, and not sacrifice, ye would not have condemned the guiltless.

Hosea 6:6
For I desired mercy, and not sacrifice; and the knowledge of God more than burnt offerings.

* * * * * * * * * *

Matthew 12:18-21 (Romans 15:12)
Behold my servant, whom I have chosen; my beloved, in whom my soul is well pleased: I will put my spirit upon him, and he shall shew judgment to the Gentiles. He shall not strive, nor cry; neither shall any man hear his voice in the streets. A bruised reed shall he not break, and smoking flax shall he not quench, till he send forth judgment unto victory. And in his name shall the Gentiles trust.

Isaiah 42:1-4
Behold my servant, whom, I uphold; mine elect, in whom my soul delighteth; I have put my spirit upon him: he shall bring forth judgment to the Gentiles. He shall not cry, nor lift up, nor cause his voice to be heard in the street. A bruised reed shall he not break, and the smoking flax shall he not quench: he shall bring forth judgment unto truth. He shall not fail nor be discouraged, till he have set judgment in the earth: and the isles shall wait for his law.

* * * * * * * * * *

Matthew 12:40
For as Jonas was three days and three nights in the whale's belly; so shall the Son of man be three days and three nights in the heart of the earth.

Jonah 1:17
Now the LORD had prepared a great fish to swallow up Jonah. And Jonah was in the belly of the fish three days and three nights.

* * * * * * * * * *

Matthew 13:14,15 (Mark 4:12; Luke 8:10; John 12:40; Acts 28:26,27)
And in them is fulfilled the prophecy of Esaias, which saith, By hearing ye shall hear, and shall not understand; and seeing ye shall see, and shall not perceive: For this people's heart is waxed gross, and their ears are dull of hearing, and their eyes they have closed; lest at any time they should see with their eyes, and hear with their ears, and should understand with their heart, and should be converted, and I should heal them.

Jeremiah 5:21
Hear now this, O foolish people, and without understanding; which have eyes, and see not; which have ears, and hear not.

Isaiah 6:9,10
And he said, Go, and tell this people, Hear ye indeed, but understand not; and see ye indeed, but perceive not. Make the heart of this people fat, and make their ears heavy, and shut their eyes; lest they see with their eyes, and hear with their ears, and understand with their heart, and convert, and be healed.

Ezekiel 12:2
Son of man, thou dwellest in the midst of a rebellious house, which have eyes to see, and see not; they have ears to hear, and hear not: for they are a rebellious house.

* * * * * * * * * *

Matthew 13:32 (Mark 4:32; Luke 13:19)
Which indeed is the least of all seeds: but when it is grown, it is the greatest among herbs, and becometh a tree, so that the birds of the air come and lodge in the branches thereof.

Ezekiel 17:23
In the mountain of the height of Israel will I plant it: and it shall bring forth boughs, and bear fruit, and be a goodly cedar: and under it shall dwell all fowl of every wing; in the shadow of the branches thereof shall they dwell.

Psalms 104:12
By them shall the fowls of the heaven have their habitation, which sing among the branches.

* * * * * * * * * *

Matthew 13:35
That it might be fulfilled which was spoken by the prophet, saying, I will open my mouth in parables; I will utter things which have been kept secret from the foundation of the world.

Psalms 78:2
I will open my mouth in a parable: I will utter dark sayings of old.

* * * * * * * * * *

Matthew 13:43
Then shall the righteous shine forth as the sun in the kingdom of their Father. Who hath ears to hear, let him hear.

Daniel 12:3
And they that be wise shall shine as the brightness of the firmament; and they that turn many to righteousness as the stars for ever and ever.

* * * * * * * * * *

Matthew 15:4 (Matthew 19:19; Mark 7:10; 10:19; Luke 18:20; Ephesians 6:2,3)
For God commanded, saying, Honour thy father and mother: and, He that curseth father or mother, let him die the death.

Exodus 20:12
Honour thy father and thy mother: that thy days may be long upon the land which the LORD thy God giveth thee.

Deuteronomy 5:16
Honour thy father and thy mother, as the LORD thy God hath commanded thee; that thy days may be prolonged, and that it may go well with thee, in the land which the LORD thy God giveth thee.

Exodus 21:17
And he that curseth his father, or his mother, shall surely be put to death.

* * * * * * * * * *

Matthew 15:8,9 (Mark 7:6,7)
This people draweth nigh unto me with their mouth, and honoureth me with their lips; but their heart is far from me. But in vain they do worship me, teaching for doctrines the commandments of men.

Isaiah 29:13
Wherefore the Lord said, Forasmuch as this people draw near me with their mouth, and with their lips do honour me, but have removed their heart far from me, and their fear toward me is taught by the precept of men.

* * * * * * * * * *

Matthew 16:27 (Romans 2:6)
For the Son of man shall come in the glory of his Father with his angels; and then he shall reward every man according to his works.

Psalms 62:12
Also unto thee, O Lord, belongeth mercy: for thou renderest to every man according to his work.

Proverbs 24:12
If thou sayest, Behold, we knew it not; doth not he that pondereth the heart consider it? and he that keepeth thy soul, doth not he know it? and shall not he render to every man according to his works?

* * * * * * * * * *

Matthew 18:16 (II Corinthians 13:1)
But if he will not hear thee, then take with thee one or two more, that in the mouth of two or three witnesses every word may be established.

Deuteronomy 19:15
One witness shall not rise up against a man for any iniquity, or for any sin, in any sin that he sinneth: at the mouth of two witnesses, or at the mouth of three witnesses, shall the matter be established.

* * * * * * * * * *

Matthew 19:4 (Mark 10:6)
And he answered and said unto them, Have ye not read, that he which made them at the beginning made them male and female.

Genesis 1:27
So God created man in his own image, in the image of God created he him; male and female created he them.

Genesis 5:2
Male and female created he them; and blessed them, and called their name Adam, in the day when they were created.

* * * * * * * * * *

Matthew 19:5 (Mark 10:7,8; I Corinthians 6:16; Ephesians 5:31)
And said, For this cause shall a man leave father and mother, and shall cleave to his wife: and they twain shall be one flesh?

Genesis 2:24
Therefore shall a man leave his father and his mother, and shall cleave unto his wife: and they shall be one flesh.

* * * * * * * * * *

Matthew 19:7 (Matthew 5:31; Mark 10:4)
They say unto him, Why did Moses then command to give a writing of divorcement, and to put her away?

Deuteronomy 24:1
When a man hath taken a wife, and married her, and it come to pass that she find no favour in his eyes, because he hath found some uncleanness in her: then let him write her a bill of divorcement, and give it in her hand, and send her out of his house.

* * * * * * * * * *

Matthew 19:18,19 (Matthew 5:21,27,43, 15:4, 22:39; Mark 7:10, 10:19, 12:31; Luke 18:20; Romans 13:9; James 2:8,11; Galatians 5:14; Ephesians 6:2,3)
He saith unto him, Which? Jesus said, Thou shalt do no murder, Thou shalt not commit adultery, Thou shalt not steal, Thou shalt not bear false witness, Honour thy father and thy mother: and, Thou shalt love thy neighbour as myself.

Exodus 20:12-16
Honour thy father and thy mother: that thy days may be long upon the land which the LORD thy God giveth thee. Thou shalt not kill, Thou shalt not commit adultery. Thou shalt not steal. Thou shalt not bear false witness against thy neighbour.

Leviticus 19:18
Thou shalt not avenge, nor bear any grudge against the children of thy people, but thou shalt love thy neighbour as thyself: I am the LORD.

Deuteronomy 5:16-20
Honour thy father and thy mother, as the LORD thy God hath commanded thee; that thy days may be prolonged, and that it may go well with thee, in the land which the LORD thy God giveth thee. Thou shalt not kill. Neither shalt thou commit adultery. Neither shalt thou steal. Neither shalt thou bear false witness against thy neighbour.

* * * * * * * * * *

Matthew 21:5 (John 12:15)
Tell ye the daughter of Sion, Behold, thy King cometh unto thee, meek, and sitting upon an ass, and a colt the foal of an ass.

Isaiah 62:11
Behold, the LORD hath proclaimed unto the end of the world, Say ye to the daughter of Zion, Behold, thy salvation cometh; behold, his reward is with him, and his work before him.

Zechariah 9:9
Rejoice greatly, O daughter of Zion; shout, O daughter of Jerusalem: behold, thy King cometh unto thee: he is just, and having salvation; lowly, and riding upon an ass, and upon a colt the foal of an ass.

* * * * * * * * * *

Matthew 21:9 (Matthew 23:39; Mark 11:9; Luke 13;35, 19:38; John 12:13)
And the multitudes that went before, and that followed, cried, saying, Hosanna to the son of David: Blessed is he that cometh in the name of the Lord; Hosanna in the highest.

Psalms 118:26
Blessed be he that cometh in the name of the LORD: we have blessed you out of the house of the LORD.

* * * * * * * * * *

Matthew 21:13 (Mark 11:17; Luke 19:46)
And said unto them, It is written, My house shall be called the house of prayer; but ye have made it a den of thieves.

Isaiah 56:7
Even them will I bring to my holy mountain, and make them joyful in my house of prayer: their burnt offerings and their sacrifices shall be accepted upon mine altar; for mine house shall be called an house of prayer for all people.

Jeremiah 7:11
Is this house, which is called by my name, become a den of robbers in your eyes? Behold, even I have seen it, saith the LORD.

* * * * * * * * * *

Matthew 21:16
And said unto him, Hearest thou what these say? And Jesus saith unto them, Yea; have ye never read, Out of the mouth of babes and sucklings thou hast perfected praise?

Psalms 8:2
Out of the mouth of babes and sucklings hast thou ordained strength because of thine enemies, that thou mightest still the enemy and the avenger.

* * * * * * * * * *

Matthew 21:33 (Mark 12:1)
Hear another parable: There was a certain householder, which planted a vineyard, and hedged it round about, and digged a winepress in it, and built a tower, and let it out to husbandmen, and went into a far country.

Isaiah 5:1,2
Now will I sing to my wellbeloved a song of my beloved touching his vineyard. My wellbeloved hath a vineyard in a very fruitful hill: And he fenced it, and gathered out the stones thereof, and planted it with the choicest vine, and built a tower in the midst of it, and also made a winepress therein: and he looked that it should bring forth grapes, and it brought forth wild grapes.

* * * * * * * * * *

Matthew 21:42 (Mark 12:10,11; Luke 20:17; Acts 4:11; I Peter 2:7)
Jesus saith unto them, Did ye never read in the scriptures, The stone which the builders rejected, the same is become the head of the corner: this is the Lord's doing, and it is marvelous in our eyes?

Psalms 118:22,23
The stone which the builders refused is become the head stone of the corner. This is the LORD's doing, it is marvelous in our eyes.

* * * * * * * * * *

Matthew 22:24 (Mark 12:19; Luke 20:28)
Saying, Master, Moses said, If a man die, having no children, his brother shall marry his wife, and raise up seed unto his brother.

Deuteronomy 25:5
If brethren dwell together, and one of them die, and have no child, the wife of the dead shall not marry without unto a stranger: her husband's brother shall go in unto her, and take her to him to wife, and perform the duty of an husband's brother unto her.

* * * * * * * * * *

Matthew 22:32 (Mark, 12:26; Luke 20:37; Acts 7:32)
I am the God of Abraham, and the God of Isaac, and the God of Jacob? God is not the God of the dead, but of the living.

Exodus 3:6
Moreover he said, I am the God of thy father, the God of Abraham, the God of Isaac, and the God of Jacob. And Moses hid his face; for he was afraid to look upon God.

Exodus 3:15
And God said moreover unto Moses, Thus shalt thou say unto the children of Israel, The Lord God of your fathers, the God of Abraham, the God of Isaac, and the God of Jacob, hath sent me unto you: this is my name for ever, and this is my memorial unto all generations.

* * * * * * * * * *

Matthew 22:37 (Mark 12:29,30,32,33; Luke 10:27)
Jesus said unto him, Thou shalt love the Lord thy God with all thy heart, and with all thy soul, and with all thy mind.

Deuteronomy 6:5
And thou shalt love the LORD thy God with all thine heart, and with all thy soul, and with all thy might.

* * * * * * * * * *

Matthew 22:39 (Matthew 19:19; Mark 12:3,33; Luke 10:27; Romans 13:9; Galatians 5:14; James 2:8)
And the second is like unto it, Thou shalt love thy neighbour as thyself.

Leviticus 19:18
Thou shalt not avenge, nor bear any grudge against the children of thy people, but thou shalt love thy neighbour as thyself: I am the LORD.

* * * * * * * * * *

Matthew 22:44 (Matthew 26:64; Mark 12:36, 14:62; Luke 20:42, 43, 22:69; Acts 2:34,35; Hebrews 1:13, 10:21,13)
The LORD said unto my Lord, Sit thou on my right hand, till I make thine enemies thy footstool?

Psalms 110:1
The LORD said unto my Lord, Sit thou at my right hand, until I make thine enemies thy footstool.

* * * * * * * * * *

Matthew 23:39 (Matthew 21:9; Mark 11:9; Luke 13:35, 19:38; John 12:13)
For I say unto you, Ye shall not see me henceforth, till ye shall say, Blessed is he that cometh in the name of the Lord.

Psalms 118:26
Blessed be he that cometh in the name of the LORD; we have blessed you out of the house of the LORD.

* * * * * * * * * *

Matthew 24:15 (Mark 13:14)
When ye therefore shall see the abomination of desolation, spoken of by Daniel the prophet, stand in the holy place, (whoso readeth, let him understand.)

Daniel 11:31
And arms shall stand on his part, and they shall pollute the sanctuary of strength, and shall take away the daily sacrifice, and they shall place the abomination that maketh desolate.

Daniel 12:11
And from the time that the daily sacrifice shall be taken away, and the abomination that maketh desolate set up, there shall be a thousand two hundred and ninety days.

* * * * * * * * * *

Matthew 24:29 (Mark 13:24,25)
Immediately after the tribulation of those days shall the sun be darkened, and the moon shall not give her light, and the stars shall fall from heaven, and the powers of the heavens shall be shaken.

Joel 2:10,31
The earth shall quake before them; the heavens shall tremble: the sun and the moon shall be dark, and the stars shall withdraw their shining: The sun shall be turned into darkness, and the moon into blood, before the great and terrible day of the LORD come.

* * * * * * * * * *

Matthew 24:31
And he shall send his angels with a great sound of a trumpet, and they shall gather together his elect from the four winds, from one end of heaven to the other.

Isaiah 27:13
And it shall come to pass in that day, that the great trumpet shall be blown, and they shall come which were ready to perish in the land of Assyria, and the outcasts in the land of Egypt, and shall worship the LORD in the holy mount at Jerusalem.

Joel 2:1
Blow ye the trumpet in Zion, and sound an alarm in my holy mountain: let all the inhabitants of the land tremble: for the day of the LORD cometh, for it is nigh at hand.

Zechariah 2:6
Ho, ho, come forth, and flee from the land of the north, saith the LORD: for I have spread you abroad as the four winds of the heaven, saith the LORD.

* * * * * * * * * *

Matthew 24:30 (Mark 13:26, 14:62; Luke 21:27; Revelation 1:7)
And then shall appear the sign of the Son of man in heaven: and then shall all the tribes of the earth mourn, and they shall see the Son of man coming in the clouds of heaven with power and great glory.

Daniel 7:13
I saw in the night visions, and, behold, one like the Son of man came with the clouds of heaven, and came to the Ancient of days, and they brought him near before him.

* * * * * * * * * *

Matthew 26:31 (Mark 14:27)
Then saith Jesus unto them, All ye shall be offended because of me this night; for it is written, I will smite the shepherd, and the sheep of the flock shall be scattered abroad.

Zechariah 13:7
Awake, O sword, against my shepherd, and against the man that is my fellow, saith the LORD of hosts: smite the shepherd, and the sheep shall be scattered: and I will turn mine hand upon the little ones.

* * * * * * * * * *

Matthew 26:64 (Matthew 22:44, 24:30; Mark 14:62; Luke 22:69)
Jesus saith unto him, Thou hast said: nevertheless I say unto you, Hereafter shall ye see the Son of man sitting on the right hand of power, and coming in the clouds of heaven.

Psalms 110:1
The LORD said unto my Lord, Sit thou at my right hand, until I make thine enemies thy footstool.

Daniel 7:13
I saw in the night visions, and, behold, one like the Son of man came with the clouds of heaven, and came to the Ancient of days, and they brought him near before him.

* * * * * * * * * *

Matthew 27:9,10
Then was fulfilled that which was spoken by Jeremy the prophet, saying, And they took the thirty pieces of silver, the price of him that was valued, whom they of the children of Israel did value.

Zechariah 11:12, 13
And I said unto them, If ye think good, give me my price; and if not, forbear. So they weighed for my price thirty pieces of silver. And the LORD said unto me, Cast it unto the potter: a goodly price that I was prised at of them. And I took the thirty pieces of silver, and cast them to the potter in the house of the LORD.

* * * * * * * * * *

Matthew 27:46 (Mark 15:34)
And about the ninth hour Jesus cried with a loud voice, saying, Eli, Eli, lama sabachthani? that is to say, My God, my God, why hast thou forsaken me?

Psalms 22:1
My God, my God, why hast thou forsaken me? Why art thou so far from helping me, and from the words of my roaring?

MARK

JESUS: THE SERVANT & SACRIFICE	
THE SON OF MAN MINISTERING	**THE SON OF MAN GIVING HIS LIFE**
John the Baptist: **1** Early ministry: **2-9**	En route to Jerusalem: **10** The final week: **11-15** Proclamation: **16**
LOCATION: Galilee & Perea	Judea & Jerusalem
OVERVIEW: Sayings & signs	Sufferings
TIME: Three-and-a-half years around A.D. 30	

FAST FACTS

AUTHOR AND SETTING:

Mark; Israel

PURPOSE:

The gospel of *Mark* was written primarily for gentile readers – particularly Roman readers. Mark desired to present Jesus as servant and sacrifice – Savior of all men.

SEEING JESUS:

Mark presents Jesus as the Son of man – ministering and giving His life as a ransom for many.

THEME VERSE:

Mark 10:45

NOTES

MARK:
SERVANT

NOTES

SEEING JESUS IN MARK

AUTHOR & SETTING

Mark means "a hammer." His gospel reflects that name as it is brief and very pointed. It is as though he wants to *hammer* the Word of God into us.

Mark's name occurs eight times in the New Testament - sometimes as Mark, or Marcus, or John-Mark. *John* was his Jewish name, and *Mark* was his Roman name.

Mark was the son of Mary, a woman of means, who lived in Jerusalem. This woman's home was the rendezvous of many Christians (Acts 12:12).

When Paul and Barnabas returned from Jerusalem to Antioch, Mark went with them (Acts 12:25). When these apostles went on their first missionary journey, they took Mark with them as a minister-attendant (Acts 13:5,13). When they reached Perga in Pamphylia, Mark left them and returned to Jerusalem.

Because of Mark's defection, Paul and Barnabas parted company when a second missionary journey was proposed, and Barnabas took Mark with him to Cyprus (Acts 15:33-39). Some years later Mark was with Peter at Babylon, which no doubt means Rome (I Peter 5:13).

Paul and Mark were reconciled, and Paul found Mark to be very profitable to him. Several years later Mark was again with Paul at Rome (Colossians 4:10,11). Finally, during his last Roman imprisonment, Paul asked Timothy to come to him and to bring Mark with him (II Timothy 4:11).

Mark was a cousin to Barnabas, and Peter was his spiritual father (Colossians 4:10; Philemon 24; I Peter 5:13).

OVERVIEW

The gospel of *Mark* was written primarily for gentile readers in general and Roman readers in particular. The Roman leaders are in view many times. Mark alone mentions Rufus and Simeon the Syrian, the father of Alexander. Mark adapts his gospel to the needs of Romans.

Matthew is adapted to the Jewish outlook, Luke to the Greek, and of course, Mark to the Roman. All three governments were based upon the idea of power; whereas, in Matthew the power of purpose is exalted, in Luke the power of thought is exalted, and in *Mark* the power of the will is exalted. These three powers answer to the outlook, respectively, of the Jew, the Greek, and the Roman.

The Romans were a people of action rather than of thought, and in addressing them Mark presents Christ as a mighty worker rather than a profound thinker. Jesus is the man who conquers by *doing*. There is in *Mark*, therefore, little discourse with much movement and accomplishment.

Three Greek words for *miracle* are used in the gospel of *Mark*:

Teras which means "a wonder":

*"For false Christs and false prophets shall rise, and shall shew signs and **wonders**, to seduce, if it were possible, even the elect"* **(Mark 13:22).**

Dunamis which means "miracle-working power":

*"And when the Sabbath day was come, he began to teach in the synagogue: and many hearing him were astonished, saying, From whence hath this man these things? and what wisdom is this which is given unto him, that even such **mighty** works are wrought by his hands?"* **(Mark 6:2).**

*"And he could there do no **mighty** work, save that he laid his hands upon a few sick folk, and healed them"* **(Mark 6:5).**

*"And king Herod heard of him; (for his name was spread abroad:) and he said, That John the Baptist was risen from the dead, and therefore **mighty** works do shew forth themselves in him"* **(Mark 6:14).**

Semelon which means "a sign":

*"And the Pharisees came forth, and began to question with him, seeking of him a **sign** from heaven, tempting him. And he sighed deeply in his spirit, and saith, Why doth this generation seek after a **sign**? Verily I say unto you, There shall no **sign** be given unto this generation"* **(Mark 8:11,12).**

*"And these **signs** shall follow them that believe; In my name shall they cast out devils; they shall speak with new tongues. And they went forth, and preached every where, the Lord working with them, and confirming the word with **signs** following. Amen"* **(Mark 16:17,20).**

There are three classifications of miracles in the gospels:

1. Miracles in the human realm:

a. The healing of the leper
b. The healing of the centurion's servant
c. The healing of Peter's mother-in-law
d. The healing of the woman with the issue of blood
e. The healing of the two blind men
f. The healing of the withered hand
g. The healing of the paralytic
h. The healing of blind Bartimaeus

NOTES

NOTES

2. **Miracles in the cosmic realm:**
   - a. Stilling of the tempest
   - b. Walking on the sea
   - c. Feeding of the 5000
   - d. Feeding of the 4000
   - e. Finding the coin in the fish's mouth
   - f. The withering of the fig tree

3. **Miracles in the spirit realm:**
   - a. Deliverance of the Gadarene demoniac
   - b. Deliverance of the blind and dumb demoniac
   - c. Deliverance of the lunatic boy
   - d. Deliverance of the Syrophenician girl
   - e. Deliverance of the dumb demoniac
   - f. The raising of Jairus' daughter

SEEING JESUS IN MARK

As the lion was the logo of Matthew, the logo of *Mark* is the ox - showing Jesus as the servant as well as the sacrifice. Mark 10:45 is the key verse which shows us *Mark's* presentation of the person and work of Jesus.

THEME VERSE

"For even the Son of man came not to be ministered unto, but to minister, and to give his life a ransom for many" **(Mark 10:45).**

OUTLINE

(Refer to maps on pages A13 and A14 in the APPENDIX)

I. **THE SON OF MAN MINISTERING -** MARK 1-9
   - A. **Much Space to Ministering in Gallilee**
     1. **John the Baptist**
     2. **Baptism of Jesus**
     3. **Temptation by Satan**
     4. **Call of Simon and Andrew**

II. **SON OF MAN GIVING HIS LIFE AS A RANSOM FOR MANY -** MARK 10-16
   - A. **On the Way to Jerusalem**
   - B. **The Final Week -** Mark 11
   - C. **His Proclamation to Every Creature -** Mark 16

THE OLD TESTAMENT QUOTED IN MARK.

Mark 1:2,3
(Matthew 3:3, 11:10; Luke 1:76, 3:4, 7:27, John 1:23)
As it is written in the prophets, Behold, I send my messenger before thy face, which shall prepare thy way before thee. The voice of one crying in the wilderness, Prepare ye the way of the Lord, make his paths straight.

Isaiah 40:3
The voice of him that crieth in the wilderness, Prepare ye the way of the LORD, make straight in the desert a highway for our God.

Malachi 3:1
Behold, I will send my messenger, and he shall prepare the way before me: and the Lord, whom ye seek, shall suddenly come to his temple, even the messenger of the covenant, whom ye delight in: behold, he shall come, saith the LORD of hosts.

* * * * * * * *

Mark 4:12 (Matthew 13;14,15; Luke 8:10; John 12:40; Acts 28:26,27)
That seeing they may see, and not perceive; and hearing they may hear, and not understand; lest at any time they should be converted, and their sins should be forgiven them.

Isaiah 6:9,10
And he said, Go, and tell this people, Hear ye indeed but understand not; and see ye indeed, but perceive not. Make the heart of this people fat, and make their ears heavy, and shut their eyes; lest they see with their eyes, and hear with their ears, and understand with their heart, and convert, and be healed.

Jeremiah 5:21
Hear now this, O foolish people, and without understanding; which have eyes, and see not; which have ears, and hear not.

Ezekiel 12:2
Son of man, thou dwellest in the midst of a rebellious house, which have eyes to see, and see not; they have ears to hear, and hear not: for they are a rebellious house.

* * * * * * * *

Mark 7:6,7 (Matthew 15:8,9)
He answered and said unto them, Well hath Esaias prophesied of you hypocrites, as it is written, This people honoureth me with their lips, but their heart is far from me. Howbeit in vain do they worship me, teaching for doctrines the commandments of men.

Isaiah 29:13
Wherefore the Lord said, Forasmuch as this people draw near me with their mouth, and with their lips do honour me, but have removed their heart far from me, and their fear toward me is taught by the precept of men.

* * * * * * * *

Mark 7:10 (Matthew 15:4, 19:19; Mark 10:19; Luke 18:20; Ephesians 6:2)
For Moses said, Honour thy father and thy mother; and, Whoso curseth father or mother, let him die the death.

Exodus 20:12
Honour thy father and thy mother: that thy days may be long upon the land which the LORD thy God giveth thee.

Exodus 21:17
And he that curseth his father, or his mother, shall surely be put to death.

Deuteronomy 5:16
Honour thy father and thy mother, as the LORD thy God hath commanded thee; that thy days may be prolonged, and that it may go well with thee, in the land which the LORD thy God giveth thee.

* * * * * * * *

Mark 8:18 (Matthew 13:14,15; Mark 4:12)
Having eyes, see ye not? and having ears, hear ye not? and do ye not remember?

Jeremiah 5:21
Hear now this, O foolish people, and without understanding; which have eyes, and see not; which have ears, and hear not.

Ezekiel 12:2
Son of man, thou dwellest in the midst of a rebellious house, which have eyes to see, and see not; they have ears to hear, and hear not: for they are a rebellious house.

Isaiah 6:9,10
And he said, Go, and tell this people, Hear ye indeed, but understand not; and see ye indeed, but perceive not Make the heart of this people fat, and make their ears heavy, and shut their eyes; lest they see

with their eyes, and hear with their ears, and understand with their heart, and convert, and be healed.

* * * * * * * *

Mark 9:44,46,48
Where their worm dieth not, and the fire is not quenched. Where their worm dieth not, and the fire is not quenched. Where their worm dieth not, and the fire is not quenched.

Isaiah 66:24
And they shall go forth, and look upon the carcases of the men that have transgressed against me: for their worm shall not die, neither shall their fire be quenched; and they shall be an abhorring unto all flesh.

* * * * * * * *

Mark 10:4 (Matthew 5:31, 19:7)
And they said, Moses suffered to write a bill of divorcement, and to put her away.

Deuteronomy 24:1
When a man hath taken a wife, and married her, and it come to pass that she find no favour in his eyes, because he hath found some uncleanness in her: then let him write her a bill of divorcement, and give it in her hand, and send her out of his house.

* * * * * * * *

Mark 10:6 (Matthew 19:4)
But from the beginning of the creation God made them male and female.

Genesis 1:27
So God created man in his own image, in the image of God created he him; male and female created he them.

Genesis 5:2
Male and female created he them; and blessed them, and called their name Adam, in the day when they were created.

* * * * * * * *

Mark 10:7,8 (Matthew 19:5; I Corinthians 6:16; Ephesians 5:31)
For this cause shall a man leave his father and mother, and cleave to his wife; And they twain shall be one flesh: so then they are no more twain, but one flesh.

Genesis 2:24
Therefore shall a man leave his father and his mother, and shall cleave unto his wife: and they shall be one flesh.

* * * * * * * *

Mark 10:19 (Matthew 5:21,27; 19:18,19; Luke 18:20; Romans 13:9; James 2:11)
Thou knowest the commandments, Do not commit adultery, Do not kill, Do not steal, Do not bear false witness, Defraud not, Honour thy father and mother.

Exodus 20:12-16
Honour thy father and thy mother: that thy days may be long upon the land which the LORD thy God giveth thee. Thou shalt not kill. Thou shalt not commit adultery. Thou shalt not steal. Thou shalt not bear false witness against thy neighbour.

Deuteronomy 5:16-20
Honor thy father and thy mother, as the LORD thy God hath commanded thee; that thy days may be prolonged, and that it may go well with thee, in the land which the LORD thy God giveth thee. Thou shalt not kill. Neither shalt thou commit adultery. Neither shalt thou steal. Neither shalt thou bear false witness against thy neighbour.

* * * * * * * *

Mark 11:9 (Matthew 21:9, 23:39; Luke 13:35, 19:38; John 12:13)
And they that went before, and they that followed, cried, saying, Hosanna; Blessed is he that cometh in the name of the Lord.

Psalms 118:26
Blessed be he that cometh in the name of the LORD: we have blessed you out of the house of the LORD.

* * * * * * * *

Mark 11:17 (Matthew 21:13; Luke 19:46)
And he taught, saying unto them, Is it not written, My house shall be called of all nations the house of prayer? but ye have made it a den of thieves.

Isaiah 56:7
Even them will I bring to my holy mountain, and make them joyful in my house of prayer: their burnt offerings and their sacrifices shall be accepted upon mine altar; for mine house shall be called an house of prayer for all people.

Jeremiah 7:11
Is this house, which is called by my name, become a den of robbers in your eyes? Behold, even I have seen it, saith the LORD.

* * * * * * * *

Mark 12:1 (Matthew 21:33)
And he began to speak unto them by parables. A certain man planted a vineyard, and set an hedge about it, and digged a place for the winefat, and built a tower, and let it out to husbandmen, and went into a far country.

Isaiah 5:1,2
Now will I sing to my wellbeloved a song of my beloved touching his vineyard. My wellbeloved hath a vineyard in a very fruitful hill: And he fenced it, and gathered out the stones thereof, and planted it with the choicest vine, and built a tower in the midst of it, and also made a winepress therein: and he looked that it should bring forth grapes, and it brought forth wild grapes.

* * * * * * * *

Mark 12:10,11 (Matthew 21:42; Luke 20:17; Act 4:11; I Peter 2:7)
And have ye not read this scripture; The stone which the builders rejected is become the head of the corner: This was the Lord's doing, and it is marvelous in our eyes?

Psalms 118:22,23
The stone which the builders refused is become the head stone of the corner. This is the LORD's doing; it is marvelous in our eyes.

* * * * * * * *

Mark 12:19 (Matthew 22:24; Luke 20:28)
Master, Moses wrote unto us, If a man's brother die, and leave his wife behind him, and leave no children, that his brother should take his wife, and raise up seed unto his brother.

Deuteronomy 25:5
If brethren dwell together, and one of them die, and have no child, the wife of the dead shall not marry without unto a stranger: her husband's brother shall go in unto her, and take her to him to wife, and perform the duty of an husband's brother unto her.

* * * * * * * *

Mark 12:26 (Matthew 22:32; Luke 20:37; Acts 7:32)
And as touching the dead, that they rise: have ye not read in the book of Moses, how in the bush God spake unto him, saying, I am the God of Abraham, and the God of Isaac, and the God of Jacob?

Exodus 3:6
Moreover he said, I am the God of thy father, the God of Abraham, the God of Isaac, and the God of Jacob. And Moses hid his face; for he was afraid to look upon God.

Exodus 3:15
And God said moreover unto Moses, Thus shalt thou say unto the children of Israel, The LORD God of your fathers, the God of Abraham, the God of Isaac, and the God of Jacob, hath sent me unto you: this is my name for ever, and this is my memorial unto all generations.

* * * * * * * *

Mark 12:29,30
(Matthew 22:37; Mark 12:32,33; Luke 10:27)
And Jesus answered him, The first of all the commandments is, Hear, O Israel; The Lord our God is one Lord: And thou shalt love the Lord thy God with all thy heart, and with all they soul, and with all thy mind, and with all thy strength: this is the first commandment.

Deuteronomy 6:4,5
Hear, O Israel: The LORD our God is one LORD: And thou shalt love the LORD thy God with all thine heart, and with all thy soul, and with all thy might.

Mark 12:31 (Matthew 22:39; Mark 12:33; Luke 10:27)
And the second is like, namely this, Thou shalt love thy neighbour as thyself. There is none other commandment greater than these.

Leviticus 19:18
Thou shalt not avenge, nor bear any grudge against the children of thy people, but thou shalt love thy neighbour as thyself: I am the LORD.

* * * * * * * *

Mark 12:32, 33
(Matthew 5:43, 22:37,39; Mark 12:29,31)
And the scribe said unto him, Well, Master, thou hast said the truth: for there is one God; and there is none other but he: And to love him with all the heart, and with all the understanding, and with all the soul, and with all the strength, and to love his neighbour as

himself, is more than all whole burnt offerings and sacrifices.

Leviticus 19:18
Thou shalt not avenge, nor bear any grudge against the children of thy people, but thou shalt love thy neighbour as thyself: I am the LORD.

Deuteronomy 4:35
Into thee it was shewed, that thou mightest know that the LORD he is God; there is none else beside him.

Deuteronomy 6:4,5
Hear, O Israel: The LORD our God is one LORD: And thou shalt love the LORD thy God with all thine heart, and with all thy soul, and with all thy might.

* * * * * * * *

Mark 12:36 (Matthew 22:44; Luke 20:42,43; Acts 2:34,35; I Corinthians 15:27; Hebrew 1:13)
For David himself said by the Holy Ghost, The LORD said to my Lord, Sit thou on my right hand, till I make thine enemies thy footstool.

Psalms 110:1
The LORD said unto my Lord, Sit thou at my right hand, until I make thine enemies thy footstool.

* * * * * * * *

Mark 13:14 (Matthew 24:15)
But when ye shall see the abomination of desolation, spoken of by Daniel the prophet, standing where it ought not, (let him that readeth understand,) then let them that be in Judea flee to the mountains.

Daniel 11:31
And arms shall stand on his part, and they shall pollute the sanctuary of strength, and shall take away the daily sacrifice, and they shall place the abomination that maketh desolate.

Daniel 12:11
And from the time that the daily sacrifice shall be taken away, and the abomination that maketh desolate set up, there shall be a thousand two hundred and ninety days.

* * * * * * * *

Mark 13:24,25 (Matthew 24:29)
But in those days after that tribulation, the sun shall be darkened, and the moon shall not give her light, And the stars of heaven shall fall, and the powers that are in heaven shall be shaken.

Joel 2:10,31
The earth shall quake before them; the heavens shall tremble: the sun and the moon shall be dark, and the stars shall withdraw their shining: The sun shall be turned into darkness, and the moon into blood, before the great and terrible day of the LORD come.

* * * * * * * *

Mark 13:26
(Matthew 24:29,30; Mark 14:62; Luke 21:27)
And then shall they see the Son of man coming in the clouds with great power and glory.

Daniel 7:13
I saw in the night visions, and, behold, one like the Son of man came with the clouds of heaven, and came to the Ancient of days, and they brought him near before him.

* * * * * * * *

Mark 14:27 (Matthew 26:31)
And Jesus saith unto them, All ye shall be offended because of me this night: for it is written, I will smite the shepherd, and the sheep shall be scattered.

Zechariah 13:7
Awake, O sword, against my shepherd, and against the man that is my fellow, saith the LORD of hosts: smite the shepherd, and the sheep shall be scattered: and I will turn mine hand upon the little ones.

* * * * * * * *

Mark 14:62
(Matthew 26:64; Mark 12:36, 13:26; Luke 22:69)
And Jesus said, I am: and ye shall see the Son of man sitting on the right hand of power, and coming in the clouds of heaven.

Psalms 110:1
The LORD said unto my Lord, Sit thou at my right hand, until I make thine enemies thy footstool.

Daniel 7:13
I saw in the night visions, and, behold, one like the Son of man came with the clouds of heaven, and came to the Ancient of days, and they brought him near before him.

LUKE

THE PERFECT HUMANITY OF JESUS			
COMING & PREPARATION	**MINISTRY IN GALILEE**	**MINISTRY IN PEREA, SAMARIA, & JUDAH**	**SUFFERING, DEATH, & RESURRECTION**
Jesus' boyhood: **1,2** Genealogy through Mary: **3** Temptation: **4**	Miracles & Teaching: **5-9**	Parables & Testings: **10-21**	The last days: **22-24**
LOCATION: Israel	Galilee	Israel	Jerusalem
OVERVIEW: Jesus' genealogy through Mary avoided a curse on Joseph's side of the family.	Among His own people He was compassionate & performed many miracles.	Among the Pharisees, He was unruffled & wise.	His closest friends deserted Him
TIME: About thirty years beginning around 4 B.C.			

FAST FACTS

AUTHOR AND SETTING:

Luke; Israel

PURPOSE:

The Greeks put a great deal of emphasis on "man," so Luke emphasized Jesus' perfect manhood, carefully and chronologically documenting His earthly ministry.

SEEING JESUS:

Matthew presented Jesus as the King; Mark revealed Him as a servant; John presented Him as the Son of God; and Luke presented Him as the perfect man...the noble teacher, friend, and helper of mankind.

THEME VERSE:

Luke 19:10

NOTES

LUKE:
SON OF MAN

NOTES

SEEING JESUS IN LUKE

AUTHOR & SETTING

Luke means "light-giving." He was a physician (Colossians 4:14). Luke was a gentile Christian and probably one of Paul's converts. He was the author of two New Testament books:

"Forasmuch as many have taken in hand to set forth in order a declaration of those things which are most surely believed among us" **(Luke 1:1).**

"The former treatise have I made, O Theophilus, of all that Jesus began both to do and teach" **(Acts 1:1).**

Luke first appears in the story which takes place at Troas:

*"And after he had seen the vision, immediately **we** endeavoured to go into Macedonia, assuredly gathering that the Lord had called **us** for to preach the gospel unto them. Therefore loosing from Troas, **we** came with a straight course to Samothracia, and the next day to Neapolis"* **(Acts 16:10,11).**

*"These going before tarried for **us** at Troas"* **(Acts 20:5).**

Luke was with Paul in both Roman imprisonments.

OVERVIEW

Luke emphasizes the perfect humanity of Jesus. The gospel was written primarily for the Greeks because of the emphasis of man.

A number of Jesus' miracles are recorded only in *Luke.* At least ten parables are recorded only in this gospel, two of which are the prodigal son and the good Samaritan.

Luke is the gospel of praise - it begins and ends with joy. The first hymns of the Church are the Magnificat (Luke 1:46-55), the Benedictus (Luke 1:68-79), the Gloria in Excelsis Deo (Luke 2:14), and the Nunc Dimittis (Luke 2:29-32).

These are the last of the Hebrew songs and the first of the Christian hymns. The words *rejoice* and *joy* occur 19 times in contrast to 26 times in Mark and Matthew combined.

This is the gospel of prayer - two parables are found here on persevering the prayer (Luke 11:5-13; 18:1-14).

There are nine instances of prayer given in Jesus' life in this book:

1. Luke 3:21 - Jesus prayed at the time of His baptism.
2. Luke 5:15,16 - Jesus prayed after a day of miracles.
3. Luke 6:12 - Jesus prayed all night before choosing His disciples.
4. Luke 9:18 - Jesus prayed before predicting His passion.
5. Luke 9:29 - Jesus prayed at his Transfiguration.
6. Luke 10:17,21 - Jesus prayed after the seventy returned.

7. Luke 11:1 - Jesus prayed before teaching the apostles to pray.
8. Luke 22:39-46 - Jesus prayed at Gethsemane.
9. Luke 23:34-46 - Jesus prayed on the Cross.

Luke gives details of Jesus' childhood.

***Luke* is also called the gospel of womanhood:**

1. Elizabeth is mentioned in chapter one.
2. Mary is mentioned in chapters one and two.
3. The widow of Nain is ,mentioned in Luke 7:12-15.
4. The women who ministered to Christ are mentioned in Luke 8:2,3.
5. Mary and Martha are mentioned in Luke 10:38-42.
6. The women who wept and followed Jesus to the Cross are mentioned in Luke 23:27-31.

This is the gospel to the whole world; Christ's ancestry is traced back to Adam (Luke 3:38).

It is believed that Luke is the only gentile writer of any books in the Bible.

Luke exhibits a professional interest in medical matters in his gospel. He refers to Jesus' healing mission; he talks about the Samaritan who helped a half-dead man - binding up his wounds and pouring wine and oil on them. Luke alone records Christ's proverb, *"...Physician, heal thyself..."* (Luke 4;23). Luke tells us that the son of the widow sat up on the bier like a patient in bed. He talks about the woman who was bowed over and could not lift herself up – but was immediately made straight.

The word *angel* is used 23 times in this gospel. There are more glimpses of the unseen world in this gospel than in any other gospel.

***Luke* resounds with angels' songs and with the music of their wings:**

1. Our Lord revealed that in the life to come the redeemed shall be equal to the angels - Luke 20:36.
2. An angel appeared to Jesus in Gethsemane and strengthened Him - Luke 22:43.
3. Certain women saw a vision of angels at the sepulcher after Jesus had rise - Luke 24:4,5,23.
4. An angel appeared to Zacharias in the Temple - Luke 1:11.
5. An angel appeared to Mary at Nazareth - Luke 1:26,27.
6. Angels appeared to the shepherds near Bethlehem - Luke 2:9.
7. Angels will accompany Jesus upon His Second Coming - Luke 9:26.
8. The angels rejoice when sinners repent - Luke 15:10.
9. Lazarus was carried by angels to Abraham's bosom - Luke 16:22.

NOTES

NOTES

SEEING JESUS IN LUKE

Matthew presents Jesus as a *king*, Mark presents Him as a servant, John presents Him as God, and Luke presents Him as a *man*. In *Luke*, Jesus is the noble teacher, friend, and helper of mankind. Jesus is the physician for the hurrt of sin. Of course, Paul spoke of Luke as *"...the beloved physician,..."* **(Colossians 4:14).**

THEME VERSE

"For the Son of man is come to seek and to save that which was lost" **(Luke 19:10).**

OUTLINE

(Refer to maps on pages A14 - A18 in the APPENDIX)

I. **THE COMING AND PREPARATION OF THE SON OF MAN -** LUKE 1-4

A. **The Only Gospel Containing the Boyhood of Jesus -** Luke 2:40-52.

B. **The Genealogy is Different in Luke Than in Matthew -** Luke 3:23-38.

1. **The "legal" line in Luke comes through Joseph - the "natural" line through Mary.**

a. Heli was probably the father of Mary.

b. A curse was pronounced upon the line of Coniah or Jehoiakim:

i. *"Is this man Coniah a despised broken idol? Is he a vessel wherein is no pleasure? wherefore are they cast out, he and his seed, and are cast into a land which they know not? O earth, earth, earth, hear the word of the LORD. Thus saith the LORD, Write ye this man childless, a man that shall not prosper in his days: for no man of his seed shall prosper, sitting upon the throne of David, and ruling any more in Judah"* **(Jeremiah 22:28-30).**

ii. *"And the sons of Jehoiakim: Jeconiah his son, Zedekiah his son"* **(I Chronicles 3:16).**

c. Christ's legal line came through David's son Solomon. Christ avoided the curse upon Coniah's descendants because He came through Mary who was a descendant of Nathan.

II. **THE MINISTRY OF THE SON OF MAN IN GALILEE -** LUKE 5-9

III. **THE MINISTRY OF THE SON OF MAN IN PEREA, SAMARIA, AND JUDAH -** LUKE 10-21

IV. **THE SUFFERING, DEATH, AND RESURRECTION OF THE SON OF MAN -** LUKE 22-24

THE OLD TESTAMENT QUOTED IN LUKE.

Luke 1:17
And he shall go before him in the spirit and power of Elias, to turn the hearts of the fathers to the children, and the disobedient to the wisdom of the just; to make ready a people prepared for the Lord.

Malachi 4:5,6
Behold, I will send you Elijah the prophet before the coming of the great and dreadful day of the LORD: And he shall turn the heart of the fathers to the children, and the heart of the children to their fathers, lest I come and smite the earth with a curse.

* * * * *

Luke 1:50
And his mercy is on them that fear him from generation to generation.

Psalms 103:17
But the mercy of the LORD is from everlasting to everlasting upon them that fear him, and his righteousness unto children's children.

* * * * *

Luke 1:53
He hath filled the hungry with good things; and the rich he hath sent empty away.

Psalms 107:9
For he satisfieth the longing soul, and filleth the hungry soul with goodness.

* * * * *

Luke 1:71
That we should be saved from our enemies, and from the hand of all that hate us.

Psalms 106:10
And he saved them from the hand of him that hated them, and redeemed them from the hand of the enemy.

* * * * *

Luke 1:76 (Matthew 11:10; Mark 1:2,3)
And thou, child, shalt be called the prophet of the Highest: for thou shalt go before the face of the Lord to prepare his ways.

Malachl 3:1
Behold, I will send my messenger, and he shall prepare the way before me: and the Lord, whom ye shall seek, shall suddenly come to his temple, even the messenger of the covenant, whom ye delight in: behold, he shall come, saith the LORD of hosts.

* * * * *

Luke 1:79 (Matthew 4:16)
To give light to them that sit in darkness and in the shadow of death, to guide our feet into the way of peace.

Isaiah 9:2
The people that walked in darkness have seen a great light: they that dwell in the land of the shadow of death, upon them hath the light shined.

* * * * *

Luke 2:23
(As it is written in the law of the Lord, Every male that openeth the womb shall be called holy to the Lord.)

Exodus 13:2
Sanctify unto me all the firstborn, whatsoever openeth the womb among the children of Israel, both of man and of beast: it is mine.

Exodus 13:12,15
That thou shalt set apart unto the LORD all that openeth the matrix, and every firstling that cometh of a beast which thou hast; the males shall be the LORD'S. And it came to pass, when Pharaoh would hardly let us go, that the LORD slew all the firstborn in the land of Egypt, both the firstborn of man, and the firstborn of beast: therefore I sacrifice to the LORD all that openeth the matrix, being males; but all the firstborn of my children I redeem.

Numbers 3:13
Because all the firstborn are mine; for on the day that I smote all the firstborn in the land of Egypt I hallowed unto me all the firstborn in Israel, both man and beast: mine shall they be: I am the LORD.

Numbers 8:17
For all the firstborn of the children of Israel are mine, both man and beast: on the day that I smote every firstborn in the land of Egypt I sanctified them for myself.

* * * * *

Luke 2:24
And to offer a sacrifice according to that which is said in the law of the Lord, A pair of turtledoves, or two young pigeons.

Leviticus 12:8
And if she not be able to bring a lamb, then she shall bring two turtles, or two young pigeons; the one for the burnt offering, and the other for a sin offering: and the priest shall make an atonement for her, and she shall be clean.

Leviticus 5:11
But if he be not able to bring two turtledoves, or two young pigeons, then he that sinned shall bring for his offering the tenth part of an ephah of fine flour for a sin offering; he shall put no oil upon it, neither shall he put any frankincense theron: for it is a sin offering.

* * * * *

Luke 2:32
A light to lighten the Gentiles, and the glory of thy people Israel.

Isaiah 42:6
I the LORD have called thee in righteousness, and will hold thine hand, and will keep thee, and give thee for a covenant of the people, for a light of the Gentiles.

Isaiah 49:6
And he said, It is a light thing that thou shouldest be my servant to raise up the tribes of Jacob, and to restore the preserved of Israel: I will also give thee for a light to the Gentiles, that thou mayest be my salvation unto the end of the earth.

* * * * *

Luke 3:4-6 (Matthew 3:3; Mark 1:3; John 1:23)
As it is written in the book of the words of Esaias the prophet, saying, The voice of one crying in the wilderness, Prepare ye the way of the Lord, make his paths straight. Every valley shall be filled, and every mountain and hill shall be brought low; and the crooked shall be made straight and the rough ways shall be made smooth; And all flesh shall see the salvation of God.

Isaiah 40:3-5
The voice of him that crieth in the wilderness, Prepare ye the way of the LORD, make straight in the desert a highway for our God. Every valley shall be exalted, and every mountain and hill shall be made low: and the crooked shall be made straight, and the rough places plain: And the glory of the LORD shall be revealed, and all flesh shall see it together: for the mouth of the LORD hath spoken it.

* * * * *

Luke 4:4 (Matthew 4:4)
And Jesus answered him, saying, It is written, That man shall not live by bread alone, but by every word of God.

Deuteronomy 8:3
And he humbled thee, and suffered thee to hunger, and fed thee with manna, which thou knewest not, neither did thy fathers know; that he might make thee know that man doth not live by bread only, but by every word that proceedeth out of the mouth of the LORD doth man live.

* * * * *

Luke 4:8 (Matthew 4:10)
And Jesus answered and said unto him, Get thee behind me, Satan: for it is written, Thou shalt worship the Lord thy God, and him only shalt thou serve.

Deuteronomy 6:13
Thou shalt fear the LORD thy God, and serve him, and shalt swear by his name.

* * * * *

Luke 4:10,11 (Matthew 4:6)
For it is written, He shall give his angels charge over thee, to keep thee: And in their hands they shall bear thee up, lest at any time thou dash thy foot against a stone.

Psalms 91:11,12
For he shall give his angels charge over thee, to keep thee in all thy ways. They shall bear thee up in their hands, lest thou dash thy foot against a stone.

* * * * *

Luke 4:12 (Matthew 4:7)
And Jesus answering said unto him, It is said, Thou shalt not tempt the Lord thy God.

Deuteronomy 6:16
Ye shall not tempt the LORD your God, as ye tempted him in Massah.

* * * * *

Luke 4:18,19 (Matthew 11:5; Luke 7:22)
The Spirit of the Lord is upon me, because he hath anointed me to preach the gospel to the poor; he hath sent me to heal the brokenhearted, to preach deliverance to the captives, and recovering of sight to the blind, to set at liberty them that are bruised, To preach the acceptable year of the Lord.

Isaiah 61:1,2
The Spirit of the Lord GOD is upon me; because the LORD hath anointed me to preach good tidings unto the meek; he hath sent me to bind up the brokenhearted, to proclaim liberty to the captives, and the opening of the prison to them that are bound; To proclaim the acceptable year of the LORD, and the day of vengeance of our God; to comfort all that mourn.

Isaiah 58:6
Is not this the fast that I have chosen? To loose the bands of wickedness, to undo the heavy burdens, and to let the oppressed go free, and that ye break every yoke?

* * * * *

Luke 7:22 (Luke 4:18)
Then Jesus answering said unto them, Go your way, and tell John what things ye have seen and heard; how that the blind see, the lame walk, the lepers are cleansed, the deaf hear, the dead are raised, to the poor the gospel is preached.

Isaiah 35:5,6
Then the eyes of the blind shall be opened, and the ears of the deaf shall be unstopped. Then shall the lame man leap as an hart, and the tongue of the dumb sing: for in the wilderness shall waters break out, and streams in the desert.

Isaiah 61:1
The Spirit of the Lord God is upon me; because the LORD hath anointed me to preach good tidings unto the meek; he hath sent me to bind up the brokenhearted, to proclaim liberty to the captives, and the opening of the prison to them that are bound.

* * * * * *

Luke 7:27 (Matthew 11:10; Mark 1:2)
This is he, of whom, it is written, Behold, I send my messenger before thy face, which shall prepare thy way before thee.

Malachi 3:1
Behold, I will send my messenger, and he shall prepare the way before me: and the Lord, whom ye seek, shall suddenly come to his temple, even the messenger of the covenant, whom ye delight in: behold, he shall come, saith the LORD of hosts.

* * * * *

Luke 8:10
(Matthew 13:14,15; Mark 4:12; John 12:40; Acts 28:26)
And he said, Unto you it is given to know the mysteries of the kingdom of God: but to others in parables; that seeing they might not see, and hearing they might not understand.

Isaiah 6:9
And he said, Go, and tell this people, Hear ye indeed, but understand not; and see ye indeed, but perceive not.

* * * * * *

Luke 10:27
(Matthew 19:19, 22:37,39; Mark 12:30,31,33; Romans 13:9; Galatians 5:14; James 2:8)
And he answering said, Thou shalt love the Lord thy God with all thy heart, and with all thy soul, and with all thy strength, and with all thy mind; and thy neighbour as thyself.

Deuteronomy 6:5
And thou shalt love the LORD thy God with all thine heart, and with all thy soul, and with all thy might.

Leviticus 19:18
Thou shalt not avenge, nor bear any grudge against the children of thy people, but thou shalt love thy neighbour as thyself: I am the LORD.

* * * *

Luke 10:28
And he said unto him, Thou has answered right: this do, and thou shalt live.

Ezekiel 20:11
And I gave them my statutes, and shewed them my judgments, which if a man do, he shall even live in them.

* * * * * *

Luke 13:19 (Matthew 13:32; Mark 4:32)
It is like a grain of mustard seed, which a man took, and cast into his garden; and it grew, and waxed a great tree; and the fowls of the air lodged in the branches of it.

Ezekiel 17:23
In the mountain of the height of Israel will I plant it: and it shall bring forth boughs, and bear fruit, and be a goodly cedar: and under it shall dwell all fowl of every wing; in the shadow of the branches thereof shall they dwell.

Psalms 104:12
By them shall the fowls of the heaven have their habitation, which sing among the branches.

* * * * *

Luke 13:27 (Matthew 7:23)
But he shall say, I tell you, I know you not whence ye are; depart from me, all ye workers of iniquity.

Psalms 6:8
Depart from me, all ye workers of iniquity, for the LORD hath heard the voice of my weeping.

* * * * *

Luke 13:35
(Matthew 21:9, 23:39; Mark 11:9, 19:38; Luke 19:38; John 12:13)
Behold, your house is left unto you desolated; and verily I say unto you, Ye shall not see me, until the time come when ye shall say, Blessed is he that cometh in the name of the Lord.

Psalms 118:26
Blessed be he that cometh in the name of the LORD; we have blessed you out of the house of the LORD.

* * * * *

Luke 18:20
(Matthew 5:21,27, 19:18,19; Mark 10:19; Romans 13:9; James 2:11)
Thou knowest the commandments, Do not commit adultery, Do not kill, Do not steal, Do not bear false witness, Honour thy father and thy mother.

Exodus 20:12-16
Honour thy father and thy mother: that thy days may be long upon the land which the LORD thy God giveth thee. Thou shalt not kill, Thou shalt not commit adultery. Thou shalt not steal. Thou shalt not bear false witness against thy neighbour.

Deuteronomy 5:16-20
Honour thy father and thy mother, as the LORD thy God hath commanded thee; that thy days may be prolonged, and that it may go well with thee, in the land which the LORD thy God giveth thee. Thou shalt not kill. Neither shalt thou commit adultery. Neither shalt thou steal. Neither shalt thou bear false witness against thy neighbour.

* * * * *

Luke 19:38
(Matthew 21:9, 23:39; Mark 11:9; Luke 13:35; John 12:13)
Saying, Blessed be the King that cometh in the name of the Lord: peace in heaven, and glory in the highest

Psalms 118:26
Blessed be he that cometh in the name of the LORD: we have blessed you out of the house of the LORD.

* * * * *

Luke 19:46 (Matthew 21:13; Mark 11:17)
Saying unto them, It is written, My house is the house of prayer: but ye have made it a den of thieves.

Isaiah 56:7
Even them will I bring to my holy mountain, and make them joyful in my house of prayer: their burnt offerings and their sacrifices shall be accepted upon mine altar; for mine house shall be called an house of prayer for all people.

Jeremiah 7:11
Is this house, which is called by my name, become a den of robbers in your eyes? Behold, even I have seen it, saith the LORD.

* * * * * *

Luke 20:17
(Matthew 21:42; Mark 12:10, 11; Acts 4:11; I Peter 2:7)
And he beheld them, and said, What is this then that is written, The stone which the builders rejected, the same is become the head of the corner?

Psalms 118:22
The stone which the builders refused is become the head stone of the corner

* * * * * *

Luke 20:28 (Matthew 22:24; Mark 12:19)
Saying, Master, Moses wrote unto us, If any man's brother die, having a wife, and he die without children, that his brother should take his wife, and raise up seed unto his brother.

Deuteronomy 25:5
If brethren dwell together, and one of them die, and have no child, the wife of the dead shall not marry without unto a stranger: her husband's brother shall go in unto her, and take her to him to wife, and perform the duty of an husband's brother unto her

* * * * *

Luke 20:37
(Matthew 22:32; Mark 12:26; Acts 7:32)
Now that the dead are raised, even Moses shewed at the bush, when he calleth the Lord the God of Abraham, and the God of Isaac, and the God of Jacob.

Exodus 3:6
Moreover he said, I am the God of thy father, the God of Abraham, the God of Isaac, and the God of Jacob. And Moses hid his face; for he was afraid to look upon God.

Exodus 3:15
And God said moreover unto Moses, Thus shalt thou say unto the children of Israel, The LORD God of your fathers, the God of Abraham, the God of Isaac, and the God of Jacob, hath sent me unto you: this is my name for ever, and this is my memorial unto all generations.

* * * * * * * * * *

Luke 20;42,43
(Matthew 22:44; Mark 12:36; Acts 2:34,35; Hebrews 1:13)
And David himself saith in the book of Psalms, The LORD said unto my Lord, Sit thou on my right hand, Till I make thine enemies thy footstool.

Psalms 110:1
The LORD said unto my Lord, Sit thou at my right hand, until I make thine enemies thy footstool.

* * * * * * * * * *

Luke 21:27
(Matthew 24:30; Mark 13:26, 14:62; Revelation 1:7)
And then shall they see the Son of man coming in a cloud with power and great glory.

Daniel 7:13
I saw in the night visions, and, behold, one like the Son of man came with the clouds of heaven, and came to the Ancient of days, and they brought him near before him.

* * * * * * * * * *

Luke 22:37
For I say unto you, that this that is written must yet be accomplished in me, And he was reckoned among the transgressors: for the things concerning me have an end.

Isaiah 53:12
Therefore will I divide him a portion with the great, and he shall divide the spoil with the strong; because he hath poured out his soul unto death: and he was numbered with the transgressors; and he bare the sin of many, and made intercession for the transgressors.

* * * * * * * * * *

Luke 22:69 (Matthew 26:64; Mark 14:62)
Hereafter shall the Son of man sit on the right hand of the power of God.

Psalms 110:1
The LORD said unto my Lord, Sit thou at my right hand, until I make thine enemies thy footstool.

* * * * * * * * * *

Luke 23:30
Then shall they begin to say to the mountains, Fall on us; and to the hills, Cover us.

Isaiah 2:19
And they shall go into the holes of the rocks, and into the caves of the earth, for fear of the LORD, and for the glory of his majesty, when he ariseth to shake terribly the earth.

Hosea 10:8
The high places also of Aven, the sin of Israel, shall be destroyed: the thorn and the thistle shall come up on their altars; and they shall say to the mountains, Cover us; and to the hills, Fall on us.

* * * * * * * * * *

Luke 23:46
And when Jesus had cried with a loud voice, he said, Father, into thy hands I commend my spirit; and having said thus, he gave up the ghost.

Psalms 31:5
Into thine hand I commit my spirit: thou hast redeemed me, O LORD God of truth.

JOHN

JESUS: THE WORD MADE FLESH			
PROLOGUE: ETERNAL WORD	**MINISTRY TO THE WORLD**	**MINISTRY TO HIS OWN**	**DEATH & RESURRECTION**
Jesus, the Word: **1**	Jesus came to save the world: **1-12**	Fulfillment of the covenant: **13-17**	Salvation is accomplished: **18-21**
LOCATION: Israel			
OVERVIEW: Using miraculous signs, John proves that *"...Jesus is the Christ, the Son of God; and that believing ye might have life through His name"* **(John 20:31).**			
TIME: Three-and-a-half years beginning around A.D. 30			

FAST FACTS

AUTHOR AND SETTING:

John; Israel

PURPOSE:

John clearly sets forth Jesus Christ in His deity in order to spark believing faith in his readers.

SEEING JESUS:

John presents seven signs to show the divinity of Jesus. *John* also gives us the seven *"I am's"* of Jesus to prove that Jesus is the Christ, the Son of God.

THEME VERSE:

John 20:30,31

NOTES

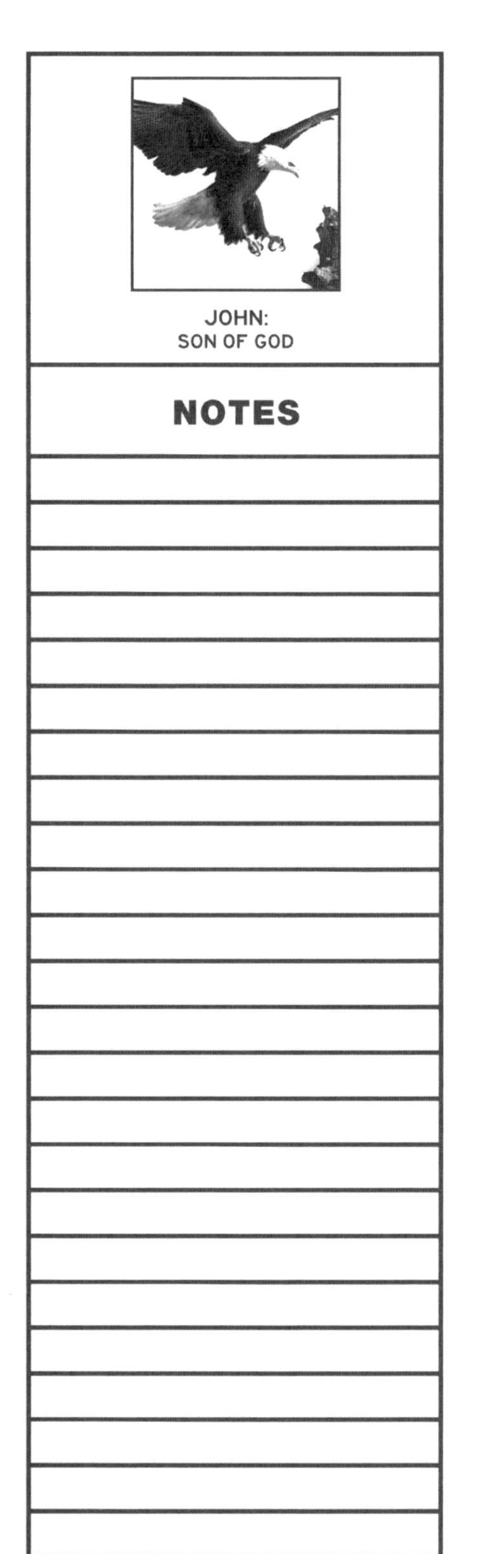

SEEING JESUS IN JOHN

AUTHOR & SETTING

John means "Jehovah is gracious." John's home was Bethsaida (John 1:44; Luke 5:10). He came from a family of four - the father and mother (Zebedee and Salome) and the two sons (James and John). The father and sons were fishermen (Matthew 4:21). Their mother, Salome, was ambitious for her sons (Matthew 20:20,21; Mark 10:35-37). There is clear evidence that the family was prosperous because the family had hired servants. John's family ministered to Jesus and the disciples of their financial substance, and they were influential in official quarters (Mark 1:20; Matthew 27:56; Luke 8:3; John 18:15,16, 19:26,27).

John was first a follower of John the Baptist, and he left John the Baptist to follow Christ (John 1:35,40).

OVERVIEW

There were at least three stages in John's fellowship with Christ:

Attachment:
"One of the two which heard John speak, and followed him, was Andrew, Simon Peter's brother" **(John 1:40).**

Discipleship:
"And going on from thence, he saw other two brethren, James the son of Zebedee, and John his brother, in a ship with Zebedee their father, mending their nets; and he called them. And they immediately left the ship and their father, and followed him" **(Matthew 4:21,22).**

Apostleship:
"And when it was day, he called unto him his disciples: and of them he chose twelve, whom also he named apostles; Simon, (whom he also named Peter,) and Andrew his brother, James and John, Philip and Bartholomew" **(Luke 6:13,14).**

John's relationship to Jesus was unique if, as conjectured, Salome was the sister of Mary, the mother of Jesus. That would make John the cousin of Jesus.

John was one of the first two *disciples* to be called (John 1:35-40).

John was one of the first *apostles* named (Matthew 4:18-22). He was one of the three privileged apostles:
"And he suffered no man to follow him, save Peter, and James, and John the brother of James"
(Mark 5:37; see also Matthew 17:1, 26:37).

John was one of the four who drew forth our Lord's great prophetic discourse: *"And as he sat upon the mount of Olives over against the temple, Peter and James and John and Andrew asked him privately, Tell us, when shall these things be? and what shall be the sign when all these things shall be fulfilled?"* **(Mark 13:3,4).**

John was one of the two sent to prepare the passover: *"And he sent Peter and John, saying, Go and prepare us the passover, that we may eat"* **(Luke 22:8).**

He was the disciple whom Jesus loved:

"Now there was leaning on Jesus' bosom one of his disciples, whom Jesus loved" **(John 13:23)**.

"When Jesus therefore saw his mother, and the disciple standing by, whom he loved, he saith into his mother, Woman, behold thy son!" **(John 19:26).**

"Then she runneth and cometh to Simon Peter, and to the other disciple, whom Jesus loved, and saith unto them, They have taken away the Lord out of the sepulchre, and we know not where they have laid him" **(John 20:2).**

"Therefore that disciple whom Jesus loved saith unto Peter, It is the Lord. Now when Simon Peter heard that it was the Lord, he girt his fisher's coat unto him, (for he was naked,) and did cast himself into the sea" **(John 21:7).**

"Then Peter, turning about, seeth the disciple whom Jesus loved following; which also leaned on his breast at supper, and said, Lord, which is he that betrayeth thee?" **(John 21:20).**

It was to John that Jesus committed the care of His mother:

"Now there stood by the cross of Jesus his mother, and his mother's sister, Mary the wife of Cleophas, and Mary Magdalene. When Jesus therefore saw his mother, and the disciple standing by, whom he loved, he saith unto his mother, Woman, behold thy son! Then saith he to the disciple, Behold thy mother! And from that hour that disciple took her unto his own home" **(John 19:25-27).**

John appears three times in the book of Acts:

In the temple: *"Now Peter and John went up together into the temple at the hour of prayer, being the ninth hour"* **(Acts 3:1).**

Before the council: *"Now when they saw the boldness of Peter and John, and perceived that they were unlearned and ignorant men, they marveled; and they took knowledge of them, that they had been with Jesus"* **(Acts 4:13).**

In Samaria: *"Now when the apostles which were at Jerusalem heard that Samaria had received the word of God, they sent unto them Peter and John"* **(Acts 8:14).**

John wrote the gospel of *John*, and eighteen years later he wrote the book of Revelation.

NOTES

NOTES

The character of John is reflected in his writings; he was retiring and reticent in disposition.

Basically John divided his gospel into revelation, rejection, and reception. All three appear in every part of the gospel.

Three are six miracles in John's gospel that only he recorded:

1. The turning of water into wine - John 2:7-9
2. The healing of the nobleman's son - John 4:49-53
3. The healing of the impotent man at Bethesda - John 5:6-9
4. The giving of sight to a man born blind - John 9:1,6,7
5. The raising of Lazarus from the dead - John 11:43,44
6. The draft of fishes - John 21:5,6

SEEING JESUS IN JOHN

In his gospel John shows that the Man of Galilee was God. The gospel of John was written for the Christian Church as a whole, for the world at large, and presents the more profound aspects of the gospel.

John gave the seven "I am's" of Jesus:

1. *"I am the Bread of Life."*
"And Jesus said unto them, I am the bread of life: he that cometh to me shall never hunger; and he that believeth on me shall never thirst" **(John 6:35).**

2. *"I am the light of the world."*
"Then spake Jesus again unto them, saying, I am the light of the world: he that followeth me shall not walk in darkness, but shall have the light of life" **(John 8:12).**

3. *"I am the door."*
"I am the door: by me if any man enter in, he shall be saved, and shall go in and out, and find pasture" **(John 10:9).**

4. *"I am the good shepherd."*
"I am the good shepherd, and know my sheep, and am known of mine" **(John 10:14).**

5. *"I am the resurrection and the life."*
"Jesus said unto her, I am the resurrection, and the life: he that believeth in me, though he were dead, yet shall he live" **(John 11:25).**

6. *"I am the way, the truth and the life."*
"Jesus saith unto him, I am the way, the truth, and the life: no man cometh unto the Father, but by me" **(John 14:6).**

7. *"I am the true vine."*
"I am the true vine, and my Father is in the husbandman" **(John 15:1).**

THEME VERSES

"And many other signs truly did Jesus in the presence of his disciples, which are not written in this book: But these are written, that ye might believe that Jesus Is the Christ, the Son of God; and that believing ye might have life through his name" **(John 20:30,31)**

OUTLINE

(Refer to maps on pages A13 and A14 in the APPENDIX)

I. **PROLOGUE - THE ETERNAL WORD -** JOHN 1

II. **CHRIST'S MINISTRY TO THE WORLD -** JOHN 1-12

III. **CHRIST'S MINISTRY TO HIS OWN -** JOHN 13-17

IV. **CHRIST'S DEATH AND RESURRECTION -** JOHN 18-21

NOTES

THE OLD TESTAMENT QUOTED IN JOHN.

John 1:23 (Matthew 3:3; Mark 1:3; Luke 3:4)
He said, I am the voice of one crying in the wilderness, Make straight the way of the Lord, as said the prophet Esaias.

Isaiah 40:3
The voice of him that crieth in the wilderness, Prepare ye the way of the LORD, make straight in the desert a highway for our God.

****

John 2:17
And his disciples remembered that it was written, The zeal of thine house hath eaten me up.

Psalms 69:9
For the zeal of thine house hath eaten me up; and the reproaches of them that reproached thee are fallen upon me.

* * * * * *

John 6:31
Our fathers did eat manna in the desert; as it is written, He gave them bread from heaven to eat.

Exodus 16:4,15
Then said the LORD unto Moses, Behold, I will rain bread from heaven for you; and the people shall go out and gather a certain rate every day, that I may prove them, whether they will walk in my law, or no. And when the children of Israel saw it, they said one to another, It is manna: for they wist not what it was. And Moses said unto them, This is the bread which the LORD hath given you to eat.

Nehemiah 9:15
And gavest them bread from heaven for their hunger, and broughtest forth water for them out of the rock for their thirst, and promisedst them that they should go in to possess the land which thou hadst sworn to give them.

Psalms 78:24
And had rained down manna upon them to eat, and had given them of the corn of heaven.

* * * * * *

John 6:45
It is written in the prophets, And they shall be all taught of God. Every man therefore that hath heard, and hath learned of the Father, cometh unto me.

Isaiah 54:13
And all thy children shall be taught of the LORD; and great shall be the peace of thy children.

Jeremiah 31:33,34
But this shall be the covenant that I will make with the house of Israel; After those days, saith the LORD, I will put my law in their inwards parts, and write it in their hearts; and will be their God, and they shall be my people. And they shall teach no more every man his neighbour, and every man his brother, saying, Know the LORD: for they shall all know me, from the least of them unto the greatest of them, saith the LORD: for I will forgive their iniquity, and I will remember their sin no more.

* * * * * *

John 10:34
Jesus answered them, Is it not written in your law, I said, Ye are gods?

Psalms 82:6
I have said, Ye are gods; and all of you are children of the most High.

* * * * * *

John 12:13
(Matthew 21:9, 23:39; Mark 11:9; Luke 13:35, 19:38)
Took branches of palm trees, and went forth to meet him, and cried, Hosanna: Blessed is the King of Israel that cometh in the name of the Lord.

Psalms 118:26
Blessed be he that cometh in the name of the LORD: we have blessed you out of the house of the LORD.

* * * * * *

John 12:15 (Matthew 21:5)
Fear not, daughter of Sion: behold, thy King cometh, sitting on an ass's colt.

Zechariah 9:9
Rejoice greatly, O daughter of Zion; shout, O daughter of Jerusalem: behold, thy King cometh unto thee: he is just, and having salvation; lowly, and riding upon an ass, and upon a colt the foal of an ass.

* * * * * *

John 12:38 (Romans 10:16)
That the saying of Esaias the prophet might be fulfilled, which he spake, Lord, who hath believed our report? and to whom hath the arm of the Lord been revealed?

Isaiah 53:1
Who hath believed our report? and to whom is the arm of the LORD revealed?

* * * * * *

John 12:40 (Matthew 13:14,15; Mark 4:12; Luke 8:10; Acts 28:26,27)
He hath blinded their eyes, and hardened their heart; that they should not see with their eyes, not understand with their heart, and be converted, and I should heal them.

Isaiah 6:9,10
And he said, Go, and tell this people, Hear ye indeed, but understand not; and see ye indeed, but perceive not. Make the heart of this people fat, and make their ears heavy, and shut their eyes; lest they see with their eyes, and hear with their ears, and understand with their heart, and convert, and be healed.

* * * * * *

John 13:18
I speak not of you all: I know whom I have chosen: but that the scripture may be fulfilled, He that eateth bread with me hath lifted up his heel against me.

Psalms 41:9
Yes, mine own familiar friend, in whom I trusted, which did eat of my bread, hath lifted up his heel against me.

* * * * * *

John 15:25
But this cometh to pass, that the word might be fulfilled that is written in their law, They hated me without a cause.

Psalms 35:19
Let not them that are mine enemies wrongfully rejoice over me: neither let them wink with the eye that hate me without a cause.

Psalms 69:4
They that hate me without a cause are more than the hairs of mine head: they that would destroy me, being mine enemies wrongfully, are mighty: then I restored that which I took not away.

* * * * * *

John 19:24
They said therefore among themselves, Let us not rend it, but cast lots for it, whose it shall be: that the scripture might be fulfilled, which saith, They parted my raiment among them, and for my vesture they did cast lots. These things therefore the soldiers did.

Psalms 22:18
They part my garments among them, and cast lots upon my vesture.

* * * * * *

John 19:36
For these things were done, that the scripture should be fulfilled, A bone of him shall not be broken.

Exodus 12:46
In one house shall it be eaten; thou shalt not carry forth ought of the flesh abroad out of the house; neither shall ye break a bone thereof.

Numbers 9:12
They shall leave none of it unto the morning, nor break any bone of it: according to all the ordinances of the passover they shall keep it.

Psalms 34:20
He keepeth all his bones: not one of them is broken.

* * * * * *

John 19:37
And again another scripture saith, They shall look on him whom they pierced.

Zechariah 12:10
And I will pour upon the house of David, and upon the inhabitants of Jerusalem, the spirit of grace and of supplications: and they shall look upon me whom they have pierced, and they shall mourn for him, as one mourneth for his only son, and shall be in bitterness for him, as one that is in bitterness for his firstborn.

ACTS

BEGINNING CHURCH HISTORY	
WITNESSING IN JERUSALEM, JUDEA, AND SAMARIA	**WITNESSING UNTO THE UTTERMOST PARTS OF THE EARTH**
Peter the leader: **1-12**	Paul takes over leadership: **13-28**
LOCATION: Jerusalem, Judea, and Samaria	The Roman Empire
OVERVIEW: The doings and teachings of Jesus Christ are now accomplished through His newborn Church which begins to endure persecution in fulfilling the Great Commission.	
TIME: A.D. 33-48	A.D. 48-62

FAST FACTS

AUTHOR AND SETTING:

Luke, Jerusalem, Judea, Samaria

PURPOSE:

Acts is the story of men and women who took the Great Commission seriously and began to spread the news of a risen Savior to the most remote corners of their known world. *Acts* is the historical link between the gospels and the espistles.

SEEING JESUS:

Jesus Christ, the resurrected Savior, is the central theme of *Acts*. Because of Luke's strong emphasis on the ministry of the Holy Spirit, perhaps this book should be titled, "The Acts of the Spirit of Christ Working in and Through the Apostles."

THEME VERSE:

Acts 1:8

NOTES

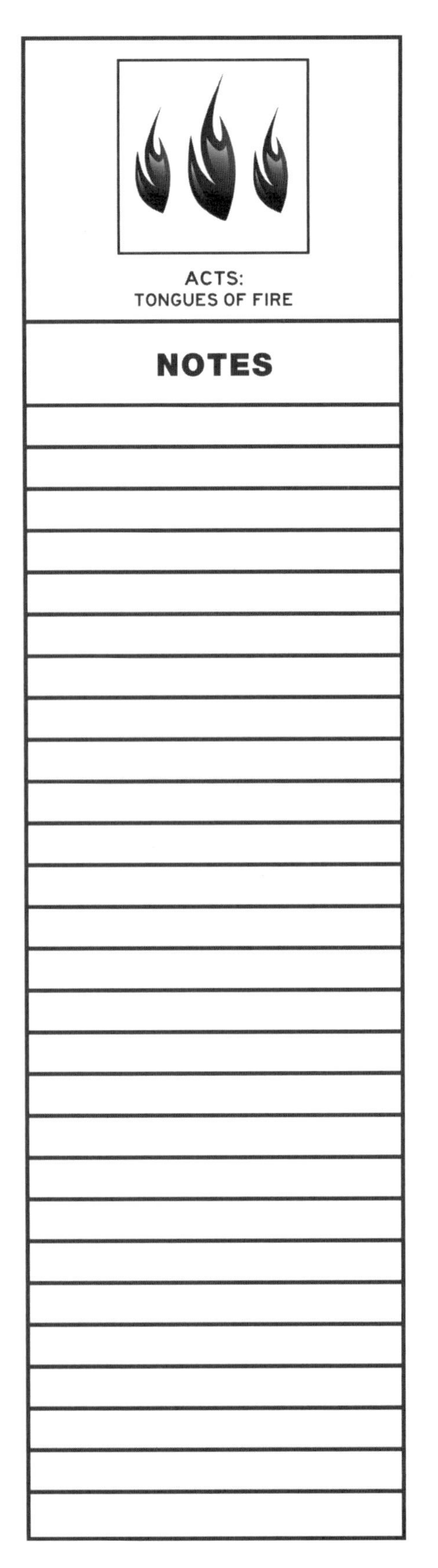

SEEING JESUS IN ACTS

AUTHOR & SETTING

Luke means "light-giving". He was a physician (Colossians 4:14). Luke was a gentile Christian and probably one of Paul's converts. He was the author of two New Testament books:

"Foreasmuch as many have taken in hand to set forth in order a declaration of those things which are most surely believed among us" **(Luke 1:1).**

"The former treatise have I made, O Theophilus, of all that Jesus began both to do and teach" **(Acts 1:1).**

Luke first appears in the story which takes place at Troas:

*"And after he had seen the vision, immediately **we** endeavoured to go into Macedonia, assuredly gathering that the Lord had called **us** for to preach the gospel unto them. Therefore loosing from Troas, **we** came with a straight course to Samothracia, and the next day to Neapolis"* **(Acts 16:10,11).**

*"These going before tarried for **us** at Troas"* **(Acts 20:5).**

Luke was with Paul in both Roman imprisonments.

OVERVIEW

Perhaps we could call the first five books of the New Testament the Pentateuch of the New Testament. Four of these books represent the person of Jesus, our Lord, while the fifth begins the first stage of Church history. Jesus is seen throughout Acts speaking and acting through His Church.

The gospel of Luke tells the story of the birth of Jesus, His childhood, His confirmation, His testing, His anointing, His teaching, His temptation, His Transfiguration, His Death, His Resurrection, and His Ascension. The two witnesses who stood by as He ascended were perhaps, Moses and Elijah.

Acts, the second book written by Luke, is a continuation of the doings and teachings of Jesus, but now the doings and teachings are accomplished through His Church, *". . . the fulness of him that filleth all in all"* (Ephesians 1:23). Acts ends with Paul in prison, but Revelation opens with the lamb on the throne.

There is always ultimate victory in God:

"I am come to send fire on the earth; and what will I, if it be already kindled? But I have a baptism to be baptized with; and how am I straitened till it be accomplished" **(Luke 12:49,50).**

We are His witnesses, His evidences, His credentials, His arguments in Jerusalem, Judea, Samaria, and the uttermost parts of the earth.

It was expedient for you and me that Jesus went away because:

1. He went away and sent us Pentecost.
2. We fulfill His commission because He went away.
3. We have assumed Him as our Lord.
4. The grouping has changed now. It used to be Peter, James, and John. Now we will see many new groupings.

In Acts 2 we begin to see the formation of the Christian Church on the day of Pentecost, 50 days after Passover. Two signs were given, one appealing to hearing, and the other appealing to sight: (1) the rushing mighty wind, and (2) the tongues of fire. The fire was a plurality in unity – the tongues were many, but the fire was one.

Those present in the Upper Room did not hear the coming of the Spirit. They heard the sound of the rushing mighty wind, the very symbol which the Lord used when He said to Nicodemus, *"The wind bloweth where it listeth,..."* **(John 3:8).**

Pentecost birthed the Church. When the Spirit came as actual life and passed into the lives of the disciples, they were each able to say, *"I am crucified with Christ: nevertheless I live; yet not I, but Christ liveth in me: and the life which I now live in the flesh I live by the faith of the Son of God, who loved me, and gave himself for me"* **(Galatians 2:20).**

The consciousness of His life was thriving through their lives. Consider the impressions made on Jerusalem:

1. Amazement
2. Perplexity
3. Criticism

The spiritual Church will always present the supernatural phenomena to the world. When Peter stood up to preach, the man who had been fearful and cringing seventy days ago was now a prophet, apostle, and evangelist with a fire of God in his heart. The Spirit was to be upon all flesh.

All the way through the Bible we find the Spirit clothing Himself with a man, clothing a man with Himself, supplying men to be cunning workers in gold and silver in the making of the Tabernacle. In the original chaos the Spirit brooded over the production of the new cosmos. The Spirit brooded over the Word made flesh in the womb of the virgin Mary. And on the day of Pentecost, the Spirit of God was poured forth on all flesh. If we are not having spiritual revelations, it is because we are not responsive to the Holy Spirit.

The book of *Acts* breaks beautifully into four segments which Jesus spoke of when He said that the disciples were to preach the gospel in (1) Jerusalem, (2) Judea, (3) Samaria, and (4) the uttermost parts of the earth. The first preaching of the gospel was in Jerusalem, then it spread by the disciples into Judea. It went on into Samaria through Philip and the deacons, plus the apostles. Then, the gospel went into the uttermost parts of the earth with Paul.

NOTES

NOTES

SEEING JESUS IN ACTS

The physical body in which Jesus *"...began both to do and teach"* **(Acts 1:1)** passed out of the apostles' sight. Jesus did not cease to be, but for their sakes His physical body vanished to make way for the new Body in which He would continue *"...to do and teach."* That Body is His Church.

There would be no book of *Acts* apart from the resurrected Christ! This is the Jesus that we see throughout this book – the living, indwelling Christ working through His Church.

THEME VERSE

"But ye shall receive power, after that the Holy Ghost is come upon you: and ye shall be witnesses unto me both in Jerusalem, and in all Judea, and in Samaria, and unto the uttermost part of the earth" **(Acts 1:8).**

OUTLINE

(Refer to maps on pages A13 and A14 in the APPENDIX.)

I. **WITNESSING IN JERUSALEM, JUDEA, AND SAMARIA -** ACTS 1-12
   A. **Peter Was the Leading Character.**

II. **WITNESSING UNTO THE UTTERMOST PARTS OF THE EARTH -** ACTS 13-28
   A. **Paul Was the Leading Character.**
   B. **The Spirit bade them go, and they went!**

THE OLD TESTAMENT QUOTED IN ACTS.

Acts 1:20
For it is written in the book of Psalms, Let his habitation be desolate, and let no man dwell therein: and his bishoprick let another take.

Psalms 69:25
Let their habitation be desolate; and let none dwell in their tents.

Psalms 109:8
Let his days be few; and let another take his office.

* * * * * *

Acts 2:17-21 (Romans 10:13)
And it shall come to pass in the last days, saith God, I will pour out of my Spirit upon all flesh: and your sons and your daughters shall prophesy, and your young men shall see visions, and your old men shall dream dreams: And on my servants and on my handmaidens I will pour out in those days of my Spirit; and they shall prophesy: And I will shew wonders in heaven above, and signs in the earth beneath; blood, and fire, and vapour of smoke: The sun shall be turned into darkness, and the moon into blood, before that great and notable day of the Lord come: And it shall come to pass, that whosoever shall call on the name of the Lord shall be saved.

Joel 2:28-32
And it shall come to pass afterward, that I will pour out my spirit upon all flesh; and your sons and your daughters shall prophesy, your old men shall dream dreams, your young men shall see visions: And also upon the servants and upon the and handmaids in those days will I pour out my spirit. And I will shew wonders in the heavens and in the earth, blood, and fire, and pillars of smoke. The sun shall be turned into darkness, and the moon into blood, before the great and the terrible day of the LORD come. And it shall come to pass, that whosoever shall call on the name of the LORD shall be delivered: for in mount Zion and in Jerusalem shall be deliverance, as the LORD hath said, and in the remnant whom the LORD shall call.

* * * * * *

Acts 2:25-31 (Acts 13:35)
For David speaketh concerning him, I foresaw the Lord always before my face, for he is on my right hand, that I should not be moved: Therefore did my heart rejoice, and my tongue was glad; moreover also my flesh shall rest in hope: Because thou will not leave my soul in hell, neither wilt thou suffer thine Holy One to see corruption. Thou hast made known to me the ways of life; thou shalt make me full of joy with thy countenance. Men and brethren, let me freely speak unto you of the patriarch David, that he is both dead and buried, and his sepulchre is with us unto this day. Therefore being a prophet, and knowing that God had sworn with an oath to him, that of the fruit of his loins, according to the flesh, he would raise up Christ to sit on his throne. He seeing this before spake of the resurrection of Christ, that his soul was not left in hell, neither his flesh did see corruption.

II Samuel 7:12,13
And when thy days be fulfilled, and thou shalt sleep with thy fathers, I will set up thy seed after thee, which shall proceed out of thy bowels, and I will establish his kingdom. He shall build an house for my name, and I will stablish the throne of his kingdom for ever.

Psalms 16:8-11
I have set the LORD always before me: because he is at my right hand, I shall not be moved. Therefore my heart is glad, and my glory rejoiceth: my flesh also shall rest in hope. For thou wilt not leave my soul in hell; neither wilt thou suffer thine Holy One to see corruption. Thou wilt shew me the path of life: in thy presence is fulness of joy; at thy right hand there are pleasures for evermore.

Psalms 89:3,4
I have made a covenant with my chosen, I have sworn unto David my servant, Thy seed will I establish for ever, and build up thy throne to all generations. Selah.

Psalms 132:11
The LORD hath sworn in truth unto David; he will not turn from it; Of the fruit of thy body will I set upon thy throne.

* * * * * *

Acts 2:34,35 (Matthew 22:44, 26:64; Mark 12:36, 14:62; Luke 20:42,43, 22:69; Hebrews 1:13, 10:12,13)
For David is not ascended into the heavens: but he saith himself, The LORD said unto my Lord, Sit thou on my right hand, Until I make thy foes thy footstool.

Psalms 110:1
The LORD said unto my Lord, Sit thou at my right hand, until I make thine enemies thy footstool.

* * * * * * * * * *

Acts 3:22 (Acts 7:37)
For Moses truly said unto the fathers, A prophet shall the Lord your God raise up unto you of your brethren, like unto me; him shall ye hear in all things whatsoever he shall say unto you.

Deuteronomy 18:15
The LORD thy God will raise up unto thee a Prophet from the midst of thee, of thy brethren, like unto me; unto him ye shall hearken.

* * * * * *

Acts 3:25 (Galatians 3:8)
Ye are the children of the prophets, and of the covenant which God made with our fathers, saying unto Abraham, And in thy seed shall all the kindreds of the earth be blessed.

Genesis 12:3
And I will bless them that bless thee, and curse him that curseth thee: and in thee shall all families of the earth be blessed.

Genesis 22:18
And in thy seed shall all the nations of the earth be blessed; because thou hast obeyed my voice.

Genesis 26:4
And I will make thy seed to multiply as the stars of heaven, and will give unto thy seed all these countries; and in thy seed shall all the nations of the earth be blessed.

Genesis 28:14
And thy seed shall be as the dust of the earth, and thou shalt spread abroad to the west, and to the east, and to the north, and to the south: and in thee and in thy seed shall all the families of the earth be blessed.

* * * * * *

Acts 4:11 (Matthew 21:42; Mark 12:10,11; Luke 20:17; I Peter 2:7)
This is the stone which was set at nought of you builders, which is become the head of the corner.

Psalms 118:22
The stone which the builders refused is become the head stone of the corner.

* * * * * *

Acts 4:24 (Acts 14:15; Revelation 10:6)
And when they heard that, they lifted up their voice to God with one accord, and said, Lord, thou art God, which hast made heaven, and earth, and the sea, and all that in them is.

Exodus 20:11
For in the six days the LORD made heaven and earth, the sea, and all that in them is, and rested the seventh day: wherefore the LORD blessed the sabbath day, and hallowed it.

Psalms 146:6
Which made heaven, and earth, the sea, and all that therein is: which keepeth truth for ever.

* * * * * *

Acts 4:25,26
Who by the mouth of thy servant David hast said, Why did the heathen rage, and the people imagine vain things? The kings of the earth stood up, and the rulers were gathered together against the Lord, and against his Christ.

Psalms 2:1,2
Why do the heathen rage, and the people imagine a vain thing? The kings of the earth set themselves, and the rulers take counsel together, against the LORD, and against his anointed, saying, Let us break their bands asunder, and cast away their cords from us.

* * * * * *

Acts 7:3
And said unto him, Get thee out of thy country and from thy kindred, and come into the land which I shall shew thee.

Genesis 12;1
Now the LORD had said unto Abram, Get thee out of thy country, and from thy kindred, and from thy father's house, unto a land that I will shew thee.

* * * * * *

Acts 7:5
And he gave him none inheritance in it, no, not so much as to set his foot on: yet he promised that he

would give it to him for a possession, and to his seed after him, when as yet he had no child.

Genesis 12:7
And the LORD appeared unto Abram, and said, Unto thy seed will I give this land: and there builded he an altar unto the LORD, who appeared unto him.

Genesis 13:15
For all the land which thou seest, to thee will I give it, and to thy seed for ever.

Genesis 17:8
And I will give unto thee, and to thy seed after thee, the land wherein thou art a stranger, all the land of Canaan, for an everlasting possession; and I will be their God.

Genesis 48:4
And said unto me, Behold, I will make thee fruitful, and multiply thee, and I will make of thee a multitude of people; and will give this land to thy seed after thee for an everlasting possession.

* * * * * *

Acts 7:6,7
And God spake on this wise, That his seed should sojourn in a strange land; and that they should bring them into bondage, and entreat them evil four hundred years. And the nation to whom they shall be in bondage will I judge, said God: and after that shall they come forth, and serve me in this place.

Genesis 15:13,14
And he said unto Abram, Know of a surety that thy seed shall be a stranger in a land that is not theirs, and shall serve them; and they shall afflict them four hundred years; And also that nation, whom, they shall serve, will I judge: and afterward shall they come out with great substance.

Exodus 3:12
And he said, Certainly I will be with thee; and this shall be a token unto thee, that I have sent thee: When thou hast brought forth the people out of Egypt, ye shall serve God upon this mountain.

Acts 7:18
Till another king arose, which knew not Joseph.

Exodus 1:8
Now there arose up a new king over Egypt, which knew not Joseph.

* * * * * *

Acts 7:27-30 (Acts 7:35)
But he that did his neighbour wrong thrust him away, saying, Who made thee a ruler and a judge over us? Wilt thou kill me, as thou didst the Egyptian yesterday? Then fled Moses at this saying, and was a stranger in the land of Madian, where he begat two sons. And when forty years were expired, there appeared to him in the wilderness of mount Sina an angel of the Lord in a flame of fire in a bush.

Exodus 2:13-15
And when he went out the second day, behold, two men of the Hebrews strove together: and he said to him that did the wrong, Wherefore smitest thou thy fellow? And he said, Who made thee a prince and a judge over us? Intendest thou to kill me, as thou killedst the Egyptian? And Moses feared, and said, Surely this thing is known. Now when Pharaoh heard this thing, he sought to slay Moses. But Moses fled from the face of Pharaoh, and dwelt in the land of Midian: and he sat down by a well.

Exodus 3:2
And the angel of the Lord appeared unto him in a flame of fire out of the midst of a bush: and he looked, and behold, the bush burned with fire, and the bush was not consumed.

* * * * * *

Acts 7:32 (Matthew 22:32; Mark 12:26; Luke 20:37)
Saying, I am the God of thy fathers, the God of Abraham, and the God of Isaac, and the God of Jacob. Then Moses trembled, and durst not behold.

Exodus 3:6
Moreover he said, I am the God of thy father, the God of Abraham, the God of Isaac, and the God of Jacob. And Moses hid his face; for he was afraid to look upon God.

Exodus 3:15
And God said moreover unto Moses, This shalt thou say into the children of Israel, the LORD God of your fathers, the God of Abraham, the God of Isaac, and the God of Jacob, hath sent me unto you: this is my name for ever, and this is my memorial unto all generations.

* * * * * *

Acts 7:33,34
Then said the Lord to him, Put off thy shoes from thy feet: for the place where thou standest is holy ground. I have seen, I have seen the affliction of my people which is in Egypt, and I have heard their groaning, and am come down to deliver them. And now come, I will send thee into Egypt.

Exodus 3:5,7,8,10
And he said, Draw not nigh hither: put off thy shoes from off thy feet, for the place whereon thou standest is holy ground. And the LORD said, I have surely seen the affliction of my people which are in Egypt, and have heard their cry by reason of their taskmasters; for I know their sorrows; And I am come down to deliver them out of the hand of the Egyptians, and to bring them up out of that land unto a good land and a large, unto a land flowing with milk and honey; unto the place of the Canaanites, and the Hittites, and the Amorites, and the Perizzites, and the Hivites, and the Jebusites. Come now therefore, and I will send thee unto Pharaoh, that thou mayest bring forth my people the children of Israel out of Egypt.

* * * * * *

Acts 7:35 (Acts 7:27)
This Moses whom they refused, saying, Who made thee a ruler and a judge? the same did God send to be a ruler and a deliverer by the hand of the angel which appeared to him in the bush.

Exodus 2:14
And he said, Who made thee a prince and a judge over us? intendest thou to kill me, as thou killedst the Egyptian? And Moses feared, and said, Surely this thing is known.

* * * * * *

Acts 7:37 (Acts 3:22)
This is that Moses, which said unto the children of Israel, A prophet shall the Lord your God raise up unto you of your brethren, like unto me; him shall ye hear.

Deuteronomy 18:15
The LORD thy God will raise up unto thee a Prophet from the midst of thee, of thy brethren, like unto me; unto him ye shall hearken.

* * * * * *

Acts 7:40
Saying unto Aaron, Make us gods to go before us: for as for this Moses, which brought us out of the land of Egypt, we wot not what is become of him.

Exodus 32:1
And when the people saw that Moses delayed to come down out of the mount, the people gathered themselves together unto Aaron, and said unto him, Up, make us gods, which shall go before us; for as for this Moses, the man that brought us up out of the land of Egypt, we wot not what is become of him.

Exodus 32:23
For they said unto me, Make us gods, which shall go before us: for as for this Moses, the man that brought us up out of the land of Egypt, we wot not what is become of him.

* * * * * *

Acts 7:42,43
Then God turned, and gave them up to worship the host of heaven; as it is written in the book of the prophets, O ye house of Israel, have ye offered to me slain beasts and sacrifices by the space of forty years in the wilderness? Yea, ye took up the tabernacle of Moloch, and the star of your god Remphan, figures which ye made to worship them: and I will carry you away beyond Babylon.

Amos 5:25-27
Have ye offered unto me sacrifices and offerings in the wilderness forty years, O house of Israel? But ye have borne the tabernacle of your Moloch and Chiun your images, the star of your god, which ye made to yourselves. Therefore will I cause you to go into captivity beyond Damascus, saith the LORD, whose name is The God of hosts.

* * * * * *

Acts 7:49,50
Heaven is my throne, and earth is my footstool: what house will ye build me? saith the Lord: or what is the place of my rest? Hath not my hand made all these things?

Isaiah 66:1,2
Thus saith the LORD, The heaven is my throne, and the earth is my footstool: where is the house that ye build unto me? and where is the place of my rest? For all those things hath mine hand made, and all those things have been, saith the LORD: but to this man will I look, even to him that is poor and of a contrite spirit, and trembleth at my word.

* * * * * *

Acts 8:32,33
The place of the scripture which he read was this, He was led as a sheep to the slaughter; and like a lamb dumb before his shearer, so opened he not his mouth: In his humiliation his judgment was taken away: and who shall declare his generation? for his life is taken from the earth.

Isaiah 53:7, 8
He was oppressed, and he was afflicted, yet he opened not his mouth: he is brought as a lamb to the slaughter, and as a sheep before her shearers is dumb, so he openeth not his mouth. He was taken from prison and from judgment: and who shall declare his generation? for he was cut off out of the land of the living: for the transgression of my people was he stricken.

* * * * * *

Acts 13:22
And when he had removed him, he raised up unto them David to be their king; to whom also he gave testimony, and said, I have found David the son of Jesse, a man after mine own heart, which shall fulfill all my will.

Psalms 89:20
I have David my servant; with my holy oil have I anointed him.

I Samuel 13:14
But now thy kingdom shall not continue: the LORD hath sought him a man after his own heart, and the LORD hath commanded him to be captain over his people, because thou hast not kept that which the LORD commanded thee.

* * * * * *

Acts 13:33 (Hebrews 1:5, 5:5)
God hath fulfilled the same unto us their children, in that he hath raised up Jesus again; as it is also written in the second psalm, Thou art my Son, this day have I begotten thee.

Psalms 2:7
I will declare the decree: the LORD hath said unto me, Thou art my Son; this day have I begotten thee.

* * * * * *

Acts 13:34
And as concerning that he raised him up from the dead, now no more to return to corruption, he said on this wise, I will give you the sure mercies of David.

Isaiah 55:3
Incline your ear, and come unto me: hear, and your soul shall live; and I will make an everlasting covenant with you, even the sure mercies of David.

* * * * * *

Acts 13:35 (Acts 2:27,31)
Wherefore he saith also in another psalm, Thou shalt not suffer thine Holy One to see corruption.

Psalms 16:10
For thou wilt not leave my soul in hell; neither wilt thou suffer thine Holy One to see corruption.

* * * * * *

Acts 13:41
Behold, ye despisers, and wonder, and perish: for I work a work in your days, a work which ye shall in no wise believe, though a man declare it unto you.

Habakkuk 1:5
Behold ye among the heathen, and regard, and wonder marvelously: for I will work a work in your days, which ye will not believe, though it be told you.

* * * * * *

Acts 13:47 (Luke 2:32)
For so hath the Lord commanded us, saying, I have set thee to be a light of the Gentiles, that thou shouldest be for salvation unto the ends of the earth.

Isaiah 42:6
I the LORD have called thee in righteousness, and will hold thine hand, and will keep thee, and give thee for a covenant of the people, for a light of the Gentiles.

Isaiah 49:6
And he said, It is a light thing that thou shouldest be my servant to raise up the tribes of Jacob, and to restore the preserved of Israel: I will also give thee for a light to the Gentiles, that thou mayest be my salvation unto the end of the earth.

* * * * * *

Acts 14:15 (Acts 4:24)
And saying, Sirs, why do ye these things? We also are men of like passions with you, and preach unto you that ye should turn from these vanities unto the living God, which made heaven, and earth, and the sea, and all things that are therein.

Exodus 20:11
For in six days the LORD made heaven and earth, the sea, and all that in them is, and rested the seventh day: wherefore the LORD blessed the sabbath day, and hallowed it.

Psalms 146:6
Which made heaven, and earth, the sea, and all that therein is: which keepeth truth for ever.

* * * * * *

Acts 15:16-18
After this I will return, and will build again the tabernacle of David, which is fallen down; and I will build again the ruins thereof, and I will set it up: That the residue of men might seek after the Lord, and all the Gentiles, upon whom my name is called, saith the Lord, who doeth all these things. Known unto God are all his works from the beginning of the world.

Amos 9:11,12
In that day will I raise up the tabernacle of David that is fallen, and close up the breaches thereof; and I will raise up his ruins, and I will build it as in the days of old: That they may possess the remnant of Edom, and of all the heathen, which are called by my name, saith the LORD that doeth this.

* * * * * *

Acts 23:5
Then said Paul, I wist not, brethren, that he was the high priest: for it is written, Thou shalt not speak evil of the ruler of thy people.

Exodus 22:28
Thou shalt not revile the gods, nor curse the ruler of thy people.

* * * * * *

Acts 28:26,27 (Matthew 13:14,15; Mark 4:12)
Saying, Go unto this people, and say, Hearing ye shall hear, and shall not understand; and seeing ye shall see, and not perceive: For the heart of this people is waxed gross, and their ears are dull of hearing, and their eyes have they closed; lest they should see with their eyes, and hear with their ears, and understand with their heart, and should be converted, and I should heal them.

Isaiah 6:9,10
And he said, Go, and tell this people, Hear ye indeed, but understand not; and see ye indeed, but perceive not. Make the heart of this people fat, and make their ears heavy, and shut their eyes; lest they see with their eyes, and hear with their ears, and understand with their heart, and convert, and be healed.

Jeremiah 5:21
Hear now this, O foolish people, and without understanding; which have eyes, and see not; which have ears, and hear not.

ROMANS

<table>
<tr><th colspan="4">SALVATION BY FAITH</th></tr>
<tr><td>INTRODUCTION TO THE GOSPEL</td><td>UNIVERSAL SINFULNESS</td><td>JUSTIFICATION BY FAITH</td><td>SANCTIFICATION</td></tr>
<tr><td>Salutation & theme: 1</td><td>"None are righteous": 2,3</td><td>Received by faith: 3
Apart from human, work, ordinances, & law: 4
Results: 5</td><td>Identification with Christ: 6
Deliverance from law & old nature: 7,8</td></tr>
</table>

GOD'S DEALING WITH ISRAEL	"OUR REASONABLE SERVICE"	CONCLUSION & PERSONAL TESTIMONY
Mercy: **9** Responsibility: **10** Remnant & gentiles: **11**	Service toward God & fellow believers: **12** Toward government & law: **13** Jews & gentiles: **14,15**	Ministry in Rome: **15** Greetings:**16**

LOCATION: The Mediterranean

OVERVIEW:
God offers His gift of righteousness to everyone who comes to Jesus Christ by faith (Romans 1:16,17).

TIME: A.D. 57

FAST FACTS

AUTHOR AND SETTING:

Paul, written from Corinth

PURPOSE:

Paul had a sixfold purpose in writing *Romans*: (1) to clarify the principle of justification by faith; (2) to explain the unbelief of Israel; (3) to commend Phoebe to the church at Rome; (4) to clarify the Mosaic Law and the new law of the Spirit of life; (5) to detail the Christian's victory over the flesh; and (6) to speak out against legalism.

SEEING JESUS:

Romans is Paul's theological explanation for the life, death, and resurrection of Jesus Christ.

NOTES

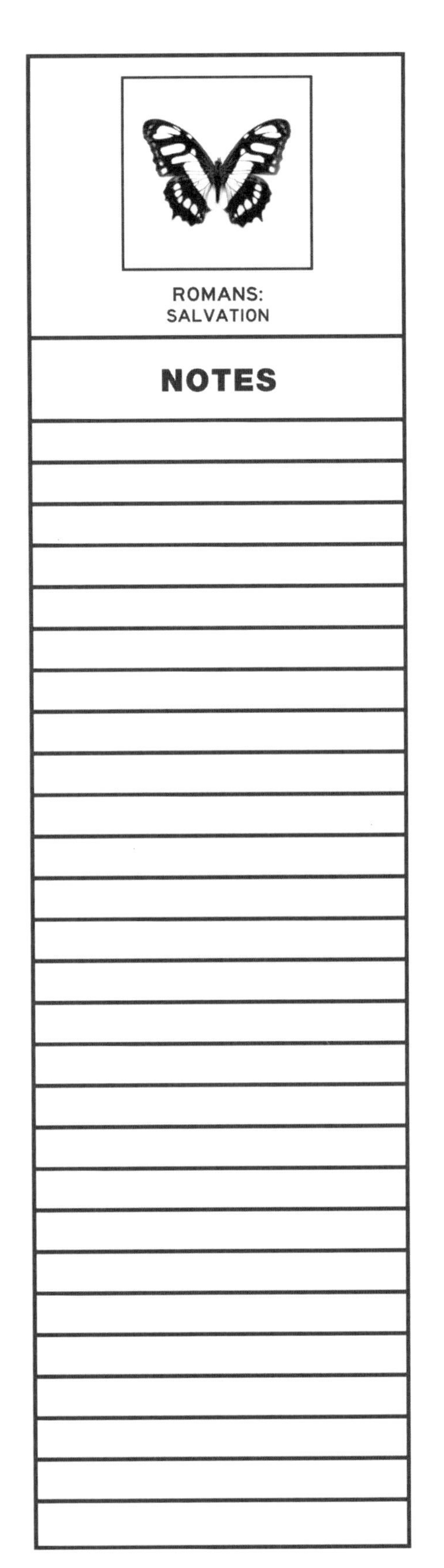

SEEING JESUS IN ROMANS

AUTHOR & SETTING

The human author of *Romans* was called *Saul*, meaning "asked of God," until the time of his clash with a Jewish false prophet named Bar-jesus (Acts 13:6-11). From that time forth Saul is referred to as *Paul*, meaning "little." He is the giant apostle of the Christian faith who considered himself *"...less than the least of all saints, ..."* **(Ephesians 3:8).** Paul dictated the book of Romans through his scribe, Tertius:

"I, Tertius, who wrote this epistle, salute you in the Lord" **(Romans 16:22).**

Paul was the human author of 13 New Testament books. Nine of these letters were written to churches, and four were written to individuals. *Chronologically* they are arranged as follows: Galatians, I Thessalonians, II Thessalonians, I Corinthians, II Corinthians, Romans, Colossians, Philemon, Ephesians, Philippians, I Timothy, Titus, and II Timothy.

Paul wrote the book of *Romans* to the saints at Rome around 58 A.D. from the house of Gaius in Corinth:

"Gaius mine host, and of the whole church, saluteth you. Erastus the chamberlain of the city saluteth you, and Quartus a brother" **(Romans 16:23)**

"I thank God that I baptized none of you, but Crispus and Gaius" **(ICorinthians 1:14).**

Evidently a businesswoman named Phoebe (KJV Phebe) delivered this letter to the saints at Rome while traveling from Corinth to Rome:

"I commend unto you Phebe our sister, which is a servant of the church which is at Cenchrea: That ye receive her in the Lord, as becometh saints, and that ye assist her in whatsoever business she hath need of you: for she hath been a succourer of many, and of myself also" **(Romans 16:1).**

OVERVIEW

Paul had six reasons for writing this letter:

He wanted to clarify the principles of justification: was it by the deeds of the law or a work of God apart from the law?

He wanted to explain the unbelief of Israel in the past, their failure in the previous dispensation, and offer a remedy for their present situation.

He wished to commend Phoebe to the church at Rome.

He wanted to clarify the issue of what constituted the Christian life - the old Mosaic Law or the new law of the spirit of life? (Romans 8)

He desired to help Roman believers understand how to have victory over the flesh by avoiding two extremes of belief in Rome at that time: (1) there is no flesh after salvation or (2) there is never any victory over the flesh until death.

Paul wanted to protect Roman Christians from the infiltration of legalism which had already made great inroads into the Roman church (Romans 13,14).

SEEING JESUS IN ROMANS

The book of *Romans* is a theological presentation of the doctrines of sin and salvation, including justification, reconciliation, and glorification. The person and work of Jesus is viewed as the foundation upon which everything in the Christian life is obtained.

NOTES

THEME VERSE

"For therein is the righteousness of God revealed from faith to faith: as it is written, The just shall live by faith" **(Romans 1:17)**

OUTLINE

(Refer to maps on pages A14-A18 in the APPENDIX.)

I. **INTRODUCTION TO THE GOSPEL OF GOD -** ROMANS 1:1-17
   - A. **Salutation -** Romans 1:1-17
   - B. **The Theme -** Romans 1:17

II. **UNIVERSAL SINFULNESS -** ROMANS 1:18-3:20
   - A. **Are We Better Than They?**
     1. *"What then? are we better than they? No, in no wise: for we have before proved both Jews and Gentiles, that they are all under sin; As it is written, There is none righteous, no, not one"* **(Romans 3:9,10).**
   - B. **By the Law Is the Knowledge of Sin**
     1. *"Now we know that what things soever the law saith, it saith to them who are under the law: that every mouth may be stopped, and all the world may become guilty before God. Therefore by the deeds of the law there shall no flesh be justified in his sight: for by the law is the knowledge of sin"* **(Romans 3:19,20)**

III. **JUSTIFICATION BY FAITH -** ROMANS 3:21-5:21
   - A. **Righteousness is Received by Faith:**
     1. *"For all have sinned, and come short of the glory of God; Being justified freely by his grace through the redemption that is in Christ Jesus"* **(Romans 3:23,24).**

NOTES

2. **Justified apart from human work** - Romans 4:1-8
3. **Apart from ordinances** - Romans 4:9-12
4. **Apart from law** - Romans 4:13-25
5. **Results** - Romans 5:1-11

B. **Contrast** - Romans 5:12-21

1. **Adam - sin, death, and condemnation**
2. **Christ - righteousness, life, and justification**

IV. **SANCTIFICATION** - ROMANS 6-9

A. **Identification With Christ In Death and Resurrection** - Romans 6:1-13

B. **Deliverance From the Law** - Romans 6:14-7:14

C. **Deliverance From the Old Nature** - Romans 8:1-4

V. **GOD'S DEALING WITH ISRAEL** - ROMANS 9-11

A. **God Exercised Mercy** - Romans 9.

B. **Israel Had a Responsibility and Failed** - Romans 10:2,3

C. **God Did Not Cast Them Away Forever** - Romans 11:1

D. **There Is Still a Remnant That Believes** - Romans 11:5

E. **Gentiles Are Warned To Learn through Experience** - Romans 11:13-22

F. **The Nation of Israel Is Yet To Be Saved** - Romans 11:25-27

G. **Doxology**

VI. **OUR REASONABLE SERVICE** - ROMANS 12-15:13

A. **Toward God** - Romans 12:1,2

B. **Toward Fellow Believers** - Romans 12:3-16

C. **Toward All Men** - Romans 12:17-21

D. **Toward Government** - Romans 13:1-7

E. **Outworking of the Law Through Love** - Romans 13:8-15:3

F. **Jews and Gentiles - One in Christ** - Romans 15:4-13

VII. **THE CONCLUSION, PERSONAL TESTIMONY, AND GREETING** - ROMANS 15:14-16:27

A. **Paul's Desire to Minister in Rome** - Romans 15:32

B. **Paul's List of Acquaintances** - Romans 16

THE OLD TESTAMENT QUOTED IN ROMANS.

Roman 1:17 (Galatians 3:11; Hebrews 10:38)
For therein is the righteousness of God revealed from faith to faith; as it is written,The just shall live by faith.

Habakkuk 2:4
Behold, his soul which is lifted up is not upright in him: but the just shall live by his faith.

* * * * * *

Romans 2:6 (Matthew 16:27)
Who will render to every man according to his deeds.

Psalms 62:12
Also unto thee, O Lord, belongeth mercy: for thou renderest to every man according to his work.

Proverbs 24:12
If thou sayest, Behold, we knew it not; doth not he that pondereth the heart consider it? and he that keepeth thy soul, doth not he know it? and shall not he render to every man according to his works?

* * * * * *

Romans 2:24
For the name of God is blasphemed among the Gentiles through you, as it is written.

Isaiah 52:5
Now therefore, what have I here, saith the LORD, that my people is taken away for nought? they that rule over them make them to howl, saith the LORD; and my name continually every day is blasphemed.

Ezekiel 36:20
And when they entered unto the heathen, whither they went, they profaned my holy name, when they said to them, These are the people of the LORD, and are gone forth out of his land.

* * * * * *

Romans 3:4
God forbid: yea, let God be true, but every man a liar; as it is written, That thou mightest be justified in thy sayings, and mightest overcome when thou art judged.

Psalms 51:4
Against thee, thee only, have I sinned, and done this evil in thy sight: that thou mightest be justified when thou speakest, and be clear when thou judgest.

* * * * * *

Romans 3:10-18
As it is written, There is none righteous, no, not one: There is none that understandeth, there is none that seeketh after God. They are all gone out of the way, they are together become unprofitable; there is none that doeth good, no, not one. Their throat is an open sepulchre; with their tongues they have used to deceit; the poison of asps is under their lips: Who mouth is full of cursing and bitterness: Their feet are swift to shed blood: Destruction and misery are in their ways: And the way of peace have they not known: There is no fear of God before their eyes.

Psalms 14:1-3
The fool hath said in his heart, There is no God. They are corrupt, they have done abominable works, there is none that doeth good. The LORD looked down from heaven upon the children of men, to see if there were any that did understand, and seek God. They are all gone aside, they are all together become filthy: there is none that doeth good, no, not one.

Psalms 53:1-3
The fool hath said in his heart, There is no God. Corrupt are they, and have done abominable iniquity: there is none that doeth good. God looked down from heaven upon the children of men, to see if there were any that did understand, that did seek God. Every one of them is gone back: they are altogether become filthy; there is none that doeth good, no, not one.

Psalms 5:9
For there is no faithfulness in their mouth; their inward part is very wickedness; their throat is an open sepulchre; they flatter with their tongue.

Psalms 140:3
They have sharpened their tongues like a serpent; adders' poison is under their lips. Selah.

Psalms 10:7
His mouth is full of cursing and deceit and fraud: under his tongue is mischief and vanity.

Isaiah 59:7-8
Their feet run to evil, and they make haste to shed innocent blood: their thoughts are thoughts of iniquity; wasting and destruction are in their paths. The way of

peace they know not; and there is no judgment in their goings: they have made them crooked paths: whosoever goeth therein shall not know peace.

Psalms 36:1
The transgression of the wicked saith within my heart, that there is no fear of God before his eyes.

* * * * * *

Romans 4:3
(Romans 4:9, 4:22; Galatians 3:6; James 2:23)
For what saith the scripture? Abraham believed God, and it was counted unto him for righteousness.

Genesis 15:6
And he believed in the LORD; and he counted it to him for righteousness.

* * * * * *

Romans 4:7,8
Saying, Blessed are they whose iniquities are forgiven, and whose sins are covered. Blessed is the man to whom the Lord will not impute sin.

Psalms 32:1,2
Blessed is he whose transgression is forgiven, whose sin is covered. Blessed is the man unto whom the LORD imputeth not iniquity, and in whose spirit there is no guile.

Romans 4:9
(Romans 4:3, 4:22, Galatians 3:6; James 2:23)
Cometh this blessedness then upon the circumcision only, or upon the uncircumcision also? for we say that faith was reckoned to Abraham for righteousness.

Genesis 15:6
And he believed in the LORD; and he counted it to him for righteousness.

* * * * * *

Romans 4:17
(As it is written, I have made thee a father of many nations,) before him whom he believed, even God, who quickeneth the dead, and calleth those things which be not as though they were.

Genesis 17:5
Neither shall thy name any more be called Abram, but thy name shall be Abraham; for a father of many nations have made thee.

Romans 4:18 (Hebrews 11:12)
Who against hope believed in hope, that he might become the father of many nations, according to that which was spoken, So shall thy seed be.

Genesis 15:5
And he brought him forth abroad, and said, Look now toward heaven, and tell the stars, if thou be able to number them: and he said unto him, So shall thy seed be.

* * * * * *

Romans 4:22
(Romans 4:3, 4:9; Galatians 3:6; James 2:23)
And therefore it was imputed to him for righteousness.

Genesis 15:6
And he believed in the LORD; and he counted it to him for righteousness.

* * * * * *

Romans 7:7 (Romans 13:9)
What shall we say then? Is the law sin? God forbid. Nay, I had not known sin, but by the law: for I had not known lust, except the law had said, Thou shalt not covet.

Exodus 20:17
Thou shalt not covet thy neighbour's house, thou shalt not covet thy neighbour's wife, nor his manservant, nor his maidservant, nor his ox, nor his ass, nor any thing that is thy neighbour's.

Deuteronomy 5:21
Neither shalt thou desire thy neighbour's wife, neither shalt thou covet thy neighbour's house, his field, or his manservant, or his maidservant, his ox, or his ass, or any thing that is thy neighbour's.

* * * * * *

Romans 8:36
As it is written, For thy sake we are killed all the day long; we are accounted as sheep for the slaughter.

Psalms 44:22
Yea, for thy sake are we killed all the day long; we are counted as sheep for the slaughter.

* * * * * *

Romans 9:7 (Hebrews 11:18)
Neither, because they are the seed of Abraham, are they all children: but, In Isaac shall thy seed be called.

Genesis 21:12
And God said unto Abraham, Let it not be grievous in thy sight because of the lad, and because of thy bondwoman; in all that Sarah hath said unto thee, hearken unto her voice; for in Isaac shall thy seed be called.

* * * * * *

Romans 9:9
For this is the word of promise, At this time will I come, and Sarah shall have a son.

Genesis 18:10
And he said, I will certainly return unto thee according to the time of life; and, lo, Sarah thy wife shall have a son. And Sarah heard it in the tent door, which was behind him.

* * * * * *

Romans 9:12
It was said unto her, The elder shall serve the younger.

Genesis 25:23
And the LORD said unto her, Two nations are in thy womb, and two manner of people shall be separated from thy bowels; and the one people shall be stronger than the other people; and the elder shall serve the younger.

* * * * * *

Romans 9:13
As it is written, Jacob have I loved, but Esau have I hated.

Malachi 1:2,3
I have loved you, saith the LORD, Yet ye say, Wherein hast thou loved us? Was not Esau Jacob's brother? saith the LORD; yet I loved Jacob, And I hated Esau, and laid his mountains and his heritage waste for the dragons of the wilderness.

* * * * * *

Romans 9:15
For he saith to Moses, I will have mercy on whom I will have mercy, and I will have compassion on whom I will have compassion.

Exodus 33:19
And he said, I will make all my goodness pass before thee, and I will proclaim the name of the LORD before thee; and will be gracious to whom I will be gracious, and will shew mercy on whom I will shew mercy.

* * * * * *

Romans 9:17
For the scripture saith unto Pharaoh, Even for this same purpose have I raised thee up, that I might shew my power in thee, and that my name might be declared throughout all the earth.

Exodus 9:16
And in very deed for this cause have I raised thee up, for to shew in thee my power; and that my name may be declared throughout all the earth.

* * * * * *

Romans 9:25 (I Peter 2:10)
As he saith also in Osee, I will call them my people, which were not my people; and her beloved, which was not beloved.

Hosea 2:23
And I will sow her unto me in the earth; and I will have mercy upon her that had not obtained mercy; and I will say to them which were not my people, Thou art my people; and they shall say, Thou art my God.

* * * * * *

Romans 9:26
And it shall come to pass, that in the place where it was said unto them, Ye are not my people; there shall they be called the children of the living God.

Hosea 1:10
Yet the number of the children of Israel shall be as the sand of the sea, which cannot be measured nor numbered; and it shall come to pass, that in the place where it was said unto them, Ye are not my people, there it shall be said unto them, Ye are the sons of the living God.

* * * * * *

Romans 9:27,28
Esaias also crieth concerning Israel, Though the number of the children of Israel be as the sand of the sea, a remnant shall be saved: For he will finish the work, and cut it short in righteousness: because a short work will the Lord make upon the earth.

Isaiah 10:22,23
For though thy people Israel be as the sand of the sea, yet a remnant of them shall return: the consumption decreed shall overflow with righteousness. For the Lord GOD of hosts shall make a consumption, even determined, in the midst of the land.

* * * * * *

Romans 9:29
And as Esaias said before, Except the Lord of Sabaoth had left us a seed, we had been as Sodoma, and been made like unto Gomorrah.

Isaiah 1:9
Except the LORD of hosts had left unto us a very small remnant, we should have been as Sodom, and we should have been like unto Gomorrah.

Deuteronomy 29:23
And that the whole land thereof is brimstone, and salt, and burning, that it is not sown, nor beareth, nor any grass growth therein, like the overthrow of Sodom, and Gomorrah, Admah, and Zeboim, which the LORD overthrew in his anger, and in his wrath.

* * * * * *

Romans 9:33 (Romans 10:11; I Peter 2:6,8)
As it is written, Behold, I lay in Sion a stumblingstone and rock of offence: and whosoever believeth on him shall not be ashamed.

Isaiah 28:16
Therefore thus saith the Lord GOD, Behold, I lay in Zion for a foundation a stone, a tried stone, a precious corner stone, a sure foundation: he that believeth shall not make haste.

Isaiah 8:14
And he shall be for a sanctuary; but for a stone of stumbling and for a rock of offence to both the houses of Israel, for a gin and for a snare to the inhabitants of Jerusalem.

* * * * * *

Romans 10:6-8
But the righteousness which is of faith speaketh on this wise, Say not in thine heart, Who shall ascend into heaven? (that is, to bring Christ down from above:) Or, Who shall descend into the deep? (that is, to bring up Christ again from the dead.) But what saith it? The word is nigh thee, even in thy mouth, and in thy heart: that is, the word of faith, which we preach.

Deuteronomy 30:12-14
It is not in heaven, that thou shouldest say, Who shall go up for us to heaven, and bring it unto us, that we may hear it, and do it? Neither is it beyond the sea, that thou shouldest say, Who shall go over the sea for us, and bring it unto us, that we may hear it, and do it? But the word is very nigh unto thee, in thy mouth, and in thy heart, that thou mayest do it.

* * * * * *

Romans 10:11 (Romans 9:33; I Peter 2:6)
For the scripture saith, Whosoever believeth on him shall not be ashamed.

Isaiah 28:16
Therefore this saith the Lord GOD, Behold, I lay in Zion for a foundation a stone, a tried stone, a precious corner stone, a sure foundation: he that believeth shall not make haste.

* * * * * *

Romans 10:13 (Acts 2:21)
For whosoever shall call upon the name of the Lord shall be saved.

Joel 2:32
And it shall come to pass, that whosoever shall call on the name of the LORD shall be delivered: for in mount Zion and in Jerusalem shall be deliverance, as the LORD hath said, and in the remnant whom the LORD shall call.

* * * * * *

Romans 10:15 (Ephesians 6:15)
And how shall they preach, except they be sent? as it is written, How beautiful are the feet of them that preach the gospel of peace, and bring glad tidings of good things!

Isaiah 52:7
How beautiful upon the mountains are the feet of him that bringeth good tidings, that publisheth peace; that bringeth good tidings of good, that publisheth salvation; that saith into Zion, Thy God reigneth.

Nahum 1:15
Behold upon the mountains the feet of him that bringeth good tidings, that publisheth peace! O Judah, keep thy solemn feasts, perform thy vows, for the wicked shall no more pass through thee; he is utterly cut off.

* * * * * *

Romans 10:16 (John 12:38)
But they have not all obeyed the gospel. For Esaias saith, Lord, who hath believed our report?

Isaiah 53:1
Who hath believed our report? and to whom is the arm of the LORD revealed?

* * * * * *

Romans 10:18
But I say, Have they not heard? Yes verily, their sound went into all the earth, and their words unto the ends of the world.

Psalms 19:4
Their line is gone out through all the earth, and their words to the end of the world. In them hath he set a tabernacle for the sun.

* * * * * *

Romans 10:19
But I say, Did not Israel know? First Moses saith, I will provoke you to jealousy by them that are no people, and by a foolish nation I will anger you.

Deuteronomy 32:21
They have moved me to jealousy with that which is not God; they have provoked me to anger with their vanities: and I will move them to jealousy with those which are not a people; I will provoke them to anger with a foolish nation.

* * * * * *

Romans 10:20
But Esaias is very bold, and saith, I was found of them that sought me not; I was made manifest unto them that asked not after me.

Isaiah 65:1
I am sought of them that asked not for me; I am found of them that sought me not: I said, Behold me, behold me, unto a nation that was not called by my name.

* * * * * *

Romans 10:21
But to Israel he saith, All day long I have stretched forth my hands unto a disobedient and gainsaying people.

Isaiah 65:2
I have spread out my hands all the day unto a rebellious people, which walketh in a way that was not good, after their own thoughts.

* * * * * *

Romans 11:3
Lord, they have killed thy prophets, and digged down thine altars; and I am left alone, and they seek my life.

I Kings 19:10
And he said, I have been very jealous for the LORD God of hosts: for the children of Israel have forsaken thy covenant, thrown down thine altars, and slain thy prophets with the sword; and I, even I only, am left; and they seek my life, to take it away.

I Kings 19:14
And he said, I have been very jealous for the LORD God of hosts: because the children of Israel have forsaken thy covenant, thrown down thine altars, and slain thy prophets with the sword; and I, even I only, am left; and they seek my life, to take it away.

* * * * * *

Romans 11:4
But what saith the answer of God unto him? I have reserved to myself seven thousand men, who have not bowed the knee to the image of Baal.

I Kings 19:18
Yet I have left me seven thousand in Israel, all the knees which have not bowed unto Baal, and every mouth which hath not kissed him.

* * * * * *

Romans 11:8
(According as it is written, God hath given them the spirit of slumber, eyes that they should not see, and ears that they should not hear;) unto this day.

Isaiah 29:10
For the LORD hath poured out upon you the spirit of deep sleep, and hath closed your eyes; the prophets and your rulers, the seers hath he covered.

Deuteronomy 29:4
Yet the LORD hath not given you an heart to perceive, and eyes to see, and ears to hear, unto this day.

* * * * * *

Romans 11:9,10
And David saith, Let their table be made a snare, and a trap, and a stumblingblock, and a recompence unto them: Let their eyes be darkened, that they may not see, and bow down their back away.

Psalms 69:22,23
Let their table become a snare before them: and that which should have been for their welfare, let it become a trap. Let their eyes be darkened, that they see not; and make their loins continually to shake.

* * * * * *

Romans 11:26,27
And so all Israel shall be saved: as it is written, There shall come out of Sion the Deliverer, and shall turn away ungodliness from Jacob: For this is my covenant unto them, when I shall take away their sins.

Isaiah 59:20,21
And the Redeemer shall come to Zion, and unto them that turn from transgression in Jacob, saith the LORD. As for me, this is my covenant with them, saith the LORD; My spirit that is upon thee, and my words which I have put in they mouth, shall not depart out of thy mouth, nor out of the mouth of thy seed, nor out of the mouth of thy seed's seed, saith the LORD, from henceforth and for ever.

Jeremiah 31:33,34
But this shall be the covenant that I will make with the house of Israel; After those days, saith the LORD, I will put my law in their inwards parts, and write it in their hearts; and will be their God, and they shall be my people. And they shall teach no more every man his neighbour, and every man his brother, saying Know the LORD: for they shall all know me, from the least of them unto the greatest of them, saith the LORD: for I will forgive their iniquity, and I will remember their sin no more.

Isaiah 27:9
By this therefore shall the iniquity of Jacob be purged; and this is all the fruit to take away his sin; when he maketh all the stones of the altar as chalkstones that are beaten in sunder, the groves and images shall not stand up.

* * * * * *

Romans 11:34 (I Corinthians 2:16)
For who hath known the mind of the Lord? Or who hath been his counsellor?

Isaiah 40:13
Who hath directed the Spirit of the LORD, or being his counsellor hath taught him?

* * * * * *

Romans 11:35
Or who hath first given to him, and it shall be recompensed unto him again?

Job 41:11
Who hath prevented me, that I should repay him? Whatsoever is under the whole heaven is mine.

* * * * * *

Romans 12:19 (Hebrews 10:30)
Dearly beloved, avenge not yourselves, but rather give place unto wrath: for it is written, Vengeance is mine; I will repay, saith the Lord.

Deuteronomy 32:35,36
To me belongeth vengeance, and recompence; their foot shall slide in due time: for the day of their calamity is at hand, and the things that shall come upon them make haste. For the LORD shall judge his people, and repent himself for his servants, when he seeth that their power is gone, and there is none shut up, or left.

* * * * * *

Romans 12:20
Therefore if thine enemy hunger, feed him; if he thirst, give him drink: for in so doing thou shalt heap coals of fire on his head.

Proverbs 25:21,22
If thine enemy be hungry, give him bread to eat; and if he be thirsty, give him water to drink: For thou shalt heap coals of fire upon his head, and the LORD shall reward thee.

* * * * * *

Romans 13:9 (Matthew 5:21,27,43, 19:18,19, 22:39; Mark 10:19, 12:31; Luke 18:20; Romans 7:7; Galatians 5:14; James 2:8,11)
For this, Thou shalt not commit adultery, Thou shalt not kill, Thou shalt not steal, Thou shalt not bear false witness, Thou shalt not covet; and if there be any other commandment it is briefly comprehended in this saying, namely, Thou shalt love thy neighbour as thyself.

Exodus 20:13-15,17
Thou shalt not kill. Thou shalt not commit adultery. Thou shalt not steal. Thou shat not covet they neighbour's house, thou shalt not covet thy neighbour's wife, nor his manservant, nor his maidservant, nor his ox, nor his ass, nor any thing that is thy neighbour's.

Deuteronomy 5:17-19, 21
Thou shalt not kill. Neither shalt thou commit adultery. Neither shalt thou steal. Neither shalt thou desire thy neighbour's wife, neither shalt thy covet thy neighbour's house, his field, or his manservant, or his maidservant, his ox, or his ass, or any thing that is thy neighbour's

Leviticus 19:18
Thou shalt not avenge, nor bear any grudge against the children of thy people, but thou shalt love thy neighbour as thyself: I am the LORD.

* * * * * *

Romans 14:11 (Philippians 2:10)
For it is written, As I live, saith the Lord, every knee shall bow to me, and every tongue shall confess to God.

Isaiah 45:23
I have sworn by myself, the word is gone out of my mouth in righteousness, and shall not return, That unto me every knee shall bow, every tongue shall swear.

* * * * * *

Romans 15:3
For even Christ pleased not himself; but, as it is written, The reproaches of them that reproached thee fell on me.

Psalms 69:7,9,20
Because for thy sake I have borne reproach; shame hath covered my face. For the zeal of thine house hath eaten me up; and the reproaches of them that reproached thee are fallen upon me. Reproach hath broken my heart; and I am full of heaviness: and I looked for some to take pity, but there was none; and for comforters, but I found none.

* * * * * *

Romans 15:9
And that the Gentiles might glorify God for his mercy; as it is written, For this cause I will confess to thee among the Gentiles, and sing unto thy name.

Psalms 18:49
Therefore will I give thanks unto thee, O LORD, among the heathen, and sing praises unto thy name.

II Samuel 22:50
Therefore I will give thanks unto thee, O LORD, among the heathen, and I will sing praises unto thy name.

* * * * * *

Romans 15:10
And again he saith, Rejoice, ye Gentiles, with his people.

Deuteronomy 32:43
Rejoice, O ye nations, with his people: for he will avenge the blood of his servants, and will render vengeance to his adversaries, and will be merciful unto his land, and to his people.

* * * * * *

Romans 15:11
And again, Praise the Lord, all ye Gentiles; and laud him, all ye people.

Psalms 117:1
O praise the LORD, all ye nations: praise him, all ye people.

* * * * * *

Romans 15:12
And again, Esaias saith, There shall be a foot of Jesse, and he that shall rise to reign over the Gentiles; in him shall the Gentiles trust.

Isaiah 11:10
And in that day there shall be a root of Jesse, which shall stand for an ensign of the people; to it shall the Gentiles seek: and his rest shall be glorious.

* * * * * *

Romans 15:21 (I Corinthians 2:9)
But as it is written, To whom he was not spoken of, they shall see: and they that have not heard shall understand.

Isaiah 52:15
So shall he sprinkle many nations; the kings shall shut their mouths at him: for that which had not been told them shall they see; and that which they had not herd shall they consider.

I CORINTHIANS

JESUS: THE WORD MADE FLESH	
CORRECTION OF CONDITIONS	**REPLY TO THEIR LETTER**
Factions & quarrelings: **1-6**	Marriage & divorce: **7** Idolatry: **8-11** Obedience: **11** Lord's Supper: **11** Spiritual gifts: **12** Gift's with love: **13** Regulations: **14** Resurrection: **15** Instruction: **16**
LOCATION: The Mediterranean	
OVERVIEW: Paul received a letter from this church; his response on the issues made Christianity practical.	
TIME: A.D. 56	

FAST FACTS

AUTHOR AND SETTING:

Paul; written from Ephesus on Paul's third missionary journey

PURPOSE:

This entire book is essentially a letter of correction based upon questions received from the Corinthians and disturbing reports Paul head about them.

SEEING JESUS:

Jesus is seen as the practical wisdom to solve all of life's difficulties.

THEME VERSE:

I Corinthians 2:16

NOTES

I CORINTHIANS:
SANCTIFIER

NOTES

SEEING JESUS IN I CORINTHIANS

AUTHOR & SETTING

First Corinthians is another one of Paul's epistles. Acts 18 describes the founding of the church at Corinth on Paul's second missionary journey. Corinth was a large city on the isthmus connecting northern and southern Greece, the capital of the Roman province of Achaia. It was an important commercial and shipping center notorious – even within Greece – for the low moral standards of its people.

Paul's epistles are in four groups:

Group one was written on his second missionary journey in 52 A.D. and consists of Galatians and I and II Thessalonians.

Group two was written on his third missionary journey in 57 A.D. and consists of I and II Corinthians and Romans. *First and Second Corinthians* give a detailed picture of a local church.

Group three was written during his first Roman imprisonment in 62-63 A.D. and consists of Colossians, Philemon, Ephesians, and Philippians.

Group four was written prior to and during his second Roman imprisonment in 66-68 A.D. and consists of I Timothy, Titus, and II Timothy.

The main subject of the epistles in group one is the return of the Lord. The main subject in group two is the gospel and its application to everyday life. Group three, called *prison epistles*, concerns the Church, -- the Body of Christ. The fourth group, the pastoral epistles, gives instruction for Christian ministry.

OVERVIEW

First Corinthians is essentially a letter of correction. Paul had heard disturbing reports and had also received a questioning letter. Paul rebuked his readers for divisions among them, immorality, lawsuits with one another, and abuse of the Lord's Supper. In chapter 15 Paul answers the Corinthians' question about the resurrection. The church at Corinth was certainly a heartache and a headache. Note, however, that in every one of Paul's epistles he has a thanksgiving statement.

In *I Corinthians* Paul gives us some wonderful examples and reasons for prayer:

1. The prayer of gratitude for the church - I Corinthians 1:2-9
2. Thanksgiving dominates the prayers of Paul - I Corinthians 1:4, 14:18, 15:5 7.

3. Paul called the Corinthians to emulate his ways which were in Christ - I Corinthians 4:17.
4. Prayer and fasting form a safeguard against the devices of Satan - I Corinthians 7:5.
5. We conquer temptation God's way - I Corinthians 10:13.
6. Prayer order must be in the church - I Corinthians 11:4,5,13.
7. Praying in the Spirit - I Corinthians 12:3.
8. Prayer with understanding – I Corinthians 14:14-17.
9. Praises for final victory - I Corinthians 15:28-57

SEEING JESUS IN I CORINTHIANS

Jesus is all we need to live the Christian life. In *I Corinthians* Paul speaks about practical wisdom for everyday living, righteousness in believers' lives, sanctification, and redemption. All of these qualities are found in Jesus and are summed up in I Corinthians 1:30: *"But of [God] are ye in Christ Jesus, who of God is made unto us wisdom, and righteousness, and sanctification, and redemption."* Jesus is also seen in this book as correcting the abuses of His Church.

THEME VERSE

"For who hath known the mind of the Lord, that he may instruct him? But we have the mind of Christ" **(I Corinthians 2:16).**

OUTLINE

(Refer to maps on pages A14-A18 in the APPENDIX.)

I. CORRECTION OF CONDITIONS WHICH HAD BEEN REPORTED TO PAUL BY THE HOUSEHOLD OF CHLOE AND OTHERS - I CORINTHIANS 1-6

A. Conditions Reported to Paul:

1. **Factions and quarreling in the church**
2. **Comparison of carnal, soulish, and spiritual Christians**
3. **Paul showed that the Lord Jesus is the foundation of the Church.**
4. **Faithfulness is necessary for God's stewards.**
5. **Paul promised to deal severely with them in person.**
6. **Paul ordered them to deal with immorality.**
7. **Prohibition against going to secular courts**
8. **They are believers bought with a price.**

NOTES

NOTES

II. **REPLY TO LETTER WHICH CORINTHIANS HAD WRITTEN -** I CORINTHIANS 7-16

A. **Concerns of the Corinthians:**

1. **Marriage and divorce -** I Corinthians 7
2. **Eating meat offered to idols -** I Corinthians 8
3. **Praise for obeying ordinances -** I Corinthians 11
4. **Rebuke for abusing the Lord's Supper -** I Corinthians 11
5. **Spiritual gifts -** I Corinthians 12
6. **Gifts exercised with love -** I Corinthians 13
7. **Regulations -** I Corinthians 14
8. **Resurrection -** I Corinthians 15
9. **Instruction for collection -** I Corinthians 16

THE OLD TESTAMENT QUOTED IN I CORINTHIANS

I Corinthians 1:19
For it is written, I will destroy the wisdom of the wise, and will bring to nothing the understanding of the prudent.

Isaiah 29:14
Therefore, behold, I will proceed to do a marvelous work among this people, even a marvellous work and a wonder: for the wisdom of their wise men shall perish, and the understanding of their prudent men shall be hid.

* * * * * *

I Corinthians 1:31 (II Corinthians 10:17)
That, according as it is written, He that glorieth, let him glory in the Lord.

Jeremiah 9:23,24
Thus saith the LORD, Let not the wise man glory in his wisdom, neither let the mighty man glory in his might, let not the rich man glory in his riches: But let him that glorieth glory in this, that he understandeth and knoweth me, that I am the LORD which exercise lovingkindness, judgment, and righteousness, in the earth: for in these things I delight, saith the LORD.

* * * * * *

I Corinthians 2:9 (Romans 15:21)
But as it is written, Eye hath not seen, nor ear heard, neither have entered into the heart of man, the things which God hath prepared for them that love him.

Isaiah 64:4
For since the beginning of the world men have not heard, nor perceived by the ear, neither hath the eye seen, O God, beside thee, what he hath prepared for him that waiteth for him.

Isaiah 52:15
So shall he sprinkle many nations; the kings shall shut their mouths at him: for that which had not been told them shall they see; and that which they had not heard shall they consider.

* * * * * *

I Corinthians 2:16 (Romans 11:34)
For who hath known the mind of the Lord, that he may instruct him? But we have the mind of Christ.

Isaiah 40:13
Who hath directed the Spirit of the LORD, or being his counselor hath taught him?

* * * * * *

I Corinthians 3:19
For the wisdom of this world is foolishness with God. For it is written, He taketh the wise in their own craftiness.

Job 5:13
*He taketh the wise in their own craftiness: and the counsel of the froward is carried headlong.** * * * * *

I Corinthians 3:20
And again, The Lord knoweth the thoughts of the wise, that they are vain.

Psalms 94:11
The LORD knoweth the thoughts of man, that they are vanity.

* * * * * *

I Corinthians 5:13
But them that are without God judgeth. Therefore put away from among yourselves that wicked person.

Deuteronomy 13:5
And that prophet, or that dreamer of dreams, shall be put to death; because he hath spoken to turn you away from the LORD your God, which brought you out of the land of Egypt, and redeemed you out of the house of bondage, to thrust thee out of the way which the LORD thy God commanded thee to walk in. So shalt thou put the evil away from the midst of thee.

Deuteronomy 17:7,12
The hands of the witnesses shall be first upon him to put him to death, and afterward the hands of all the people. So thou shalt put the evil away from among you. And the man that will do presumptuously, and will not hearken unto the priest that standeth to minister there before the LORD thy God, or unto the judge, even that man shall die: and thou shalt put away the evil from Israel.

Deuteronomy 19:19
Then shall ye do unto him, as he had thought to have done unto his brother: so shalt thou put the evil away from among you.

Deuteronomy 22:24
Then ye shall bring them, both out unto the gate of that city, and ye shall stone them with stones that they

die; the damsel, because she cried not, being in the city; and the man, because he hath humbled his neighbour's wife: so thou shalt put away evil from among you.

Deuteronomy 24:7
If a man be found stealing any of his brethren of the children of Israel, and maketh merchandise of him, or selleth him; then that thief shall die; and thou shalt put evil away from among you.

* * * * * *

I Corinthians 6:16 (Matthew 19:5; Mark 10:7,8; Ephesians 5:31)
What? Know ye not that he which is joined to an harlot is one body? for two, saith he, shall be one flesh.

Genesis 2:24
Therefore shall a man leave his father and his mother, and shall cleave unto his wife: and they shall be one flesh.

* * * * * *

I Corinthians 9:9 (I Timothy 5:18)
For it is written in the law of Moses, Thou shalt not muzzle the mouth of the ox that treadeth out the corn, Doth God take care for oxen?

Deuteronomy 25:4
Thou shalt not muzzle the ox when he treadeth out the corn.

* * * * * *

I Corinthians 10:7
Neither be ye idolaters, as were some of them; as it is written, The people sat down to eat and drink, and rose up to play.

Exodus 32:6
And they rose up early on the morrow, and offered burnt offerings, and brought peace offerings; and the people sat down to eat and to drink, and rose up to play.

* * * * * *

I Corinthians 10:26
For the earth is the Lord's, and the fullness thereof.

Psalms 24:1
The earth is the Lord's, and the fullness thereof; the world, and they that dwell therein.

Psalms 50:12
If I were hungry, I would not tell thee: for the world is mine, and the fullness thereof.

* * * * * *

I Corinthians 14:21
In the law it is written, With men of other tongues and other lips will I speak unto this people; and yet for all that will they not hear me, saith the Lord.

Isaiah 28:11,12
For with stammering lips and another tongue will he speak to this people. To whom he said, This is the rest wherewith ye may cause the weary to rest; and this is the refreshing: yet they would not hear.

* * * * * *

I Corinthians 15:27
For he hath put all things under his feet. But when he saith all things are put under him, it is manifest that he is excepted, which did put all things under him.

Psalms 8:6
Thou madest him to have dominion over the works of thy hands; thou hast put all things under his feet.

* * * * * *

I Corinthians 15:32
If after the manner of men I have fought with beasts at Ephesus, what advantageth it me, if the dead rise not? Let us eat and drink; for to morrow we die.

Isaiah 22:13
And behold joy and gladness, slaying oxen, and killing sheep, eating flesh, and drinking wine: let us eat and drink; for to morrow we shall die.

* * * * * *

I Corinthians 15:45
And so it is written, The first man Adam was made a living soul; the last Adam was made a quickening spirit.

Genesis 2:7
And the LORD God formed man of the dust of the ground, and breathed into his nostrils the breath of life; and man became a living soul.

* * * * * *

I Corinthians 15:54
So when this corruptible shall have put on incorruption, and this mortal shall have put on

immortality, then shall be brought to pass the saying that is written, Death is swallowed up in victory.

Isaiah 25:8
He will swallow up death in victory; and the Lord GOD will wipe away tears from off all faces; and the rebuke of his people shall he take away from off all the earth: for the LORD hath spoken it.

* * * * * *

I Corinthians 15:55
O death, where is thy sting? O grave, where is thy victory?

Hosea 13:14
I will ransom them from the power of the grave; I will redeem them from death: O death, I will be thy plagues; O grave, I will be thy destruction: repentance shall be hid from mine eyes.

II CORINTHIANS

THE DEFENSE OF PAUL'S AUTHORITY		
MISSIONARY PRINCIPLES	**CHRISTIAN STEWARDSHIP**	**VINDICATION OF MINISTRY**
Rejoicing: **1,2** Contrasting Old & New Covenants: **3-7**	Giving: **8,9**	Commendations: **10-12** Visions & revelations: **12** Greetings: **13**
LOCATION: The Mediterranean		
OVERVIEW: Paul's character is examined	Preparation for Macedonian ministry	Imminence of Paul's Corinthian visit
TIME: A.D. 56		

FAST FACTS

AUTHOR AND SETTING:

Paul; Macedonia

PURPOSE:

In this letter Paul showed how beautifully the work of Christ reconciles God to man and how the work of the Holy Spirit reconciles man to God. This was a letter of encouragement.

SEEING JESUS:

Jesus is seen in *II Corinthians* as encouraging the young church no matter what their trials. Jesus shows them how to triumph.

THEME VERSE:

II Corinthians 1:20

NOTES

II CORINTHIANS:
APOSTLE

NOTES

SEEING JESUS IN II CORINTHIANS

AUTHOR & SETTING

Acts 19:21,22 and 20:1 tell how Paul left Ephesus where he wrote I Corinthians. At Troas he had a rendezvous with Titus (the bearer of Paul's first letter to the I Corinthians). Paul told Titus to meet him back at Troas for a report of the reception of his letter. He became anxious when Titus didn't show, and even though an effectual door of ministry was opened to him, Paul left Macedonia. Titus found him and met him there.

On learning about the reception of his first letter, Pail wrote the second letter and sent it by Titus. *Second Corinthians* grew out of the report of Titus. Titus said that the Corinthians received Paul's first letter well, but he also reported that there was much fear and trembling among the people.

Titus told Paul how the man involved in fornication repented. The Corinthians had begun to take an offering, but it was not finished. Titus reported that some of the believers were unequally yoked with unbelievers. A mortal combat was going on in Paul's letters.

Titus, along with two others who were to help with the collection, carried the second letter to Corinth.

OVERVIEW

Second Corinthians opens a window into Paul's heart. In this letter Paul shows how very beautifully the work of Christ reconciles God to man and how the work of ht Holy Spirit reconciles man to God. Paul wrote a letter of encouragement to the Corinthians. He wanted them to go from trials to triumph.

Paul dealt at length with his ministry:

1. It was commended of God (II Corinthians 3:1)
2. It was of the New Testament, not of the Old Testament (II Corinthians 3:6-8)
3. It was a ministry of glory and righteousness (II Corinthians 3:9-11)
4. It was a ministry of hope, light, and liberty (II Corinthians 3:12-17).
5. It was a ministry of constant transformation (II Corinthians 3:18).
6. It was an honest ministry (II Corinthians 4:1,2).
7. It was an unselfish ministry (II Corinthians 4:3-6).

8. It was a ministry of power (II Corinthians 4:7).

9. It was a ministry of suffering (II Corinthians 4:8-12).

10. It was a bold and faithful ministry (II Corinthians 4:3-15).

11. It was a ministry of eternal things (II Corinthians 4:16-18).

12. It was a ministry of the future (II Corinthians 5:1-8).

13. It was a hard-working ministry to please God (II Corinthians 5:9-13).

14. It was a ministry of reconciliation (II Corinthians 5:14-19).

15. It was an entreating ministry (II Corinthians 5:20,21; 6:1,2).

16. It was a blameless and approved ministry (II Corinthians 6:3-10).

17. It was a human and compassionate ministry (II Corinthians 6:11-13).

18. It was a separated ministry (II Corinthians 6:14-18).

19. It was a clean ministry (II Corinthians 7:1).

20. It was a healing ministry longing for fellowship (II Corinthians 7:2-4).

21. It was a human ministry subject to human fears and discouragement (II Corinthians 7:5-7).

22. It was a human ministry with ordinary emotions and feelings (II Corinthians 7:8-15).

Second Corinthians 8,9 shows the great collection for the poor saints at Jerusalem.

The following facts help us understand the collection:

1. There were many poor people in Jerusalem.

2. Wealthier Christians donated in order to have a relief fund distributed by the disciples.

3. In connection with these funds were the tragedies of Ananias and Sapphira (Acts 5).

4. There were prior complaints about the office of the deacon.

NOTES

NOTES

Acts 11:27-30 tells of the great dearth. The Antioch church took a relief collection. This is the first account of relief collections (Galatians 2:10; I Corinthians 16:1-4; Romans 15:25-28; Acts 20:4, 24:17).

Two continents participated: all the churches in Asia Minor, Macedonia, and Achaia took part. There was a series of collections taken to meet the need of the believers in Jerusalem because of the extreme dearth that occurred there. Among those who aided Paul in this effort were Trophimus and Tychicus.

There were eight rules that governed the collections:

1. It had to be taken on the first day of the week (I Corinthians 16:2).
2. The donor must first have given himself to the Lord (II Corinthians 8:5).
3. It was necessary to abound in the grace of giving (II Corinthians 8:7).
4. Pledges were made (II Corinthians 8:11).
5. It was according to what a man had (II Corinthians 8:12).
6. It was to be voluntary (II Corinthians 8:12).
7. It was to be deliberate (II Corinthians 9:7).
8. It was to be cheerfully done (II Corinthians 9:7).

Trustworthy men were counted as collecting agents. The churches themselves appointed the messengers who had charge - II Corinthians 8:19-23.

Their zeal for pledges had provoked others - II Corinthians 9:2. Shame would follow if the pledges were not redeemed - II Corinthians 9:3,4.

The major subjects of II Corinthians are (1) the two covenants (II Corinthians 1-3), (2) the gospel ministry (II Corinthians 4,5), (3) the ministry of reconciliation (II Corinthians 6,7), (4) the great collection (II Corinthians 8,9), and (5) Paul's reply to his enemies (II Corinthians 10-12).

Romans shows the mind of Paul, but II Corinthians shows his heart.

SEEING JESUS IN II CORINTHIANS

Jesus is seen in *II Corinthians* as encouraging the young church no matter what their trials. Christ is -

Our comfort:
"For as the sufferings of Christ abound in us, so our consolation also aboundeth by Christ" **(II Corinthians 1;5).**

Our triumph:
"Now thanks be unto God, which always causeth us to triumph in Christ, and maketh manifest the savour of his knowledge by us in every place" **(II Corinthians 2:14).**

Our Lord:
"For we preach not ourselves, but Christ Jesus the Lord; and ourselves your servants for Jesus' sake" **(II Corinthians 4:5).**

Our glory:
"For God, who commanded the light to shine out of darkness, hath shined in our hearts, to give the light of the knowledge of the glory of God in the face of Jesus Christ" **(II Corinthians 4:6).**

Our judge:
"For we must all appear before the judgment seat of Christ; that every one may receive the things done in his body, according to that he hath done, whether it be good or bad" **(II Corinthians 5:10).**

Our reconciliation:
"To wit, that God was in Christ, reconciling the world unto himself, not imputing their trespasses unto them; and hath committed unto us the word of reconciliation" **(II Corinthians 5:19).**

Our substitute:
"For [God] hath made [Jesus] to be sin for us, who knew no sin; that we might be made the righteousness of God in him" **(II Corinthians 5:21).**

Our gift:
"Thanks be unto God for his unspeakable gift" **(II Corinthians 9:15).**

Our master:
"Do ye look on things after the outward appearance? If any man trust to himself that he is Christ's, let him of himself think this again, that, as he is Christ's, even so are we Christ's" **(II Corinthians 10:7).**

Our strength:
"And he said unto me, My grace is sufficient for thee: for my strength is made perfect in weakness. Most gladly therefore will I rather glory in my infirmities, that the power of Christ may rest upon me" **(II Corinthians 12:9).**

NOTES

NOTES

THEME VERSE

"For all the promises of God in him are yea, and in him Amen, unto the glory of God by us" **(II Corinthians 1:20).**

OUTLINE

(Refer to maps on pages A14-A18 in the APPENDIX.)

I. **MISSIONARY PRINCIPLES AND PRACTICES OF THE APOSTLE PAUL –** II CORINTHIANS 1-7
   - A. **Rejoiced at Triumph in Christ -** II Corinthians 2:14
   - B. **Contrasted Ministry of Old and New Covenants -** II Corinthians 3:6-18

II. **CHRISTIAN STEWARDSHIP -** II CORINTHIANS 8,9
   - A. **Christian Giving -** II Corinthians 8:1-8
     1. **Exhorted for liberality**

III. **VINDICATION OF PAUL'S APOSTLESHIP AND MINISTRY -** II CORINTHIANS 10-13
   - A. **Came Against Accusation -** II Corinthians 10-13
     1. **Commended himself -** II Corinthians 11,12
     2. **Showed his labors and sufferings -** II Corinthians 11:16-33
   - B. **Visions and Revelations -** II Corinthians 12:1-10
   - C. **Intention To Visit Them Again -** II Corinthians 12:19-13:10
   - D. **Closed With Greetings and Benedictions**

THE OLD TESTAMENT QUOTED IN II CORINTHIANS

II Corinthians 4:13
We having the same spirit of faith, according as it is written, I believed, and therefore have I spoken; we also believe, and therefore speak.

Psalms 116:10
I believed, therefore have I spoken: I was greatly afflicted.

* * * * * *

II Corinthians 6:2
(For he saith, I have heard thee in a time accepted, and in the day of salvation have I succoured thee: behold, now is the accepted time; behold, now is the day of salvation).

Isaiah 49:8
Thus saith the LORD, In an acceptable time have I heard thee, and in a day of salvation have I helped thee: and I will preserve thee, and give thee for a covenant of the people, to establish the earth, to cause to inherit the desolate heritages.

* * * * * *

II Corinthians 6:16
And what agreement hath the temple of God with idols? for ye are the temple of the living God; as God hath said, I will dwell in them, and walk in them; and I will be their God, and they shall be my people.

Leviticus 26:12
And I will walk among you, and will be your God, and he shall be my people.

Ezekiel 37:27
My tabernacle also shall be with them: yea, I will be their God, and they shall be my people.

* * * * * *

II Corinthians 6:17
Wherefore come out from among them, and be ye separate, saith the Lord, and touch not the unclean thing; and I will receive you.

Isaiah 52:11
Depart ye, depart ye, go ye out from thence, touch no unclean thing; go ye out of the midst of her; be ye clean, that bear the vessels of the LORD.

Jeremiah 51:45
My people, go ye out of the midst of her, and deliver ye every man his soul from the fierce anger of the LORD.

* * * * * *

II Corinthians 8:15
As it is written, He that had gathered much had nothing over; and he that had gathered little had no lack.

Exodus 16:18
And when they did mete it with an omer, he that gathered much had nothing over, and he that gathered little had no lack; they gathered every man according to his eating.

* * * * * *

II Corinthians 9:9
As it is written, He hath dispersed abroad; he hath given to the poor: his righteousness remaineth for ever.

Psalms 112:9
He hath dispersed, he hath given to the poor; his righteousness endureth for ever; his horn shall be exalted with honour.

* * * * * *

II Corinthians 10:17 (I Corinthians 1:31)
But he that glorieth, let him, glory in the Lord.

Jeremiah 9:24
But let him that glorieth glory in this, that he understandeth and knoweth me, that I am the LORD which exercise lovingkindness, judgment, and righteousness, in the earth: for in these things I delight, saith the LORD.

* * * * * *

II Corinthians 13:1 (Matthew 18:16)
This is the third time I am coming to you. In the mouth of two or three witnesses shall every word be established.

Deuteronomy 19:15
One witness shall not rise up against a man for any iniquity, or for any sin, in any sin that he sinneth: at the mouth of two witnesses, or at the mouth of three witnesses, shall the matter be established.

GALATIANS

<table>
<tr><td colspan="3">THE CHARTER OF LIBERTY</td></tr>
<tr><td>DEFENSE OF APOSTOLIC & PERSONAL AUTHORITY</td><td>EXPLANATION OF THE GOSPEL & DOCTRINES</td><td>APPLICATION TO PRACTICAL CHRISTIAN LIVING</td></tr>
<tr><td>Ministry: 1
Personal: 2</td><td>Spiritual children of Abraham: 3
Children of God: 4</td><td>Sanctification: 5
“Glory in the Cross”: 6</td></tr>
<tr><td colspan="3">LOCATION: Galatia - province of Rome</td></tr>
<tr><td>OVERVIEW:
Proofs of Paul’s gospel</td><td>Theological explanation of Paul’s gospel</td><td>Practical application of Paul’s gospel</td></tr>
<tr><td colspan="3">TIME: A.D. 49</td></tr>
</table>

FAST FACTS

AUTHOR AND SETTING:

Paul; perhaps written in Syrian Antioch

PURPOSE:

Eight basic doctrines are discussed in *Galatians*: (1) Christians can fall from grace and return to legalism; (2) this gospel is a direct revelation from God; (3) justification is by faith alone: (4) living victoriously; (5) the Holy Spirit places us into the Body of Christ; (6) Moses' law is completely abolished; (7) backsliders must return to grace and be restored; and (8) those who return to lawkeeping are obliged to observe the whole law.

SEEING JESUS:

Jesus is represented in *Galatians* as our liberator – delivering the believer from sin, law, and self.

THEME VERSE:

Galatians 2:20

NOTES

GALATIANS:
LIBERTY

NOTES

SEEING JESUS IN GALATIANS

AUTHOR & SETTING

The book of *Galatians* was written by Paul to correct the fickle Galatians from further backsliding and from following the legalistic Judaizers from Judea. It also covers the relationship of Christians to the new covenant.

OVERVIEW

There are basically eight doctrines in *Galatians*:

1. Christians can fall from grace and return to legalism.
2. Paul's gospel was a revelation direct from God.
3. Justification is by faith alone without the law.
4. Christians can live victoriously over sin.
5. The Holy Spirit places us into the Body of Christ.
6. The law of Moses is completely abolished.
7. Backsliders must return to grace and can be restored.
8. All who go back to law-keeping are under obligation to observe the whole law.

SEEING JESUS IN GALATIANS

The crucified Christ is at the center of our freedom from the law, from the curse of sin, and from our sinful nature:

"O foolish Galatians, who hath bewitched you, that ye should not obey the truth, before whose eyes Jesus Christ hath been evidently set forth, crucified among you?" **(Galatians 3:1).**

THEME VERSE

"I am crucified with Christ: nevertheless I live; yet not I, but Christ liveth in me: and the life which I now live in the flesh I live by the faith of the Son of God, who loved me, and gave himself for me" **(Galatians 2:20)**

OUTLINE

(Refer to maps on pages A14-A18 in the APPENDIX.)

I. PAUL'S DEFENSE OF APOSTOLIC AUTHORITY - GALATIONS 1,2 **- PERSONAL**

A. Paul Defended His Apostolic Authority:

1. *"But I certify you, brethren, that the gospel which was preached of me is not after man. For I neither received it of man, neither was I taught it, but by the revelation of Jesus Christ"* **(Galatians 1:11,12).**

II. PAUL'S EXPLANATION OF THE GOSPEL - GALATIANS 3,4 **- DOCTRINAL**

A. All Who Believe Are Spiritual Children of Abraham

B. If You Are Under the Law, You are Under the Curse:

1. *"For as many as are of the works of the law are under the curse: for it is written, Cursed is every one that continueth not in all things which are written in the book of the law to do them. But that no man is justified by the law in the sight of God, it is evident: for, The just shall live by faith. And the law is not of faith: but, The man that doeth them shall live in them"* **(Galatians 3:10-12).**

2. The True purpose of the law is to show man his need of a Savior:

a. *"Wherefore the law was our schoolmaster to bring us unto Christ, that we might be justified by faith"* **(Galatians 3:24).**

C. Christ Has Redeemed Us From the Curse of the Law:

1. *"Christ hath redeemed us from the curse of the law, being made a curse for us: for it is written, Cursed is every one that hangeth on a tree"* **(Galatians 3:13).**

D. Those Who Believe in Jesus Are Sons of God:

1. *"For ye are all the children of God by faith in Christ Jesus"* **(Galatians 3:26).**

2. *"To redeem them that were under the law, that we might receive the adoption of sons"* **(Galatians 4:5).**

III. PAUL'S APPLICATION OF THE GOSPEL TO CHRISTIAN LIVING - GALATIONS 5,6 **- PRACTICAL**

A. Sanctification is by Faith:

1. *"If we live in the Spirit, let is also walk in the Spirit"* **(Galatians 5:25).**

B. The Flesh Produces Sin – the Spirit Produces Life:

1. *"But the fruit of the Spirit is love, joy, peace, longsuffering, gentleness, goodness, faith, Meekness, temperance: against such there is no law"* **(Galatians 5:22,23).**

NOTES

NOTES

C. **Christians Glory In the Cross:**

1. *"But God forbid that I should glory, save in the cross of our Lord Jesus Christ, by whom the world is crucified unto me, and I unto the world"* **(Galatians 6:14).**

THE OLD TESTAMENT QUOTED IN GALATIANS

Galatians 3:6 (Romans 4:3,9,22; James 2:23)
Even as Abraham believed God, and it was accounted to him for righteousness.

Genesis 15:6
And he believed in the LORD; and he counted it to him for righteousness.

* * * * *

Galatians 3:8 (Acts 3:25)
And the scripture, foreseeing that God would justify the heathen through faith, preached before the gospel unto Abraham, saying, In thee shall all nations be blessed.

Genesis 12:3
And I will bless them that bless thee, and curse him that curseth thee: and in thee shall all families of the earth be blessed.

Genesis 22:18
And in thy seed shall all the nations of the earth be blessed; because thou hast obeyed my voice.

Genesis 26:4
And I will make thy seed to multiply as the stars of heaven, and will give unto thy seed all these countries; and in thy seed shall all the nations of the earth be blessed.

Genesis 28:14
And thy seed shall be as the dust of the earth, and thou shalt spread abroad to the west, and to the east, and to the north, and to the south: and in thee and in thy seed shall all the families of the earth be blessed.

* * * * *

Galatians 3:10
For as many as are of the works of the law are under the curse: for it is written, Cursed is every one that continueth not in all things which are written in the book of the law to do them.

Deuteronomy 27:26
Cursed be he that confirmeth not all the words of this law to do them. And all the people shall say, Amen.

* * * * *

Galatians 3:11 (Romans 1:17; Hebrews 10:37,38)
But that no man is justified by the law in the sight of God, it is evident: for, The just shall live by faith.

Habakkuk 2:4
Behold, his soul which is lifted up is not upright in him: but the just shall live by his faith.

* * * * *

Galatians 3:12
And the law is not of faith: but, The man that doeth them shall live in them.

Leviticus 18:5
Ye shall therefore keep my statutes, and my judgments: which if a man do, he shall live in them: I am the LORD.

* * * * *

Galatians 3:13
Christ hath redeemed us from the curse of the law, being made a curse for us: for it is written, Cursed is every one that hangeth on a tree.

Deuteronomy 21:23
His body shall not remain all night upon the tree, but thou shalt in any wise bury him that day; (for he that is hanged is accursed of God;) that thy land be not defiled, which the LORD thy God giveth thee for an inheritance.

* * * * *

Galatians 4:27
For it is written, Rejoice, thou barren that bearest not; break forth and cry, thou that travailest not: for the desolate hath many more children than she which hath an husband.

Isaiah 54:1
Sing, O barren, thou that didst not bear; break forth into singing, and cry aloud, thou that didst not travail with child: for more are the children of the desolate than the children of the married wife, saith the LORD.

* * * * *

Galatians 4:30
Nevertheless what saith the scripture? Cast out the bondwoman and her son: for the son of the bondwoman shall not be heir with the son of the freewoman.

Genesis 21:10
Wherefore she said unto Abraham, Cast out this bondwoman and her son: for the son of this bondwoman shall not be heir with my son, even with Isaac.

* * * * *

Galatians 5:14 (Matthew 5:43, 19:19, 22:39; Mark 12:31,33; Luke 10:27; Romans 13:9; James 2:8)
For all the law is fulfilled in one word, even in this; Thou shalt love thy neighbour as thyself.

Leviticus 19:18
Thou shalt not avenge, nor bear any grudge against the children of thy people, but thou shalt love thy neighbour as thyself: I am the LORD.

EPHESIANS

RECEIVING YOUR INHERITANCE		
BELIEVER'S POSITION IN CHRIST	**BELIEVER'S CONDUCT IN THE WORLD**	**STANDING AS CONQUERORS**
Rights in Christ: **1,2** Mystery & prayer: **3**	Walking in victory: **4,5** Practical relationships: **6**	"The winner's circle": **6**
LOCATION: Written from prison in Rome to the church at Ephesus		
OVERVIEW: Unity in Christ	Responsibilities of Christianity	Position of victory
TIME: A.D. 60-61		

FAST FACTS

AUTHOR AND SETTING:

Paul; Roman prison

PURPOSE:

The believer has a responsibility to walk in accordance with his heavenly calling in Christ Jesus (*Ephesians 4:1*). Believers must be aware of their position in Christ as a basis of their everyday life.

SEEING JESUS:

Christ is the center in Whom all things unite and the bond Who unites all things.

THEME VERSE:

Ephesians 1:8,9

NOTES

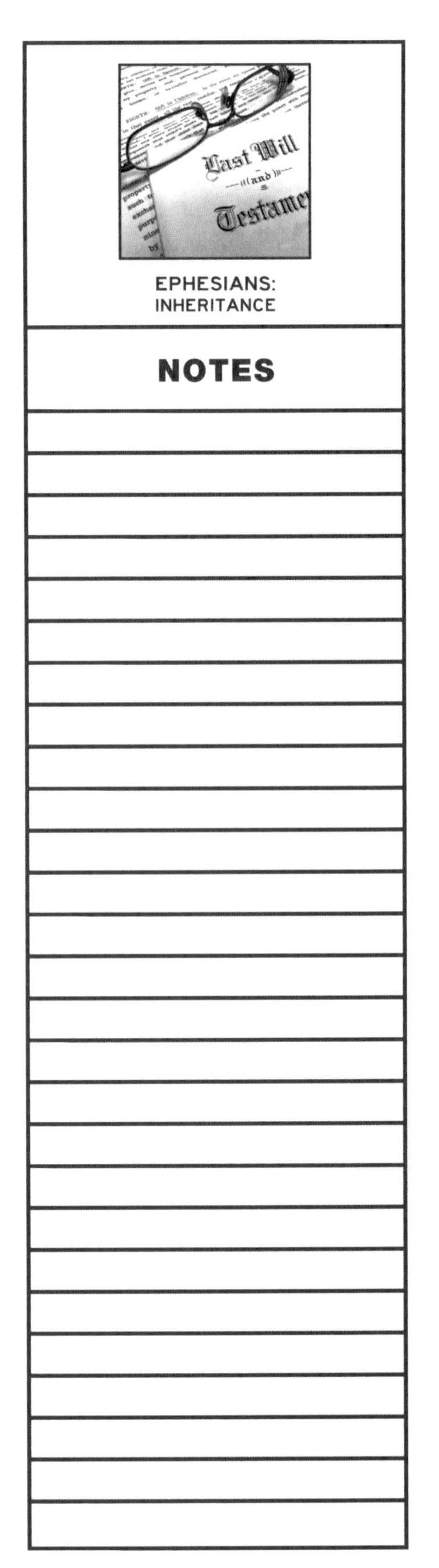

SEEING JESUS IN EPHESIANS

AUTHOR & SETTING

This epistle was written while Paul was in a Roman prison:

"For this cause I Paul, the prisoner of Jesus Christ for you Gentiles" **(Ephesians 3:1).**

"I therefore, the prisoner of the Lord, beseech you that ye walk worthy of the vocation wherewith ye are called" **(Ephesians 4:1).**

"For which I am an ambassador in bonds: that therein I may speak boldly, as I ought to speak" **(Ephesians 6:20).**

The book of *Ephesians* has a close similarity with the book of Colossians. Keep in mind that Paul spent three years at Ephesus (Act 18,20).

OVERVIEW

The key thought in the book of *Ephesians* is the gathering together of all things in Jesus Christ. Christ is the center in Whom all things unite and the bond Who unites all things.

There is disunity in (1) nature, (2) man, (3) beast and man (4) nations, (5) ideology, and (6) Jew and gentile. All disunity can become unity when all men and all powers are united in Christ.

In the first three chapters, Paul deals with the concept of unity in Christ. In chapters 4, 5, and 6 Paul tells how God will bring all this to pass.

Christ is God's instrument of reconciliation. The Church is Christ's instrument of reconciliation.

Unity is beautifully expressed in this book:

One Body
One Spirit
One hope
One Lord
One faith
One baptism
One Father

The three major words of this book are *"sit," "walk," "stand."*

Our position is first to *sit* in heavenly places possessing our inheritance as co-heirs with Christ. From sitting we can *walk* according to His calling. Lastly, we *stand* as a conqueror on this earth.

SEEING JESUS IN EPHESIANS

There are nine important terms in *Ephesians* chapter 1 that refer to what Christ has done for us:

Blessed us
Chosen us
Predestinated us
Made us accepted
Redeemed us
Abounded toward us
Made known unto us
Given us an Inheritance
Sealed us

The term, "in Christ," or its equivalent, is used by Paul over 30 times in this book. It is because of the believer's position *in Christ* that he can walk worthy of the Lord on a daily basis.

THEME VERSE

"Wherein he hath abounded toward us in all wisdom and prudence; Having made known unto us the mystery of his will, according to his good pleasure which he hath purposed in himself" **(Ephesians 1:8,9).**

OUTLINE

(Refer to maps on pages A14-A18 in the APPENDIX.)

I. THE BELIEVER'S POSITION IN CHRIST - EPHESIANS 1-3

- **A. We are Seated Together in Heavenly Places.**
- **B. We Have Salvation -** Ephesians 1:1,2.
- **C. We Have All Spiritual Blessings -** Ephesians 1:3-14.
- **D. We Have Been Chosen by the Father -** Ephesians 1:3-6.
  1. **Redeemed by the Son -** Ephesians 1:7-12
  2. **Sealed by the Holy Spirit -** Ephesians 1:13,14
- **E. Ephesians Has Two Great Prayers by Paul:**
  1. **The first prayer is for full experiential knowledge of God -** Ephesians 1:15-23.
     - a. In the close of this prayer, the Church is called the Body of Christ.
  2. **The second prayer is for the believer to be strengthened by the Holy Spirit -** Ephesians 3:14-21.
- **F. Salvation by Grace -** Ephesians 2:1-10
  1. **What we were in the past:**

NOTES

NOTES

a. *"And you hath he quickened, who were dead in trespasses and sins; Wherein in time past ye walked according to the course of this world, according to the prince of the power of the air, the spirit that now worketh in the children of disobedience: Among whom also we all had our conversation in times past in the lusts of our flesh, fulfilling the desires of the flesh and of the mind; and were by nature the children of wrath, even as others"* **(Ephesians 2:1-3).**

2. **What we are in the present:**

   a. *"But God, who is rich in mercy, for his great love wherewith he loved us, Even when we were dead in sins, hath quickened us together with Christ, (by grace ye are saved;) And hath raised us up together, and made us sit together in heavenly places in Christ Jesus"* **(Ephesians 2:4-6).**

3. **What we shall be in the future:**

   a. *"That in the ages to come he might shew the exceeding riches of his grace in his kindness toward us through Christ Jesus. For by grace are ye saved through faith; and that not of yourselves: it is the gift of God: Not of works, lest any man should boast. For we are his workmanship, created in Christ Jesus unto good works, which God hath before ordained that we should walk in them"* **(Ephesians 2:7-10).**

G. **Oneness of Jews and Gentiles in Christ -** Ephesians 2:11-22

1. **What gentiles were without Christ:**

   a. *"Wherefore remember, that ye being in time past Gentiles in the flesh, who are called Uncircumcision by that which is called the Circumcision in the flesh made by hands; That at that time ye were without Christ, being aliens from the commonwealth of Israel, and strangers from the covenants of promise, having no hope, and without God in the world"* **(Ephesians 2:11,12).**

2. **Body of Christ is composed of Jews and gentiles -** Ephesians 2:13-18

3. **Body of Christ is also called a *building* -** Ephesians 2:19-22

   a. Jesus is the chief corner stone:

      i. *"The stone which the builders refused is become the head stone of the comer"* **(Psalms 118:22).**

H. **Revelation of the Mystery -** Ephesians 3:1-12:

1. *"That the Gentiles should be fellow heirs, and of the same body, and partakers of his promise in Christ by the gospel"* **(Ephesians 3:6).**

I. **Second Prayer**

1. **Strength in the inner man to comprehend the full measure of Christ's love -** Ephesians 3:14-21.

II. **THE BELIEVER'S CONDUCT IN THE WORLD -** EPHESIANS 4-6

A. **Walk According to Your High Calling:**

1. **A worthy walk -** Ephesians 4:1-16
2. **A different walk -** Ephesians 4:17-32
3. **A loving walk -** Ephesians 5:1-14
4. **A wise walk -** Ephesians 5:15-6:9
5. **A Holy Spirit-empowered walk -** Ephesians 5:18:

   a. *"And be not drunk with wine, wherein is excess; but be filled with the Spirit."*

6. **A walk that results in praise and thanksgiving -** Ephesians 5:19,20:

   a. *"Speaking to yourselves in psalms and hymns and spiritual songs, singing and making melody in your heart to the Lord; Giving thanks always for all things unto God and the Father in the name of our Lord Jesus Christ."*

7. **It is a walk that works in practical relationships in life.**

B. **A Christian Walk is a Warfare -** Ephesians 6:10-20

1. **Put on the whole armor of God -** Ephesians 6:10-17
2. **Engage in prayer -** Ephesians 6:18-20

C. **Close Greeting -** Ephesians 6:21-24

1. **Mentions Tychicus, the bearer of the epistle**

III. **HAVING DONE ALL, WE STAND AS CONQUERORS.**

NOTES

THE OLD TESTAMENT QUOTED IN EPHESIANS.

Ephesians 2:17
And came and preached peace to you which were afar off, and to them that were nigh.

Isaiah 57:19
I create the fruit of the lips; Peace, peace to him that is far off, and to him that is near, saith the LORD; and I will heal him.

* * *

Ephesians 4:8
Wherefore he saith, When he ascended up on high, he led captivity captive, and gave gifts unto men.

Psalms 68:18
Thou hast ascended on high, thou hast led captivity captive: thou hast received gifts for men; yea, for the rebellious also, that the LORD God might dwell among them.

* * *

Ephesians 4:25
Wherefore putting away lying, speak every man truth with his neighbour: for we are members one of another.

Zechariah 8:16
These are the things that ye shall do;: Speak ye every man the truth to his neighbour; execute the judgment of truth and peace in your gates.

* * *

Ephesians 4:26
Be ye angry, and sin not: let not the sun go down upon your wrath.

Psalms 4:4
Stand in awe, and sin not: commune with your own heart upon your bed, and be still. Selah

* * *

Ephesians 5:31
(Matthew 19:5; Mark 10:7; I Corinthians 6:16)
For this cause shall a man leave his father and mother, and shall be joined unto his wife, and they two shall be one flesh.

Genesis 2:24
Therefore shall a man leave his father and his mother, and shall cleave unto his wife: and they shall be one flesh.

* * *

Ephesians 6:2,3 (Matthew 15:4; Mark 7:10)
Honour thy father and mother; which is the first commandment with promise; That it may be well with thee, and thou mayest live long on the earth.

Exodus 20:12
Honour thy father and thy mother: that thy days may be long upon the land which the LORD thy God giveth thee.

Exodus 21:17
And he that curseth his father, or his mother, shall surely be put to death.

Deuteronomy 5:16
Honour thy father and thy mother, as the LORD thy God hath commanded thee; that thy days may be prolonged, and that it may go well with thee, in the land which the LORD thy God giveth thee.

* * *

Ephesians 6:14,15 (Romans 10:15)
Stand therefore, having your loins girt about with truth, and having on the breastplate of righteousness; And your feet shod with the preparation of the gospel of peace.

Isaiah 11:5
And righteousness shall be the girdle of his loins, and faithfulness the girdle of his reins.

Isaiah 52:7
How beautiful upon the mountains are the feet of him that bringeth good tidings, that publisheth peace; that bringeth good tidings of good, that publisheth salvation; that saith unto Zion, Thy God reigneth!

Isaiah 59:17
For he put on righteousness as a breastplate, and an helmet of salvation upon his head; and he put on the garments of vengeance for clothing, and was clad with zeal as a cloke.

* * *

Ephesians 6:17
And take the helmet of salvation, and the sword of the Spirit, which is the word of God.

Isaiah 59:17
For he put on righteousness as a breastplate, and an helmet of salvation upon his head; and he put on the garments of vengeance for clothing, and was clad with zeal as a cloke.

Hosea 6:5
Therefore have I hewed them by the prophets; I have slain them by the words of my mouth; and thy judgments are as the light that goeth forth.

PHILIPPIANS

PATTERNING AFTER JESUS	
THE EPISTLE OF JOY	**CHRIST'S PORTRAYAL**
Attitude: **1** The mind of Christ: **2** Encouraging to walk: **3**	Believer's life: **1** Believer's example: **2** Believer's faith & hope: **3** Believer's strength: **4**
LOCATION: Under house arrest in Rome	
OVERVIEW: It was the power of Christ within Paul that gave him contentment.	
TIME: A.D. 62	

FAST FACTS

AUTHOR AND SETTING:

Paul; under house arrest in Rome

PURPOSE:

Paul explains how we can have joy in difficult circumstances.

SEEING JESUS:

Christ is our life *(Philippians 1:21)*, or model of humility *(Philippians 2:5)*, and our power *(Philippians 4:13)*.

THEME VERSE:

Philippians 2:2

NOTES

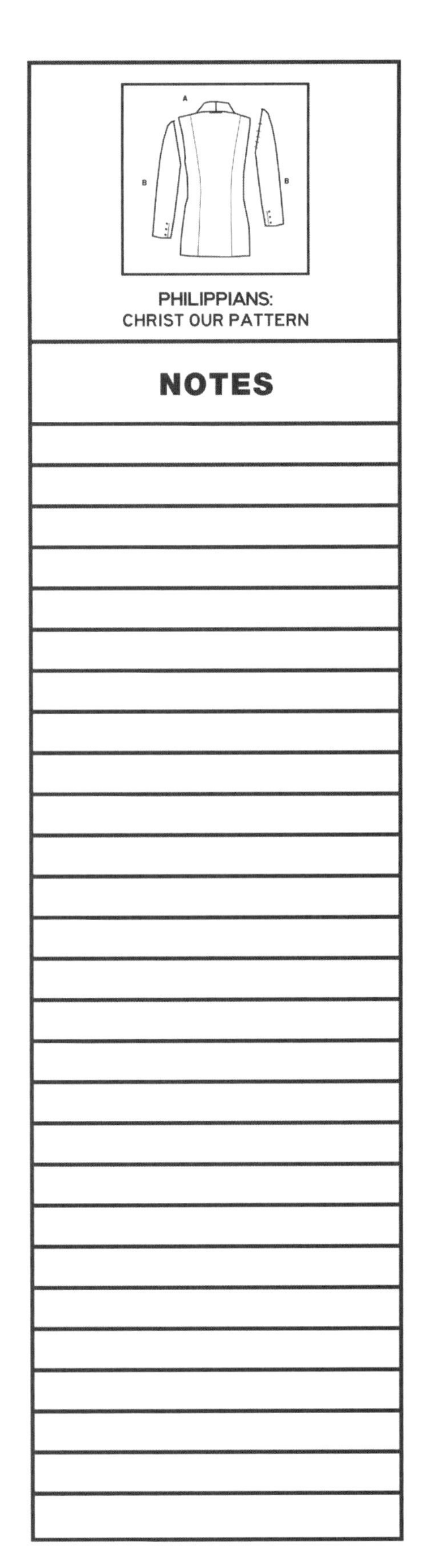

SEEING JESUS IN PHILIPPIANS

AUTHOR & SETTING

The establishing of the church at Philippi is recorded in Acts 16.

Paul, the author of this book, mentions joy, rejoicing, or gladness 19 times in his letter to this church. Paul's circumstances, however, were not joyous; he was a prisoner of Rome under house arrest. Paul wanted to go to Rome as a preacher, not as a prisoner. He learned, however, to be joyful in difficult circumstances:

"And Paul dwelt two whole years in his own hired house, and received all that came in unto him, Preaching the kingdom of God, and teaching those things which concern the Lord Jesus Christ, with all confidence, no man forbidding him"
(Acts 28:30,31).

OVERVIEW

In this book, Paul explains how we can have joy in difficult circumstances. The key to the joyous Christian life that Paul found was the renewing of his mind in God's Word. *Mind* is used 10 times and *think*, 5 times.

Here are the thieves that can rob you of your joy:

1. Circumstances
2. People
3. Things
4. Worry
5. Wrong thinking

What will maintain your joy?

1. The single mind - Philippians 1
2. The submissive mind - Philippians 2
3. The spiritual mind - Philippians 3
4. The secure mind - Philippians 4

We must surrender our minds to Christ daily. A person's joy cannot be stolen if he has a single mind toward Christ.

The Christian life is not a *playground* - it's a *battleground.*

There are 3 weapons given in this book:

1. **The Word of God** (Sword of the Spirit)
2. **Prayer**
3. **Suffering** (experience)

It was the power of Christ within Paul that gave him contentment. Nature itself depends on hidden resources; trees draw from the earth. Paul depended on the power working in him.

Suggestions to help keep victory in your life:

1. Surrender your mind to the Lord daily.
2. Let the Holy Spirit renew your mind through the Word.
3. During the day *mind your mind.*
4. As you serve others you will have a joyful mind.

In Philippians 3:12-16 we have the essentials for winning the race:

1. Divine dissatisfaction:

"Not as though I had already attained, either were already perfect: but I follow after, if that I may apprehend that for which also I am apprehended of Christ Jesus. Brethren, I count not myself to have apprehended..." **(Philippians 3:12,13).**

2. Devotion:

"... but this one thing I do, ..." **(Philippians 3:13).**

3. Direction:

"... forgetting those things which are behind, and reaching forth unto those things which are before" **(Philippians 3:13).**

4. Determination:

"I press toward the mark for the prize of the high calling of God in Christ Jesus" **(Philippians 3:14).**

5. Discipline:

"Let us therefore, as many as be perfect, be thus minded: and if in any thing ye be otherwise minded, God shall reveal even this unto you. Nevertheless, whereto we have already attained, let us walk by the same rule, let us mind the same thing" **(Philippians 3:15,16).**

NOTES

NOTES

SEEING JESUS IN PHILIPPIANS

Jesus is seen as...

...the believer's life:
"For to me to live is Christ, and to die is gain" **(Philippians 1:21).**

...the believer's example of humility:
"Let this mind be in you, which was also in Christ Jesus: Who, being in the form of God, thought it not robbery to be equal with God" **(Philippians 2:5,6).**

...the giver of our glorified body:
Who shall change our vile body, that it may be fashioned like unto his glorious body, according to the working whereby he is able even to subdue all things unto himself" **(Philippians 3:21).**

...the believer's strength:
"I can do all things through Christ which strengtheneth me" **(Philippians 4:13).**

THEME VERSE

"Fulfill ye my joy, that ye be likeminded, having the same love, being of one accord, of one mind" **(Philippians 2:2).**

OUTLINE

(Refer to maps on pages A14-A18 in the APPENDIX.)

I. THE EPISTLE OF JOY

- A. **Paul's Joy Flowed From the Lord.**
- B. **Paul's Attitude Toward the Philippians**
  1. **Thanksgiving**
  2. **He desired to see them -** Philippians 1:3-11.
  3. **He told his circumstances.**
- C. **Paul Encouraged Believers To Have the Mind of Christ -** Philippians 2:1-11.
- D. **Paul Encouraged Their Walk -** Philippians 3:17-21.

II. CHRIST'S PORTRAYAL

- A. **He is the Believer's Life -** Philippians 1.
- B. **He is the Believer's Example -** Philippians 2.
- C. **He is the Believer's Faith and Hope -** Philippians 3.
- D. **He is the Believer's Strength -** Philippians 4.

THE OLD TESTAMENT QUOTED IN PHILIPPIANS

Philippians 2:10 (Romans 14:11)
That at the name of Jesus every knee should bow, of things in heaven, and things in earth, and things under the earth.

Isaiah 45:23
I have sworn by myself, the word is gone out of my mouth in righteousness, and shall not return, That unto me every knee shall bow, every tongue shall swear.

NOTES

COLOSSIANS

JESUS CHRIST: THE HEAD OF THE CHURCH		
DOCTRINE--CHRIST'S PREEMINENCE DECLARED	**DANGER--CHRIST'S PREEMINENCE DEFENDED**	**DUTY--CHRIST'S PREEMINIENCE DEMONSTRATED**
Redemption, creation, the church, & ministry: **1**	Beware of philosophies, legalism, & disciplines: **2**	Purity & fellowship--at home & at work: **3** Witness & service: **4**
LOCATION: Roman prison		
OVERVIEW: God's mystery revealed.		God's mystery lived out.
TIME: A.D. 60-61		

FAST FACTS

AUTHOR AND SETTING:

Paul; Roman prison

PURPOSE:

Colossians was written to people who looked at their horoscopes for guidance. It was written to answer the relationship between diet and spiritual living. It was written to show that God speaks to us through His Word. It was also written to show that eastern religions have nothing to offer born-again believers.

SEEING JESUS:

Colossians emphasizes Christ as the head of the Body.

THEME VERSE:

Colossians 1:18

NOTES

COLOSSIANS:
HEAD OF THE BODY

NOTES

SEEING JESUS IN COLOSSIANS

AUTHOR & SETTING

Colossians was written to Paul to answer some important questions. It was written to people who looked at their horoscopes for guidance. It was written to answer the relationship between diet and spiritual living. It was also written to show that God speaks to us through His Word; and lastly, it was written to show that Eastern religions have nothing to offer born-again believers.

Colosse was one of the three cities located about 100 miles inland from Ephesus. The other two cities were Laodicea and Hierapolis (Colossians 4:13,16). Colosse was the meeting point of the east and the west. All kinds of philosophies mingled in this cosmopolitan area. This city is never mentioned in the book of Acts because Paul did not start the Colossian church, nor did he ever visit it. He heard of their faith (Colossians 1:4,9), but he never saw the believers personally:

"For I would that ye knew what great conflict I have for you, and for them at Laodicea, and for as many as have not seen my face in the flesh" **(Colossians 2:1).**

The church at Colosse was an outgrowth of Paul's three-year ministry in Ephesus (Acts 19, 20:17-38). During Paul's ministry at Ephesus, at least two men from Colosse were brought to faith in Jesus Christ - Epaphras and Philemon.

OVERVIEW

The Colossian assembly was predominantly gentile in its membership. Heresy threatened the peace and purity of the Colossian church because it tried to combine Eastern philosophy and Jewish legalism with elements of an early form of what Bible scholars call *Gnosticism* (from the Greek word, "gnosis," meaning "to know"). *"Agnostic"* means "one who does not know." Gnostics were supposed to be the people "in the know."

Paul warned his readers:

"Beware lest any man spoil you through philosophy and vain deceit, after the tradition of men, after the rudiments of the world, and not after Christ" **(Colossians 2:8).**

There are three things Paul warns about:

1. *"... lest any man should beguile you...* **(Colossians 2:4).**
2. *"... lest any man spoil you..."* **(Colossians 2:8).**
3. *"Let no man therefore judge you..."* **(Colossians 2:16).**

The difference between the books of Ephesians and *Colossians* is that Ephesians emphasizes the Body of Christ, and *Colossians* emphasizes Christ as the Head of the Body.

SEEING JESUS IN COLOSSIANS

Christ is seen on virtually every page of this book:

He is the image of God (Colossians 1:15).
He is the head of the Church (Colossians 1:18).
He is the believer's hope of glory (Colossians 1:27).
He is the head of all principalities and powers (Colossians 2:10).
He is seated on the right hand of God (Colossians 3:1).
He is all in all (Colossians 3:11).

NOTES

THEME VERSE

"And he is the head of the body, the church: who is the beginning, the firstborn from the dead; that in all things he might have the preeminence" **(Colossians 1:18).**

OUTLINE

(Refer to maps on pages A14-A18 in the APPENDIX.)

I. **DOCTRINE - CHRIST'S PREEMINENCE DECLARED -** COLOSSIANS 1
   - A. **In the Gospel Message -** Colossians 1:1-12
   - B. **In Redemption -** Colossians 1:13,14
   - C. **In Creation -** Colossians 1:15-17
   - D. **In the Church -** Colossians 1:18-23
   - E. **In Paul's Ministry -** Colossians 1:24-29

II. **DANGER - CHRIST'S PREEMINENCE DEFENDED -** COLOSSIANS 2
   - A. **Beware of Empty Philosophies -** Colossians 2:1-10.
   - B. **Beware of Religious Legalism -** Colossians 2:11-17.
   - C. **Beware of Man-made Disciplines -** Colossians 2:18-23.

III. **DUTY - CHRIST'S PREEMINENCE DEMONSTRATED -** COLOSSIANS 3,4
   - A. **In Personal Purity -** Colossians 3:1-11
   - B. **In Christian Fellowship -** Colossians 3:12-17
   - C. **In the Home -** Colossians 3:18-21
   - D. **In Daily Work -** Colossians 3:22-4:1
   - E. **In Christian Witness -** Colossians 4:2-16
   - F. **In Christian Service -** Colossians 4:17,18

THE OLD TESTAMENT QUOTED IN COLOSSIANS:
NOT FOUND

I THESSALONIANS

A FAMILY LETTER	
PAUL REMEMBERS	**PAUL EXHORTS**
Birth of the church: **1** Nurturing: **2** Establishing: **3**	Walking in holiness, harmony, honesty, & hope: **4** Helpfulness: **5**
LOCATION: Written to the church in Thessalonica from Corinth	
OVERVIEW: Historical review	Future events
TIME: A.D. 51	

FAST FACTS

AUTHOR AND SETTING:

Paul; Corinth

PURPOSE:

Paul seeks to show how the return of Jesus Christ should affect our lives and our conduct within the local church.

SEEING JESUS:

First Thessalonians represents Jesus as the returning Lord *(I Thessalonians 4:13-5:11)*.

THEME VERSE:

I Thessalonians 5:9

NOTES

I & II THESSALONIANS:
GLORY

NOTES

SEEING JESUS IN I THESSALONIANS

AUTHOR & SETTING

We know, of course, that the apostle Paul wrote this letter to the church at Thessalonica. This ancient city was originally named *Therma* for the many hot springs adjacent to it. When Rome conquered Macedonia in 168 B.C., the city was made the capital of the entire province. In Paul's day 200,000 people lived there, most of them Greeks, but also many Romans and a strong Jewish minority.

Today Thessalonica has a population of about 300,000. It is one of the few cities that has survived from the New Testament era of apostolic ministry. It served as an important ally base during World War I, and in World War II it was captured by the German army. The Jewish population of about 60,000 persons was deported or exterminated. Thessalonica is an important industrial and commercial city in modern Greece and is second to Athens in population.

Paul went to Macedonia in response to a vision he received in which a man from Macedonia called for help (Acts 16:9). Paul eventually reached Thessalonica and ministered in the synagogue for three Sabbaths, and the Lord worked in power (Acts 17:1-9). Paul's time there was not particularly a lengthy one. His ministry, however, was strong enough that he left behind a thriving church. When he left for Athens, Paul told Timothy and Silas to remain there and help the new church, and then to join him later (Acts 17:14). When they were reunited Paul sent Timothy back to Thessalonica in his stead because he was unable to travel there himself (I Thessalonians 2:17,18). Timothy was to encourage the Christians and to assure them of Paul's love and concern.

It was when Timothy rejoined Paul at Corinth and gave him the report on the new church that Paul wrote *I Thessalonians*.

OVERVIEW

The two major themes in *I* and *II Thessalonians* are the return of Jesus Christ and the ministry of the local church. In these two letters Paul shows the prophetical and the practical. Paul insisted that the doctrine of the return of Jesus Christ must be more than a doctrine - it must be dynamic in our lives and in the ministry of our churches. The background of the Thessalonian church is in Acts 17:1-15.

Paul's purpose in writing this letter was to ground the Thessalonians in the doctrine of Christian faith, especially in reference to Christ's return. He encouraged them to live holy lives. They were confused about the return of Jesus, and he endeavored to straighten them out.

Some believers thought that the day of the Lord had arrived because of their intense persecution, but Paul showed them otherwise. He also corrected some of the weaknesses in the church. The members were not respecting and honoring their spiritual leadership as they should. A pastor doesn't demand respect, but he commands respect.

First Thessalonians is a letter from a spiritual father to his spiritual children. Paul pictured the church as a family. The word "brethren" or "brother" is used 19 times in the first letter and 9 times in the second. Each New Testament letter is a special message of blessing. Romans emphasizes the righteousness of God, I Corinthians focuses on the wisdom of God, II Corinthians on the comfort of God, Galatians on the freedom of God, Ephesians stresses the wealth of the Christian, Philippians is the joy letter, Colossians presents the preeminence of Christ, and I and *II Thessalonians* is a message of the return of Jesus Christ and how this doctrine should affect our lives.

SEEING JESUS IN I THESSALONIANS

Jesus is clearly seen as the believer's salvation - both now and at His Second Coming.

"For God hath not appointed us to wrath, but to obtain salvation by our Lord Jesus Christ, Who died for us, that, whether we wake or sleep, we should live together with him" **(I Thessalonians 5:9,10).**

NOTES

NOTES

THEME VERSE

"For God hath not appointed us to wrath, but to obtain salvation by our Lord Jesus Christ" **(I Thessalonians 5:9).**

OUTLINE

(Refer to maps on pages A14-A18 in the APPENDIX.)

I. **PAUL REMEMBERS -** I THESSALONIANS 1-3
   A. **How the Church was Born -** I Thessalonians 1
   B. **How the Church Was Nurtured -** I Thessalonians 2
   C. **How the Church Was Established -** I Thessalonians 3

II. **PAUL EXHORTS -** I THESSALONIANS 4,5
   A. **How the Church Should Walk:**
      1. **In holiness -** I Thessalonians 4:1-8
      2. **In harmony -** I Thessalonians 4:9,10
      3. **In honesty -** I Thessalonians 4:11,12
      4. **In hope -** I Thessalonians 4:13-5:11
      5. **In helpfulness -** I Thessalonians 5:12-28

THE OLD TESTAMENT QUOTED IN I THESSALONIANS: NOT FOUND

II THESSALONIANS

CLARIFYING THE SECOND COMING		
ENCOURAGEMENT & SUFFERINGS	**ENLIGHTENMENT & TEACHING**	**ENABLEMENT IN LIVING**
Praise, promise, & prayer: **1**	Man of sin, Son of God, & child of God: **2**	Obey, follow, & discipline: **3**
LOCATION: Written from Corinth to the church at Thessalonica		
OVERVIEW: Thanksgiving and assurance for believers	End-time details	Practical considerations
TIME: A.D. 51		

FAST FACTS

AUTHOR AND SETTING:

Paul: written from Corinth

PURPOSE:

Second Thessalonians was written to correct certain wrong ideas and wrong practices related to the doctrine of the Lord's return.

SEEING JESUS:

The Second Coming of Jesus is given much attention in this book. Thanks to Paul's letters we are not ignorant of the details surrounding this blessed event!

THEME VERSE:

II Thessalonians 2:16,17

NOTES

I & II THESSALONIANS:
GLORY

NOTES

SEEING JESUS IN II THESSALONIANS

AUTHOR & SETTING

Paul went to Macedonia in response to a vision he received in which a man from Macedonia called for help (Acts 16:9). Paul eventually reached Thessalonica and ministered in the synagogue for three Sabbaths, and the Lord worked in power (Acts 17:1-9). Paul's time there was not particularly a lengthy one. His ministry, however, was strong enough that he left behind a thriving church. When he left for Athens, Paul told Timothy and Silas to remain there and help the new church, and then to join him later (Acts 17:14). When they were reunited Paul sent Timothy back to Thessalonica in his stead because he was unable to travel there himself (I Thessalonians 2:17,18). Timothy was to encourage the Christians and to assure them of Paul's love and concern.

It was when Timothy rejoined Paul at Corinth and gave him the report on the new church that Paul wrote I Thessalonians. He wrote *II Thessalonians* just a short time later to correct certain wrong ideas and wrong practices related to the doctrine of the Lord's return.

OVERVIEW

Four times in his letter Paul gives thanks for the way the church responded to his ministry. The characteristics of this church make it ideal. They were an elect people (II Thessalonians 1:1-4). The word *church* in verse one means "a called out people."

Whenever you read about a call in the Bible, it indicates divine election. God is calling out a people from this world (Acts 15:13-18). Seven times in John 17 our Lord referred to believers as those whom the Father gave to Him out of this world. That is a good description of the Church. They are not only an elect people, but they are also an exemplary people (II Thessalonians 1:5-7). Why? Because they have received the Word, they have followed their spiritual leaders, and they have suffered for Christ in turning from idols to serve the *living* God.

Psalms 115 gives a very good description of what it is like to worship an idol. Christians, however, are children of the *living* God (Romans 9:26). Their bodies are the temples of the *living* God (II Corinthians 6:16). They are indwelt by the Spirit of the *living* God (II Corinthians 3:3). The Church is a church of the *living* God (I Timothy 3:15), and for His Church, God is preparing the city of the *living* God (Hebrews 12:22). Our *living* God is giving us a *living* hope through the resurrection of His Son, Jesus Christ (I Peter 1:3).

These believers angered their friends and relatives, and this led to their persecution. They also encouraged other people. They were an enthusiastic people (II Thessalonians 1:8). Their work of faith and love showed they were receivers and givers. They certainly were an expectant people (II Thessalonians 1:9,10).

CONTRAST OF I AND II THESSALONIANS

I Thessalonians 4:13-18	II Thessalonians 1
Christ returns in the air.	Christs returns to earth.
He comes secretly for the Church.	He comes openly.
Believers escape the Tribulation judgment.	
Occurs at an undisclosed time.	Occurs at the end of the Tribulation period - "Day of the Lord."

There are two aspects of the Lord's return: (1) Christ will come in the air *for* His Church (I Thessalonians 4:13-18). This will usher in a period of tribulation on the earth (I Thessalonians 5:1-3); (2) at the close of this period, He will return to the earth *with* His Church (II Thessalonians 1:5-10). He will defeat His enemies and set up His kingdom (Revelation 19:11-21).

We need to be looking daily for the return of Jesus Christ. Paul greatly encouraged the Thessalonians. He said that if we appreciate the Word with our hearts, appropriate the Word with our minds, and apply the Word with our wills, then the whole person will be controlled by God's Word. God will give us the victory. Paul encouraged his readers again and again: "Don't give up! You have the Word of God within you, the people of God around you, and the glory of God before you. There is no need to give up."

SEEING JESUS IN II THESSALONIANS

Second Thessalonians clarifies the events leading up to the "day of Christ" (II Thessalonians 2:2).
Jesus' Second Coming will bring salvation to Christians (II Thessalonians 2:13) but terrible judgment to unbelievers (II Thessalonians 1:7-9).

NOTES

NOTES

THEME VERSES

"Now our Lord Jesus Christ himself, and God, even our Father, which hath loved us, and hath given us everlasting consolation and good hope through grace, Comfort your hearts, and establish you in every good word and work"
(II Thessalonians 2:16,17).

OUTLINE

(refer to maps on pages A14-A18 in the APPENDIX.)

I. **ENCOURAGEMENT AND SUFFERING -** II THESSALONIANS 1
   - A. **Praise -** II Thessalonians 1:1-4
   - B. **Promise -** II Thessalonians 1:5-10
   - C. **Prayer -** II Thessalonians 1:11,12

II. **ENLIGHTENMENT AND TEACHING -** II THESSALONIANS 2
   - A. **How the Man of Sin Appears -** II Thessalonians 2:1-7
   - B. **How the Son of God Appears -** II Thessalonians 2:8-12
   - C. **How the Child of God Should Live -** II Thessalonians 2:13-17

III. **ENABLEMENT IN LIVING -** II THESSALONIANS 3
   - A. **Obey the Word -** II Thessalonians 3:1-6
   - B. **Follow Our Example -** II Thessalonians 3:7-9
   - C. **Discipline the Unruly -** II Thessalonians 3:10-15
   - D. **Closing Benediction -** II Thessalonians 3:16-18

THE OLD TESTAMENT QUOTED IN II THESSALONIANS: NOT FOUND

I TIMOTHY

HOW TO BE A GOOD PASTOR				
SOUND DOCTRINE	**PRAYER & WORSHIP**	**CHURCH OFFICERS**	**APOSTASY**	**PASTORAL OVERSIGHT**
The Word: **1**	Public prayer: **2**	Responsibilities: **3**	Godliness: **4**	Rebuke: **5** Fight: **6**
LOCATION: Written to Timothy at Ephesus between Paul's first and second Roman imprisonment.				
OVERVIEW: Warning concerning false doctrine	Instructions concerning worship	Qualifications for officers	Duties toward others	Godly relationships and personal admonitions
TIME: A.D. 62-63				

FAST FACTS

AUTHOR AND SETTING:

Paul; written from Macedonia to Ephesus

PURPOSE:

There are basically two purposes behind the writing of this book: (1) to help you understand the ministry of the local church, and (2) to encourage you to never give up.

SEEING JESUS:

In *I Timothy* Jesus is our shepherd and our pastor. He is God ***"... manifest in the flesh, justified in the Spirit, seen of angels, preached unto the Gentiles, believed on in the world, received up into glory"*** **(I Timothy 3:16).**

THEME VERSE:

I Timothy 3:15

NOTES

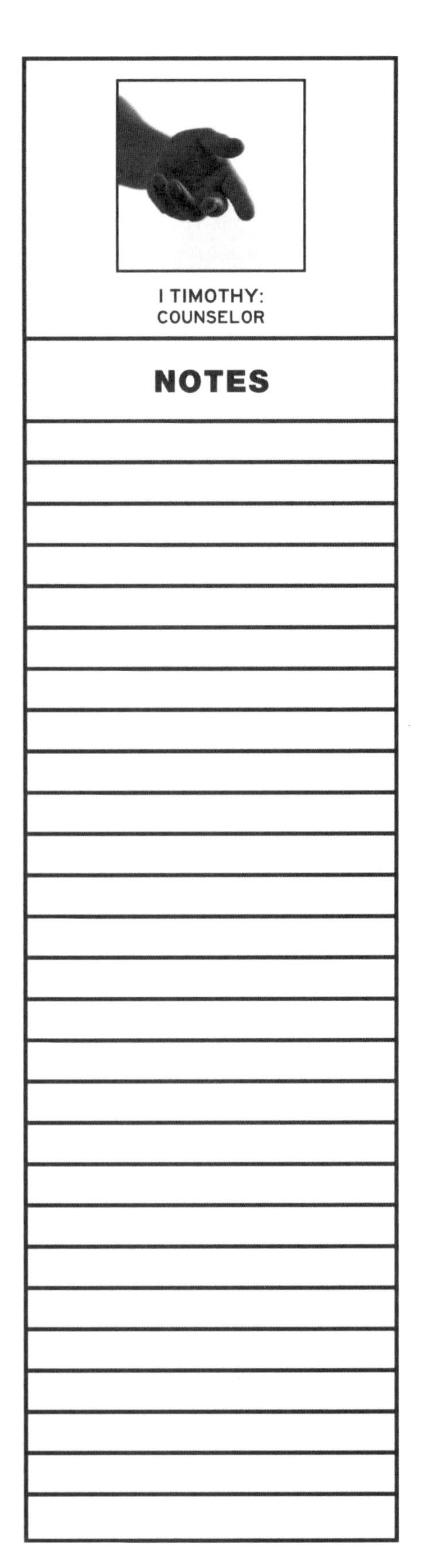

SEEING JESUS IN I TIMOTHY

AUTHOR & SETTING

The author of *I* and *II Timothy*, of course, is Paul. This first epistle was probably written between Paul's first and second Roman imprisonments. Timothy had been left at the church in Ephesus and was not happy there - it was very, very difficult. Paul admonished him to, "Be faithful. It's always too soon to quit." In fact, Paul used the word, "*pistos*," or "faithful," 17 times in *I* and *II Timothy* and Titus.

There are basically two purposes behind the writing of this book:

1. To help you understand the ministry of the local church
2. To encourage you to never give up

The circumstances surrounding the writing of this book begin when Paul was arrested in Jerusalem in A.D. 57 and was kept in prison for two years (Acts 21:19; 26:32). His voyage to Rome to be tried before Caesar started around September A.D. 59. Following the shipwreck, after a three-month wait on Malta, he arrived in Rome in A.D. 60 (Acts 27,28). There he lived in a rented house and ministered. Paul wrote *I Timothy* and Titus after his first acquittal in Rome. Around A.D. 65 he was arrested again and put into a dungeon. It was then that he wrote II Timothy, his last letter.

OVERVIEW

This is one of the three short letters called *pastoral epistles*. In *I* and *II Timothy* instructions are given for overseeing a church. In *I Timothy*, Paul dealt with a Christian's behavior in the house of God.

Timothy is first mentioned in Acts 16:1:

"Then came he to Derbe and Lystra: and, behold, a certain disciple was there, named Timotheus, the son of a certain woman, which was a Jewess, and believed; but his father was a Greek."

The name *Timothy*, means "honoring God." Timothy lived in Lystra. Paul visited there twice on his first missionary journey. When Paul returned to Lystra on his second journey, he decided to take Timothy with him as a companion and helper. Timothy is mentioned often in the New Testament.

Timothy was brought up in a religious home:

***"When I call to remembrance the unfeigned faith that is in thee, which dwelt first in thy grandmother Lois, and thy mother Eunice; and I am persuaded that in thee also"* (II Timothy 1:5).**

Paul led Timothy to Christ:

"Unto Timothy, my own son in the faith: Grace, mercy, and peace, from God our Father and Jesus Christ our Lord" **(I Timothy 1:2).**

Timothy was of mixed parentage; his mother was a Jewess and his father was a Greek. Local leaders recommended Timothy to Paul who added him to his missionary staff (Acts 16:1-5).

Paul often reminded Timothy that he was chosen for the ministry:

"This charge I commit unto thee, son Timothy, according to the prophecies which went before on thee, that thou by them mightest war a good warfare" **(I Timothy 1:18).**

"Neglect not the gift that is in thee, which was given thee by prophecy, with the laying on of the hands of the presbytery" **(I Timothy 4:14).**

Timothy was faithful to the Lord:

"For this cause have I sent unto you Timotheus, who is my beloved son, and faithful in the Lord, who shall bring you into remembrance of my ways which be in Christ, as I teach everywhere in every church" **(I Corinthians 4:17).**

Timothy had a deep concern for God's people:

"For I have no man like-minded, who will naturally care for your state. For all seek their own, not the things which are Jesus Christ's. But ye know the proof of him, that, as a son with the father, he hath served with me in the gospel" **(Philippians 2:20-22).**

Timothy, however, was easily discouraged, and he had some physical problems:

"Drink no longer water, but use a little wine for the stomach's sake and thine often infirmities" **(I Timothy 5:23).**

Timothy was not receiving proper respect from his church members, and Paul taught him how to receive this respect. Paul instructed him how to deal with age differences and how to deal with various classes of people in the church. The number one thing Paul emphasized was that Timothy must be strong in the Word and strong in teaching his people the Word.

NOTES

NOTES

SEEING JESUS IN I TIMOTHY

Paul gives us a beautiful picture of Jesus in this letter:

"For there is one God, and one mediator between God and men, the man Christ Jesus" **(I Timothy 2:5).**

"And without controversy great is the mystery of godliness: God was manifest in the flesh, justified in the Spirit, seen of angels, preached unto the Gentiles, believed on in the world, received up into glory"
(I Timothy 3:16).

THEME VERSE

"But if I tarry long, that thou mayest know how thou oughtest to behave thyself in the house of God, which is the church of the living God, the pillar and ground of the truth" **(I Timothy 3:15).**

OUTLINE

(Refer to maps on pages A14-A18 in the APPENDIX.)

I. **SOUND DOCTRINE -** I TIMOTHY I
   - A. **Resist False Doctrine.**
   - B. **The Word is Our Salvation.**

II. **PRAYER AND WORSHIP -** I TIMOTHY 2
   - A. **A Public Prayer**

III. **CHURCH OFFICERS -** I TIMOTHY 3

IV. **APOSTASY -** I TIMOTHY 4
   - A. **Set an Example of Godliness.**
   - B. **Give Attention to Scriptures, Exhortation, and Teaching.**

V. **PASTORAL OVERSIGHT -** I TIMOTHY 5,6
   - A. **Rebuke False Teachers.**
   - B. **Fight the Good Fight of Faith:**
     1. *"Fight the good fight of faith, lay hold on eternal life, whereunto thou art also called, and hast professed a good profession before many witnesses"* **(I Timothy 6:12).**
     2. *"O Timothy, keep that which is committed to thy trust, avoiding profane and vain babblings, and oppositions of science falsely so called"* **(I Timothy 6:20).**

We see Jesus as our great Shepherd and pastor of the sheep. His care and His concern for the local church is found in *I* and *II Timothy*.

THE OLD TESTAMENT QUOTED IN I TIMOTHY.

I Timothy 5:18 (I Corinthians 9:9)
For the scripture saith, Thou shalt not muzzle the ox that treadeth out the corn. And, The labourer is worthy of his reward.

Deuteronomy 25:4
Thou shalt not muzzle the ox when he treadeth out the corn.

NOTES

II TIMOTHY

PAUL'S LAST WILL AND TESTAMENT		
APOSTASY	**EXHORTATIONS FOR OTHERS**	**HELP FOR PERILOUS TIMES**
Manifestation & cure: **1**	Seven pictures of ministry: **2**	Strengthening: **3**
LOCATION: In prison in Rome - awaiting execution		
OVERVIEW: Paul the messenger would die, but God's message would live on through Timothy and the Christians trained under Paul's ministry.		
TIME: A.D. 67		

FAST FACTS

AUTHOR AND SETTING:

Paul; Roman prison

PURPOSE:

Paul needed Timothy to take the leadership of the churches. This letter is Paul's final instructions for equipping Timothy in God's work.

SEEING JESUS:

We see Jesus as the *Good Shepherd* showing His *under-shepherds* how to act and how to behave in the house of God.

THEME VERSE:

II Timothy 3:17

NOTES

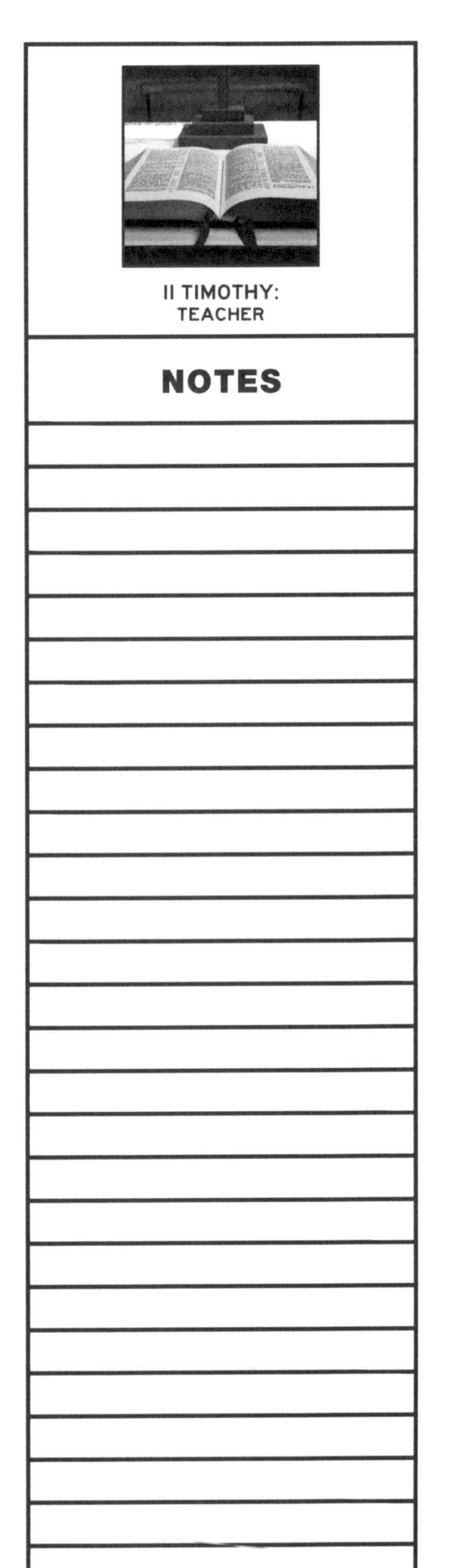

SEEING JESUS IN II TIMOTHY

AUTHOR & SETTING

This epistle was written by Paul while he was in prison expecting to be executed:

"For I am now ready to be offered, and the time of my departure is at hand" **(II Timothy 4:6).**

Most of Paul's associates were gone, and only Luke was at his side to assist him. Paul sent Tychicus to replace Timothy at Ephesus so that Timothy might join Paul at Rome:

"Do thy diligence to come shortly unto me. And Tychicus have I sent to Ephesus" **(II Timothy 4:9,12).**

OVERVIEW

Paul needed Timothy to take the leadership of the churches. Timothy needed three attributes for this ministry: courageous enthusiasm, shameless suffering, and spiritual loyalty. These are all presented in chapter one.

In chapter two Paul helped Timothy to avoid an identity crisis by presenting seven pictures of the Christian minister.

Paul showed Timothy:

The steward
The solider
The athlete
The farmer
The workman
The vessel
The servant.

Paul showed Timothy that the ministry is no place for a loafer.

Paul's emphasis in chapter three is *knowledge* and *responsibility*. Paul gave Timothy instruction for the perilous times: he was to turn away from false teaching. Paul showed Timothy the signs of false teachers and their converts: they were simply imitators. Paul told Timothy to follow those who were true: their lives would be open for all to see, they would teach true doctrine, they would practice what they preach, their purpose would be to glorify God, they would be willing to suffer, and above all, they would continue in God's Word.

Paul's advice for pastors in *I* and *II Timothy* includes a tremendous emphasis upon the Word.

Paul refers to 17 people in II Timothy 4. Paul won souls and made friends. Paul gave Timothy his final admonitions and called out the names of special friends and workmen in the gospel.

Paul, the messenger, would die; but the message God gave him would live. God buries His workman, but His work goes on.

Again, Paul was saying to us through *II Timothy,* "It's always too soon to quit."

SEEING JESUS IN II TIMOTHY

We see Jesus as the Good Shepherd showing His *under shepherds* how to act and how to behave in the house of God.

THEME VERSE

"That the man of God may be perfect, thoroughly furnished unto all good works" **(II Timothy 3:17).**

OUTLINE

(Refer to maps on pages A14-A18 in the APPENDIX.)

I. APOSTASY - II TIMOTHY 1

A. Its Manifestation:

1. *"This thou knowest, that all they which are in Asia be turned away from me; of whom are Phygellus and Hermogenes"* **(II Timothy 1:15).**
2. *"For Demas hath forsaken me, having loved this present world, and is departed unto Thessalonica; Crescens to Galatia, Titus unto Dalmatia"* **(II Timothy 4:10)**

B. Its Cure:

1. *"Hold fast the form of sound words, which thou hast heard of me, in faith and love which is in Christ Jesus"* **(II Timothy 1:13).**

II. EXHORTATIONS TO ENTRUST TO OTHERS - II TIMOTHY 2

A. The Faithful Steward

B. The Courageous Solider

C. The Careful Athlete

D. The Persevering Farmer

E. The Diligent Worker

F. The Clean Vessel

NOTES

NOTES

G. **The Gentle Servant**

III. **HELP FOR PERILOUS TIMES -** II TIMOTHY 3

A. **Continue in the Word.**

IV. **FINAL CHARGE TO TIMOTHY -** II TIMOTHY 4

A. **Take the Strengthening of God's Word:**

1. *"Notwithstanding the Lord stood with me, and strengthened me; that by me the preaching might be fully known, and that all the Gentiles might hear; and I was delivered out of the mouth of the lion"* **(II Timothy 4:17).**

2. *"And the Lord shall deliver me from every evil work, and will preserve me unto his heavenly kingdom: to whom be glory for ever and ever, Amen"* **(II Timothy 4:18).**

THE OLD TESTAMENT QUOTED IN II TIMOTHY: NOT FOUND

TITUS

"ZEALOUS OF GOOD WORKS"	
THREE RESPONSIBILITIES	**HOW TO HAVE A HEALTHY CHURCH**
Preach the Word, ordain elders, silence false teachers: **1**	Older & younger saints, slaves & citizens, problem people: **2,3**
LOCATION: Written by Paul from Macedonia to Crete	
OVERVIEW: Greetings and warnings concerning false teachers	Advice concerning ministry
TIME: Around A.D. 65	

FAST FACTS

AUTHOR AND SETTING:

Paul; written from Macedonia to Crete

PURPOSE:

In this book Paul gives Titus instructions for pastoring the church at Crete.

SEEING JESUS:

"Looking for that blessed hope, and the glorious appearing of the great God and our Savior Jesus Christ; Who gave himself for us, that He might redeem us from all iniquity, and purify unto himself a peculiar people, zealous of good works" **(Titus 2:13,14).**

THEME VERSE:

Titus 2:11-14

NOTES

TITUS:
PASTOR / SHEPHERD

NOTES

SEEING JESUS IN TITUS

AUTHOR & SETTING

Titus means "nurse, one who rears." In this book Paul gives Titus instructions for pastoring the church at Crete:

"For this cause left I thee in Crete, that thou shouldest set in order the things that are wanting, and ordain elders in every city, as I had appointed thee" **(Titus 1:5).**

OVERVIEW

Titus is similar to I and II Timothy. The phrase that is used again and again in *Titus* is "good works":

*"In all things shewing thyself a pattern of **good works**: in doctrine shewing uncorruptness, gravity, sincerity. Who gave himself for us, that He might redeem us from all iniquity, and purify unto himself a peculiar people, zealous of **good works**"* **(Titus 2:7,14).**

*"This is a faithful saying, and these things I will that thou affirm constantly, that they which have believed in God might be careful to maintain **good works**. These things are good and profitable unto men. And let our's also learn to maintain **good works** for the necessary uses, that they be not unfruitful"* **(Titus 3:8,14).**

Titus is mentioned 13 times in the Pauline epistles.

Titus was a Greek believer:

"But neither Titus, who was with me, being a Greek, was compelled to be circumcised" **(Galatians 2:3).**

Titus had served Paul on special assignments to Corinth (II Corinthians 7:13,14; 8:6,16,23; 12:18). He had been converted through Paul's personal ministry:

"To Titus, mine own son after the common faith: Grace, mercy, and peace, from God the Father and the Lord Jesus Christ our Savior" **(Titus 1:4).**

Timothy was also converted by Paul:

"Unto Timothy, my own son in the faith: Grace, mercy, and peace, from God our Father and Jesus Christ our Lord" **(I Timothy 1:2).**

Paul commended Titus, saying, *"... he is my partner and fellow helper concerning you: ..."* **(II Corinthians 8:23).** Titus' pastorate at Crete was very trying because he had a difficult flock. He was young, but he was not given to the ailments or timidity of Timothy.

Jews from Crete were present on the day of Pentecost, and they had carried the gospel back to their native land (Acts 2:11).

Paul left Titus at Crete to correct two wrongs:
(1) unrighteousness among the Cretans and (2) false teachers who were trying to mix the law with the gospel of grace. Many of the gentiles were abusing the message of grace and turning it into license.

This book is basically a condensed version of Paul's first letter to Timothy.

SEEING JESUS IN TITUS

Jesus is seen as our "blessed hope" (Titus 2:13) and our "Saviour" (Titus 3:6).

THEME VERSE

"For the grace of God that bringeth salvation hath appeared to all men, Teaching us that, denying ungodliness and worldly lusts, we should live soberly, righteously, and godly, in this present world; Looking for that blessed hope, and the glorious appearing of the great God and our Saviour Jesus Christ: Who gave himself for us, that he might redeem us from all Iniquity, and purify unto himself a peculiar people, zealous of good works" **(Titus 2:11-14).**

OUTLINE

(Refer to maps on pages A14-A18 in the APPENDIX.)

I. **TITUS HAD THREE RESPONSIBILITIES -** TITUS 1
   - **A. Preach God's Word**
   - **B. Ordain Qualified Elders**
   - **C. Silence False Teachers**

II. **HOW TO HAVE A HEALTHY CHURCH -** TITUS 2,3
   - **A. Older Saints**
   - **B. Younger Saints**
   - **C. Christian Slaves**
   - **D. Christians as Citizens**
   - **E. Problem People**
   - **F. Conclusion**

THE OLD TESTAMENT QUOTED IN TITUS: NOT FOUND

NOTES

PHILEMON

PAYING ANOTHER'S DEBT	
CONDEMNED BY LAW, BUT SAVED BY GRACE	
Greetings: **1-8** Intercession: **9-16**	Imputation: **17,18** Salutations: **19-25**
LOCATION: Written by Paul in a Roman prison to Philemon in Colossae	
OVERVIEW: An appeal for Philemon to receive back Onesimus, a runaway slave	
TIME: Around A.D. 60	

FAST FACTS

AUTHOR AND SETTING:

Paul; Roman Prison

PURPOSE:

Paul presents 14 arguments as to why Philemon should receive Onesimus back.

SEEING JESUS:

This epistle shows the doctrine of imputation - the paying of a debt by one for another. We can certainly see the picture of Jesus Christ Who paid the price for us.

THEME VERSE:

Philemon 6

NOTES

PHILEMON:
COMPASSIONATE FRIEND

NOTES

SEEING JESUS IN PHILEMON

AUTHOR & SETTING

Philemon means "affectionate." *Philemon* is an appeal letter, probably the greatest appeal letter you've ever read. Onesimus was a runaway slave belonging to Philemon. He had probably stolen from Philemon in addition to running away from him. Paul, the author of this letter, appealed to Philemon to receive his slave back.

Onesimus had been transformed. He had come to Rome and by divine appointment had met with Paul. Paul led him to Christ. Paul eventually sent Onesimus back 1,000 miles with the very letter in his hand that would either bring him reprieve or possible death. Tychicus accompanied Onesimus back to Philemon.

Slavery was very prevalent in that day. Many were born as slaves, and sometimes parents even sold their children as slaves to alleviate their poverty. Some people were captured in war and made slaves, while some were caught by piracy and kidnapping and made slaves. We don't know why Onesimus was a slave, but we do know that he who is the Lord's slave is the Lord's freeman (I Corinthians 7:22).

After Paul had led him to Christ, Onesimus stayed and ministered to Paul. Onesimus could not run from his sin, however, and his day of reckoning was at hand.

Two pictures were given of Onesimus. Paul first described him as someone who *"... in time past was to thee unprofitable, ..."* (Philemon 11). Paul's second description reversed the first by saying, *"... but now profitable to thee and to me"* (Philemon 11). Onesimus was a changed man. His name means "one who gives pleasure, advantage, and profit." The Greek word for "unprofitable" is *achrestos*. The Greek word for "profitable" is *euchrestos*. *Chrestos* means "useful." When Paul put "eu" in front of the word, it meant "completely useful."

When a man comes to Jesus, he is transformed from waste to wealth. He fits well into the family of God. Paul called Onesimus a beloved brother who had once been a slave but who had become the Lord's freeman:

***"For he that is called in the Lord, being a servant, is the Lord's freeman; likewise also he that is called, being free is Christ's servant"* (I Corinthians 7:22).**

Paul was Onesimus' spiritual father. Paul speaks to Philemon in this appeal letter and tells him that Onesimus is his son, his brother, his heart, and his own self.

OVERVIEW

Paul presents 14 arguments to Philemon:

1. Show your love to Onesimus as you do to all the saints.
2. Paul asked this on his own authority.
3. Wave the authority of being a master over the slave and free him for love's sake.
4. Paul uses the fact that he is old and a prisoner to persuade Philemon.
5. Paul mentioned his own spiritual relationship to Philemon and to Onesimus - Paul had begotten them both in the Lord.
6. Paul said, "Your forgiveness of Onesimus is profitable for both of us."
7. Paul appealed on the basis of his own strong affection for Philemon.
8. Paul said that he denied himself in sending Onesimus back.
9. Philemon need not fear that Onesimus would ever run away again.
10. Onesimus was not a servant now; he was a brother.
11. Paul said, "Receive him as you would me."
12. Paul promised satisfaction for the debt - he would pay it himself.
13. Philemon's forgiveness of Onesimus would give Paul joy and comfort.
14. Paul concluded, "I have confidence in you, Philemon."

Who could resist such an appeal? I'm sure that Philemon released Onesimus from his slavery.

SEEING JESUS IN PHILEMON

This epistle shows the doctrine of imputation - the paying of a debt by one for another. We can certainly see the picture of Jesus Christ Who paid the price for us. Our sins were put upon Him; our debts were upon him; Jesus freely took them to set us free. Paul was willing to take the debts of Onesimus in order that Onesimus be set free; it is a beautiful picture of Jesus Christ.

NOTES

NOTES

THEME VERSE

"That the communication of thy faith may become effectual by the acknowledging of every good thing which is in you in Christ Jesus" **(Philemon 6).**

OUTLINE

(Refer to maps on pages A14-A18 in the APPENDIX.)

I. AN APPEAL

A. It Begins With a Greeting.

B. Paul Intercedes for Onesimus.

C. The Doctrine of Imputation:

1. *"If thou count me therefore a partner, receive him as myself. If he hath wronged thee, or oweth thee ought, put that on mine account"* **(Philemon 17,18).**
2. **Our sins were put on Jesus' account.**

THE OLD TESTAMENT QUOTED IN PHILEMON: NOT FOUND

HEBREWS

CHRISTIANITY IS BETTER		
SUPERIORITY OF CHRIST	**SUPERIORITY OF PRIESTHOOD OF CHRIST**	**EXHORTATION TO FAITH, HOPE, & LOVE**
Christ is better than angels & Moses: **1-3**	The service of Jesus Christ: **4-9**	Living the Christian life: **10-13**
LOCATION: Probably written to believers in Rome		
OVERVIEW: The exhaulted person of Jesus	The better ministry of Jesus	The Christian's better walk of faith
TIME: Around A.D. 68		

FAST FACTS

AUTHOR AND SETTING:

Unknown

PURPOSE:

This book explains the superiority of the Lord Jesus Christ over Judaism to Hebrew believers who were tempted to return to their Jewish religion.

SEEING JESUS:

The picture of Jesus here, of course, is that He is "better" than *everything* of the Old Covenant - He is the best!

THEME VERSE:

Hebrews 9:15

NOTES

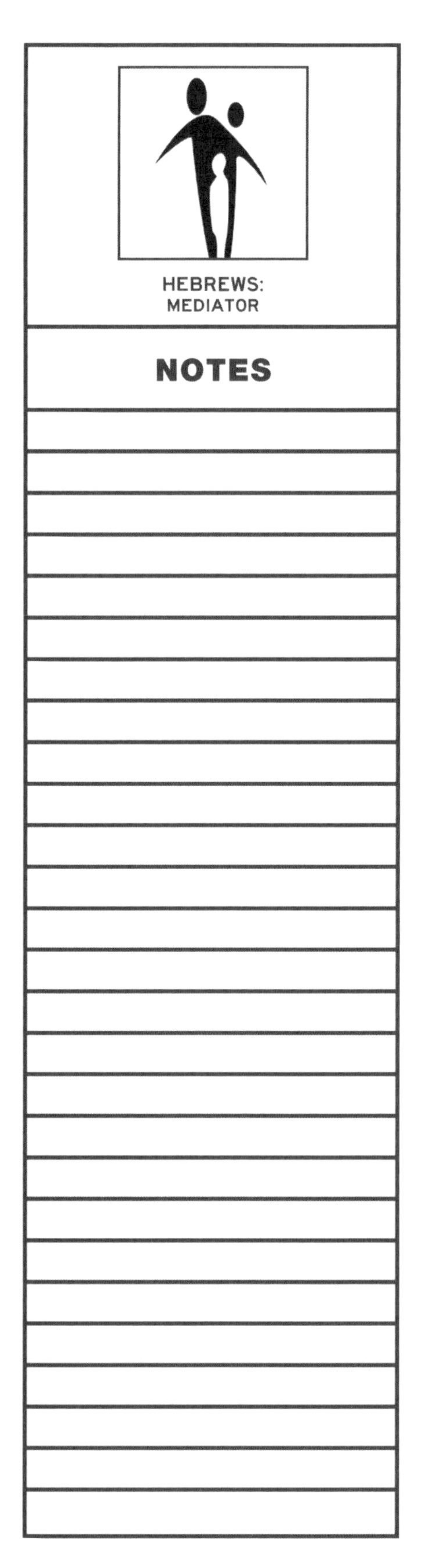

SEEING JESUS IN HEBREWS

AUTHOR & SETTING

We do not know who wrote the book of *Hebrews*. Some have suggested that Paul was its author, while others argue for Apollos, Luke, Priscilla, or Barnabas. It is also not clear to whom the letter was written, although most scholars hold to the view that it was written to Jewish believers living in Rome (because of the statement in Hebrews 13:24 regarding *"They of Italy..."* who sent greetings to the recipients of the letter).

It seems clear from the content of this letter that those who read it were suffering persecution and considering returning to the Jewish faith with its rituals and sacrifices for sin. The book of Hebrews explains the superiority of the Lord Jesus Christ over Judaism. This epistle contains numerous quotes from the Old Testament, and it was written before the destruction of Jerusalem.

OVERVIEW

The key word in *Hebrews* is unquestionably the word, "better."

"Better" occurs 13 times in the King James version of the epistle:

1. Christ was "... made so much better than the angels..." (Hebrews 1:4).
2. "... we are persuaded better things of you..." (Hebrews 6:9).
3. "... the less is blessed of the better" (Hebrews 7:7).
4. "... the bringing in of a better hope..." (Hebrews 7:19).
5. "... Jesus made a surety of a better testament" (Hebrews 7:22).
6. "... he is the mediator of a better covenant..." (Hebrews 8:6).
7. "... established upon better promises" (Hebrews 8:6).
8. "... better sacrifices..." (Hebrews 9:23).
9. "... a better and an enduring substance" (Hebrews 10:34).
10. "... a better country, ..." (Hebrews 11:16).
11. "... a better resurrection" (Hebrews 11:35).
12. "God having provided some better thing for us..." (Hebrews 11:40).
13. "... the blood of sprinkling, that speaketh better things than that of Abel" (Hebrews 12:24).

Another important thought is contained in those verses which mention "partaker":

1. *"... as the children are partakers of flesh and blood, he also himself likewise took part of the same..."* (Hebrews 2:14).
2. *"... holy brethren, partakers of the heavenly calling..."* (Hebrews 3:1).
3. *"For we are made partakers of Christ, ..."* (Hebrews 3:14).
4. *"... were made partakers of the Holy Ghost"* (Hebrews 6:4).
5. *"But if ye be without chastisement, whereof all are partakers, ..."* (Hebrews 12:8).
6. *"... but he for our profit, that we might be partakers of his holiness"* (Hebrews 12:10).

Much consideration and emphasis is given also to heaven and heavenliness:

1. The heavens are the works of God's hands (Hebrews 1:10).
2. Believers are partakers of the heavenly calling (Hebrews 3:1).
3. Jesus has passed into the heavens (Hebrews 4:14).
4. Believers have tasted of the heavenly gift (Hebrews 6:4).
5. Christ, in His high priesthood, was made higher than the heavens (Hebrews 7:26).
6. The throne of the Majesty is in the heavens (Hebrews 8:1).
7. There is a copy and shadow of heavenly things (Hebrews 8:5).
8. The copies of the things in the heavens were purified (Hebrews 9:23).
9. There are heavenly things (Hebrews 9:23).
10. Christ entered into heaven itself (Hebrews 9:24).
11. The descendants of Abraham are as many as the stars in the sky (Hebrews 11:12).
12. Christians desire a heavenly country (Hebrews 11:16).
13. Christians have come unto the heavenly Jerusalem (Hebrews 12:22).
14. The church of the firstborn is written in heaven (Hebrews 12:23).
15. God speaks from heaven (Hebrews 12:25).
16. God will shake the earth and heaven (Hebrews 12:26).

NOTES

NOTES

A striking characteristic of Hebrews is the contrasts which it presents:

1. God's Son is set in contrast with the angels (Hebrews 1,2).
2. Jesus is contrasted with Moses (Hebrews 3:1-11).
3. The "rest" of Canaan is contrasted with the "rest" of God (Hebrews 3:12-4:13).
4. Christ and Aaron are contrasted (Hebrews 4:14-5:10).
5. Babyhood and maturity are contrasted (Hebrews 5:11-14).
6. Apostasy and faithfulness are contrasted (Hebrews 6).
7. The Melchizedek priesthood is contrasted with the Aaronic priesthood (Hebrews 7).
8. The old and new covenants are set in contrast (Hebrews 8).
9. The offerings of the law and Christ are contrasted (Hebrews 9:10-18).
10. The differences between punishment under the law and punishment under grace are noted (Hebrews 10:19-39).
11. Vital faith and empirical sight are set in bold contrast (Hebrews 11).
12. True sons and spiritual bastards are sorrowfully distinguished (Hebrews 12:5-13).
13. Earthly and heavenly congregations and cities are set in contrast (Hebrews 12:18-29).
14. Old and new altars are set one against the other (Hebrews 13:10-15).

Hebrews includes more than 35 Old Testament quotations. It was written to save people from apostasy. Every teaching necessary to the Christian faith is implicit in Hebrews.

SEEING JESUS IN HEBREWS

The picture of Jesus here, of course, is that He is "better" than *everything* of the Old Covenant -- He is the best!

THEME VERSE

"And for this cause he is the mediator of the new testament, that by means of death, for the redemption of the transgressions that were under the first testament, they which are called might receive the promise of eternal inheritance" **(Hebrews 9:15).**

OUTLINE

(Refer to maps on pages A14-A18 in the APPENDIX.)

I. **SUPERIORITY OF CHRIST** - HEBREWS 1-3
   - A. **Christ is Better than Angels.**
   - B. **Christ is Better than Moses.**

II. **SUPERIORITY OF THE PRIESTHOOD OF CHRIST** - HEBREWS 4-9

III. **EXHORTATION TO FAITH, HOPE, AND LOVE** - HEBREWS 10-13

NOTES

THE OLD TESTAMENT QUOTED IN HEBREWS.

Hebrews 1:5 (Hebrews 5:5; Acts 13:33)
For unto which of the angels said he at any time, Thou art my Son, this day have I begotten thee? And again, I will be to him a Father, and he shall be to me a Son?

Psalms 2:7
I will declare the decree: the LORD hath said unto me, Thou art my Son; this day have I begotten thee.

II Samuel 7:14
I will be his father, and he shall be my son. If he commit iniquity, I will chasten him with the rod of men, and with the stripes of the children of men.

* * *

Hebrews 1:7
And of the angels he saith, Who maketh his angels spirits, and ministers a flame of fire.

Psalms 104:4
Who maketh his angels spirits; his ministers a flaming fire.

* * *

Hebrews 1:8,9
But into the Son he saith, Thy throne, O God, is for ever and ever: a sceptre of righteousness is the sceptre of thy kingdom. Thou has loved righteousness, and hated iniquity: therefore God, even thy God, hath anointed thee with the oil of gladness above thy fellows.

Psalms 45:6,7
Thy throne, O God, is for ever and ever: the sceptre of thy kingdom is a right sceptre. Thou lovest righteousness, and hatest wickedness: therefore God, thy God, hath anointed thee with the oil of gladness above thy fellows.

* * *

Hebrews 1:10-12
And, Thou, Lord, in the beginning hast laid the foundation of the earth, and the heavens are the works of thine hands. They shall perish; but thou remainest; and they all shall wax old as doth a garment; And as a vesture shalt thou fold them up, and they shall be changed: but thou art the same, and thy years shall not fail.

Psalms 102:25-27
Of old hast thou laid the foundation of the earth; and the heavens are the work of thy hands. They shall perish, but thou shalt endure: yea, all of them shall wax old like a garment; as a vesture shalt thou change them, and they shall be changed: But thou art the same, and thy years shall have no end.

* * *

Hebrews 1:13 (Matthew 22:44; Hebrews 10:12,13)
But to which of the angels said he at any time, Sit on my right hand, until I make thine enemies thy footstool?

Psalms 110:1
The LORD said unto my LORD, Sit thou at my right hand, until I make thine enemies thy footstool.

* * *

Hebrews 2:6-8
But one in a certain place testified, saying, What is man, that thou art mindful of him? or the son of man, that thou visitest him? Thou madest him a little lower than the angels; thou crownedst him with glory and honour, and didst set him over the works of thy hands: Thou hast put all things in subjection under his feet. For in that he put all in subjection under him, he left nothing that is not put under him. But now we see not yet all things put under him.

Psalms 8:4-6
What is man, that thou art mindful of him? and the son of man, that thou visitest him? For thou hast made him a little lower than the angels; and hast crowned him with glory and honour. Thou madest him to have dominion over the works of thy hands; thou has put all things under his feet.

* * *

Hebrews 2:12
Saying, I will declare thy name unto my brethren, in the midst of the church will I sing praise unto thee.

Psalms 22:22
I will declare thy name unto my brethren: in the midst of the congregation will I praise thee.

* * *

Hebrews 2:13
And again, I will put my trust in him. And again, Behold I and the children which God hath given me.

II Samuel 22:3
The God of my rock; in him will I trust: he is my shield, and the horn of my salvation, my high tower, and my refuge, my saviour; thou savest me from violence.

Isaiah 8:17,18
And I will wait upon the LORD, that hideth his face from the house of Jacob, and I will look for him. Behold, I and the children whom the LORD hath given me are for signs and for wonders in Israel from the LORD of hosts, which dwelleth in mount Zion.

* * *

Hebrews 3:7-11 (Hebrews 3:15, 4:3,5,7)
Wherefore (as the Holy Ghost saith, To day if ye will hear his voice. Harden not your hearts, as in the provocation, in the day of temptation in the wilderness: When your fathers tempted me, proved me, and saw my work forty years. Wherefore I was grieved with that generation, and said, They do always err in their heart; and they have not known my ways. So I sware in my wrath, They shall not enter into my rest.)

Psalms 95:7-11
For he is our God; and we are the people of his pasture, and the sheep of his hand. To day if ye will hear his voice, Harden not your heart, as in the provocation, and as in the day of temptation in the wilderness: When your fathers tempted me, proved me, and saw my work. Forty years long was I grieved with this generation, and said, it is a people that do err in their heart, and they have not known my ways: Unto whom I sware in my wrath that they should not enter into my rest.

* * *

Hebrews 3:15 (Hebrews 3:7,8, 4:7)
While it is said, To day if ye will hear his voice, harden not your hearts, as in the provocation.

Psalms 95:7,8
For he is our God; and we are the people of his pasture, and the sheep of his hand. To day if ye will hear his voice, Harden not your heart, as in the provocation, and as in the day of temptation in the wilderness.

* * *

Hebrews 4:3 (Hebrews 3:11, 4:5)
For we which have believed do enter into rest, as he said, As I have sworn in my wrath, if they shall enter into my rest: although the works were finished from the foundation of the world.

Psalms 95:11
Unto whom I sware in my wrath that they should not enter into my rest.

* * *

Hebrews 4:4
For he spake in a certain place of the seventh day on this wise, And God did rest the seventh day from all his works.

Genesis 2:2
And on the seventh day God ended his work which he had made; and he rested on the seventh day from all his work which he had made.

* * *

Hebrews 4:5 (Hebrews 3:11, 4:3)
And in this place again, If they shall enter into my rest.

Psalms 95:11
Unto whom I sware in my wrath that they should not enter into my rest.

* * *

Hebrews 4:7 (Hebrews 3:7,8,15)
Again, he limiteth a certain day, saying in David, To day, after so long a time; as it is said, To day if ye will hear his voice, harden not your hearts.

Psalms 95:7,8
For he is our God; and we are the people of his pasture, and the sheep of his hand. To day if ye will hear his voice, Harden not your heart, as in the provocation, and as in the day of temptation in the wilderness.

* * *

Hebrews 5:5 (Hebrews 1:5)
So also Christ glorified not himself to be made an high priest; but he that said unto him, Thou art my Son, to day have I begotten thee.

Psalms 2:7
I will declare the decree: the LORD hath said unto me, Thou art my Son; this day have I begotten thee.

* * *

Hebrews 5:6 (Hebrews 7:17,21)
As he saith also in another place, Thou art a priest for ever after the order of Melchizedec.

Psalms 110:4
The LORD hath sworn, and will not repent. Thou art a priest for ever after the order of Melchizedec.

* * *

Hebrews 6:14
Saying, Surely blessing I will bless thee, and multiplying I will multiply thee.

Genesis 22:17
That in blessing I will bless thee, and in multiplying I will multiply thy seed as the stars of the heaven, and as the sand which is upon the sea shore; and thy seed shall possess the gate of his enemies.

* * *

Hebrews 7:17 (Hebrews 5:6, 7:21)
For he testifieth, Thou art a priest for ever after the order of Melchisedec.

Psalms 110:4
The LORD hath sworn, and will not repent, Thou art a priest for ever after the order of Melchizedec.

* * *

Hebrews 7:21 (Hebrews 5:6, 7:17)
(For those priests were made without an oath; but this with an oath by him that said unto him, The Lord sware and will not repent, Thou art a priest for ever after the order of Melchizedec.)

Psalms 110:4
The LORD hath sworn, and will not repent, Thou art a priest for ever after the order of Melchizedek.

* * *

Hebrews 8:5
Who serve unto the example and shadow of heavenly things, as Moses was admonished of God when he was about to make the tabernacle: for, See, saith he, that thou make all things according to the pattern shewed to thee in the mount.

Exodus 25:40
And look that thou make them after their pattern, which was shewed thee in the amount.

* * *

Hebrews 8:8-12 (Hebrews 10:16,17)
For finding fault with them, he saith, Behold, the days come, saith the Lord, when I will make a new covenant with the house of Israel and with the house of Judah: Not according to the covenant that I made with their fathers in the day when I took them by the hand to lead them out of the land of Egypt; because they continued not in my covenant, and I regarded them not, saith the LORD. For this is the covenant that I will make with the house of Israel after those days, saith the LORD: I will put my laws into their mind, and write them in their hearts: and I will be to them a God, and they shall be to me a people: And they shall not teach every man his neighbour, and every man his brother, saying, Know the Lord: for all shall know me, from the least to the greatest. For I will be merciful to their unrighteousness, and their sins and their iniquities will I remember no more.

Jeremiah 31:31-34
Behold, the days come, saith the LORD, that I will make a new covenant with the houses of Israel, and with the house of Judah: Not according to the covenant that I made with their fathers in the day that I took them by the hand to bring them out of the land of Egypt; which my covenant they brake, although I was an husband unto them, saith the LORD: But this shall be the covenant that I will make with the house of Israel; After those days, saith the Lord, I will put my law in their inward parts, and write it in their hearts; and will be their God, and they shall be my people. And they shall teach no more every man his neighbour, and every man his brother, saying, Know the LORD: for they shall all know me, from the least of them unto the greatest of them, saith the LORD: for I will forgive their iniquity, and I will remember their sin no more.

* * *

Hebrews 9:20
Saying, This is the blood of the testament which God hath enjoined unto you.

Exodus 24:8
And Moses took the blood, and sprinkled it on the people, and said, Behold the blood of the covenant, which the LORD hath made with you concerning all these words.

* * *

Hebrews 10:5-9
Wherefore when he cometh into the world, he saith, Sacrifice and offering thou wouldst not, but a body hast thou prepared me: In burnt offerings and sacrifices for sin thou hast had no pleasure. Then said I, Lo, I come (in the volume of the book it is written of me) to do thy will, O God. Above when he said, Sacrifice and offering and burnt offerings and offering for sin thou wouldst not, neither hadst

pleasure therein; which are offered by the law; Then said he, Lo, I come to do thy will. O God. He taketh away the first, that he may establish the second.

Psalms 40:6-8
Sacrifice and offering thou didst not desire; mine ears hast thou opened: burnt offering and sin offering hast thou not required. Then said I, Lo, I come: in the volume of the book it is written of me, I delight to do thy will, O my God: yea, thy law is within my heart.

* * *

Hebrews 10:12,13
(Matthew 22:44; Hebrews 1:13)
But this man, after he had offered one sacrifice for sins for ever, sat down on the right hand of God; From henceforth expecting till his enemies be made his footstool.

Psalms 110:1
The LORD said unto my LORD, Sit thou at my right hand, until I make thine enemies thy footstool.

* * *

Hebrews 10:16,17 (Hebrews 8:10,12)
This is the covenant that I will make with them after those days, saith the Lord, I will put my laws into their hearts, and in their minds will I write them: And their sins and iniquities will I remember no more.

Jeremiah 31:33-34
But this shall be the covenant that I will make with the house of Israel; After those days, saith the LORD, I will put my law in their inward parts, and write it in their hearts; and will be their God, and they shall be my people. And they shall teach no more every man his neighbour, and every man his brother, saying, Know the LORD: for they shall all know me, from the least of them unto the greatest of them, saith the LORD: for I will forgive their iniquity, and I will remember their sin no more.

* * *

Hebrews 10:27
But a certain fearful looking for of judgment and fiery indignation, which shall devour the adversaries.

Isaiah 26:11
LORD, when thy hand is lifted up, they will not see: but they shall see, and be ashamed for their envy at the people; yea, the fire of thine enemies shall devour them.

* * *

Hebrews 10:30 (Romans 12:19)
For we know him that hath said, Vengeance belongeth unto me, I will recompense, saith the Lord. And again, The Lord shall judge his people.

Deuteronomy 32:35,36
To me belongeth vengeance, and recompence; their foot shall slide in due time: for the day of their calamity is at hand, and the things that shall come upon them make haste. For the LORD shall judge his people, and repent himself for his servants, when he seeth that their power is gone, and there is none shut up, or left.

* * *

Hebrews 10:37,38 (Romans 1:17; Galatians 3:11)
For yet a little while, and he that shall come will come, and will not tarry. Now the just shall live by faith: but if any man draw back, my soul shall have no pleasure in him.

Habakkuk 2:3,4
For the vision is yet for an appointed time, but at the end it shall speak, and not lie: though it tarry, wait for it; because it will surely come, it will not tarry. Behold, his soul which is lifted up is not upright in him: but the just shall live by his faith.

* * *

Hebrews 11:5
By faith Enoch was translated that he should not see death; and was not found, because God had translated him: for before his translation he had this testimony, that he pleased God.

Genesis 5:24
And Enoch walked with God: and he was not; for God took him.

* * *

Hebrews 11:12 (Romans 4:18)
Therefore sprang there even of one and him as good as dead, so many as the stars of the sky in multitude, and as the sand which is by the sea shore innumerable.

Genesis 22:17 (Genesis 15:5)
That in blessing I will bless thee, and in multiplying I will multiply thy seed as the stars of the heaven, and as the sand which is upon the sea shore; and thy seed shall possess the gate of his enemies.

* * *

Hebrews 11:18 (Romans 9:7)
Of whom it was said, That in Isaac shall thy seed be called.

Genesis 21:12
And God said unto Abraham, Let it not be grievous in thy sight because of the lad, and because of thy bondwoman; in all that Sarah hath said unto thee, hearken unto her voice; for in Isaac shall thy seed be called.

* * *

Hebrews 12:5,6
And ye have forgotten the exhortation which speaketh unto you as unto children, My son, despise not thou the chastening of the Lord, nor faint when thou art rebuked of him: For whom the Lord loveth he chasteneth, and scourgeth every son whom he receiveth.

Proverbs 3:11,12
My son, despise not the chastening of the LORD; neither be weary of his correction: For whom the LORD loveth he correcteth; even as a father the son in whom he delighteth.

* * *

Hebrews 12:20
For they could not endure that which was commanded. And if so much as a beast touch the mountain, it shall be stoned, or thrust through with a dart.

Exodus 19:12,13
And thou shalt set bounds unto the people round about, saying, Take heed to yourselves, that ye go not up into the mount, or touch the border of it: whosoever toucheth the mount shall be surely put to death: There shall not an hand touch it, but he shall surely be stoned, or shot through; whether it be beast or man, it shall not live: when the trumpet soundeth long, they shall come up to the mount.

* * *

Hebrews 12:21
And so terrible was the sight, that Moses said, I exceedingly fear and quake.

Deuteronomy 9:19
For I was afraid of the anger and hot displeasure, wherewith the LORD was wroth against you to destroy you. But the LORD hearkened unto me at that time also.

* * *

Hebrews 12:26
Whose voice then shook the earth: but now he hath promised, saying, Yet once more I shake not the earth only, but also heaven.

Haggal 2:6
For thus saith the LORD of hosts; Yet once, it is a little while, and I will shake the heavens, and the earth, and the sea, and the dry land.

* * *

Hebrews 13:5
Let your conversation be without covetousness; and be content with such things as ye have: for he hath said, I will never leave thee, nor forsake thee.

Deuteronomy 31:6
Be strong and of a good courage, fear not, nor be afraid of them: for the LORD thy God, he it is that doth go with thee; he will not fail thee, nor forsake thee.

* * *

Hebrews 13:6
So that we may boldly say, The Lord is my helper, and I will not fear what man shall do unto me.

Psalms 118:6
The LORD is on my side; I will not fear: what can man do unto me?

JAMES

BE A VICTOR—NOT A VICTIM	
SPIRITUAL MATURITY	**FIVE MARKS OF MATURITY**
Growing up in Christ: **1-4**	Patience in testing: **1** Relationships: **2** Self-control: **3** Peacemakers: **4** Prayer for troubles: **5**
LOCATION: Written from Jerusalem	
OVERVIEW: Genuine faith will produce real changes in a person's conduct and character; the absence of change is a symptom of a dead faith	
TIME: Around A.D. 46 - perhaps the first New Testament writing	

FAST FACTS

AUTHOR AND SETTING:

James; from Jerusalem to Jews abroad

PURPOSE:

Utilizing wisdom akin to that found in Proverbs, *James* develops the theme of the characteristics of true faith. Jesus' half-brother deals with five basic problems faced by all Christians: impatience in difficulties (1:1-4); talking, but not living, the truth (2:14); control of the tongue (3:1); fighting and coveting (4:1); and collecting material toys (5:1).

SEEING JESUS:

Jesus is our wisdom for Christian maturity. James refers to his half-brother as the "Lord Jesus Christ" *(James 1:1, 2:1)* and anticipates the Second Coming *(James 5:7,8)*.

THEME VERSE:

James 1:25

NOTES

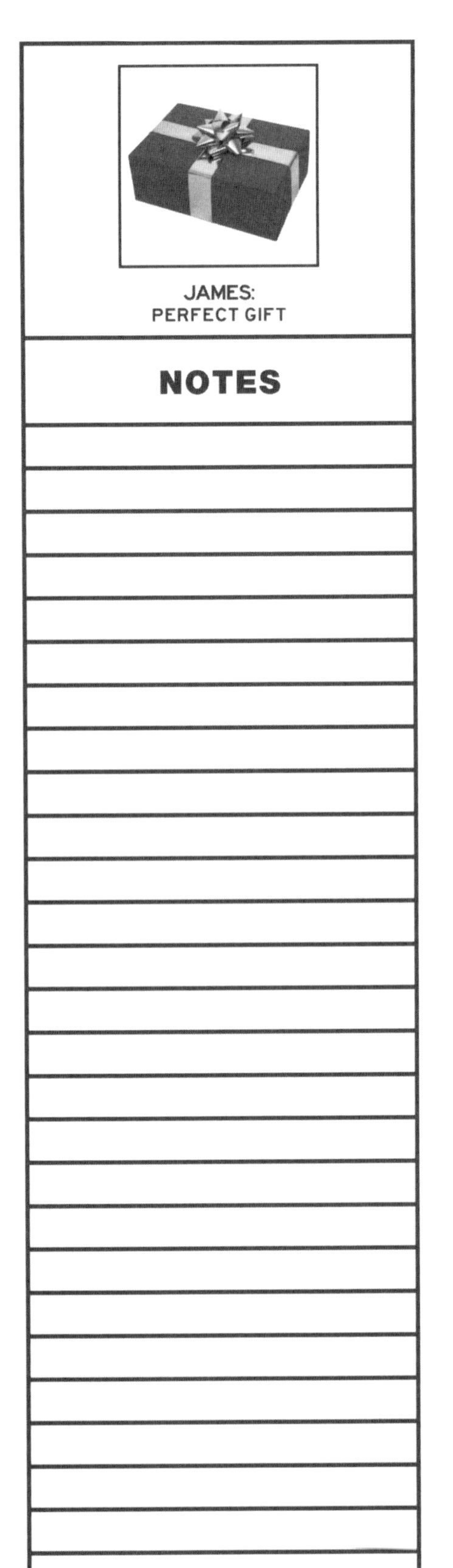

SEEING JESUS IN JAMES

AUTHOR & SETTING

James is the Greek form of *Jacob*, meaning "supplanter." He was a half-brother of Jesus and called himself *"... a servant of God and of the Lord Jesus Christ, ..."* (James 1:1). From the first verse it is also apparent that James was writing to Jews scattered outside of Jerusalem. This book is considered the Proverbs of the New Testament because of the wisdom it contains.

OVERVIEW

James deals with five basic problems faced by all Christians:

1. Impatience in difficulties - James 1:1-4
2. Taking, but not living, the truth - James 2:14
3. Control of the tongue - James 3:1
4. Fighting and coveting - James 4:1
5. Collecting material toys - James 5:1

The message of *James* is "Be a victor - not a victim."

Tremendous emphasis is put on wisdom and maturity in God. At the beginning of his book, James, the half-brother of Jesus, does not make a claim of being related to Jesus by natural birth but by supernatural birth - by being born again. James calls himself the servant of Jesus rather than the half-brother of Jesus.

In chapter one James tells how to turn trials into triumphs. He gives us special ways to come through trials and temptations; we are told to look ahead at what can come out of temptation; we are told to look *around* at God's goodness; and we are told to look *within* at God's power - Christ within, the hope of glory. *James* reveals how Christians can be deceived and drawn away; deception brings disobedience, and disobedience brings death. We are given the opportunity in chapter one to choose a coffin or a crown - whoever endures temptations will receive a crown.

In chapter two James discusses three kinds of faith. There is *dead* faith, which is faith that speaks with the mouth but never has action to go with the mouth. This kind of faith basically involves only head knowledge or reasoning. There is also *demonic* faith, for James says that even the devils believe and tremble. These two kinds of faith, however, are not what God is wanting for our lives. God wants *dynamic* faith. This faith involves the whole man; it involves the mind and the emotions and the will. Dynamic faith produces dynamic works, and James uses the stories of Abraham and Rahab to illustrate this truth.

In chapter three James explains how the tongue is unruly and perhaps the greatest troublemaker we have. The tongue can run unchecked like a fire, or it can overcome contrary forces if it is used correctly. The tongue also has the power to delight; it can be a fresh fountain, and it can be a tree of life. However, our tongues will not speak words of life unless we feed the roots of our trees. Proverbs 4:23 explains it this way: *"Keep thy heart with all diligence; for out of it are the issues of life."* We need to feed our root system, our hearts, with God's Word and daily allow God to control our words.

Chapter four is the war chapter. God shows us five kinds of wars - class wars, employment wars, church wars, personal wars, and internal wars. Fortunately, James gives us a way to overcome all these wars and to experience peace in all five areas.

In chapter five James says that money talks and prayer talks. In this chapter James deals with trouble - trouble with your employer and trouble in all kinds of situations and circumstances. A mature Christian knows what to do in trouble - pray. There is a lot of praying in this chapter; in fact, seven times James mentions prayer and the power of prayer. There is prayer for the suffering, for the sick, for the nation, and for straying people.

James is a powerful book, a book of wisdom for daily living.

SEEING JESUS IN JAMES

Jesus is the wisdom of God, and this little book is full of godly wisdom. James refers to his half-brother as *"... the Lord Jesus Christ, ..."* (James 1:1) and speaks of Christ's Second Coming (James 5:8,9).

NOTES

NOTES

THEME VERSE

"But whoso looketh into the perfect law of liberty, and continueth therein, he being not a forgetful hearer, but a doer of the work, this man shall be blessed in his deed" **(James 1:25).**

OUTLINE

(Refer to maps on pages A14-A18 in the APPENDIX.)

I. **THE THEME OF JAMES: SPIRITUAL MATURITY -** JAMES 1-4

II. **FIVE MARKS OF MATURITY**

- A. **Patience in Testing** - James 1
  1. **Trials on the outside** - James 1:1-12
  2. **Temptations on the inside** - James 1:13-27
- B. **A Mature Christian Practices Truth in Relationship** - James 2
  1. **Faith and love** - James 2:1-13
  2. **Faith and works** - James 2:14-26
- C. **Power Over the Tongue** - James 3
  1. **Exhortations**
- D. **A Peacemaker - Not a Troublemaker** - James 4
  1. **Three wars** - James 4:1-3
  2. **Three enemies** - James 4:4-7
  3. **Three admonitions** - James 4:8-17
- E. **Prayer for Our Troubles** - James 5
  1. **Economic troubles** - James 5:1-9
  2. **Physical troubles** - James 5:10-16
  3. **International troubles** - James 5:17,18
  4. **Church troubles** - James 5:19,20

James is a wonderful book to lead Christians into spiritual maturity. Looking into the mirror of God's Word is sometimes like the first time a savage looks into a mirror; he is startled when he sees himself, and he breaks the mirror. In the same way, some people get mad at the pastor when he speaks the truth and they see themselves for what they really are. James wants you to look into the Word, see the truth, and not turn your back upon it. Receive God's Word, and let it work in your life.

THE OLD TESTAMENT QUOTED IN JAMES

James 2:8 (Matthew 19:19; Romans 13:9)
If ye fulfill the royal law according to the scripture, Thou shalt love thy neighbour as thyself, ye do well.

Leviticus 19:18
Thou shalt not avenge, nor bear any grudge against the children of thy people, but thou shalt love thy neighbour as thyself: I am the LORD.

* * *

James 2:11 (Matthew 5:21,27, 19:18; Mark 10:19; Luke 18:20; Romans 13:9)
For he that said, Do not commit adultery, said also, Do not kill. Now if thou commit no adultery, yet if thou kill, thou art become a transgressor of the law.

Exodus 20:13,14
Thou shalt not kill, Thou shalt not commit adultery.

Deuteronomy 5:17,18
Thou shalt not kill. Neither shalt thou commit adultery.

* * *

James 2:23 (Romans 4:3,9,22; Galatians 3:6)
And the scripture was fulfilled which saith, Abraham believed God, and it was imputed unto him for righteousness: and he was called the Friend of God.

Genesis 15:6
And he believed in the Lord; and he counted it to him for righteousness.

Isaiah 41:8
But thou, Israel, art my servant, Jacob whom I have chosen, the seed of Abraham my friend.

* * *

James 4:6 (I Peter 5:5)
But he giveth more grace. Wherefore he saith, God resisteth the proud, but giveth grace unto the humble.

Proverbs 3:34
Surely he scorneth the scorners: but he giveth grace unto the lowly.

I PETER

THE APOSTLE OF HOPE		
GOD'S GRACE & GOD'S CHARACTER	**GOD'S GRACE & RELATIONSHIPS**	**GOD'S GRACE & RIGHTEOUS SUFFERING**
Hope, holiness, & brotherly love: **1**	Civil authorities, employers, home, & church: **2**	Christ's example: **4**
LOCATION: Rome (Babylon)		
OVERVIEW: Encouragement in trials	Submission in life	Hope in suffering
TIME: Around A.D. 63 - just prior to the fire of Rome in A.D. 64		

FAST FACTS

AUTHOR AND SETTING:

Peter; Roman prison

PURPOSE:

Peter wrote to encourage his readers to be good witnesses to their persecutors and to remember that their suffering would lead to glory.

SEEING JESUS:

The Resurrection of Jesus from the dead is the Christian's living hope despite suffering in this world *(I Peter 1:3).*

THEME VERSE:

I Peter 1:3

NOTES

I PETER:
CORNERSTONE

NOTES

SEEING JESUS IN I PETER

AUTHOR & SETTING

We are told immediately who wrote this letter:

"Peter, an apostle of Jesus Christ..." **(I Peter 1:1).**

Peter had once been called *Simon* before Jesus changed his name. In the gospel of John, we read of Simon (which means "listening" or "wavering") being brought to Jesus by his brother Andrew:

"He [Andrew] first findeth his own brother Simon, and saith unto him, We have found the Messias, which is, being interpreted, the Christ. And he brought him to Jesus. And when Jesus beheld him, he said, Thou art Simon the son of Jona: thou shalt be called Cephas, which is by interpretation, A stone"
(John 1:41,42).

Simon was a "wavering" one who, through the grace of God, would become a rock - a pillar in the Church.

The New Testament letter of I Peter offers genuine hope in the darkest hour of suffering and persecution. The occasion for the writing of this letter seems to be both literally and figuratively the "fiery trial" that was about to begin for Christians in Rome (where Peter was), which would eventually spread to believers living throughout Asia. First Peter was probably written around 63 A.D. just prior to the great fire of Rome during Nero's reign as Caesar. Nero blamed the fire on the new sect called Christians, and thus began horrible punishment and suffering for believers - first in Rome and then throughout the Roman Empire.

The Holy Spirit gave Peter advanced warning of the trials and suffering awaiting Christians, and, through this *apostle of hope*, the Lord prepared the Church to appropriate the true grace of God in turning their suffering into glory.

OVERVIEW

In I Peter we have a letter of encouragement; the theme of *suffering* runs throughout Peter's letter; but so also does the theme of *glory*. Peter gives us a marvelous equation: Christian suffering + God's grace = glory. Thus Peter is known as the *apostle of hope*.

There are basically five reasons for suffering: circumstances, sin, Satan, relationships, and righteousness. Each type of suffering requires a different kind of response by us, and God's Word reveals different benefits that follow suffering IF we respond in the right way.

Trials and temptations come in all shapes and sizes, which is just what Peter tells us in the first chapter:

"Wherein ye greatly rejoice, though now for a season, if need be, ye are in heaviness through ***manifold temptations****"* **(I Peter 1:6).**

But Peter wrote a beautiful verse to complement these "manifold temptations":

"As every man hath received the gift, even so minister the same one to another; as good stewards of the ***manifold grace*** *of God"* **(I Peter 4:10).**

Grace will take care of temptation. There are different portions of grace for various sizes of temptation. If you hold up your hand, you will see that your little finger is smaller than your middle finger. Likewise, there are different sizes of temptations. Your little finger could represent small temptations, and your middle finger could be tall temptations.

Now look at your other hand, and see it as God's manifold grace. He has just the right-sized grace to go with the little temptation, and just the right amount of grace to match the tall temptation. Do you know how to receive this grace? When you put your hands together (matching trials with God's grace), your hands are in the right position for prayer, and prayer will bring God's grace into your suffering!

SEEING JESUS IN I PETER

Jesus is the "chief corner stone":

"Wherefore also it is contained in the scripture, Behold, I lay in Sion a chief corner stone, elect, precious: and that believeth on him shall not be confounded" **(I Peter 2:6).**

Jesus is seen in this book as our example:

"For even hereunto were ye called; because Christ also suffered for us, leaving us an example, that ye should follow his steps" **(I Peter 2:21).**

Jesus is our Shepherd:

"For ye were as sheep going astray; but are now returned unto the Shepherd and Bishop of your souls" **(I Peter 2:25).**

NOTES

NOTES

THEME VERSE

"Blessed be the God and Father of our Lord Jesus Christ, which according to his abundant mercy hath begotten us again unto a lively hope by the resurrection of Jesus Christ from the dead" **(I Peter 1:3).**

OUTLINE

(Refer to maps on pages A14-A18 in the APPENDIX.)

I. **GOD'S GRACE AND HOPE -** I PETER 1:1-12

II. **GOD'S GRACE AND HOLINESS -** I PETER 1:13-21

III. **GOD'S GRACE AND BROTHER LOVE -** I PETER 1:22-25

IV. **GOD'S GRACE AND SPIRITUAL MATURITY -** I PETER 2:1-10

V. **THE GRACE OF GOD AND RELATIONSHIPS - PART I -** I PETER 2:11-25

VI. **THE GRACE OF GOD AND RELATIONSHIPS - PART II -** I PETER 3:1-13

VII. **SUFFERING AND THE WILL OF GOD -** I PETER 3:14-22

VIII. **RIGHTEOUS SUFFERING AND THE SEPARATED LIFE -** I PETER 4:1-19

IX. **LEADERSHIP IN TIMES OF SUFFERING -** I PETER 5:1-14

THE OLD TESTAMENT QUOTED IN I PETER.

I Peter 1:16
Because it is written, Be ye holy; for I am holy.

Leviticus 11:44
For I am the LORD your God: ye shall therefore sanctify yourselves, and ye shall be holy; for I am holy: neither shall ye defile yourselves with any manner of creeping thing that creepeth upon the earth.

Leviticus 19:2
Speak unto all the congregation of the children of Israel; and say unto them: Ye shall be holy; for I the LORD your God am holy.

Leviticus 20:7
Sanctify yourselfes therefore, and be ye holy; for I am the LORD your God.

* * *

I Peter 1:24,25
For all flesh is as grass, and all the glory of man as the flower of grass. The grass withereth, and the flower thereof falleth away. But the word of the Lord endureth for ever. And this is the word which by the gospel is preached unto you.

Isaiah 40:6-8
The voice said, Cry, And he said, What shall I cry? All flesh is grass, and all the goodliness thereof is as the flower of the field: The grass withereth, the flower fadeth: because the spirit of the LORD bloweth upon it: surely the people is grass.

* * *

I Peter 2:6,8 (Romans 9:33, 10:11)
Wherefore also it is contained in the scripture, Behold, I lay in Sion a chief corner stone, elect, precious: and he that believeth in him shall not be confounded. And a stone of stumbling, and a rock of offence, even to them which stumble at the word, being disobedient: whereunto also they were appointed.

Isaiah 8:14
And he shall be for a sanctuary; but for a stone of stumbling and for a rock of offence to both the houses of Israel, for a gin and for a snare to the inhabitants of Jerusalem.

Isaiah 28:16
Therefore thus saith the Lord God, Behold, I lay in Zion for a foundation a stone, a tried stone, a precious corner stone, a sure foundation: he that believeth shall not make haste.

* * *

I Peter 2:7 (Matthew 21:42)
Unto you therefore which believe he is precious: but unto them which be disobedient, the stone which the builders disallowed, the same is made the head of the corner.

Psalms 118:22
The stone which the builders refused is become the head stone of the corner.

* * *

I Peter 2:9
But ye are a chosen generation, a royal priesthood, an holy nation, a peculiar people; that ye should shew forth the praises of him who hath called you out of darkness into his marvellous light.

Exodus 19:5,6
Now therefore, if ye will obey my voice indeed, and keep my covenant, then ye shall be a peculiar treasure unto me above all people: for all the earth is mine: And ye shall be unto me a kingdom of priests, and an holy nation. These are the words which thou shalt speak unto the children of Israel.

Isaiah 43:20,21
The beast of the field shall honour me, the dragons and the owls; because I give waters in the wilderness, and rivers in the desert, to give drink to my people, my chosen. This people have I formed for myself; they shall shew forth my praise.

* * *

I Peter 2:10 (Romans 9:25)
Which in time past were not a people, but are now the people of God: which had not obtained mercy, but now have obtained mercy.

Hosea 1:6,9,10
And she conceived again, and bare a daughter. And God said unto him, Call her name Lo-ruhamah: for I will no more have mercy upon the house of Israel; but I will utterly take them away. Then said God, Call his name Lo-ammi: for ye are not my people, and I will not be your God. Yet the number of the children of Israel shall be as the sand of the sea, which cannot

be measured nor numbered; and it shall come to pass, that in the place where it was said unto them, Ye are not my people, there it shall be said unto them, Ye are the sons of the living God.

Hosea 2:23
And I will sow her unto me in the earth; and I will have mercy upon her that had not obtained mercy; and I will say to them which were not my people, Thou art my people; and they shall say, Thou Art my God.

* * *

I Peter 2:22
Who did no sin, neither was guile found in his mouth.

Isaiah 53:9
And he made his grave with the wicked, and with the rich in his death; because he had done no violence, neither was any deceit in his mouth.

* * *

I Peter 3:10-12
For he that will love life, and see good days, let him refrain his tongue from evil, and his lips that they speak no guile: Let him eschew evil, and do good; let him seek peace, and ensure it. For the eyes of the Lord are over the righteous, and his ears are open unto their prayers: but the face of the Lord is against them that do evil.

Psalms 34:12-16
What man is he that desireth life, and loveth many days, that he may see good? Keep thy tongue from evil, and thy lips from speaking guile. Depart from evil, and do good; seek peace, and pursue it. The eyes of the LORD are upon the righteous, and his ears are open unto their cry. The face of the LORD is against them that do evil, to cut off the remembrance of them from the earth.

* * *

I Peter 3:14
But and if ye suffer for righteousness' sake, happy are ye; and be not afraid of their terror, neither be troubled.

Isaiah 8:12,13
Say ye not, A confederacy, to all them to whom this people shall say, A confederacy; neither fear ye their fear, nor be afraid. Sanctify the LORD of hosts himself; and let him be your fear, and let him be your dread.

* * *

I Peter 4:18
And if the righteous scarcely be saved, where shall the ungodly and the sinner appear?

Proverbs 11:31
Behold, the righteous shall be recompensed in the earth: much more the wicked and the sinner.

* * *

I Peter 5:5 (James 4:6)
Likewise, ye younger, submit yourselves unto the elder. Yea, all of you be subject one to another, and be clothed with humility: for God resisteth the proud, and giveth grace to the humble.

Proverbs 3:34
Surely he scorneth the scorners: but he giveth grace unto the lowly.

II PETER

KNOWING & GROWING IN CHRIST		
EXPLANATION: KNOWLEDGE OF CHRIST	**EXAMINATION: FALSE TEACHERS**	**EXHORTATION: TRUE CHRISTIANS**
Knowledge - gift, growth, & ground: **1**	Condemnation, character, claims, & outcome: **2**	"The day of the Lord": **3**
LOCATION: From Roman prison to believers scattered in Asia Minor		
OVERVIEW: How to grow in Christ	How to spot false doctrines	How to prepare for the future
TIME: A.D. 64-66		

FAST FACTS

AUTHOR AND SETTING:

Peter; Roman Prison

PURPOSE:

This book shows that there cannot be a static position in Christ, but we must keep on growing.

SEEING JESUS:

The "Lordship" of Jesus Christ is paramount in *II Peter.* Through His power believers were granted all things pertaining to life and godliness; through His knowledge they received glory and virtue; through His promises they were made partakers of the divine nature.

THEME VERSE:

II Peter 1:4

NOTES

II PETER:
THE WAY

NOTES

SEEING JESUS IN II PETER

AUTHOR & SETTING

Peter wrote this letter to the same believers addressed in I Peter. Here in *II Peter* the emphasis is on the knowledge of God. Peter opens with *"Grace and peace be multiplied unto you through the knowledge of God, and of Jesus our Lord"* **(II Peter 1:2).** In the closing salutation he says, *"But grow in grace, and in the knowledge of our Lord and Saviour Jesus Christ..."* **(II Peter 3:18).**

OVERVIEW

Throughout this epistle we will see an emphasis on knowledge. Through the power of Christ, believers were granted all things pertaining to life and godliness. Through His knowledge they received glory and virtue. Through His promises they were made partakers of the divine nature.

In II Peter 1:5-8 we see the cultivation of the Christian graces and virtues through which you will not be unfruitful in the knowledge of Lord Jesus Christ.

Knowledge here means "full and complete knowledge."

This book shows that there cannot be a static position in our Christ, but we must keep on growing in order to maintain our spiritual position.

SEEING JESUS IN II PETER

Peter tells us that the knowledge of our Lord and Savior Jesus Christ is the pathway to Christian maturity. Peter also looks forward to Christ's Second Coming (II Peter 3:10).

THEME VERSE

"Whereby are given unto us exceeding great and precious promises: that by these ye might be partakers of the divine nature, having escaped the corruption that is in the world through lust" **(II Peter 1:4).**

OUTLINE

(Refer to maps on pages A14-A18 in the APPENDIX.)

I. **EXPLANATION - THE KNOWLEDGE OF CHRIST -** II PETER 1:1-21
   - A. **The Gift of Knowledge -** II Peter 1:1-4
   - B. **The Growth of Knowledge -** II Peter 1:5-11
   - C. **The Ground of Knowledge -** II Peter 1:12-21

II. **EXAMINATION - THE FALSE TEACHERS -** II PETER 2:1-22
   - A. **Their Condemnation -** II Peter 2:1-9
   - B. **Their Character -** II Peter 2:10-17
   - C. **Their Claims -** II Peter 2:18,19
   - D. **Their Outcomes -** II Peter 2:20-22

III. **EXHORTATION - THE TRUE CHRISTIAN -** II PETER 3:1-21

THE OLD TESTAMENT QUOTED IN II PETER.

II Peter 2:22
But it is happened unto them according to the true proverb. The dog is turned to his own vomit again; and the sow that was washed to her wallowing in the mire.

Proverbs 26:11
As a dog returneth to his vomit, so a fool returneth to his folly.

NOTES

I JOHN

FELLOWSHIP IN THE FATHER'S KINGDOM				
FATHER'S FAMILY	**GOD IS LIGHT**	**CHILDREN OF GOD**	**GOD IS LOVE**	**CLOSING EXHORTATION**
Introduction: **1**	Fellowship: **1,2**	By His love: **3**	More fellowship: **4**	Purpose of writing: **5**
LOCATION: Written from Ephesus by the apostle John				
OVERVIEW: Fellowhip in the light	Obedience means love	The practice of love	Testing spirits and genuineness of love	The assurance of love
TIME: Around A.D. 90				

FAST FACTS

AUTHOR AND SETTING:

John, Ephesus

PURPOSE:

First John encourages us to leave our old life and walk in our new life. This book deals with worldliness.

SEEING JESUS:

Jesus is seen as the "Word of life" *(I John 1:1)*, or "advocate" *(I John 2:1)*, and "the Christ" *(I John 2:22)*. The blood of Jesus cleanses us from all sin *(I John 1:7)*.

THEME VERSE:

I John 1:5

NOTES

I JOHN:
LOVE

NOTES

SEEING JESUS IN I JOHN

AUTHOR & SETTING

The writer of this book is John, the apostle. He is the author of the gospel of John and the book of Revelation. *First John* was probably written shortly before Revelation. The theme, of course, is fellowship in the Father's kingdom. John used two beautiful expressions to describe God: love and light.

OVERVIEW

John used three themes throughout the five chapters: obedience, love, and truth. A spirit-controlled mind knows and understands truth, a spirit-controlled heart feels love, and a spirit-controlled will inclines us to obedience; this book deals with spirit, soul, and body.

Our life begins with sonship and continues in fellowship. There is always an enemy to our new life in Jesus, and that enemy is sin. The secret of victory over sin is to walk in the light. This book deals with obedience to God Who is love and God Who is light.

There are basically three motives for obedience: because we *must* obey, because we *need* to obey, or because we *want* to obey. A slave obeys because he *must* obey, an employee obeys because he *needs* to obey, but a Christian obeys his Father because he *wants* to obey. Baby Christians must constantly be warned or rewarded, but mature Christians listen to God's Word and obey it simply because they love Him. This, of course, is the victory over sin.

First John encourages us to leave our old life and walk in our new life. This book deals with worldliness. Worldliness is not so much a matter of *activity* as it is an *attitude*. Worldliness not only affects your response to the love of God, but it also affects your response to the *will* of God:

"And the world passeth away, and the lust thereof: but he that doeth the will of God abideth for ever" **(I John 2:17).**

John exposes the world system which uses three devices to trap Christians: the lust of flesh, the lust of the eyes, and the pride of life. These same devices trapped Eve back in the garden. Worldliness creeps in upon a believer; it is a gradual process:

First, *friendship* of the world develops:

"Ye adulterers and adulteresses, know ye not that the friendship of the world is enmity with God? whosoever therefore will be a friend of the world is the enemy of God" **(James 4:4).**

Next, the Christian becomes *spotted* by the world:

"Pure religion and undefiled before God and the Father is this, To visit the fatherless and widows in their affliction, and to keep himself unspotted from the world" **(James 1:27).**

Thirdly, the believer becomes *conformed* to the world:

"And be not conformed to this world: but be ye transformed by the renewing of your mind, that ye may prove what is that good, and acceptable, and perfect, will of God" **(Romans 12:2).**

And fourthly, he becomes *condemned* with the world:

"But when we are judged, we are chastened of the Lord, that we should not be condemned with the world" **(I Corinthians 11:32).**

There are basically three kinds of Christians listed in the local church family: the fathers, the young men, and the little children. Please note that young men are the conquerors; God was warning His family about conflict between light and darkness, love and hatred, and truth and error. *First John* is a book of contrast and conflicts dealing with the essentials of the Christian life.

SEEING JESUS IN I JOHN

John tells us of the present ministry of Jesus:

"If we confess our sins, he is faithful and just to forgive us our sins, and to cleanse us from all unrighteousness" **(I John 1:9).**

John puts special emphasis on the fact that Jesus is the Christ:

"Who is a liar but he that denieth that Jesus is the Christ? He is antichrist, that denieth the Father and the Son" **(I John 2:22).**

THEME VERSE

"This then is the message which we have heard of him, and declare unto you, that God is light, and in him is no darkness at all" **(I John 1:5).**

OUTLINE

(Refer to maps on pages A14-A18 in the APPENDIX.)

I. **INTRODUCTION - STATEMENT OF THE THEME: FELLOWSHIP IN THE FATHER'S FAMILY -** I JOHN 1:1-4

II. **FELLOWSHIP WITH GOD WHO IS LIGHT -** I JOHN 1:5-2:29

III. **THE CHILDREN OF GOD BY HIS LOVE -** I JOHN 3:1-4:6

IV. **FELLOWSHIP WITH GOD WHO IS LOVE -** I JOHN 4:7-5:12

V. **PURPOSE OF WRITING AND CLOSING EXHORTATION -** I JOHN 5:13-21

THE OLD TESTAMENT QUOTED IN I JOHN: NOT FOUND

NOTES

II JOHN

TRUTH AT HOME AND AT CHURCH		
WE MUST KNOW THE TRUTH	**WE MUST WALK IN THE TRUTH**	**WE MUST ABIDE IN THE TRUTH**
Love in truth & live in truth: **1-3**	Truth, love, & obedience: **4-6**	Wrong doctrine & wrong living: **7-11**

LOCATION: Ephesus

OVERVIEW:
We must have fellowship with Christians, but we must not have fellowship with false teachers.

TIME: A.D. 90

FAST FACTS

AUTHOR AND SETTING:

John; Ephesus

PURPOSE:

False teachers were present in the church and even in the believers' homes. John warned against anything false in the home and in the church.

SEEING JESUS:

Refuting the prevalent (and heretical) Gnostic doctrine that "a divine being cannot take on human flesh," John emphasizes that those who do not confess Jesus Christ as coming in the flesh (verse 7) are deceivers who must be avoided. You must abide in the "doctrine of Christ" (verse 9) to have a relationship with God.

THEME VERSE:

II John 5

NOTES

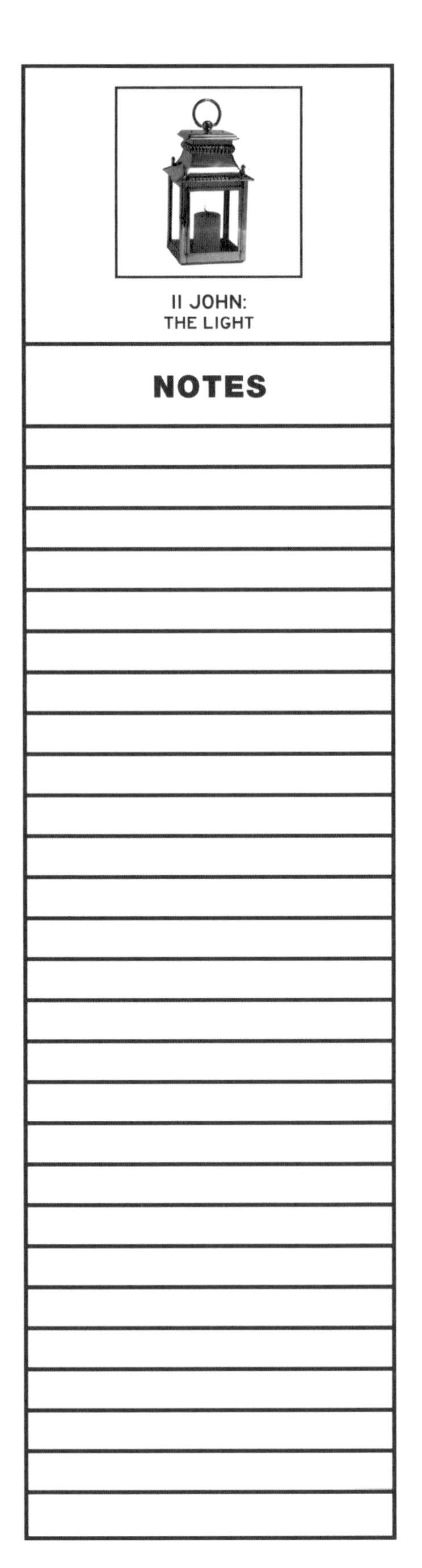

SEEING JESUS IN II JOHN

AUTHOR & SETTING

John is the author; the occasion of the writing of this book seems to be the preeminence of false teachers. Apostate teachers had not only invaded the church, but they also had invaded the homes. Titus had faced a similar situation in Crete:

"For there are many unruly and vain talkers and deceivers, specially they of the circumcision: Whose mouths must be stopped, who subvert whole houses, teaching things which they ought not, for filthy lucre's sake" **(Titus 1:10,11).**

"For of this sort are they which creep into houses, and lead captive silly women laden with sins, led away with diverse lusts" **(II Timothy 3:6).**

This brief letter was written to a godly mother and her children. John probably had a specific family and congregation in mind. He warned against anything false in the home and in the church.

OVERVIEW

In the first four verses of this epistle, John uses the word, *"truth,"* five times. Truth has to do with reality, especially the reality of the gospel of Jesus Christ. When people love *in truth*, they love because of the gospel. When something is *for the truth's sake*, it is for the sake of the gospel. When greetings come *in truth and in love*, the word, *"truth,"* is used to describe an intellectual harmony with the moral action of love. Love is truth in human action, and truth is love in regard to the order of things. Love abides in us, and it shall be with us forever.

John makes certain that he mentions love before he warns against deceivers. His special burden is that Christians love one another. Deceivers will come, controversies will persist, but true believers will still have an atmosphere of love. Love can win where arguments fail. Love in a controversial situation is respect for the sincerity of another's mind. It forgives felonious opinions as well as wrong motives.

John repeated what he said in the first epistle about the heretics whom he identifies as antichrists. When deceivers come, believers must be aware. The test of truth is to abide in the teachings of Christ; this is to abide in the Father and the Son.

This letter reveals the close tie between church leaders and the Christian laymen of the first century. Even when serious error arose, the faithful ones held together in bonds of love, truth, and joy. Homes were opened to traveling ministers as a mark of love and appreciation.

SEEING JESUS IN II JOHN

In a short letter of only 13 versus, John makes three direct references to Jesus:

"Grace be with you, mercy, and peace, from God the Father, and from the Lord Jesus Christ, the Son of the Father, in truth and love" **(II John 3).**

"For many deceivers are entered into the world, who confess not that Jesus Christ is come in the flesh. This is a deceiver and an antichrist" **(II John 7).**

"Whosoever transgresseth, and abideth not in the doctrine of Christ, hath not God. He that abideth in the doctrine of Christ, he hath both the Father and the Son" **(II John 9).**

THEME VERSE

And now I beseech thee, lady, not as though I wrote a new commandment unto thee, but that which we had from the beginning, that we love one another" **(II John 5).**

OUTLINE

(Refer to maps on pages A14-A18 in the APPENDIX.)

I. WE MUST KNOW THE TRUTH - II JOHN 1-3

- **A. Truth is Used Four Times in the Salutation.**
- **B. We Know the Truth.**
  - **1. We love in truth.**
  - **2. We live for truth's sake.**

II. WE MUST WALK IN THE TRUTH - II JOHN 4-6

- **A. This Commandment is Used Five Times in These Verses.**
  - **1. The commandment to love is new by example.**
  - **2. Love and obedience go together.**
  - **3. Truth, love, and obedience are united.**
  - **4. We don't live in a *vicious* circle, but a *victorious* circle of love, truth, and obedience.**

III. WE MUST ABIDE IN THE TRUTH - II JOHN 7-11.

- **A. Truth and Life Go Together; Wrong Doctrine and Wrong Living Go Together.**
  - **1. There is danger in going *back*.**
  - **2. There is danger in going *ahead*.**
  - **3. There is danger in going *with*.**

IV. CONCLUSION - II JOHN 12,13

THE OLD TESTAMENT QUOTED IN II JOHN: NOT FOUND

NOTES

III JOHN

THE PROSPEROUS SOUL		
GAIUS	**DIOTREPHES**	**DEMETRIUS**
Walked in truth: **1-8**	Resisted the truth: **9-11**	Received a good report of the truth: **12-14**
LOCATION: Ephesus		
OVERVIEW: Hospitality in the church	Sinful ambitions	Praise of men and of God
TIME: A.D. 90		

FAST FACTS

AUTHOR AND SETTING:

John; Ephesus

PURPOSE:

John wrote to Gaius to thank him for receiving the traveling "missionaries" whom he had sent out.

SEEING JESUS:

Jesus is mentioned in verse seven, speaking of those missionaries who went out *"... for his [Jesus'] name's sake..."*

THEME VERSE:

III John 2

NOTES

III JOHN: PROSPERITY

NOTES

SEEING JESUS IN III JOHN

AUTHOR & SETTING

John uses the endearing title, "Beloved," which in the Greek appears ten times in these three epistles. Even when John sternly exhorts and rebukes the Christians, he never loses his tenderness for the ones to whom he is writing. John speaks of his reader as the one *"... whom I love in the truth"* **(III John 1).**

OVERVIEW

John prays for Gaius' prosperity in health and in soul. Gaius was a leader, but it appears that he was not an aggressive leader (verse 11). He tended to fall in line with the status quo rather than create trouble. John exhorted him to *"... follow not that which is evil, but that which is good"* **(III John 11).**

Third John emphasizes three men: Gaius, Diotrephes, and Demetrius.

SEEING JESUS IN III JOHN

John's only direct reference to Jesus is in verse 7:

"Because that for his name's sake they went forth, taking nothing of the Gentiles" **(III John 7).**

The frequent references to truth point to Jesus Who is the truth!

THEME VERSE

"Beloved, I wish above all things that thou mayest prosper and be in health, even as thy soul prospereth" **(III John 2).**

OUTLINE

(Refer to maps on pages A14-A18 in the APPENDIX.)

I. **GAIUS, WHO WALKED IN TRUTH -** III JOHN 1-8

II. **DIOTREPHES, WHO RESISTED THE TRUTH -** III JOHN 9-11

III. **DEMETRIUS, WHO HAD A GOOD REPORT OF THE TRUTH -** III JOHN 12-14

THE OLD TESTAMENT QUOTED IN III JOHN: NOT FOUND

JUDE

FIGHTING FOR THE FAITH			
INTRODUCTION & EXHORTATION	**EXAMPLES OF APOSTASY**	**DESCRIPTION OF FALSE TEACHERS**	**INSTRUCTION & COMFORT**
"Contending": **1-4**	"Remembrance": **5-7**	"Woe": **8-19**	"Keep": **20-25**
LOCATION: Jerusalem			
OVERVIEW: Warning of apostasy		Winning over apostasy	
TIME: Around A.D. 70			

FAST FACTS

AUTHOR AND SETTING:

Jude; Jerusalem

PURPOSE:

Jude's greatest desire was to keep people from failing spiritually; he believed in contending for the faith that was delivered to the saints.

SEEING JESUS:

In *Jude* we see that Jesus is our spiritual anchor.

THEME VERSE:

Jude 3

NOTES

JUDE:
GUIDE

NOTES

SEEING JESUS IN JUDE

AUTHOR & SETTING

The book of *Jude* is apostasy unmasked. *Jude* comes from the word *Judas*, which means "proceeding." The disciple Judas was the greatest apostate. Jude, the half-brother to Jesus, makes no claim to his natural birth. His true identity lies in his spiritual birth. Jude calls himself a servant of Jesus Christ, putting his heavenly relationship far above his earthly relationship. The book opens with Jude calling the readers *"beloved."*

OVERVIEW

Jude's great desire was to keep people from falling spiritually; he was contending for the faith that was delivered to the saints. Jude emphasizes mercy, peace, and love. Mercy looks *upward*, peace looks *inward*, and love looks *outward*.

There are three major characteristics of an apostate:

He is ungodly.
He turns grace into lasciviousness.
He denies that Jesus is Lord.

Apostasy is a downward progression because it is an absence of reverence for God, a twisting of the doctrine of grace, and a denial of Jesus as Lord. Enoch foretold the apostate's doom before the flood (Jude 14,15), and Jesus agreed (Matthew 13:24-30,38).

Apostasy is nothing new. In Jude 11 we read of the example of Cain. The Jewish nation also fell away from God. Angels fell, as did the gentile cities of Sodom and Gomorrah. Every falling away came because of sin.

Israel's failure is a warning to the Church. Judgment is coming. Light is ahead for some - for others, darkness. When people fall away from Christ, ultimately they fall into fleshly sins. They are asleep to the truth, and they set aside Christ as their Lord and Master.

Three examples from the past are given:

1. Cain - a tiller of the soil
2. Balaam - a prophet
3. Korah (KJV Core) - a prince in Israel

There was the way of Cain, the *error* of Balaam, and the *rebellion* of Korah. The way of Cain was to ignore the shedding of blood; the error of Balaam was allowing money to be more important than God's will; and the rebellion of Korah was lust for power.

Jude uses five word pictures for this apostasy:

The earth. Apostates are like hidden rocks - unseen dangers.

The air. Apostates are like clouds without water - offering false promises and carried by the wind or evil spirits.

The trees. Apostates are like trees that are dead to the fruit of profession and dead to the root of possession.

The sea. Apostates are like wild waves - putting forth wasted efforts.

The starry heavens. Apostates are like wandering stars - aimless in their course.

The wonderful contrasts are that instead of dangerous rocks, we can be living stones; instead of waterless clouds, we can be sources of living water; instead of dead trees, we can be trees of righteousness; instead of raging waves, we can be like peaceful rivers; and instead of wandering stars, we can shine as the stars forever and ever.

SEEING JESUS IN JUDE

In *Jude* we see that Jesus is our spiritual anchor. We can keep ourselves in the love of God; we can build ourselves up on our most holy faith by praying in the Spirit; we can let the Word of grace build us up; and we can keep looking for Christ's return. Jesus has given us the *anchors* that keep us anchored to Him.

THEME VERSE

"Beloved, when I gave all diligence to write unto you of the common salvation, it was needful for me to write unto you, and exhort you that ye should earnestly contend for the faith which was once delivered unto the saints" **(Jude 3).**

OUTLINE

(Refer to maps on pages A14-A18 in the APPENDIX.)

I. **INTRODUCTION AND EXHORTATION -** JUDE 1-4
   A. **The Special Word is "Contend" -** Jude 3.

II. **HISTORICAL EXAMPLES OF APOSTASY -** JUDE 5-7
   A. **The Special Word is "Remembrance" -** Jude 5.

III. **DESCRIPTION OF FALSE TEACHERS -** JUDE 18,19
   A. **The Special Word is "Woe" -** Jude 11.

IV. **INSTRUCTION AND COMFORT -** JUDE 20-25
   A. **The Special Word is "Keep" -** Jude 21,24

THE OLD TESTAMENT QUOTED IN JUDE: NOT FOUND

NOTES

REVELATION

THE FINAL CHAPTER OF A LOVE STORY		
GLORIFIED CHRIST	**SEVEN CHURCHES**	**END-TIME EVENTS**
Vision of Jesus: **1**	Letters: **2,3**	Fulfillment: **4-22**
LOCATION: Island of Patmos in the Aegean Sea		
OVERVIEW: The victorious Christ	Church-age characteristics	We win!
TIME: Around A.D. 95		

FAST FACTS

AUTHOR AND SETTING:

John; Island of Patmos

PURPOSE:

John wanted to inform and encourage Christians regarding God's ultimate victory over evil.

SEEING JESUS:

We see Jesus *revealed* in this book!

THEME VERSE:

Revelation 1:1,2

NOTES

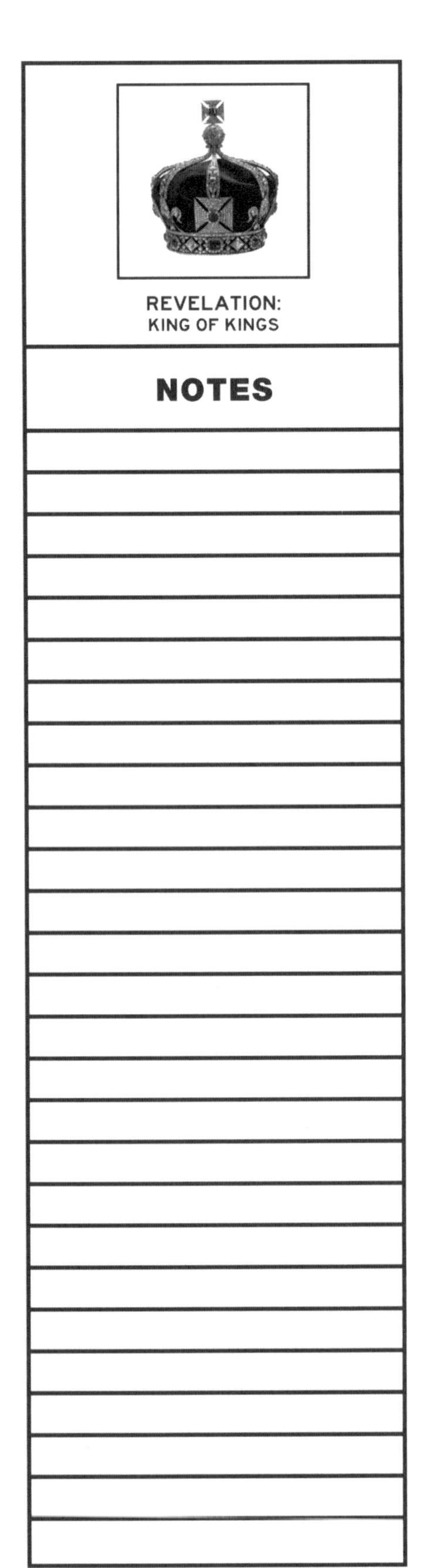

SEEING JESUS IN REVELATION

AUTHOR & SETTING

The book of *Revelation* presents a panoramic view of history from the time of its author, John, to eternity future. *Revelation* is partly historical and partly prophetical. John received this vision on the isle of Patmos, a rocky island in the Aegean Sea.

Revelation is the last chapter of a love story. The Bible is a great love story between God and man. *Revelation* means "an unveiling," and we see Jesus unveiled in this book.

OVERVIEW

The first verse in *Revelation* speaks of *"... things which must shortly come to pass; ..."* A prophecy is more than history written in advance; it is the completion of a story. Daniel tells a story of the nations; Ezekiel tells a story of the Jews; *Revelation* is the wrap-up of both of these stories. *Revelation* is basically a continuation of the book of Acts.

Prophetic language always falls in two groups: literal and figurative. *Revelation* contains much figurative language in types and symbols.

***Revelation* opens with messages to seven churches, which many feel represent the seven church ages:**

Ephesus - the apostolic age

Smyrna - the church of persecution (about the second century)

Pergamos - the church of imperial favor (when Constantine embraced the church along with the idolatry of his age)

Thyatira - the church of apathy

Sardis - the church of reformation

Philadelphia - the latter-day outpouring of the church age

Laodicea - the lukewarm church at the end of this age

Revelation was written for the Church. That is why I believe the church ages are represented by the seven churches. *Revelation* is not only for the Church, it is also about the Church. The Jews are not directly mentioned in this book except in chapter 17 where 144,000 have become Christians.

Revelation differs from the other books in the Bible in the way it was revealed. It was revealed directly to John through a vision, and he was told exactly what to write and what not to write.

There are various types of symbols used in *Revelation* along with the meaning of many of the symbols. For example, we read about candlesticks, stars, a woman, a manchild, a dragon, a beast, and a harlot. Symbols were used because this book was written in perilous times for Christians, and it was safer to hide a message within symbolic imagery. The purpose was not to confuse Christians, but to inform and encourage them regarding God's ultimate victory over evil.

Revelation involves redemption; it involves the restoration of everything that was lost by sin, including man, the soul, the body, the human race, and the earth. The process of redemption has now been committed to the Church. The history of the Church is the history of redemption as it applies to the soul of man. Redemption involves the soul, the body, and the earth:

"And when these things begin to come to pass, then look up, and lift up your heads; for your redemption draweth nigh" **(Luke 21:28).**

"And not only they, but ourselves also, which have the firstfruits of the Spirit, even we ourselves groan within ourselves, waiting for the adoption, to wit, the redemption of our body" **(Romans 8:23).**

"And grieve not the holy Spirit of God, whereby ye are sealed unto the day of redemption" **(Ephesians 4:30).**

Redemption is the restoration of everything that was lost; the story of Revelation is described by some in three words:

Generation
Degeneration
Regeneration

Regeneration appears only two times in the Bible, referring to the soul of Titus and to the earth:

"Not by works of righteousness which we have done, but according to his mercy he saved us, by the washing of regeneration, and renewing of the Holy Ghost" **(Titus 3:5).**

"And Jesus said unto them, Verily I say unto you, That ye which have followed me, in the regeneration when the Son of man shall sit in the throne of his glory, ye also shall sit upon twelve thrones, judging the twelve tribes of Israel" **(Matthew 19:28).**

Regeneration is applied to the *soul* because there has been degeneration, and there must be a restoration to the original perfect state by a washing and a renewing.

Regeneration is applied to the *earth* because it has degenerated far below the perfection of the original creation and has to be restored.

Regeneration is *not* applied to the body of the saints; our bodies are not to be restored to their original state because they would

NOTES

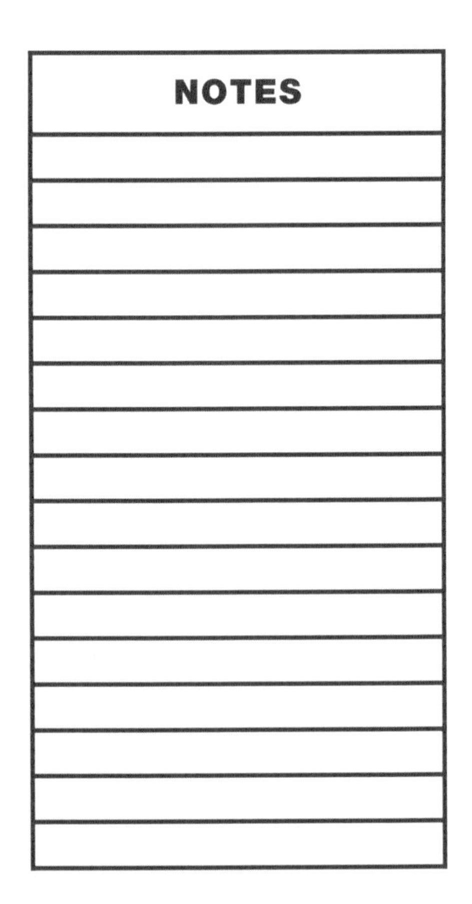

then be subject to death again. Instead, our bodies are to be changed and glorified. The body is sown a natural body, and it will be raised as a spiritual body (I Corinthians 15:44).

***Revelation* completes the story that Genesis began:**

1. Genesis tells how the earth was subject to the curse because of sin. *Revelation* shows the new earth where there is no more curse.

2. In Genesis we see light coming from the sun. In *Revelation* the Lord God is the light of the holy city.

3. In Genesis dominion is given to man - only to pass into the hands of Satan. In *Revelation* dominion is restored to the saints who inherit the earth.

4. In Genesis God plants the tree of life for man to eat and live. In *Revelation* the tree of life is seen growing again, and the leaves are for the healing of the nations.

5. In Genesis Satan appears and is victorious. In *Revelation* Satan appears again, but this time he is defeated by the blood of the Lamb!

All the major judgments that come upon the earth have fire in them.

THE SEVEN ROOMS OF REVELATION:

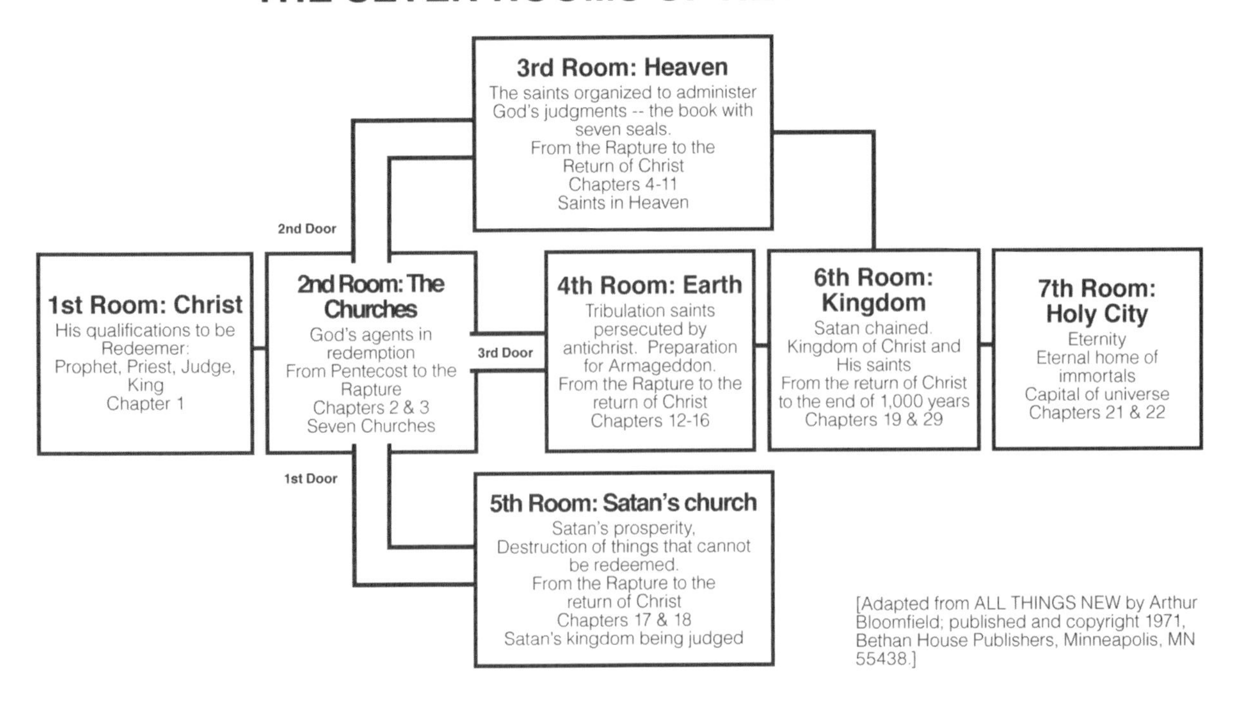

In the first room we see Christ and His qualifications to be our Redeemer. He is shown as a *Prophet* - the faithful witness. Because of His atonement, He stands in the midst of candlesticks clothed with a *priestly* robe. His hair is white. As a *Savior* and *King* He has eyes like fire and feet like brass - the King sits in judgment.

The second room comprises chapters 2 and 3. This room is devoted to the church ages. The churches are God's servants and agents in the program of redemption.

Notice that the second room has three outlets. One door opens downward to the wicked woman, Jezebel, of the Thyatira church and to the harlot woman of chapter 17. Another door opens to the fourth room which reveals the Antichrist and the experiences of those who were left behind at the Rapture. The second door leads to the third room and the scene in heaven immediately after the resurrection. Rooms 3, 4 and 5 occupy the same space because the events are happening at the same time.

The fifth room has no outlet because everything in it will be destroyed. We see the mystery of evil and its destruction.

The sixth room is the kingdom room. Here we are allowed to gaze upon the climax of the ages. But before the revelation of Christ on the earth, there is a ceremony in heaven which involves the saints - the Marriage Supper of the Lamb.

The seventh room is the last and most glorious room - the very sanctuary of God. Here, in detail, is pictured the eternal home of the saints. Here are things our eyes have not seen, nor our ears heard, nor our hearts and minds imagined! It is so marvelous.

SEEING JESUS IN REVELATION

This entire book is *"The Revelation of Jesus Christ..."* (Revelation 1:1). Here are some of the more straightforward pictures of Jesus:

"And from Jesus Christ, who is the faithful witness, and the first begotten of the dead, and the prince of the kings of the earth. Unto him that loved us, and washed us from our sins in his own blood" **(Revelation 1:5).**

"And when I saw him, I feel at his feet as dead. And he laid his right hand upon me, saying unto me, Fear not; I am the first and the last: I am he that liveth, and was dead; and, behold, am alive for evermore. Amen; and have the keys of hell and of death" **(Revelation 1:17,18).**

NOTES

NOTES

"And unto the angel of the church in Thyatira write; These things saith the Son of God, who hath his eyes like unto a flame of fire, and his feet are like fine brass" **(Revelation 2:18).**

"And to the angel of the church in Philadelphia write; These things saith he that is holy, he that is true, he that hath the key of David, he that openeth, and no man shutteth; and shutteth, and no man openeth" **(Revelation 3:7).**

"And unto the angel of the church of the Laodiceans write; These things saith the Amen, the faithful and true witness, the beginning of the creation of God" **(Revelation 3:14).**

"And one of the elders saith unto me, Weep not: behold, the Lion of the tribe of Juda, the Root of David, hath prevailed to open the book, and to loose the seven seals thereof. And I beheld, and, lo, in the midst of the throne and of the four beasts, and in the midst of the elders, stood a Lamb as it had been slain, having seven horns and seven eyes, which are the seven Spirits of God sent forth into all the earth" **(Revelation 5:5,6).**

"And I saw another mighty angel come down from heaven, clothed with a cloud: and a rainbow was upon his head, and his face was as it were the sun, and his feet as pillars of fire" **(Revelation 10:1).**

"And I saw heaven opened, and behold a white horse; and he that sat upon him was called Faithful and True, and in righteousness he doth judge and make war" **(Revelation 19:11).**

"And he was clothed with a vesture dipped in blood: and his name is called The Word of God" **(Revelation 19:13).**

"And he hath on his vesture and on his thigh a name written, KING OF KINGS, AND LORD OF LORDS" **(Revelation 19:16).**

"I am Alpha and Omega, the beginning and the end, the first and the last" **(Revelation 22:13).**

"I Jesus have sent mine angel to testify unto you these things in the churches. I am the root and the offspring of David, and the bright and morning star" **(Revelation 22:16).**

The overall picture here is one of the VICTORIOUS JESUS!

THEME VERSE

"The revelation of Jesus Christ, which God gave unto him, to shew unto his servants things which must shortly come to pass; and he sent and signified it by his angel unto his servant John: Who bare record of the word of God, and of the testimony of Jesus Christ, and of all things that he saw" **(Revelation 1:1,2).**

OUTLINE

(Refer to maps on pages A14-A18 in the APPENDIX.)

I. **THE VISION OF THE GLORIFIED CHRIST -** REVELATION 1

II. **THE LETTERS TO THE SEVEN CHURCHES -** REVELATION 2,3

III. **THE END-TIME EVENTS -** REVELATION 4-22

NOTES

THE OLD TESTAMENT QUOTED IN REVELATION.

Revelation 1:7
(Matthew 24:30; Mark 13:26; Luke 21:27)
Behold, he cometh with clouds; and, every eye shall see him, and they also which pierced him; and all kindreds of the earth shall wail because of him. Even so. Amen.

Daniel 7:13
I saw in the night visions, and, behold, one like the Son of man came with the clouds of heaven, and came to the Ancient of days, and they brought him near before him.

Zechariah 12:10
And I will pour upon the house of David, and upon the inhabitants of Jerusalem, the spirit of grace and of supplications: and they shall look upon me whom they have pierced, and they shall mourn for him, as one mourneth for his only son, and shall be in bitterness for him, as one that is in bitterness for his firstborn.

* * *

Revelation 2:26,27
And he that overcometh, and keepeth my works unto the end, to him will I give power over the nations: And he shall rule them with a rod of iron; as the vessels of a potter shall they be broken to shivers: even as I received of my Father.

Psalms 2:8,9
Ask of me, and I shall give thee the heathen for thine inheritance, and the uttermost parts of the earth for thy possession. Thou shalt break them with a rod of iron; thou shalt dash them in pieces like a potter's vessel.

* * *

Revelation 4:8
And the four beasts had each of them six wings about him; and they were full of eyes within: and they rest not day and night, saying, Holy, holy, holy, Lord God Almighty, which was, and is, and is to come.

Isaiah 6:3
And one cried unto another, and said, Holy, holy, holy, is the LORD of hosts: the whole earth is full of his glory.

* * *

Revelation 10:6 (Acts 4:24, 14:15)
And sware by him that liveth for ever and ever, who created heaven, and the things that therein are, and the earth, and the things that therein are, and the sea, and the things which are therein, that there should be time no longer.

Psalms 146:6
Which made heaven, and earth, the sea, and all that therein is: which keepeth truth for ever.

* * *

Revelation 18:7
How much she hath glorified herself, and lived deliciously, so much torment and sorrow give her: for she saith in her heart, I sit a queen, and am no widow, and shall see no sorrow.

Isaiah 47:5,7
Sit thou silent, and get thee into darkness. O daughter of the Chaldeans: for thou shalt no more be called, The lady of kingdoms. And thou saidst, I shall be a lady for ever: so that thou didst not lay these things to thy heart, neither didst remember the latter end of it.

* * *

Revelation 19:2
For true and righteous are his judgments: for he hath judged the great whore, which did corrupt the earth with her fornication, and hath avenged the blood of his servants at her hand.

Psalms 19:9
The fear of the LORD is clean, enduring for ever: the judgments of the LORD are true and righteous altogether.

* * *

Revelation 19:3
And again they said, Alleluia. And her smoke rose up for ever and ever.

Isaiah 34:10
It shall not be quenched night nor day; the smoke thereof shall go up for ever: from generation to generation it shall lie waste; none shall pass through it for ever and ever.

BIBLIOGRAPHY

Dake, Finis Jennings. DAKE'S ANNOTATED REFERENCE BIBLE. Lawrenceville: Dake Bible Sales, Inc., 1963.

Lockyer; Herbert Sr. NELSON'S ILLUSTRATED BIBLE DICTIONARY. Nashville: Thomas Nelson Publishers, 1986.

Strong, James. STRONG'S EXHAUSTIVE CONCORDANCE COMPACT EDITION. Grand Rapids: Baker Book House, 1981.

Wilkinson, Bruce and Kenneth Boa. TALK THRU THE BIBLE. Nashville: Thomas Nelson Publishers, 1983.

Young, Robert. YOUNG'S ANALYTICAL CONCORDANCE TO THE BIBLE. Grand Rapids: Wm. B. Eerdmans Publishing Company, 1964.

___________. THE BETHANY PARALLEL COMMENTARY ON THE NEW TESTAMENT. Minneapolis: Bethany House Publishers, 1983.

___________. THE BETHANY PARALLEL COMMENTARY ON THE OLD TESTAMENT. Minneapolis: Bethany House Publishers, 1985.

APPENDIX

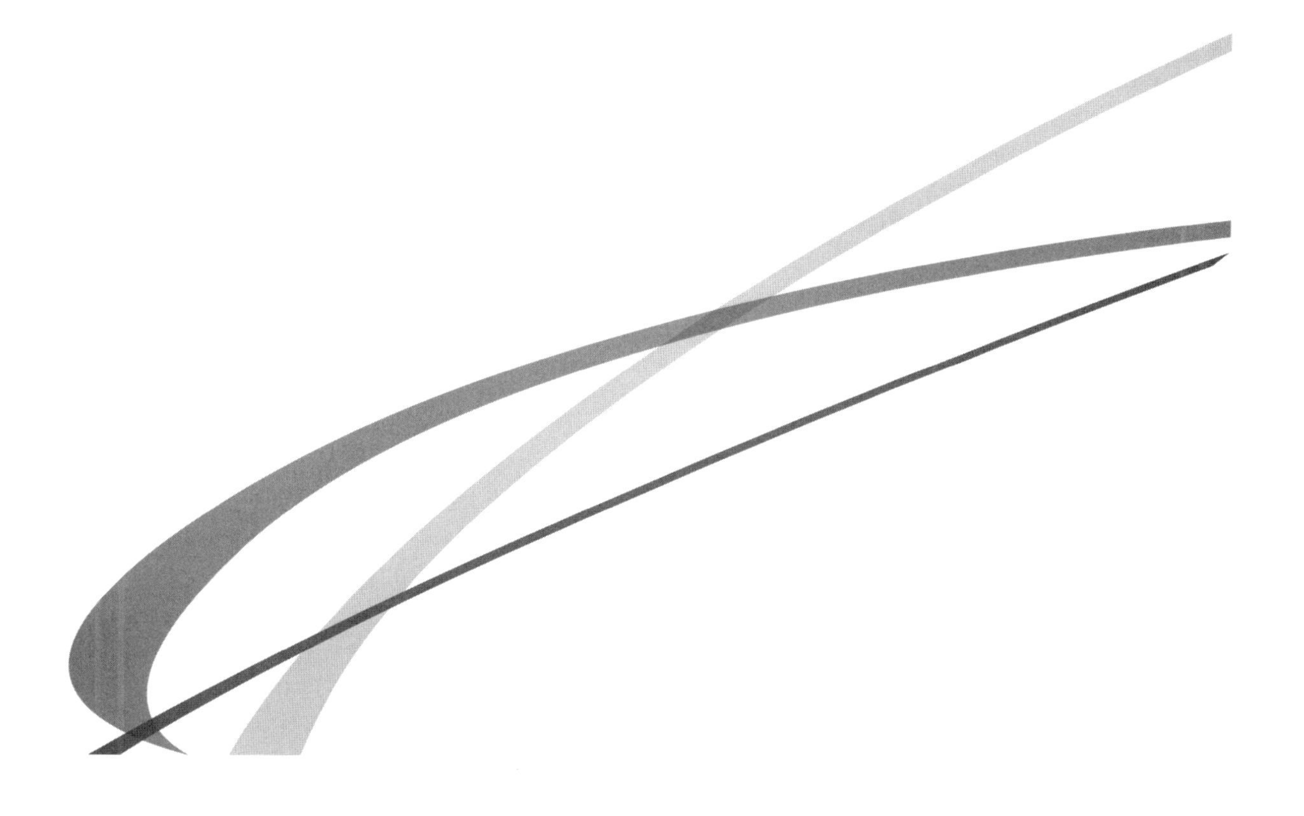

Setting for the Pentateuch

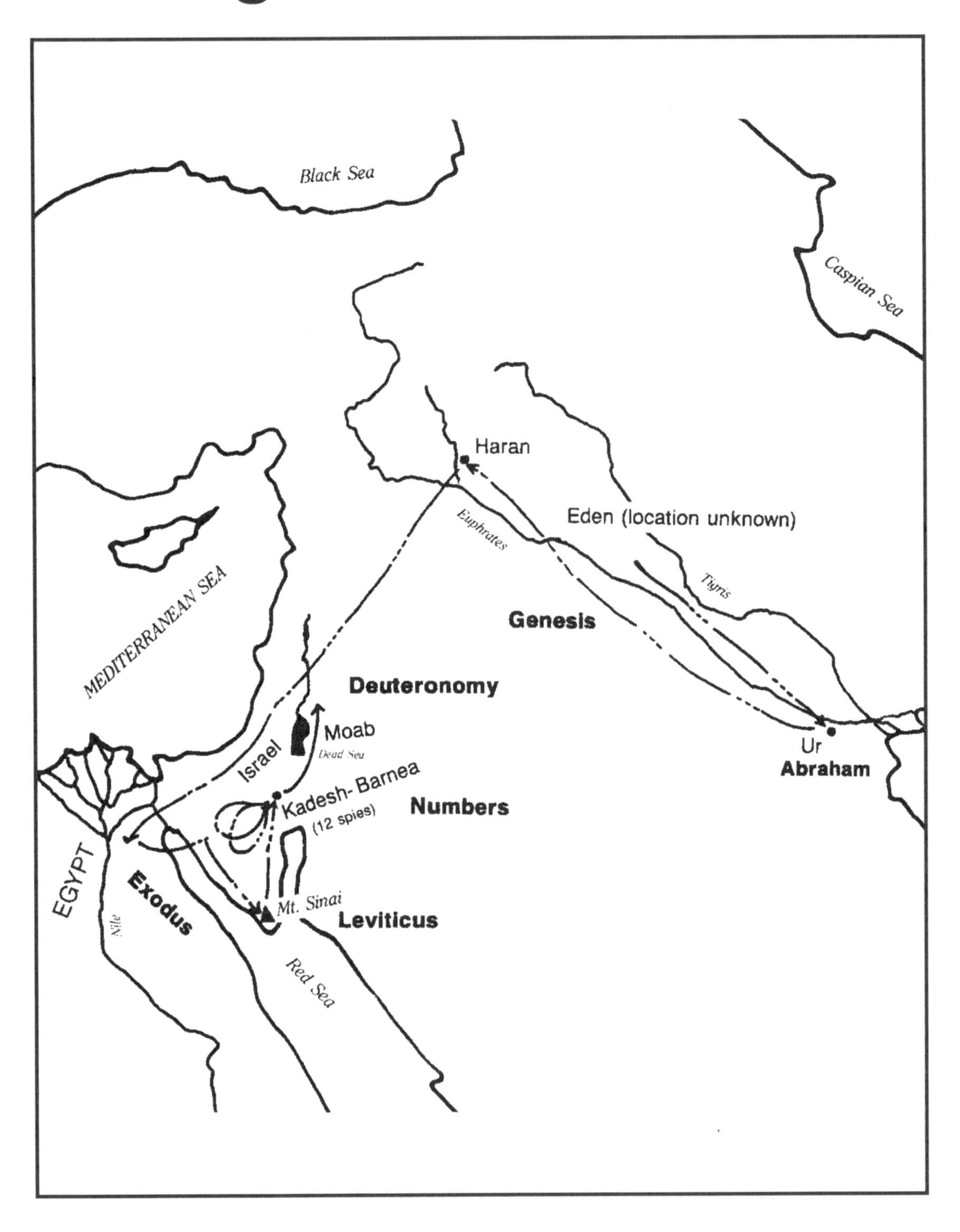

Geography of Genesis

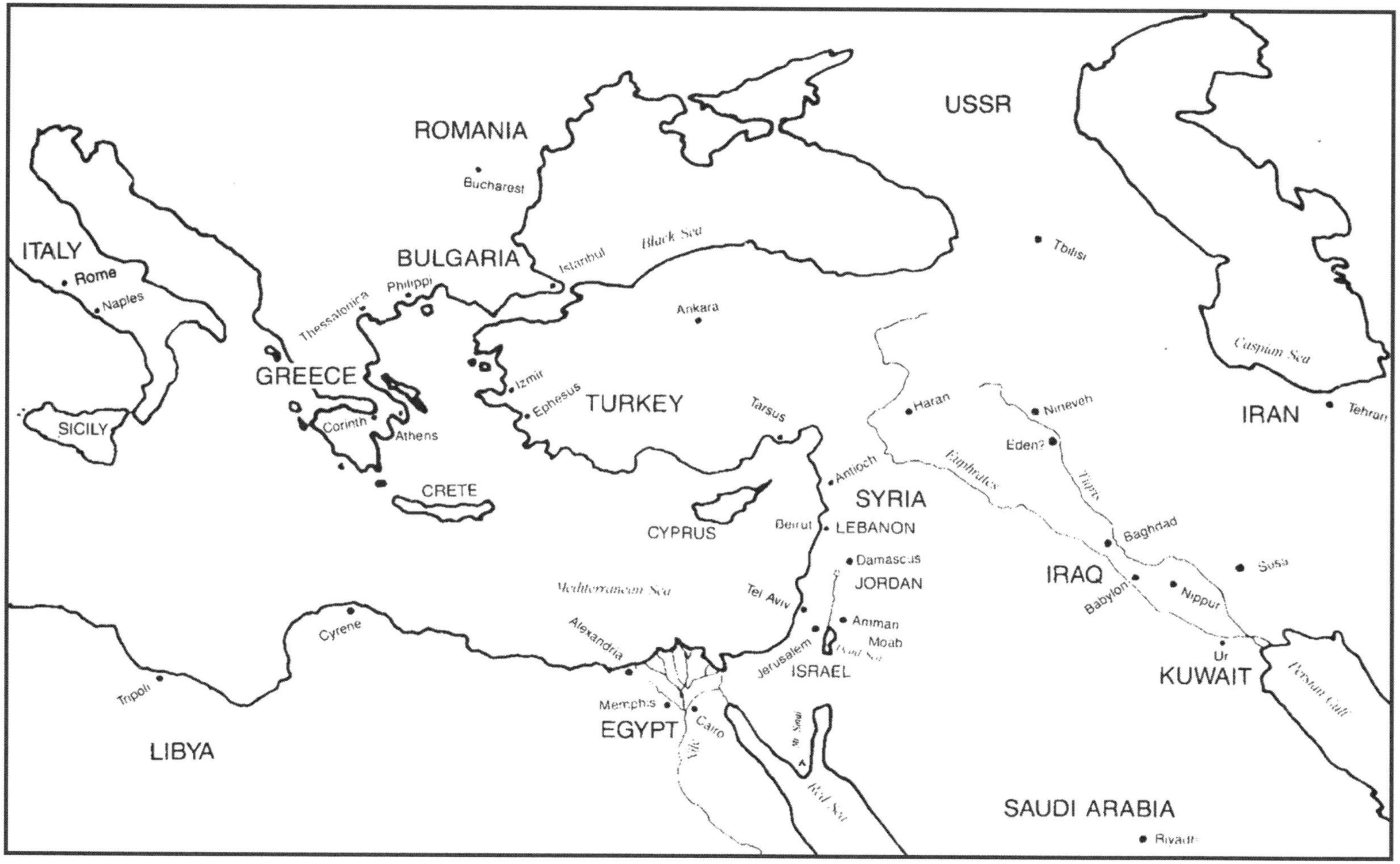

ITALY
Rome
Naples
SICILY
ROMANIA
Bucharest
BULGARIA
Philippi
Thessalonica
Istanbul
Black Sea
GREECE
Corinth
Athens
CRETE
Izmir
Ephesus
TURKEY
Ankara
Tarsus
USSR
Tbilisi
Caspian Sea
IRAN
Tehran
Haran
Nineveh
Eden?
Euphrates
Tigris
Antioch
SYRIA
Beirut
LEBANON
CYPRUS
Damascus
JORDAN
Mediterranean Sea
Tel Aviv
Amman
Moab
Dead Sea
Jerusalem
ISRAEL
Baghdad
Susa
IRAQ
Babylon
Nippur
Ur
KUWAIT
Persian Gulf
Cyrene
Tripoli
LIBYA
Alexandria
Memphis
EGYPT
Cairo
Nile
Mt. Sinai
Red Sea
SAUDI ARABIA
Riyadh

God Calls Abraham

(Genesis 12)

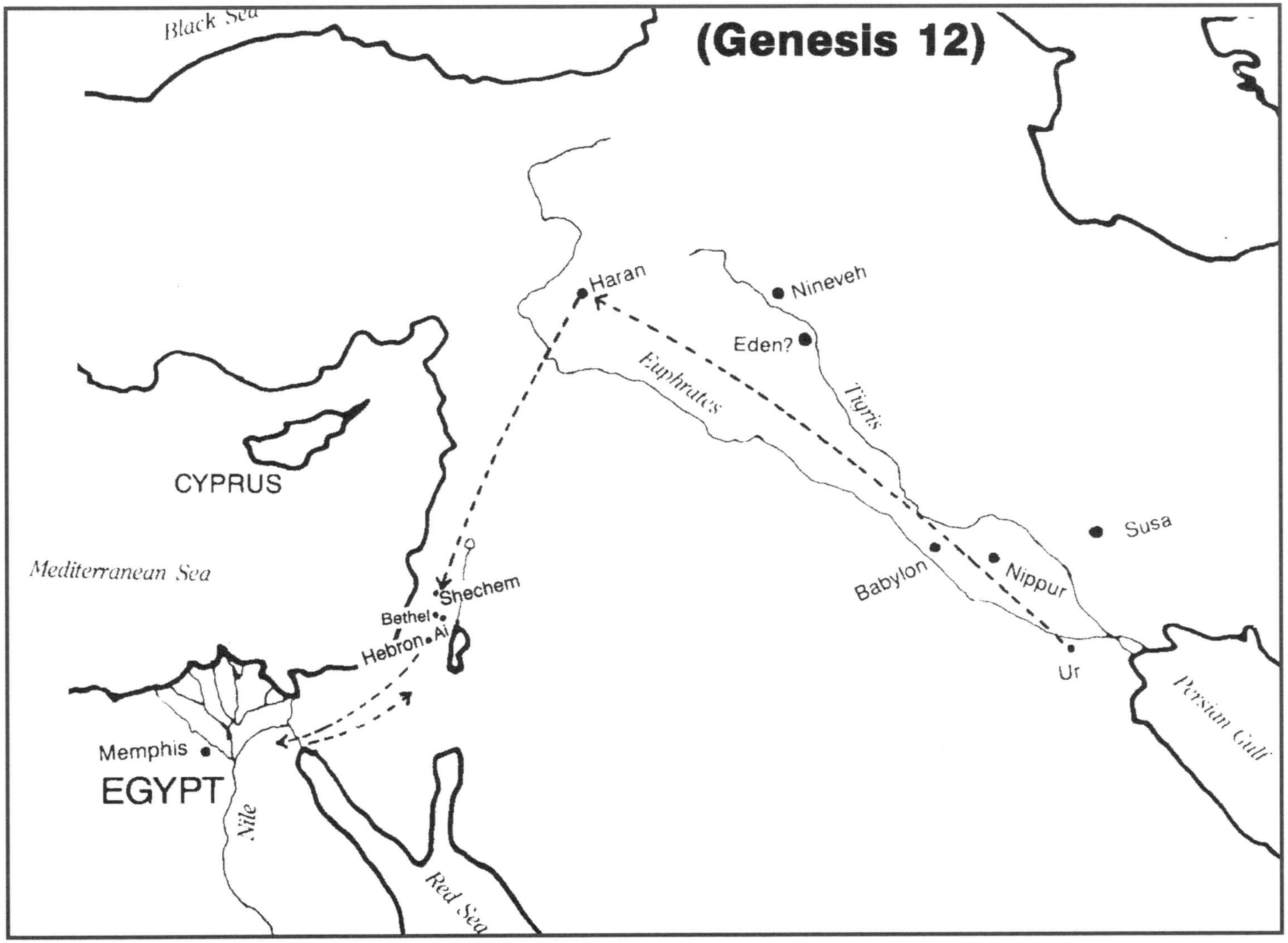

From Egypt to the Promised Land

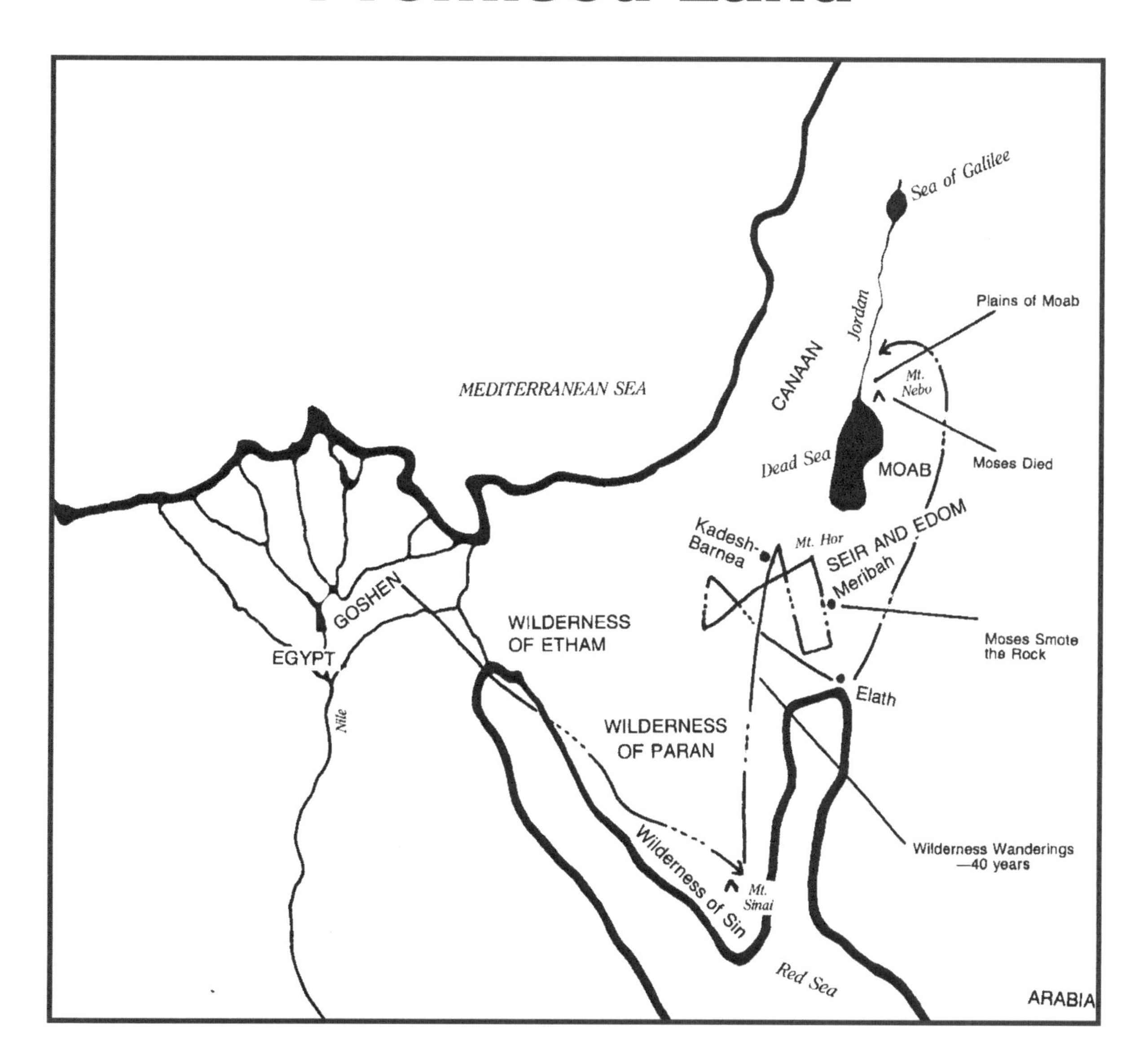

Cities of Refuge

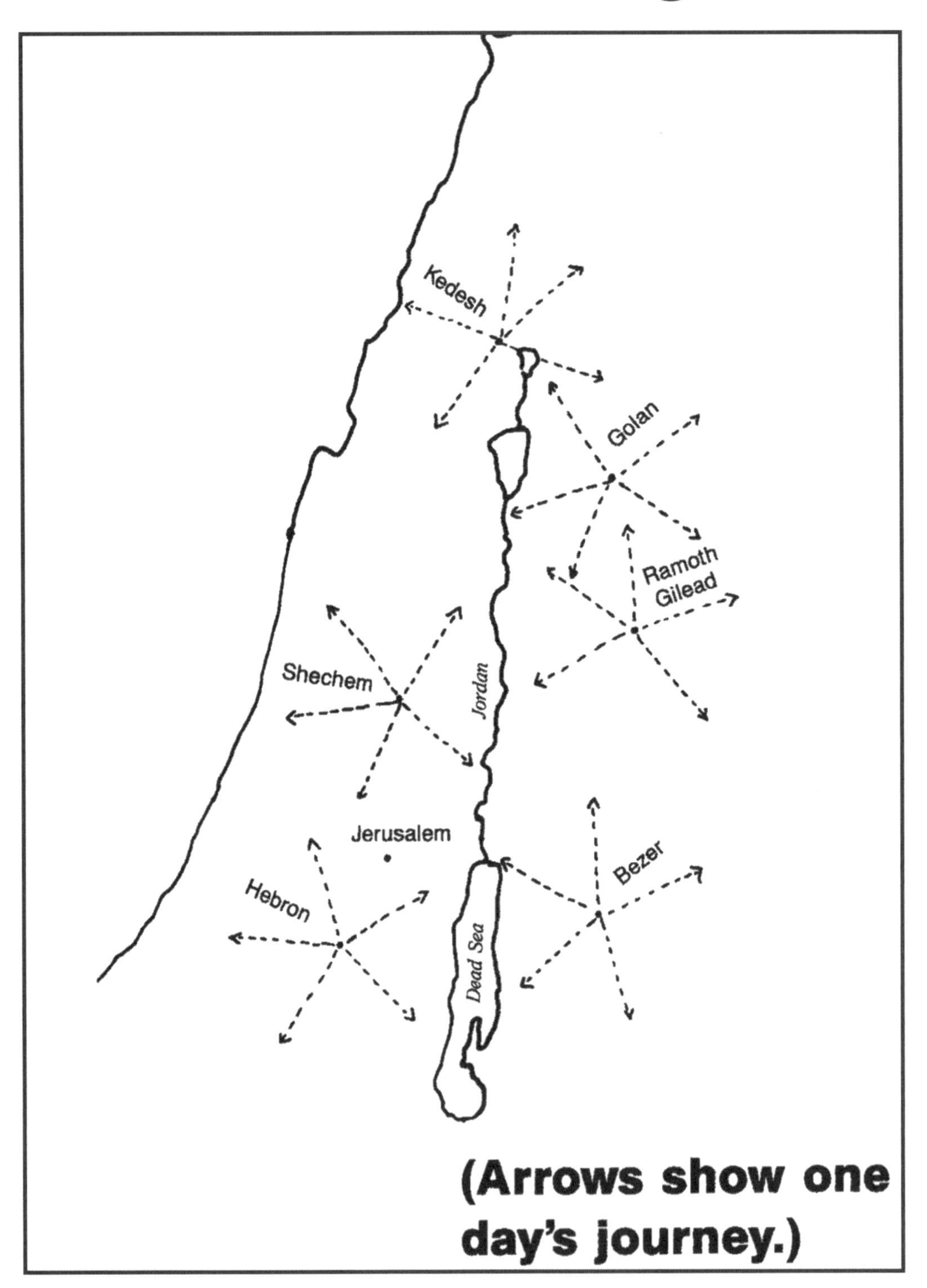

Old Testament Geography

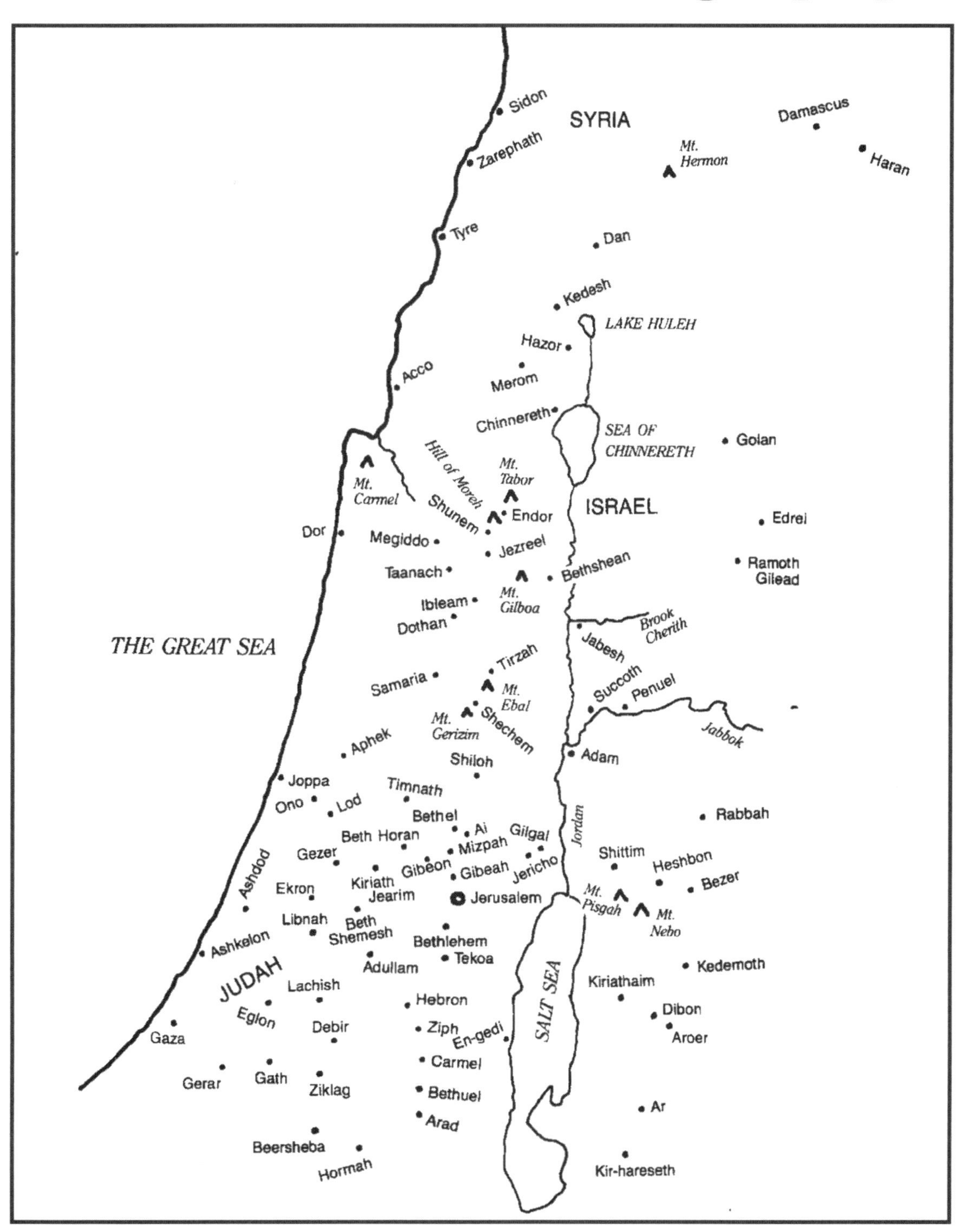

The Divided Kingdom

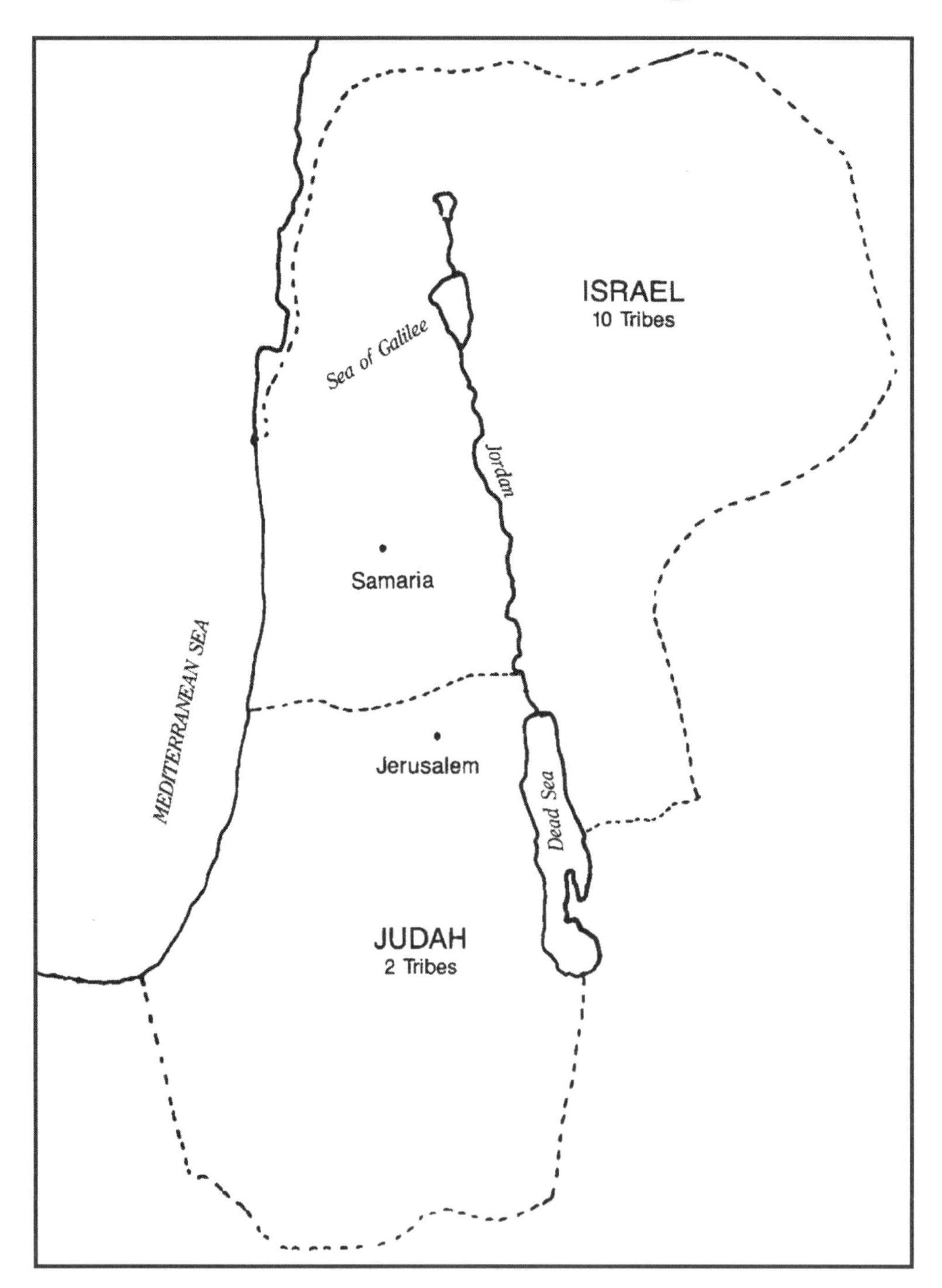

Assyrian Captivity

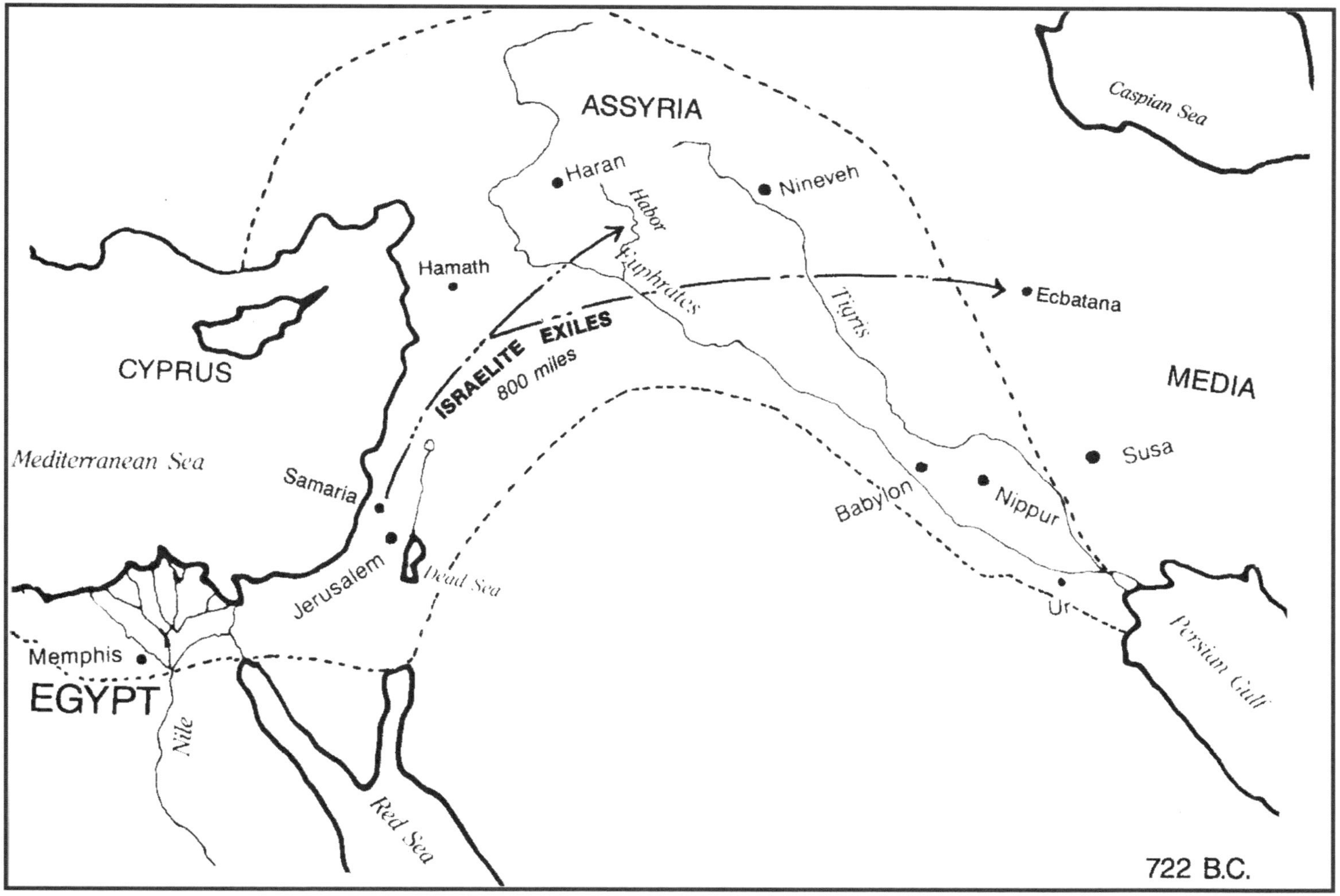

ASSYRIA
Caspian Sea
Haran
Habor
Nineveh
Hamath
Euphrates
Ecbatana
Tigris
ISRAELITE EXILES
800 miles
CYPRUS
MEDIA
Mediterranean Sea
Samaria
Susa
Babylon
Nippur
Jerusalem
Dead Sea
Ur
Persian Gulf
Memphis
EGYPT
Nile
Red Sea
722 B.C.

Babylonian Captivity

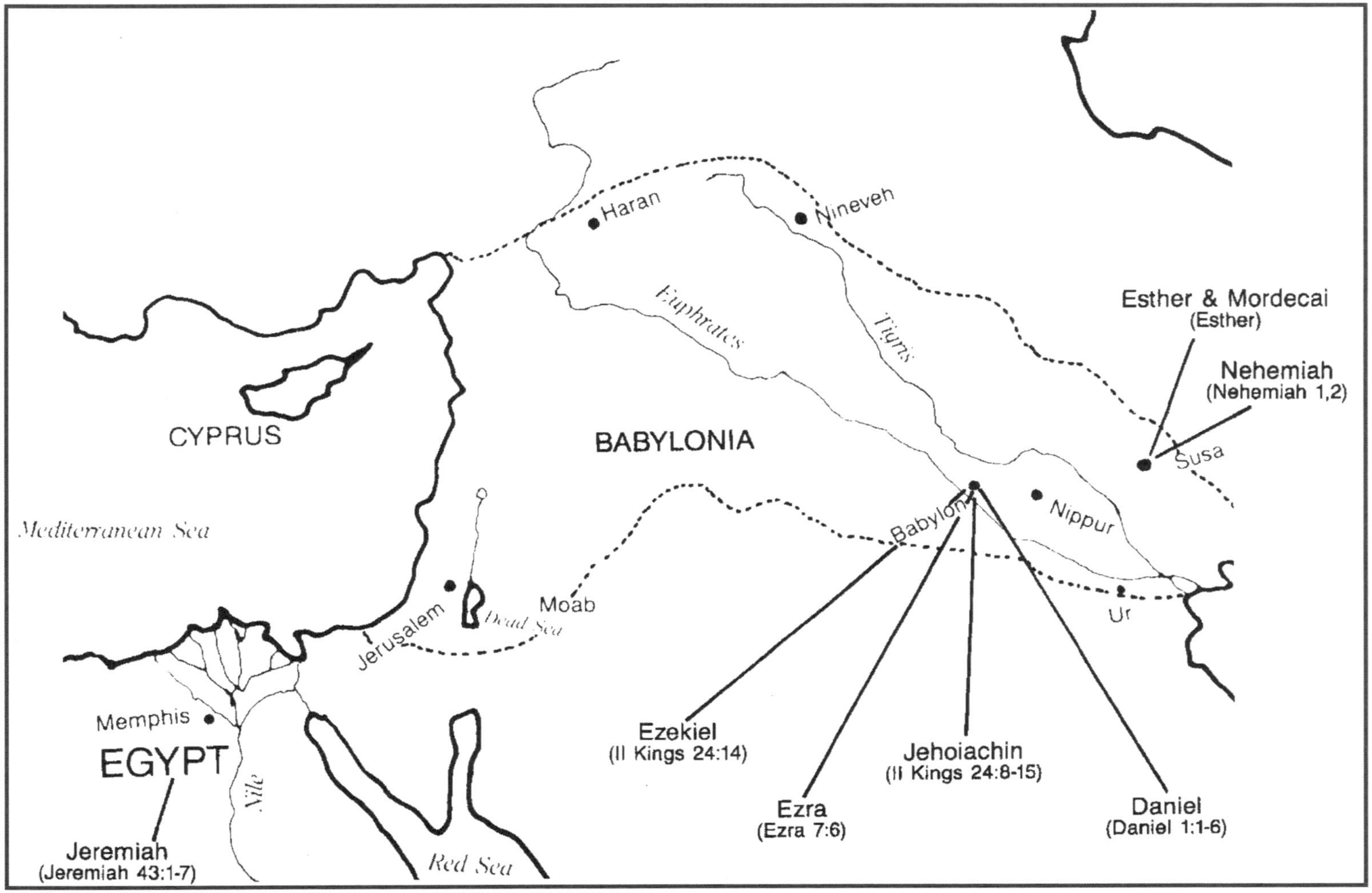

Return From Captivity

MEDIA
Haran
Nineveh
ELAM
Susa
CYPRUS
Mediterranean Sea
Euphrates
Tigris
Babylon
Nippur
Jerusalem
Dead Sea
Moab
BABYLONIA
Ur
Memphis
EGYPT
Nile
Red Sea

1. Zerubbabel (Ezra 1:11—Sheshbazzar)
2. Ezra (Ezra 7:1-6)
3. Nehemiah (Nehemiah 2:1-11)

Birth & Early Travels of Jesus

(Matthew 2:1-23)

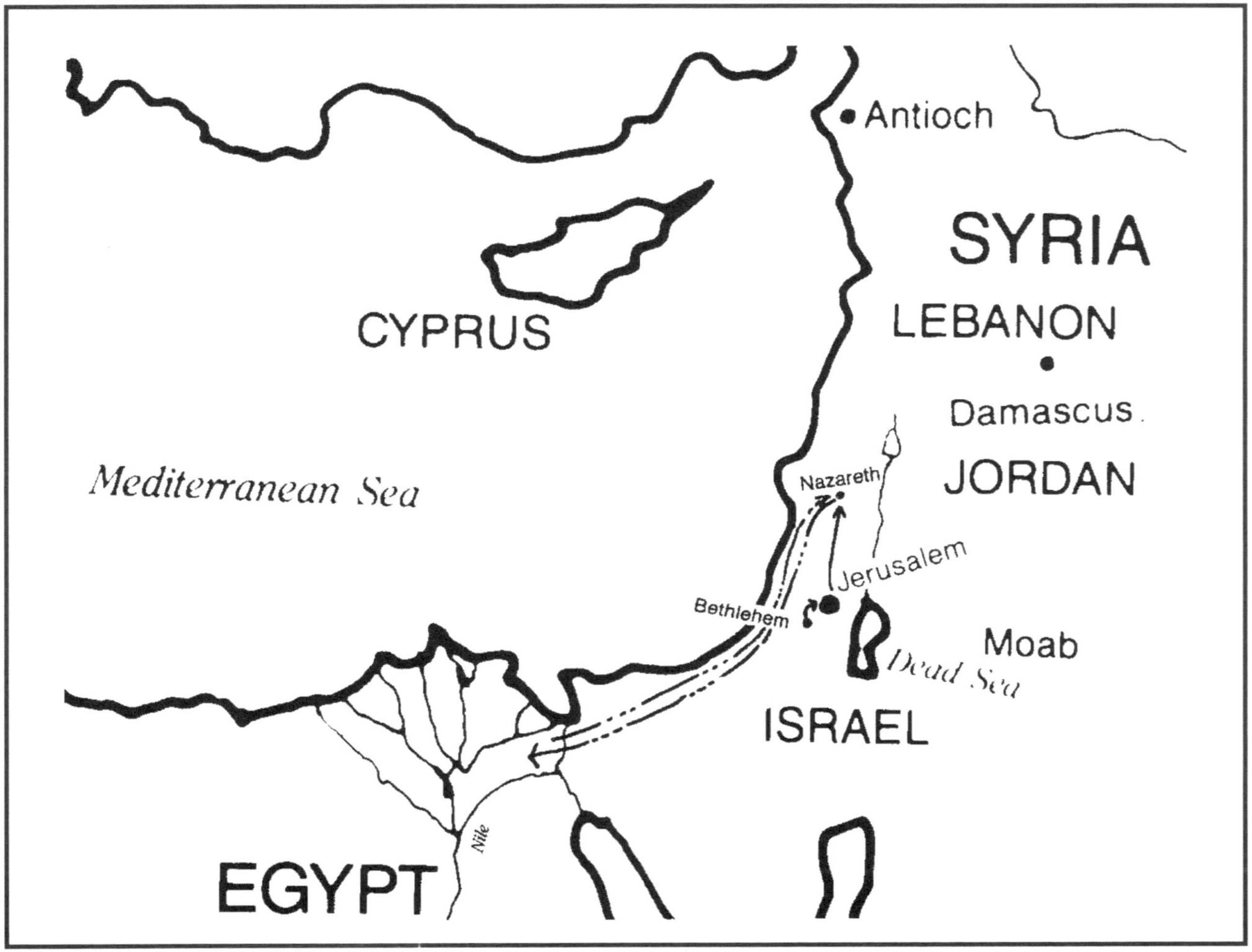

New Testament Geography

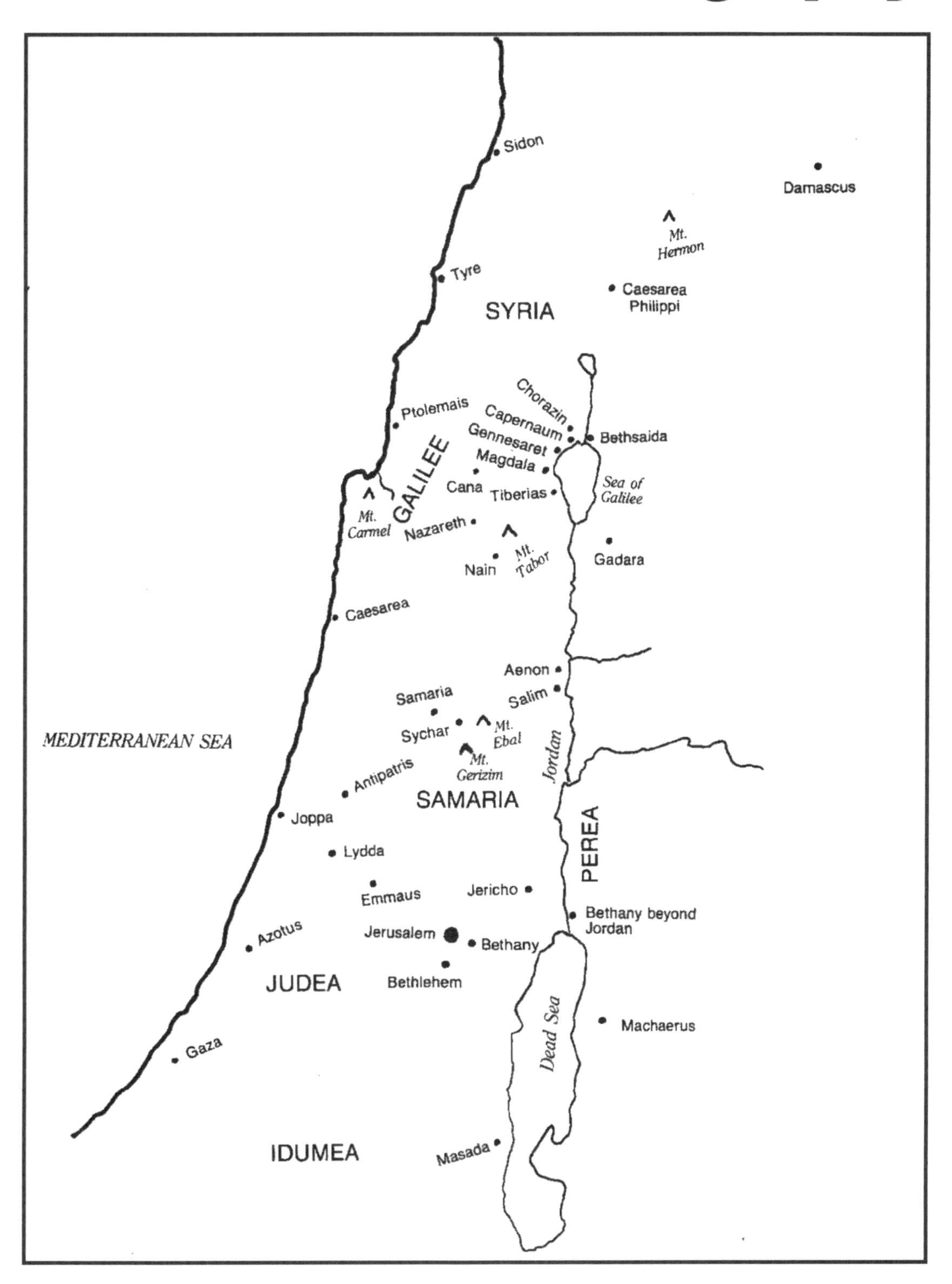

Sidon
Damascus
Mt. Hermon
Tyre
Caesarea Philippi
SYRIA
Chorazin
Ptolemais
Capernaum
Gennesaret
Bethsaida
GALILEE
Magdala
Cana
Tiberias
Sea of Galilee
Mt. Carmel
Nazareth
Mt. Tabor
Nain
Gadara
Caesarea
Aenon
Samaria
Salim
Sychar
Mt. Ebal
MEDITERRANEAN SEA
Mt. Gerizim
Jordan
Antipatris
SAMARIA
Joppa
PEREA
Lydda
Emmaus
Jericho
Bethany beyond Jordan
Azotus
Jerusalem
Bethany
JUDEA
Bethlehem
Dead Sea
Machaerus
Gaza
IDUMEA
Masada

Travels of Paul after His Conversion

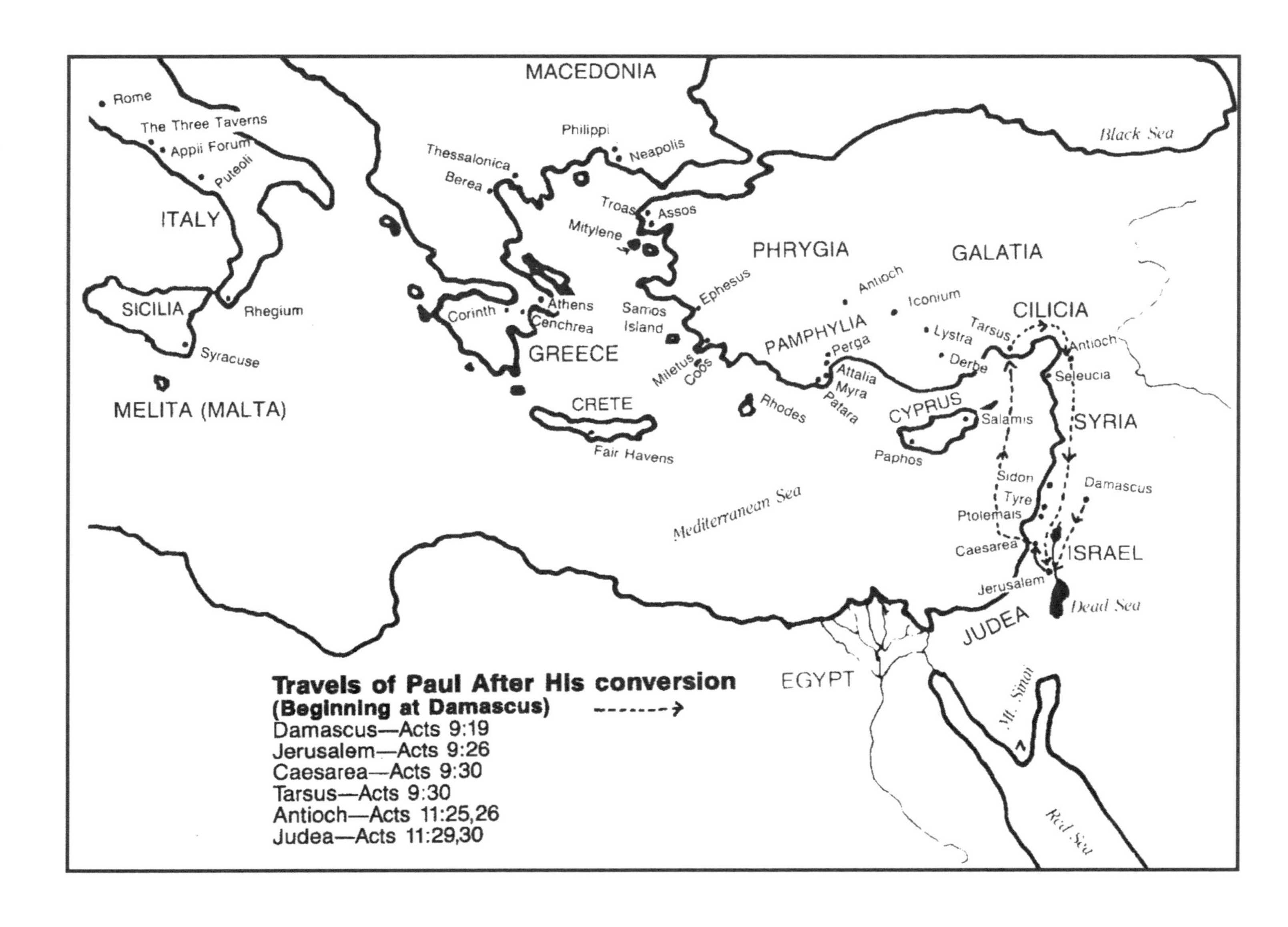

Paul's First & Second Missionary Journeys

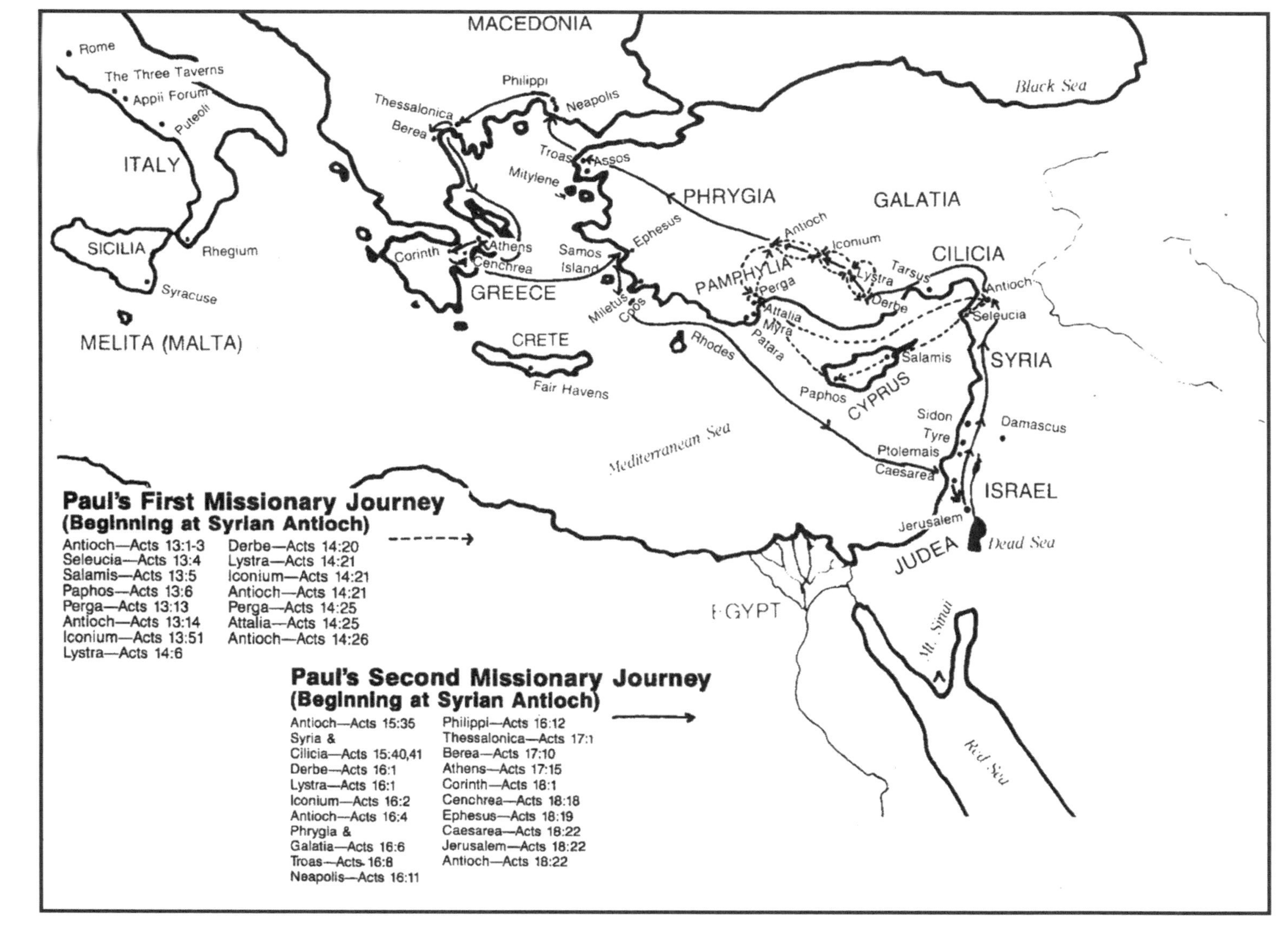
MACEDONIA
Rome
The Three Taverns
Appii Forum
Puteoli
ITALY
SICILIA
Rhegium
Syracuse
MELITA (MALTA)
Philippi
Neapolis
Thessalonica
Berea
Troas
Assos
Mitylene
Corinth
Athens
Cenchrea
Samos Island
GREECE
CRETE
Fair Havens
Ephesus
Miletus
Coos
Rhodes
PHRYGIA
GALATIA
Black Sea
Antioch
Iconium
Lystra
Derbe
Tarsus
CILICIA
PAMPHYLIA
Perga
Attalia
Myra
Patara
Antioch
Seleucia
Salamis
SYRIA
Paphos
CYPRUS
Sidon
Tyre
Ptolemais
Caesarea
Damascus
Mediterranean Sea
ISRAEL
Jerusalem
Dead Sea
JUDEA
EGYPT
Mt. Sinai
Red Sea
Paul's First Missionary Journey
(Beginning at Syrian Antioch)
Antioch—Acts 13:1-3
Seleucia—Acts 13:4
Salamis—Acts 13:5
Paphos—Acts 13:6
Perga—Acts 13:13
Antioch—Acts 13:14
Iconium—Acts 13:51
Lystra—Acts 14:6
Derbe—Acts 14:20
Lystra—Acts 14:21
Iconium—Acts 14:21
Antioch—Acts 14:21
Perga—Acts 14:25
Attalia—Acts 14:25
Antioch—Acts 14:26
Paul's Second Missionary Journey
(Beginning at Syrian Antioch)
Antioch—Acts 15:35
Syria & Cilicia—Acts 15:40,41
Derbe—Acts 16:1
Lystra—Acts 16:1
Iconium—Acts 16:2
Antioch—Acts 16:4
Phrygia & Galatia—Acts 16:6
Troas—Acts 16:8
Neapolis—Acts 16:11
Philippi—Acts 16:12
Thessalonica—Acts 17:1
Berea—Acts 17:10
Athens—Acts 17:15
Corinth—Acts 18:1
Cenchrea—Acts 18:18
Ephesus—Acts 18:19
Caesarea—Acts 18:22
Jerusalem—Acts 18:22
Antioch—Acts 18:22

Paul's Third Missionary Journey & Paul's Journey to Rome

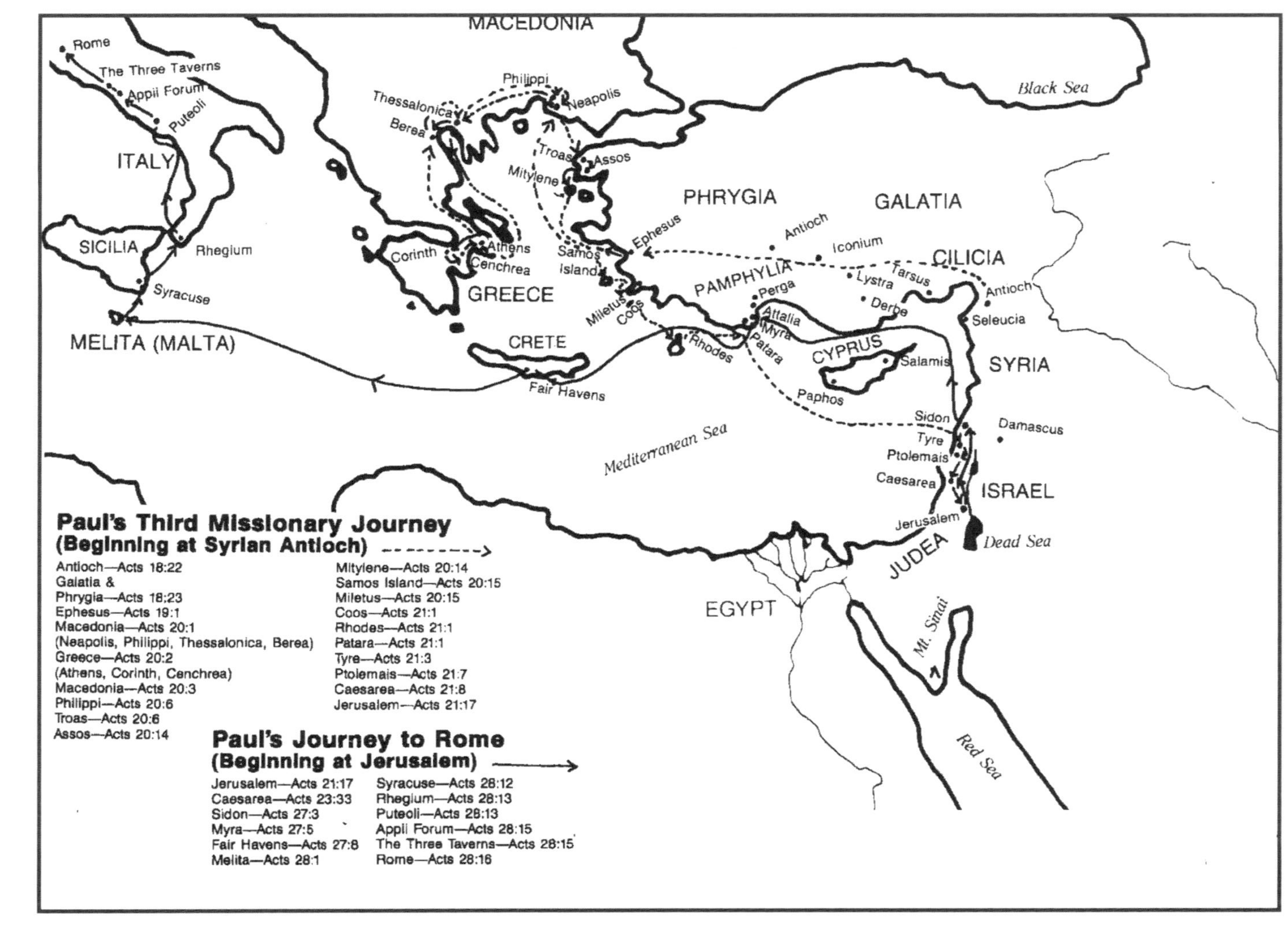
MACEDONIA
Rome
The Three Taverns
Appii Forum
Puteoli
ITALY
SICILIA
Rhegium
Syracuse
MELITA (MALTA)
Philippi
Thessalonica
Berea
Neapolis
Troas
Assos
Mitylene
Corinth
Athens
Cenchrea
GREECE
Samos Island
Miletus
Coos
CRETE
Fair Havens
Black Sea
PHRYGIA
GALATIA
Ephesus
Antioch
Iconium
CILICIA
Tarsus
Lystra
Derbe
PAMPHYLIA
Perga
Attalia
Myra
Patara
Rhodes
CYPRUS
Salamis
Paphos
Antioch
Seleucia
SYRIA
Sidon
Tyre
Ptolemais
Caesarea
Damascus
ISRAEL
Jerusalem
JUDEA
Dead Sea
Mediterranean Sea
EGYPT
Mt. Sinai
Red Sea
Paul's Third Missionary Journey
(Beginning at Syrian Antioch)
Antioch—Acts 18:22
Galatia &
Phrygia—Acts 18:23
Ephesus—Acts 19:1
Macedonia—Acts 20:1
(Neapolis, Philippi, Thessalonica, Berea)
Greece—Acts 20:2
(Athens, Corinth, Cenchrea)
Macedonia—Acts 20:3
Philippi—Acts 20:6
Troas—Acts 20:6
Assos—Acts 20:14
Mitylene—Acts 20:14
Samos Island—Acts 20:15
Miletus—Acts 20:15
Coos—Acts 21:1
Rhodes—Acts 21:1
Patara—Acts 21:1
Tyre—Acts 21:3
Ptolemais—Acts 21:7
Caesarea—Acts 21:8
Jerusalem—Acts 21:17
Paul's Journey to Rome
(Beginning at Jerusalem)
Jerusalem—Acts 21:17
Caesarea—Acts 23:33
Sidon—Acts 27:3
Myra—Acts 27:5
Fair Havens—Acts 27:8
Melita—Acts 28:1
Syracuse—Acts 28:12
Rhegium—Acts 28:13
Puteoli—Acts 28:13
Appii Forum—Acts 28:15
The Three Taverns—Acts 28:15
Rome—Acts 28:16

New Testament Letters

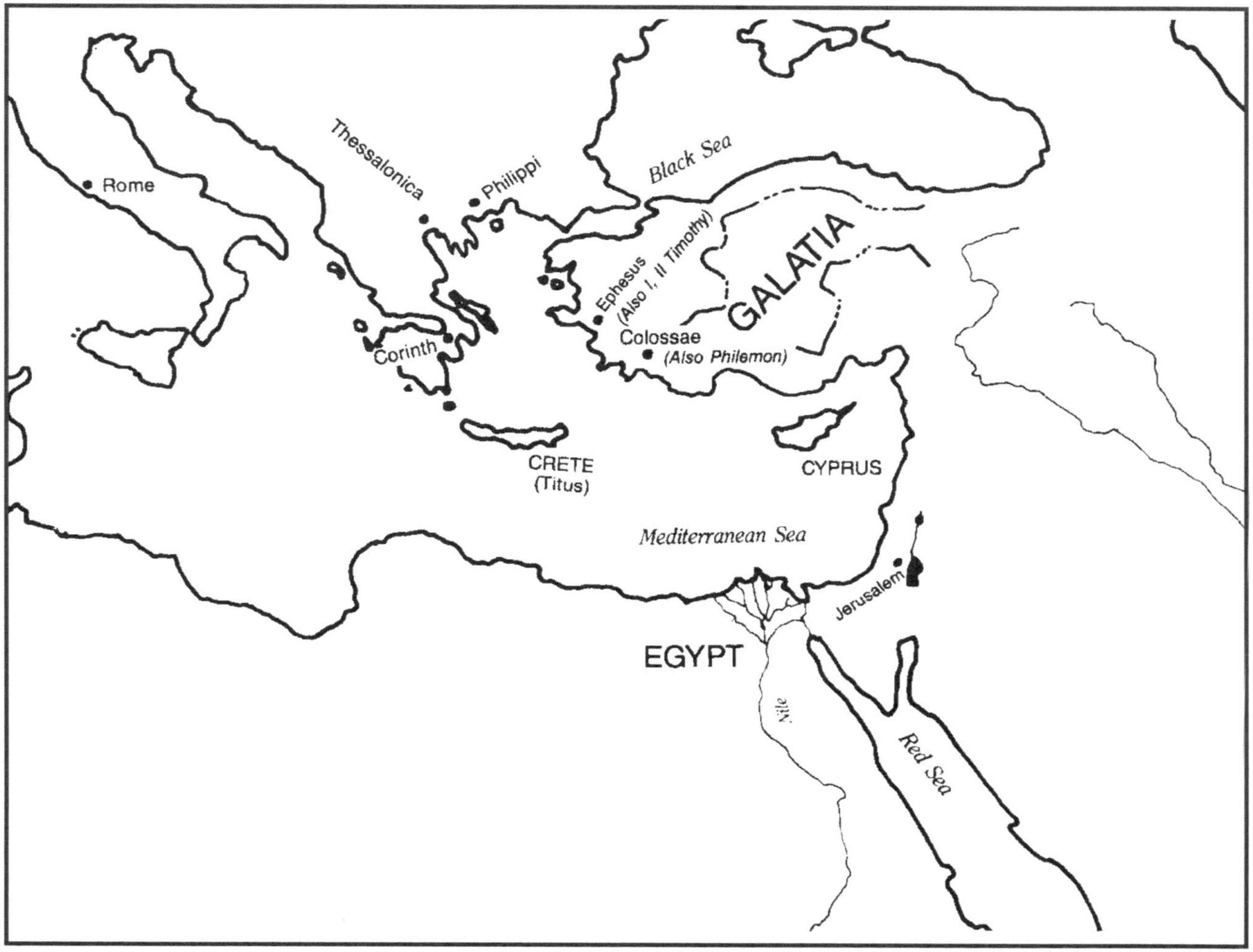

Rome
Thessalonica
Philippi
Black Sea
Ephesus
(Also I, II Timothy)
GALATIA
Colossae
(Also Philemon)
Corinth
CRETE
(Titus)
CYPRUS
Mediterranean Sea
Jerusalem
EGYPT
Nile
Red Sea